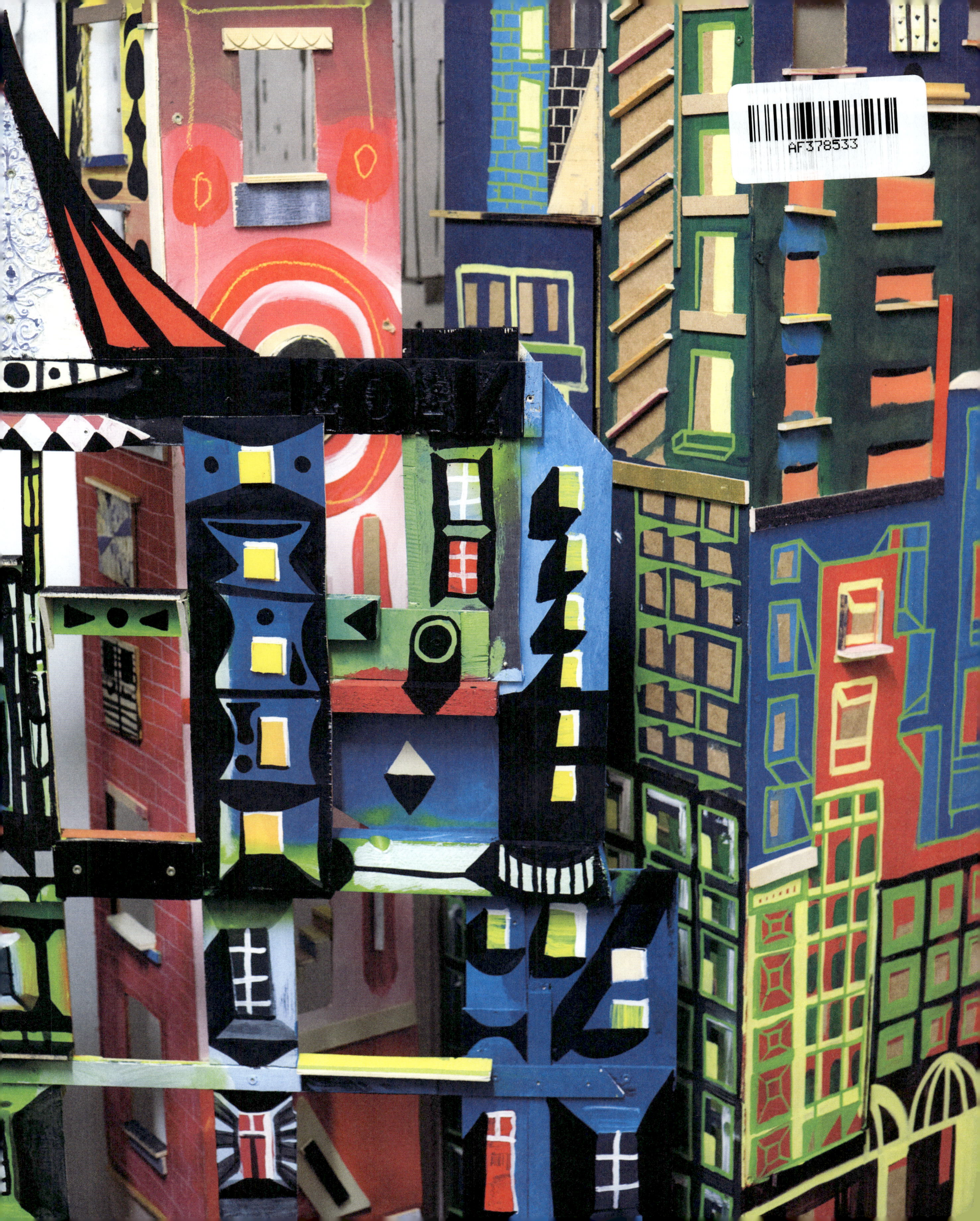

AF378533

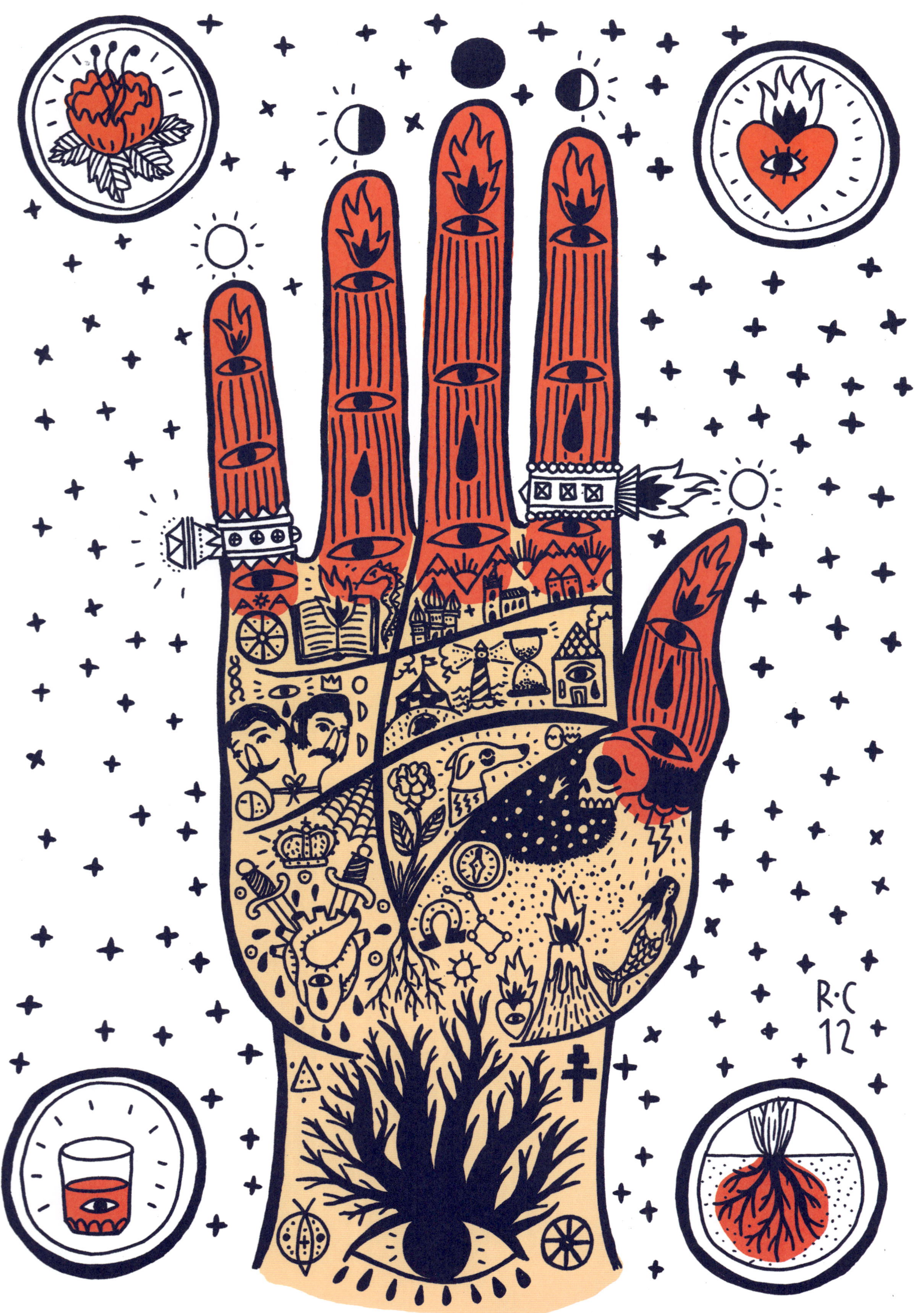

Make Your Mark

The New Urban Artists

Tristan Manco

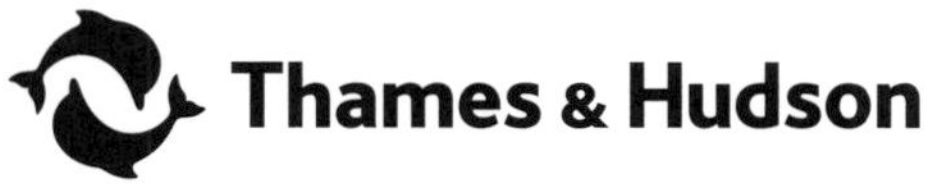

Thames & Hudson

First published in the United Kingdom in 2016 by
Thames & Hudson Ltd, 181A High Holborn,
London WC1V 7QX

Make Your Mark: The New Urban Artists © 2016
Thames & Hudson Ltd

Text © 2016 Tristan Manco

Design by Samuel Clark
www.bytheskydesign.com

British Library Cataloguing-in-Publication Data
A catalogue record for this book is available from
the British Library

ISBN 978-0-500-29218-1

Printed and bound in China by C&C Offset Printing
Co. Ltd

To find out about all our publications, please visit
www.thamesandhudson.com. There you can
subscribe to our e-newsletter, browse or download
our current catalogue, and buy any titles that are
in print.

For my dad Luis Manco

P. 1
**44flavours, with
Jan Brokop and
Hans Staden**
Untitled, c. 2010
Mixed-media
installation
Dimensions variable

P. 2
Ricardo Cavolo
Life Hand, 2013
Screenprint
55 × 50 cm
(21⅝ × 19¾ in.)

BELOW
Rob Sato
Remains, 2012
Watercolour on
Arches paper
Dimensions unknown

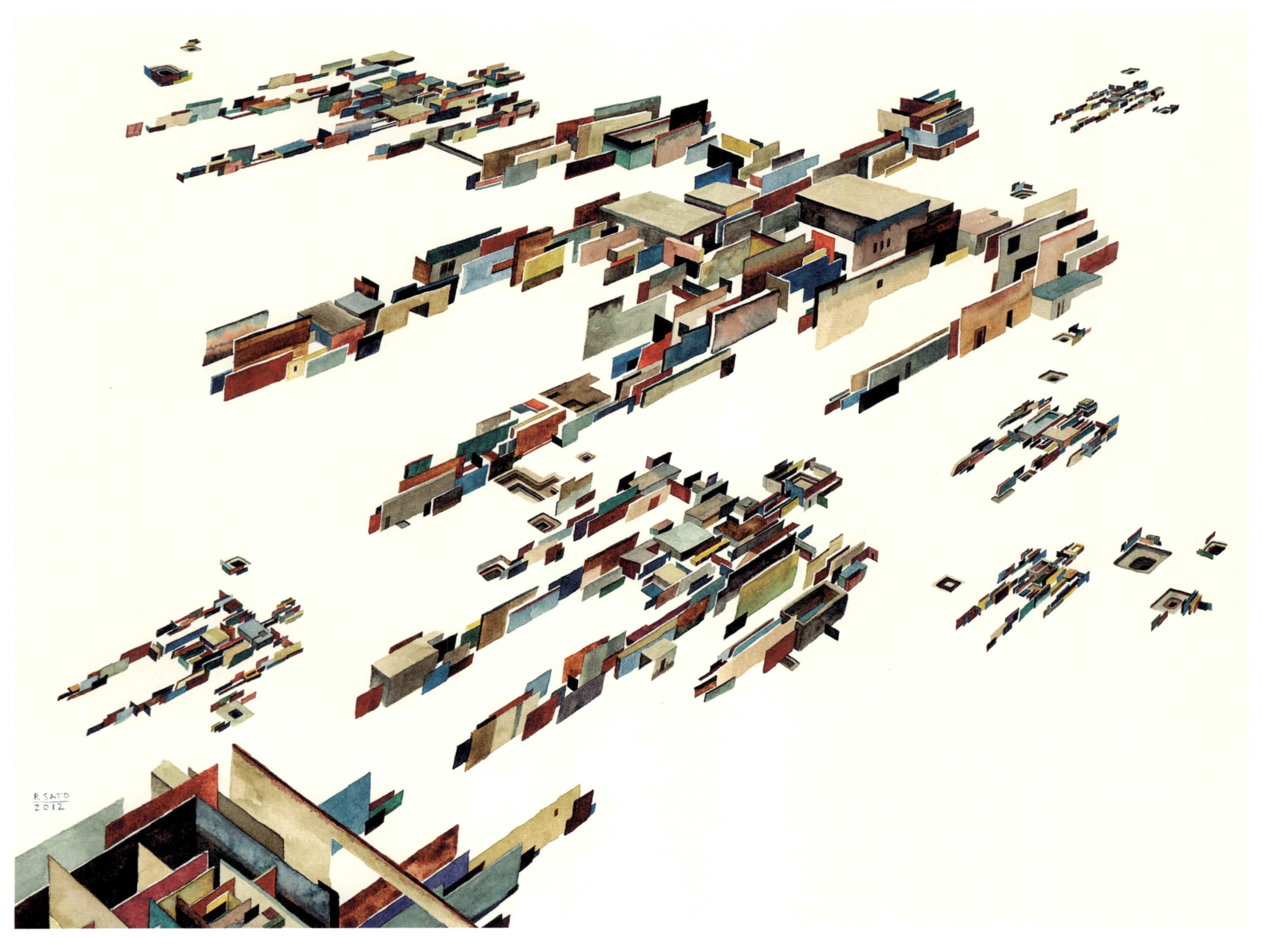

Contents

Introduction

To make one's mark is to make a difference or to have a significant effect on something, whether it is within society or creative realms. We can make our mark in our endeavours, our actions and in our choices. Making your mark is a central and guiding principle in art; it is the impression or feeling that an artwork evokes in the viewer, and the dialogue between the two that follows. It is the passion to create and to express oneself, to explore and challenge ideas.

The uniqueness of an artwork lies in its distinctive visual character or quality, a combination of message and medium that is the hallmark of its maker. It could be a certain approach to conveying a subject, or the use of specific materials or techniques that sets one work apart from another. To make your mark as an artist, therefore, requires not only the drive to make an impact with one's ideas but also to develop a clear visual language and approach in communicating them. There are no hard or fast rules as to how this 'mark' or style might be developed, with there being seemingly limitless and endlessly fascinating directions an artist might take.

To explore this theme, *Make Your Mark* focuses its attention on the particular journeys of forty-five contemporary artists from around the world, who make – and break – their own rules when it comes to creating and disseminating their art. With independence, passion

Ibrahim Ahmed III
Untitled, from the series
'There is No Clash', 2015
Mixed media on canvas
Dimensions unknown

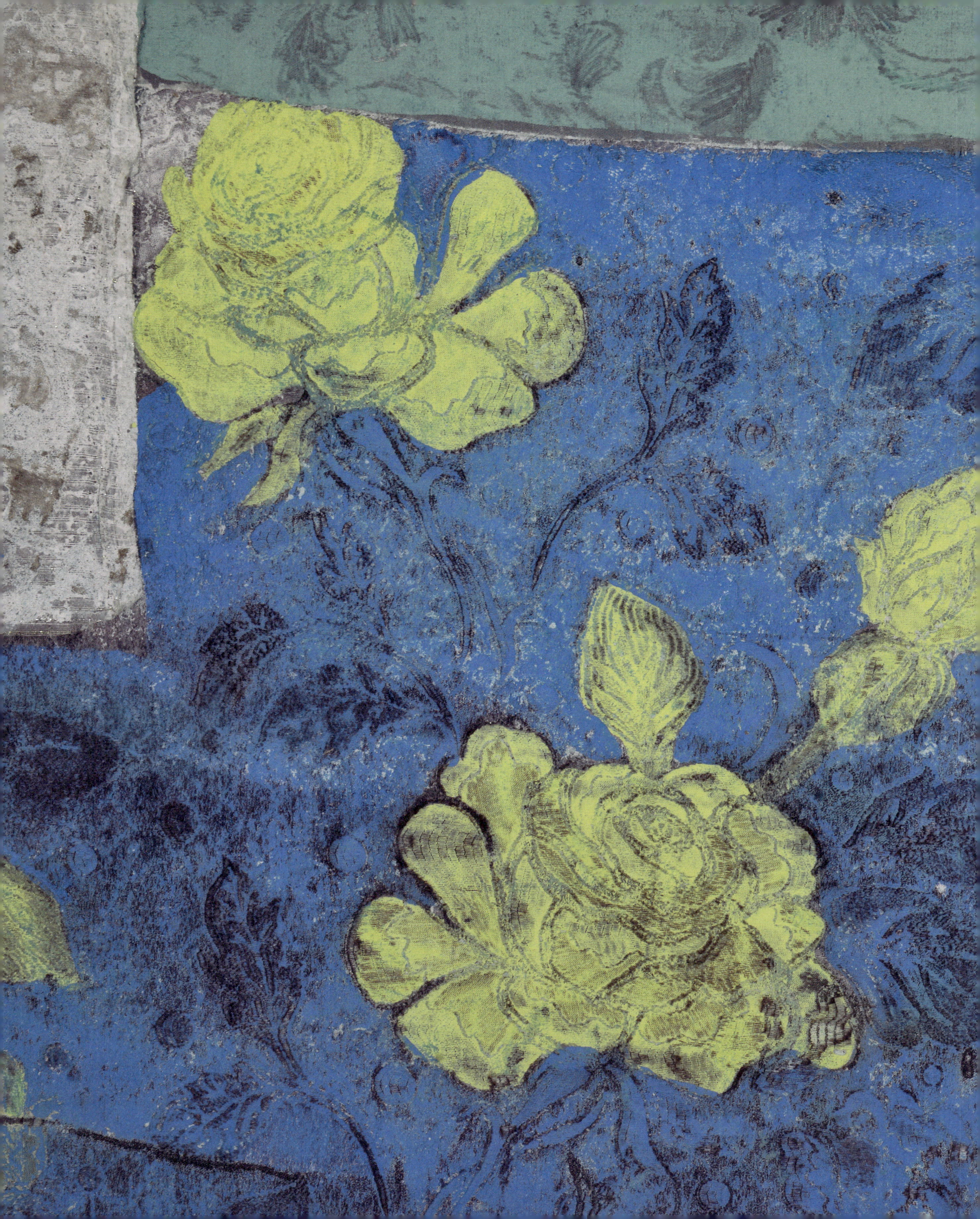

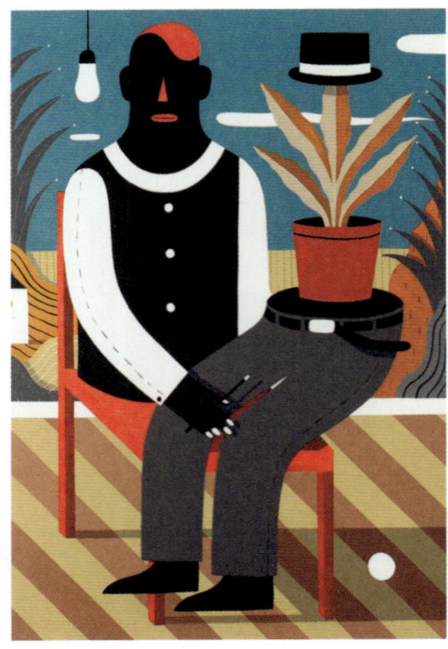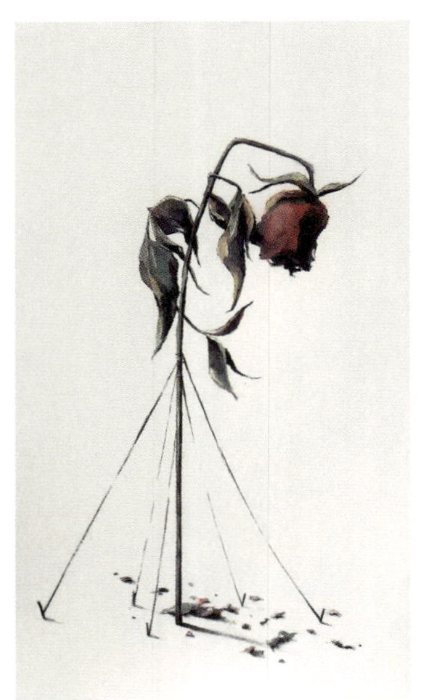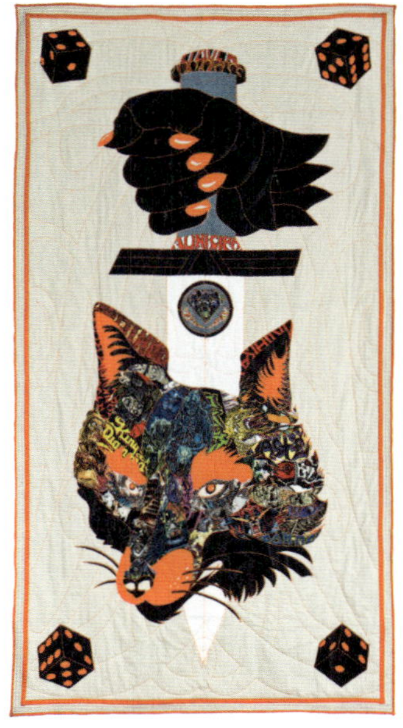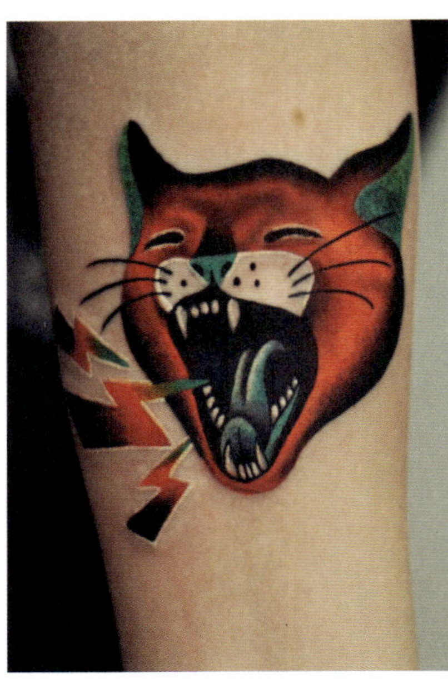

Agostino Iacurci
Half and Half, 2015
Acrylic on canvas
150 × 200 cm (59⅛ × 78¾ in.)

Pejac
Gulliver, 2013
Acrylic and watercolour
on paper
45 × 27 cm (17¾ × 10⅝ in.)

Ben Venom
All Bets are OFF!, 2013
Handmade quilt with heavy
metal T-shirts, denim and
leather
149.8 × 276.8 cm (59 × 109 in.)

David Côté
Tattoo design, 2015

João Ruas
Study from the artist's
sketchbook, c. 2013
Pencil on paper
Dimensions unknown

Raymond Lemstra
Randy Maelstrom, 2014
Sculpture in wood
50 × 70 × 50 cm
(19¾ × 27⅝ × 19¾ in.)

Carlos Donjuán
Cinelli Boys, 2014
Mixed media on Arches paper
55.9 × 76.2 cm (22 × 30 in.)

and thoughtfulness they exemplify this broad ideal of establishing a distinctive 'mark' to entice and intrigue the viewer. In this book they are hailed as 'the new urban artists', the term 'urban' being used in the broadest sense here to encompass a contemporaneous, liberated and alternative art culture. 'Urban art' usually implies work that is influenced by street art and graffiti culture, and artists who use the urban environment as their platform. However, some of the makers included in this book are not necessarily 'urban artists' and do not ordinarily make street art. Instead, they are informed by contemporary urban life, and allow their experiences of it to infiltrate their work.

It could be argued that urban art is a recent trend that seems to have tapped into the zeitgeist. Certainly its influence can be felt across the creative spheres, with museums and galleries reflecting on and engaging with the genre, and in the way particular styles associated with it are filtering into other areas, such as advertising, illustration and design. Urban art is, by nature, eclectic, bringing together people from all walks of life, from fine artists to graphic designers to graffiti artists, enabling new alliances and influences to form. The urban art

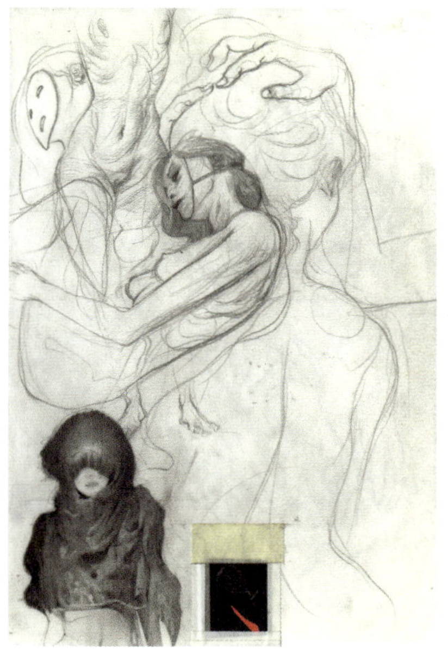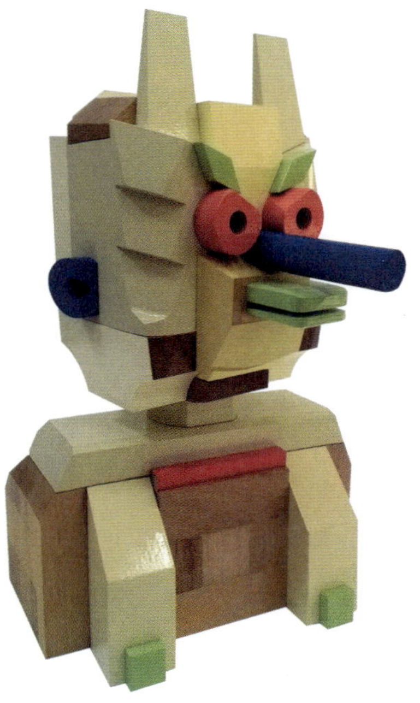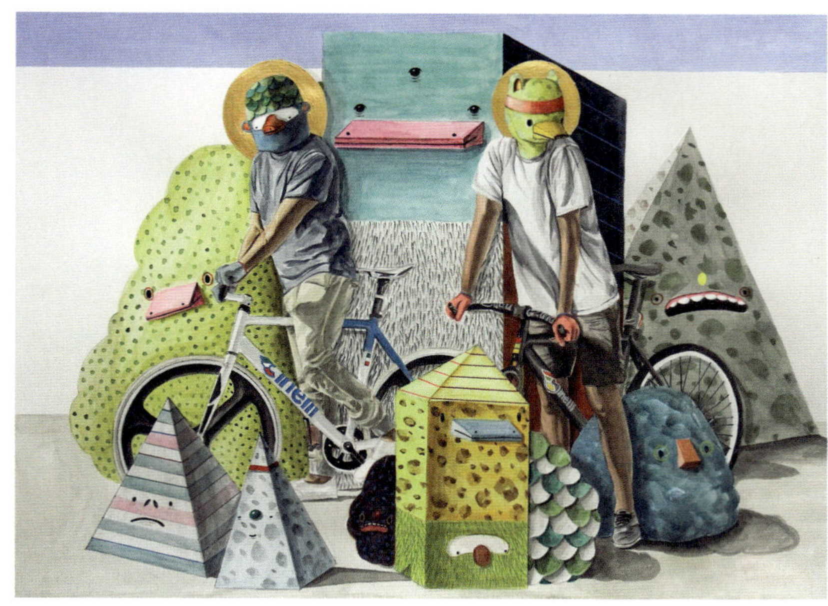

movement has been a catalyst for experimentation and innovation. It is a place where graffiti artists are inspired to become sculptors, designers to become painters or all of these things in one go.

Urban art has it roots in a long history of tradition and innovation, much of which contemporary street artists still acknowledge, by referring to the genre's particular codes and aesthetics in their output. However, its scope is now widening, with increasingly progressive and stylistically rich works being produced. Similarly, artworks made in the studio are becoming just as revered as those on the street, with the phrase 'urban art' extending to them also, since they are made in much the same spirit as their external counterparts. With the street no longer being the only environment in which urban artists work, their art has become more about a particular outlook – a freedom of expression, a sort of 'wildness' and openness to experimentation. It has been guided by the applying of the DIY attitude to other forms, bringing with it an exhilarating, informal and collective approach to making and presenting art. This movement, if it can yet be called one, has seen artists breaking with tradition in terms of the ways they disseminate their art – finding unconventional and interesting ways in which to work with galleries and institutions, sharing their work online and being responsible for the proliferation of many street art and mural festivals worldwide.

Urban artists display an inherent level of optimism, adopting a positive attitude to painting on the street, where of course their work may be removed within minutes. Thankfully the documentation of urban art through social media has been its saving grace. By sharing works with a vast audience online, artists can extend their 'mark', often reaching viewers within real time, or just moments after a piece is finished. For those makers for whom experiencing the context of the work is integral to its message, such forums are of course inherently limiting. However, the positives must outweigh the negatives – blogs and other such forums are essential to the connectedness of the artistic community and fundamental to many of these artists in achieving an audience for their output.

In embracing this philosophy of what it means to 'make your mark', included in this book are many extraordinary artists who express

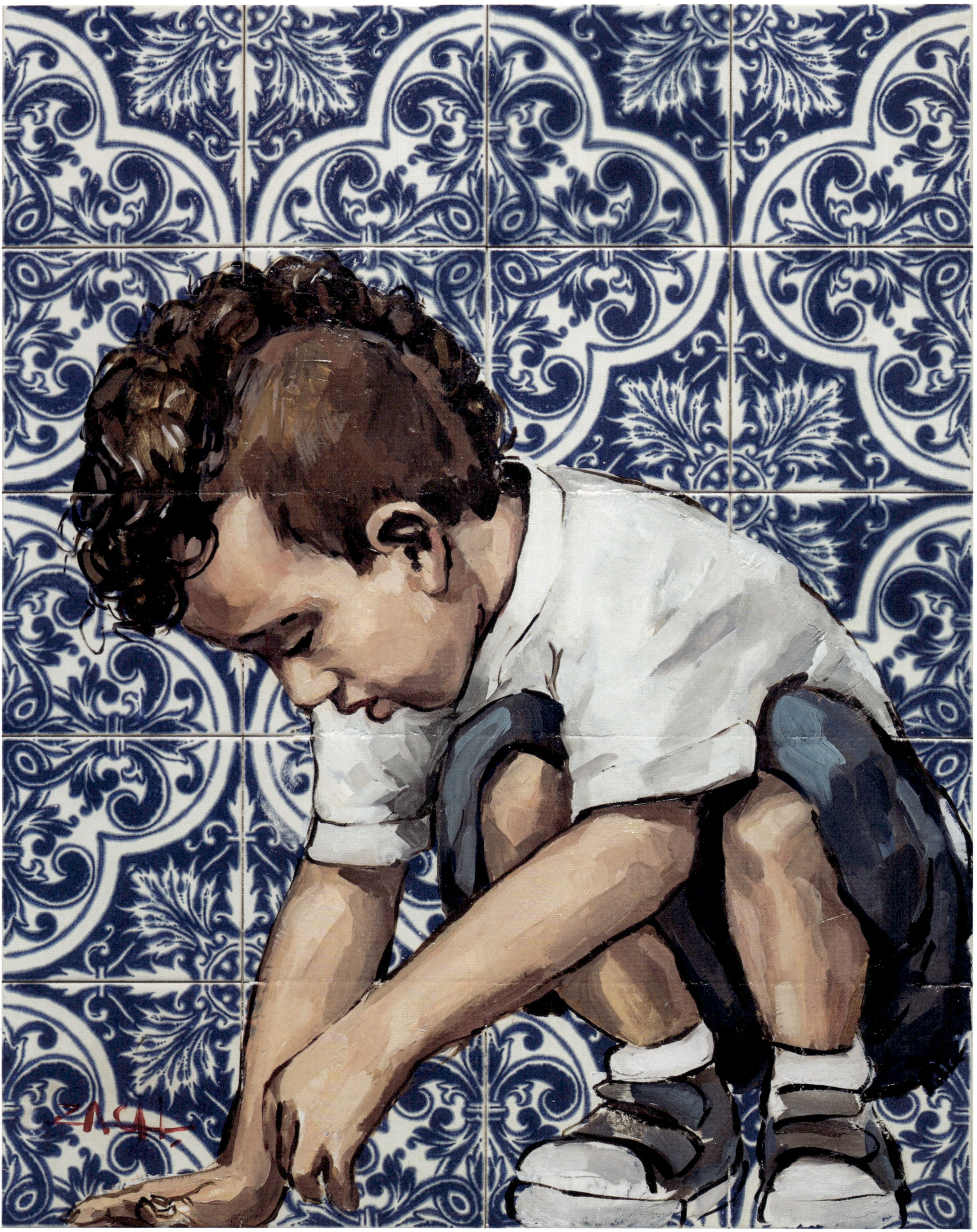

shared concerns, and who are similarly independent in honing their craft. Collectively their practice spans a wide variety of subject-matter, techniques and use of materials: from the playful and punchy tattoo-inspired illustrations of Spanish artist Ricardo Cavolo to the more gentle Neoclassical tones of Brazilian painter João Ruas, the vast murals of the Argentinian muralist Pastel or the extraordinarily intricate drawings of Dutch artist Raymond Lemstra. They are drawn together by their diversity, their imagination, attitude and application. They also display exceptional determination and ingenuity and are uncompromising when it comes to staying true to their vision.

Make Your Mark is a rallying call for artists to embrace this ethos of originality in both concept and craftsmanship. It is an appeal to make art using traditional techniques by hand through drawing, painting and making, but also to propel them forward in truly innovative and imaginative ways that captivate and make us look again. Essentially our focus is on the 'new', works that are fresh and unique. Even if we accept that there is no such thing as absolute originality, it is interesting to see how different artists distil ideas and how their particular experiences and influences unfold in their work. No two artists take the same artistic journey; their passions, backgrounds and motivations bring them to sometimes entirely different conclusions.

This book is divided into three thematic chapters – 'Draw', 'Paint' and 'Make'. However, the lines between these groupings are blurred, with the artists being equally at home in any one of them. Many defy such categories, for example, the Colombian artist Jim Pluk, whose work shifts seamlessly from the comic book to collage and canvas.

The artists in this book sustain their art in multiple ways, using alternative and independent channels to connect with an audience, and displaying a personal vision and mode of expression that is not lost to commercial pressure. Their practice is, as far as possible, integrated into a way of life that is supported by a larger independent art community. Essentially the different platforms, techniques and ways the artists place and share their art are as much part of their practice as is the making of their work.

Ernest Zacharevic
Untitled, from the series 'Floor is Lava', 2015
Oil and mixed media on canvas
Dimensions unknown

44flavours
Untitled, c. 2014
Mixed media
Dimensions unknown

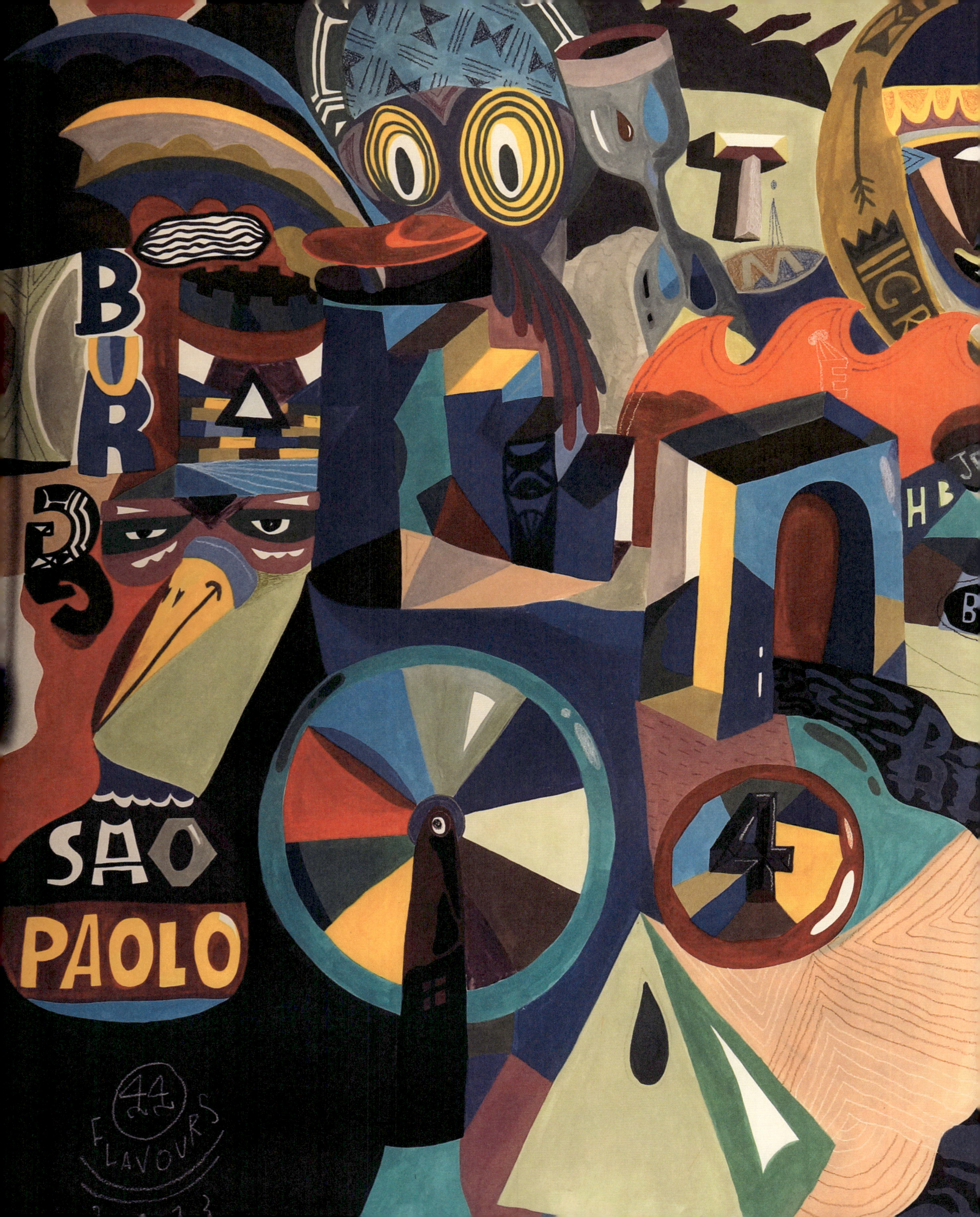
BUR
SAO
PAOLO
44
FLAVOURS
4

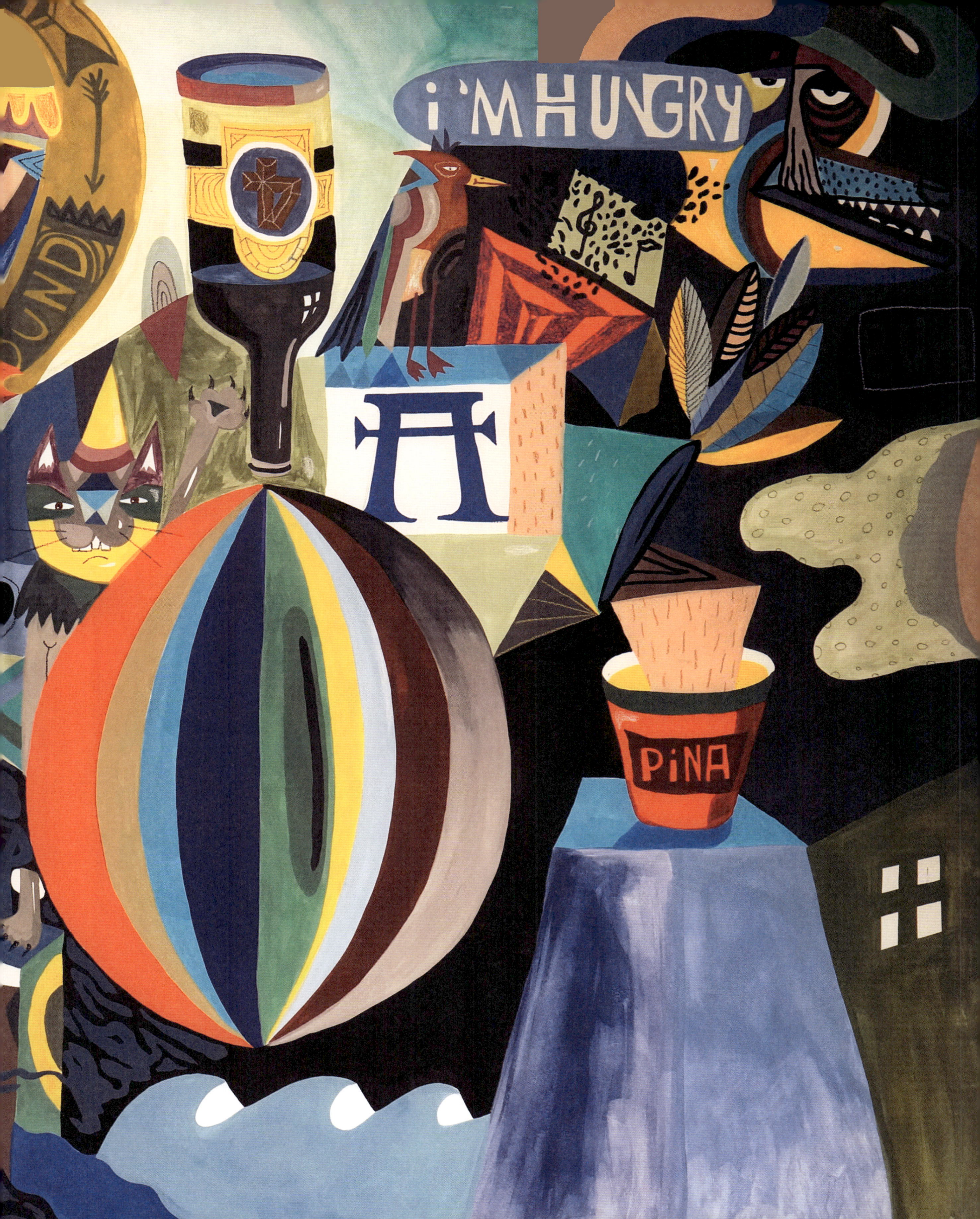

i'M HUNGRY
PiNA

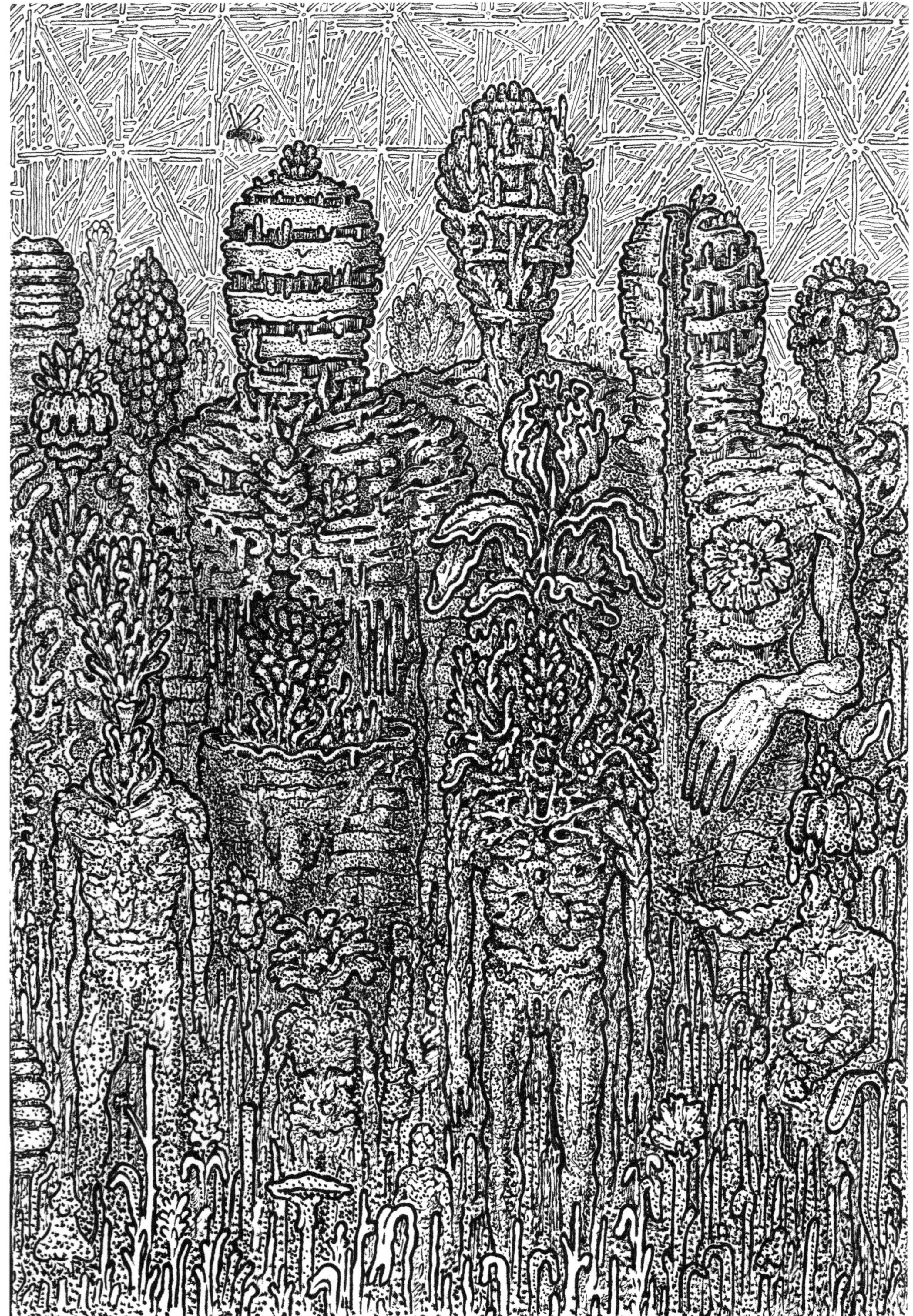

Draw

From the moment – as children – we open our first pack of crayons and then proceed to redecorate our parents' kitchen with them, drawing is the most natural and intuitive way into art-making. It is how we learn to make our mark both literally and creatively. For artists, the joy of drawing often stems from the visceral pleasure it provides and the access it gives to the imagination first unlocked during childhood. This pleasure is evident in the work of the artists included in this chapter, all of whom present us with a fascinating spectrum of approaches to the form. Even in the simplest drawing we can see how each has created their own distinct language of line, visual vocabulary and mastery of technique.

One might assume that all possible new approaches to drawing have been exhausted. However, as the work of the artists in this chapter shows, this age-old technique is being revived afresh through new interpretations. Using methods such as cross-hatching or combining fine gradation with contemporary shapes or unusual subject-matter in their illustrations, artists such as Raymond Lemstra and Ugo Gattoni have re-enlivened the form, as have the other artists (presented here through various means). The laborious processes they deploy in their drawing work seem counterintuitive to the contemporary context in which they are made, but also signify a sort of antidote to 'digital fatigue', coupled with a reburgeoning admiration for this tradition. By referencing the history of drawing the artists pay tribute to the sensibilities of another age: as can be seen in Lemstra's use of aged paper and 1920s typography, which give his work a

vintage feel, or in Gattoni's drawings which, with their balanced proportions and studied precision, express a nod to the Neoclassical. In the digital era, work like this stands out.

With the proliferation of Instagram, Pinterest and other online image-sharing platforms it is interesting to note how some artists appear to be attracted to a visual heritage that, conversely, is pre-Internet, even pre-photography. They share nostalgia for a time in which drawing was in its ascendancy; when, for instance, newspapers were illustrated by hand-drawn etchings rather than by photographs or pixels on a smartphone. Even if the artists in this chapter embrace digital media or are proficient in digital drawing, their subject-matter can often convey the spirit of something far more archaic. This can be seen in the work of artists such as Irena Zablotska from the Ukraine, whose work recalls folkloric iconography, but which she produces in both digital format and media such as pen, coloured pencil and paint. By the same token, the drawings of Canadian artist Bonar have an almost medieval character, like the fantastical illuminations found in the encyclopedias of the middle ages, conjured up by the artists of that time from hearsay and imagination.

Each of the artists in this chapter display a remarkable inventiveness in their drawing, whether in terms of a particular style or idiosyncratic fusion of influences. Equally, they might experiment with format or technique, as can be seen in Gattoni's vast architecturally themed panoramas, which are drawn either on paper or walls, or in the application of bespoke techniques, such as the multi-processed drawing and monoprint methods of the British artist Mark Francis Williams. With their alternative backgrounds, experiences and influences, each artist has naturally developed a novel approach to mark making, as is displayed by the smooth lines

Bonar
Forest People, 2015
Ink on paper
Dimensions unknown

and curvilinear forms of Danish artist Rune Fisker, the curved isometric shapes of New Zealand-based artist and illustrator T-Wei and the loose strokes and blocks of colour used by Austrian graffiti artist Mafia. For them, the quality or aesthetic of their mark is significant to their message, something that Williams likens to 'the way a note is played in music…. The distinctiveness of the line, dot, smear or scratch, which articulates and engineers the narrative of a piece.'

The process of drawing is evolutionary. Throughout this chapter rough and finished drawings are illustrated, and it is possible to see how sketches develop from thumbnails into finished works, how ideas germinate and how visual choices have been made along the way. Drawing – often perceived only as a preparatory process in the making of artworks in other media – is now becoming increasingly valued as an art form in its own right. Across visual fields from illustration to fine art, awards, exhibitions and art fairs, such as 'Drawing Now Paris', are being solely dedicated to the form.

In this chapter, drawing is celebrated, with incredibly accomplished and inspiringly diverse examples. To provide a more comprehensive view of their oeuvre, also shown are works by these artists in other media, encompassing sculpture, tattoo design, printmaking, painting – on canvas and walls – to illustrate how the qualities of their drawing work translates into other forms.

More than half of the artists featured here have a background in or work with graffiti, street art or mural painting, as well as making pieces in the studio. The lines between these areas are blurred; with some makers aligning themselves with a more classic or post-graffiti sensibility, such as Mafia and fellow Austrian, Knarf – who often paint spontaneous pieces, sometimes incorporating the letter styles of traditional graffiti, as well as making more intricate murals – while the largely figurative output of the artists Aryz and Sainer, from Spain and Poland respectively, aligns itself more closely with the new muralist movement, with both making works on a vast scale. Something else that this chapter hones in on is how their experiences as street artists filter into their other endeavours. How, for instance, do the expressive qualities and sense of freedom born from working outside, often in an improvised fashion, become manifest in the studio? While each artist takes a particular stance in this respect, a symbiotic relationship appears to emerge between the visual language, methodology and processes that play out in both arenas.

Each of the artists in this chapter brings a broad mix of styles to the genres in which they work. For instance, French artist Bault and Spanish artist Dulk create wonderfully stylized character-based pieces with a comic art sensibility. Both makers are drawn towards animals as a theme; Bault's vision verges on the fantastical while also dwelling on ecological themes, whereas Dulk's output has a surreal fairytale quality. Comic art permeates the work of the artists selected here in other ways, too. One example is Aryz, whose output alludes to the work of contemporary graphic novel artists, such as Miguelanxo Prado (b. 1958) or Shaun Tan (b. 1974), but also demonstrates his knowledge of classical art and a practice based in observational work. His sketchbooks are a delight to see, in terms of how he transitions between his drawings and colour studies in paint. Comic art in a more narrative form is also represented by the inclusion of Colombian artist Jim Pluk, who produces wordless stories based on human observation; a humorous take on people's foibles and their experiences of modern life. Representing another form of visual culture growing in importance, namely tattoo art, is the work of Canadian artist David Côté. Through his sketches and finished tattoos it can be seen how drawings are embodied and brought to life.

Drawing is a powerful tool for communicating concepts and narratives that cannot quite be put into words. The artists in this chapter use this tool in numerous ways – enticing us through line and shade, delighting us with unexpected contrasts or juxtapositions and surprising us by breaking with pictorial convention and creating refreshingly original images. Their work can be extraordinarily accomplished and yet still remain low tech and accessible, allowing the viewer to connect with it in an honest and direct fashion. Today, we can teach a computer to draw but it cannot reveal the human spirit in the same way these artists can.

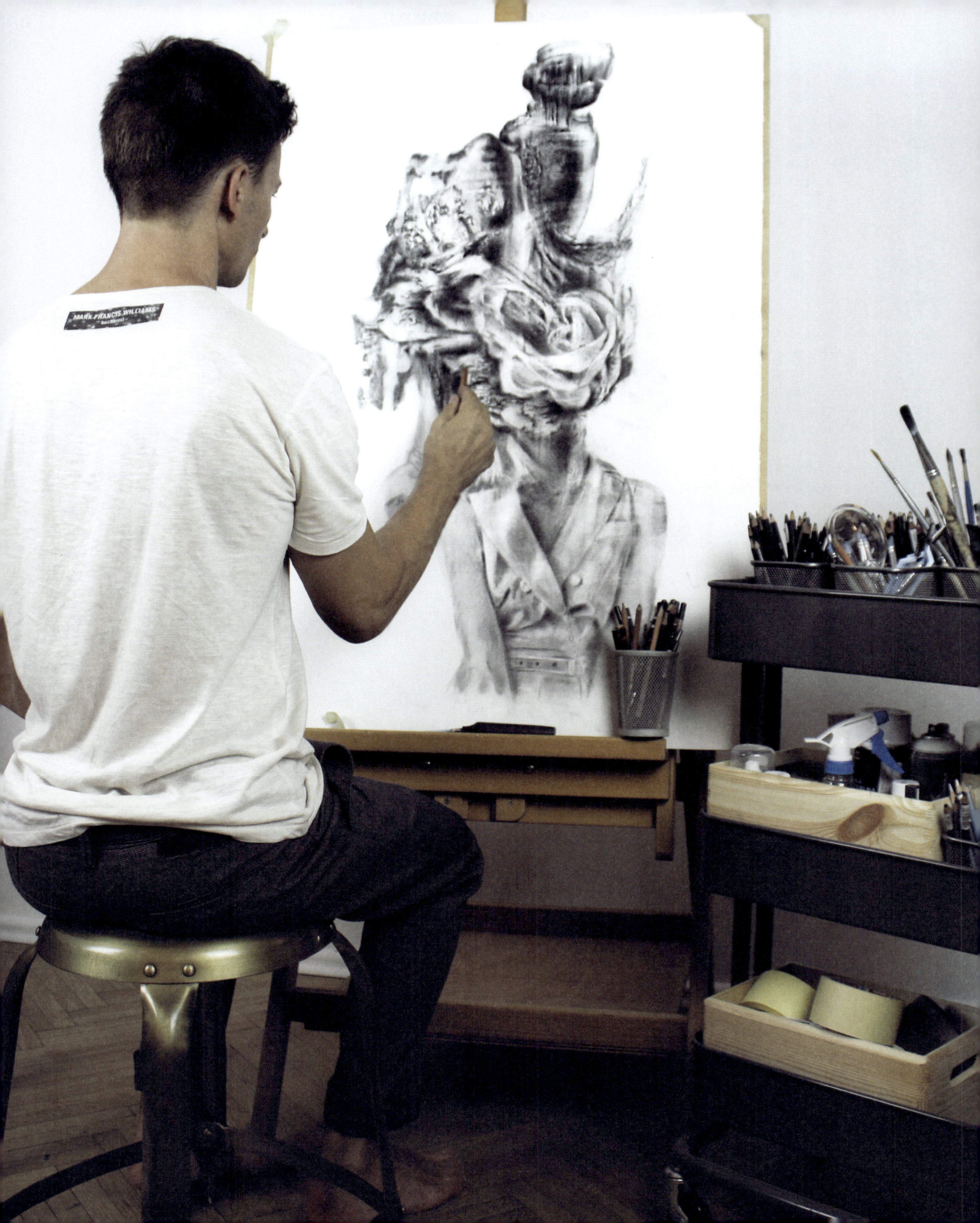

Aryz
Since he began making his characteristic oversized murals,

Barcelona-born Aryz has gained a deserved reputation for being an exceptional talent. At just twenty-six he has amassed an extraordinary collection of work in locations around the world, including Spain, Portugal, Scandinavia, Poland and the US, as well as receiving critical acclaim for the exhibitions of his paintings and sculptures in Spain and the US.

Part of Aryz's charm is that his subject-matter is unpredictable; other than a predilection for the skull as a motif, themes range from the sublime to the ridiculous – an idyllic scene populated with Greek gods, still lifes, a horse on a bicycle, a peacock wearing a bow tie, dancing ostriches – all painted on the façades of lived-in and derelict buildings. There is a dry irony and absurdity to his choice of imagery, while at the same time a sense of pathos or melancholy. His approach,

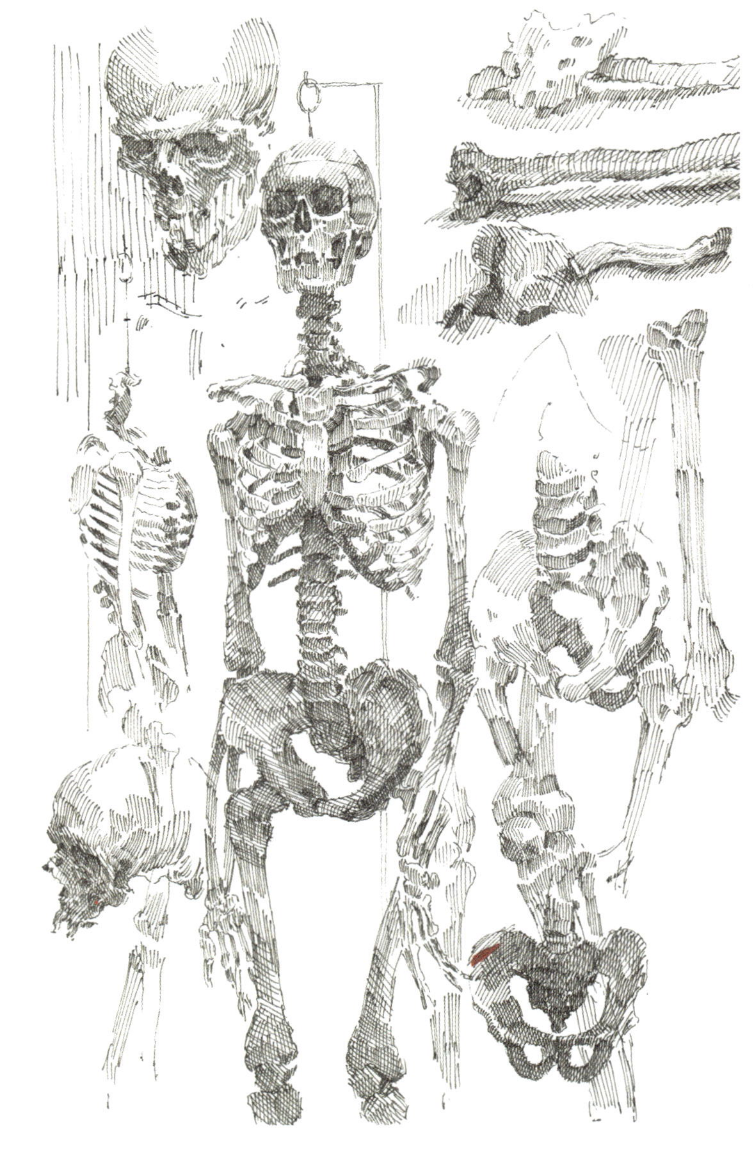

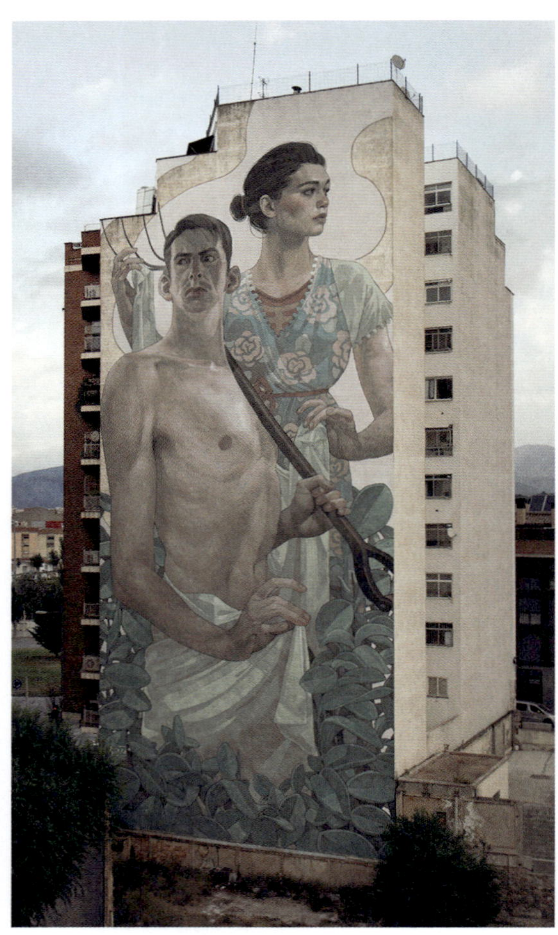

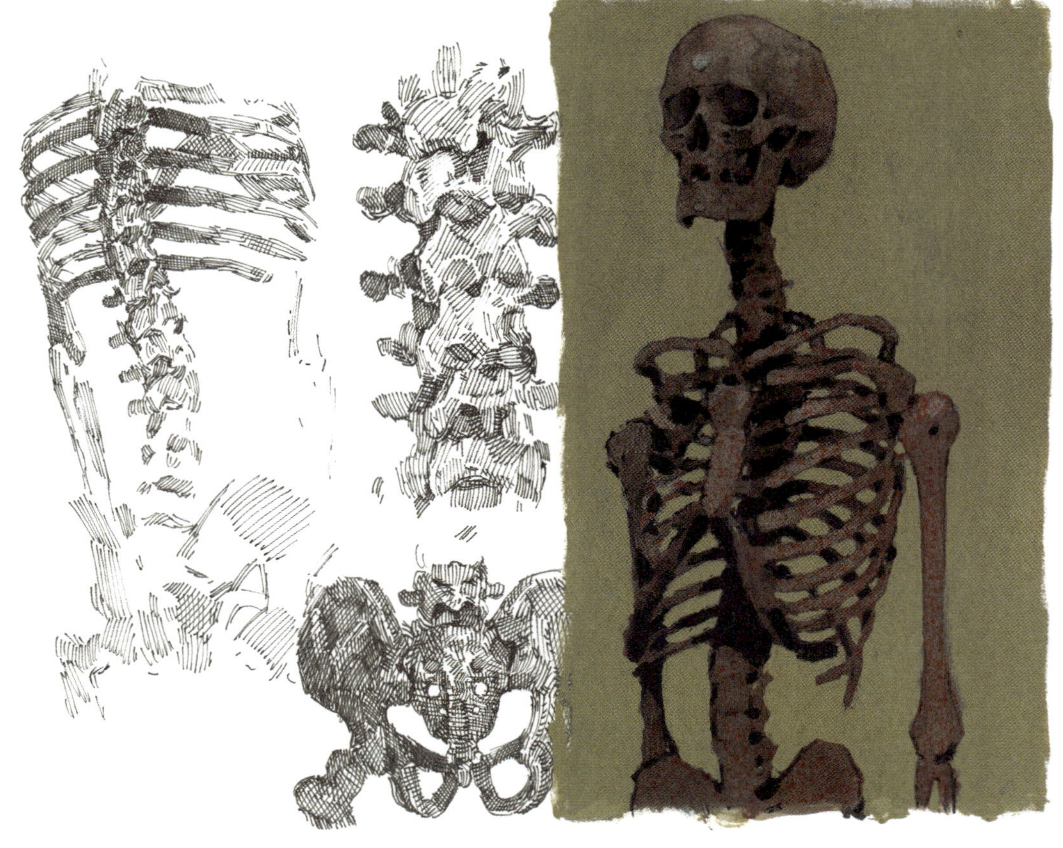

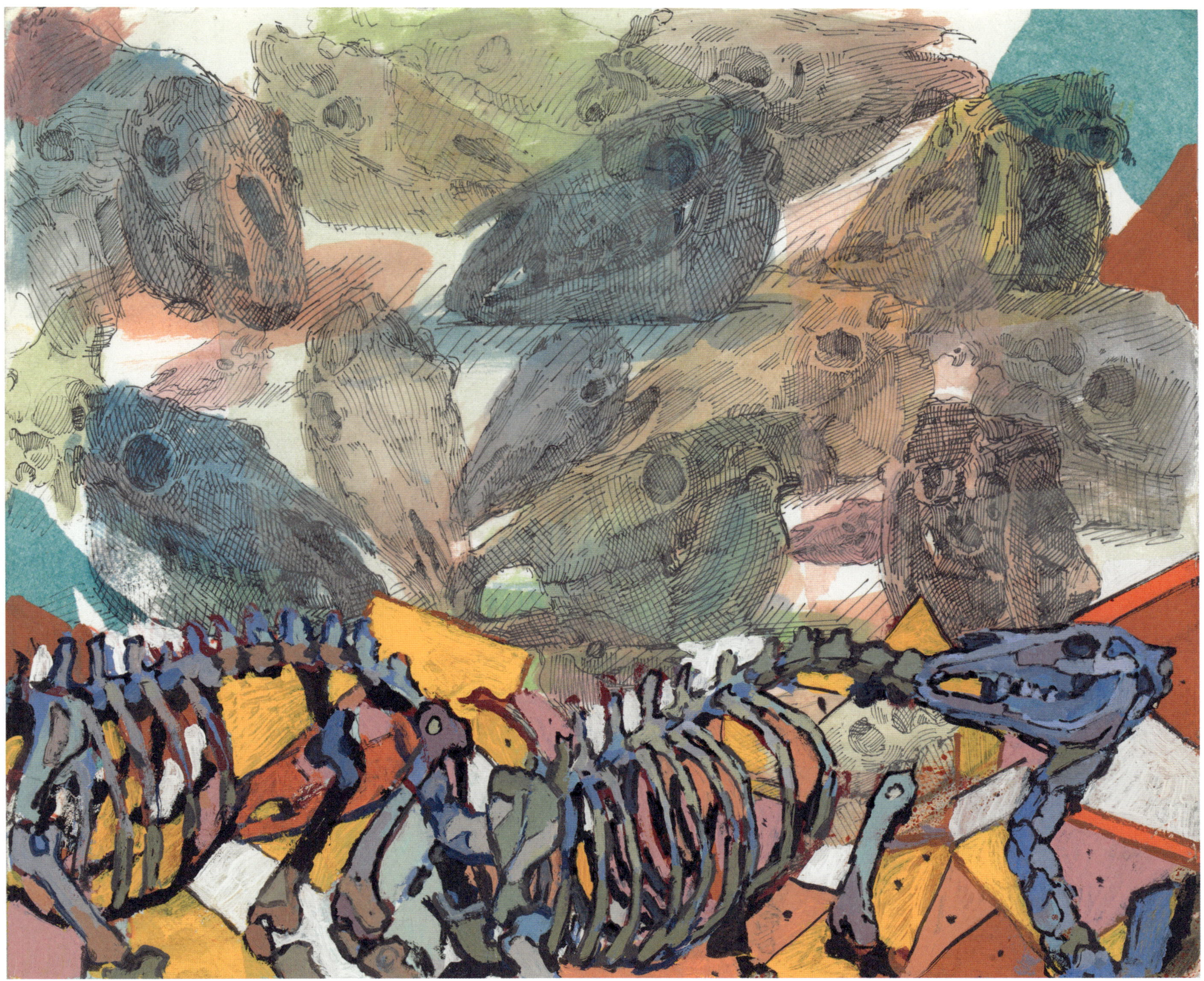

Pages from the artist's
sketchbook, 2012

Untitled, mural in
Granollers, Spain, 2014
House paint
Dimensions unknown

Pages from the artist's
sketchbook, 2012

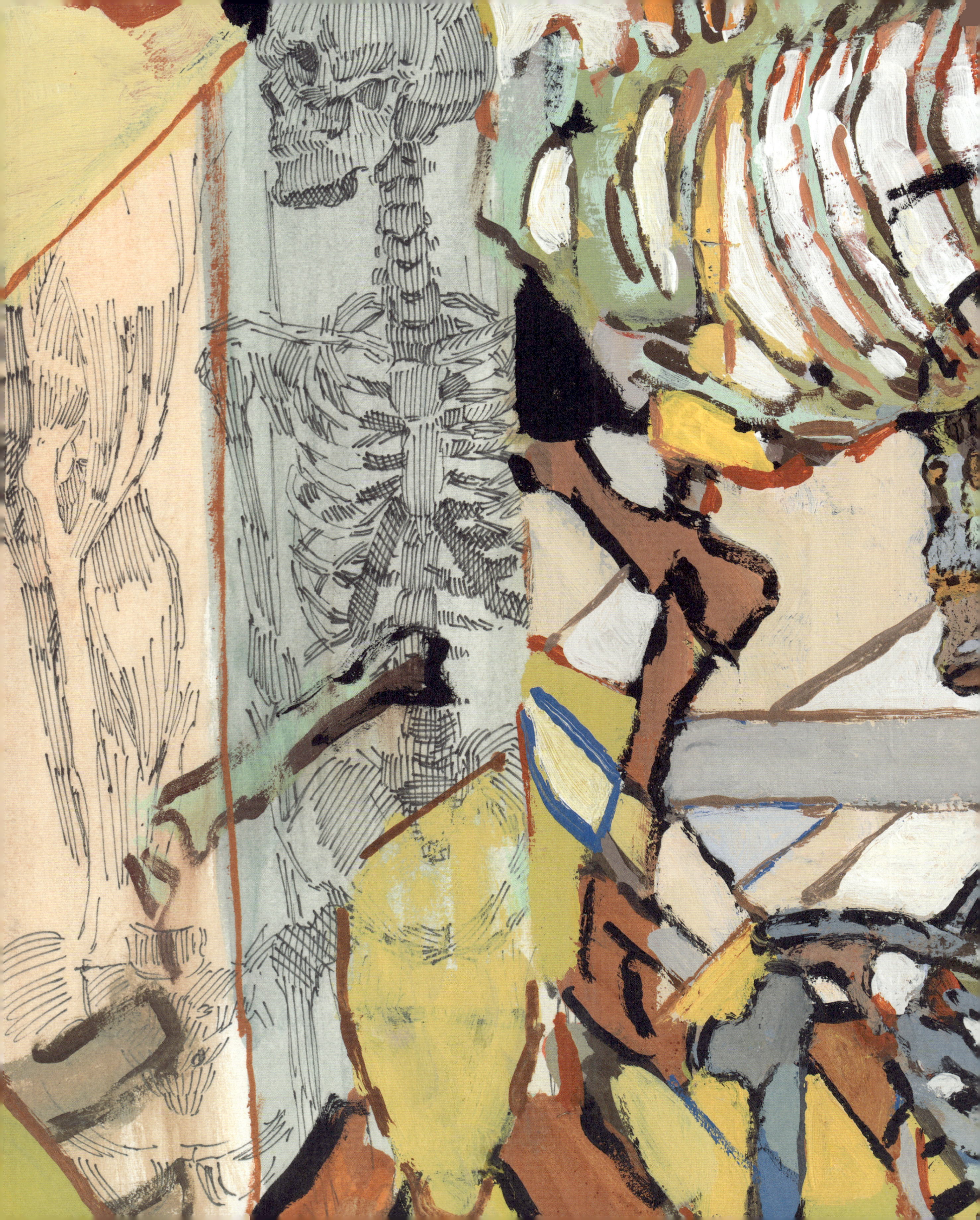

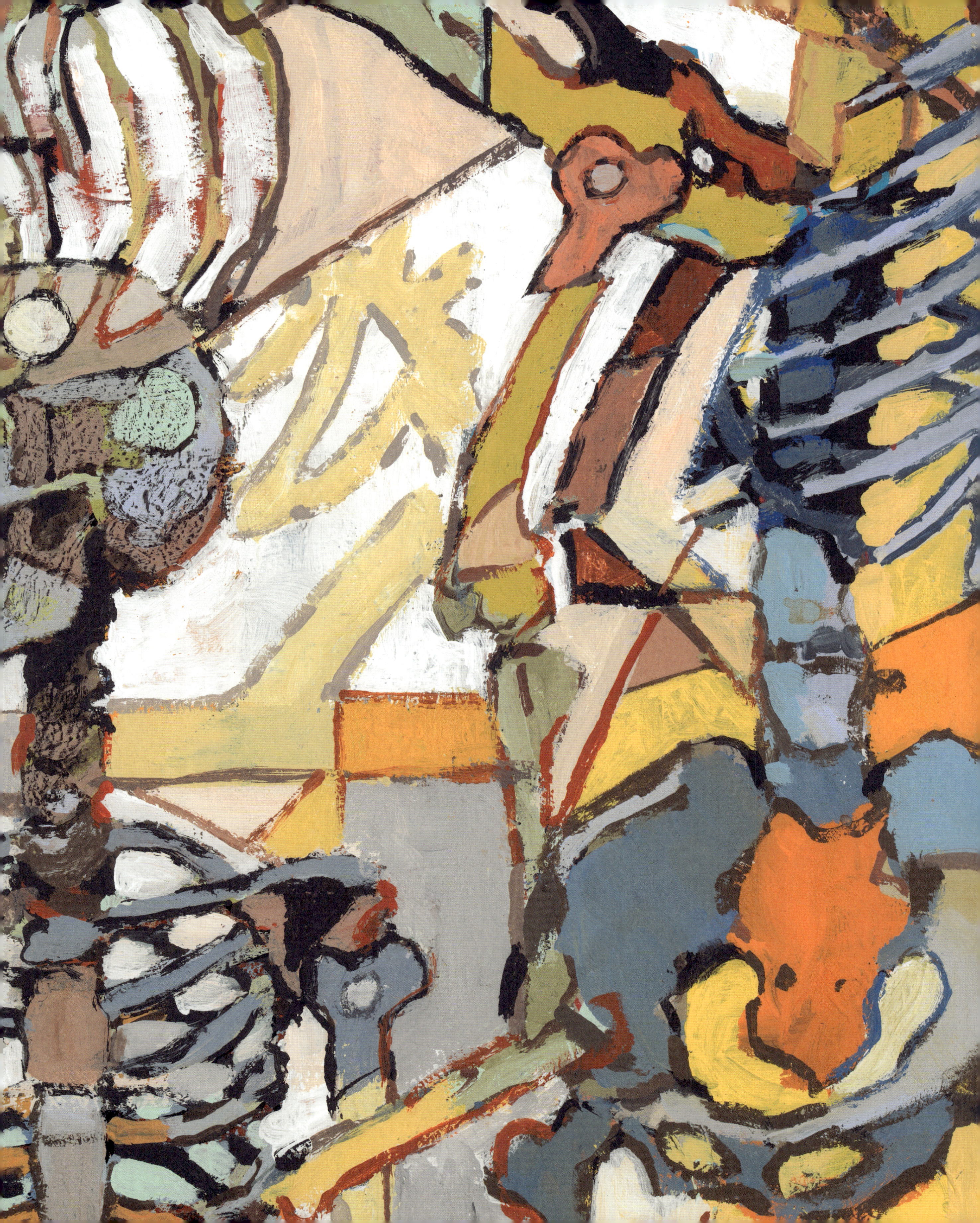

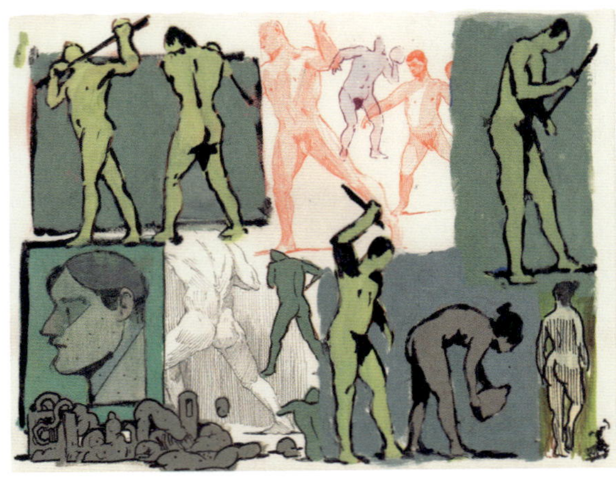
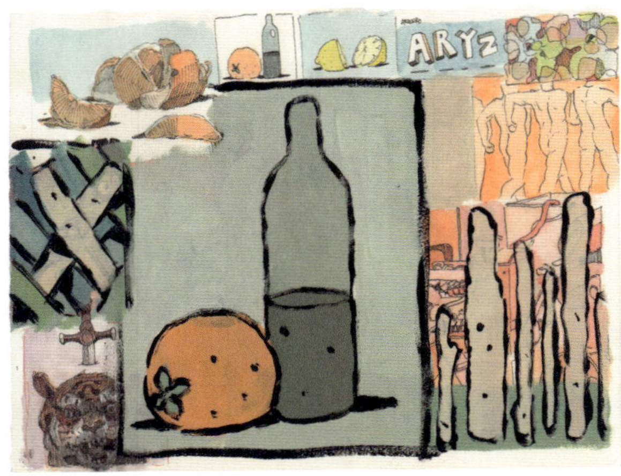
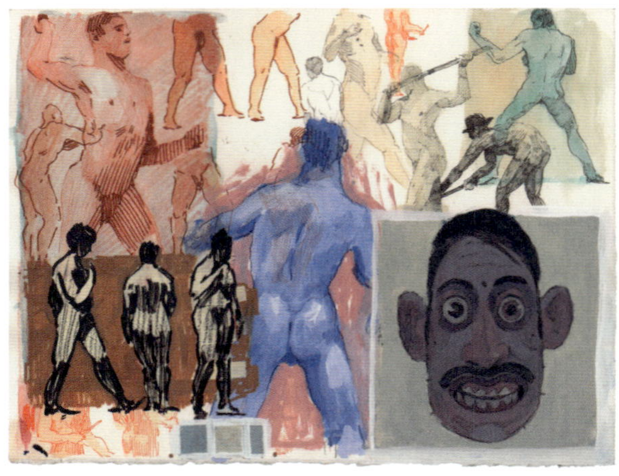
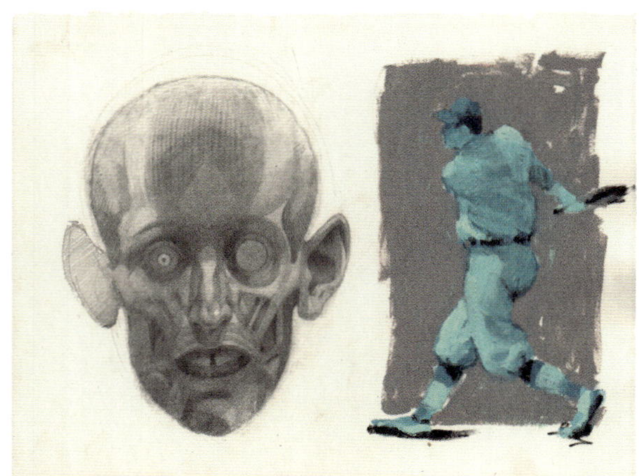

ABOVE, BELOW AND OPPOSITE
**Pages from the artist's
sketchbook, 2013–14**

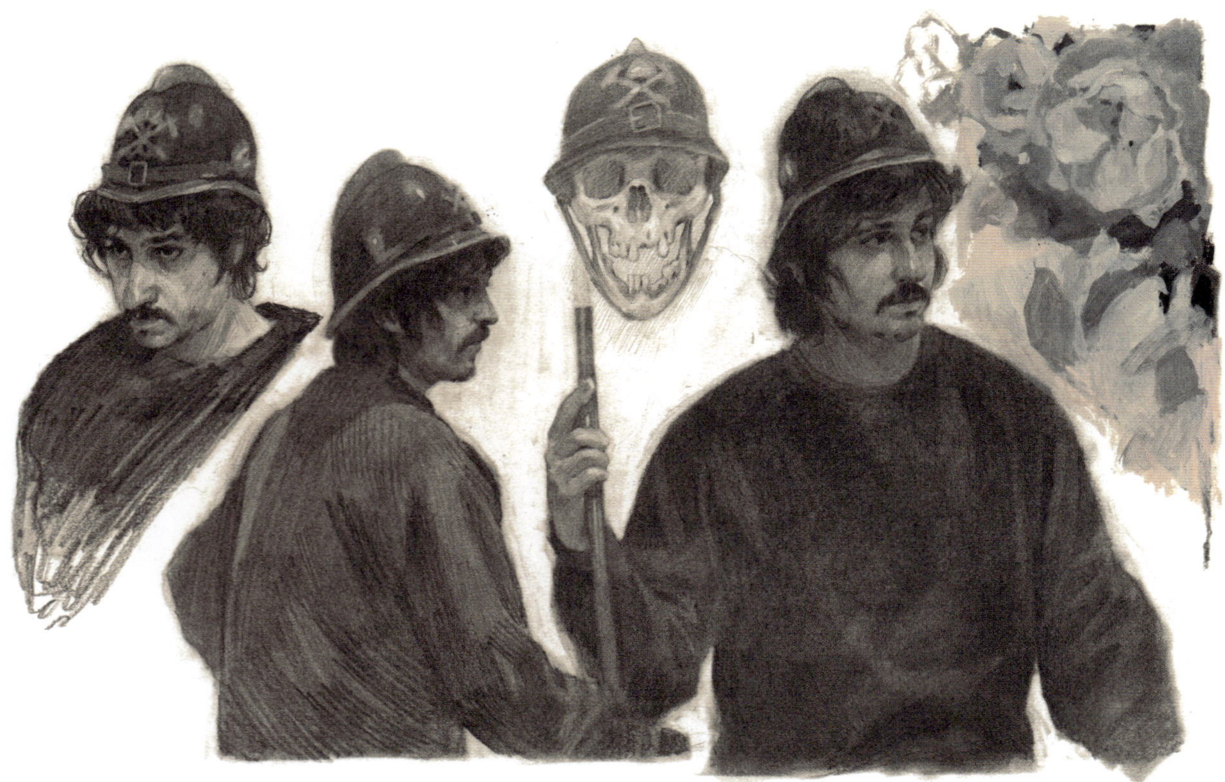

he claims, is instinctual rather than conceptually led, and he prioritizes colour and composition over ideas. Aryz's colour palette developed naturally – when he first started making murals he did so in abandoned factories, using recycled pastel-coloured house paint, to which he later added black. The result was an overall grey, muted tone quite unlike the bright palette to which street art typically lends itself.

In addition to making highly detailed and intricate murals, Aryz is also an illustrator; and underlying this practice is an accomplished draftsmanship. Drawing on the work of the Old Masters in his characteristic cross-hatching style, he experiments with volume, light and shade. In his line work he has developed a natural understanding of anatomy, as well as forms found in the natural world, which he then further stylizes. Aryz's sketches – loose brushstrokes of desaturated colours that follow strong lines – are condensed versions of what later comes to life on the canvas or wall, illustrating well the artist's transition from drawing to painting within his practice.

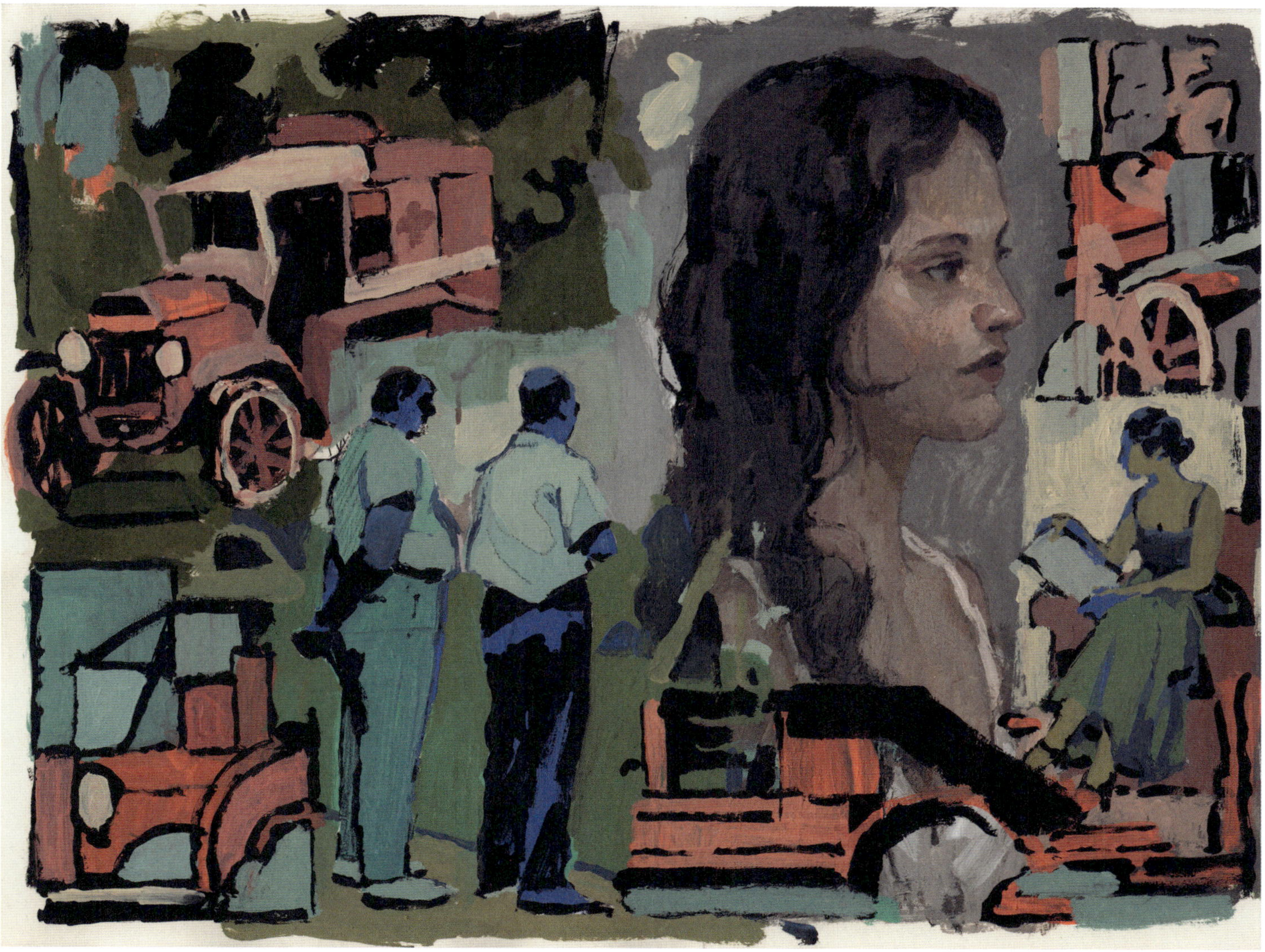

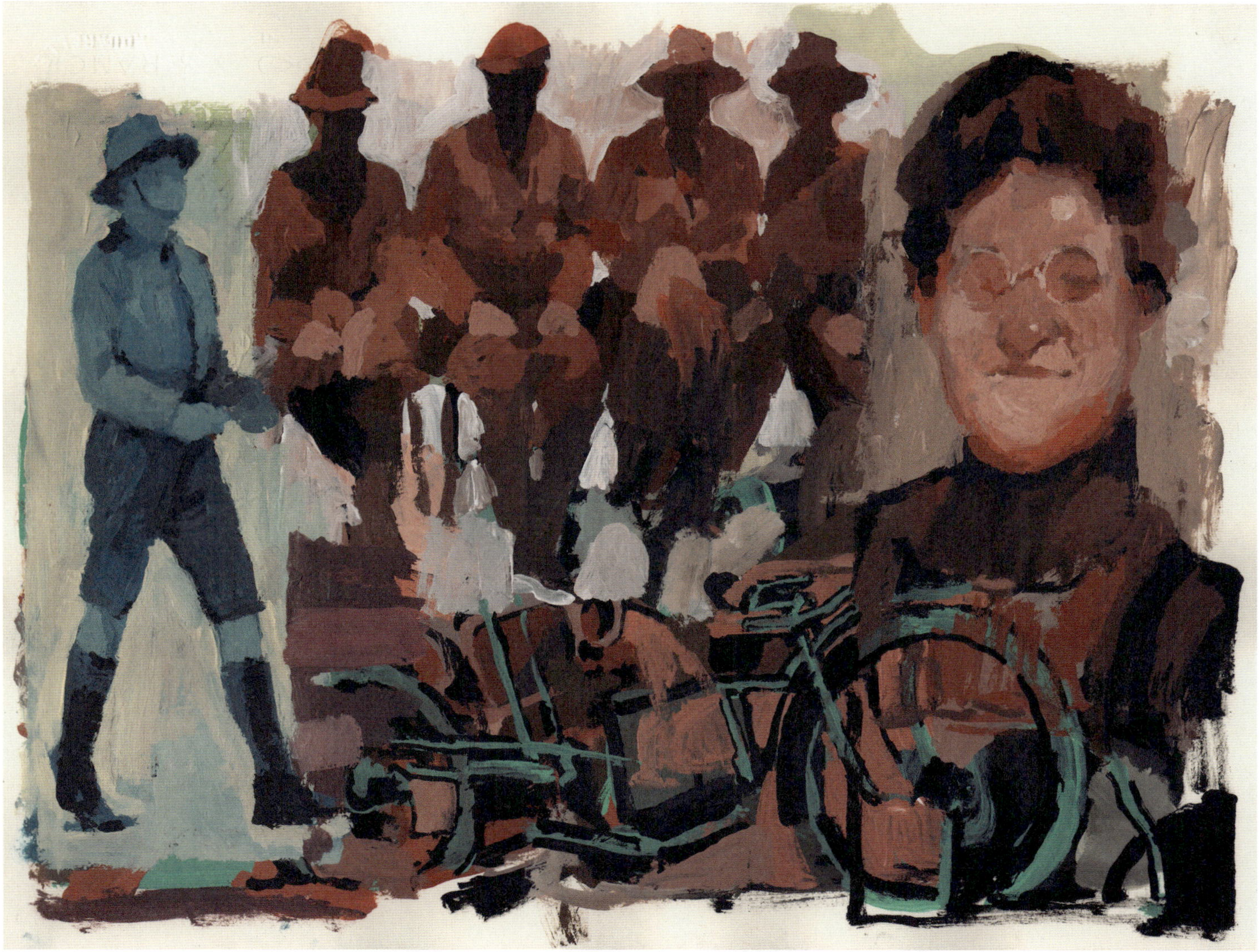

Bault

Renowned for his astonishingly inventive street paintings that feature a carnival of strange, hybrid characters, such as four-legged boats transporting unconventional creatures, toucans with wheels for feet and figures with oversized heads and limbs, Paris-based Bault's whirlwinds of weirdness are painted prolifically by the artist both in urban and rural locations.

Working alone, and in collaboration with other street artists, such as Perk and Friend, Bault started making graffiti work in 1998, a practice that has formed the backbone of his output ever since. He studied at the Avignon Fine Arts School and the Decorative Arts School in Strasbourg, and since then has developed a career in studio art, graphic design and video. All these disciplines find in common his love of detail and the influence of Surrealism, tribal art and the French *bande dessinée* comic strip aesthetic.

Whether working on walls, paper or canvas, Bault blots marks of colour on to the surface, into which he 'cuts shapes' to reveal the subject. In these works, he claims, he is forging 'links between very

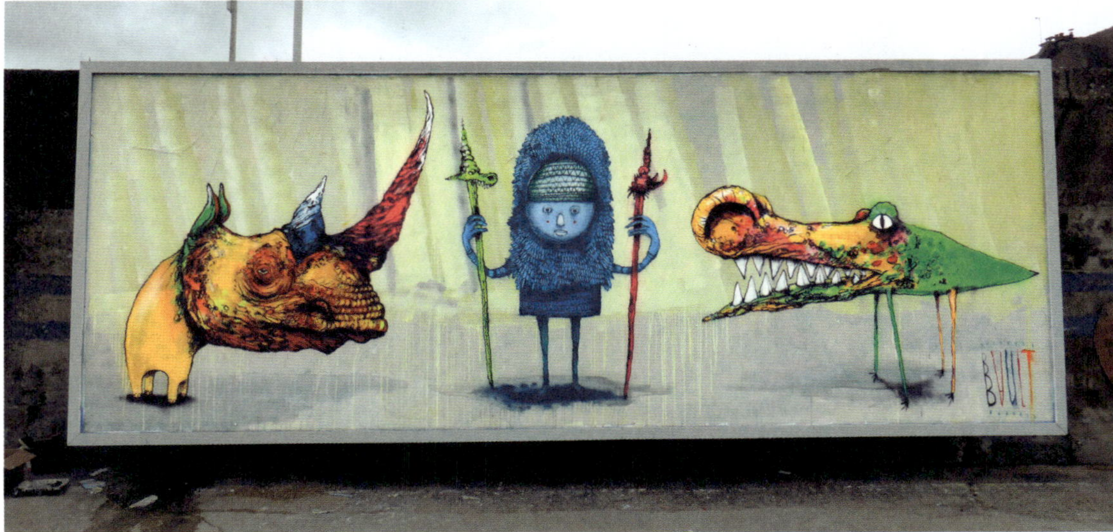

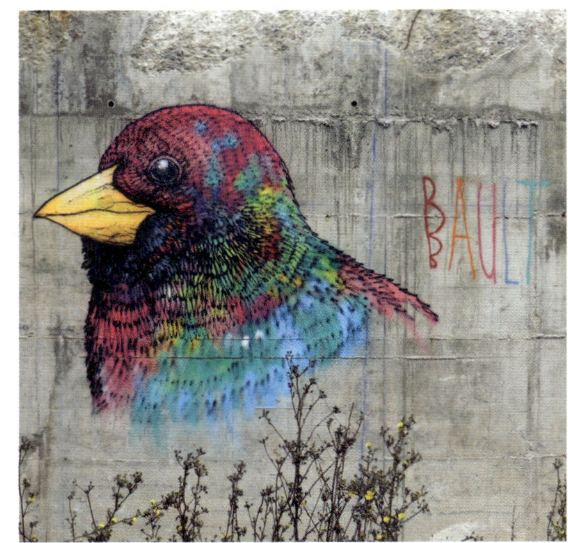

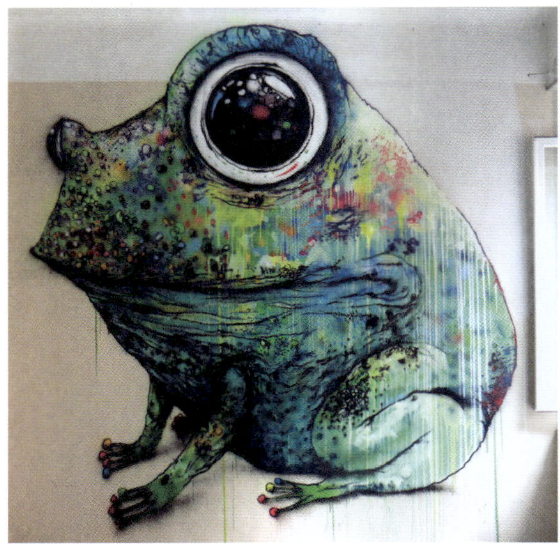

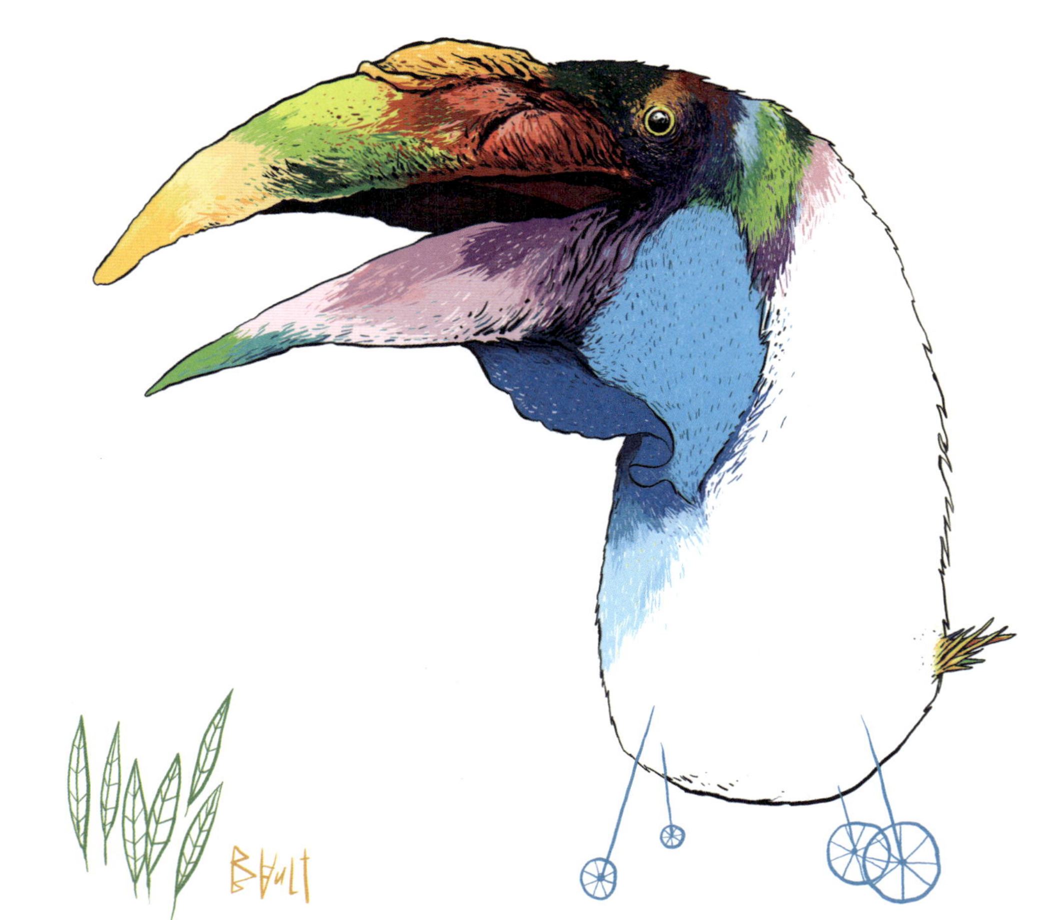

CLOCKWISE FROM TOP
Festival of Rain, mural in Arromanche, Normandy, France, 2014
Spray paint and acrylic
400 × 800 cm
(157½ × 315 in.)

Frog, mural commissioned by 'L'Expo de Ouf 3', Nîmes, France, 2014
Spray paint and acrylic
250 × 350 cm
(98½ × 174⅛ in.)

Tuk Tuk, 2014
Offset print
60 × 60 cm
(23⅝ × 23⅝ in.)

Bird, mural in Rodez, France, 2014
Spray paint
100 × 100 cm
(39⅜ × 39⅜ in.)

OPPOSITE
Owl, 2014
Offset print
80 × 60 cm
(31½ × 23⅝ in.)

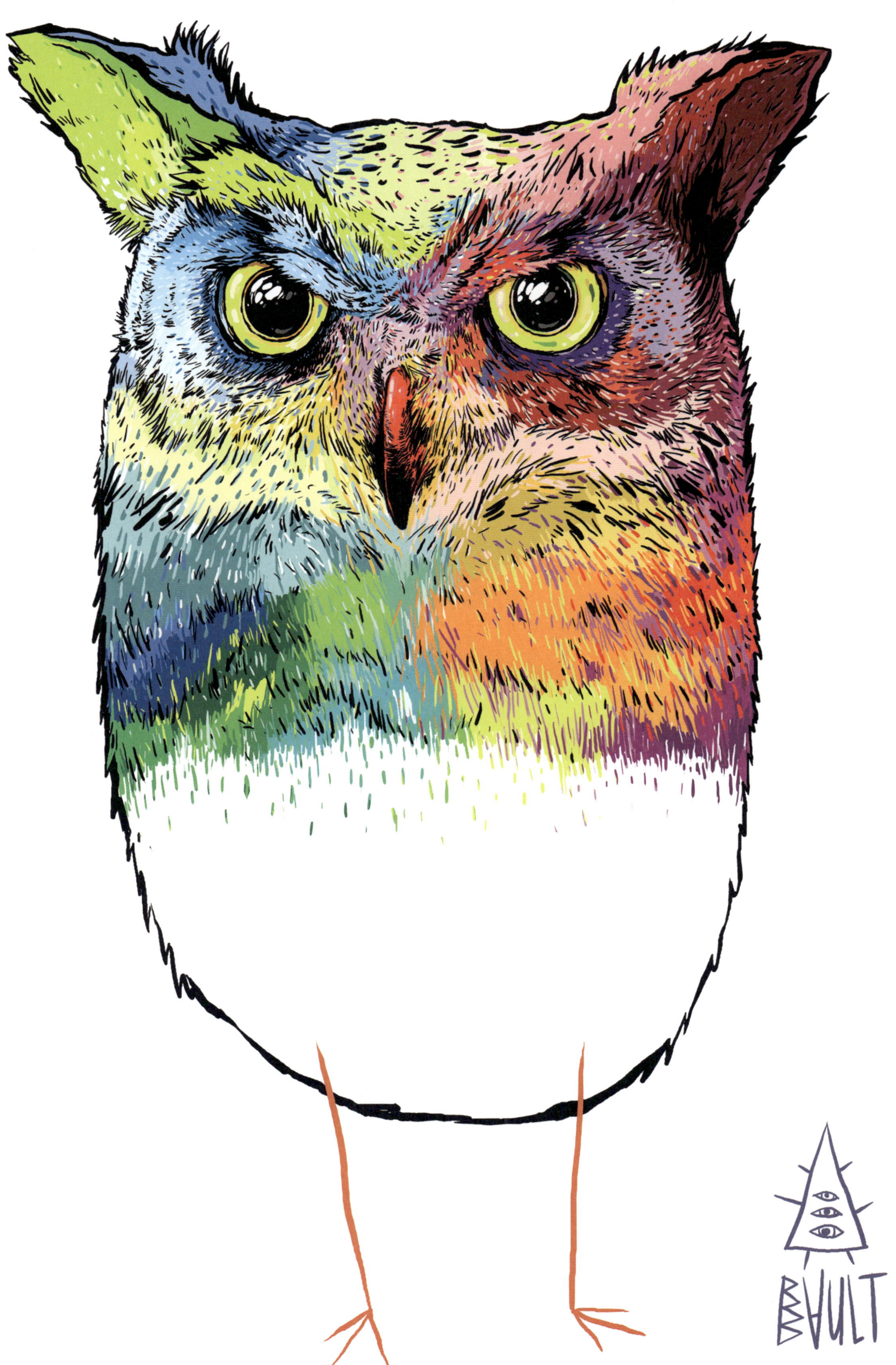

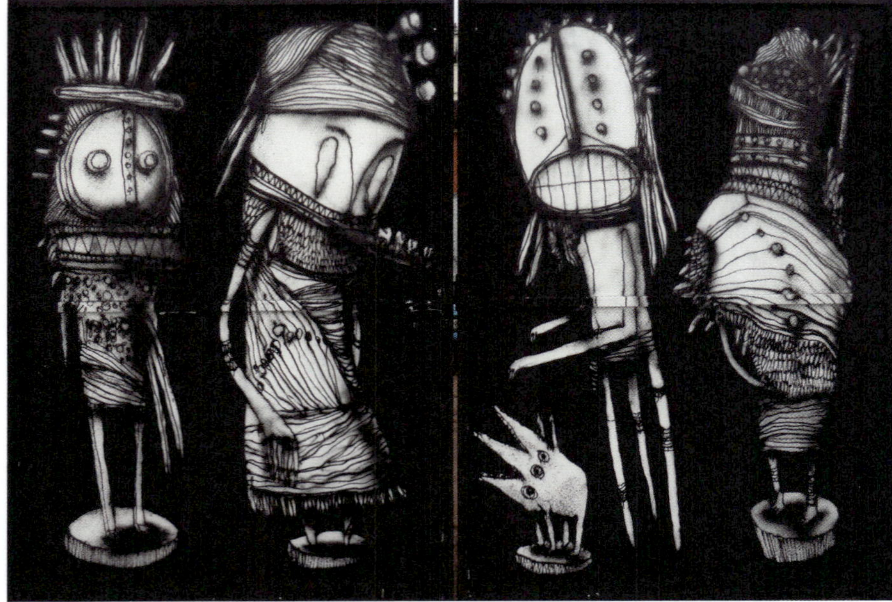

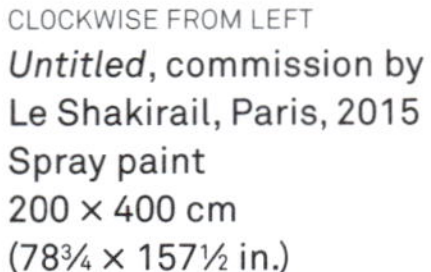

Untitled, commission by
Le Shakirail, Paris, 2015
Spray paint
200 × 400 cm
(78¾ × 157½ in.)

Jelly Fish, 2014
Acrylic on metal
40 × 20 cm (15¾ × 7⅞ in.)

Fire Maker, 2014
Acrylic on paper
40 × 20 cm (15¾ × 7⅞ in.)

Boat to Somewhere, 2015
Acrylic and spray paint
on paper
80 × 60 cm (31½ × 23⅝ in.)

Pandemist, 2015
Acrylic and spray paint
on metal
45 × 30 cm (17¾ × 11¾ in.)

Rain Maker, 2015
Acrylic and spray paint
on metal
45 × 30 cm (17¾ × 11¾ in.)

OPPOSITE, CLOCKWISE FROM TOP RIGHT
Coral Fish, 2015
Acrylic and graphite on paper
80 × 60 cm (31½ × 23⅝ in.)

Pandemist, 2015
Acrylic and graphite on paper
80 × 60 cm (31½ × 23⅝ in.)

Microcosme, 2015
Acrylic and graphite on paper
80 × 60 cm (31½ × 23⅝ in.)

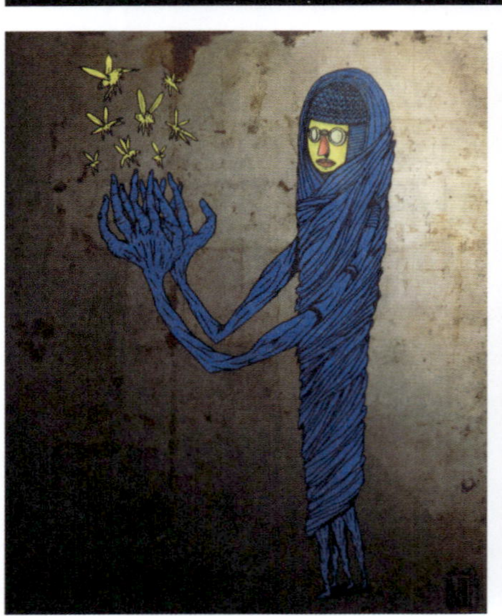

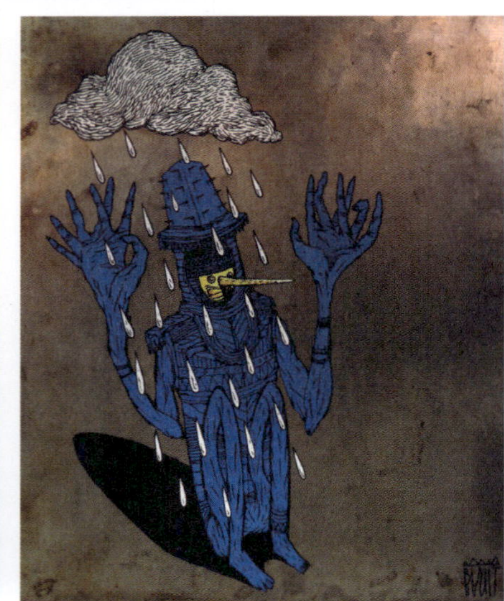

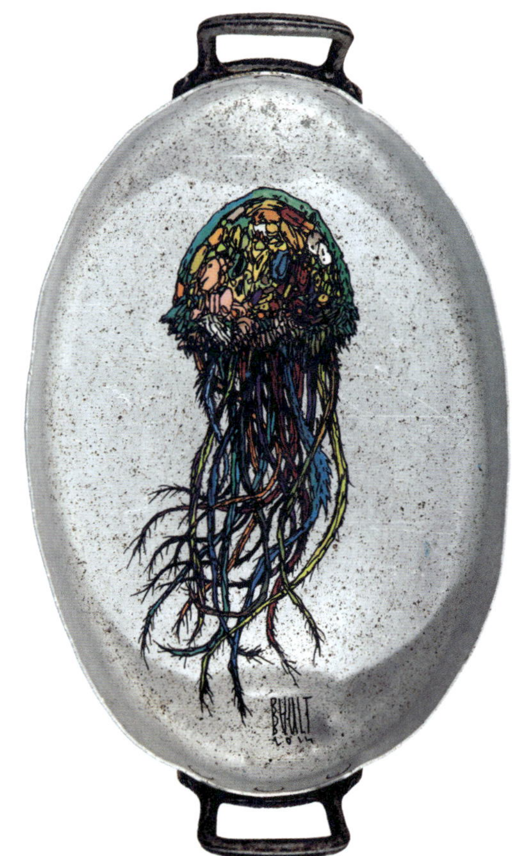

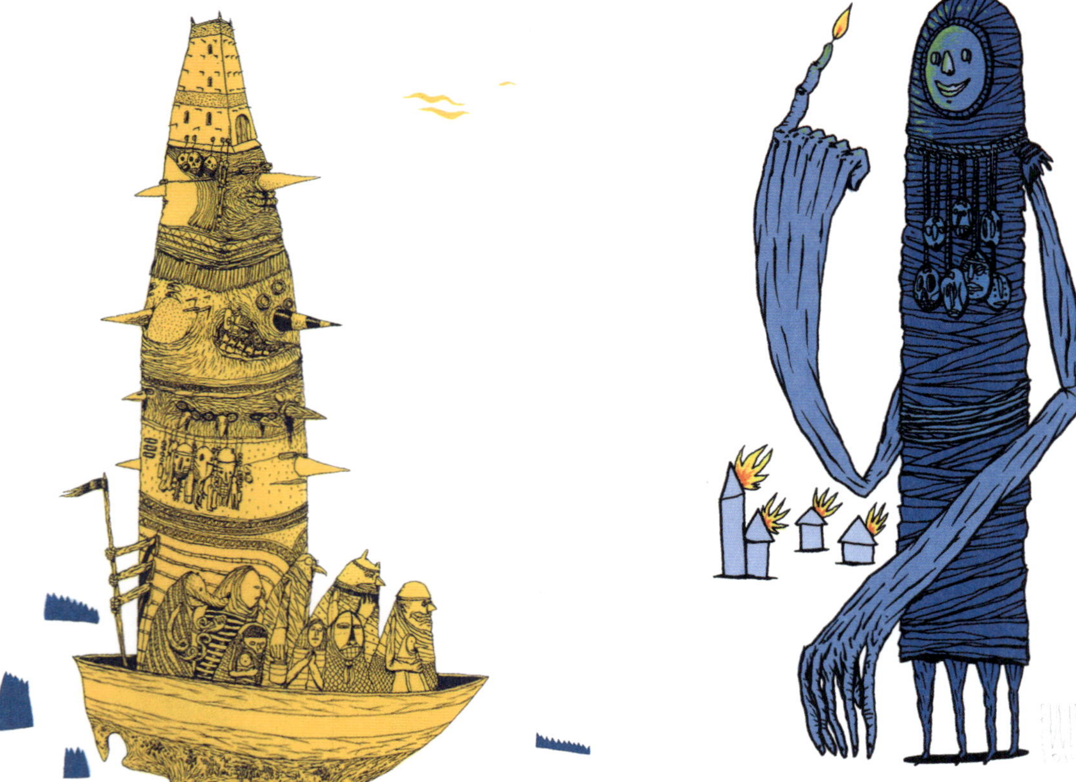

naive representation, abstraction, contrasted with
more realistic or designed parts; it's like narrating
different stories or making a break or juxtaposition
within the narration or, sometimes, just a discussion
between noisy graphics and light spaces.'

A pervading theme throughout is the relationship
between humans and animals; elements of which are
combined into surprising amalgamations that reflect
upon ecology and the fragility of the natural world.
More recent events, such as the terrorist attack at the
offices of Charlie Hebdo in Paris in 2015, have caused
him to reveal other concerns, namely social intolerance
and integration, themes that he explores with a sense
of irony, using symbols such as fetishes and voodoo
statues to signify marginalized social groups.

Bault likes to experiment with media – Chinese ink,
wood, feathers – and with technique, often using his
fingers alone to make marks. He also deploys a pen
tablet in his drawings, since it allows him more freedom
to edit his work. Whether working by hand or employing
digital media, the act of drawing and painting, he feels,
takes him back to basics: 'When you paint a wall, there
is the freedom of movement, the apprehension of space
that is unique. It's like going back to the ancient cave
paintings. I'm a caveman with an iPhone.'

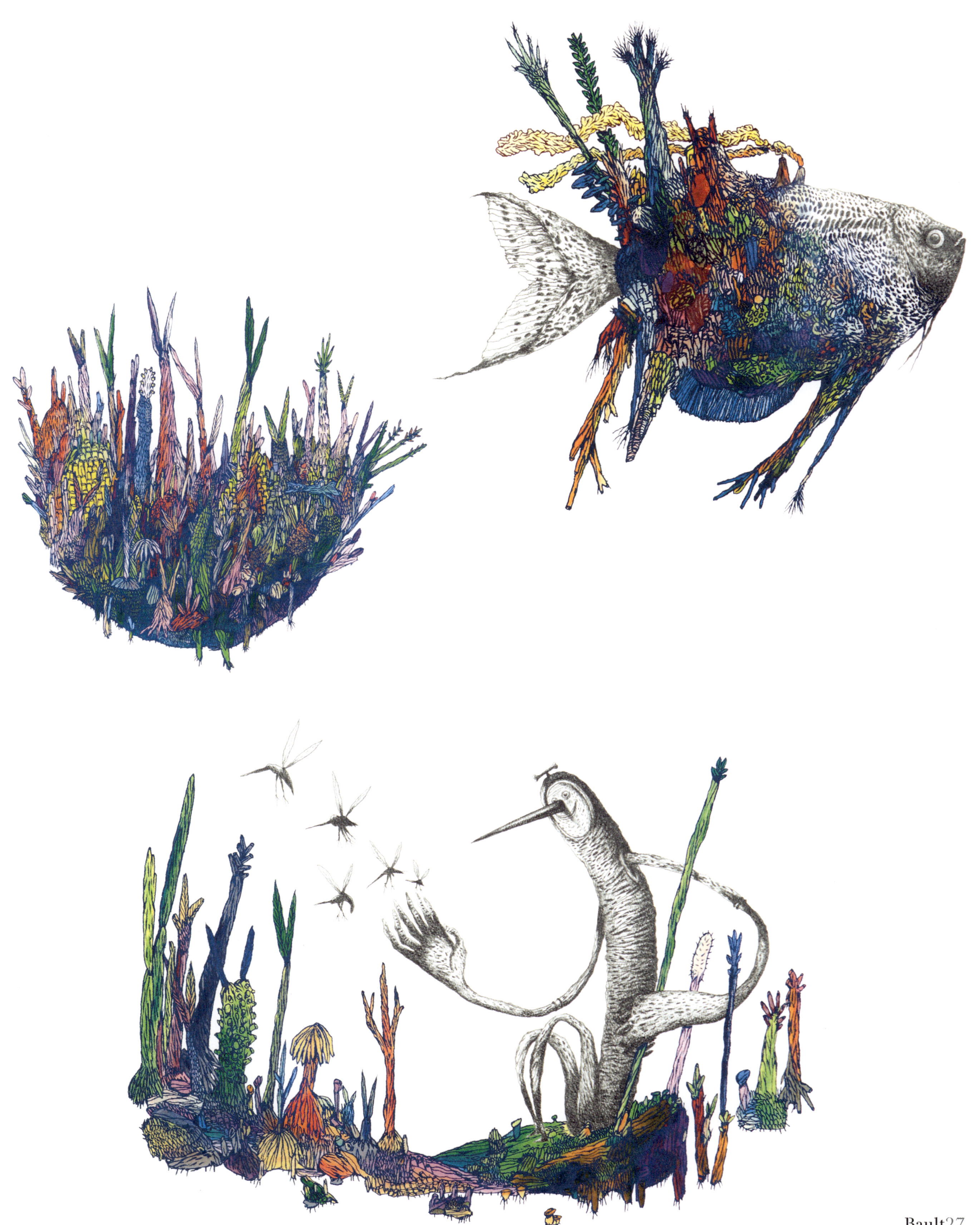

Bault27

Bonar

Part of a new generation of exciting young artists emerging from Montreal's creative scene,

Bonar (aka Olivier Bonnard) claims among his influences Pop, Surrealism and lowbrow art. His work is vastly inventive, complex and multifaceted and he works prolifically in many different media, such as illustration, painting, mural art, animation and, most recently, sculpture. Having studied animation for six years, graduating from the Cégep du Vieux Montréal in 2010, Bonar has since gone on to direct a number of shorts in his career as animator. As an artist he aims to continuously challenge himself and to step out of his comfort zone: 'I don't want to be known for one thing. Doing the same stuff over and over without exploring seems boring to me, I try to keep it alive.'

In all of his endeavours Bonar strives for autonomy, restricting commissions only to those that spark his interest and allow him some freedom of expression: 'If I feel like doing something dark, I do it, I don't try to please.' He likes to break with visual convention, injecting unusual sinewy forms and a distinctive colour palette into his fabulously strange and unexplained

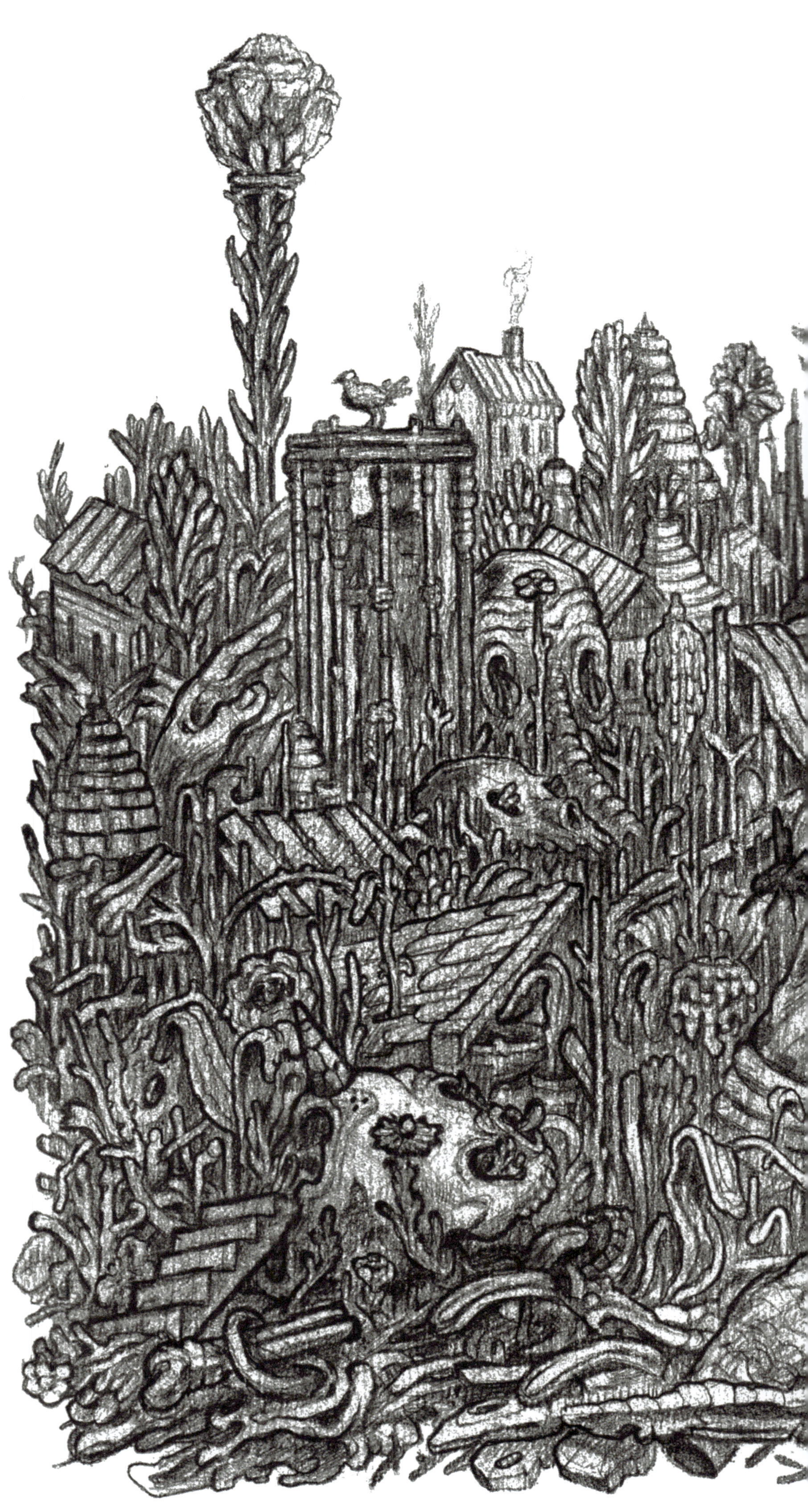

Garden, 2014
Pencil on paper
11 × 16 cm (4⅜ × 6⅜ in.)

The Murder of Mr Plant, 2014
Pencil on paper
70 × 55 cm (27⅝ × 21⅝ in.)

Guard, 2014
Acrylic on paper
75 × 45 cm (29½ × 17¾ in.)

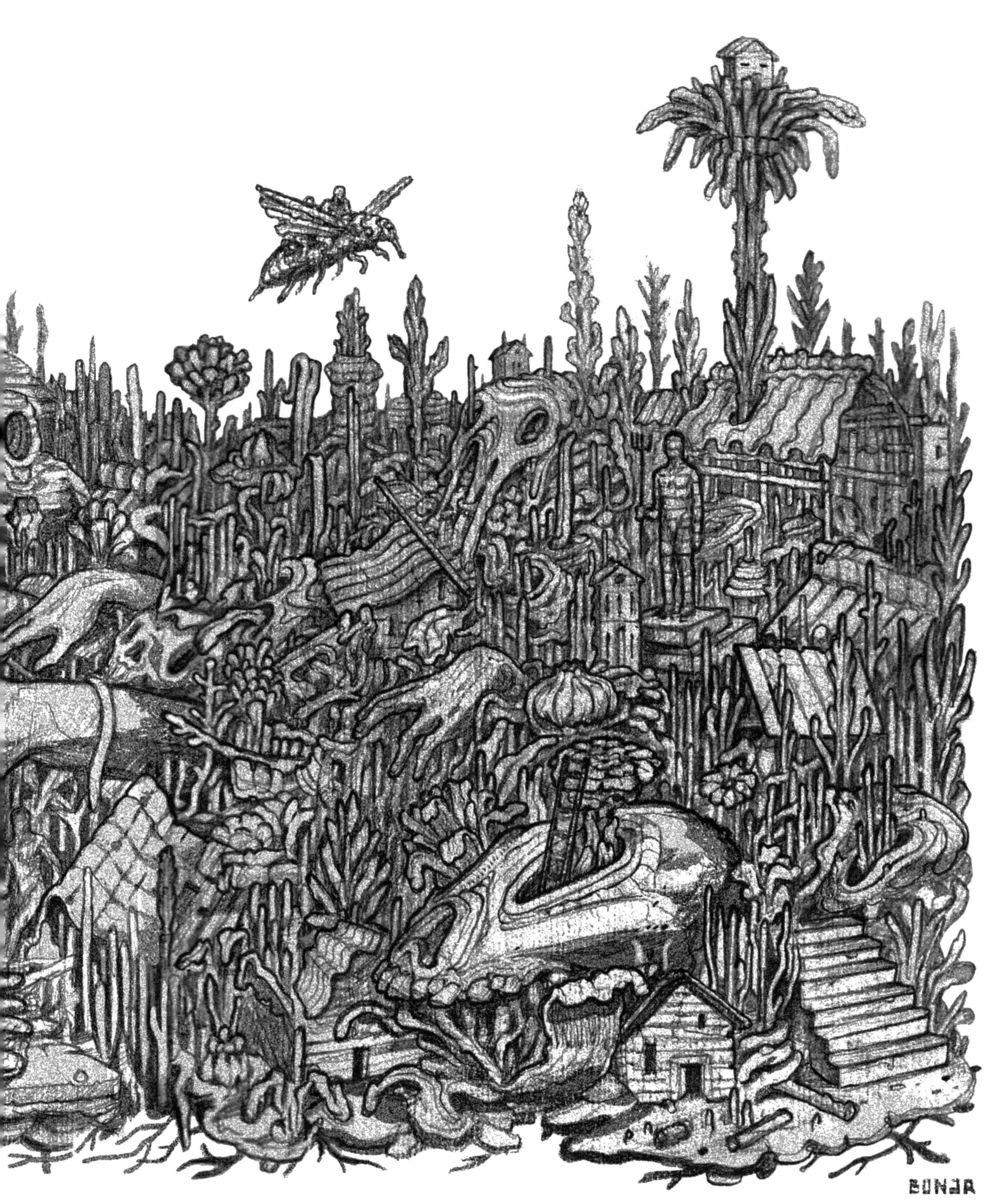

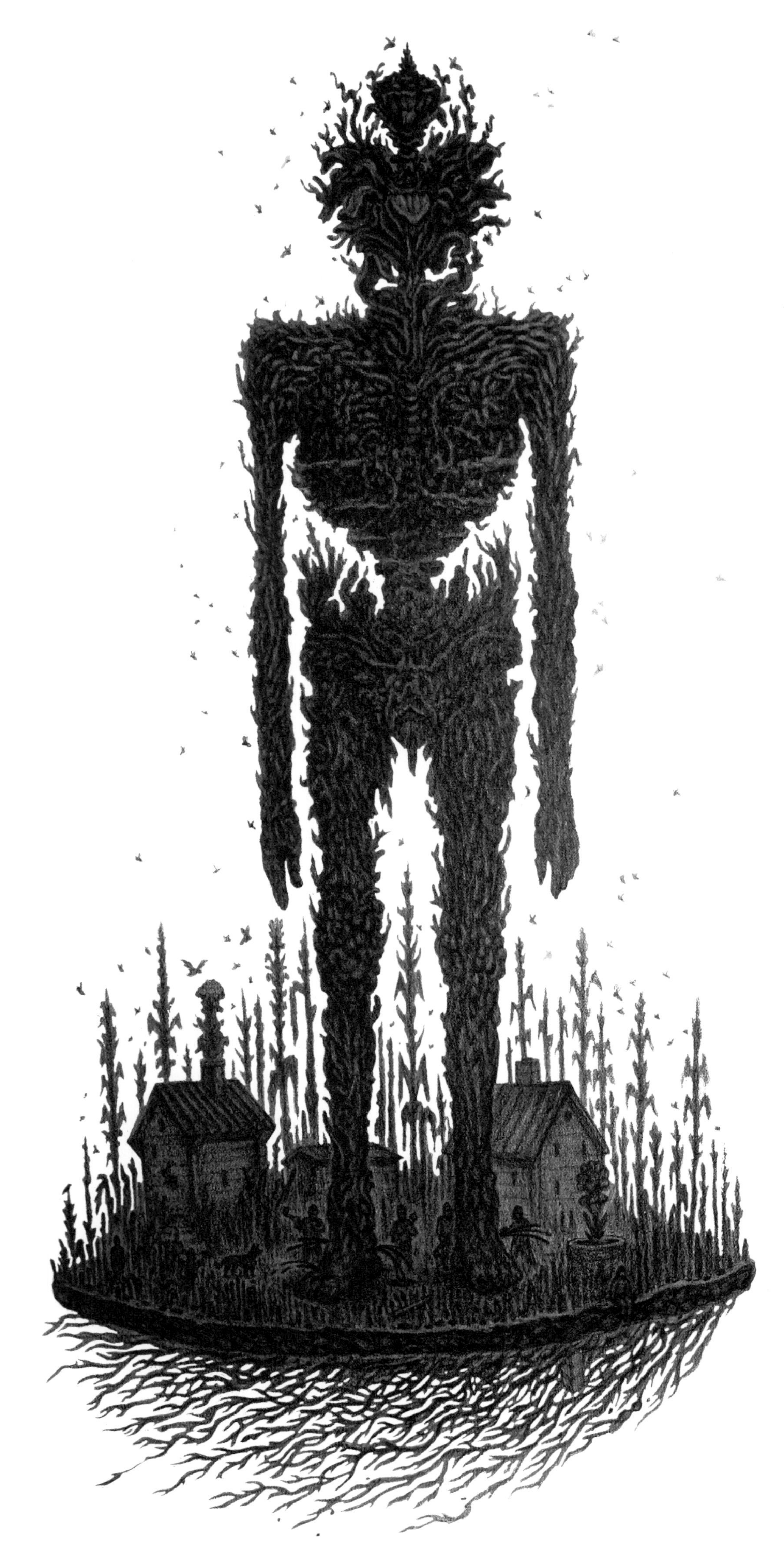

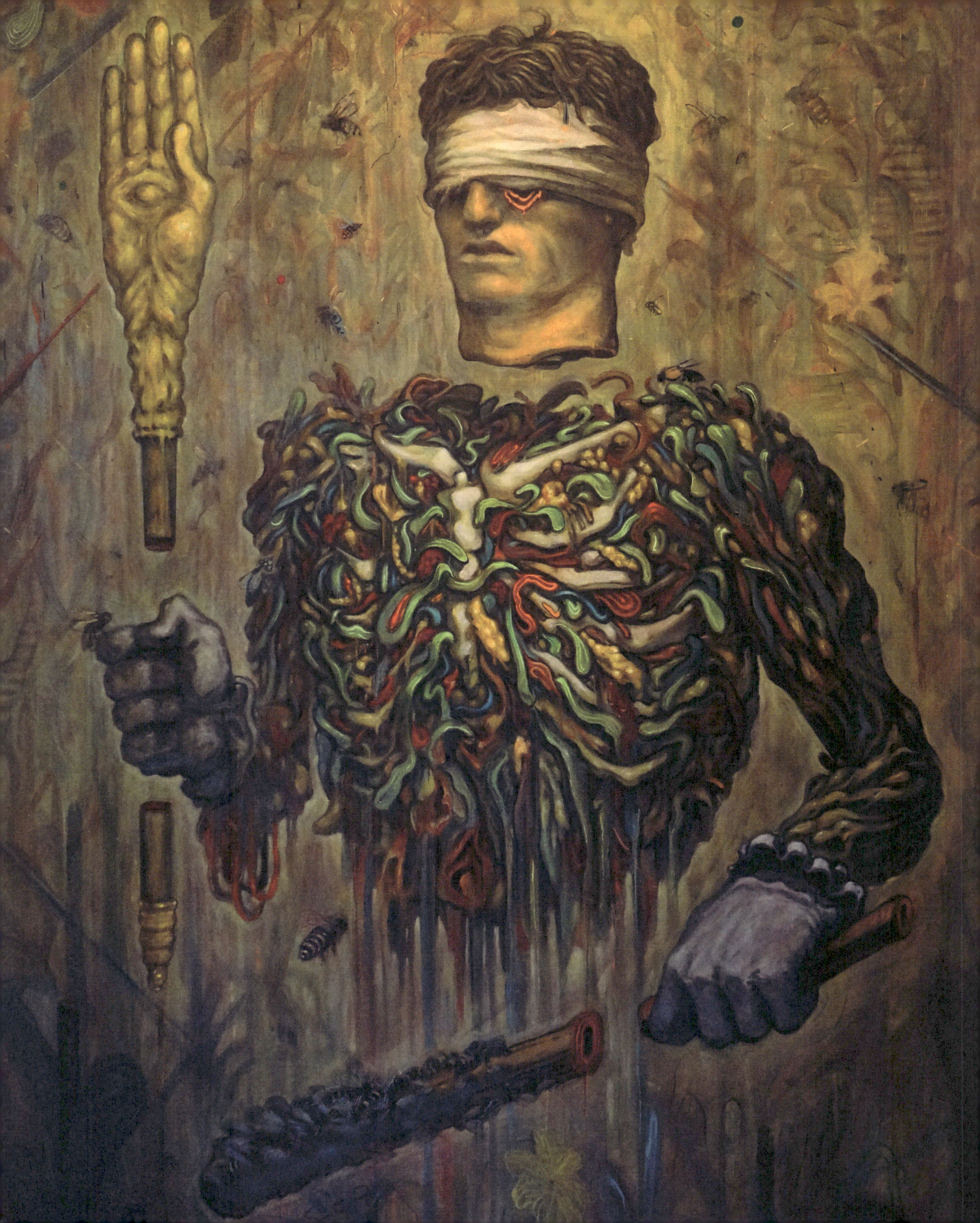

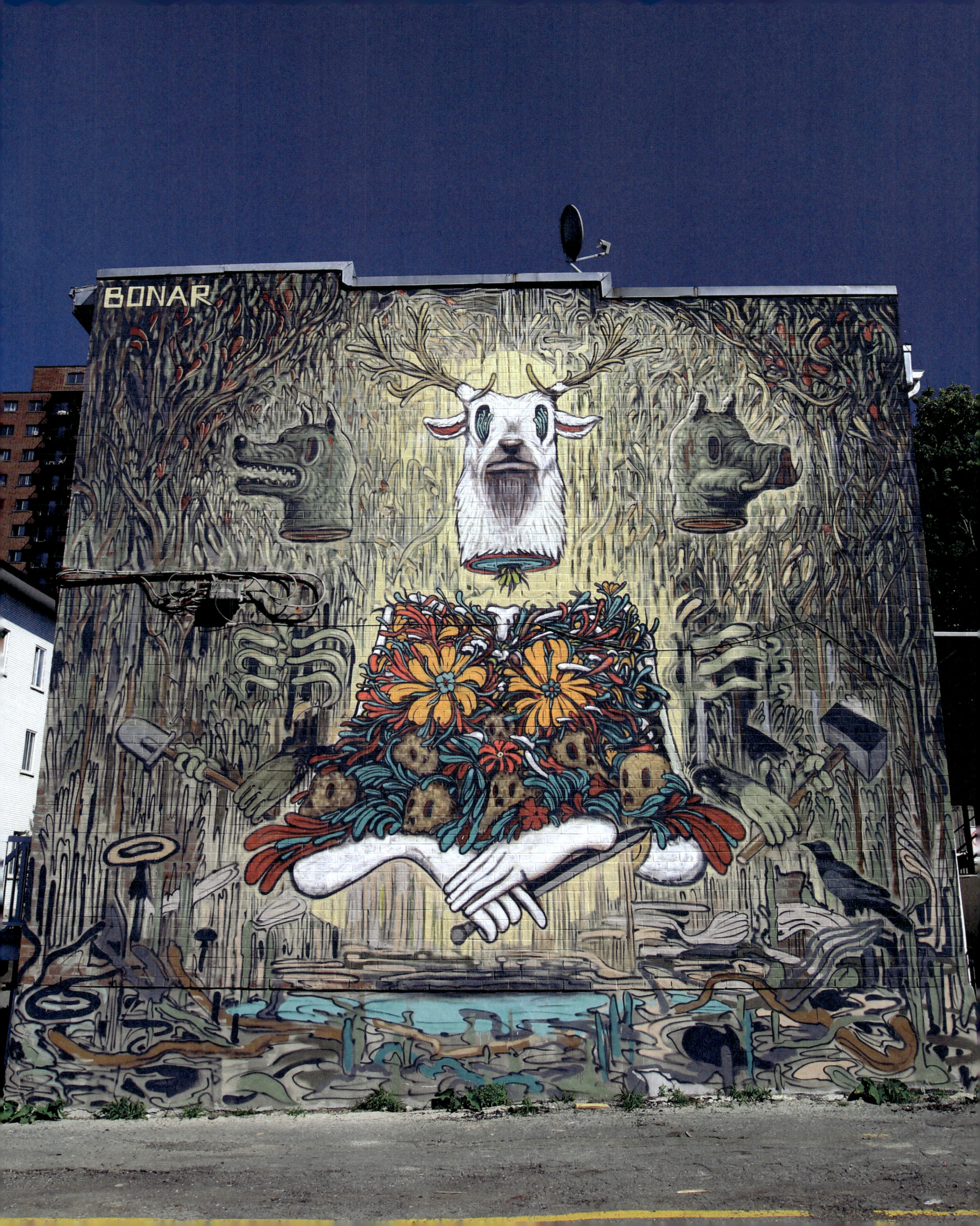
BONAR

narratives, which in part reference the language of comic art, but elsewhere hint at mythology and folklore. Everything about Bonar's output feels fresh, both in terms of style and technique, with his visual world evolving into an ever-more immersive and multi-dimensional experience as he becomes more accomplished as an artist. While he has enviable skills both as a painter and a draughtsman, it is his drawings in particular that have a striking organic quality: 'What I enjoy about drawing is that it's relaxing but can be highly technical at the same time, and with just a line you can speak volumes. The possibilities of the line are infinite.'

Using the moniker 'Bonar' for his wall-based works and murals, he likes to keep a low profile and rarely ever gives interviews. Similarly, he isn't attached to a commercial gallery, works only on private commissions and infrequently produces exhibitions. However, far from being a solitary figure, Bonar is very much a part of the city's art scene, curating group shows of work by other artists, and taking part in collaborations such as 'En Masse', a collective of Montreal-based artists who make predominantly black-and-white murals throughout the city.

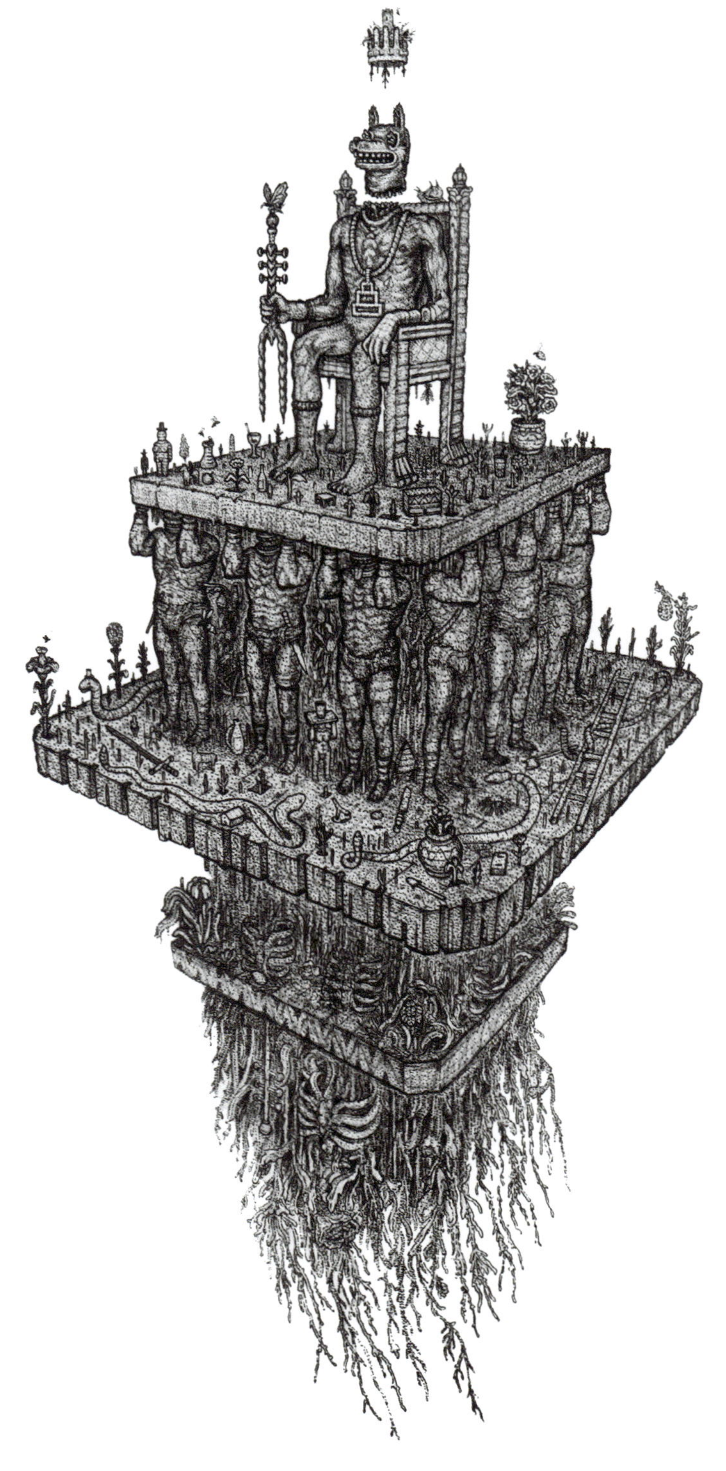

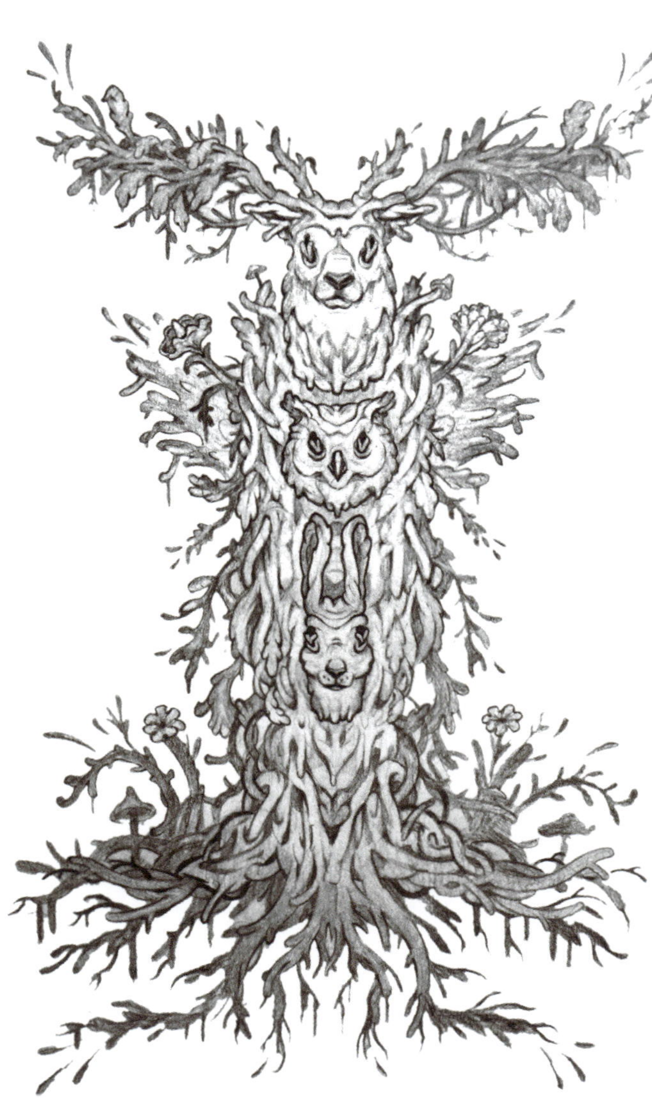

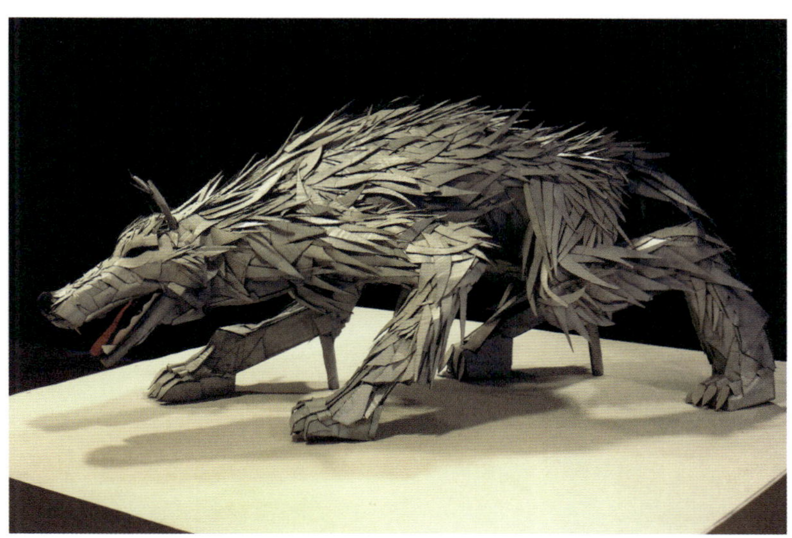

David Côté

A young artist from Montreal, who is fast becoming a rising star in the tattoo world,

David Côté has a long waiting list for his stunning artworks. He now tours the globe, taking up short residencies at numerous tattoo stores and conventions. When not travelling Côté can be found residing at the Imperial Tattoo Connexion store in Montreal.

Côté is part of a new generation of tattoo artists who, while respecting the traditions of the genre, are pushing the form in new directions. This is evidenced in the originality of his designs, which employ vibrant Pop colours, flat geometric shapes and few visible outlines, all flavoured with a Surrealist and psychedelic sensibility.

A number of factors underpin Côté's fascination with tattoo art. As a child he was transfixed by his uncle's tattoos; and, while training as a graphic designer (a profession he later abandoned as a career, finding it too formal a discipline for his creative impulses), body art continued to intrigue him as an art form. He first started making designs for tattoos when a friend admired his drawings and asked him to make an artwork for his hand. After much persuasion, and in spite of having no experience, he agreed. He then embarked on a full apprenticeship and the rest is history.

Tattooing as an art form appeals to Côté because it appears to have no boundaries or limits, while at

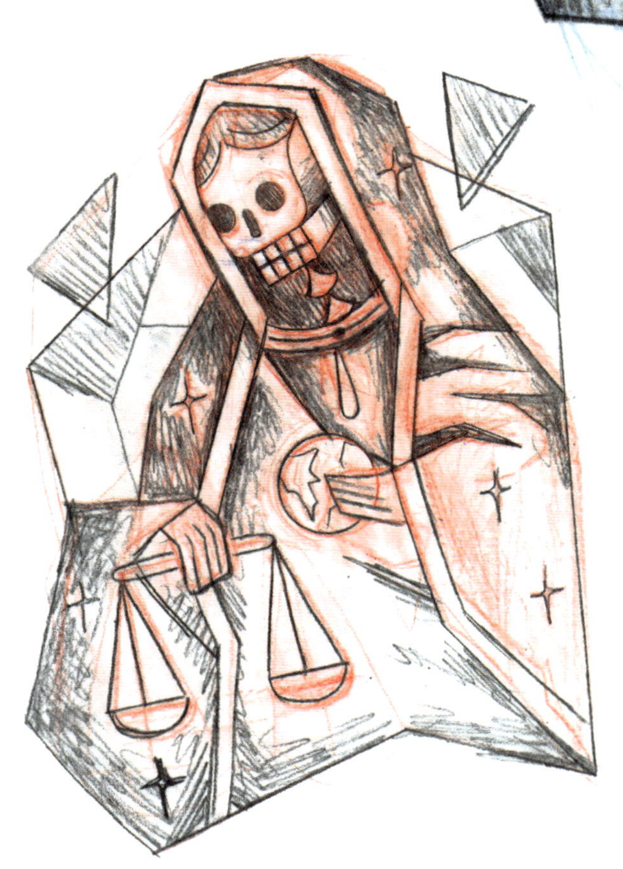

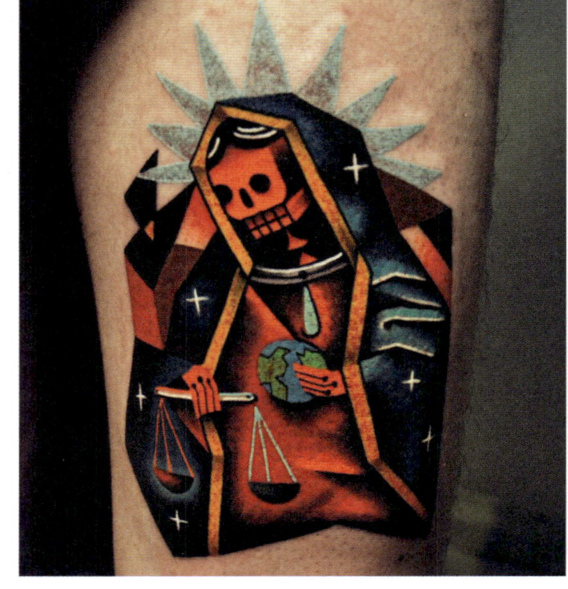

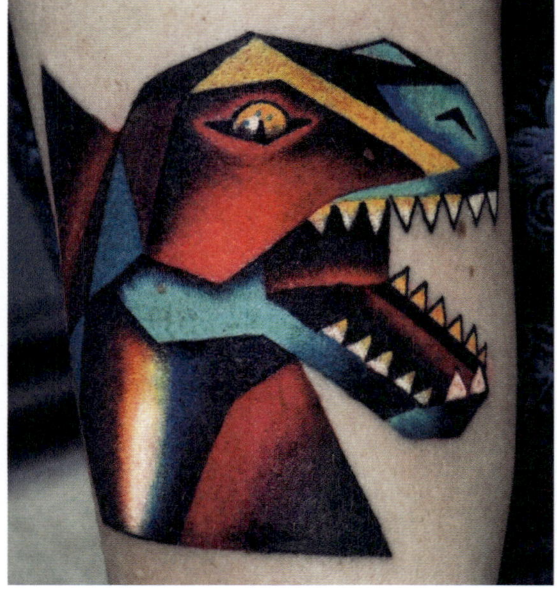

A selection of tattoo
studies and designs, 2015

OPPOSITE
Tattoo designs, 2015

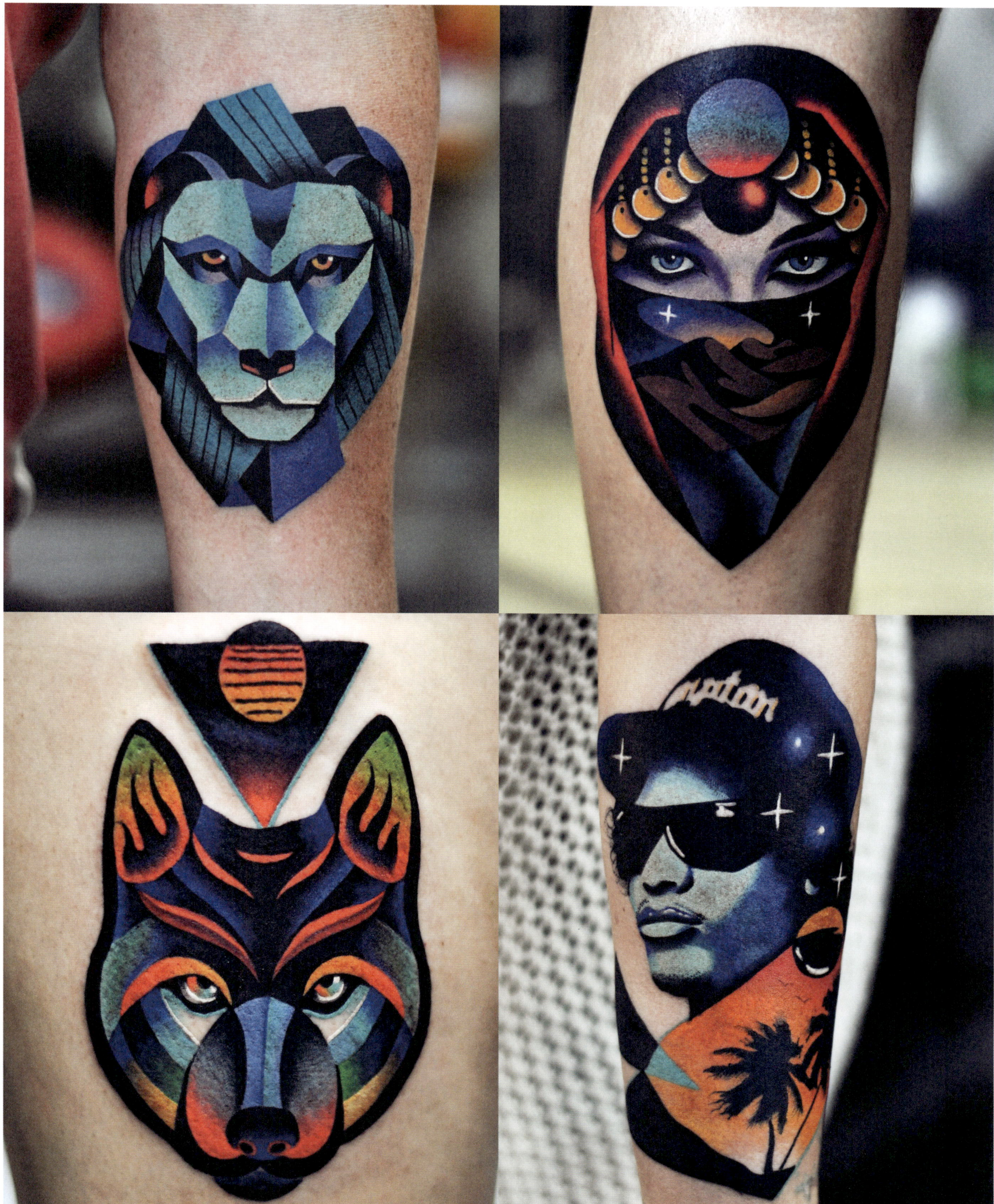

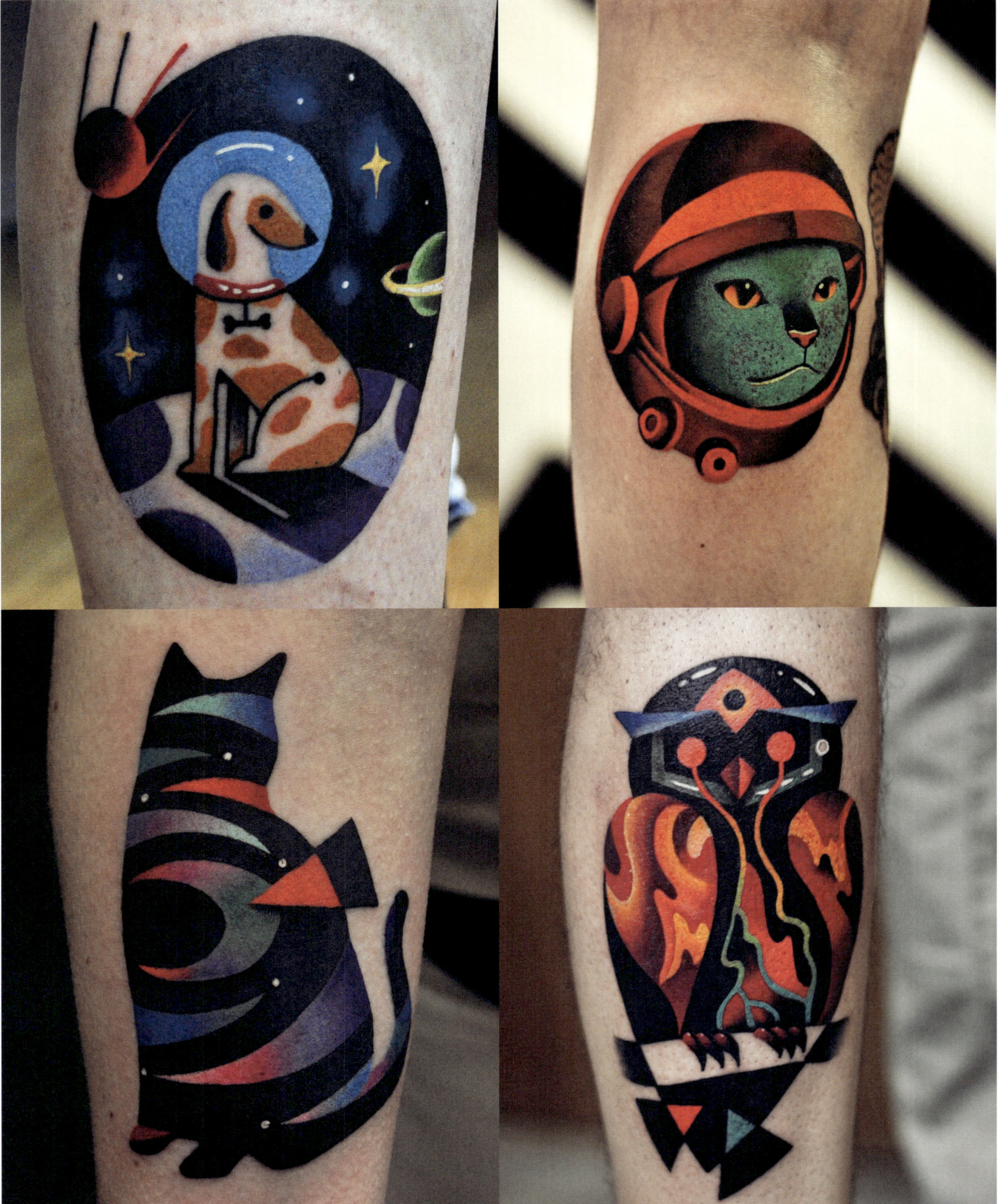

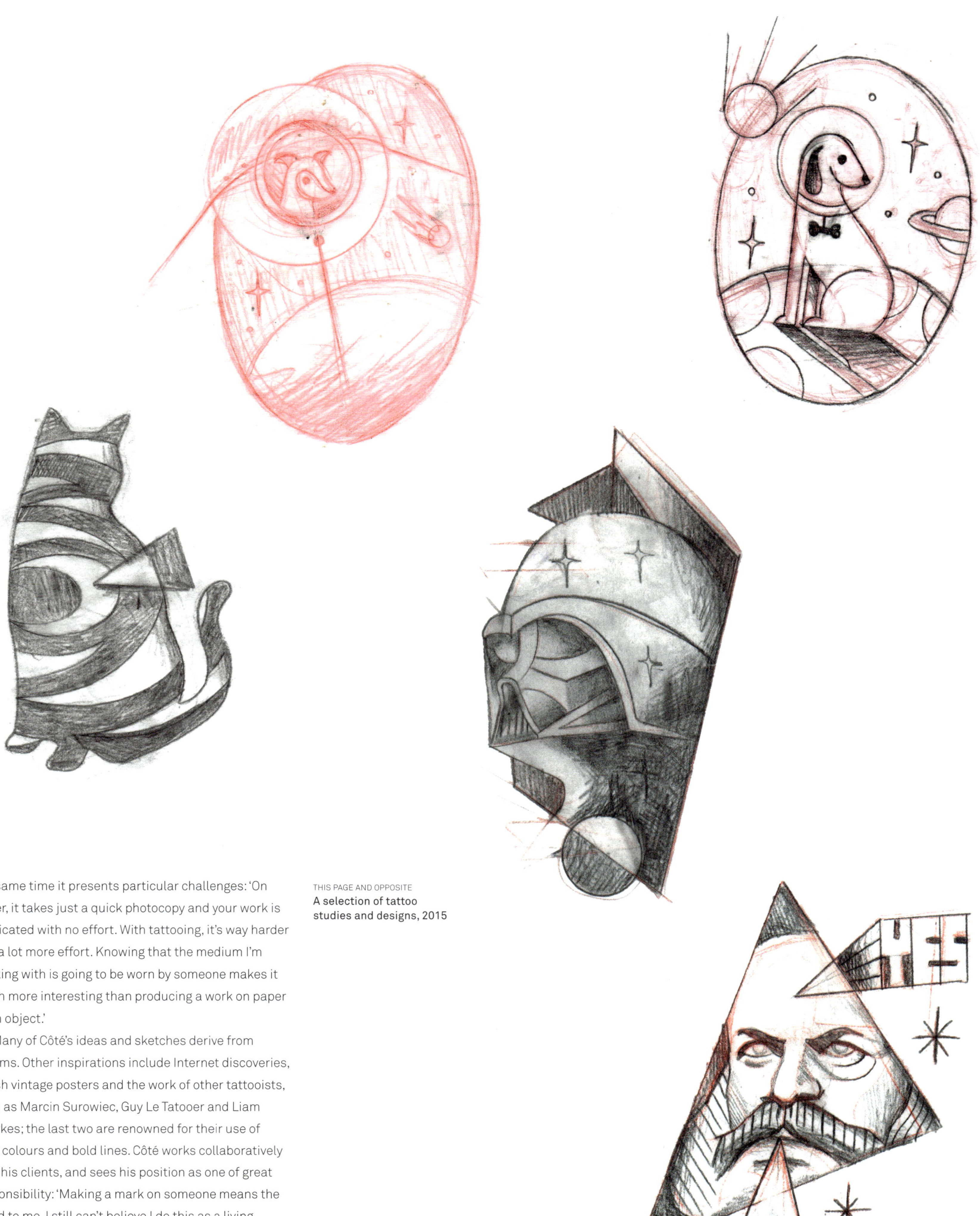

the same time it presents particular challenges: 'On paper, it takes just a quick photocopy and your work is duplicated with no effort. With tattooing, it's way harder and a lot more effort. Knowing that the medium I'm working with is going to be worn by someone makes it much more interesting than producing a work on paper or an object.'

Many of Côté's ideas and sketches derive from dreams. Other inspirations include Internet discoveries, Polish vintage posters and the work of other tattooists, such as Marcin Surowiec, Guy Le Tatooer and Liam Sparkes; the last two are renowned for their use of dark colours and bold lines. Côté works collaboratively with his clients, and sees his position as one of great responsibility: 'Making a mark on someone means the world to me. I still can't believe I do this as a living. I would have never guessed that people would actually be that interested in my artworks.'

THIS PAGE AND OPPOSITE
A selection of tattoo studies and designs, 2015

Dulk

A young Valencian artist whose unique brand of burlesque Surrealism is executed in a wide range of media, Dulk (aka Antonio Segura Donat) brings an unstoppable energy to all that he does. His practice includes studio painting, murals, illustration and sculpture, all of which is executed with a sense of fun and imagination. Central to his work is a mastery of comic art forms, such as the language of characterization, scenery and line work. Working within a graphic visual code comes as second nature to him; the result being meticulous and arresting drawings in which disparate elements are impossibly coupled within dreamlike narratives.

Another important foundation to Dulk's work is his love of animals of all kinds, which feature in some way in almost all of his output. Having grown up on his father's farm surrounded by beasts of all kinds, he became

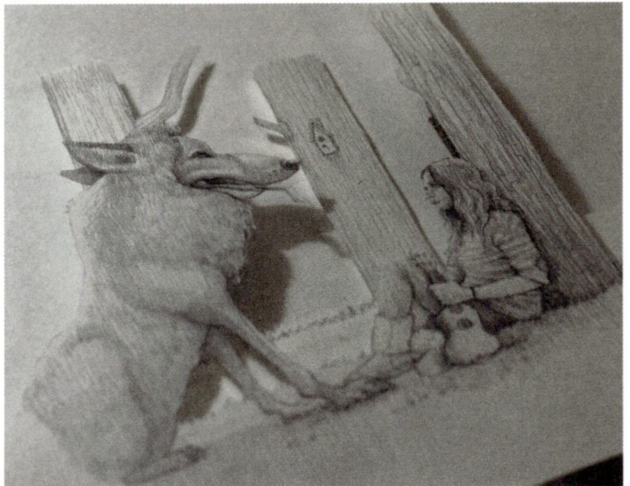
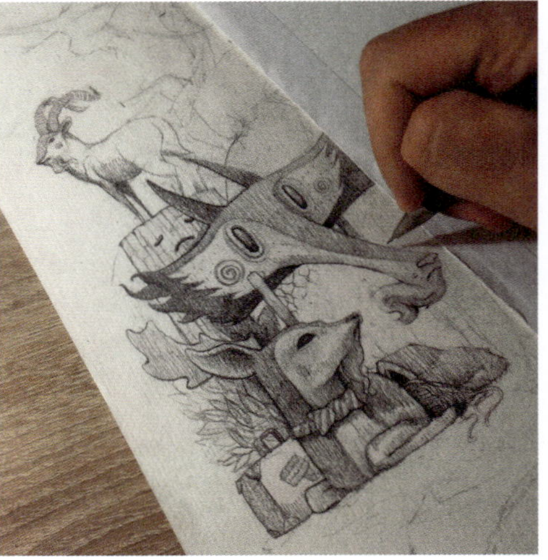
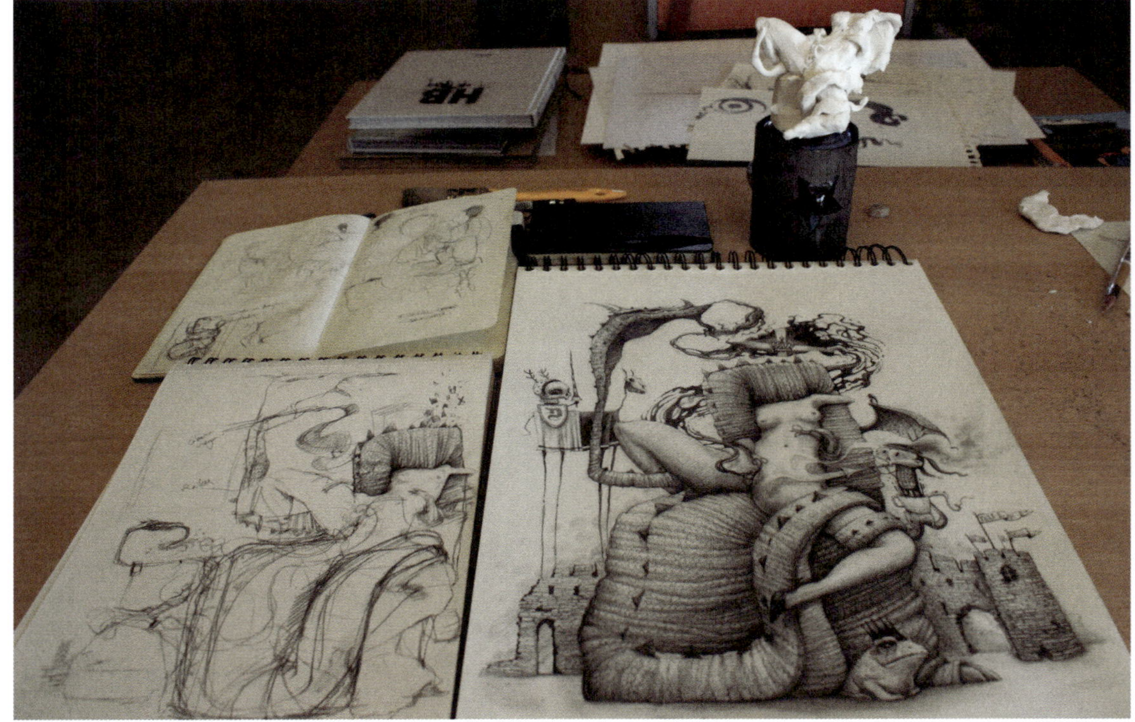

CLOCKWISE FROM TOP LEFT
Study for Moron Police's
*Defenders of the Small
Yard* album, detail, 2014
Pencil on paper
Dimensions unknown

Study for *Tribute to the
Iberian Wildlife*, 2014
Pencil on paper
Dimensions unknown

Study for *Fuego Cruzado*, 2014
Pencil on paper
Dimensions unknown

Study for *Defenders of the
Small Yard*, 2014

OPPOSITE
*The Nightmare in
Wonderland*, 2015
Pencil on paper
70 × 50 cm (27⅝ × 19⅝ in.)

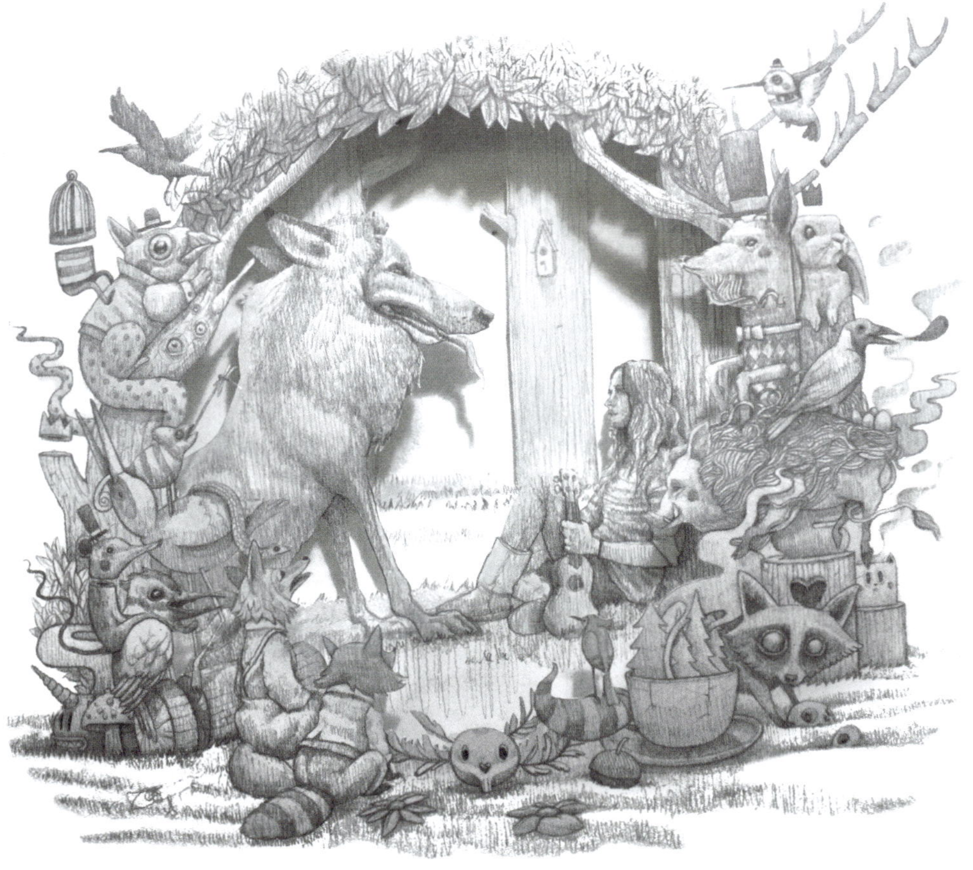

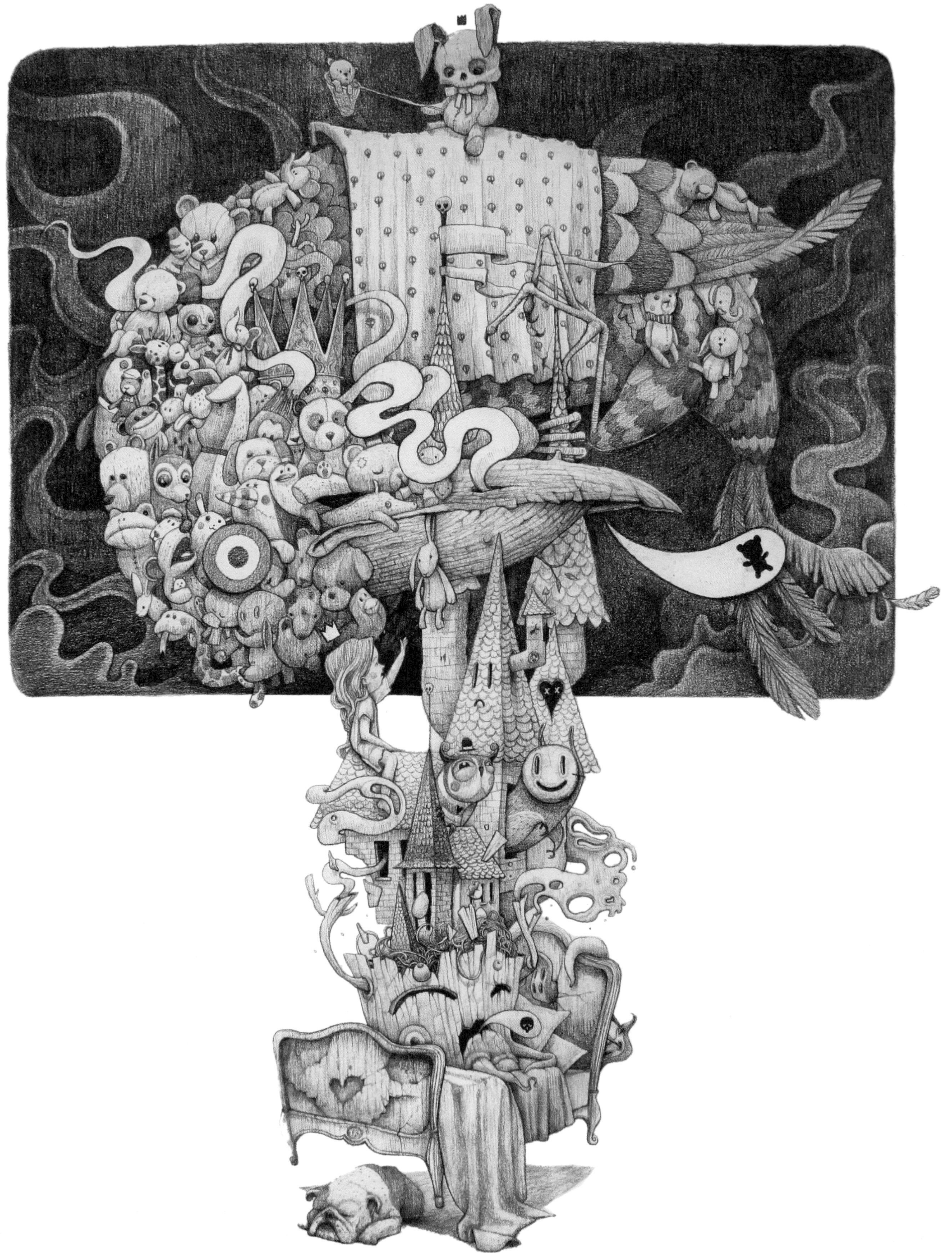

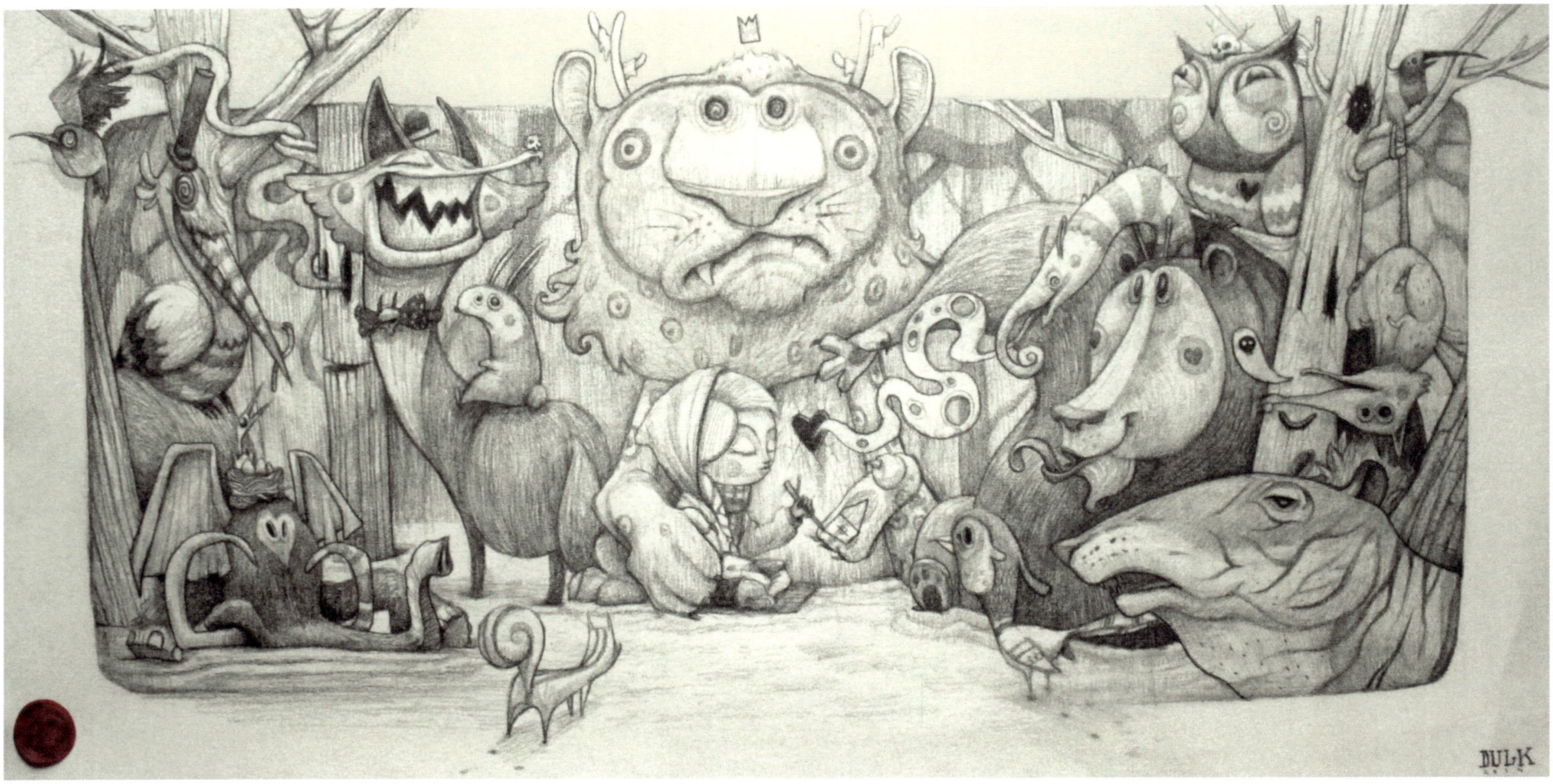

BULK

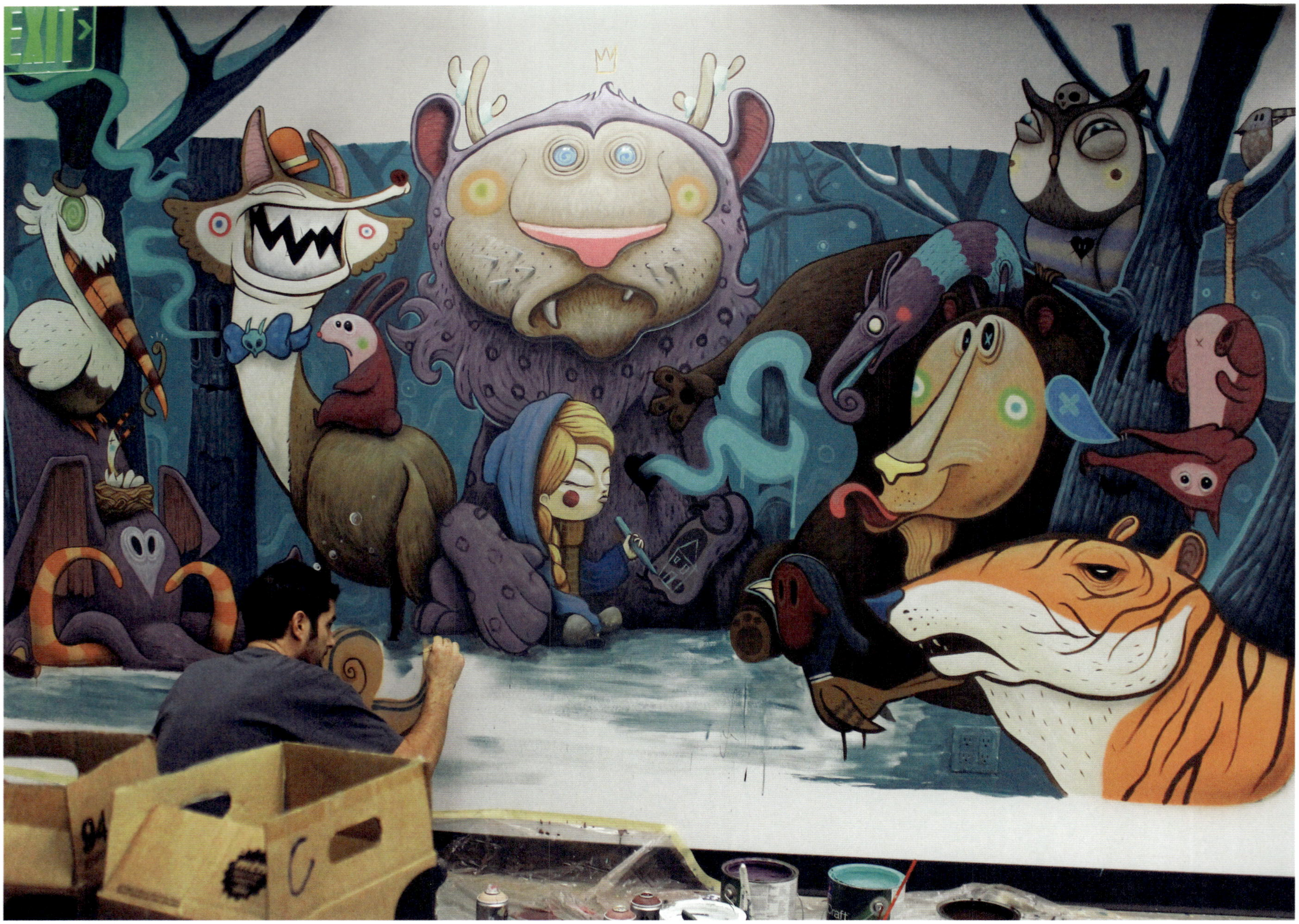

EXIT >

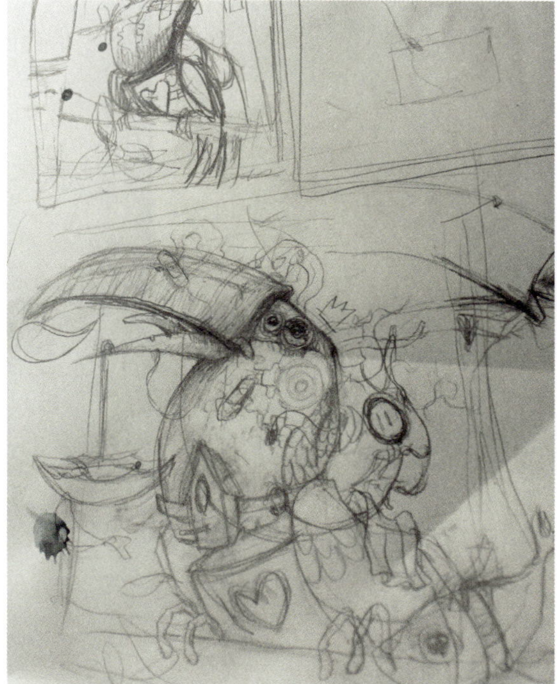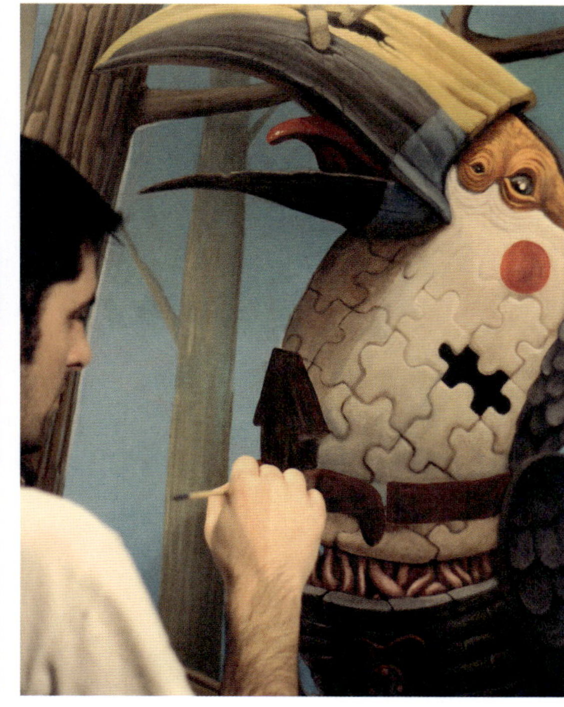

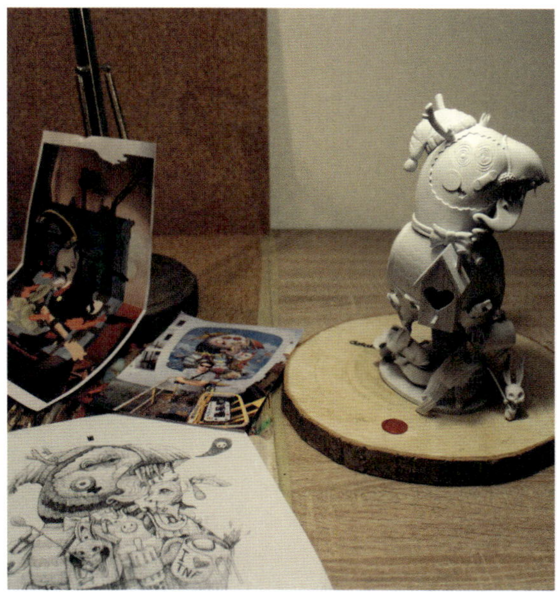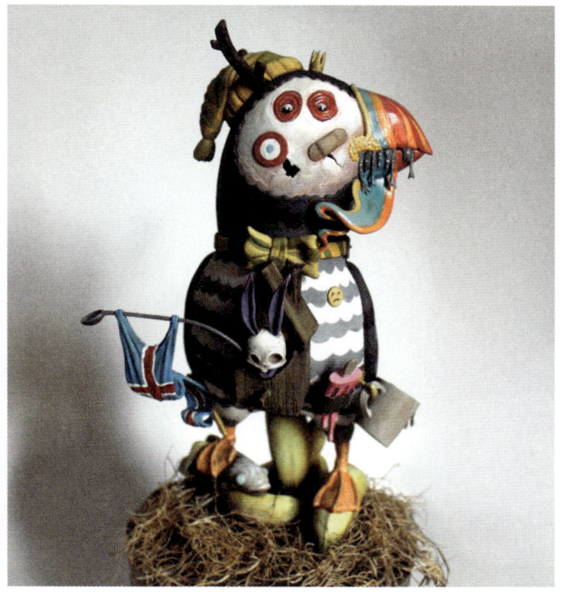

obsessed with and fascinated by them. As a child he also used to trawl through old encyclopedias, and began drawing exotic creatures such as elephants and tigers from the studies he found there. Drawing forms the basis of all of Dulk's work and he considers the pencil to be his emblem: 'I really like working in pencil because it brings uniformity to my work. My illustrations are packed with information and pencil work brings this all together, structurally underpinning the colour and introducing an elegance and readability to my work.'

The spray can, which was introduced to him when he was eighteen by a friend, has had a similar captivating effect. This friend also suggested he adopt the moniker Dulk, a name under which he has worked ever since. At around the same time he encountered the work of the Dutch painter, Hieronymus Bosch (c. 1450–1516), which triggered in him a great sense of imagination and freedom, in particular a desire to focus on storytelling, using his dreams and daily experiences as a source of inspiration. As an artist, he says, it is important 'to have your own brand, your own style. Each person is different and each artist has to be too. Sharing our own vision of the world as art makes known the feelings of an artist. I think of style as an extension of personality.'

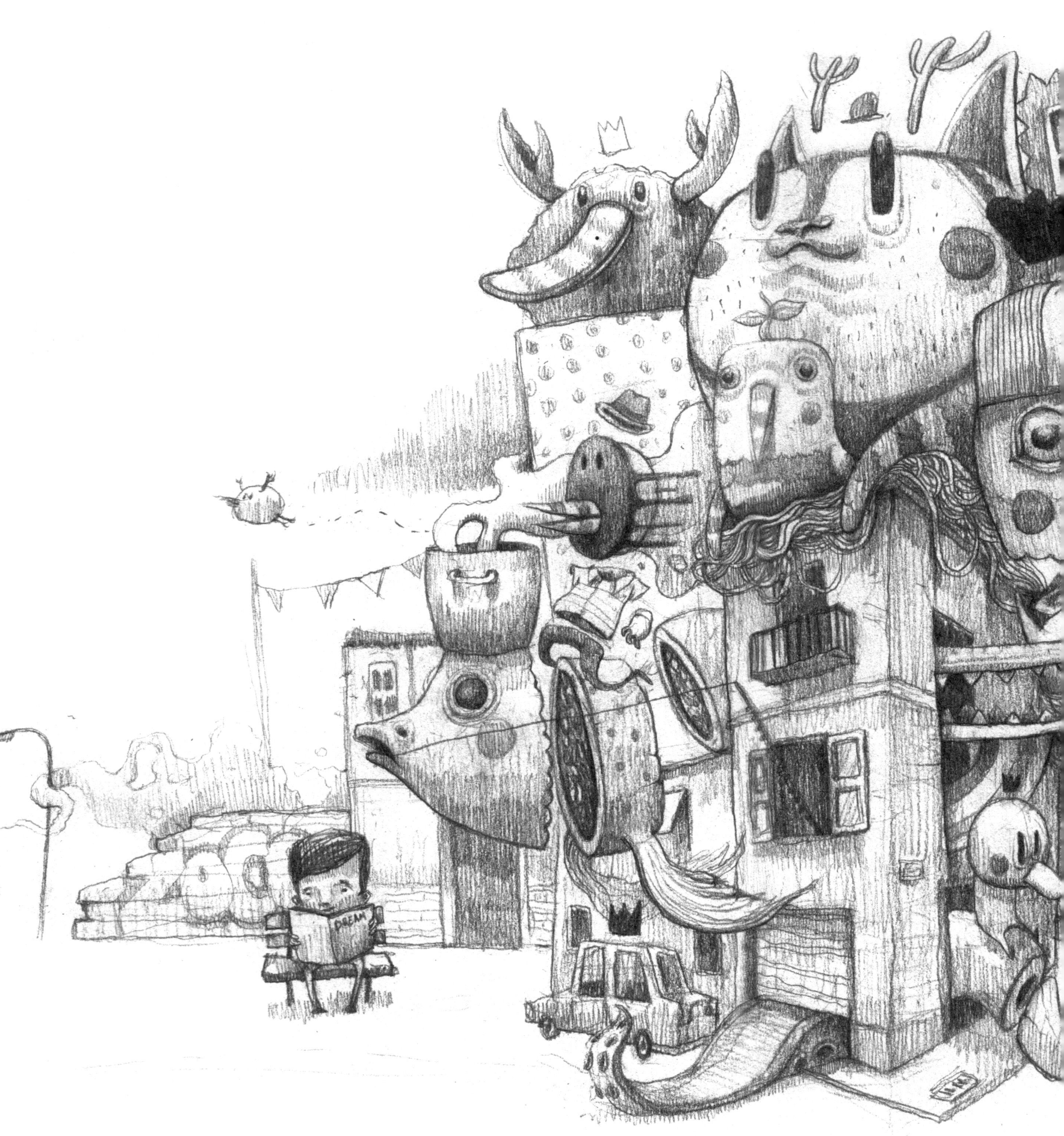
DREAM

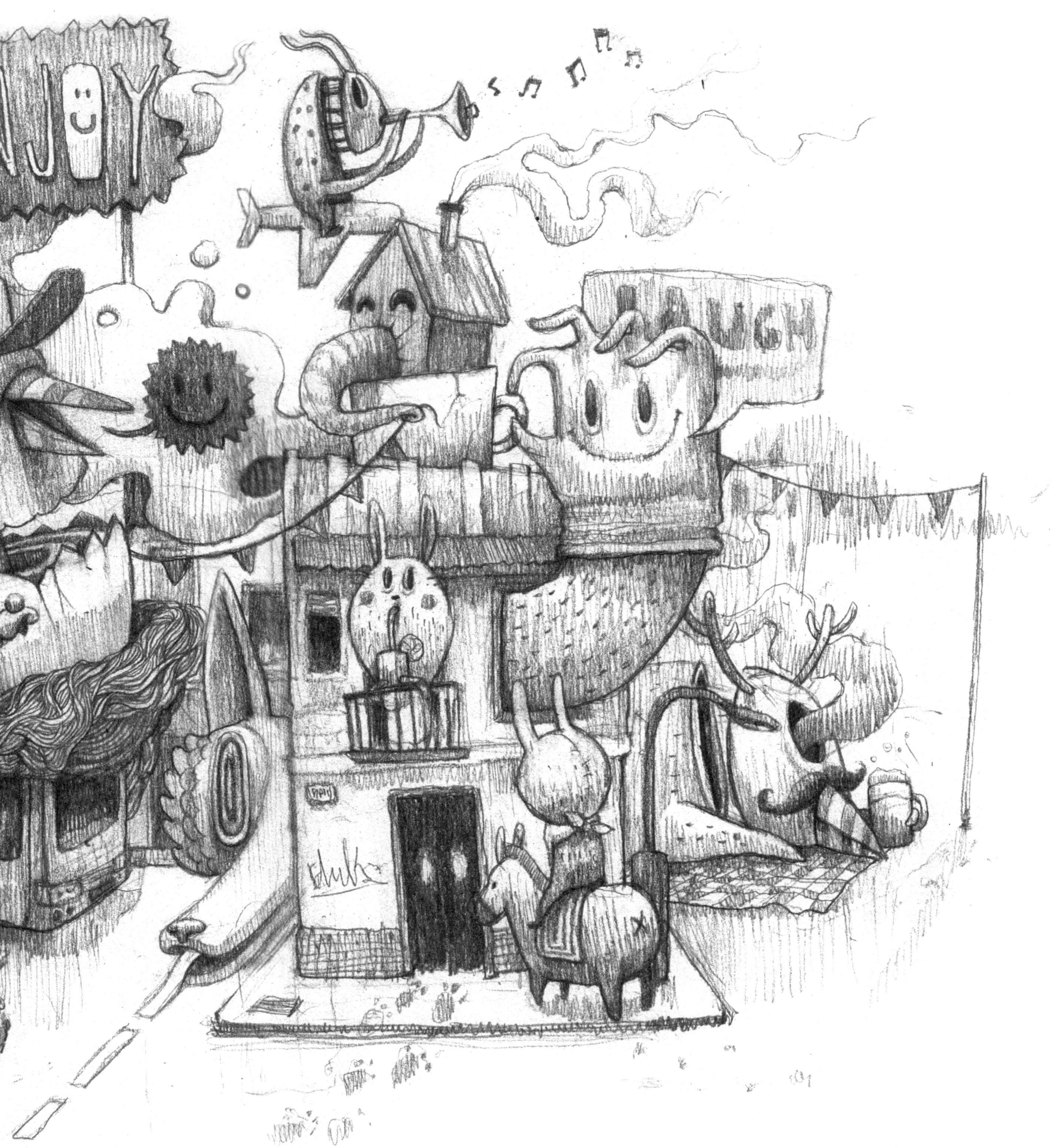
ENJOY
LAUGH

Rune Fisker
Concerned with wordless narratives,

often drawn with a fine line in monochrome, to which colour is sometimes added, are the remarkable works of the Copenhagen-based artist and animator, Rune Fisker. Like scenes from a Surreal film noir, mysterious protagonists enter into each frame, playing a part in a story that is somehow hidden from sight, and that has no logical or related sequence.

Fisker's work is like a fiendish puzzle, one in which the viewer is presented with snapshots, or visual clues, that enable them to navigate his fictional universe. The artist himself admits that what those clues might mean is not always certain: 'I like that what I draw can surprise me, and I'm often not quite sure what the story is. They are like riddles: "Why is he running around with a head in a box? Who does the head belong to, and why is there furniture floating around him?" – all questions to which I often don't have the answer.'

As his work has evolved, his characters' expressions have been almost entirely elided, replaced instead by shrouded or contorted abstract faces. Without their features serving as a distraction, Fisker feels he has more freedom to explore the other aspects of his draughtsmanship, and in particular let the stories themselves (whatever they may be) take centre-stage.

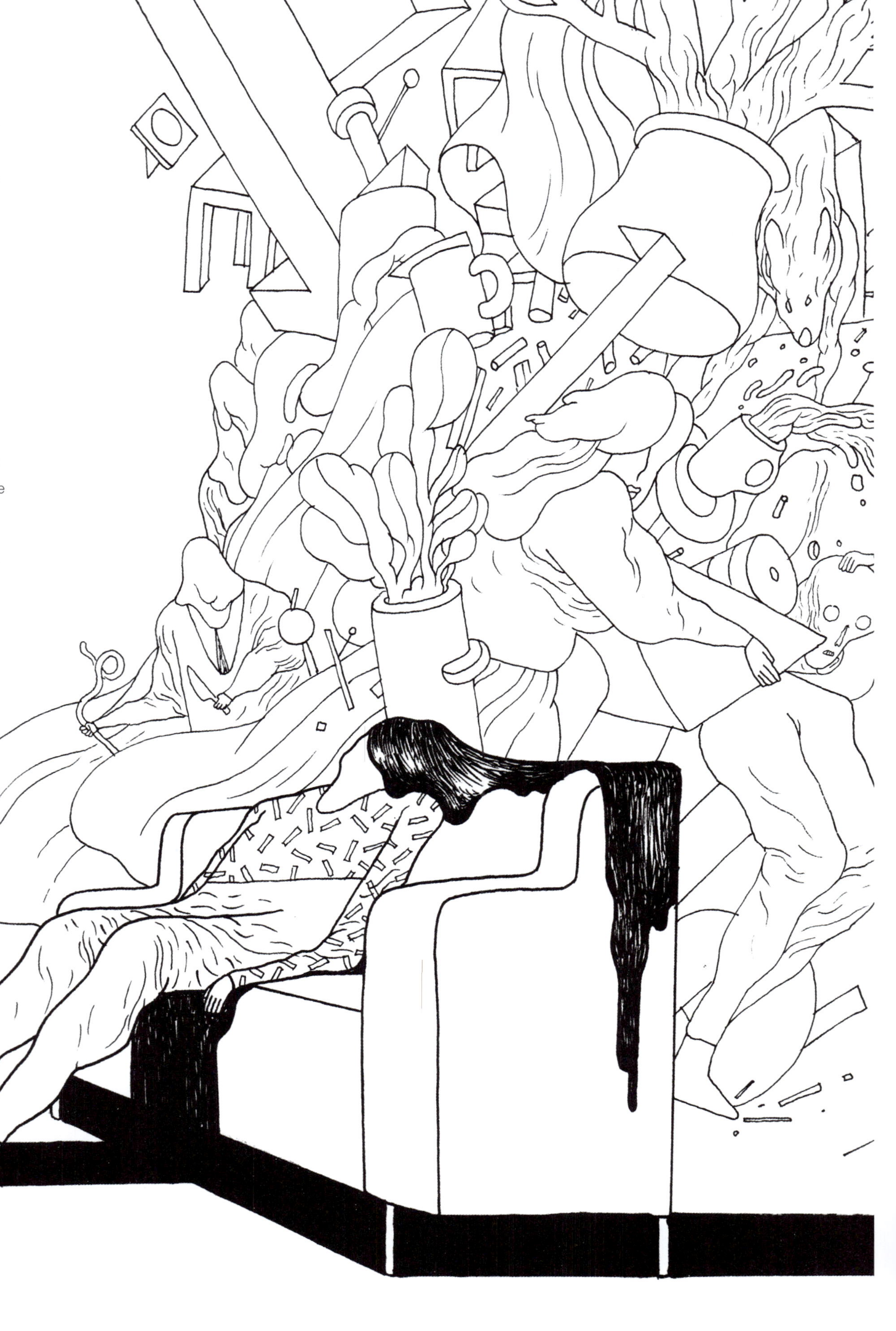

Untitled, c. 2014
Pen on paper
Dimensions unknown

OPPOSITE, CLOCKWISE FROM TOP LEFT
The End, 2015
Giclée print with archival ink
48.3 × 32.9 cm (19 × 13 in.)

Untitled, 2015
Pen on paper
Dimensions unknown

One Fine Spring Day, commission by Spectrum Object, 2015
Pen on paper
Dimensions unknown

Untitled, c. 2014
Pen on paper
Dimensions unknown

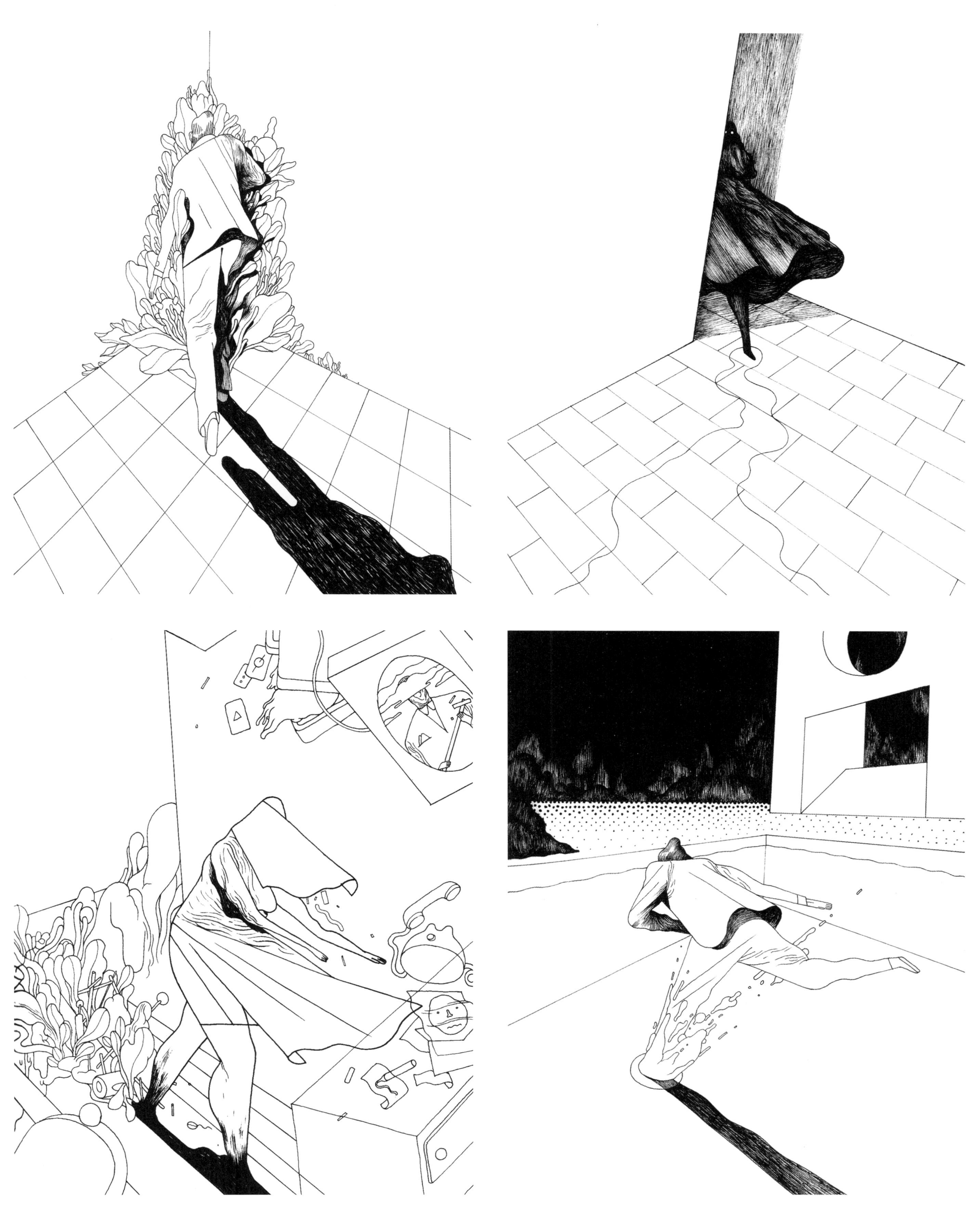

Part of the beauty of Fisker's work lies in his mastery of line, which is characteristically both angular and organic, with his twisted and poised figures adding tension and drama to each composition. The comic books that he read as a child – Hergé's *The Adventures of Tintin*, the works of Jean-Claude Mézières (b. 1938) and Moebius (1938–2012) – as well as the precision and simplicity found in the linear style of artists such as Joost Swarte (b. 1947) all find resonance, although Fisker's work is more dark and brooding in tone.

Fisker also collaborates with his brother Esben, and together they run the small design and production company, Benny Box, specializing in animation design and motion graphics. The brothers produce their own animations as well as title sequences for such acclaimed Danish television series as 'Borgen' (2010–). This practice feeds back into his drawing work, a process of which he explains: 'When you work with moving images you come to appreciate well-timed movements – I like to try to capture that with my drawings. I like for them to appear as a still from a movie or animation might.'

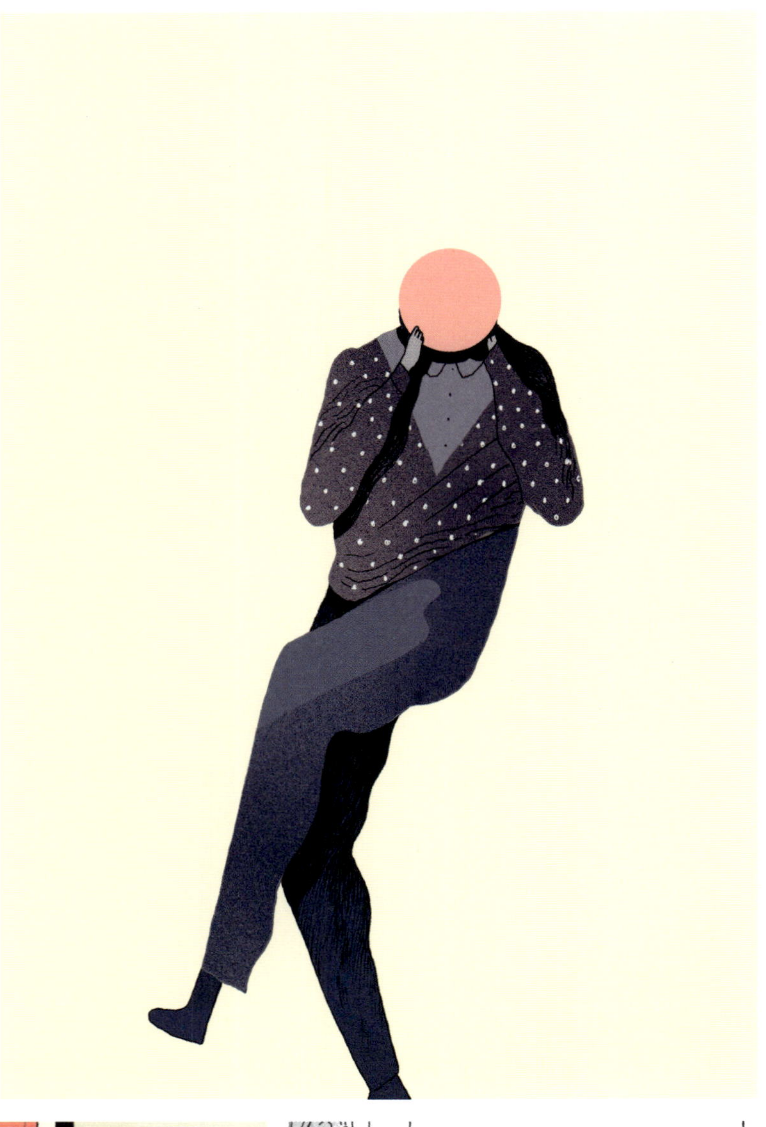

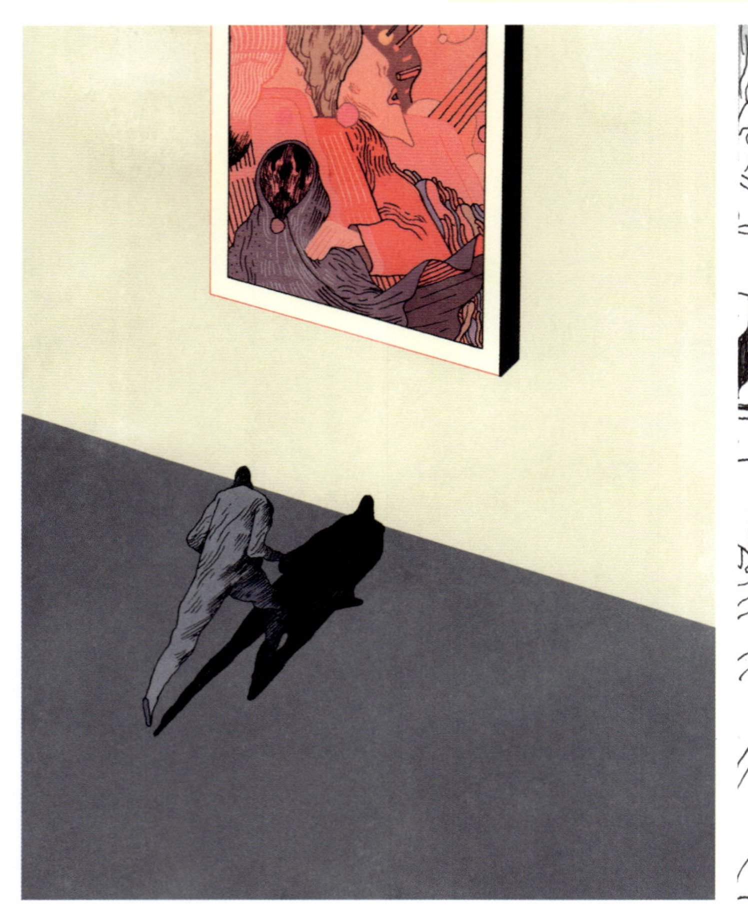

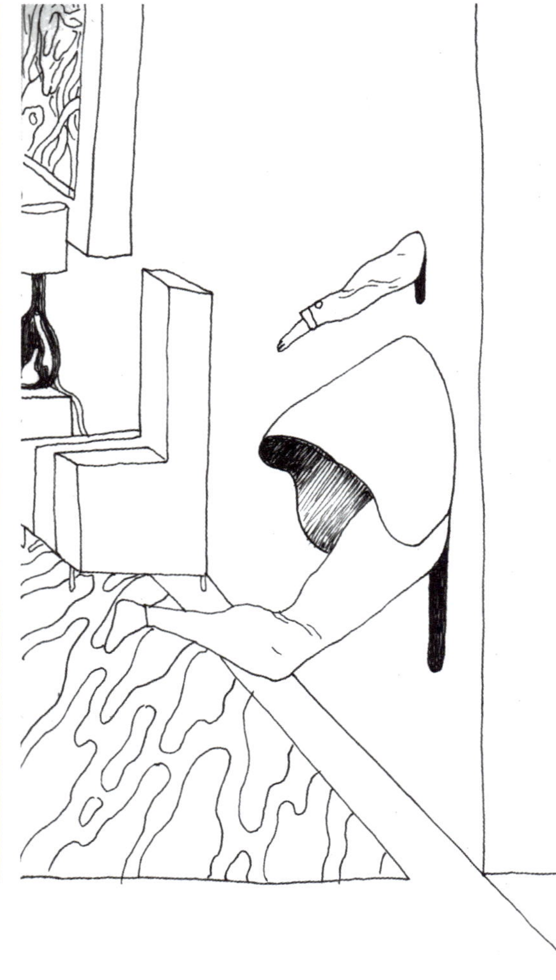

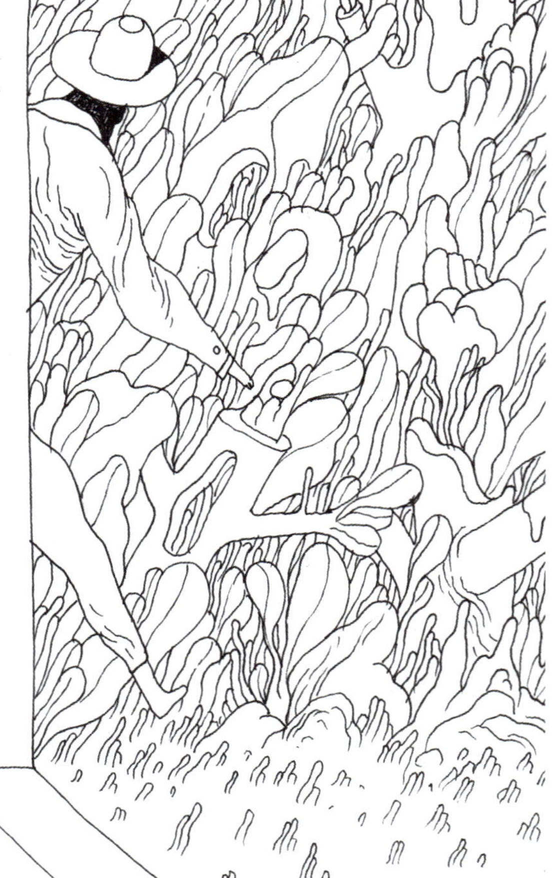

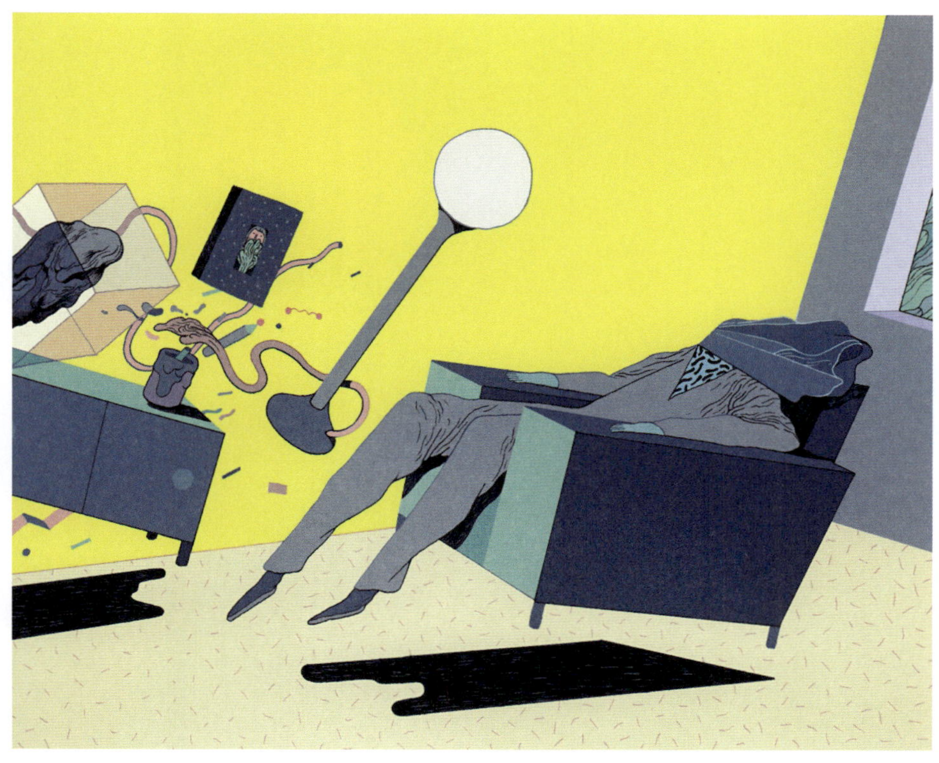

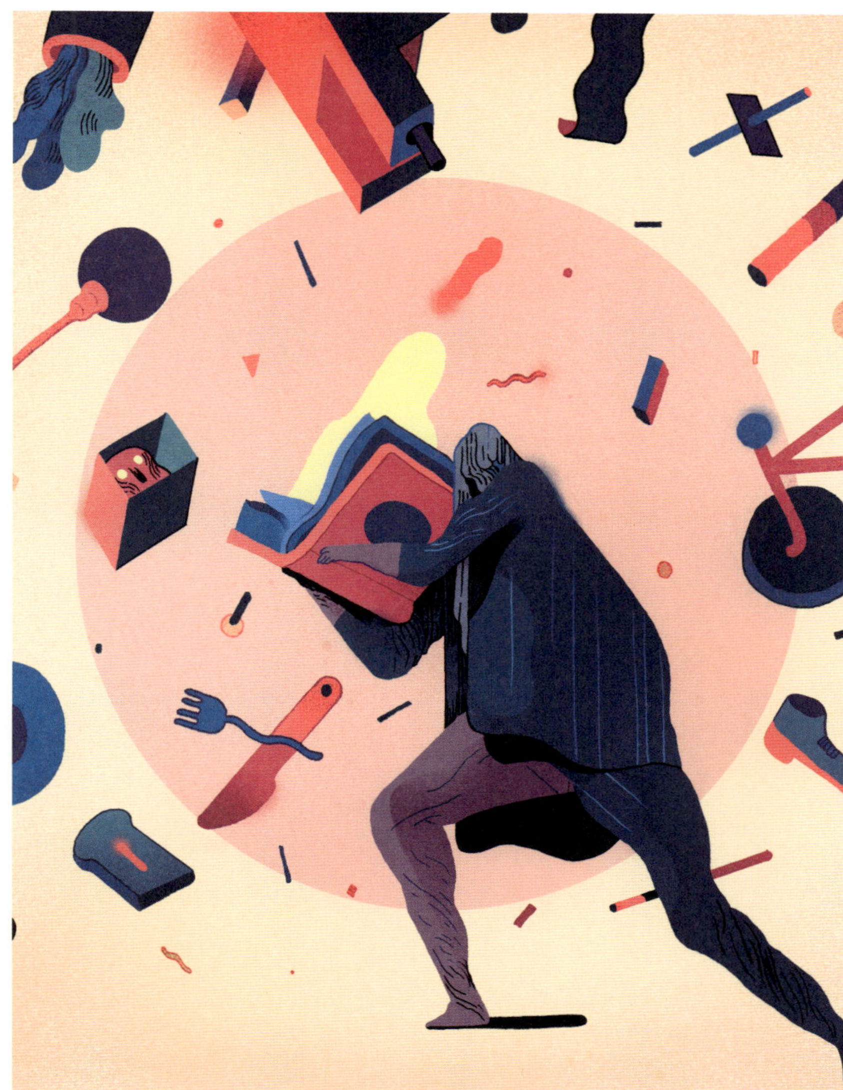

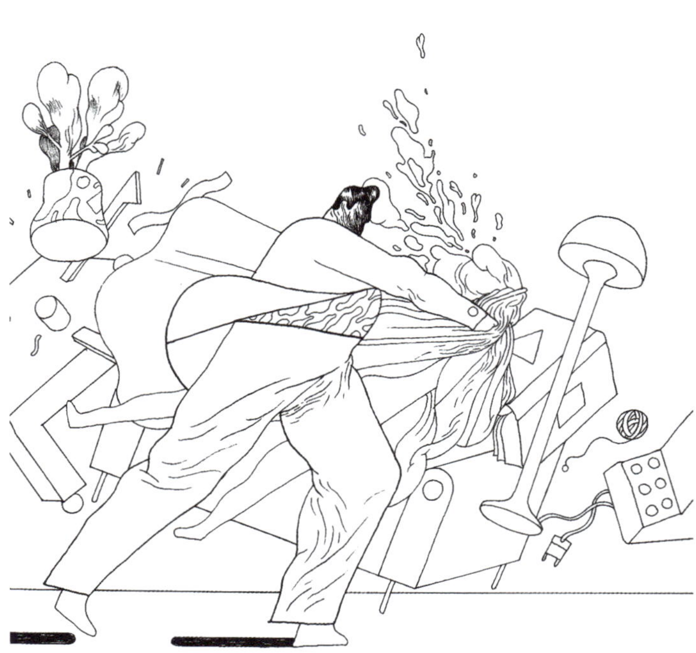

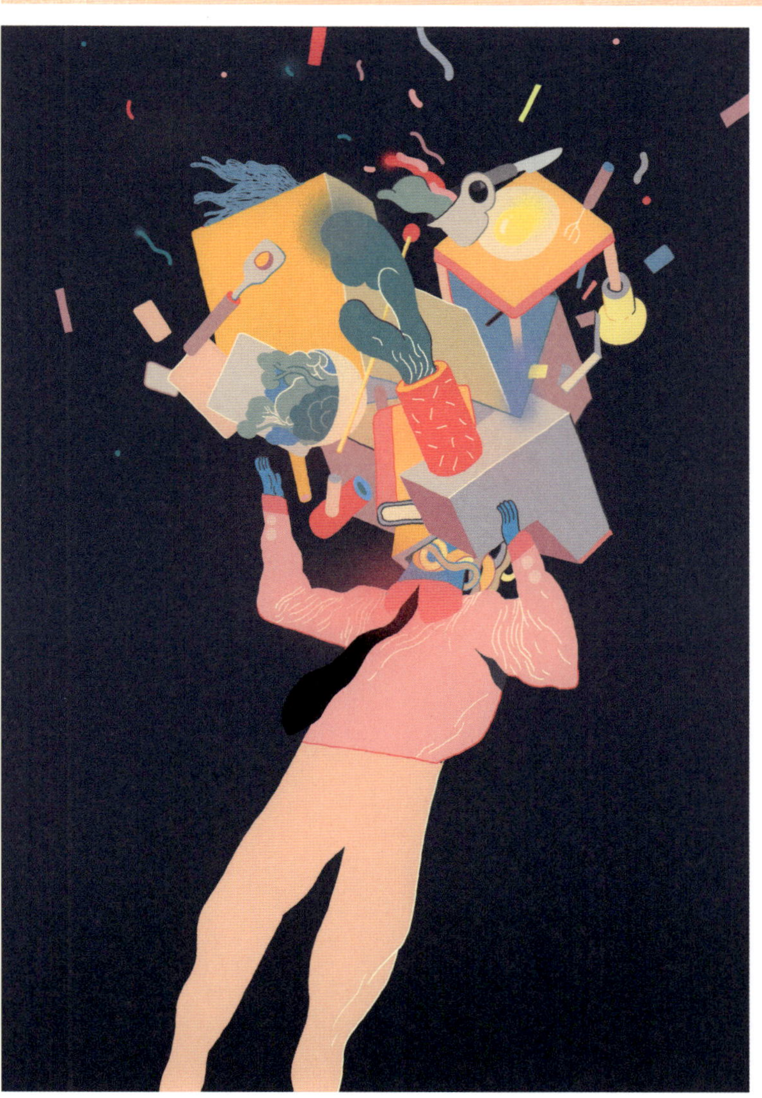

Ugo Gattoni

Exhibiting an incredible attention to detail in his work,

French artist Ugo Gattoni has a stupendously packed and accomplished portfolio. His skilful use of line, shade and texture, and the way in which his drawings are luxuriously filled with intricate or complex elements, is mind-boggling.

Having studied graphic design at the EPSAA in Paris in 2010, Gattoni decided soon after to make his way in the world as an illustrator and artist. His first major exhibition included an impressive landscape drawing of approximately 2 × 10 m (6 × 33 ft), executed solely with a black fine-liner pen. Since then he has become especially known for his signature cityscapes, which are crammed full of acutely observed details, humour and Surrealist gestures.

Gattoni has an avid following and receives many commissions. In 2012 he took part in a live drawing project in collaboration with the French illustrator McBess at the Hayward Gallery in London. The same year, and inspired by the London Olympics, he undertook another magnum opus in the form of his first publication, *Bicycle*, a concertina-style book that imagines a cycle race through the streets of London. In this instance, however, the racers are not only athletes but also 'cycle couriers, commuters, bankers, delivery boys, mums with kids, youths on stolen mountain bikes…fashionistas and hipsters on fixed-gear bikes'.

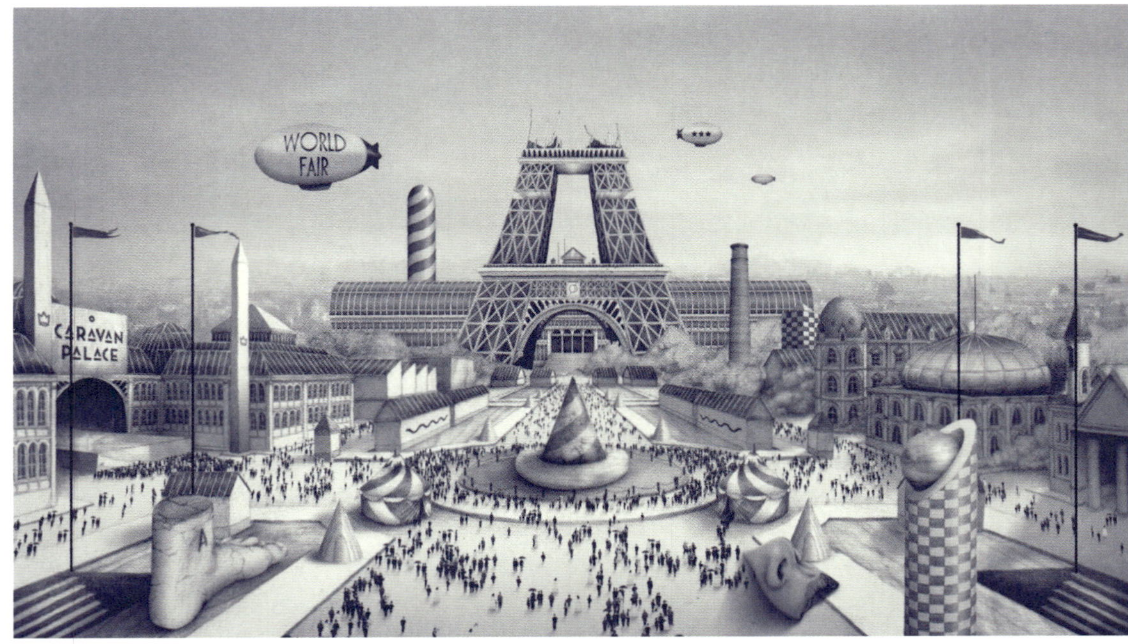

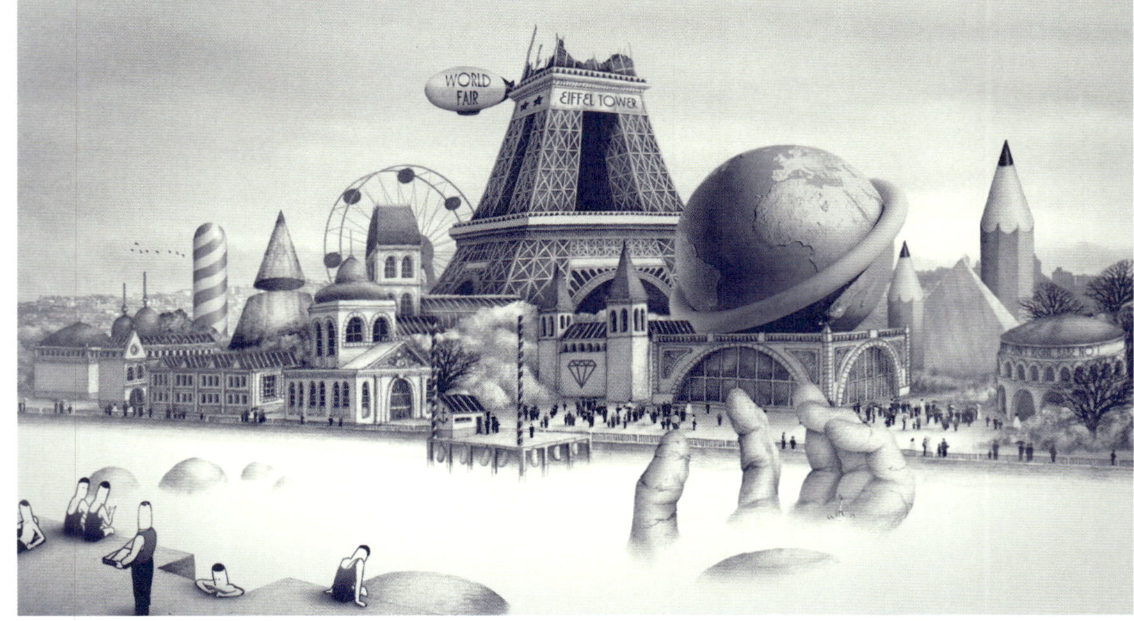

Artwork for Caravan Palace's
Panic album, 2012
Pencil on paper
Dimensions unknown

Artwork for *Panic*, 2012
Pencil on paper
Dimensions unknown

Copains, 2013
Pencil on paper
Dimensions unknown

OPPOSITE
Laocoon, 2013
Pencil on paper
Dimensions unknown

OVERLEAF
Ultra Copains, detail, 2012
Ink on paper
41 × 500 cm (16⅛ × 196⅞ in.)

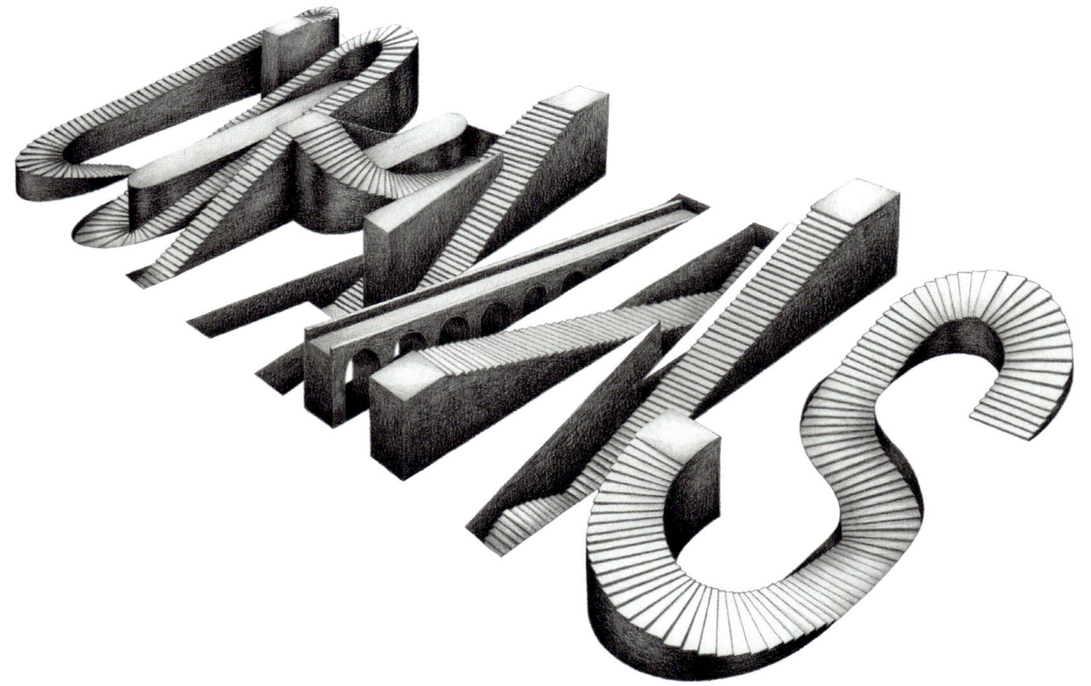

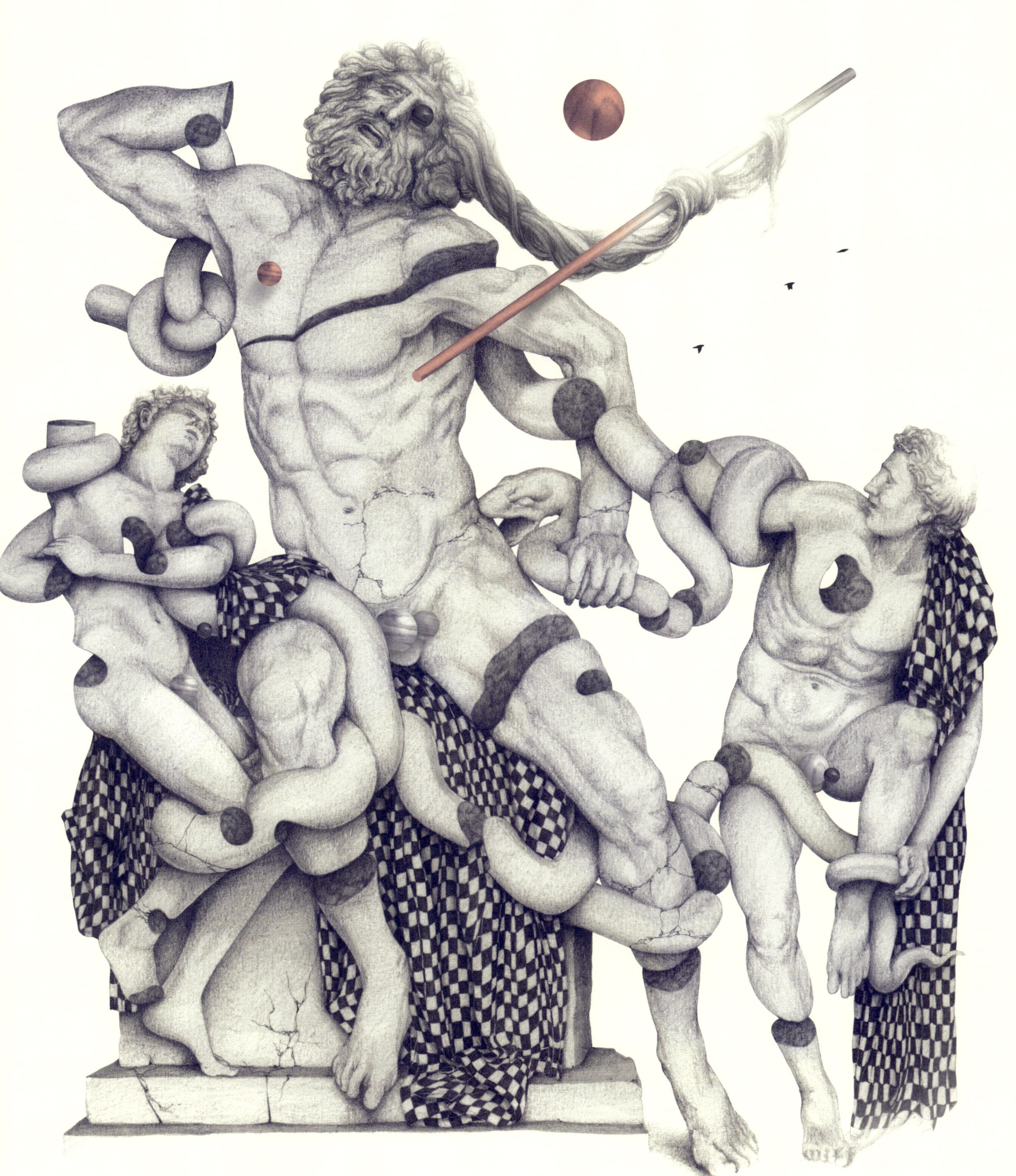

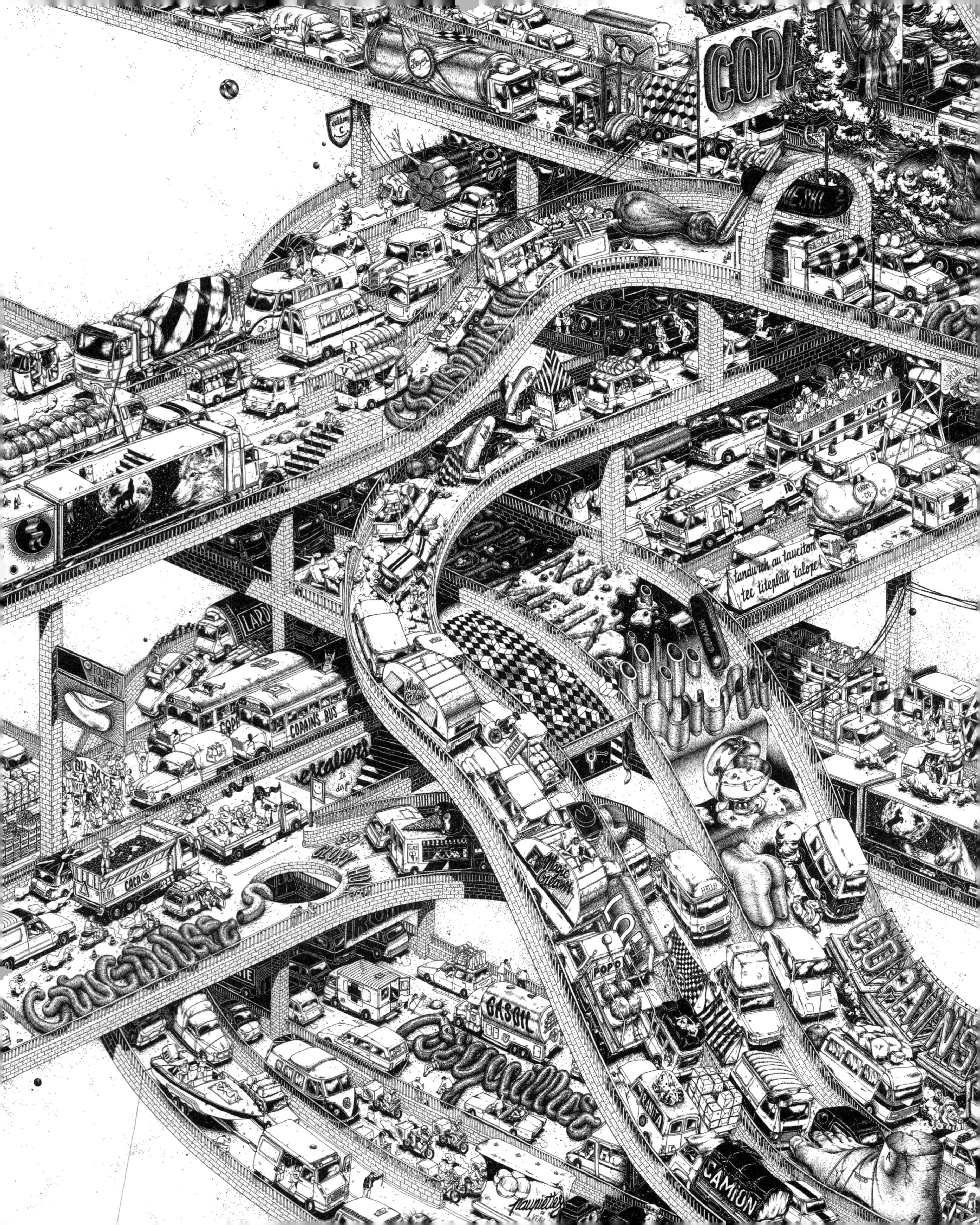

COPAIN
COPAINS BUS
COPAINS
COPAINS
GASOIL
CAMION

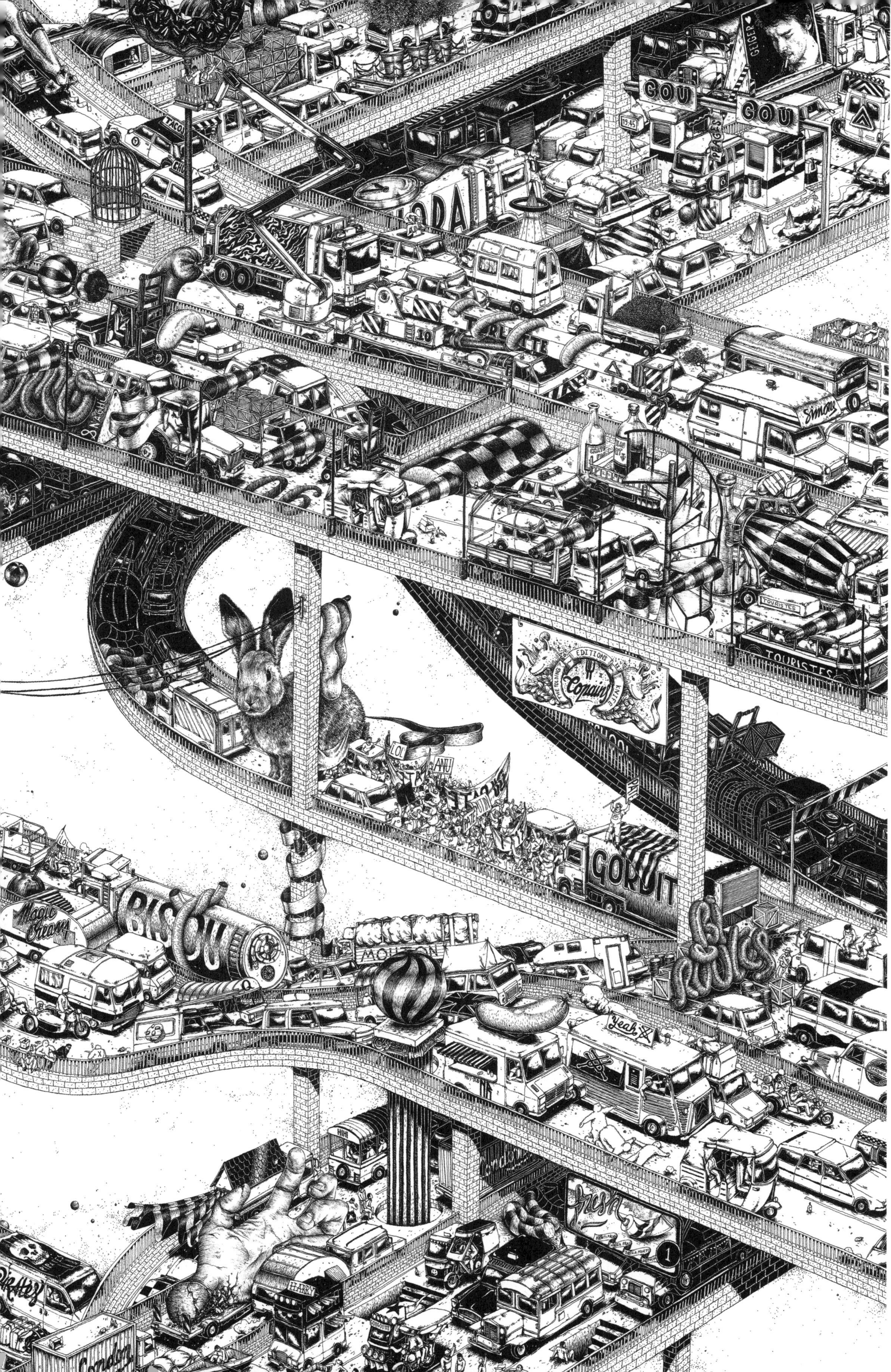

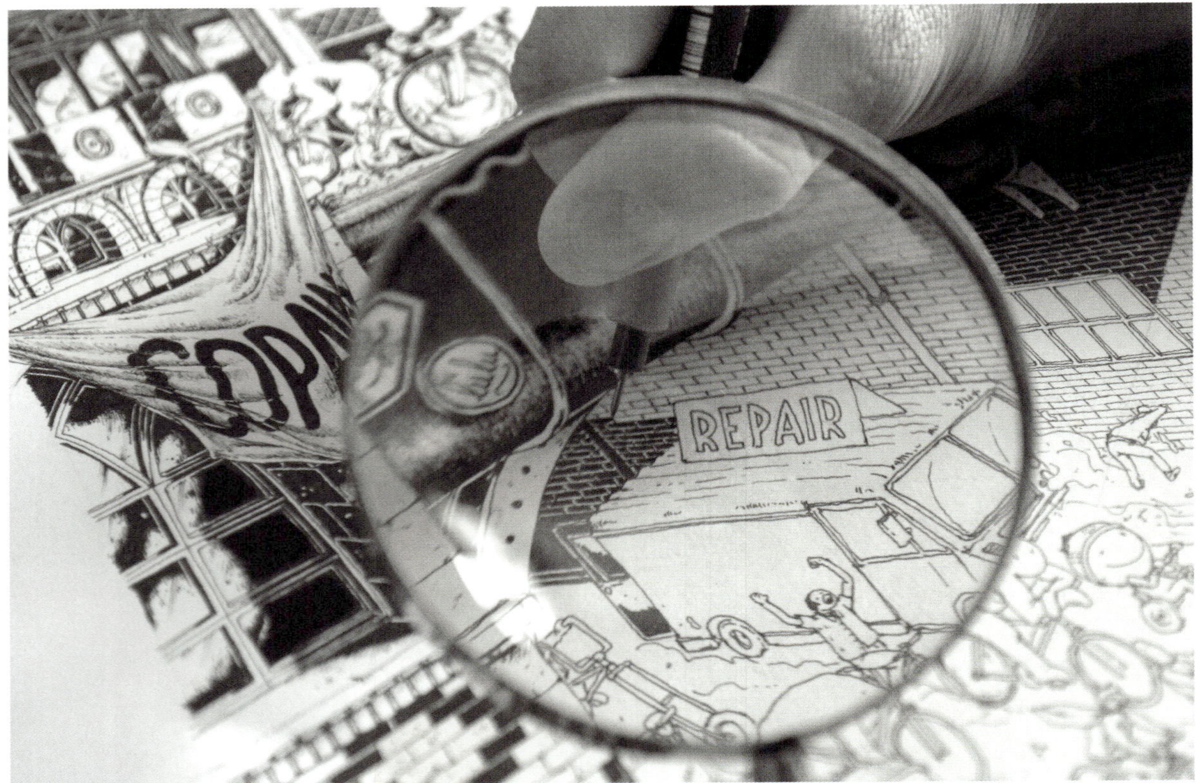

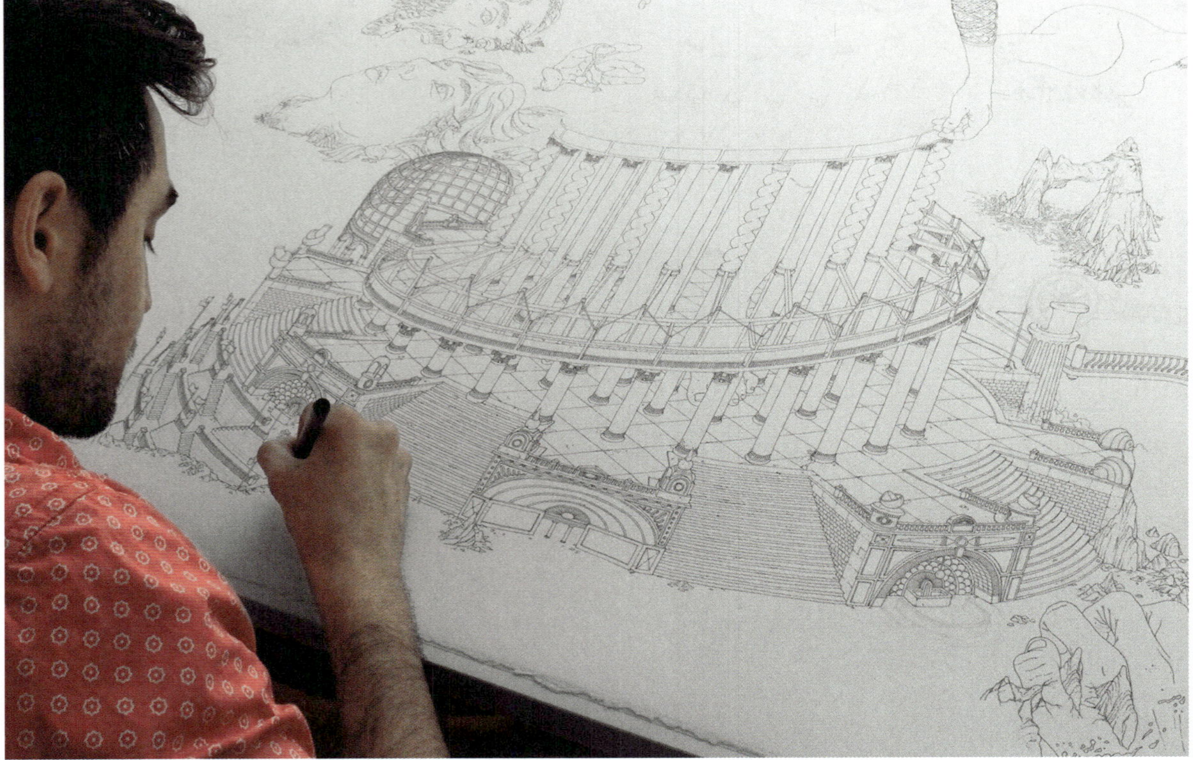

Drawn only with a rotring Rapidograph pen, this continuous scene combines absurd scenarios with meticulously detailed architecture, all rendered with audacious ambition, commitment and a clear love of drawing. *Bicycle* became the calling card for Gattoni's work and allowed him free reign to develop his visual universe without constraints.

Describing the driving force behind his work he says, 'I draw things from daily life, such as friends, places I love...The drawings immerse people in a universe, as actors rather than spectators. I love that there are several levels of interpretation: first we see a huge highway then, as we get closer, a traffic jam, and then the interaction between the different characters; a walk into the scenes that compose the story.'

In addition to the stimuli that daily life provides, Gattoni cites as inspiration the painters Michelangelo (1475–1564), Hieronymus Bosch (c. 1450–1516) and Salvador Dalí (1904–1989), as well as Greek Mythology and architecture – he frequently experiments with architectural forms, representing materials such as wood, marble and stone.

Ultra Copains, detail, 2012

The artist at work.

Untitled, c. 2012
Pencil on paper
Dimensions unknown

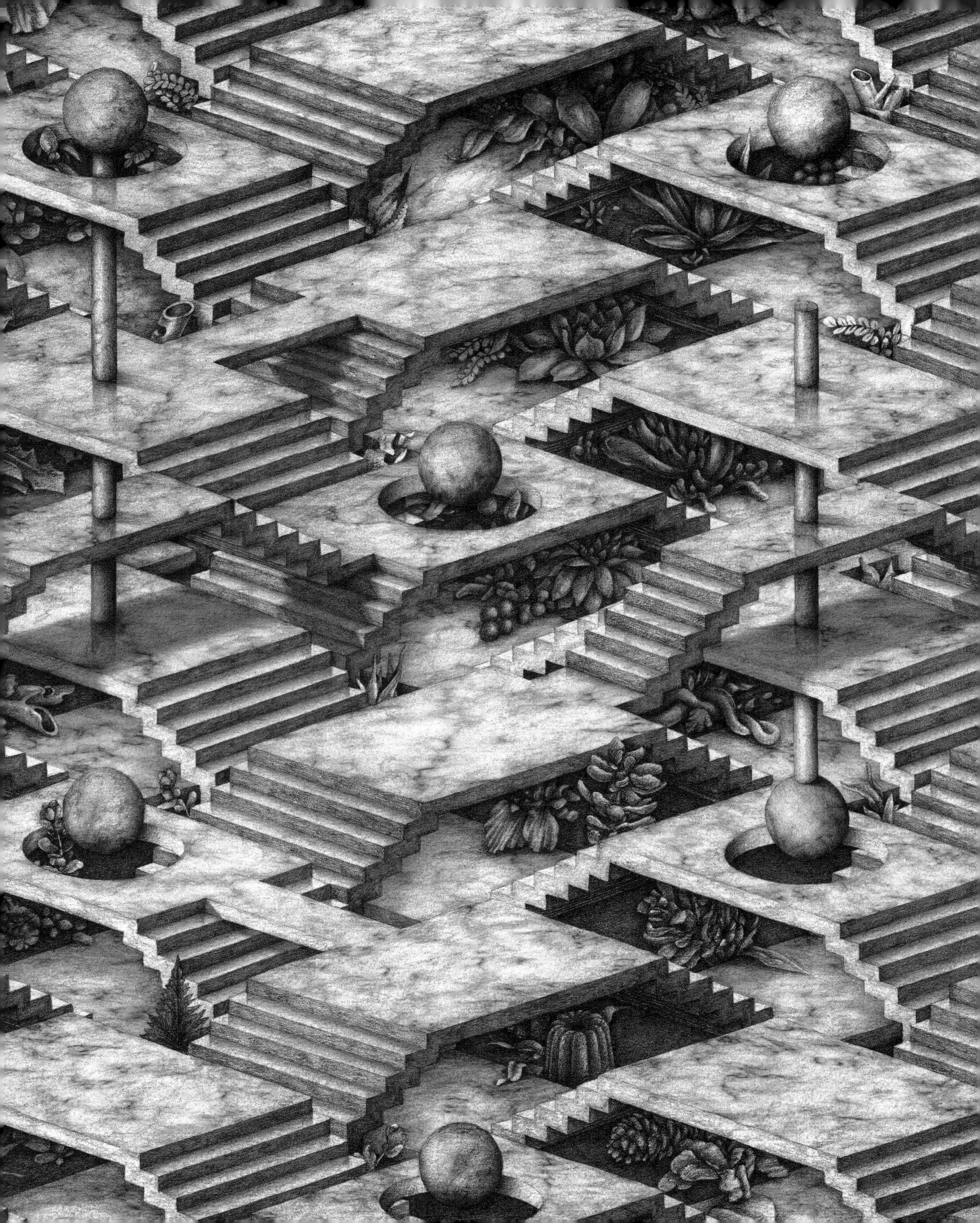

Knarf
Refreshingly bold and dynamic,

Knarf's stylistic innovations evince great maturity in an artist who is still only in his twenties. Having painted murals since the age of fourteen, he also has a degree in sculpture and is currently studying graphic arts and printmaking at the Academy of Fine Arts Vienna. It is this combination of both formal and informal practice that drives his art, resulting in endeavours that encompass a wide range of materials and formats, such as street posters, murals and zines.

The initial attraction of graffiti to Knarf was its illicit nature, but he soon began to appreciate other aspects of the form, taking into consideration, for example, its relationship to its context, all the while not being too precious about the legacy of the end product. Rather than following trends, he combines medium, context and subject-matter in original and thought-provoking ways. He surprises the viewer, making drawings with a loose, frenzied energy and creating shapes that are abstract, organic and gestural. His expressive brushstrokes at times hint at landscapes or the forms and features of creatures, while his printed paste-ups are large-scale, mixing pattern with an unexpected variety of imagery; all of which is wonderfully raw and unfettered.

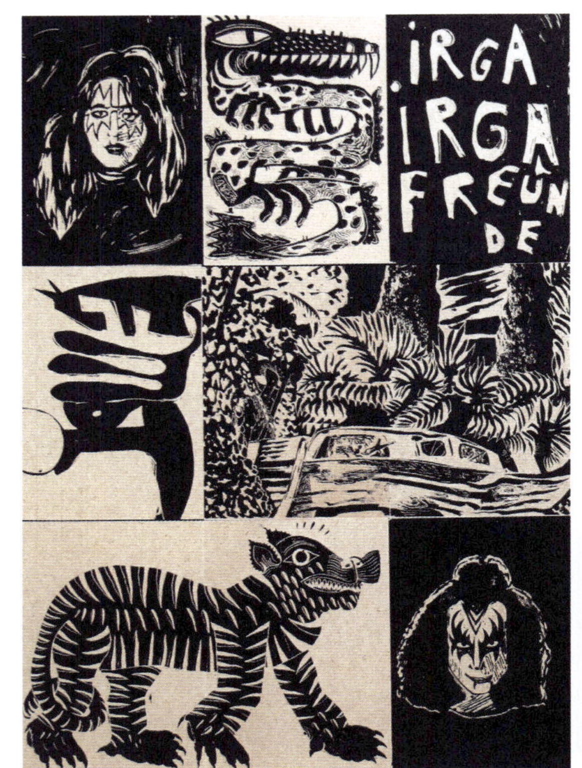

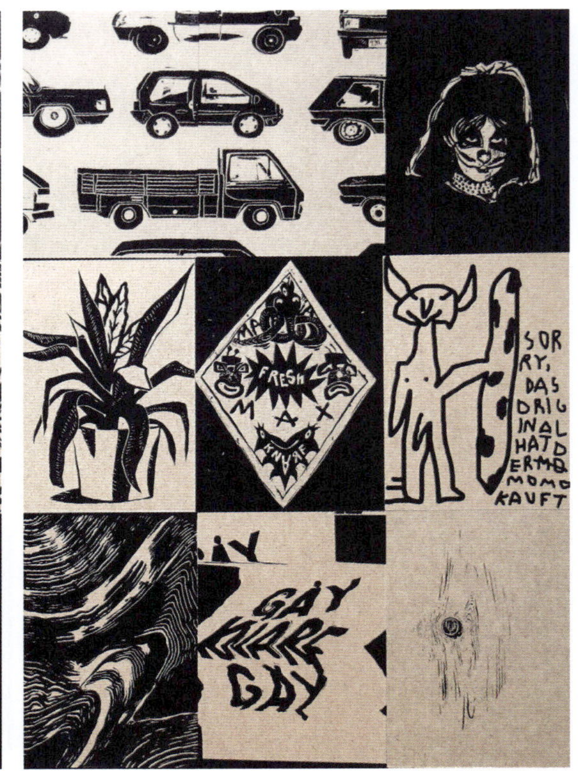

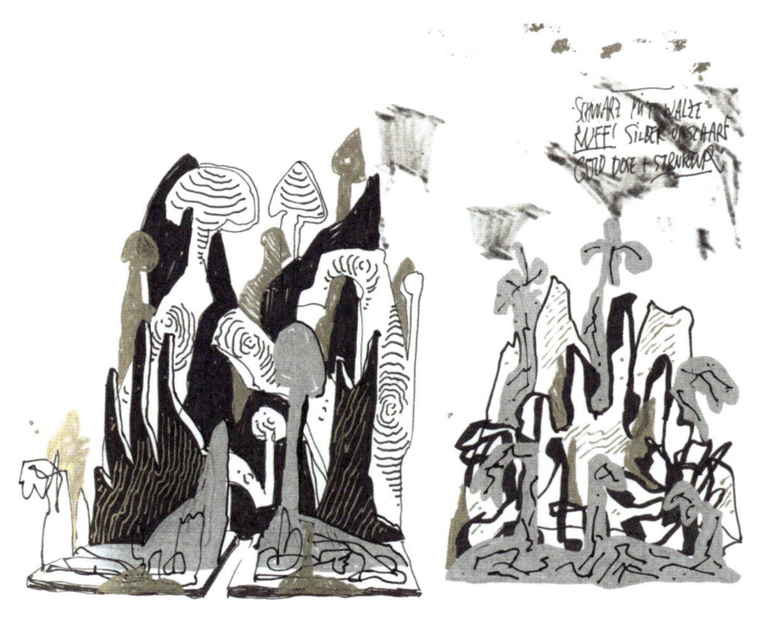

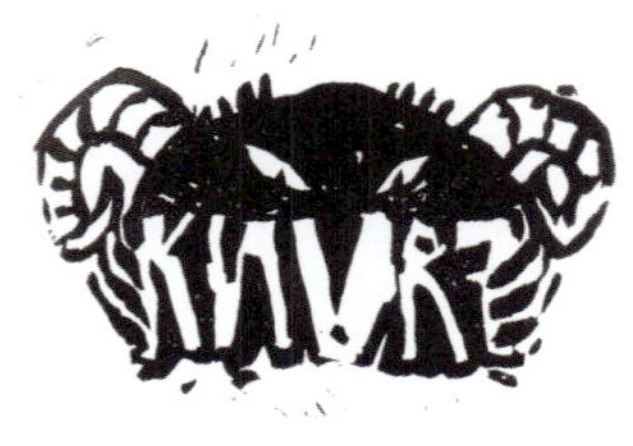

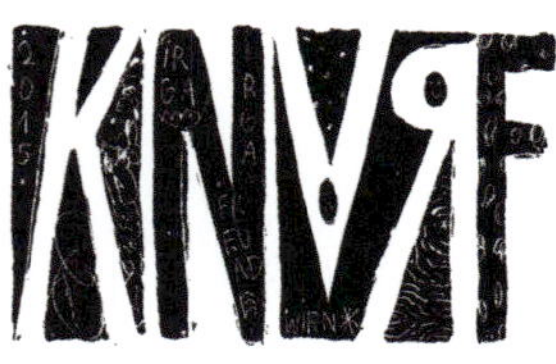

TOP
Untitled, from the series
'Irga Irga Freunde', 2015
Silkscreen on wood
63 × 45 cm (24⅞ × 17¾ in.)

CENTRE AND FAR RIGHT
**Pages from the artist's
sketchbook,** *c.* **2014
Mixed media
Dimensions unknown**

ABOVE AND RIGHT
**Knarf logostamps, 2014–15
Linocut
3 × 5 cm (11⅞ × 19¾ in.)**

OPPOSITE
**Drawings from the artist's
sketchbook, 2015
Mixed media
71 × 101 cm
(28 × 39½ in.) each**

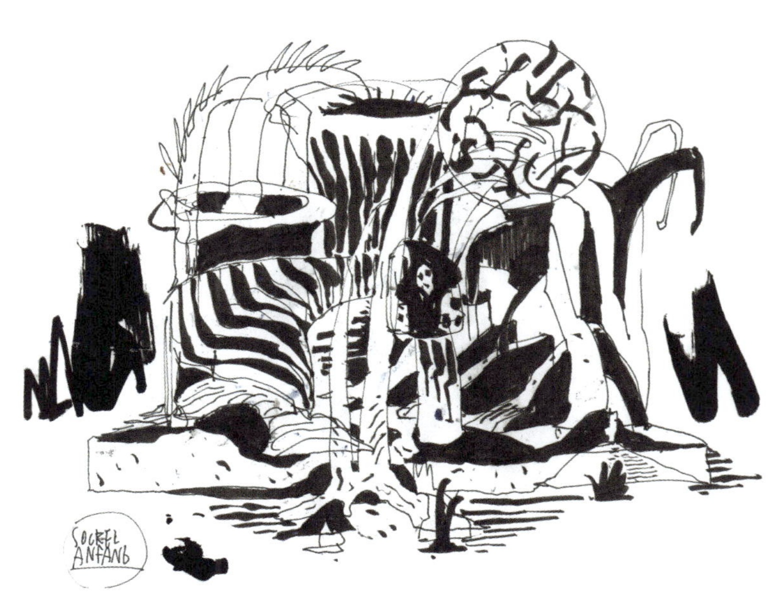

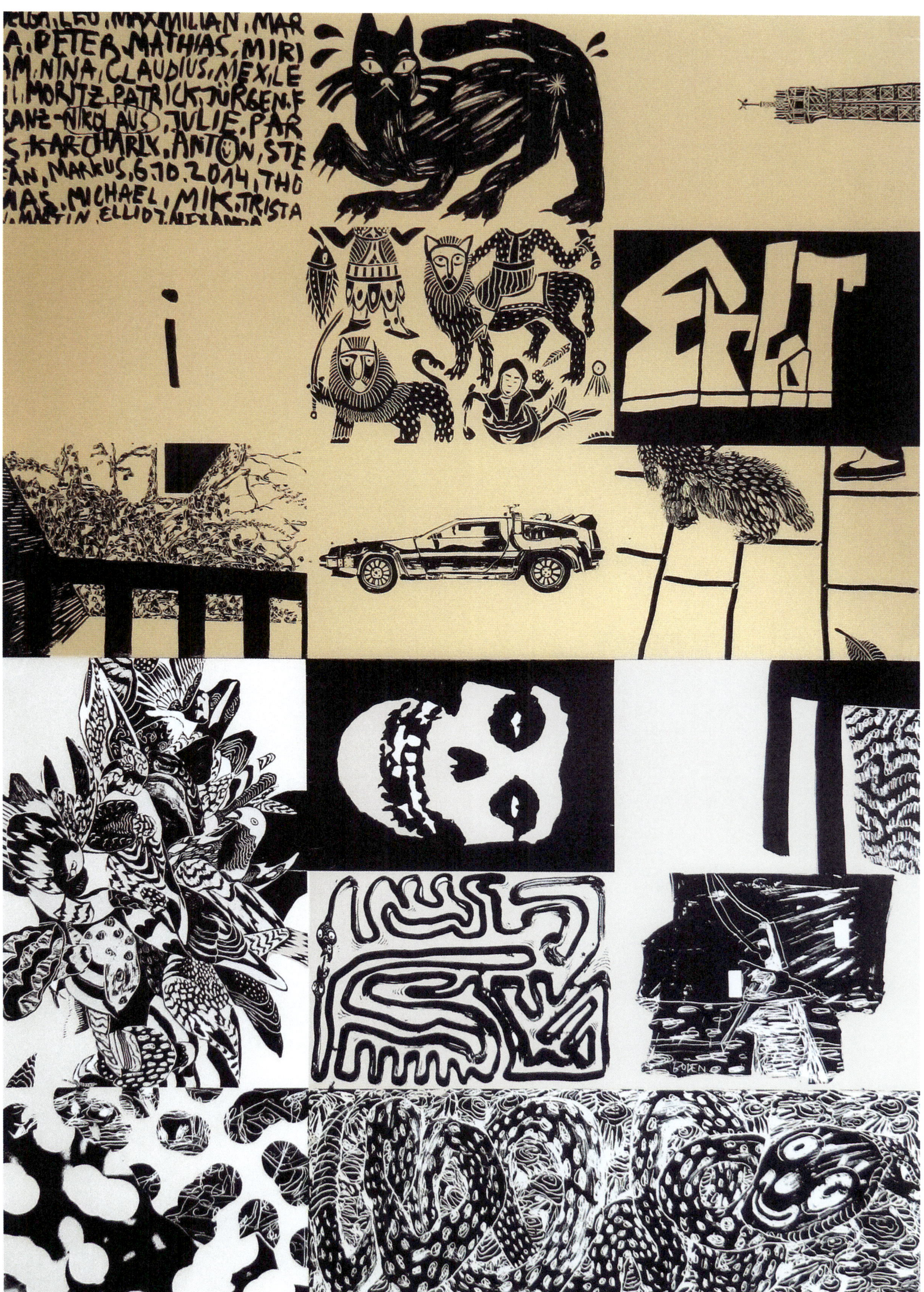
GALILEO MAXIMILIAN MAR
A PETER MATHIAS MIRI
M NINA CLAUDIUS MEXILE
MORITZ PATRICK JÜRGEN F
ANZ NIKOLAUS JULIE PAR
S KARCHARLY ANTON STE
AN MARKUS 6.10.2014 THO
MAS MICHAEL MIK TRISTA
MARTIN ELLIOT ALEXANDA
ERFURT

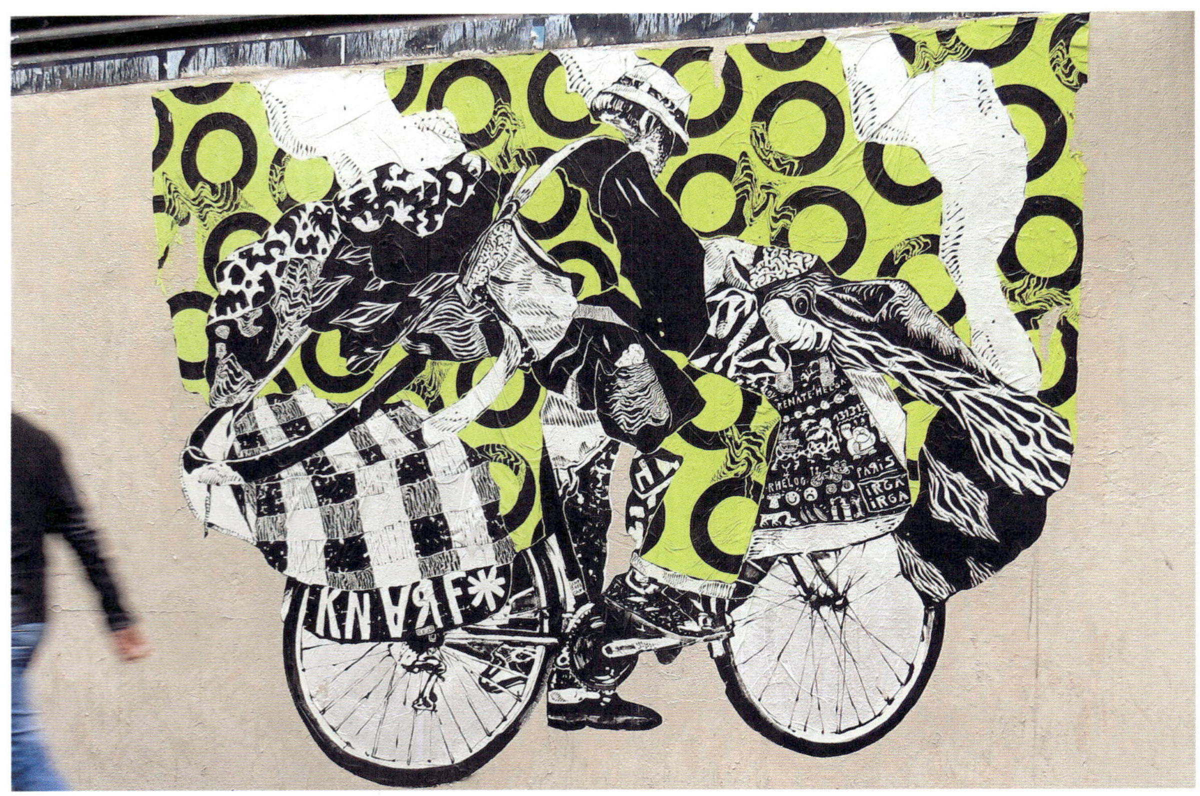

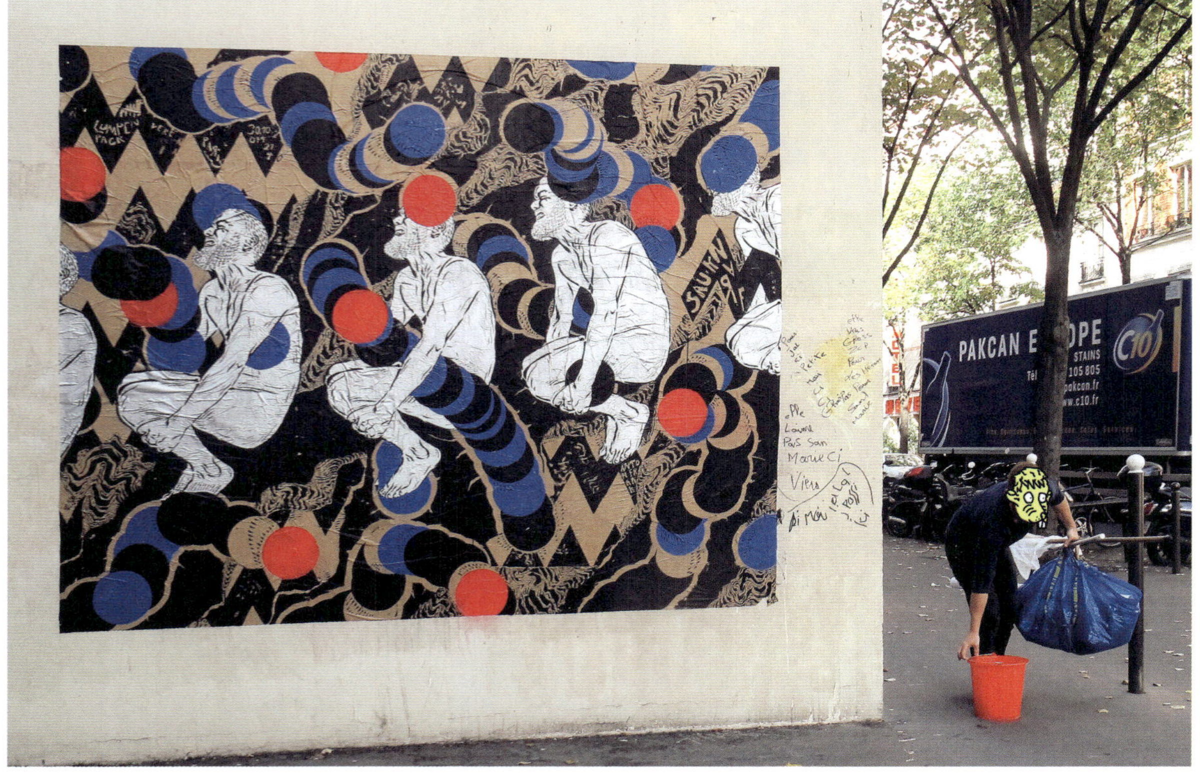

Untitled, mural in Paris, 2014
Acrylic on paper
200 × 300 cm
(78¾ × 118⅛ in.)

Knarf in collaboration with
MeerSau
Untitled, mural in Paris, 2014
Acrylic on paper
200 × 300 cm
(78¾ × 118⅛ in.)

OPPOSITE
Knarf in collaboration
with Nychos
Cockfight, 2015
Screenprint on paper
85 × 64 cm (33½ × 25¼ in.)

Drawing is central to Knarf's varied creative outlets and in particular sketchbooks are a safe arena in which to try out new ideas, such as his studies for wall works. In 2011, as an exercise, he made one drawing every day for a year in an A4 sketchbook, in all kinds of media. The result was the limited-edition book *365 Bildgeschichten*, published by the Inoperable Gallery in Vienna to accompany the exhibition 'My Year Has 365 Pages'.

Along with the artists Mafia (see pages 64–67), Fresh Max and Shida, Knarf is part of the IRGA IRGA Crew, which in 2014 founded the organization WANDBLATT. The group produces books and zines, including a magazine of the same title, *ein WANDBLATT aus Wien*, and through exhibitions and wall-based projects showcases the work of up-and-coming graffiti artists. With a low-fi, spontaneous energy, WANDBLATT is a vibrant space in which to experiment.

Whether drawing, making linocuts or leaving tags in hidden locations, somehow Knarf's productivity merges together into a seemingly spontaneous riot of forms that continue to leave a lasting impression.

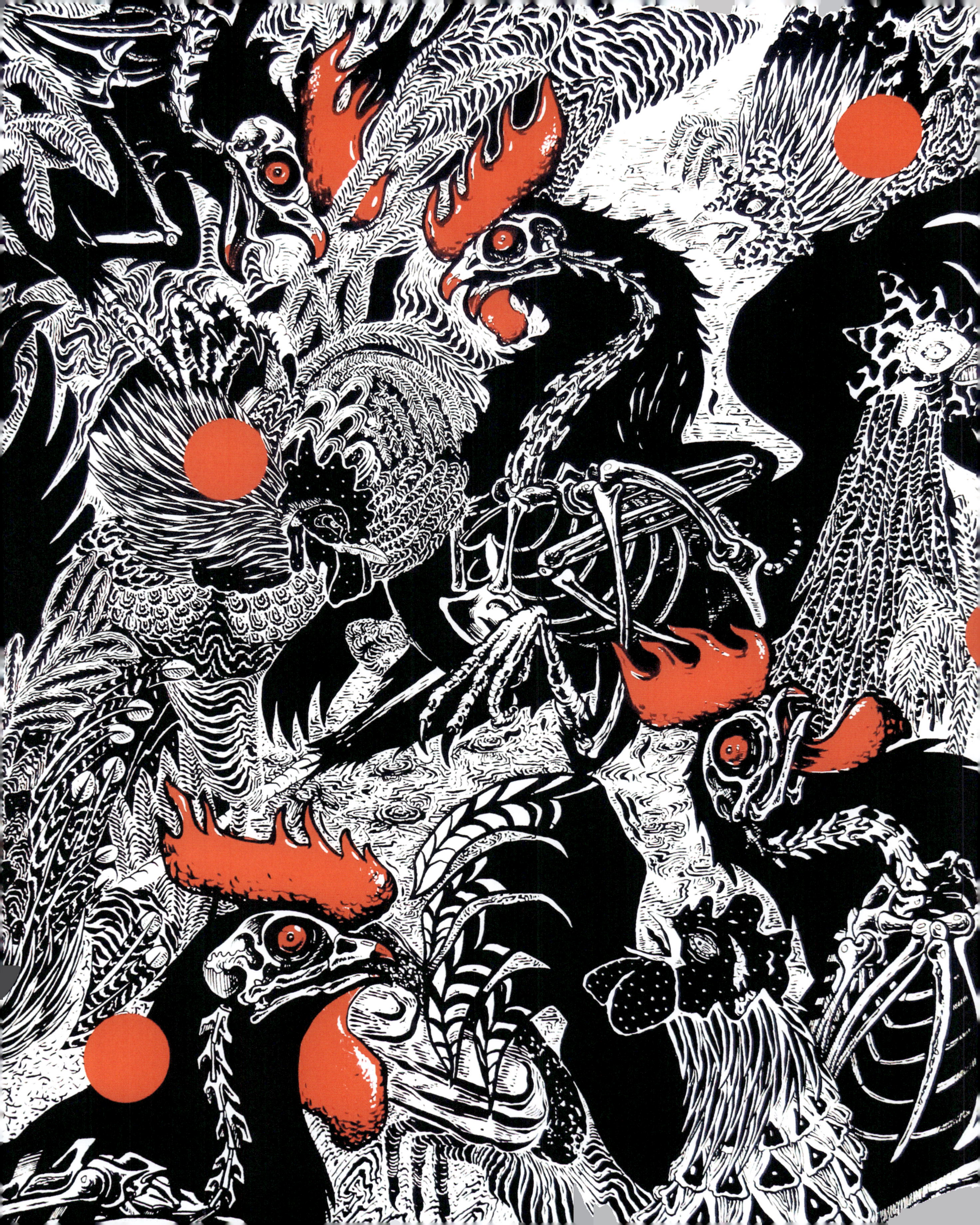

Raymond Lemstra

Transporting us to an alternative dimension, one in which 'future-primitive' characters inhabit a universe described with a meticulous delicacy, is the work of Dutch artist Raymond Lemstra. Encountering his drawings is rather like discovering an ethnographical manuscript in an antique bookstore in another galaxy faraway, if that were at all possible.

Lemstra's characters make reference to the language of primitive art in their accentuated and decorated features, however, the method he deploys to execute them is anything but archaic – involving a highly laborious technique of cross-hatching with pencil, which is then tinted with watercolour. There is an inherent clash of intent in the way Lemstra uses refined craftsmanship and traditional materials to describe such curious and random forms. 'I very much enjoy the slow and laboursome process,' he explains, 'These moments of pure dedication to the work are peaceful

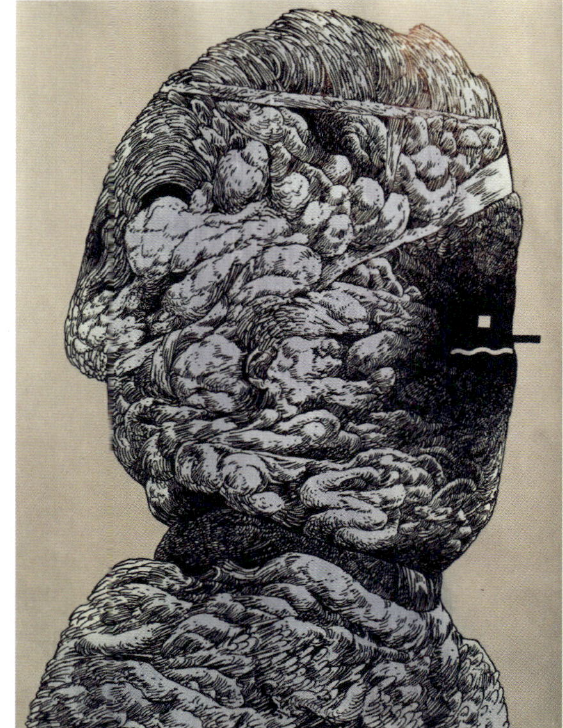

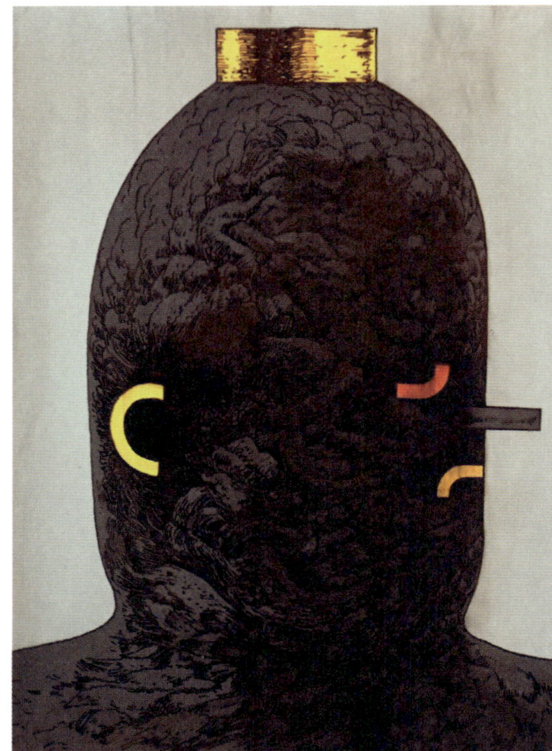

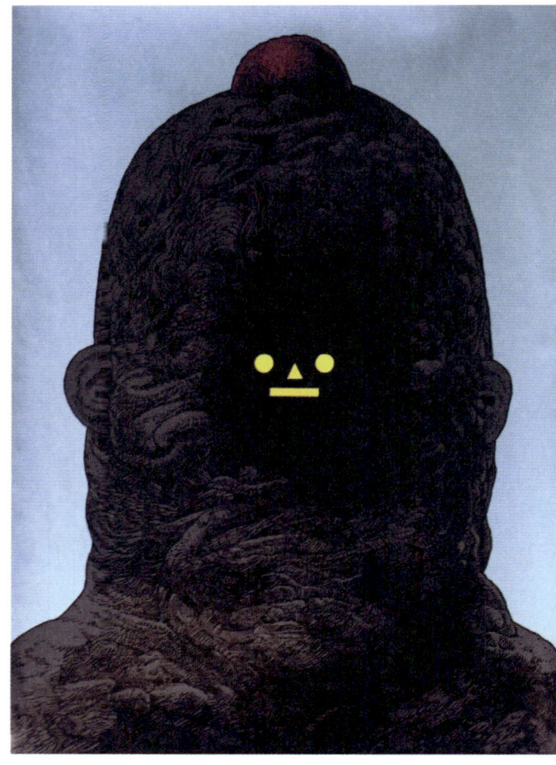

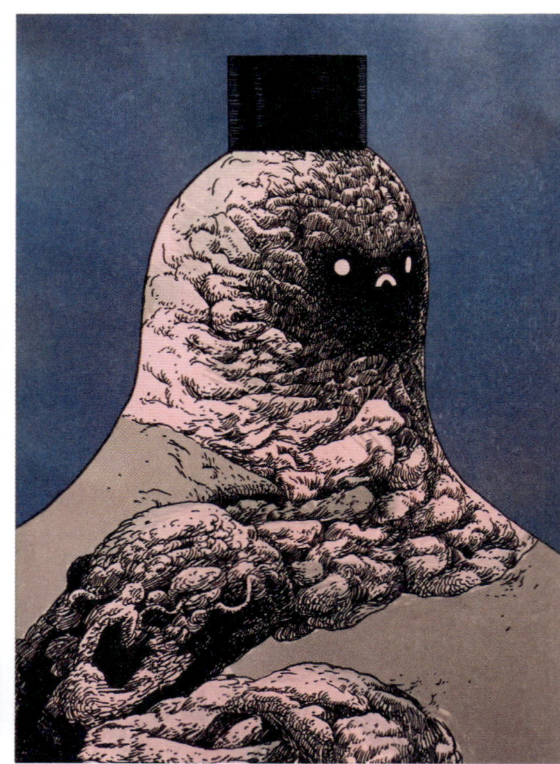

Untitled, four works from the series 'Crumbs', 2015
Ink on paper
Dimensions unknown

OPPOSITE
Untitled, from 'Crumbs'
Ink on paper
Dimensions unknown

OVERLEAF
Untitled, works commissioned by *Nobrow*, issue no. 9, 2014
Graphite, chalk and coloured pencil on paper
26 × 18 cm
(10¼ × 4⅝ in.) each

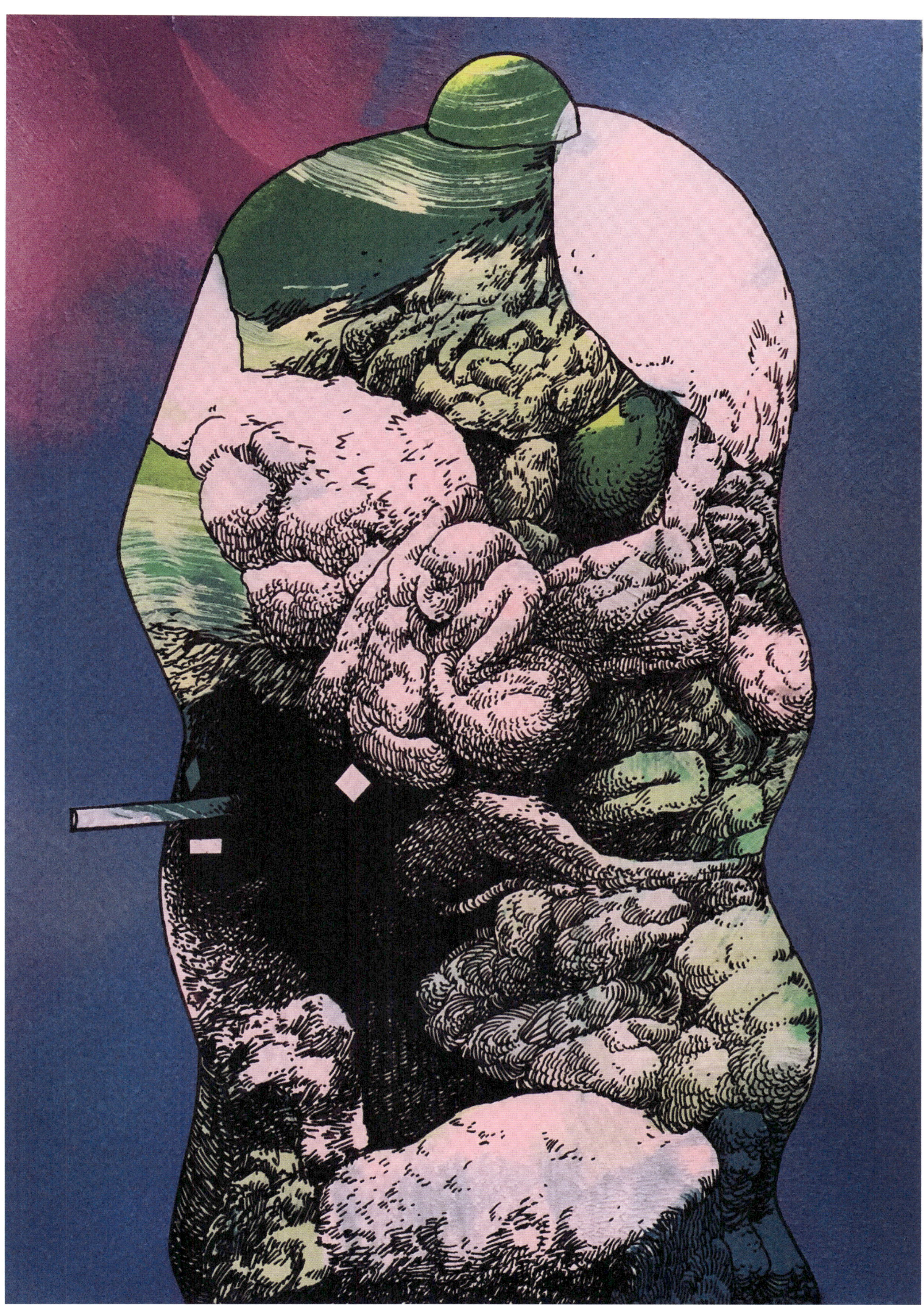

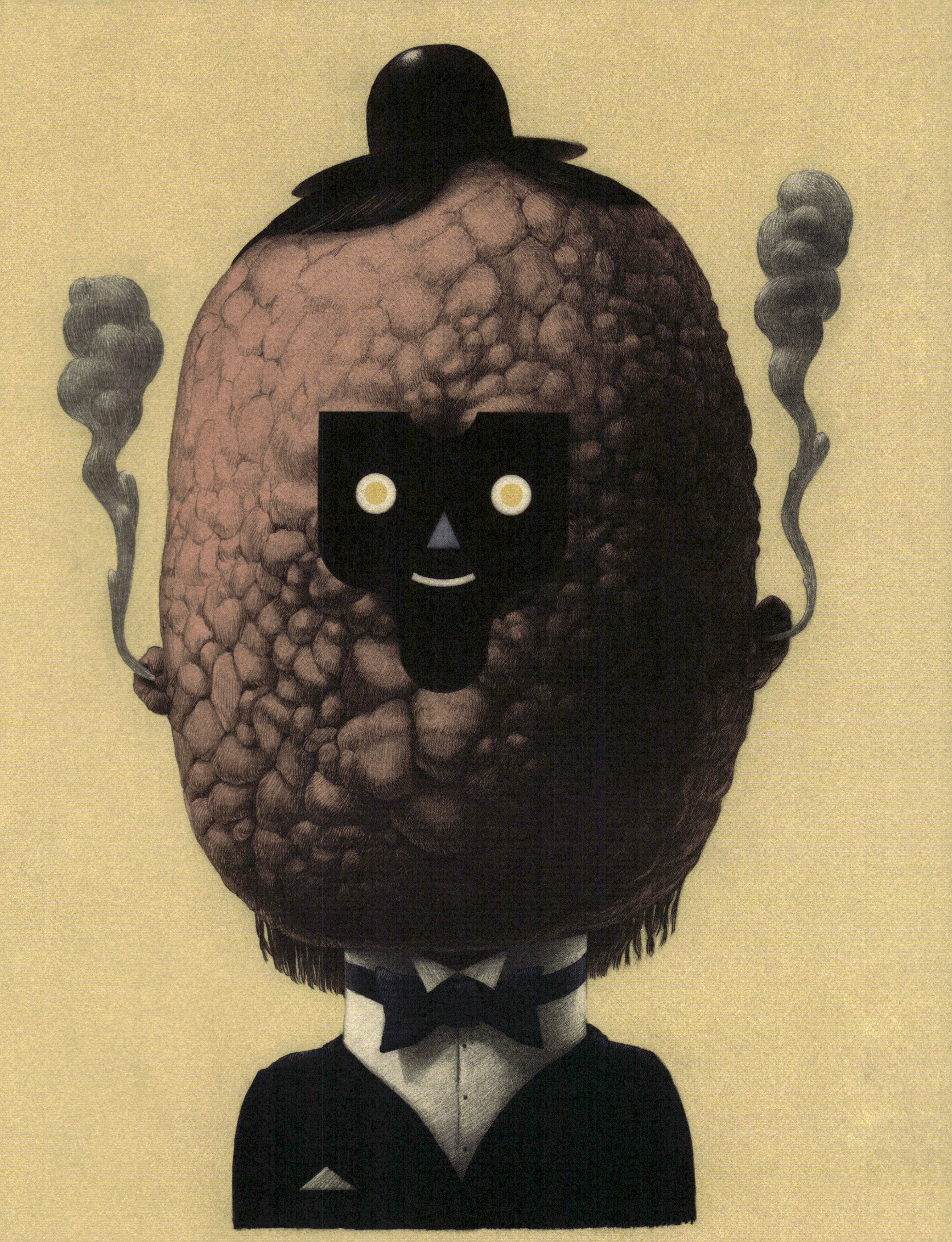

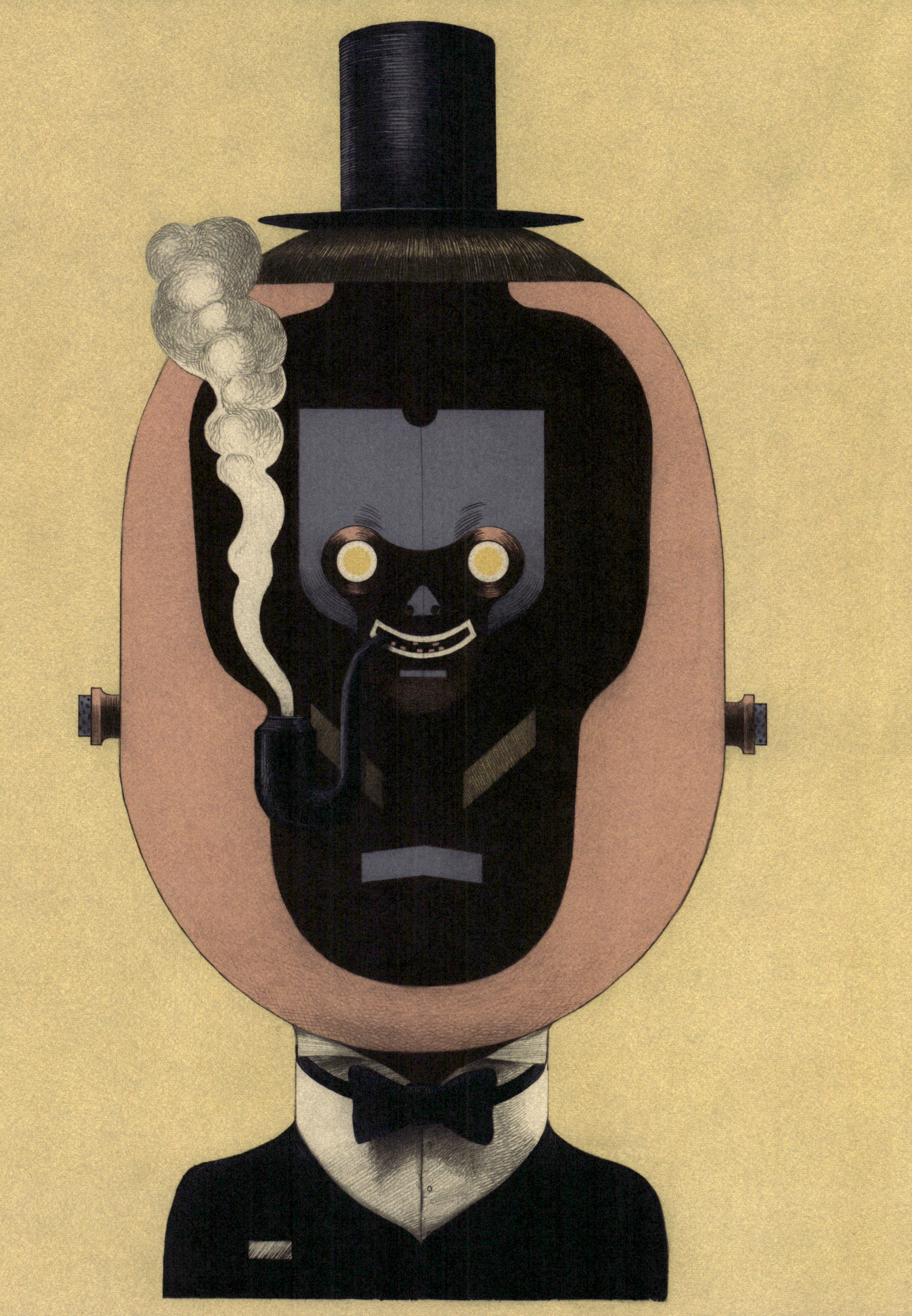

moments for me, I treasure them…it's mostly a process
of slow moulding and the weighing up of shapes and
overall aesthetics.'

Besides the incongruities in Lemstra's use
of technique and subject-matter are the visual
juxtapositions. In his compositions sombre characters
can be found wearing formal attire or smoking, yet they
have the exaggerated features of futurist sculptures,
are adorned with tribal markings or comprise
unusual organic textures and forms. Of these bizarre
combinations the artist comments, 'When I draw
characters I imagine that the subjects have spent their
whole morning dressing up in order to look their best for
the event of being frozen in time…. I am interested in the
stories the image suggests, as well as the "choices" that
the characters appear to have made, such as wearing
elaborate smoking gear, all of which invite the viewer
to apply their own associations.'

Each new body of work is guided by its own set of
aesthetics. For example, in the series 'Crumbs' the
distinct characters possess similar physiognomies,
and Lemstra's minimal use of background colour and
detailed line work throughout reconciles the series as
a whole. Lemstra explains how most of his characters
come into existence via his 'strict rules for creating
and combining shapes. In this process I refer to the
aesthetics of geometry, the golden ratio, or just my gut
instinct. I usually feel that I am ruining an empty sheet
of paper with my first lines, but after some extensive
effort I bring it back to a balanced whole.'

Snout, 2014
Graphite on paper
18 × 26 cm (4⅝ × 10¼ in.)

OPPOSITE
Pearl, 2014
Graphite on paper
26 × 18 cm (10¼ × 4⅝ in.)

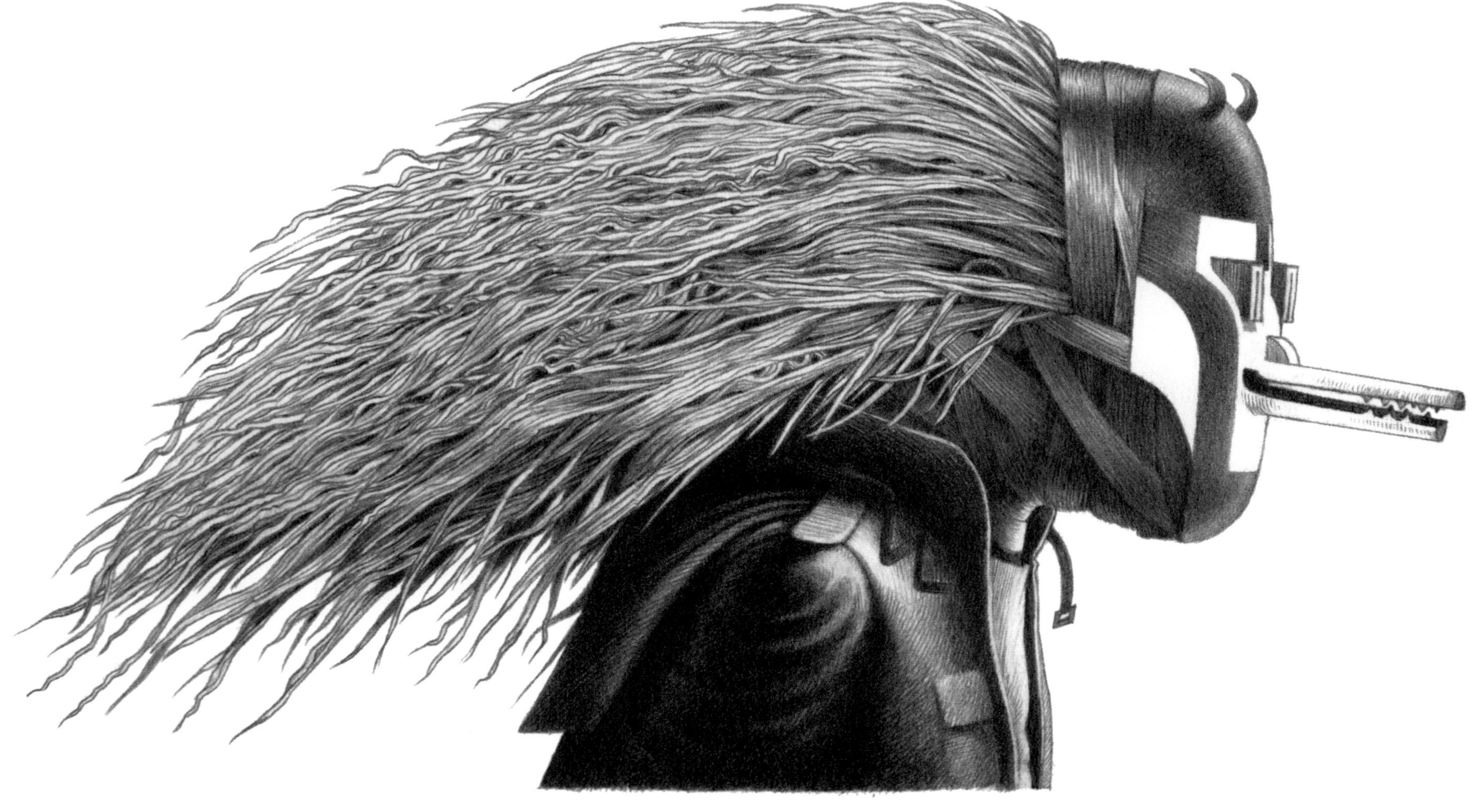

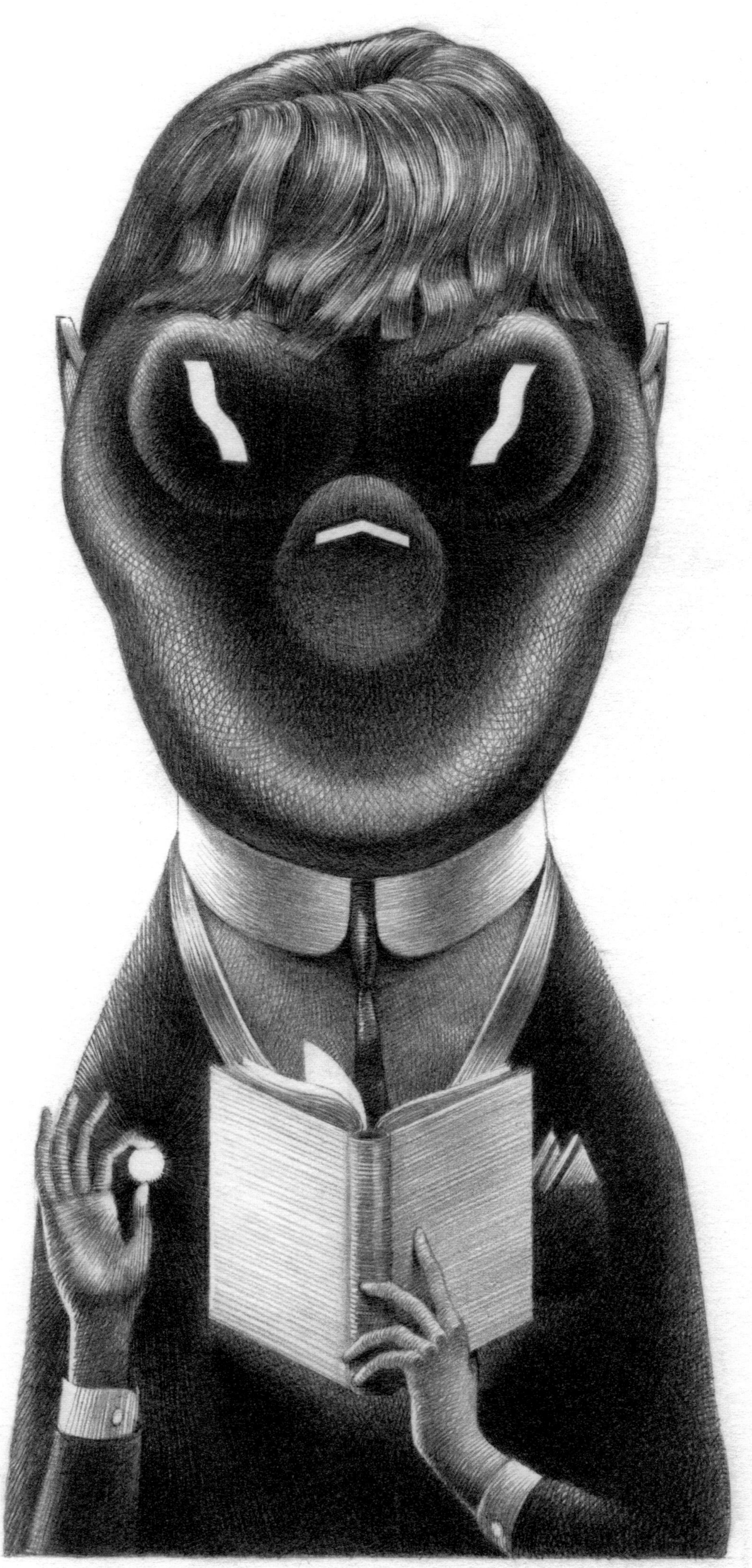

Mafia

Renowned for his avant-garde style, Mafia

(who also goes under the moniker of Tabak) is an up-and-coming artist and graffiti writer based in Vienna. Mafia has been his principal tag since taking up graffiti letter-writing ten years ago, while he adopts Tabak for the purpose of the works that depart from this tradition. Both his street art and studio pieces are a hybrid of letter-based forms – in his words a 'microcosmos' of visual elements – that seek to deconstruct the realms of contemporary art and graffiti, whether it be in the form of glyphs broken down into planes of colour, rough over-painting, geometric shapes or the more recognizable motifs of Modernist-style nudes, tropical plants and comic characters.

The rough textures, jazzy motifs and fluid, overlaid lines that he uses bring a feverish energy and spontaneity to his mark making. In Mafia's propensity to use grey palettes and abstract forms his work has some resemblance to the paintings of Georges Braque (1882–1963), with the recurring leaf motif an incidental nod to Henri Matisse (1869–1954). However one reads into the work, its mix of influences – from Modernism, Italo disco, superheroes and 1980s cartoons – come together in a bizarre runaway train of thought. In his studio work he uses materials such as felt-tip markers to complement his raw style. In addition to graffiti, Mafia's studio practice also takes inspiration from old comics, magazines and work by the painters Philip Guston (1913–1980) and Sol LeWitt (1928–2007).

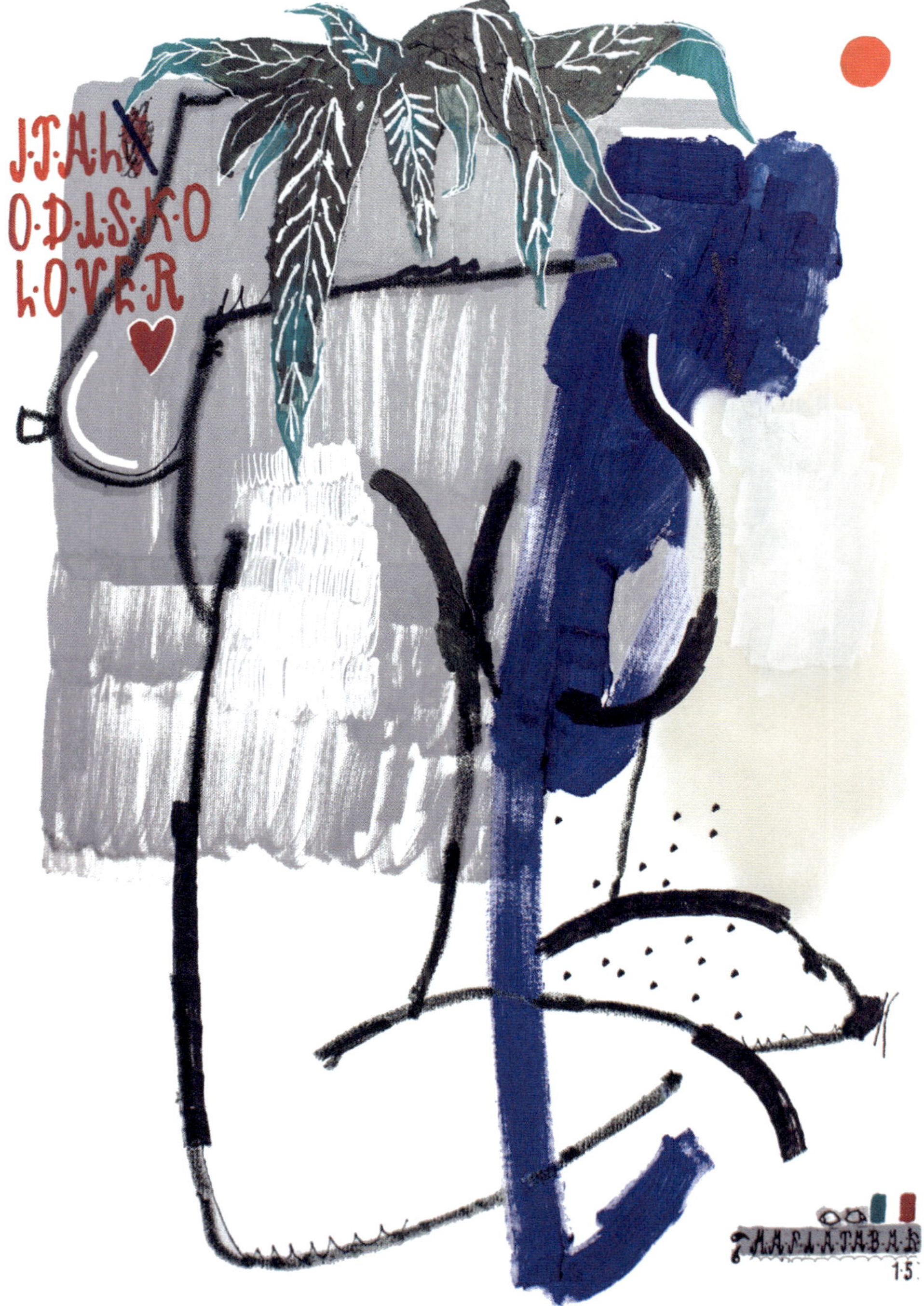

Nude, 2015
Acrylic on canvas
70 × 50 cm (27⅝ × 19⅝ in.)

OPPOSITE
Blue Nudes, 2015
Felt pen on paper
40 × 30 cm (15⅝ × 11⅞ in.)

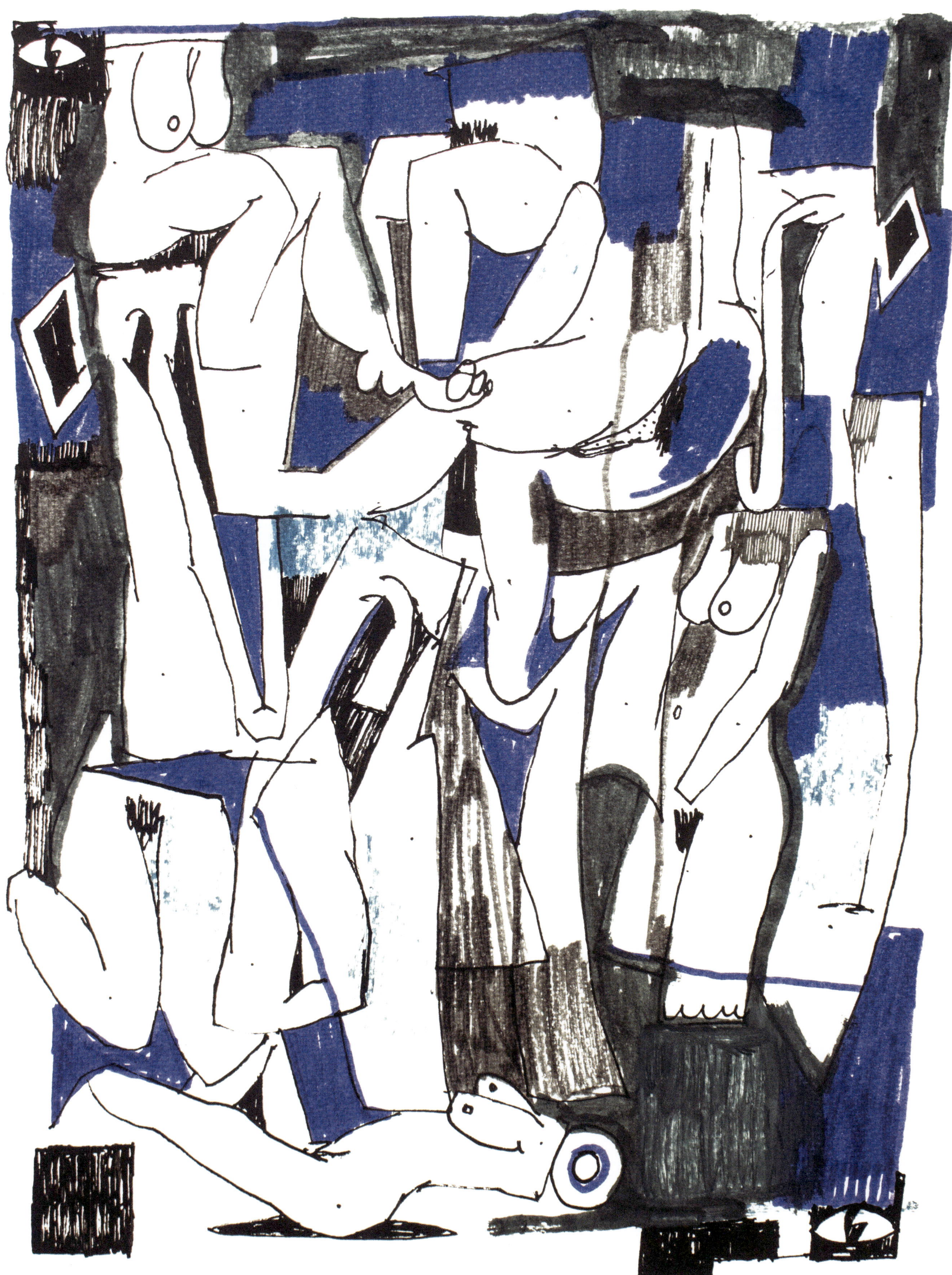

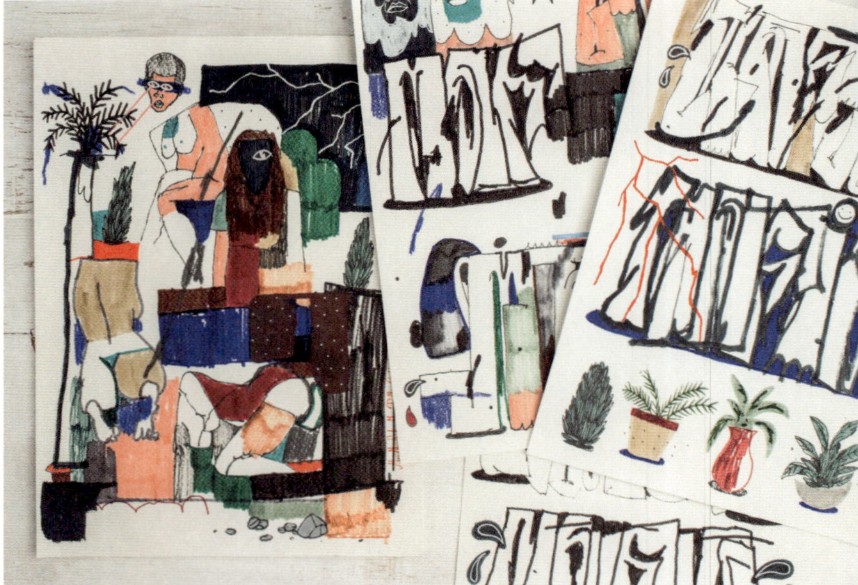

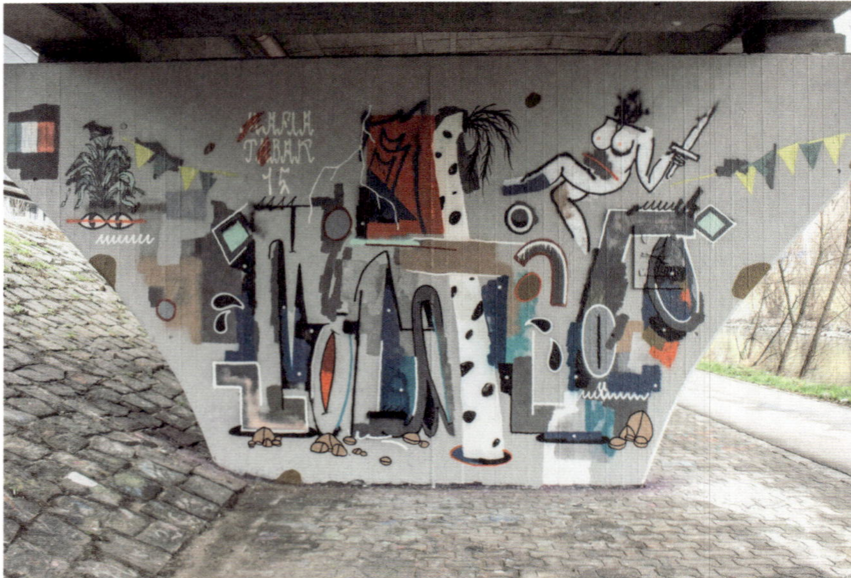

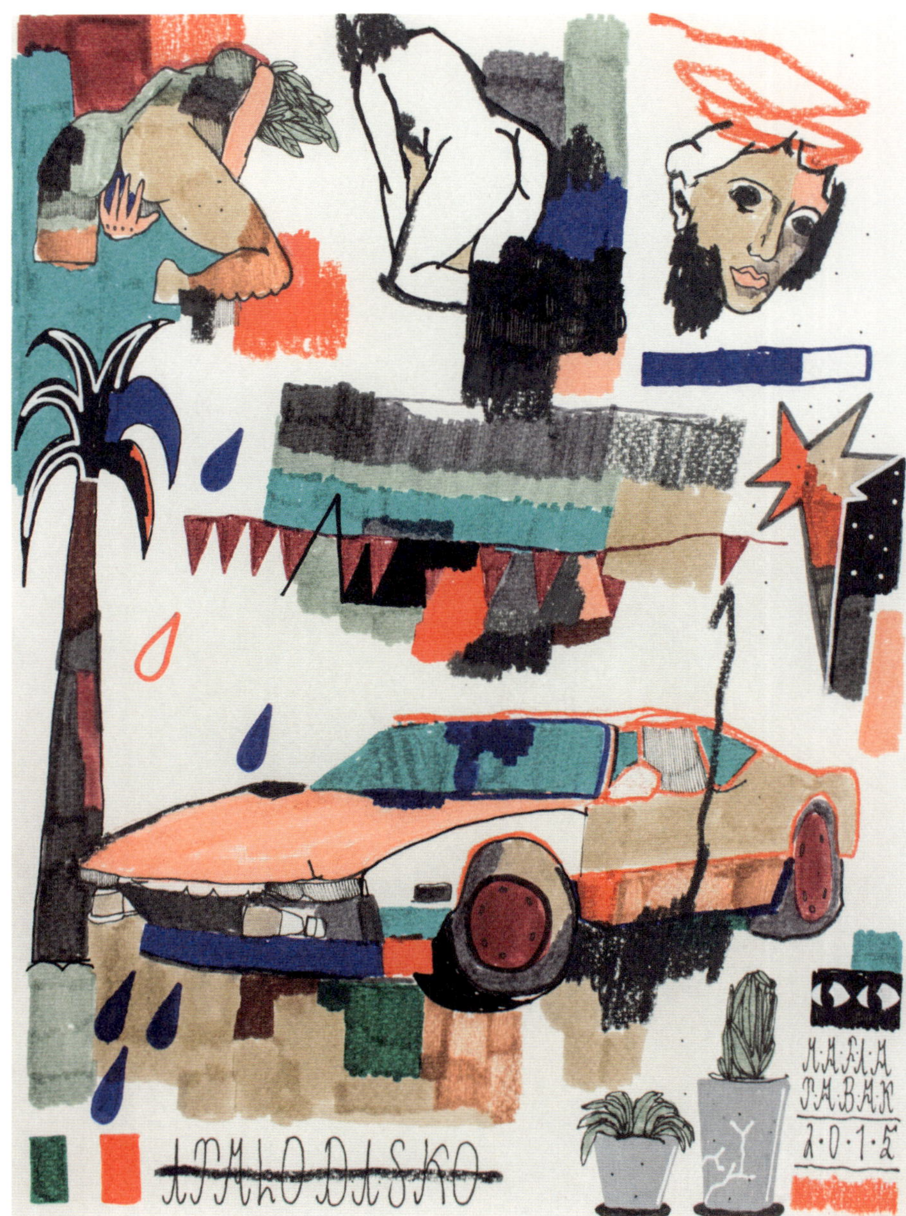

The backbone of this visual feast is his early graffiti work, as he explains: 'You have to learn the basics and your position in one game before you can begin to create your own style.' Traditional graffiti, however, he perceives as being distinct from his own practice: 'It just exists on trains, freights and abandoned areas and in the streets. It doesn't need any explanation because it is what it is. All my canvas stuff, drawings, murals and prints are another way of expressing myself, which is, of course, all influenced by my graffiti background.' Mafia adopts some of the clichés and forms commonly found in graffiti art, but reinterprets them, breaking them down into disparate elements to allow new forms to evolve.

Mafia is also part of the IRGA IRGA Crew with the artists Knarf (see pages 54–57), Fresh Max and Shida. As a group they regularly organize events and exhibitions as well as publish the magazine *ein WANDBLATT aus Wien*, a format in which like-minded artists can present their work. Both he and Knarf are enrolled at the Academy of Fine Arts Vienna, where they have had the opportunity to experiment with numerous printing processes, putting them to use in *WANDBLATT* and in their own posters and zines.

CLOCKWISE FROM TOP LEFT
Preliminary studies, 2014
Acrylic and felt pen
on paper
Dimensions variable

Untitled, 2014
Acrylic and felt pen
on paper
40 × 30 cm
(15⅝ × 11⅞ in.)

Untitled, mural in Portland,
Oregon, 2015
Mixed media
Dimensions unknown

OPPOSITE
Untitled, 2015
Acrylic on paper
177.8 × 127 cm (70 × 50 in.)

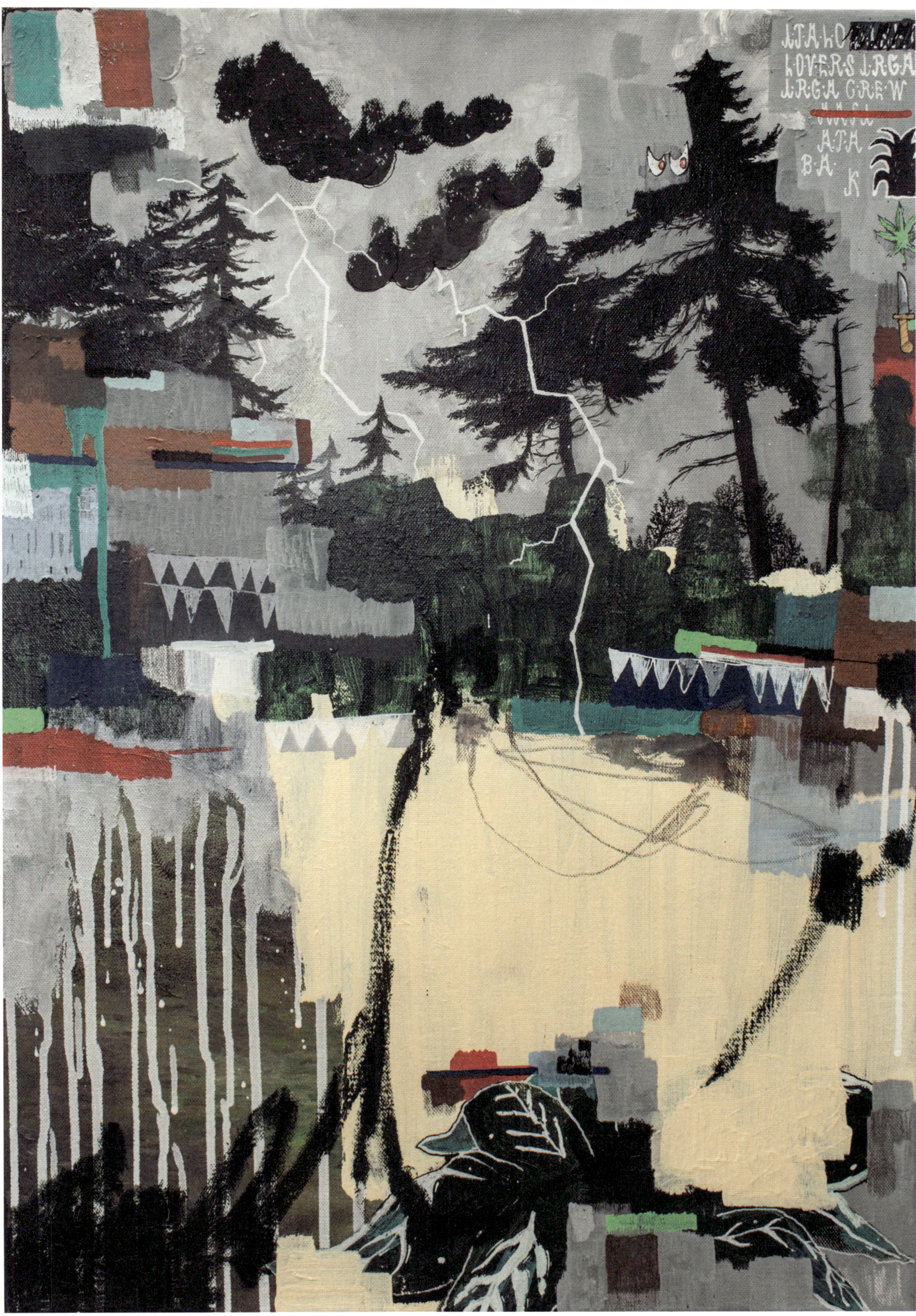
ITALO
LOVERS IRGA
IRGA CREW
MMCI
ATA
BA   K

Morcky

With a background in graffiti and street art, the illustrations, paintings and animations of the

Italian artist Morcky (aka Marco Galmacci) have both Constructivist and futuristic intimations. Living and working in Amsterdam since 2002, his multifaceted portfolio is an enviable mix of styles and achievements: he has exhibited worldwide, is a founder of the collective 'Hello, Savants!', has created music videos for the singer-songwriter Anouk and DJ Roger Sanchez, as well as making animations that have been featured at international festivals such as ResFest in the US and OneDotZero in the UK. In 2012 he produced his first graphic novel, *InsideOut: A Galactic Adventure*, which brought to life in fiction some of the characters he has been developing in his animations.

No. 3, from the series 'Concrete Dreams', 2014
Ink on paper
30 × 30 cm (11⅞ × 11⅞ in.)

OPPOSITE
Work in progress for
Fase 2 – Evoluzione, for 'Concrete Dreams', 2014
Pencil and acrylic on canvas
150 × 100 cm (59⅛ × 39⅜ in.)

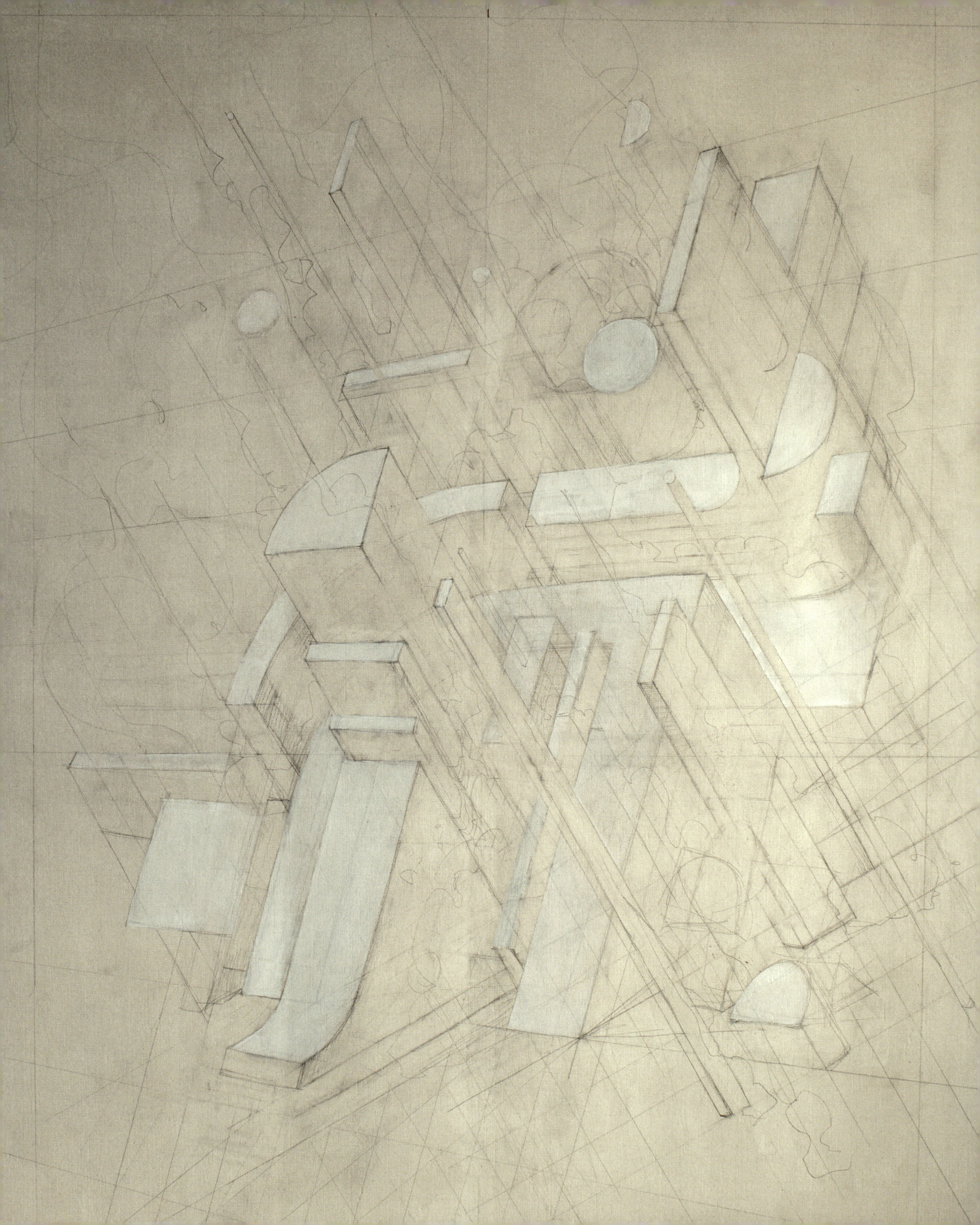

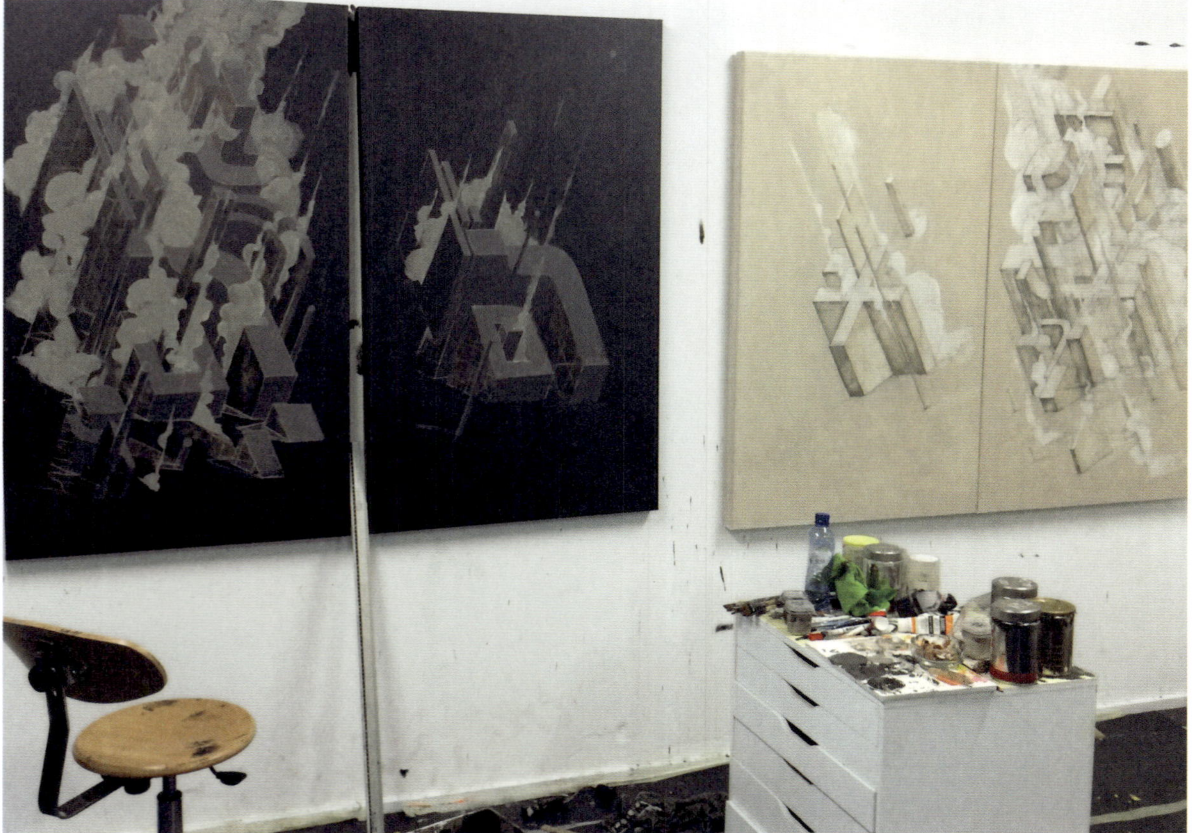

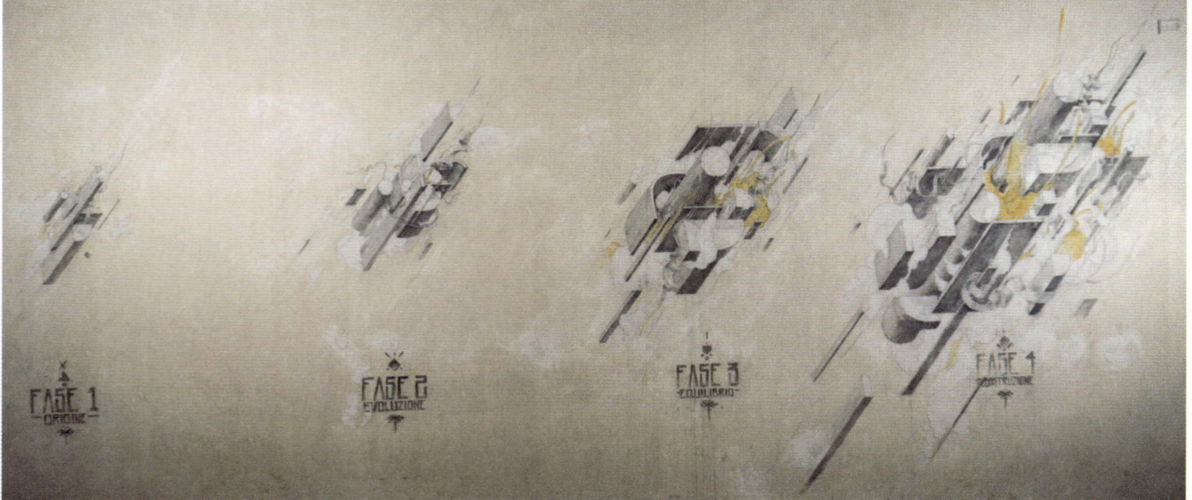

There are two predominant features to Morcky's art: his use of characters and the exploration of architectural space – subjects that sometimes appear separately and at others in harmony, in juxtapositions reminiscent of retro-futurist Utopian worlds, which are rendered in a beautifully muted colour palette. With a wonderful use of line, which recalls the highly influential and avant-garde French comic artist Moebius, as well as other figures associated with the *bande dessinée* comic art genre, Morcky plays with visual perspectives and expectations. Architecture becomes type, the mechanical becomes organic and geometric blocks of composition seem to float away as if in a Constructivist painting. Attracted to both complex and minimalist forms, he seeks to make these elements cohabit within a single, synchronized space. This approach is exemplified in a recent series of paintings he produced for the exhibition, 'Concrete Dreams', at the Original Dampkring Gallery in Amsterdam in 2014. 'Concrete Dreams' began life as studies of letters in three-dimensions, which then gradually became more abstract. The intention, he says, was to 'capture solid structures in dynamic poses…to suggest a moment suspended in time. To create this feeling I had to be really strict with the perspectives and shapes of the masses, so I introduced organic elements like smoke and ribbons to create an interplay of geometric accuracy and instinctive freehand drawing.' The effect is otherworldly, conjuring up a vision of a fantasy cyberspace with a twentieth-century futurist aesthetic.

Despite living and working in Amsterdam, Morcky maintains his connection to his hometown of Perugia, organizing collaborations between the city's artists, artisans and craftspeople. Underlying this is a passion to learn through collaboration: 'I believe that creativity and originality happen when you blend together all your experiences, knowledge and techniques. I think that's a duty for every artist.'

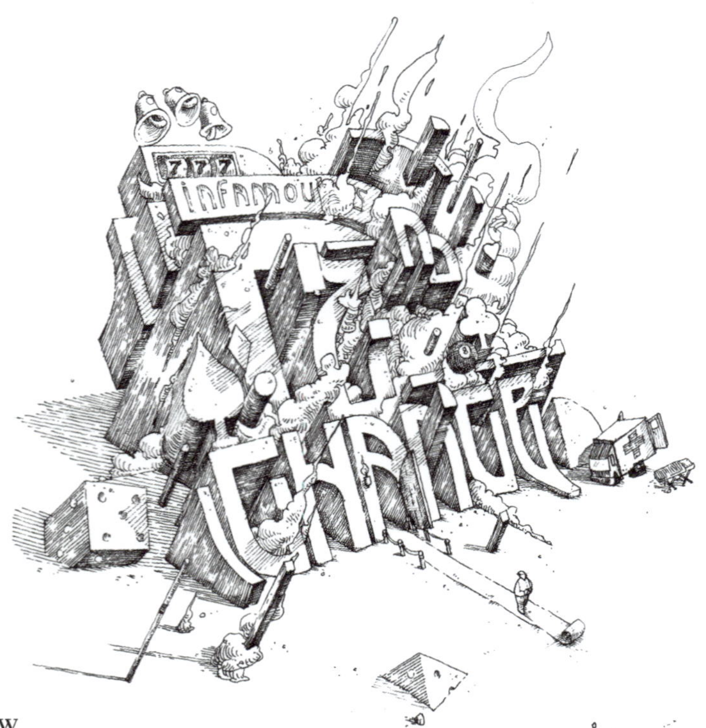

Works from 'Concrete Dreams' in the studio.

Untitled, from 'Concrete Dreams'
Pencil and acrylic on wall
250 × 900 cm (78¾ × 354⅜ in.)

Second Chance, 2014
Ink on paper
50 × 50 cm (19¾ × 19¾ in.)

OPPOSITE, CLOCKWISE FROM TOP LEFT
Phase 2 – Evolution, from 'Concrete Dreams'
Pencil and acrylic on canvas
150 × 100 cm (59⅛ × 39⅜ in.)

Phase 1 – Origin, from 'Concrete Dreams'
Pencil and acrylic on canvas
130 × 80 cm (51¼ × 31½ in.)

Untitled, from 'Concrete Dreams'
Ink on paper
30 × 30 cm (11⅞ × 11⅞ in.)

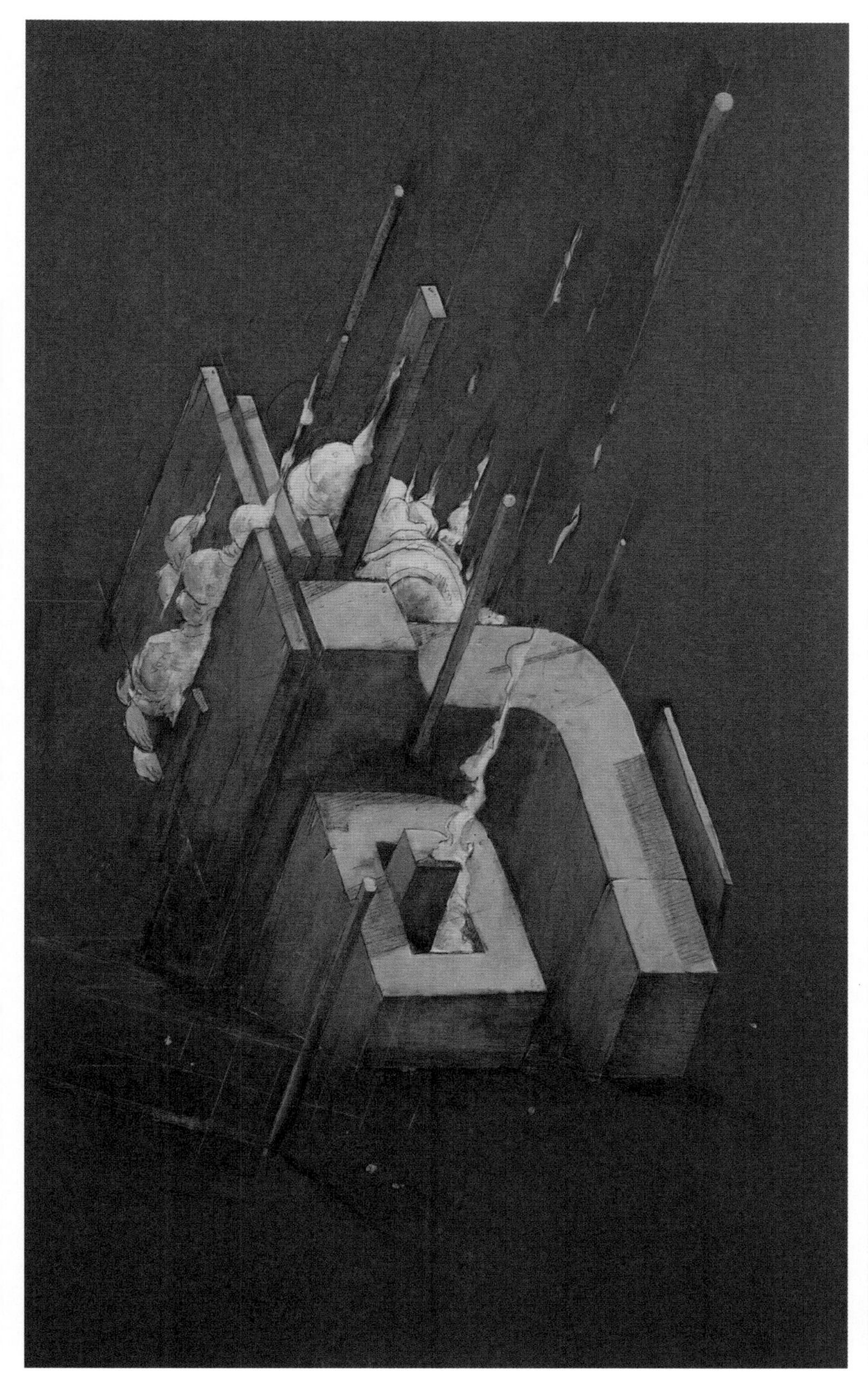

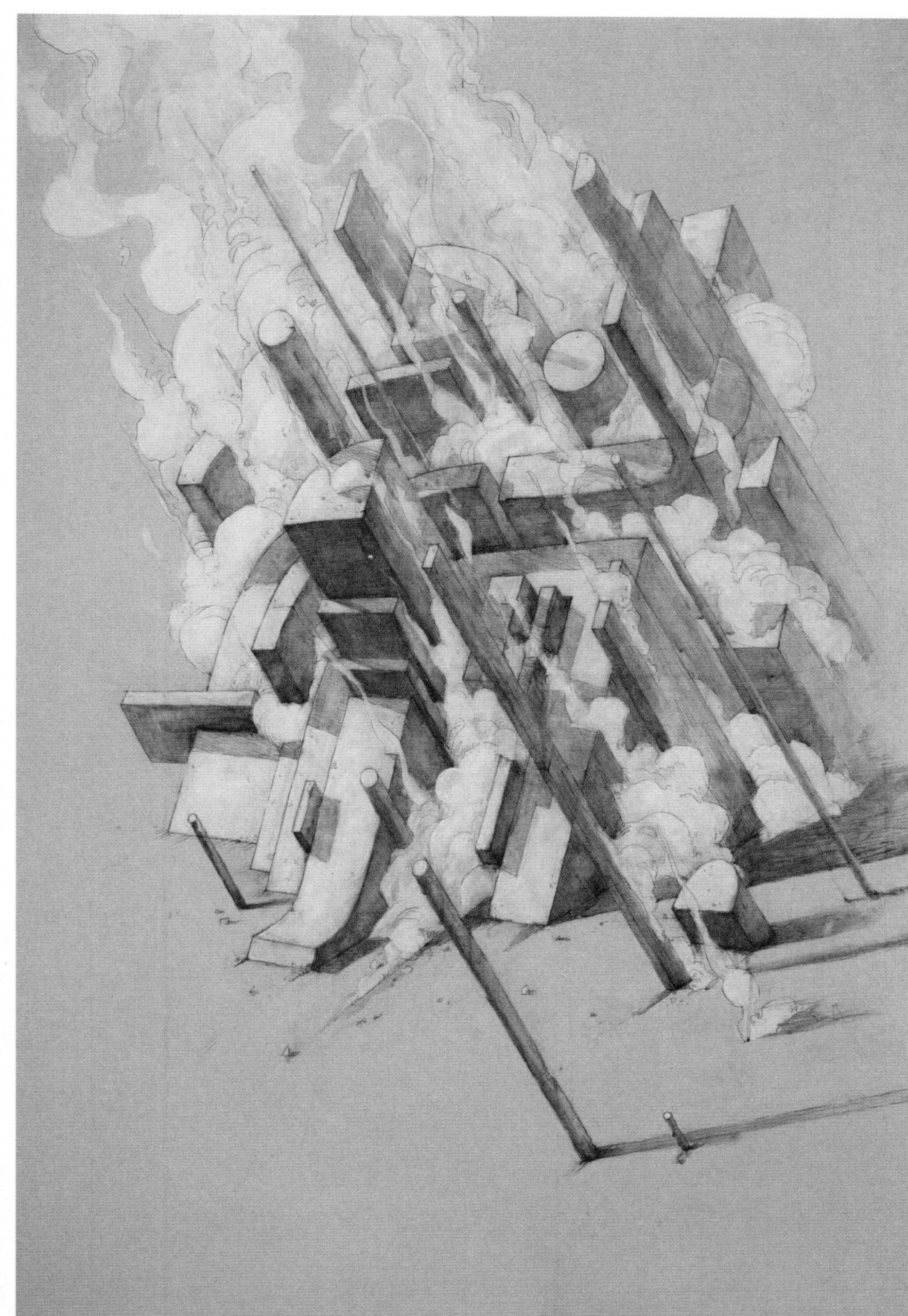

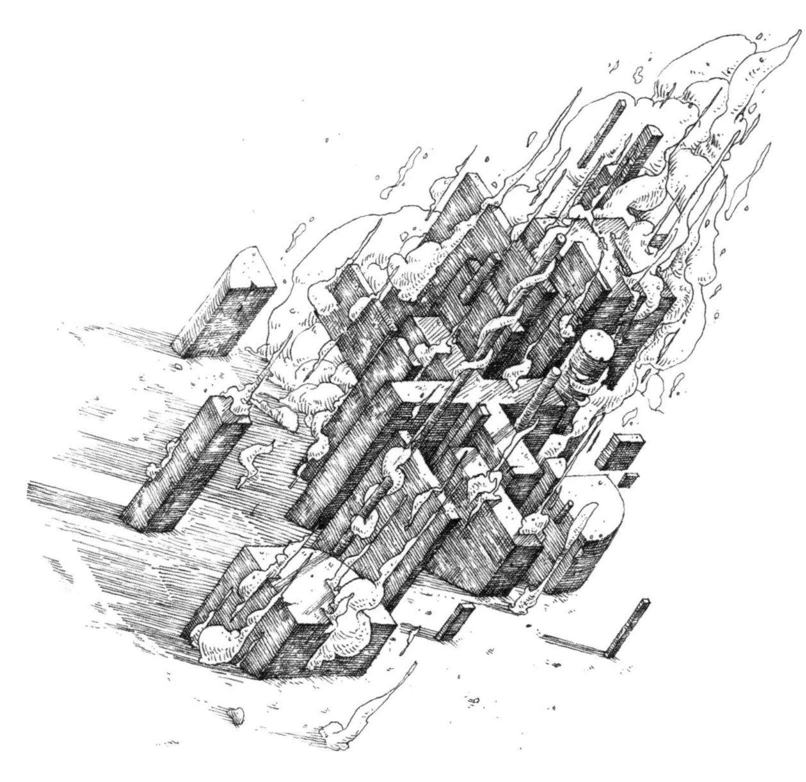

Morcky71

Jim Pluk

Overflowing with energy, wit and charm,

the work of Colombian artist Jim Pluk is both prodigious and varied. He has published numerous books for children, while his comics and illustrations have reached audiences in France, Germany, Iceland, Peru, Argentina and Colombia. His drawings, paintings and collages have also been exhibited internationally, in locations such as Spain, Mexico, Argentina, the US and Hong Kong. Comprising loose lines and freewheeling forms, his style seems infinitely adaptable and appealing to all. What makes his work continually exciting and surprising is the range of his materials – pencil, pen, watercolour, biro, acrylic and Photoshop – as well as his trademark compositions in black and white.

Pluk's work resonates with the viewer; his animals, children or adults are entangled in narratives that communicate everyday situations, relationships, feelings and desires, things to which we can all relate. Pluk chooses not to populate these narratives with text: 'I like the silence,' he says, 'and I also like that this lack of text allows everyone to understand the comics without the limit of language. Sometimes they are very upbeat, at others, a bit dark and melancholic. I like not to limit myself with subjects.'

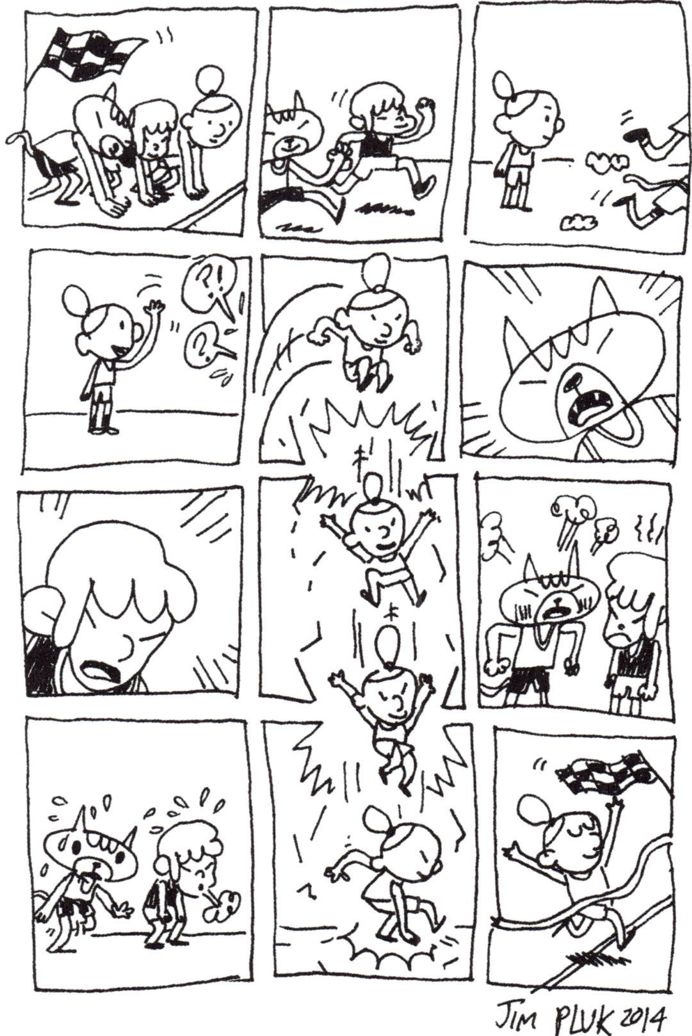

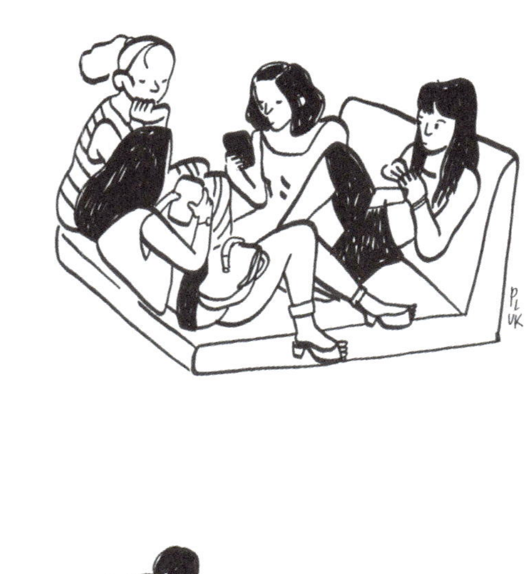

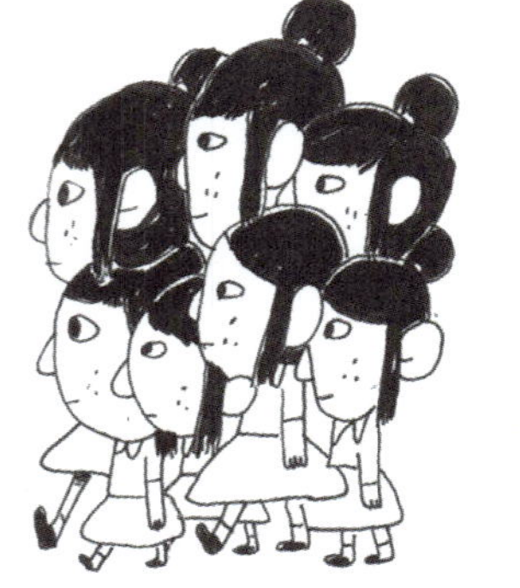

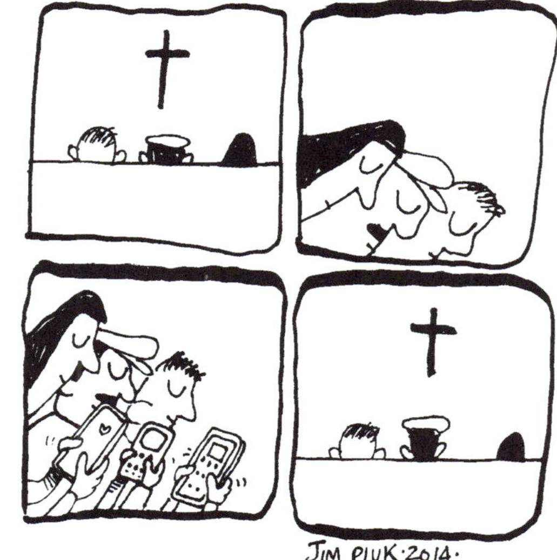

CLOCKWISE FROM TOP
Untitled, 2014
Ink on paper
18 × 12 cm (7⅛ × 4¾ in.)

Untitled, 2014
Ink on paper
14 × 14 cm (5½ × 5½ in.)

Untitled, 2014
Ink on paper
10 × 15 cm (4 × 5⅞ in.)

Untitled, 2014
Ink on paper
14 × 18 cm (5½ × 7⅛ in.)

OPPOSITE
Untitled, 2014
Ecoline and ink on paper
10 × 15 cm (4 × 5⅞ in.)

Untitled, 2014
Pen marker and ink
on paper
14 × 14 cm (5½ × 5½ in.)

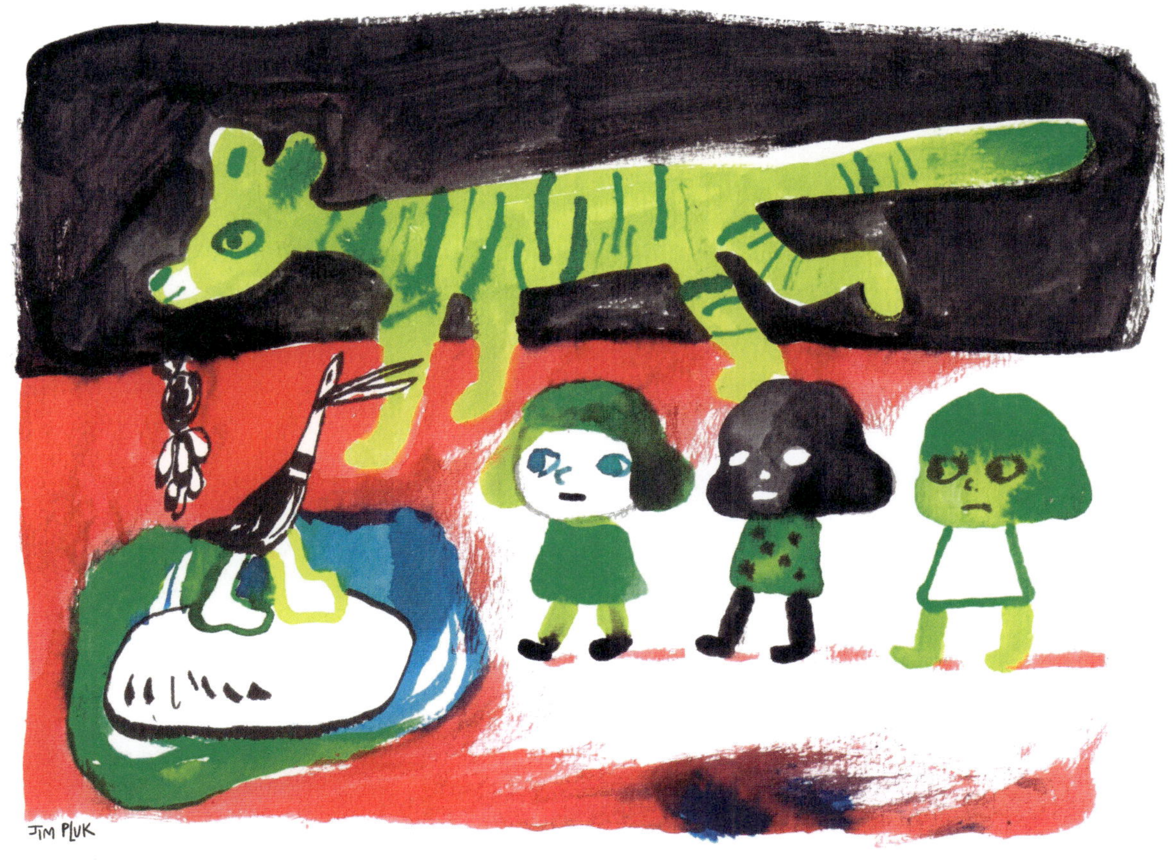

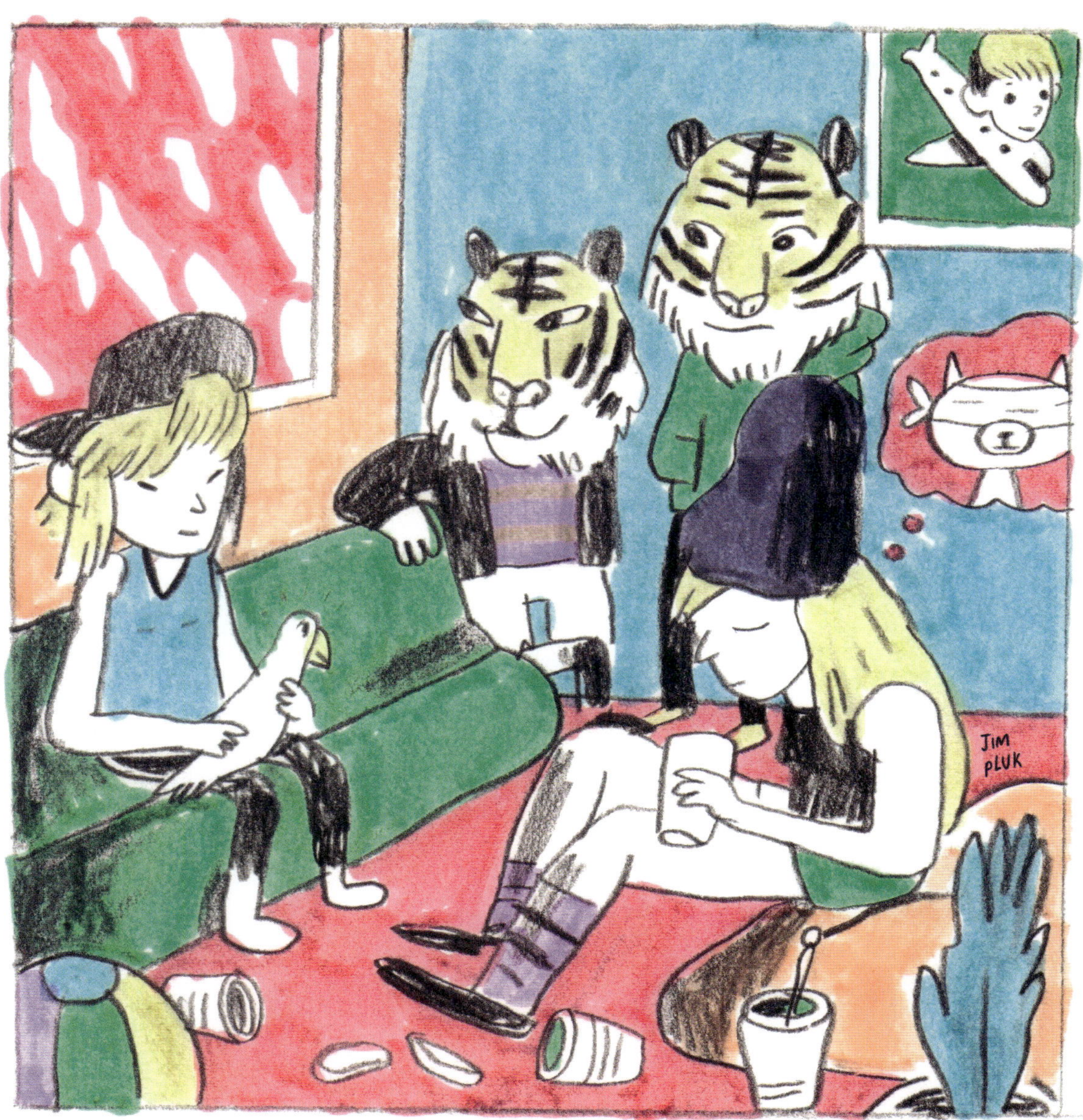

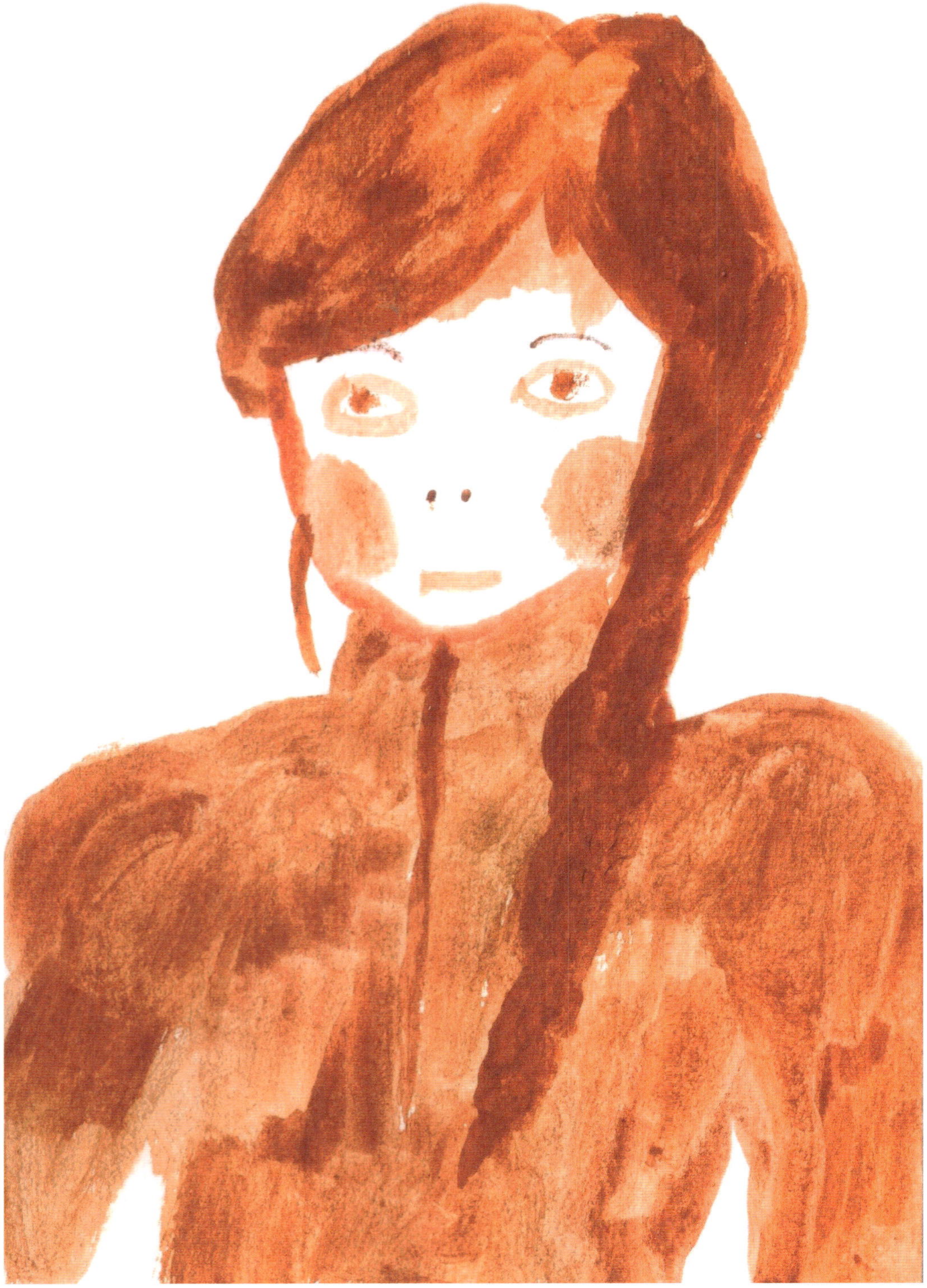

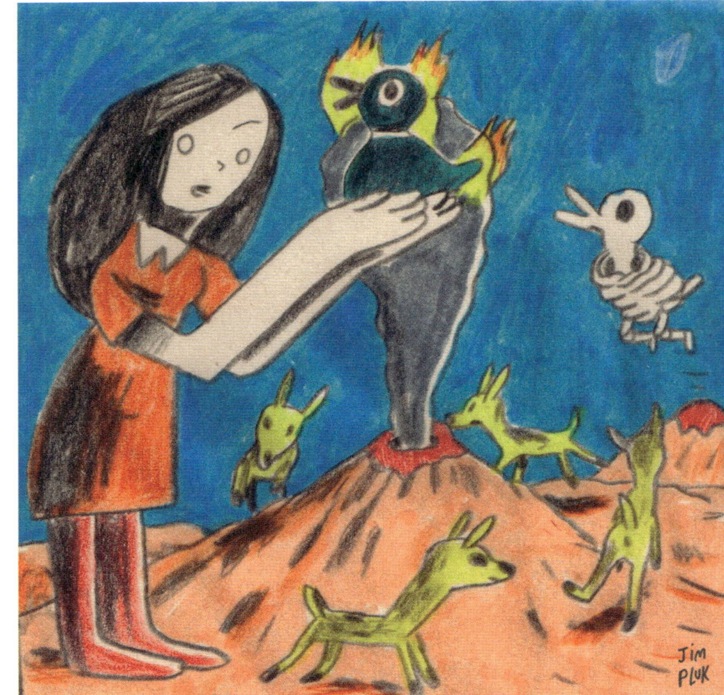

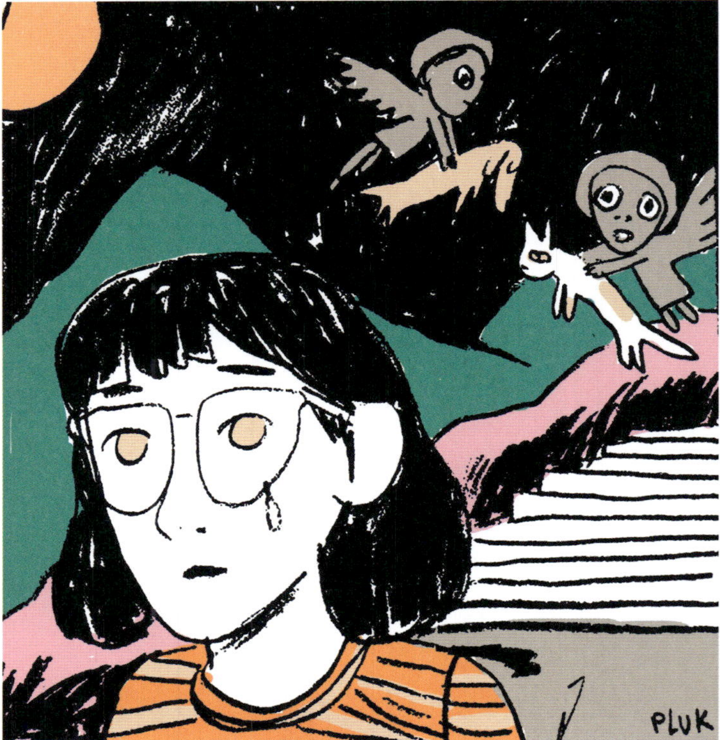

Pluk also works with La Escuelita de los Andes, a Colombian organization through which he offers free comic and drawing workshops for children. He feels that he learns more from working with children than he does with professional artists, which then feeds back in to his output. Although Pluk primarily draws and paints, he occasionally produces collages, photographs and mural paintings, and is always armed with a pencil, paper and camera. Whenever he feels saturated or exhausted by one method he will switch to another: 'I turn to another technique, as a way to rest.' Of his practice overall he states: 'I'm not trying to produce something new or original or to be innovative. I am trying to create in order to communicate what's inside, in my soul. I'm doing it to express myself, to live, to be free. I could not live if I couldn't draw!'

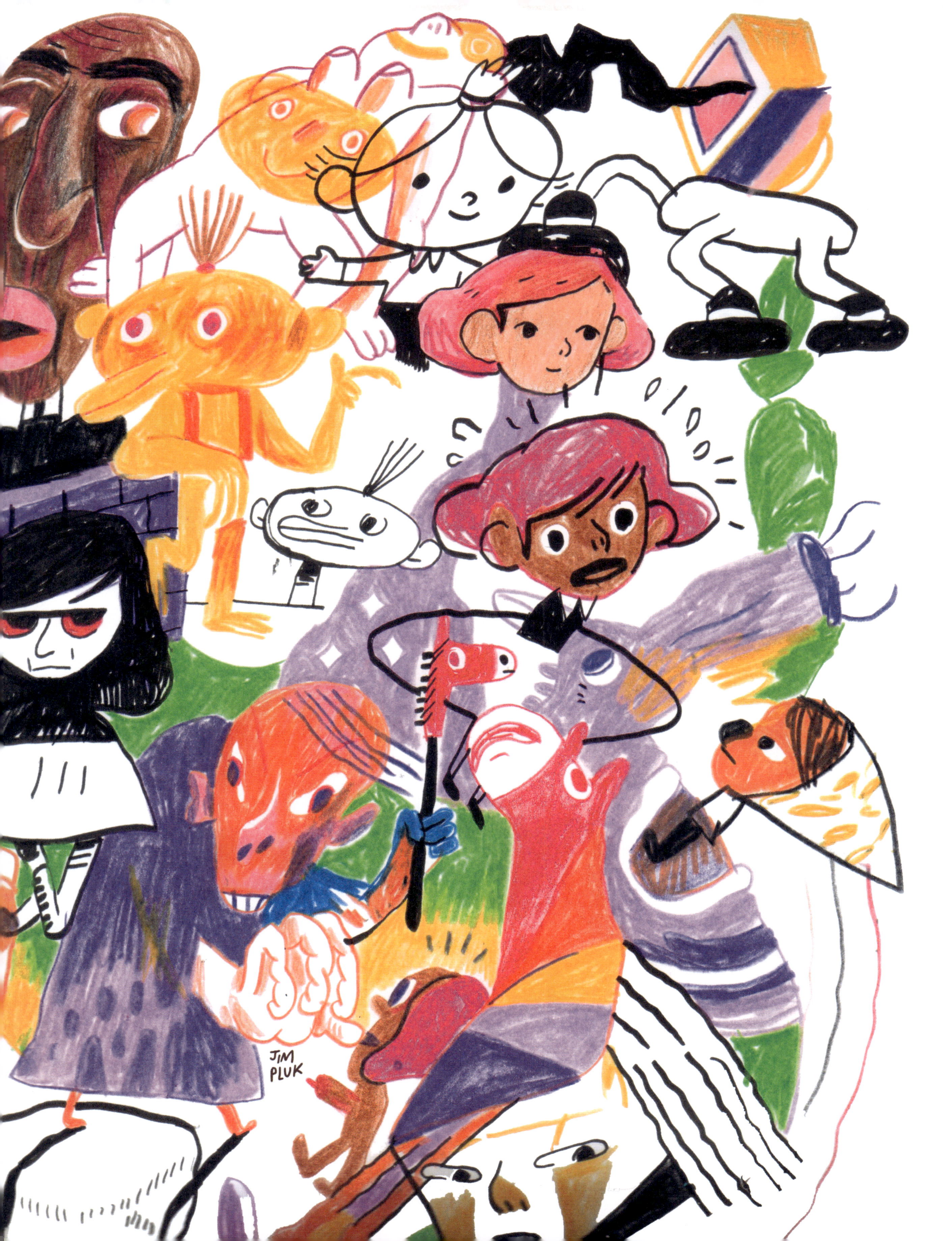

Sainer

Best known for his epic murals,

the Polish artist Sainer works both on his own and in partnership with the artist Bezt, as part of the Etam Cru. Made with consummate skill, his works are a tour de force, showcasing a mastery of colour, light and shadow in a style that amalgamates realism with comic stylization. In those featuring figures, Sainer demonstrates a superb eye for anatomy, arranging characters in dramatic and carefully poised positions with an enviable knowledge of musculature. In addition to these mammoth mural undertakings, drawing at a small scale is one of his favourite ways to work. His sketchbooks are filled with location drawings from life, some of which are extraordinarily detailed, while others are looser compositions for illustrations, paintings or murals. He uses fine lines and various shading methods, such as cross-hatching, and introduces soft grainy textures into his drawings to breathe life into them.

Sainer's journey into art as a profession is partly accidental. His overriding passion was initially football, a sport that he played professionally until the age of seventeen, only ceasing due to an injury in 2001.

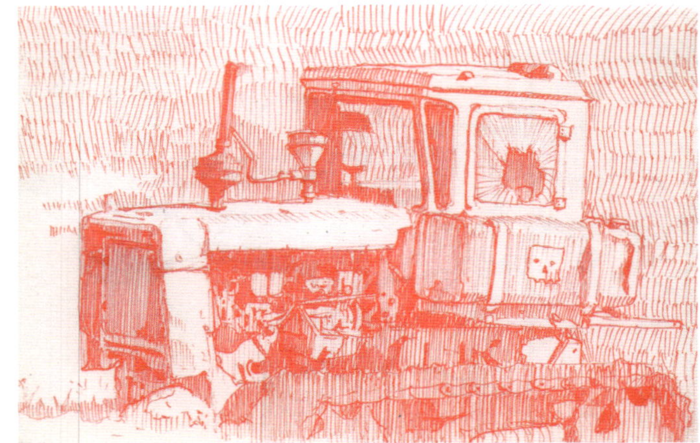
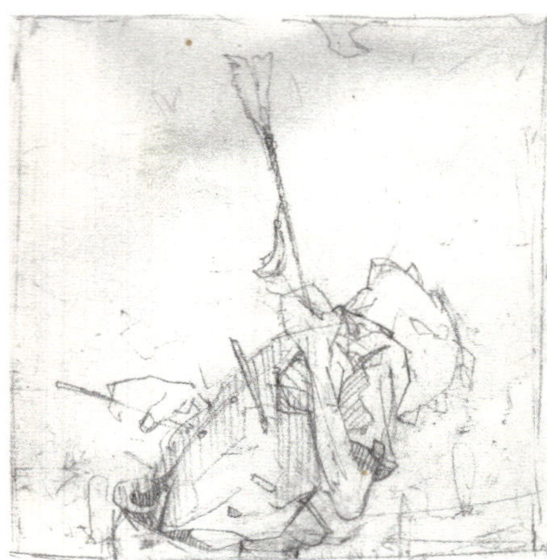

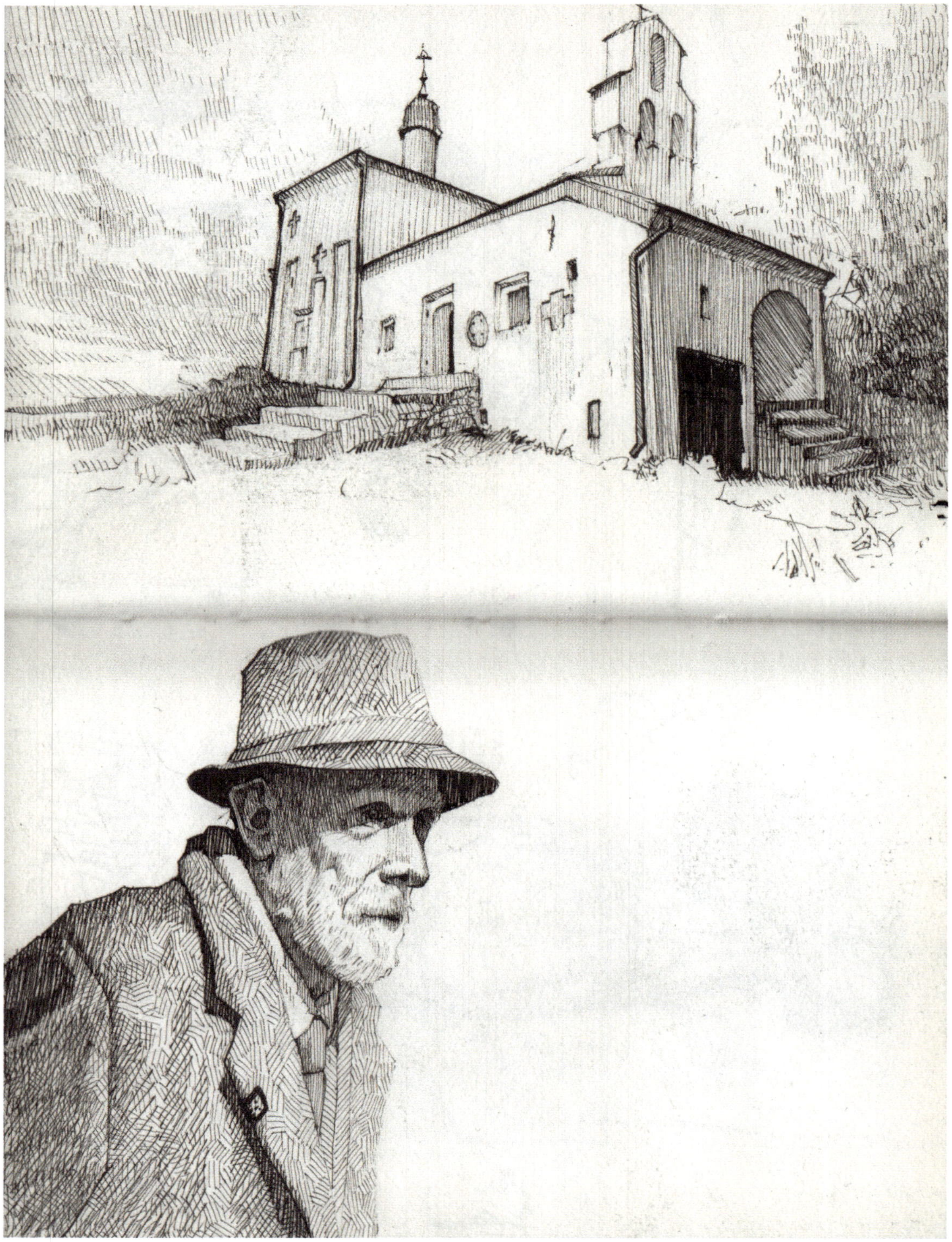

Pages from the artist's
sketchbook, *c.* 2014
Pencil on paper
Dimensions unknown

OPPOSITE
Untitled, 2014
Mixed media
Dimensions unknown

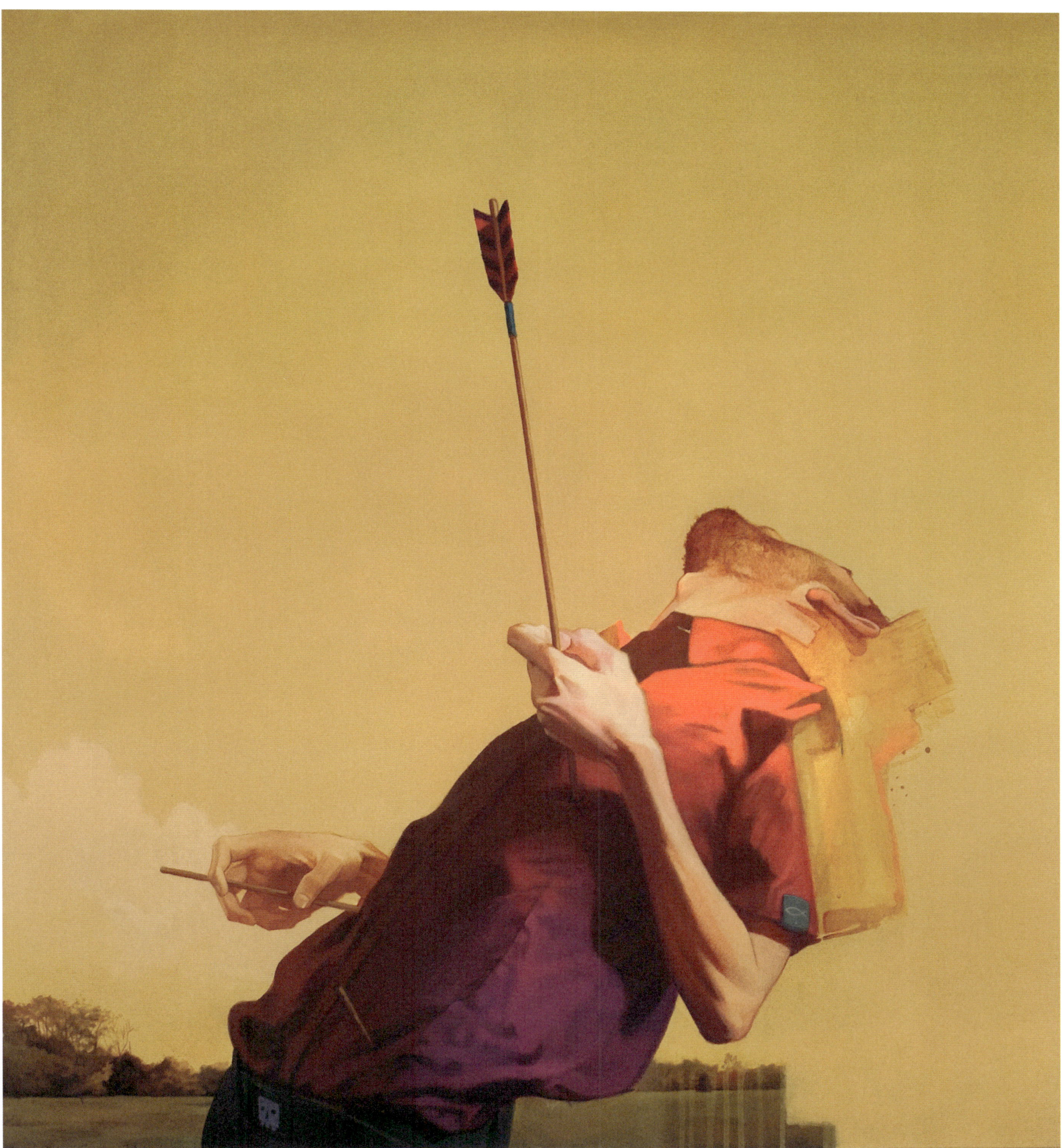

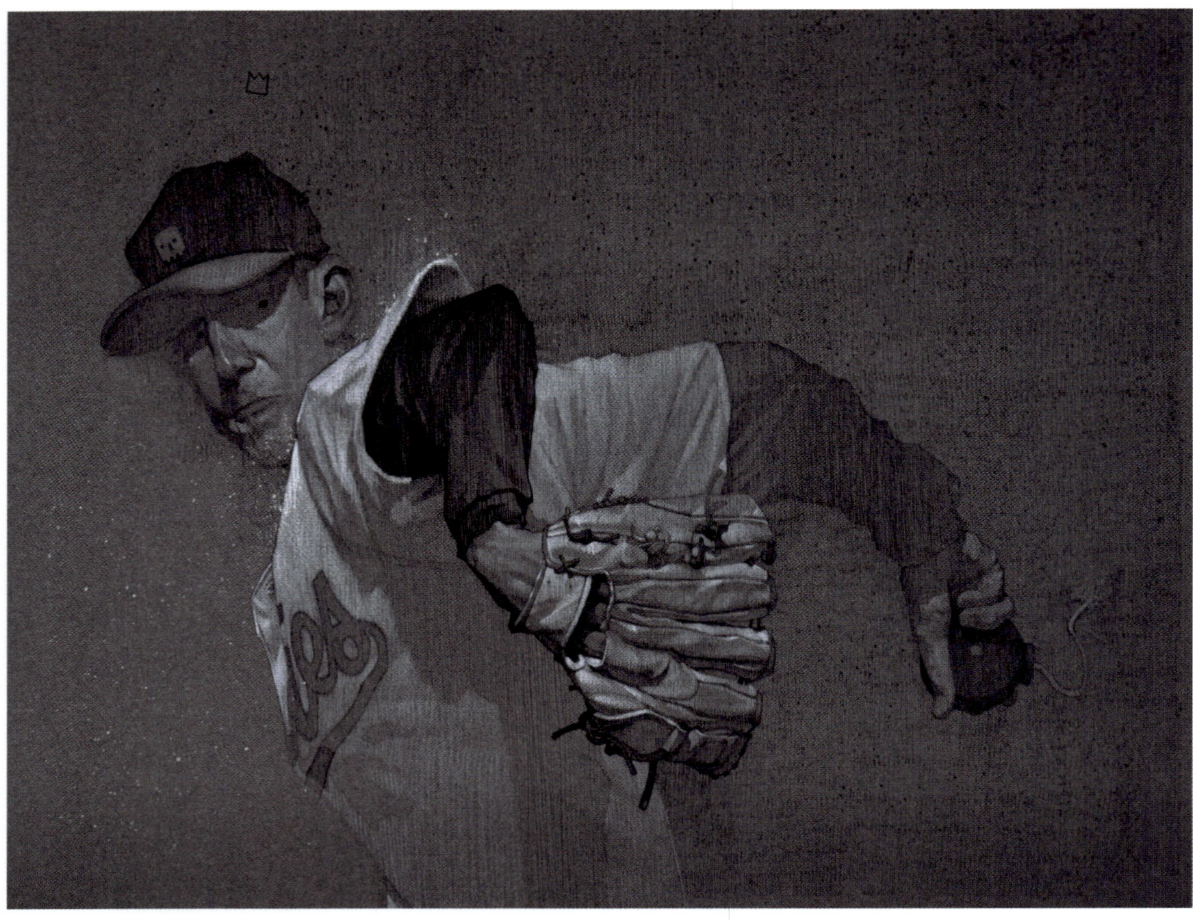

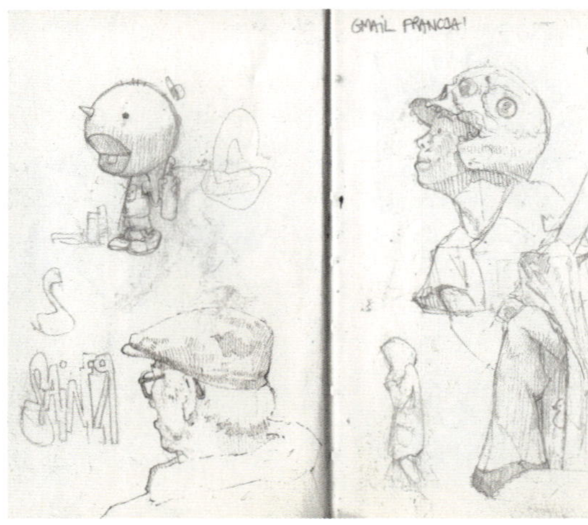

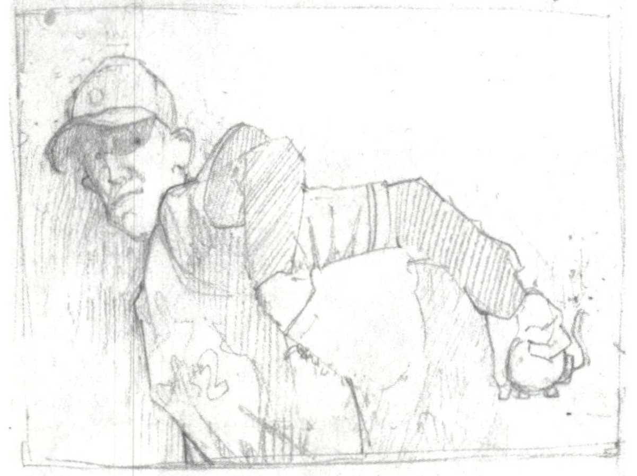

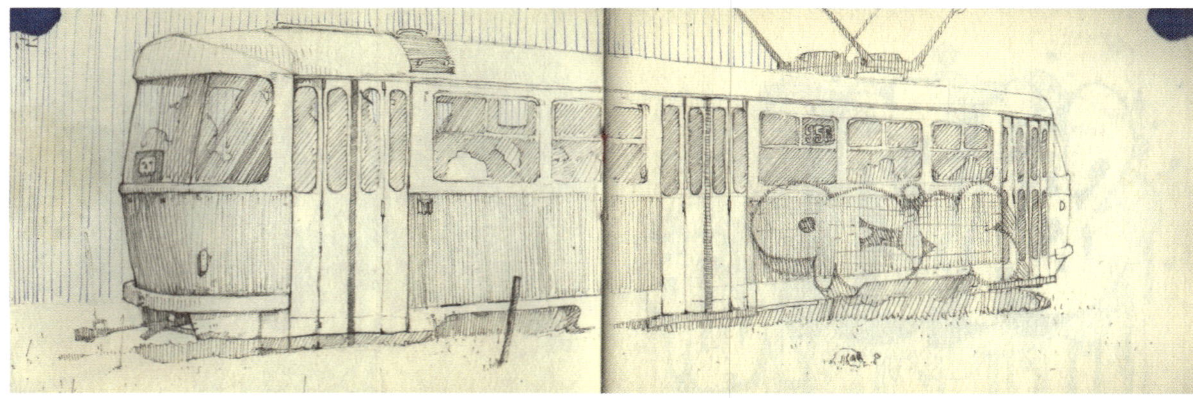

Football's loss was the art world's gain. With more time on his hands Sainer spent most of his hours endlessly drawing. He became interested in graffiti and began to practise with a spray can in abandoned spaces. As a child he had always been fascinated by cartoons and would often redraw characters, but in these later years he also looked to what was happening on the street and his love of hip-hop culture for inspiration. Study at the Strzeminski Academy of Art in Lodz soon beckoned, which is where he met Bezt, with whom he has collaborated ever since.

While classic graffiti remains an inspiration for Sainer, his work is predominantly character-based. He likes to think of his compositions in terms of movie stills – moments in time suspended – and balances his figures with other elements to create harmonic configurations. As Sainer summarizes of his work: 'For me the most important thing is to keep having fun, but at the same time working hard so as not to be stuck in the same place and making the same stamp everywhere.' Having already developed such a distinct and diverse body of work, Sainer is clearly one to watch.

TOP
Untitled, 2015
Graphite on paper
71 × 102 cm (28 × 40 in.)

CENTRE AND ABOVE
Pages from the artist's
sketchbook, *c.* 2014
Pencil on paper
Dimensions unknown

OPPOSITE
Untitled, 2015
Graphite on paper
102 × 71 cm (40 × 28 in.)

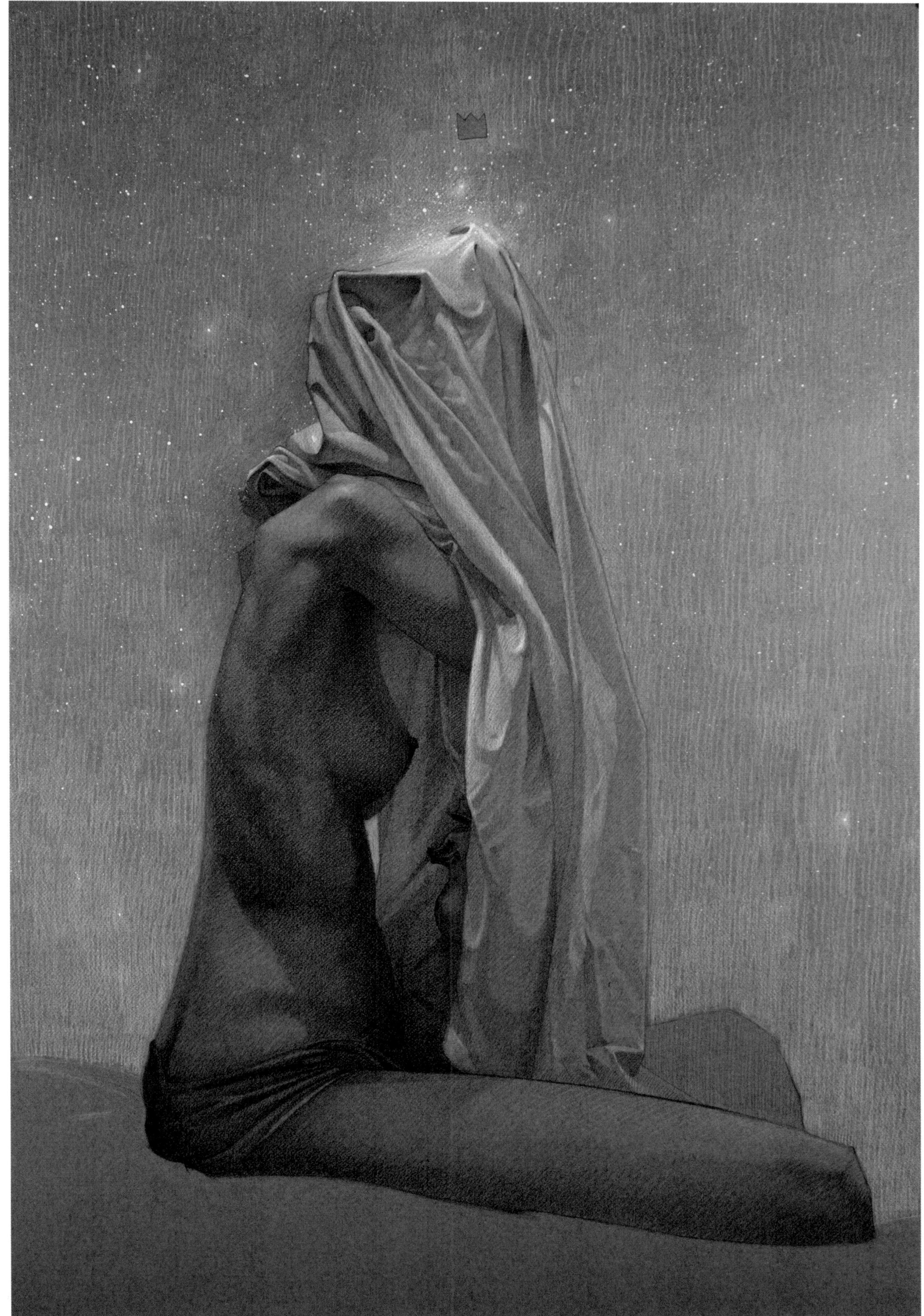

T-Wei

Being able to earn a living from your art without compromise is a delicate balance,

of which New Zealand-based artist and illustrator T-Wei (aka Tien Hee) is a great example. Supporting himself through freelance illustration, such as character design and game animation, he has retained an art practice that is satisfyingly experimental and completely unchained to commercial constraints. His personal paintings, posters and illustrations are full of curiously spliced, diced and mutated characters, and are spaces in which anything could happen; pigeons are sandwiched into burger buns, bulldog tongues become a new flavour of ice cream and electrically powered children are crossed with alligators. These completely free-associative images are a playful mish-mash of the cutesy and the grotesque, in which the artist's imagination has been free to run wild.

Having trained in animation and illustration T-Wei still considers himself as being self-taught, since much of the work he produced at university was stylistically tangential to what was being taught. Not finding in this environment the support he felt he needed, he began posting work on Internet forums such SatelliteSoda and Ledheavy, using the feedback provided by his peers to propel him forward in ways he had not before considered.

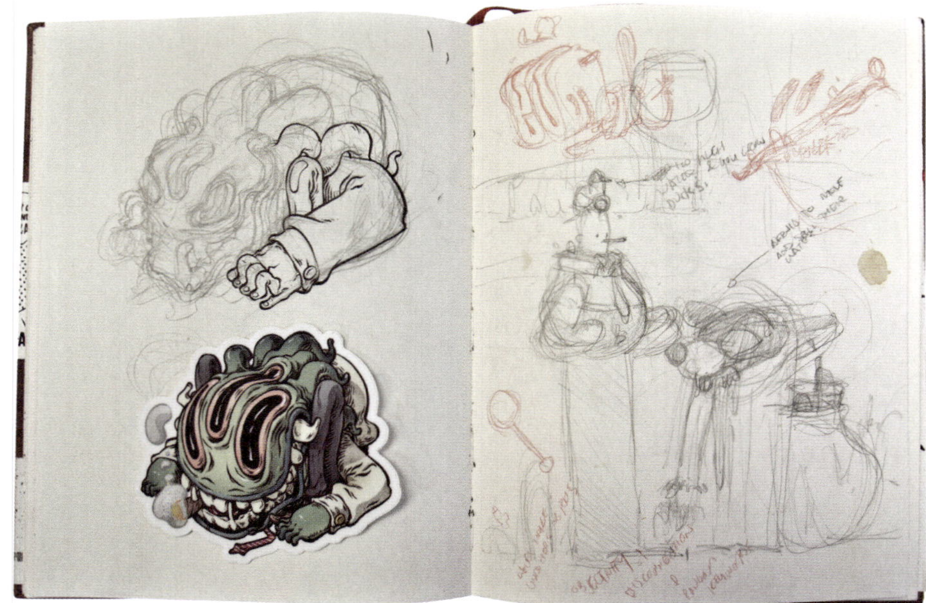

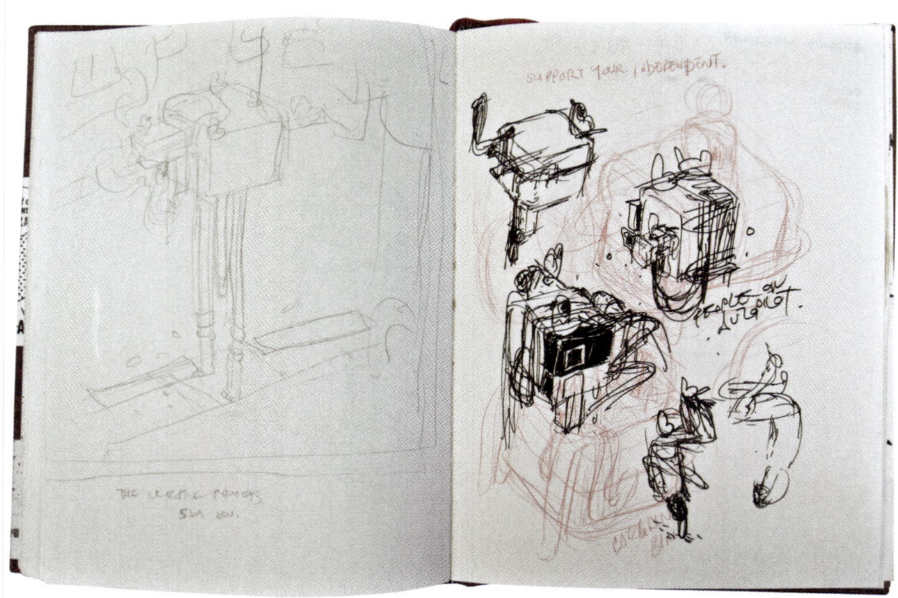

ABOVE
Pages from the artist's sketchbook, 2014
Ink and graphite on paper
21 × 18 cm
(8¼ × 7⅛ in.) each

BELOW LEFT
Alligator Child, 2014
Ink on paper
29.7 × 42 cm
(11⅝ × 16⅝ in.)

BELOW RIGHT
Leftovers, 2014
Mixed media
Dimensions unknown

OPPOSITE
Curiosity Cabinet, 2014
Mixed media
42 × 42 cm (16⅝ × 16⅝ in.)

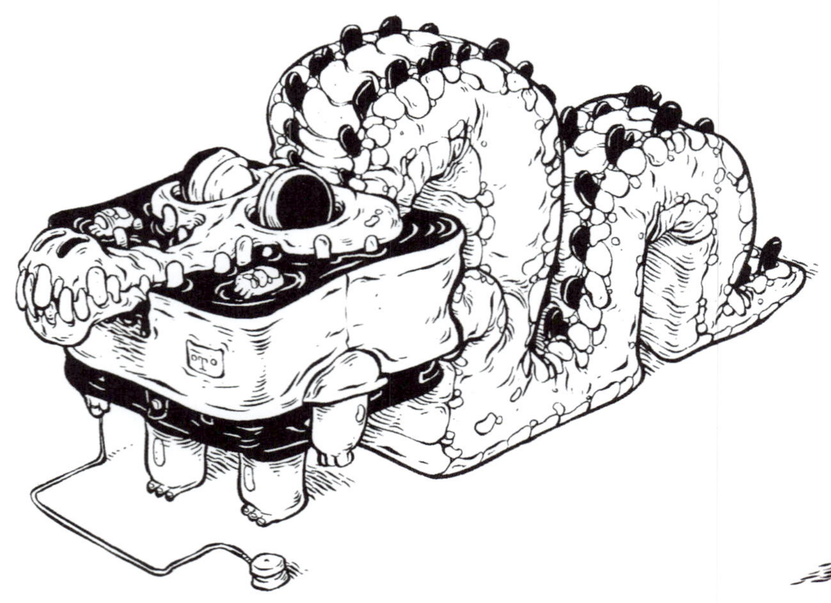

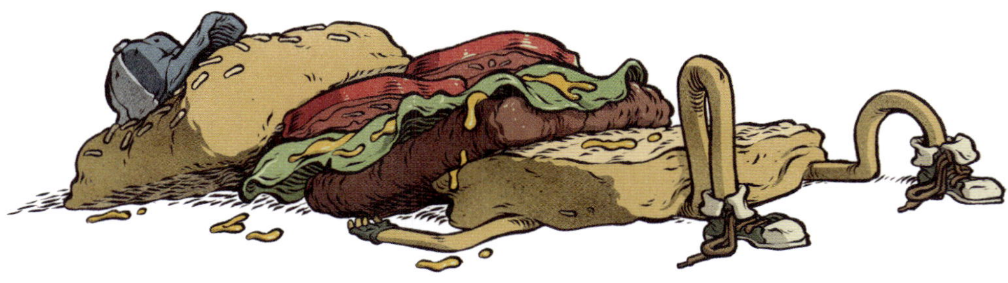

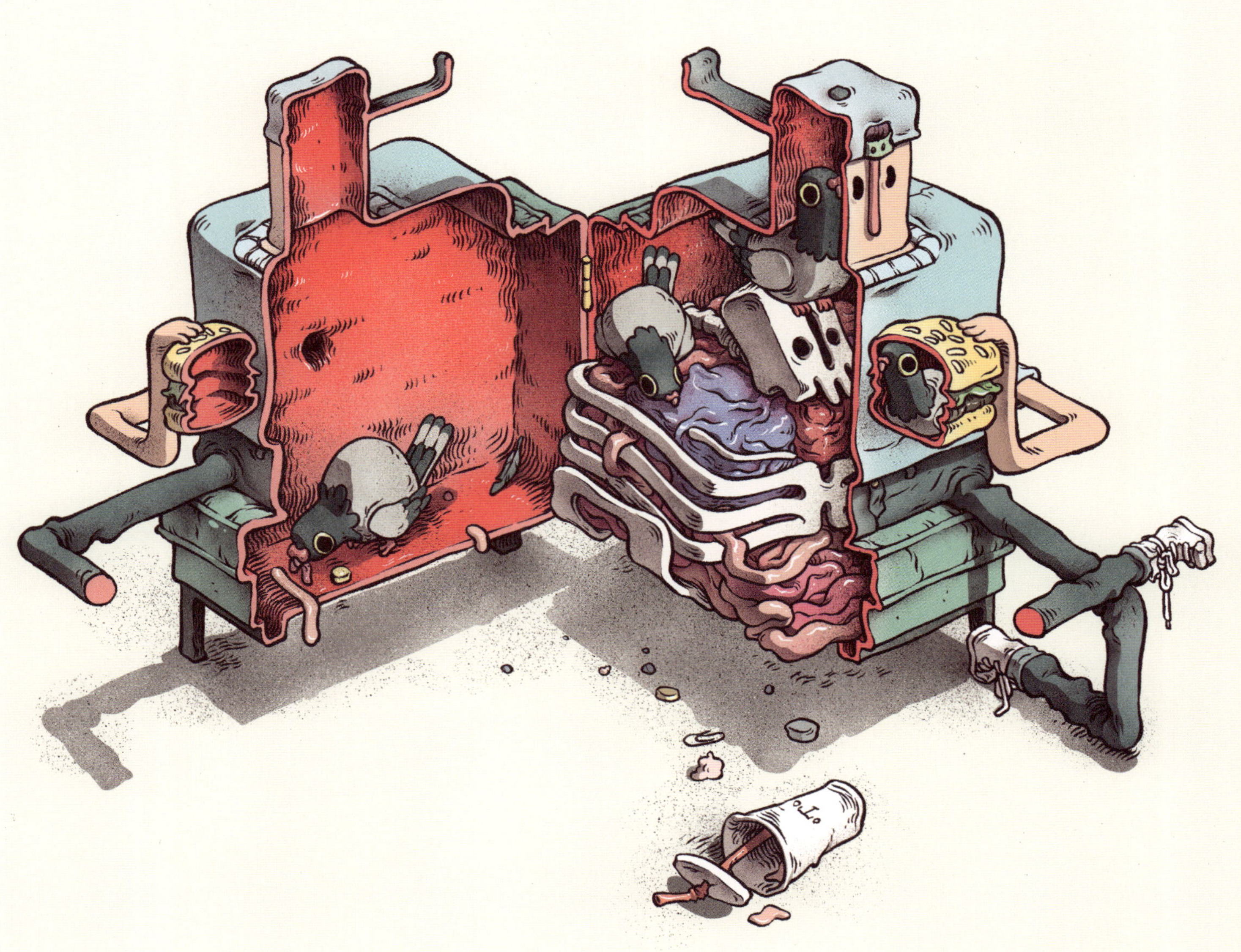

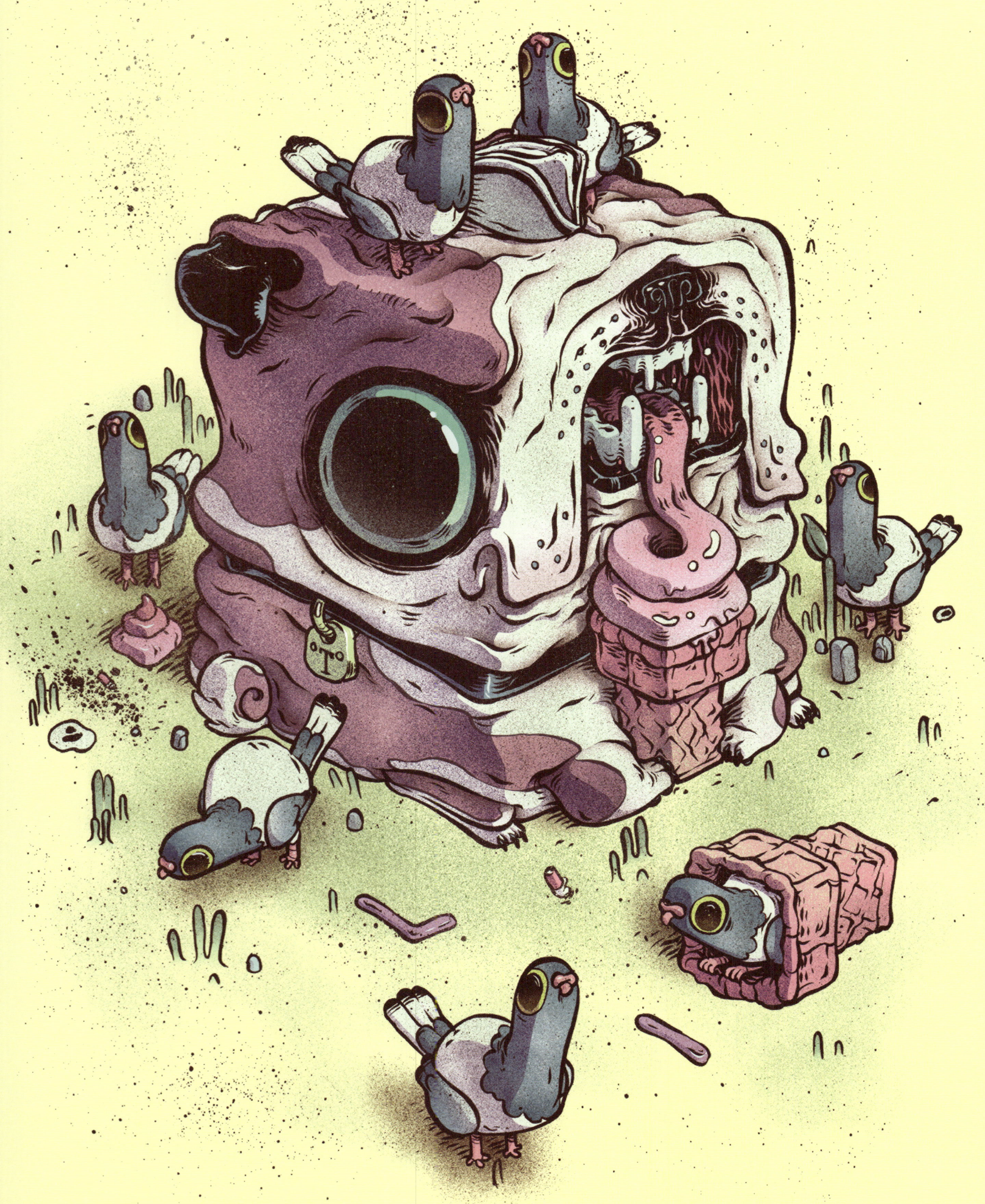

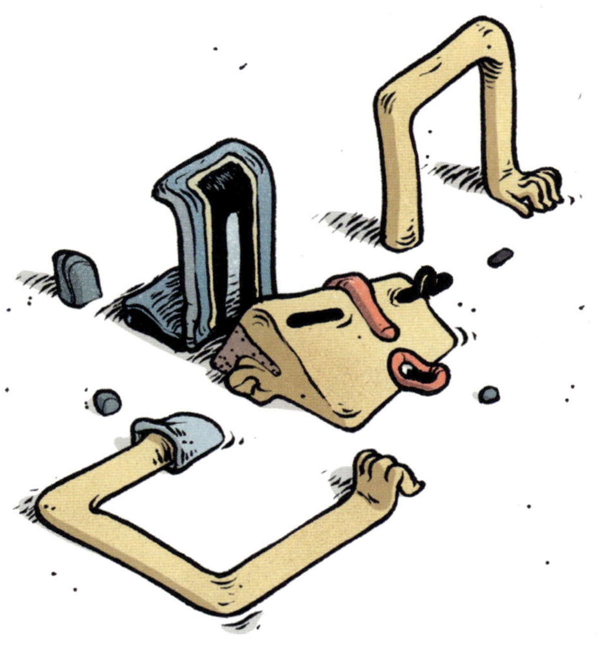

Entering into T-Wei's comic world is rather like discovering a new television channel, one where Saturday morning cartoons have been allowed to roam free, untamed and pushed to Ren-and-Stimpy-style extremes. Figures are stretched, squashed and pulled apart for kicks in scenes that are bizarre and squeamish. In more recent work there is also a digital, retro-gaming aesthetic, which is achieved via the use of isometric projection, making his characters seem more object-like in appearance. They become 'he-man figures or Lego dudes that exist in this minute world that you can't quite immerse yourself in…these little weirdoes and allegories reflect what's going on in your own day-to-day existence. It's a bit addictive.'

Explaining his inspirations he professes to be both in awe of and frustrated by his artistic heroes but nonetheless they spur him on in his work: 'There's a feeling I get when I look at art that I like. It's sort of a mix of happiness and wanting to throw up that both energizes and demoralizes. This is the feeling I want to instill in the people that see my work.'

T-Wei has a worldwide following, with works being featured in art magazines such as *Hi-Fructose* and the Pictoplasma *Character Portraits* (2014) book.

OPPOSITE
The Ice-Cream Man, 2015
Mixed media
Dimensions unknown

ABOVE
How Do You Feel Today?,
2014
Mixed media
Dimensions unknown

RIGHT
We're all Screaming, 2014
Acrylic on wood
160 × 160 cm
(62⅞ × 62⅞ in.)

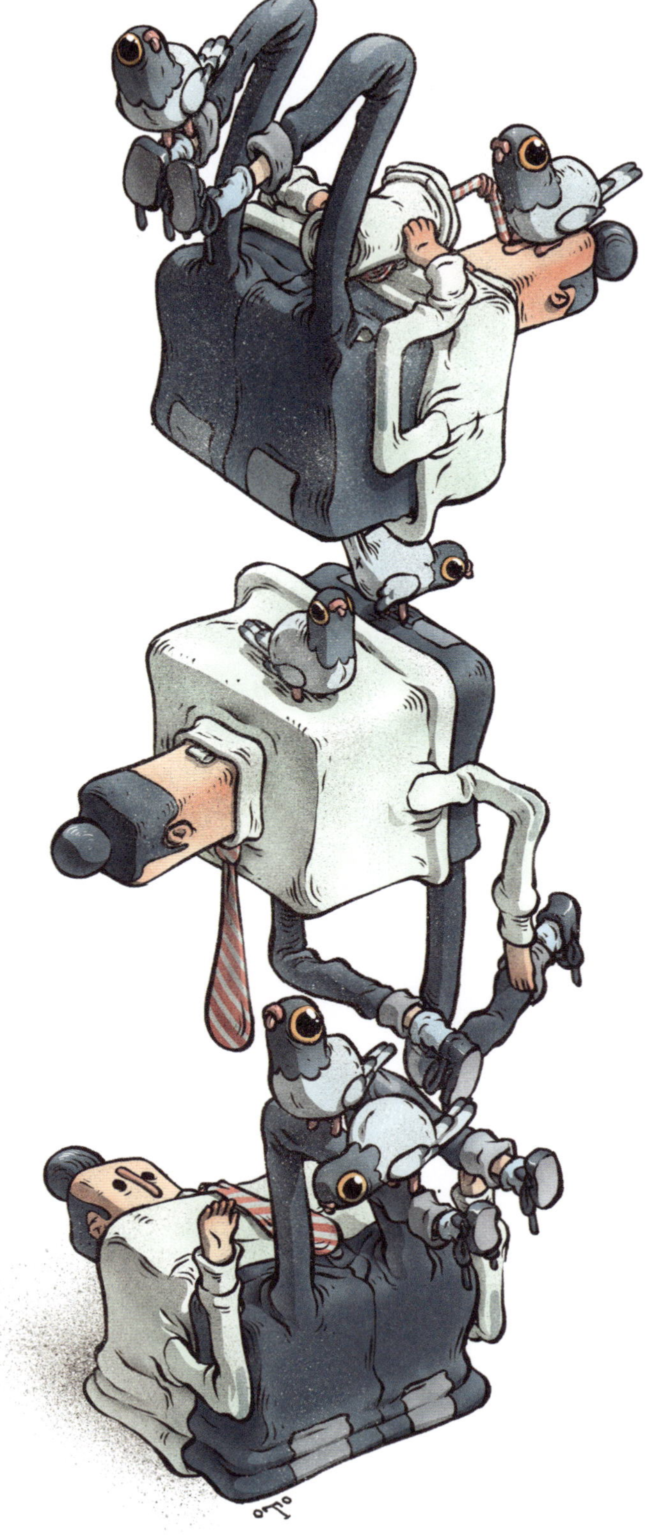

Mark Francis Williams

A British artist who trained at the Chelsea School of Art in London,

Mark Francis Williams now lives and works in Bucharest in Romania, where the city and its people have become a major muse for his work. His techniques are experimental, involving drawing, photography and ping, which he uses to achieve ephemeral and eroded effects, which in turn relate to the transience of life and the passage of time marked upon the city.

As he explains, 'I live in a building, constructed in the 1930s, whose fascias are eroding and dishevelled. The whole city has an air of impermanence, in part because of the general aesthetic…. This is in strong contrast to the synthetic environments of the newly erected shopping malls and middle-class suburbs, yet, rather than being dispiriting or depressing, these older districts actually feel more authentic, more alive and are to some degree an acceptance of the passing of time.' In response, Williams's practice is focused on this theme of transience and corrosion, primarily involving figurative work, in which he seeks to achieve a visual harmony between the 'stable and the unstable', both as a concept and as a process.

Works in progress, 2014

Brake, 2014
Charcoal on
heavyweight paper
100 × 70 cm
(39⅜ × 27⅝ in.)

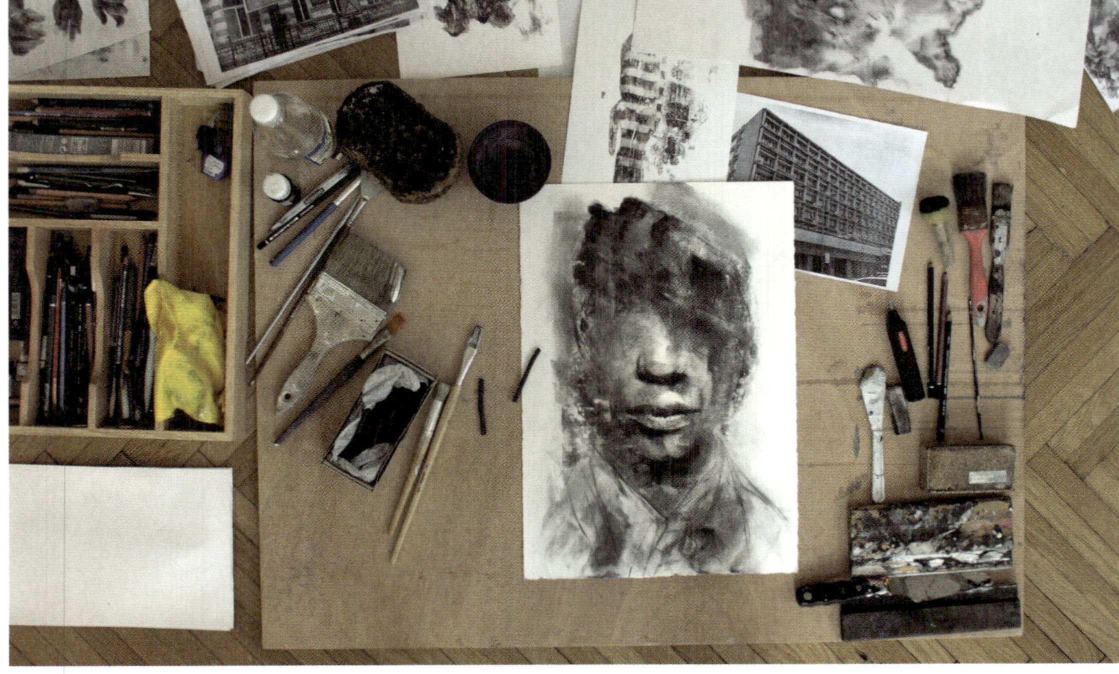

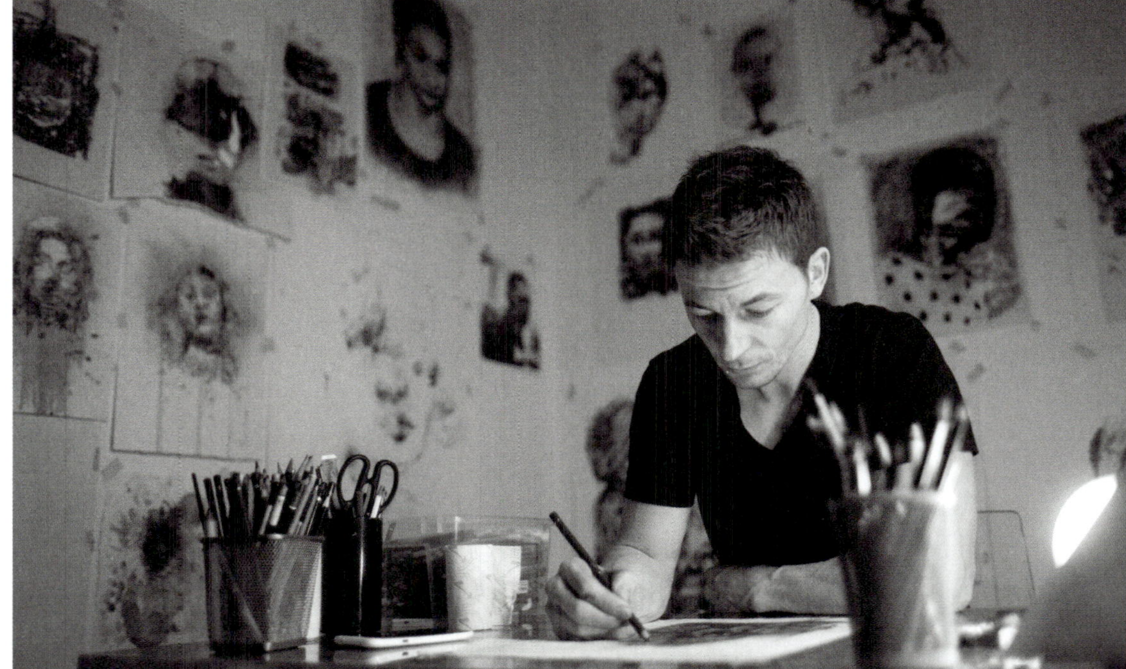

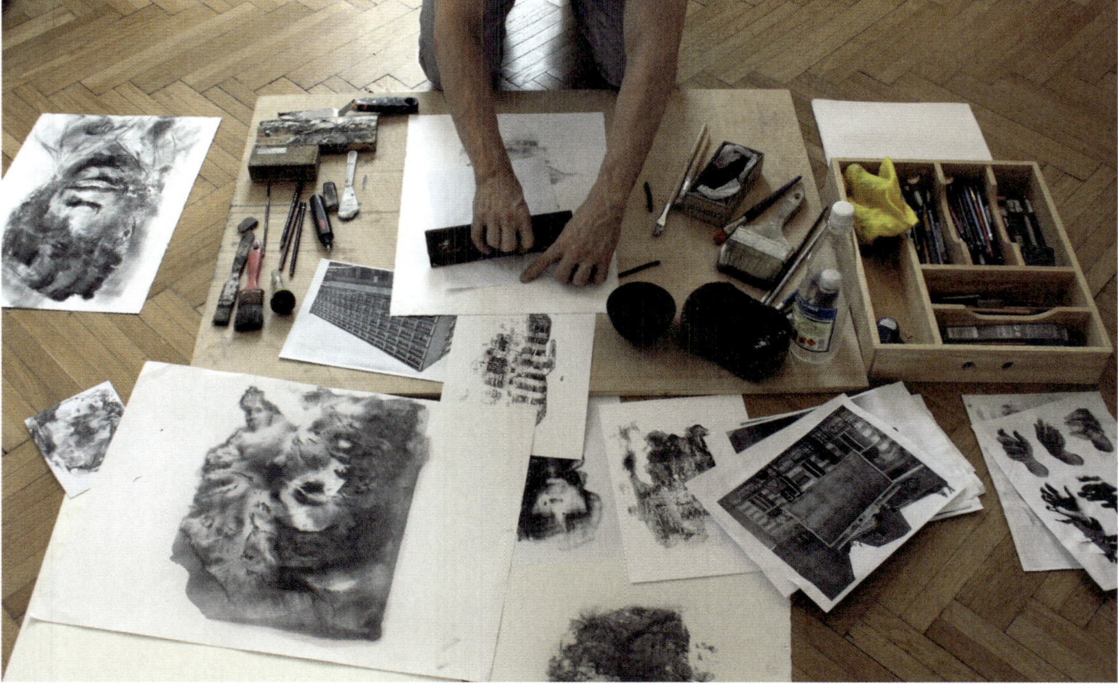

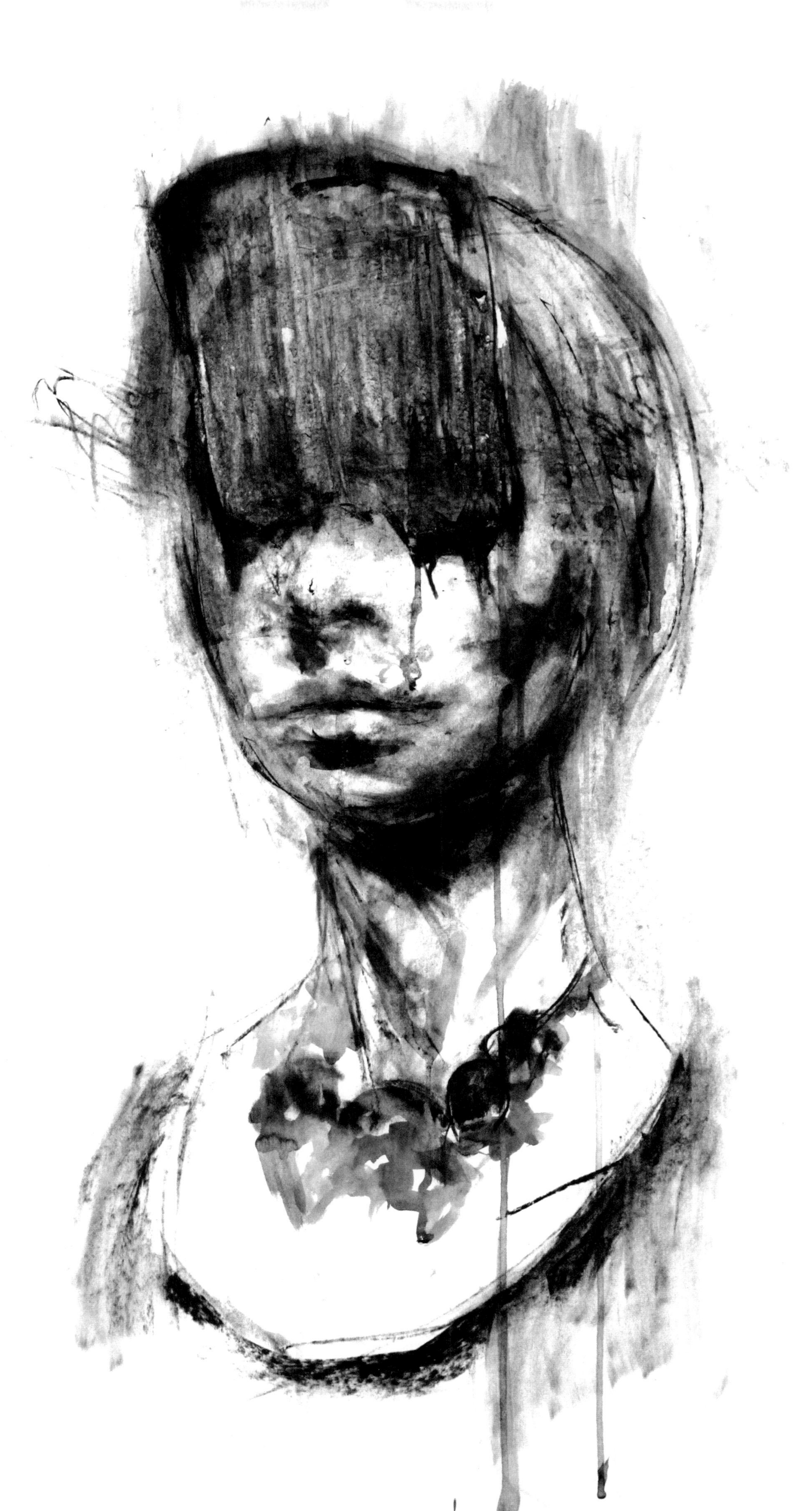

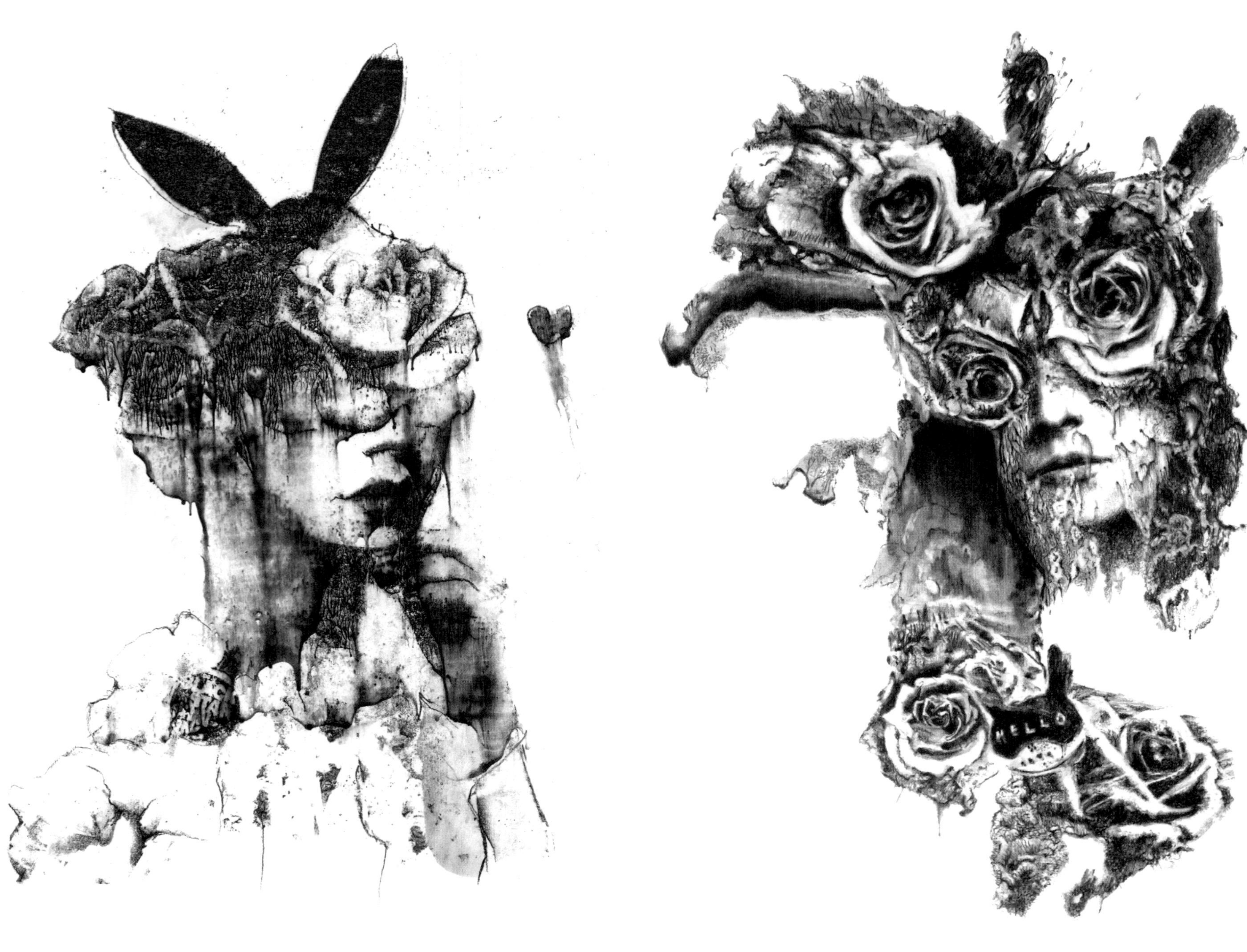

Flower Head, c. 2014
Monoprint on paper
100 × 70 cm (39⅜ × 27⅝ in.)

Flower Head II, 2014
Graphite and charcoal on
Fabriano heavyweight paper
100 × 70 cm (39⅜ × 27⅝ in.)

Untitled, 2013
Monoprint on paper
45 × 30 cm (17⅝ × 11⅞ in.)

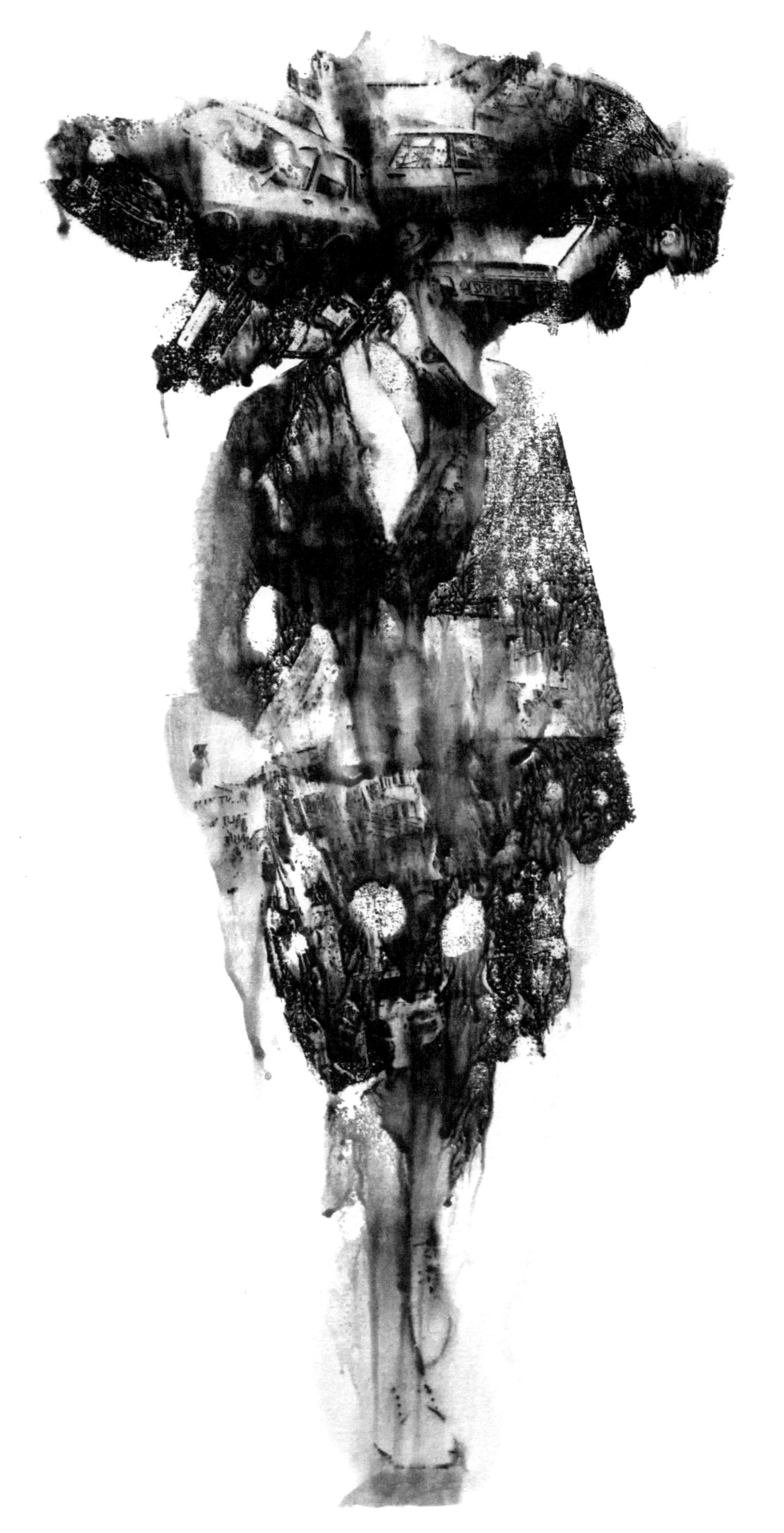

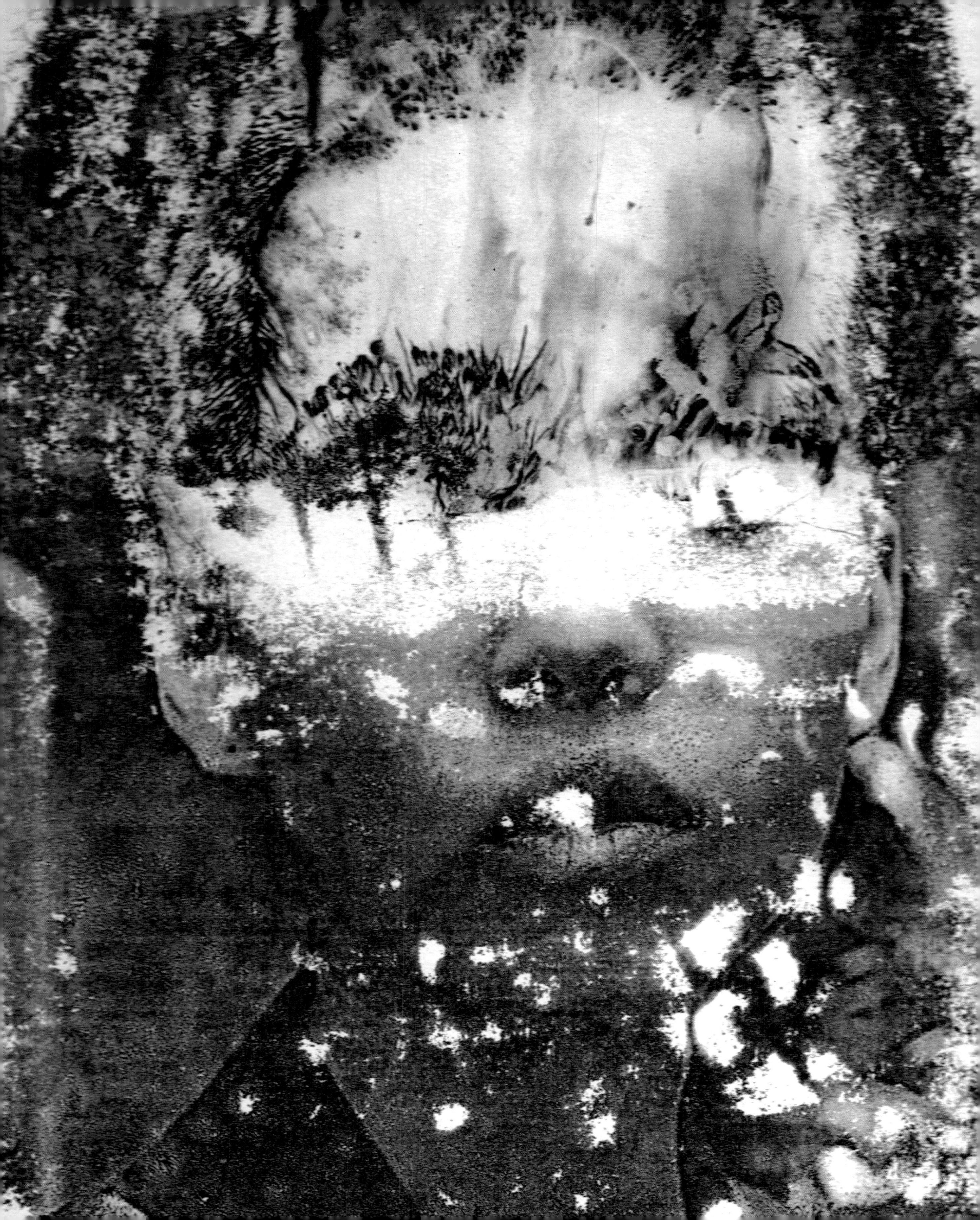

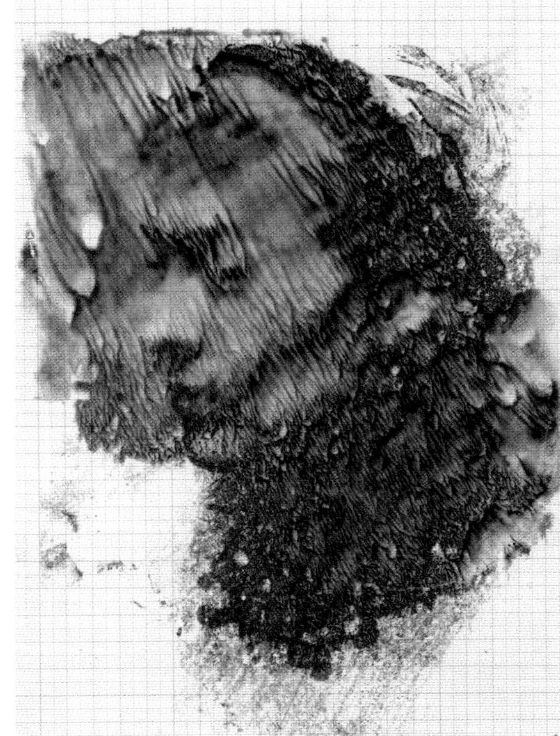
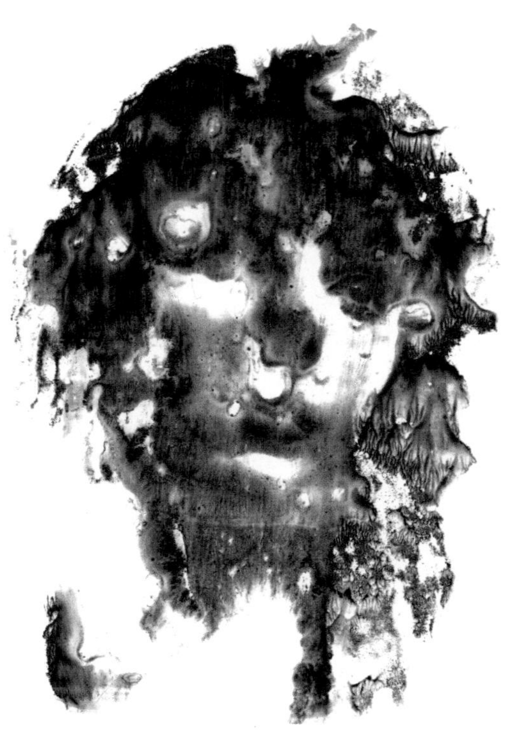
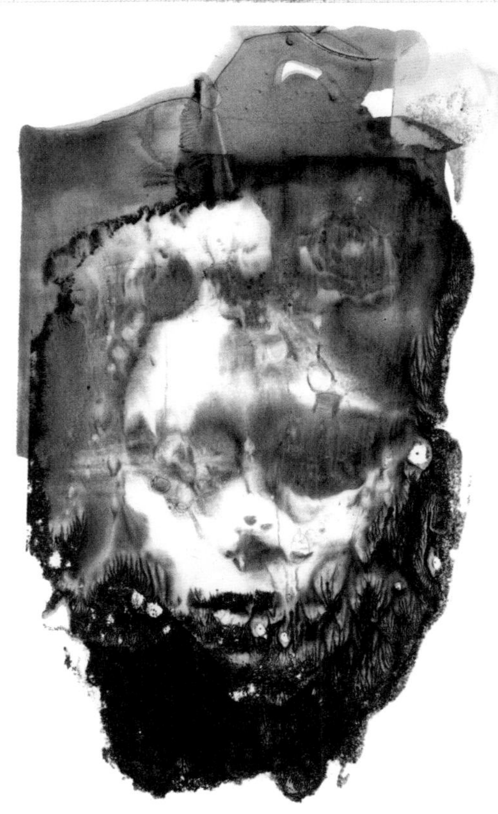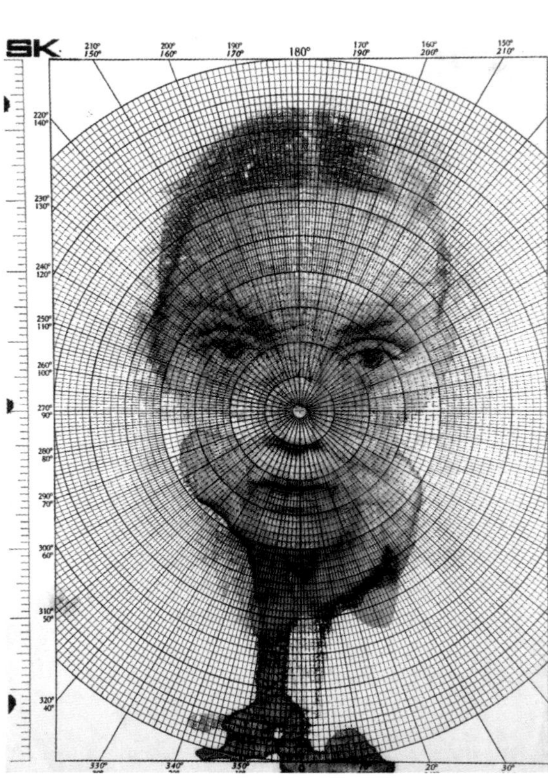

Williams encourages the element of chance in his work, allowing happy accidents to unfold as he combines numerous print and drawing techniques. Initially each work starts with photographs taken from the streets of Bucharest, which are then collaged together. He then paints and draws directly onto the photos, makes prints from them and uses solvents to scrape, push, press, drip, drag and make splashes, further eroding the image. Finally they are torn, collaged and reshot and the whole process repeated over. Occasionally, Williams will experiment further, dragging a paintbrush or an eraser through the image, to see how it might change through the exclusion of certain details. Of this process he explains, 'I feel I am dealing with an image that is much more alive and far less descriptive. To some degree I want to create a "found" object.'

The resulting images have a dreamlike quality that is heightened by their evasive and fleeting nature, and it is this idea of transience that he wishes to exploit, 'in opposition to the deluded belief that we are at the end of history, and that globalization and capitalism is the height of human endeavour'.

OPPOSITE
Untitled, 2013
Monoprint on paper
45 × 30 cm (17⅝ × 11⅞ in.)

CLOCKWISE FROM TOP LEFT
Untitled, 2013
Monoprint on graph paper
45 × 30 cm (17⅝ × 11⅞ in.)

Untitled, 2013
Monoprint on paper
45 × 30 cm (17⅝ × 11⅞ in.)

Untitled, 2013
Monoprint on graph paper
45 × 30 cm (17⅝ × 11⅞ in.)

Untitled, 2014
Monoprint on paper
45 × 30 cm (17⅝ × 11⅞ in.)

Irena Zablotska

Magical and curious are the colourful and naive illustrations and paintings

of the Ukrainian artist Irena Zablotska (or Joulu). Her visual worlds are at times psychedelic, comprising vibrant pattern and colour combinations from which strange scenes populated by hybrid creatures emerge. Zablotska's narratives have a folkloric or mythical quality and she cites Ukrainian naive art – in particular the work of the artist Maria Pryimachenko (1909–1997) – childhood books and cartoons as significant influences.

Zablotska's calling as an artist and illustrator came after initially training as a Geographic Information Systems (GIS) engineer. Not relishing the prospect of working in the field, she instead learnt the skill of web design, an area that she found fascinating. After working for a number of software enterprises in her home city of Lviv, she eventually formed her own company, which provided the independence she craved. It was around this time that she became acquainted with a group of local street artists and, inspired by the freedom and energy she felt that they were radiating, made the move into making her own art. Initially, this took the form of digital illustration. 'Soon after that,' she says, 'curators started inviting me to exhibit my work, and I suddenly realized that my art was actually appreciated by people, especially by some of the artists I had looked up to for so long.'

Pages from the artist's
sketchbook, 2014
Pencil and ink on paper
Dimensions unknown

The Four, 2014
Pastel and pencil on paper
40 × 30 cm (15⅝ × 11⅞ in.)

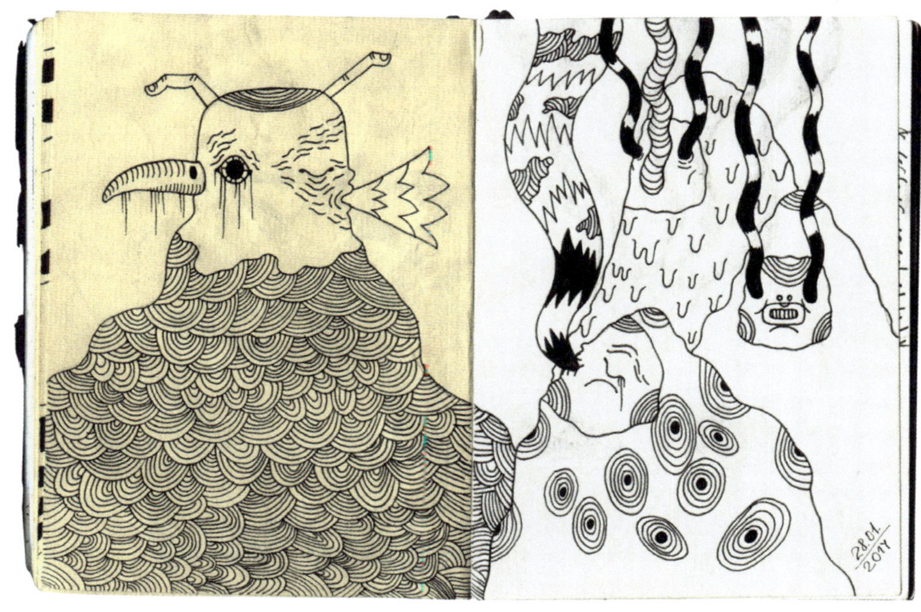

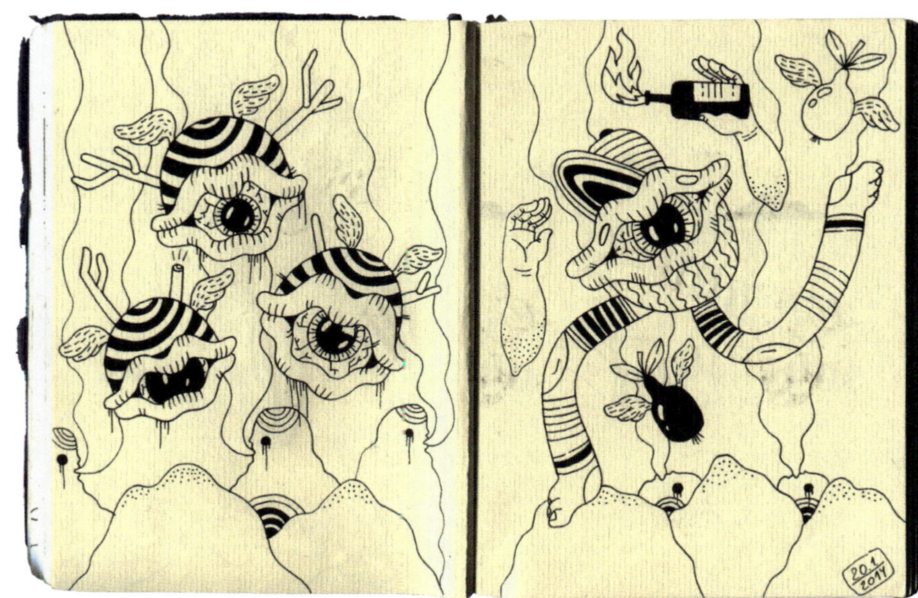

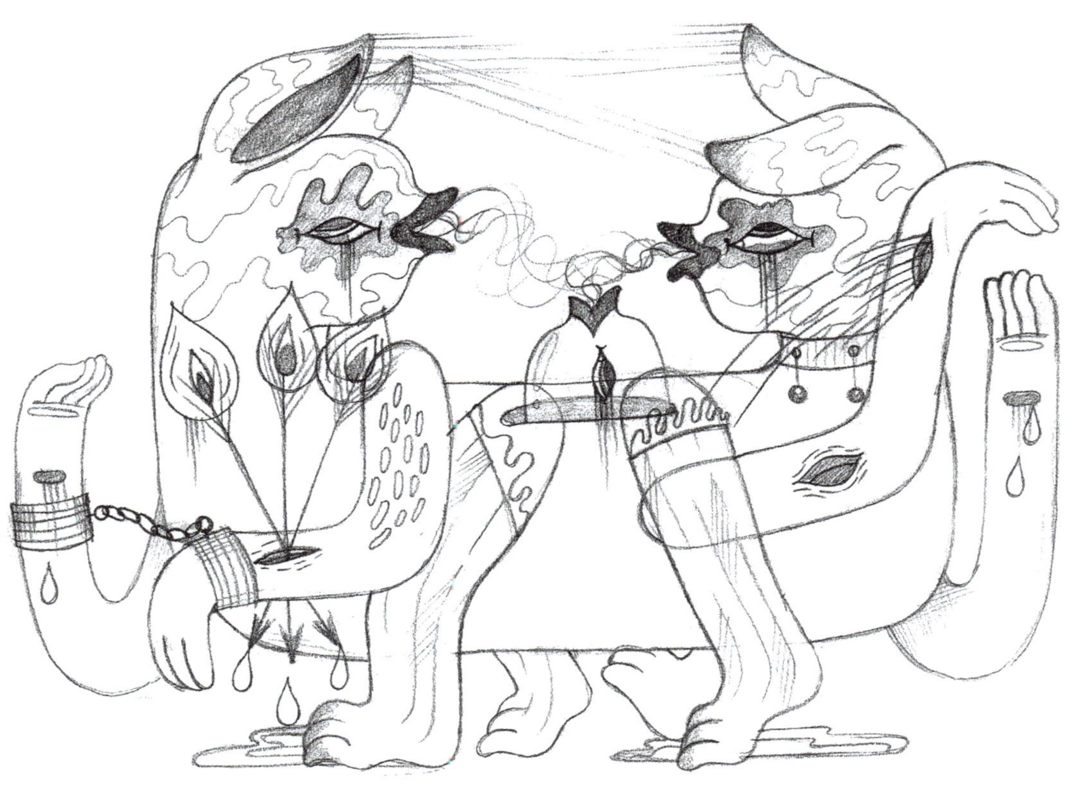

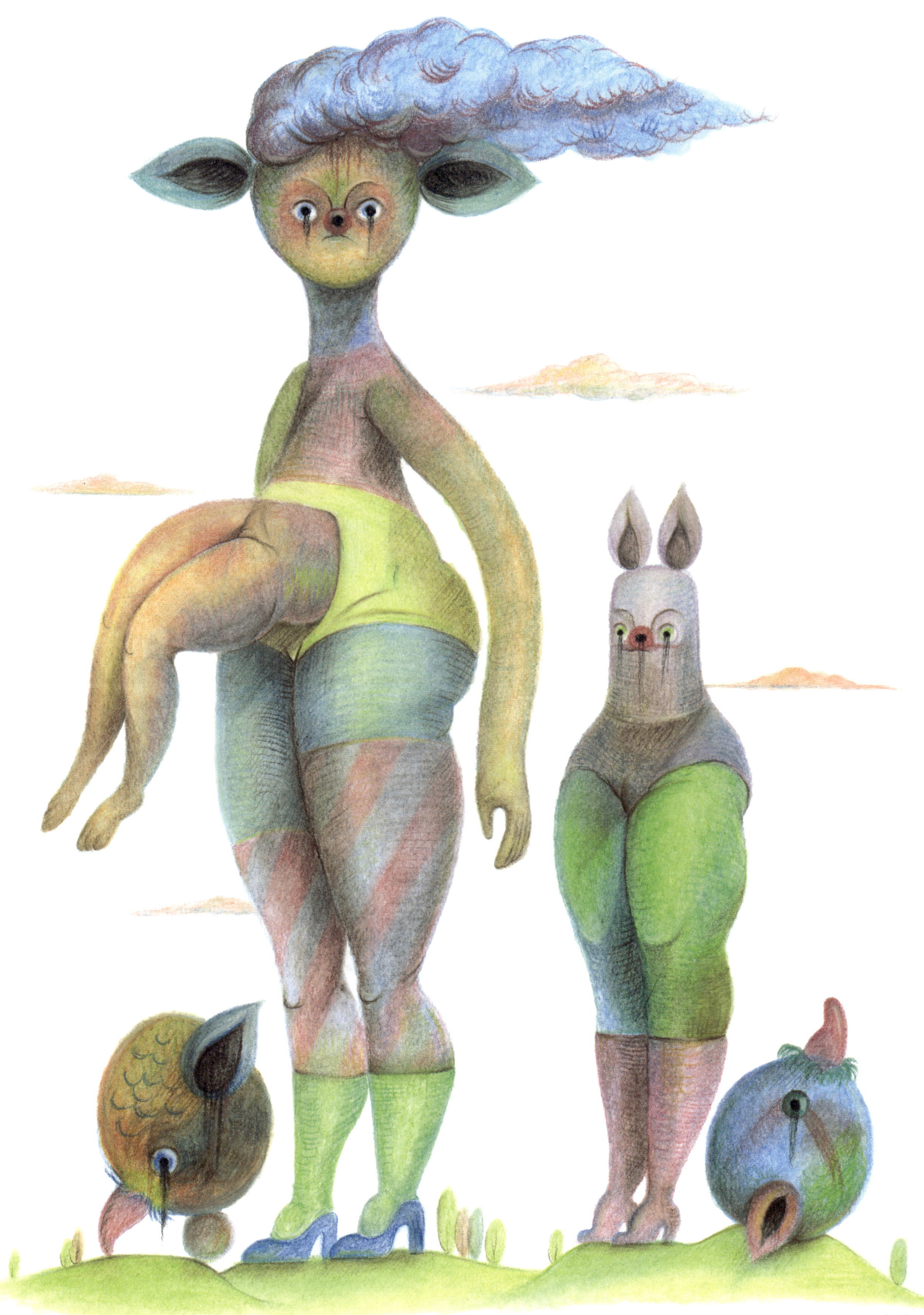

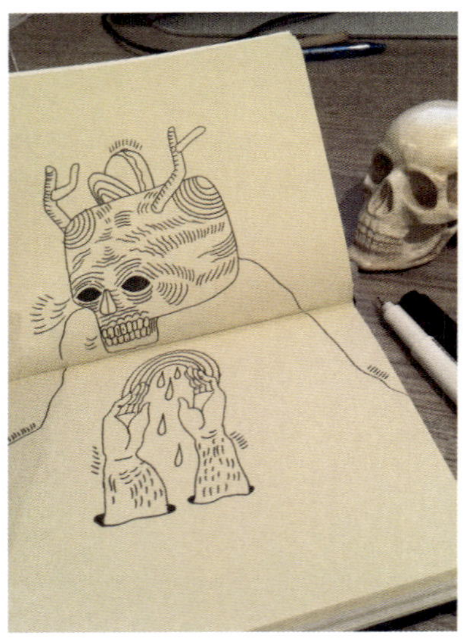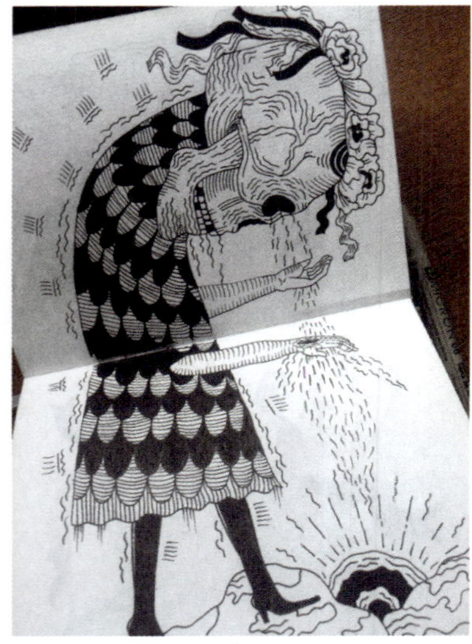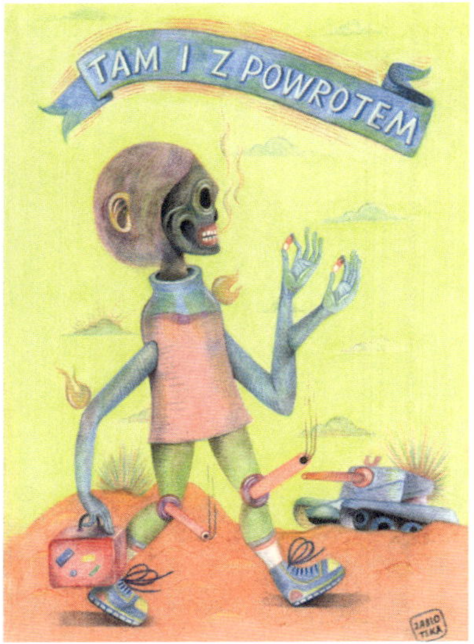

FAR LEFT AND BELOW
Pages from the artist's
sketchbook, 2014
Pencil and ink on paper
Dimensions unknown

LEFT
Round Trip, 2014
Mixed media on paper
Dimensions unknown

OPPOSITE
Pages from the artist's
sketchbook, 2014
Pencil and ink on paper
Dimensions unknown

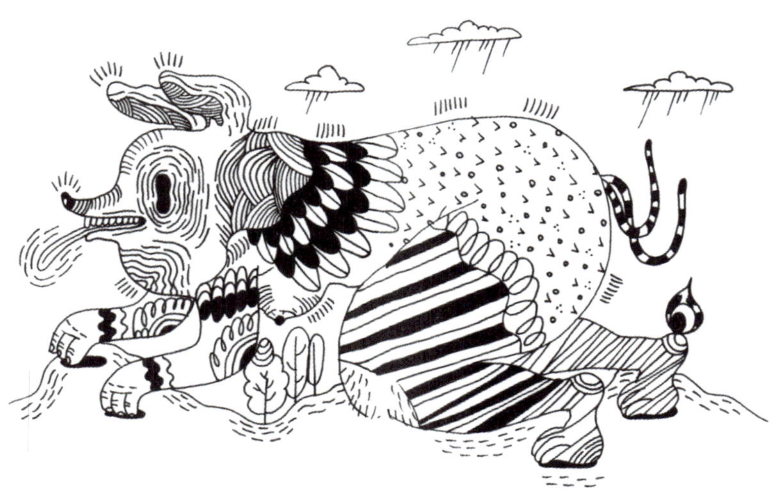

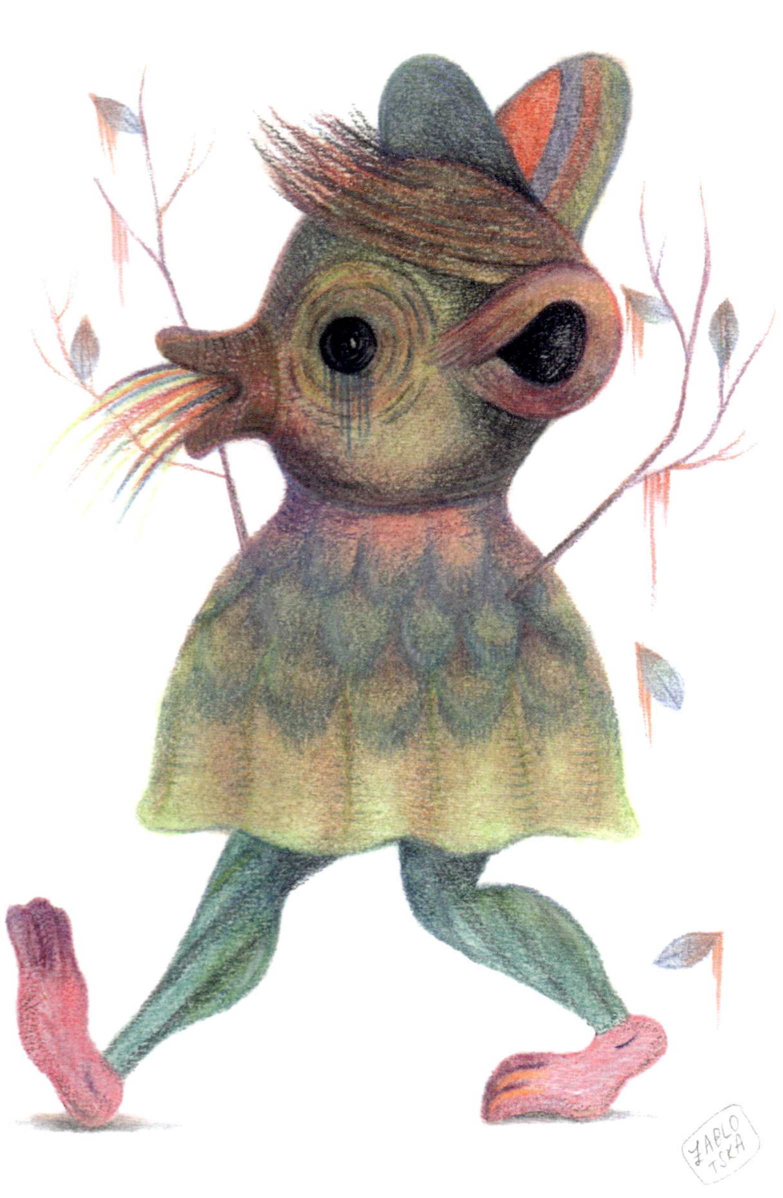

Today website design, more specifically website illustration, still forms part of her professional output. However, more frequently print works and private commissions are being demanded by her clients. In her commercial work she exerts as much creative freedom as she can, sometimes including secret symbols, the meaning of which is known only to her or her contemporaries. An example is a recurring character whose right ear is bigger than the left – a motif deployed by the artist to represent herself.

Zablotska's work reaches people in different ways, whether it is the forms and colours that they are enticed by or her narratives, which are often are interpreted in a manner the artist did not intend: 'I was once surprised to hear', she says, 'that one of my frightening illustrations, as I see it, was seen to be so appealing that it might be used as a children's illustration.'

Zablotska is proud of her Ukrainian heritage and the recent crisis in her home country has been a great influence on her practice. 'I have an entire sketchbook filled with works that are directly connected with these events. When they started shooting innocent people in Kiev, I couldn't do anything but listen to the news and draw.'

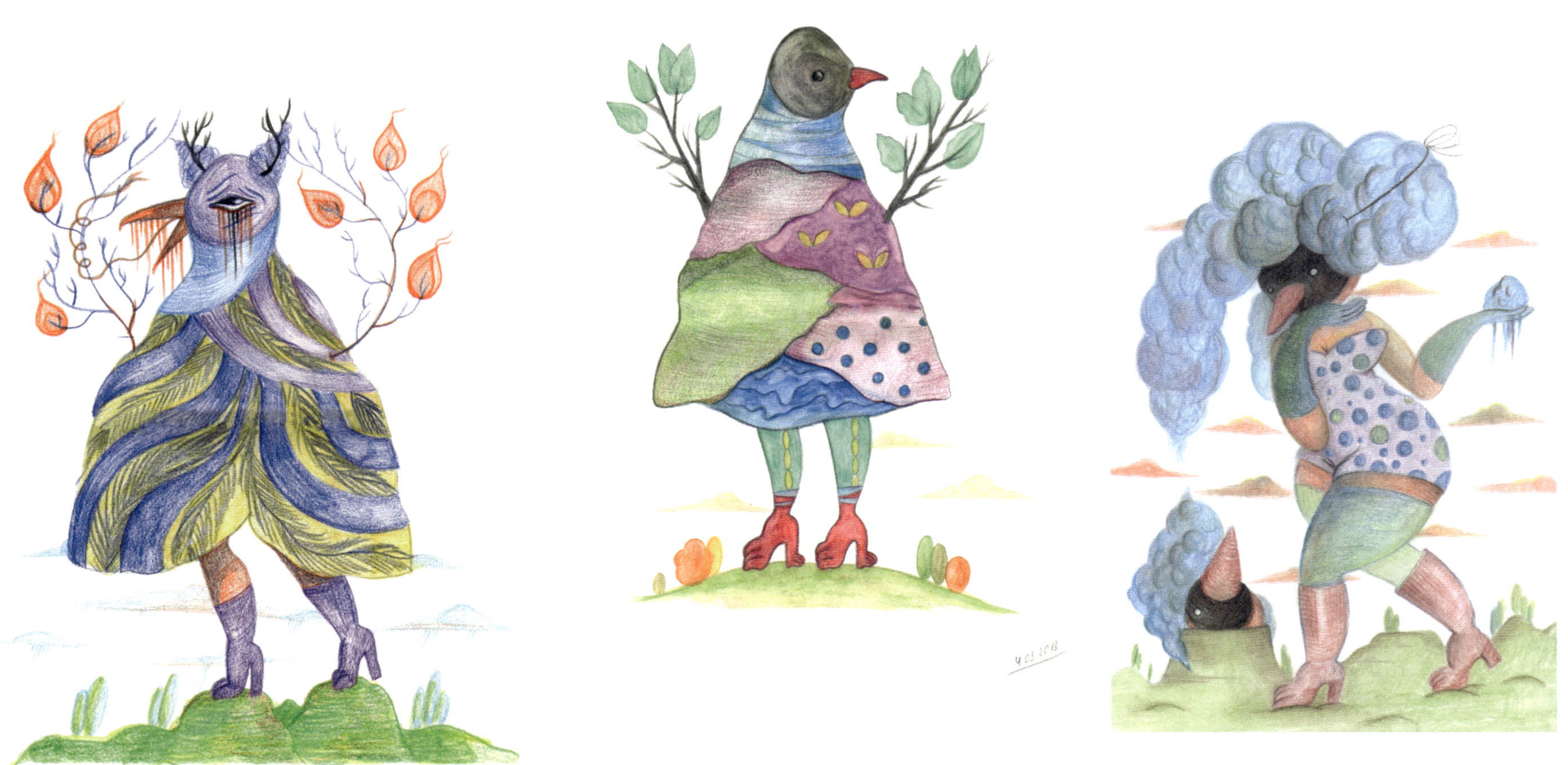

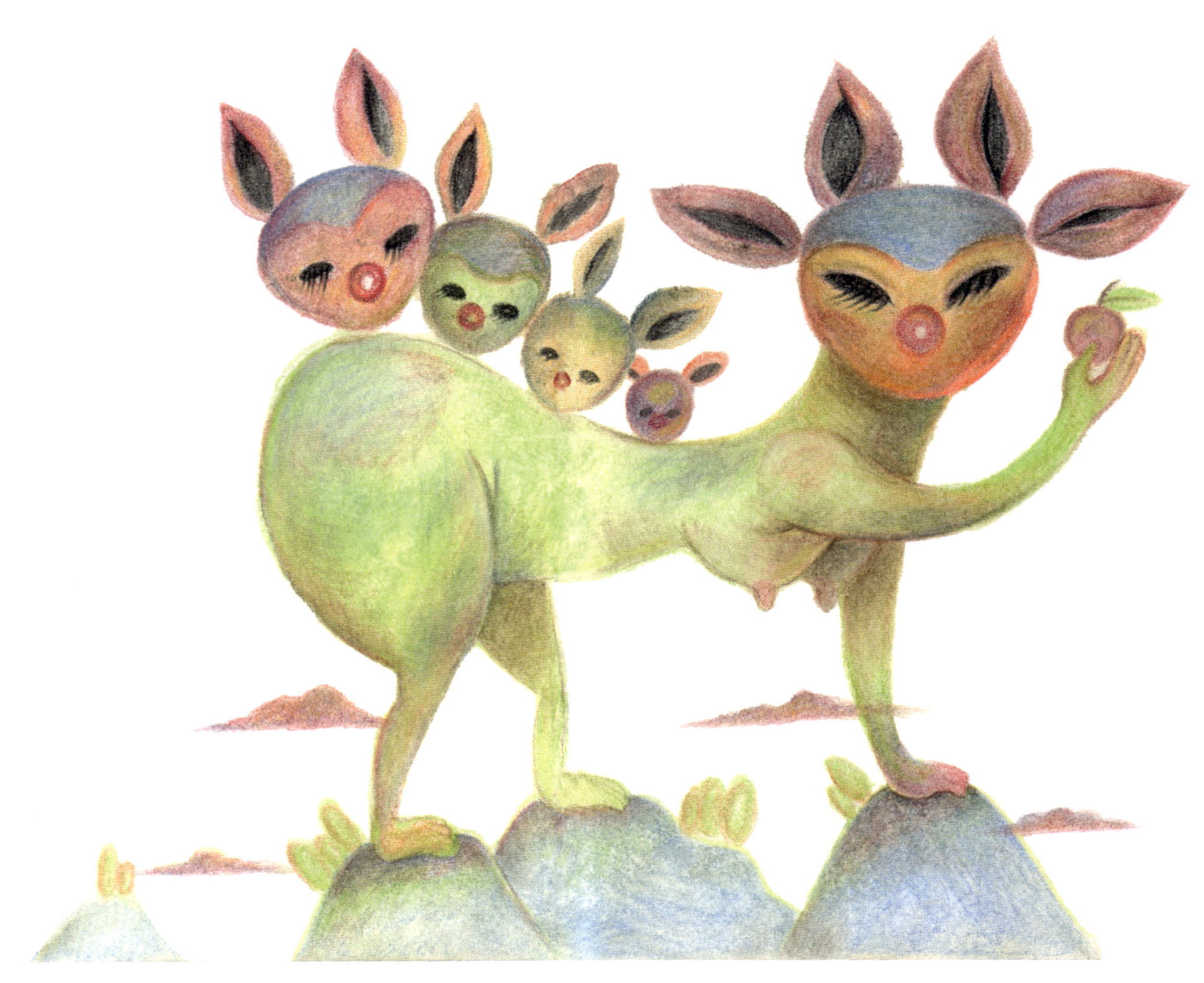

Irena Zablotska93

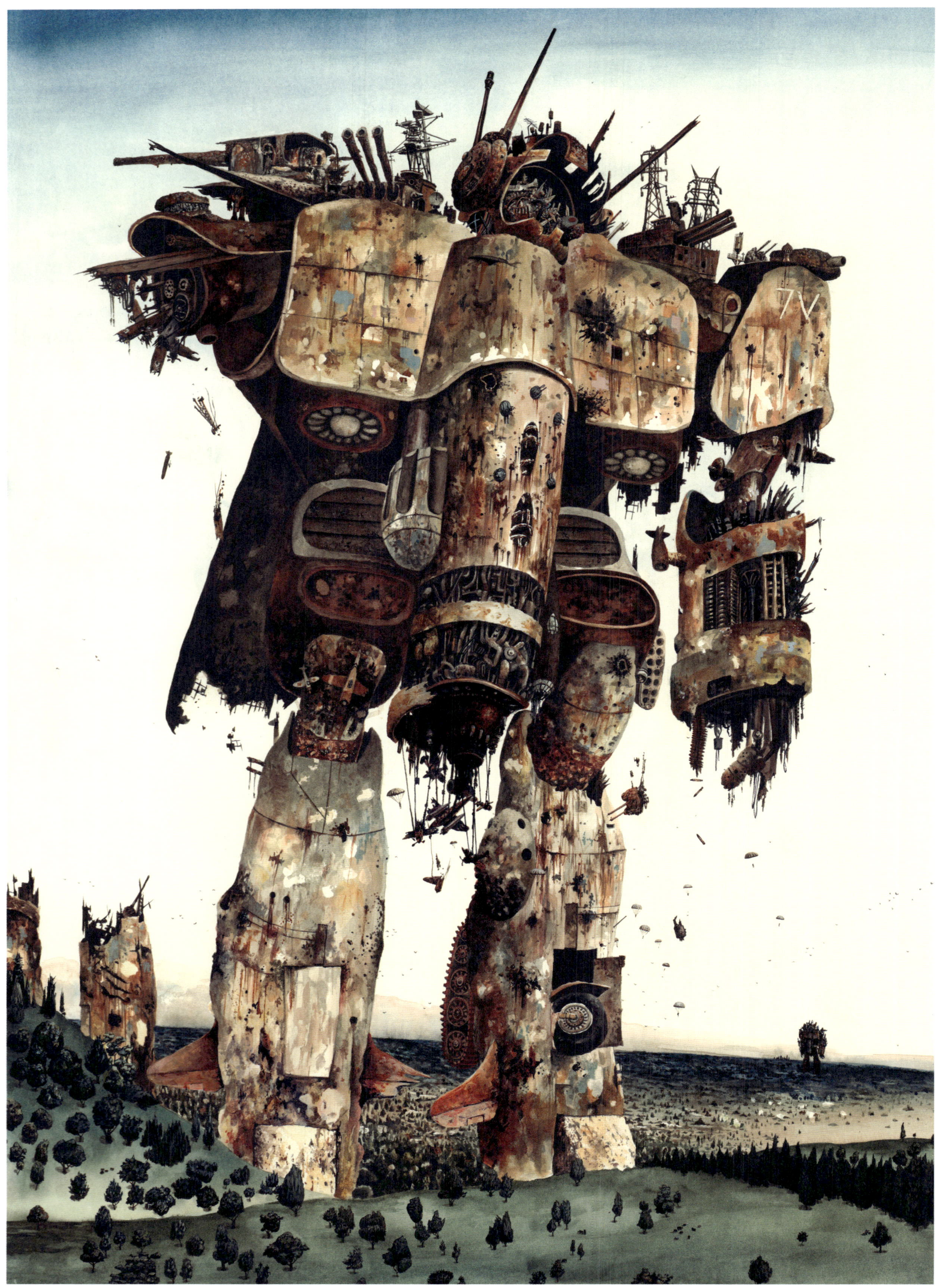

Paint

Perhaps more than any other medium, painting holds a continual fascination. The term itself evokes the archetype of the struggling or famous artist, of iconic galleries and museums and the bewildering sums that are paid for the world's most revered masterpieces. Even as the field of contemporary art has fragmented to include a vast array of media and practices, painting still holds a mystique for many. In spite of its historical and cultural legacy there is also something very democratizing about the medium, it is an essential material and technique to which we all have access and that we could use to express ourselves should we so wish. At its most basic level, paint – whether watercolour, acrylic, oil or spray – in the hands of an artist is the key to a language of colour and form.

In this chapter, artists who follow this primary proclamation in painting – to be uninhibited in their approach, to create work that captivates and energizes – are championed. They have a refreshing and overarching honesty, and bring personality and directness to their art, connecting intuitively to the viewer and drawing them in to their world. While, as we have seen in the previous chapter, the artists have been brought together underneath the umbrella of 'urban art', a good number maintain a practice outside street art, working with contemporary art galleries, as commercial illustrators or producing limited-edition prints for sale online or through other commercial outlets. The majority of these painters, however, work both in the public realm and in the studio. They are united in their independent and progressive stance; uncompromising in the format and content of their production, and often unconventional in the way they exhibit work or collaborate with the institutions that do so on their behalf; they are at ease with experimentation and unfazed by working across a multitude of genres or media. This free and unburdened approach is typified, for example, in the distinctive format and scale of the watercolours of Los Angeles-based Rob Sato, or in the way Bolivian artist Luciano Calderon merges together the high- and lowbrow, integrating popular vernacular art forms into his exhibitions, from hand-knitted Bolivian ski-mask-style hats to painted vinyl street signage. Similarly, British artist Danny Fox has exhibited his work in pubs and tattoo shops – as an antidote to the context of the conventional white cube. Within this broad church of artists there is a marked tendency to break with convention.

By showing primarily painting in this chapter is not to say that it represents the entirety of an artist's oeuvre, although it does serve to put such work into focus. The artists selected here often adopt multiple media, such as fine art, illustration and mural painting and therefore have a diverse range of reference points, influences and outcomes, while also being united in the practice of painting as a way of responding to contemporary life. Influences vary from artist to artist – from literature to comics, modern art to tattoo art, primitive art to graffiti, with there being no hard or fast rules as to which materials they might use or where they might display their art.

In the work shown here, street art and graffiti feed in to fine art and back again, as the American artist Zio Ziegler summarizes of his practice: 'A lot of my early influences came from graffiti. The idea of having the boldest spot, an interesting and provocative surface, the most visual traffic, and the fastest read for a piece while still maintaining complexity that doesn't disappoint under scrutiny.' Graffiti culture has, over the decades, developed a vast lexicon of visual language – letter styles, drop shadows, optical tricks, fades and deconstructed freestyle forms, figures and characters – to make an impact. Through tagging or signature marks, graffiti is its own form of mark making, with artists becoming recognized for their

Rob Sato
Pastoral in a Future Passed, c. 2014
Watercolour on paper
Dimensions unknown

characteristic approach towards subject-matter, quality of line or use of symbols.

The street painters profiled in this chapter have similarly developed all manner of gestural marks with spray paint and brushes. An example is the New York-based artist Cern, who builds up his images with a wonderful array of dynamic marks – quickly sprayed arched lines, daubed and scraped layers of house paint, washes, drips and highlights – to create paintings that are full of life and interest. Although street painting relies on the artist's improvisational abilities, it also requires visual planning to achieve the right composition. This can be seen in the work of artists such as El Curiot and Le Super Demon, who both live and work in Mexico City, and create intricate patterns that reference the sacred geometry and forms found in pre-Colombian art, native handicrafts and folk art.

Rather than simply being a fashionable preoccupation, a principal factor in the choice to make art in public spaces is the dialogue it allows between the context and the viewer. With this in mind Argentinian muralist Pastel creates lush, flora-filled murals that feature local native species, to remind us of the significance of the natural world. Of his approach he states, 'I like to feel that we [as artists] build public spaces, and not as a selfish act of painting, otherwise we'll become an extra tool of chaos and gentrification.' In other ways artists such as the Lithuanian Ernest Zacharevic, who lives and works in Malaysia, use the street as a stage, sometimes integrating objects found there as props to instigate a narrative or to create the illusion that they are being used by his painted protagonists, as in the example of his two children riding an abandoned bicycle. Similarly, Barcelona-based Pejac is known for his situational *trompe l'oeil* illusions that have political, social or environmental undertones. Skilfully realized, they play with the notion that nothing is quite as it seems – as in his Tokyo piece, *Everyone is an Artist*, in which a stencilled figure of a woman throws a pail of water out on to the street, accidentally recreating the iconic Hokusai wave – and suggest that art can be found in the everyday.

Part of the charm of Zacharevic's and Pejac's work is how their realism is illusory, where the real and the imagined seamlessly blend. In contrast, the Italian artist Agostino Iacurci uses bold flat colours, often at a monumental scale, to distinguish between his work and its surroundings. His is a universal language, made accessible through a strong sense of narrative and colour. In divergence to Iacurci's straightforward geometric forms are the paintings of the Russian artist Marat Danilyan, who fuses abstraction and realism in the form of deconstructed figures in muted pastel shades. As these examples show, urban art is not necessarily universal in its appearance even if it is so in appeal.

Counterbalancing the artists who work outside are several who are mostly studio based, and who operate at a different pace, scale and use of technique. This can be seen in the exquisite executions in gouache and watercolour of Brazilian artist João Ruas, or the equally refined paintings of Tokyo-based artist Fuco Ueda, who uses traditional Japanese techniques and materials in her work. Both of these artists adopt customary techniques, which they transform through their particular contemporary visions.

Invariably, the artists in this chapter are mindful of the fact that they are both contributing and in debt to the history of painting. Given the immense legacy and history of the form, and with so many great Old and Modern Masters having come before, it can be daunting to follow in such a revered tradition. For example, Ueda's work owes much to the influence of centuries of Japanese art, and yet there is a great confidence and originality in her interpretation of this heritage. We see this also in the work of British painter Danny Fox, who is fearless about his own influences, which include the greats of Modern Art, Pablo Picasso (1881–1973) and Henri Matisse (1869–1954). It is with determination, obsession and authenticity that this new generation of artists is now pushing paint to its limits in terms of technique, application and concept.

A number of the artists featured here are self-taught, and display non-conformist and independent tendencies, while also demonstrating an admirable sense of self-determination in producing their art. They are energetic rule-breakers, often feverishly prolific, making paintings that are unique and captivating. Some are led by their materials, such as the American artist Rob Sato: 'The paintings tend to be better when I let the emotional impact of the visuals and the joy of the materials lead the way.' While others try not to let this be a guiding force, as Zacharevic reflects: 'I always try to focus on the content and the context of my work and not to limit myself by a medium.' Evidently their use of materials, subject-matter and context are all elements between which the artists must negotiate a balance.

Fuco Ueda
Garden of Silence, 2014
Acrylic on canvas
72 × 50 cm (28½ × 19½ in.)

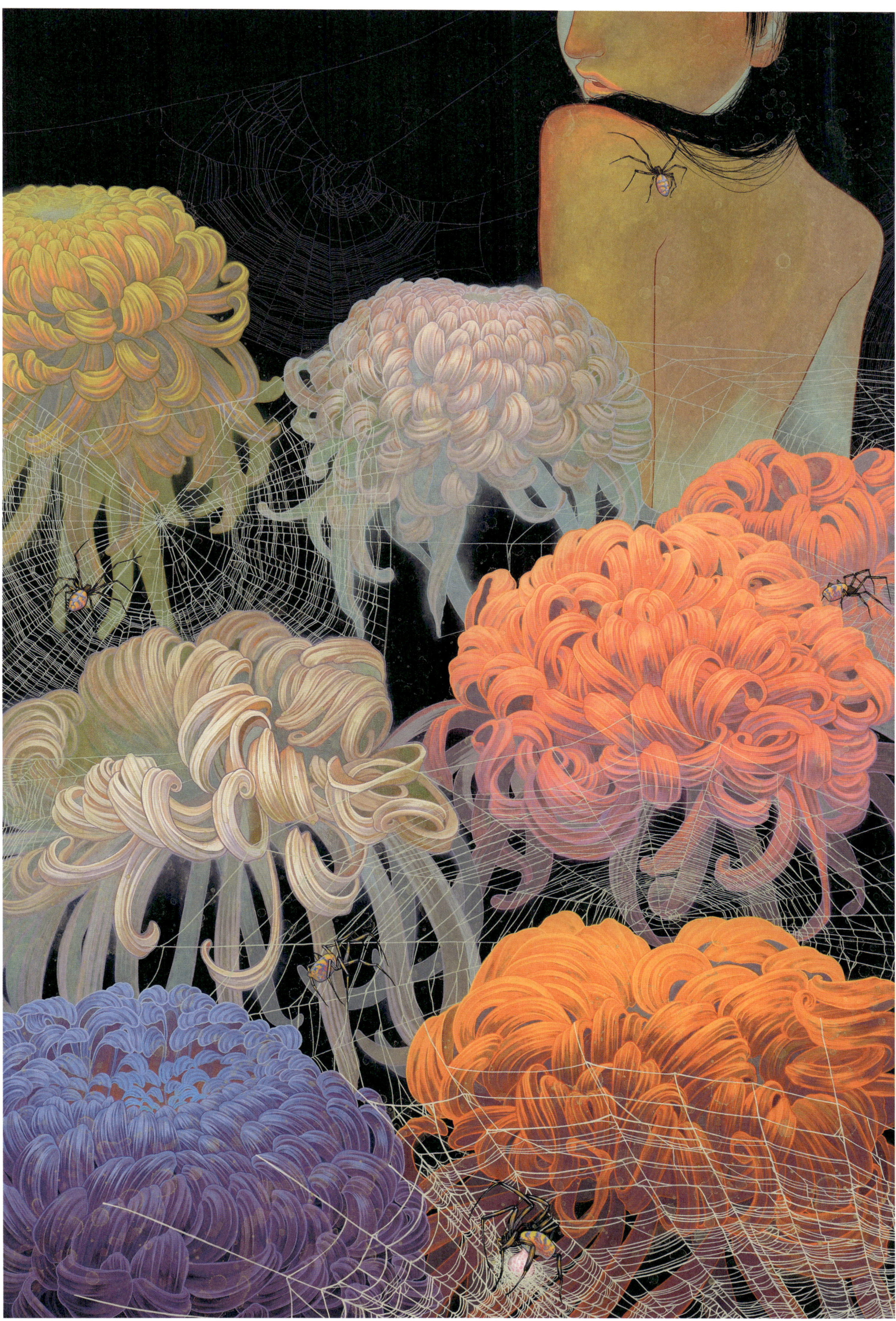

Luciano Calderon

Borrowing from Bolivian folk art, handicrafts and *arte popular*, such as sign painting and other commercial art, are the paintings of the Bolivian artist Luciano Calderon.

Now dividing his time between the affluent and immaculate city of Bern in Switzerland, and the chaotic and sprawling urban centre of El Alto in Bolivia, Calderon studied graphic design at the School of Design Bern and Biel, graduating in 2007. It was at this time that he began considering Bolivian *arte popular* in relation to his own output, especially his typographic work, which was evolving into something more akin to the raw and untutored styles he had encountered in El Alto, rather than the influences to which he had been exposed in Switzerland. Drawn to this art form due to its 'authenticity', functionality and predominantly hand-crafted aesthetic, Calderon's transition from graphic design to contemporary art was gradual, a move that involved a fusing together of text, image and painting. It is the rich visual language of the typography and colour palette employed by the local painters and shop owners of El Alto in their signs in particular that Calderon seems

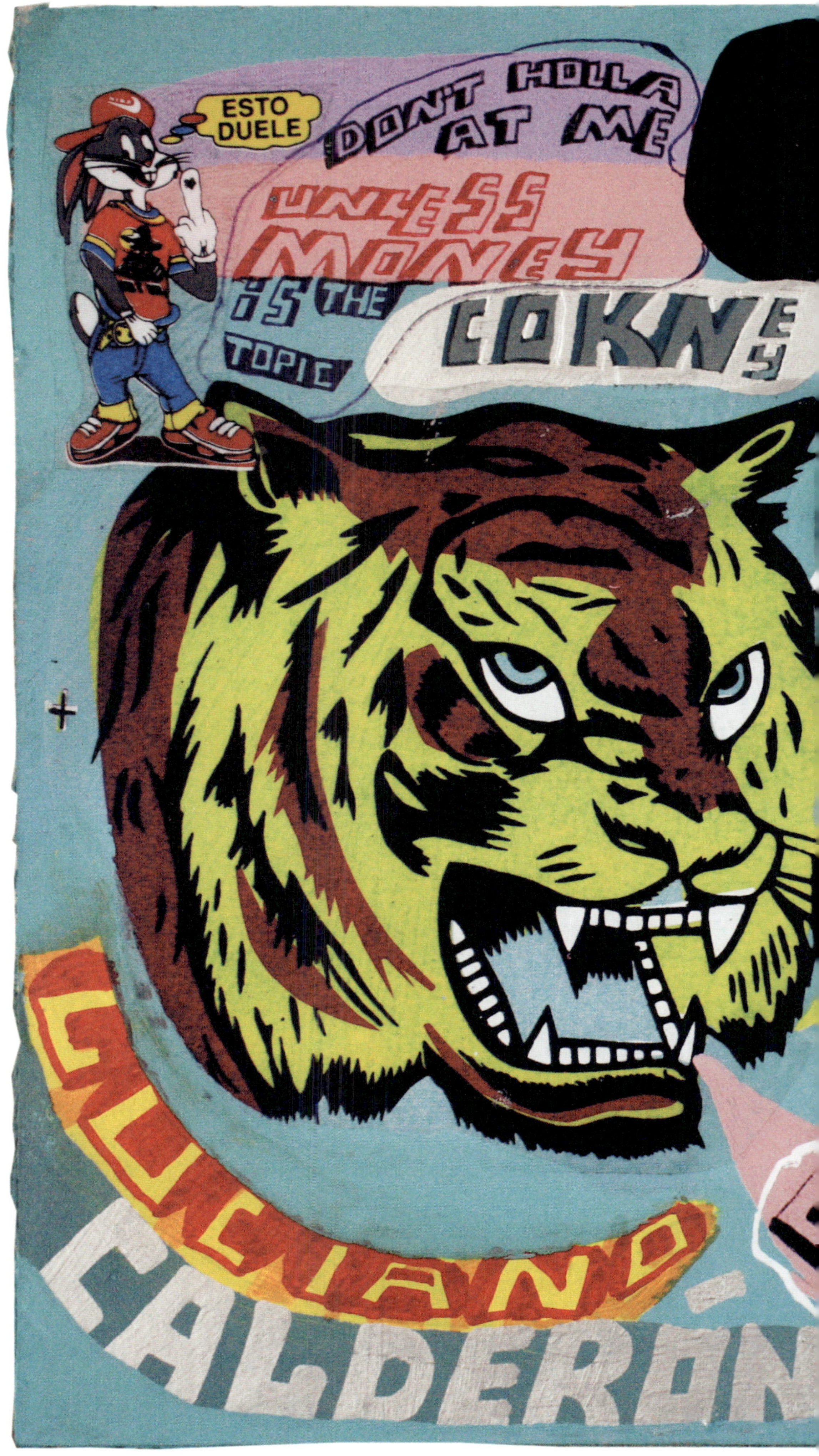

Tigre, 2013
Mixed media on cardboard
26 × 40 cm (10¼ × 15¾ in.)

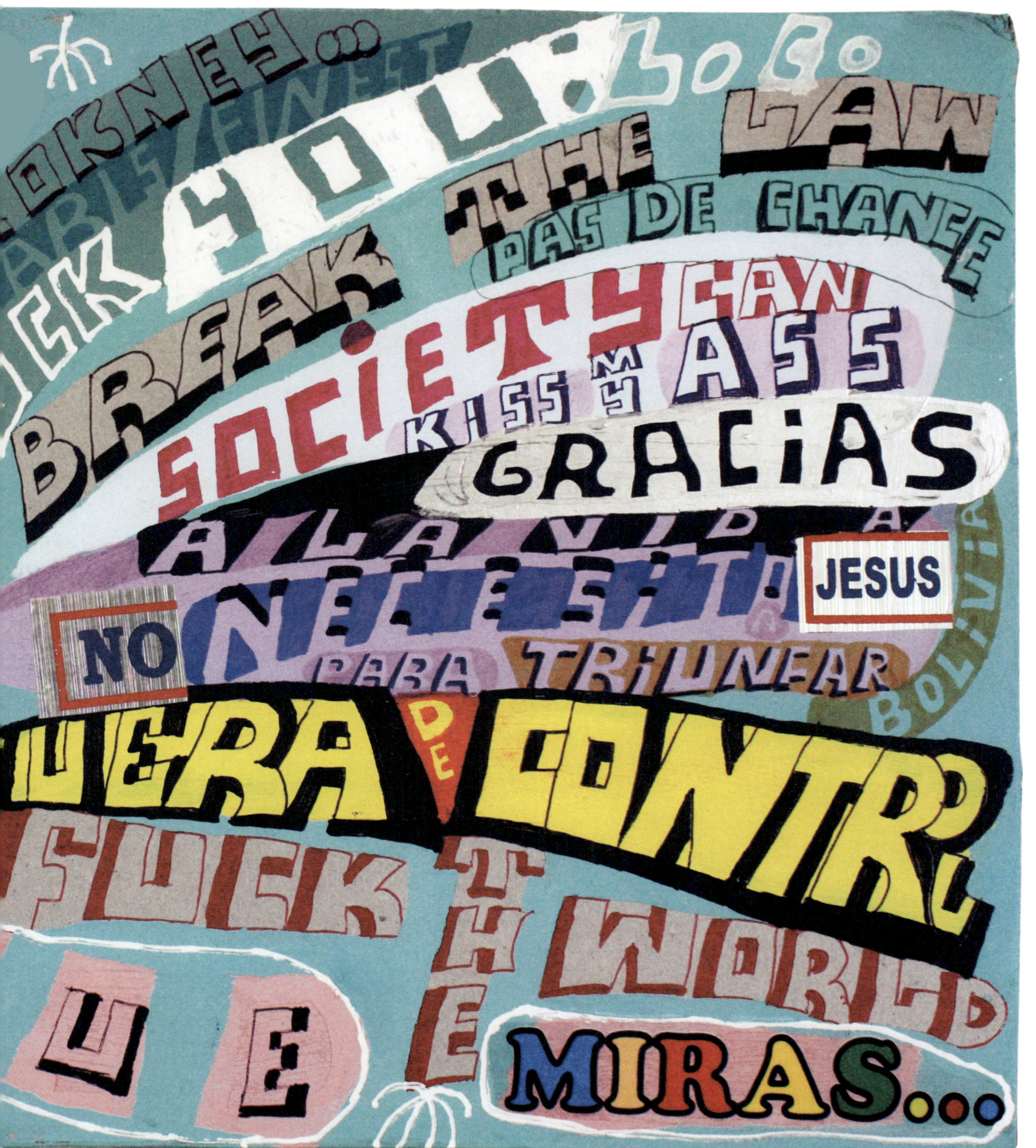
BREAK YOUR... THE LAW
PAS DE CHANCE
SOCIETY CAN KISS MY ASS
GRACIAS
A LA VIDA
JESUS
NO
PARA TRIUNFAR
BOLIVIA
FUERA DE CONTROL
FUCK THE WORLD
MIRAS...

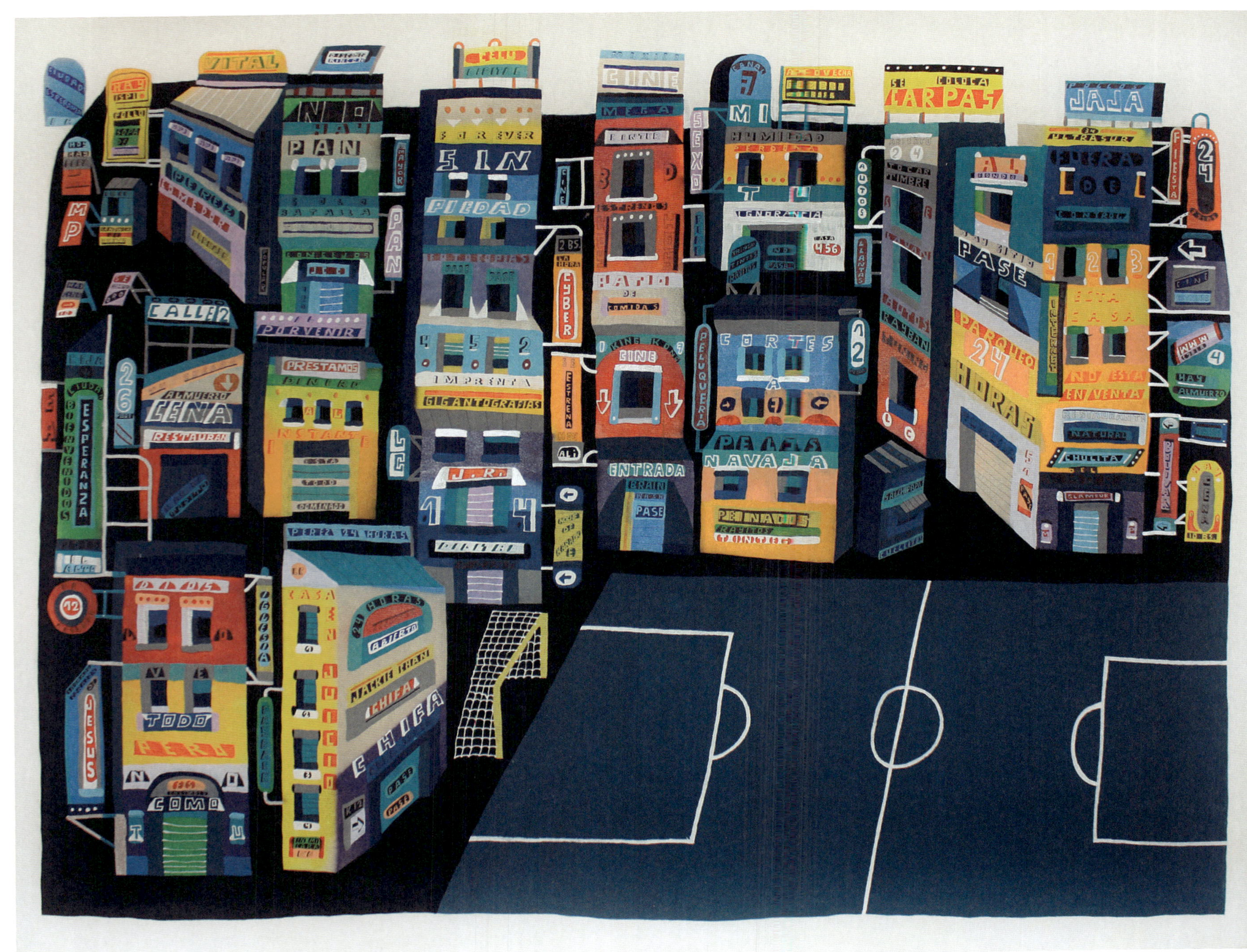

Ciudad Esquina, 2015
Mixed media on canvas
150 × 200 cm (59 × 79 in.)

OPPOSITE
Ciudad Azul, 2015
Mixed media on canvas
150 × 200 cm (59 × 79 in.)

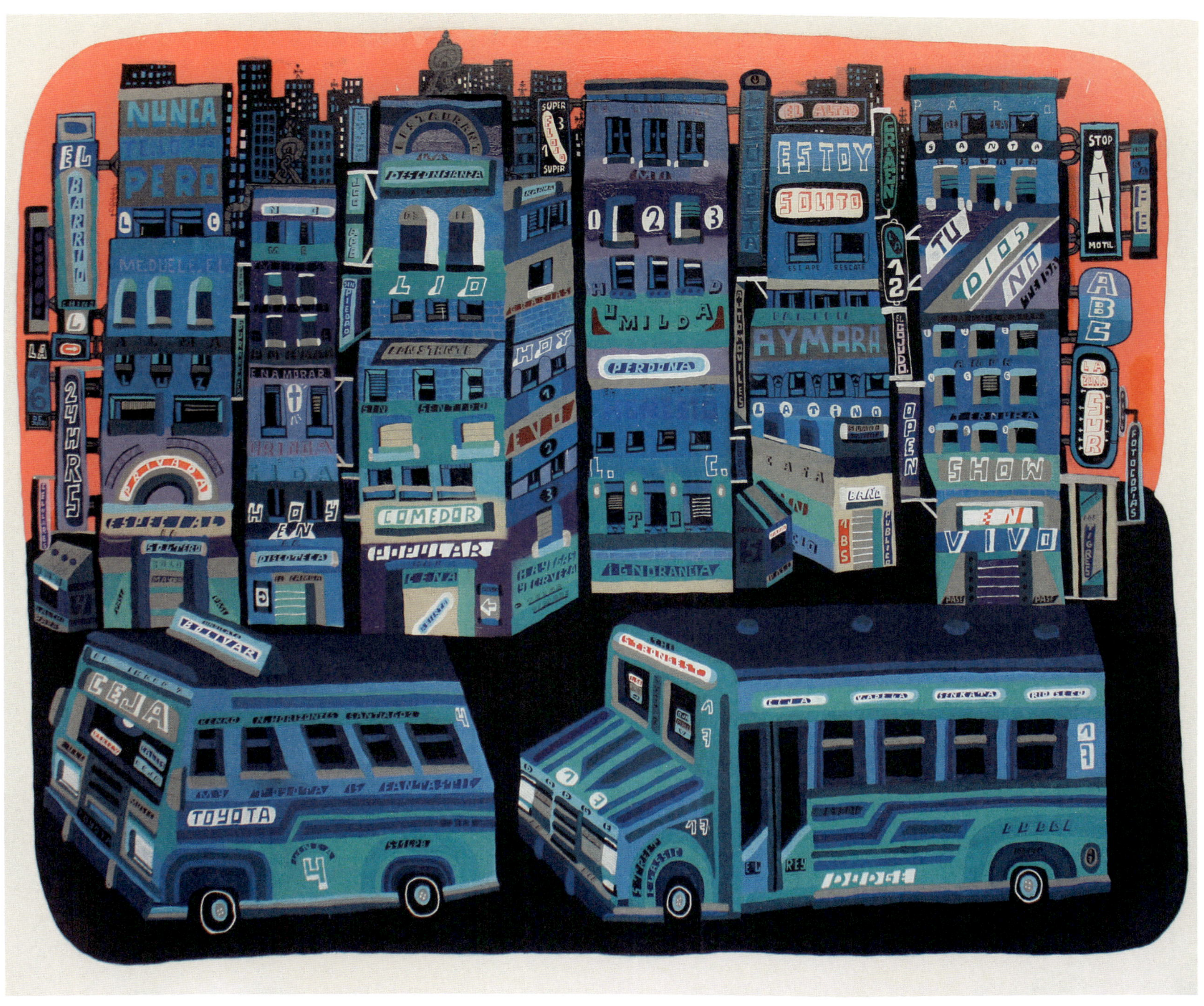

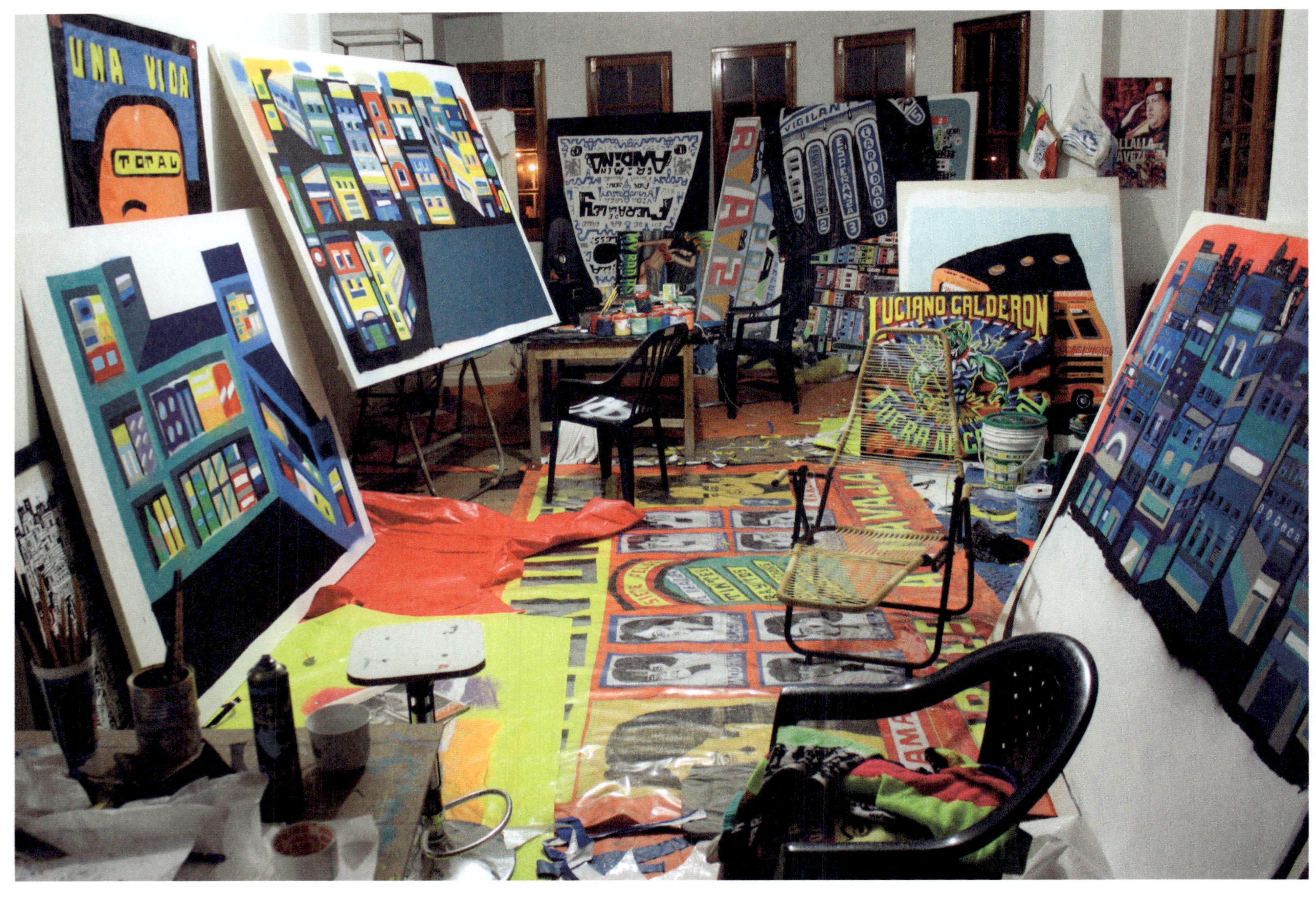

The artist's studio.

to adopt in his work, although rather than simply producing pastiches he reinterprets this art form to communicate concerns about contemporary society at large. Social and political issues – such as police corruption, homelessness or the gentrification of urban spaces – all find a platform for expression in his compositions, but not to the detriment of their craft-like aesthetic, which is prominent throughout.

The contemporary art scene in Bolivia is still in its infancy, which, as Calderon notes, has much to do with the fact that usually only the privileged are able to make art, with economic pressures dictating that most people must work from a young age in order to support their families. As he sums up, 'Sadly art in Bolivia is not for everybody and that's why I think its so amazing that at the same time you find it everywhere, on every corner and on every sign.'

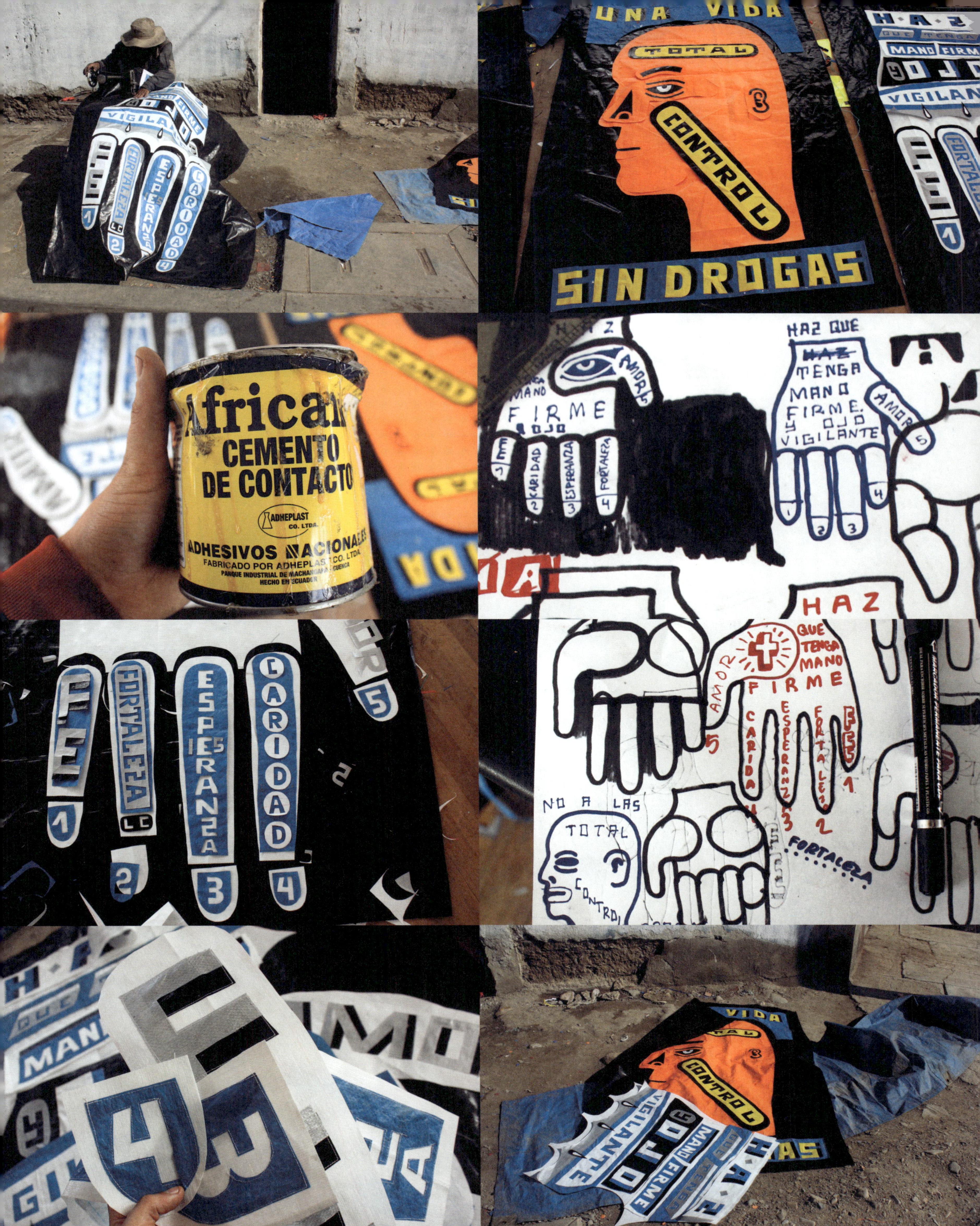
MANO
VIGILA
FORTALEZA
ESPERANZA
CARIDAD
1
2
3
UNA VIDA
HAZ
QUE TENGA
MANO FIRME
OJO
VIGILAN
TOTAL
CONTROL
SIN DROGAS
African
CEMENTO
DE CONTACTO
ADHEPLAST
CO. LTDA.
ADHESIVOS NACIONALES
FABRICADO POR ADHEPLAST CO. LTDA.
PARQUE INDUSTRIAL DE MACHANGARA · CUENCA
HECHO EN ECUADOR
HAZ
TENGA
MANO
FIRME
Y
OJO
VIGILANTE
AMOR
FIRME
OJO
CARIDAD
ESPERANZA
FORTALEZA
AMOR
HAZ QUE
HAZ
AMOR
1
2
3
4
5
FE
FORTALEZA
LC
ESPERANZA
CARIDAD
1
2
3
4
5
HAZ
QUE TENGA
MANO
FIRME
AMOR
CARIDAD
ESPERANZA
FORTALEZA
FE
NO A LAS
TOTAL
CONTROL
FORTALEZA
5
4
3
2
1
MANO
FORTALEZA
4
3
AMOR
VIDA
CONTROL
VIGILANTE
MANO FIRME
OJO
HAZ

Ricardo Cavolo

Like an illustrative superhero, leaving behind a trail of his trademark light flashes and sweeping comets,

the Spanish artist Ricardo Cavolo launches a force of positivity through his art. Bursting with colour, energy and symbolism, Cavolo's work is upbeat, even when the subject-matter concerns the challenges that life brings. His work is powerful but not overpowering, and rich with detail.

Born into an artistic family, Cavolo's idea of fun as a child was to spend his days drawing alongside his father (who is also a painter) and listening to music, something he now happily does for a living. Initially, his professional career encompassed working as an art director at several advertising agencies before discovering that there was an audience for his own work, after which he became a freelance illustrator. Since then his output has featured in all manner of illustrative outlets such as posters, tarot cards, maps and book covers and has included large-scale murals, painted on and in buildings, trains and even a disused aeroplane (for Glastonbury Festival). Most recently he wrote and

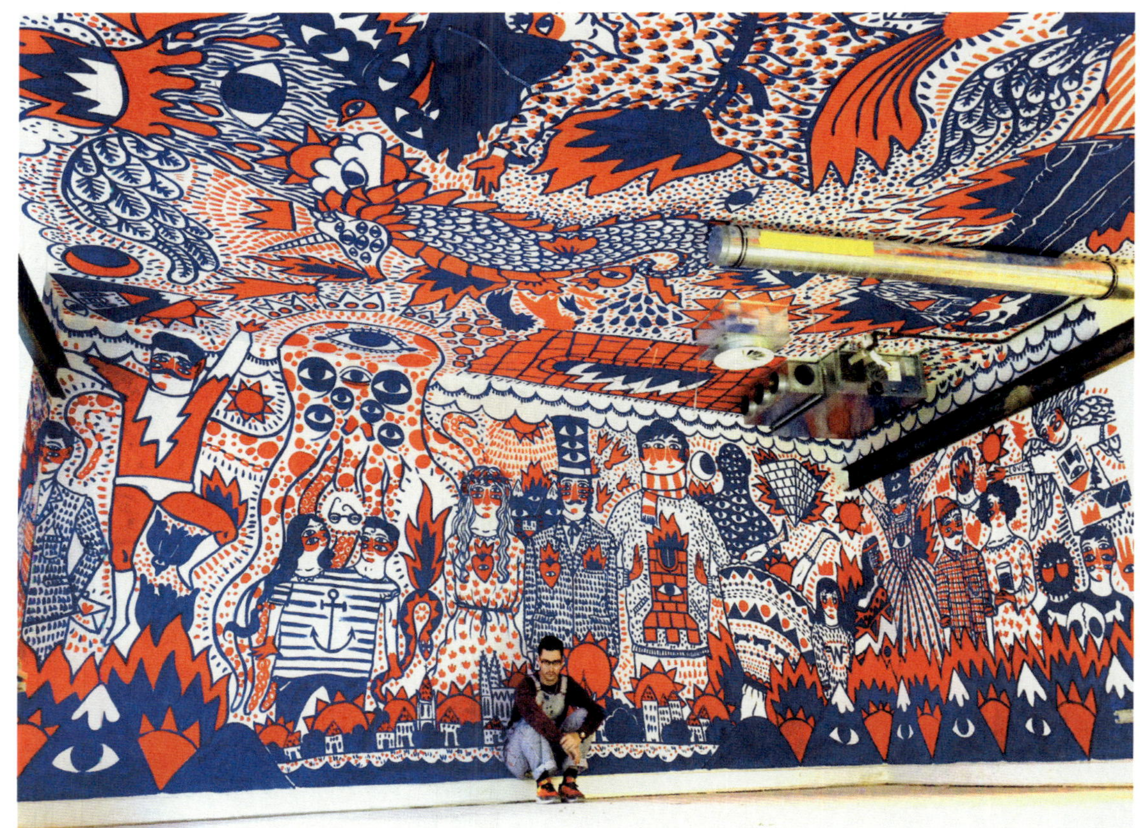

Untitled, mural commissioned by
Urban Outfitters, Cologne, 2013
Mixed media
Dimensions variable

Study for Tattoo Flashes, 2011
Pencil on paper
Dimensions unknown

Study for Frida, 2014
Pencil on paper
Dimensions unknown

OPPOSITE
Yorokobu, 2012
Watercolour and ink on paper
Dimensions unknown

OVERLEAF LEFT
Frida, 2014
Watercolour and ink
on paper
Dimensions unknown

OVERLEAF RIGHT
Ecce Homo, 2012
Watercolour and ink
on paper
Dimensions unknown

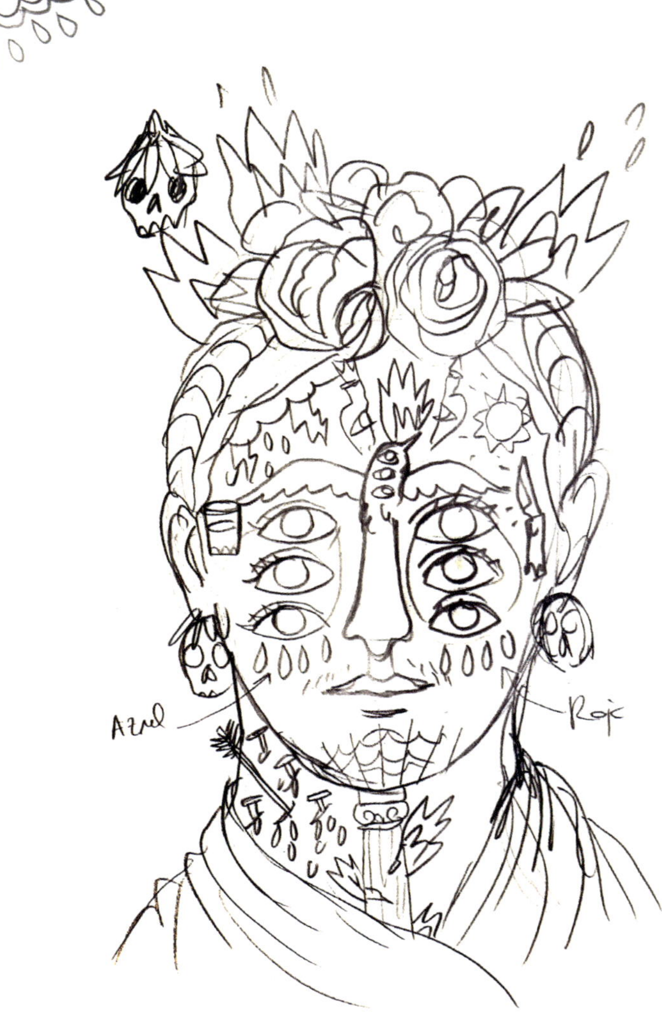

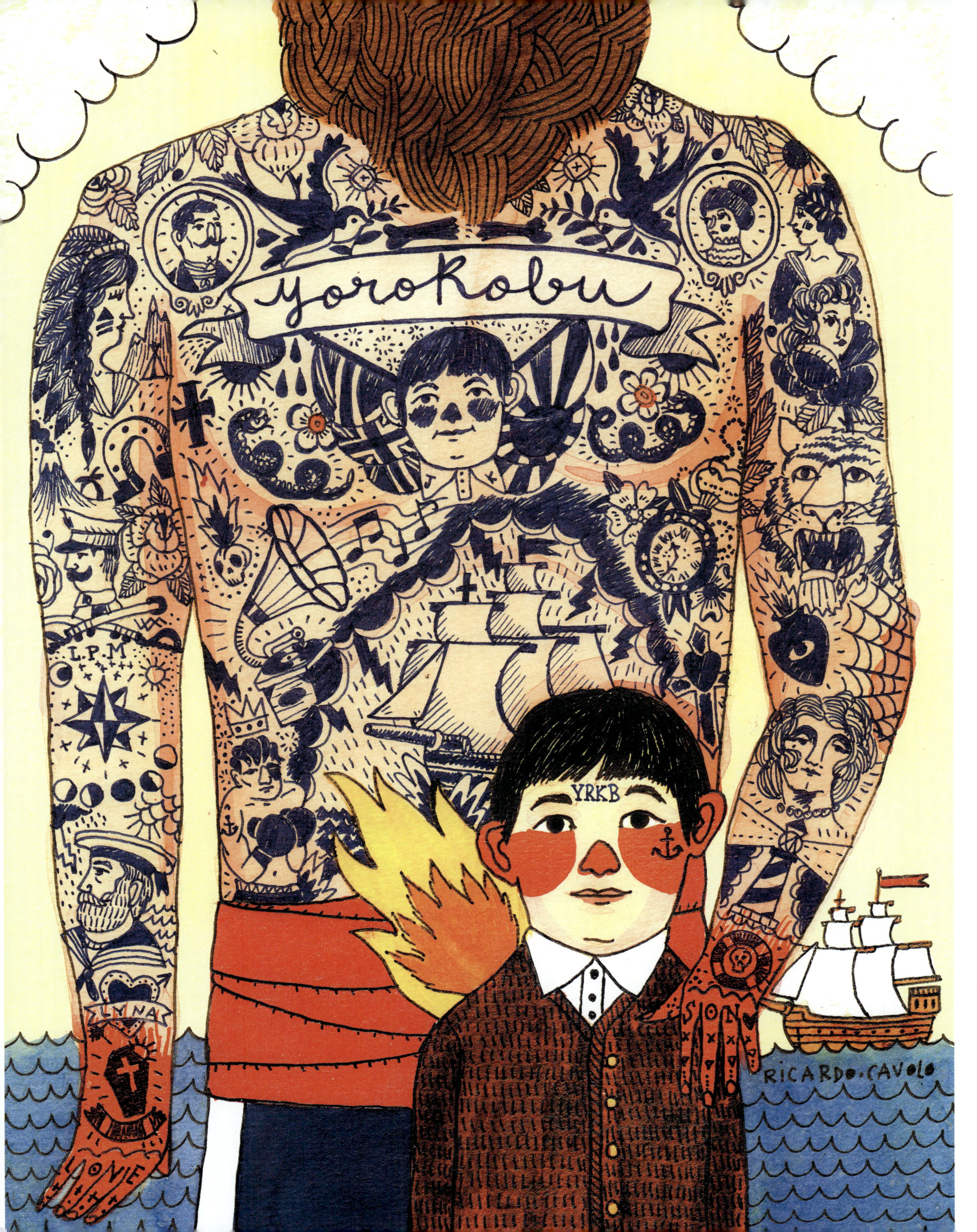

YoroKobu
YRKB
LPM
RICARDO·CAVOLO

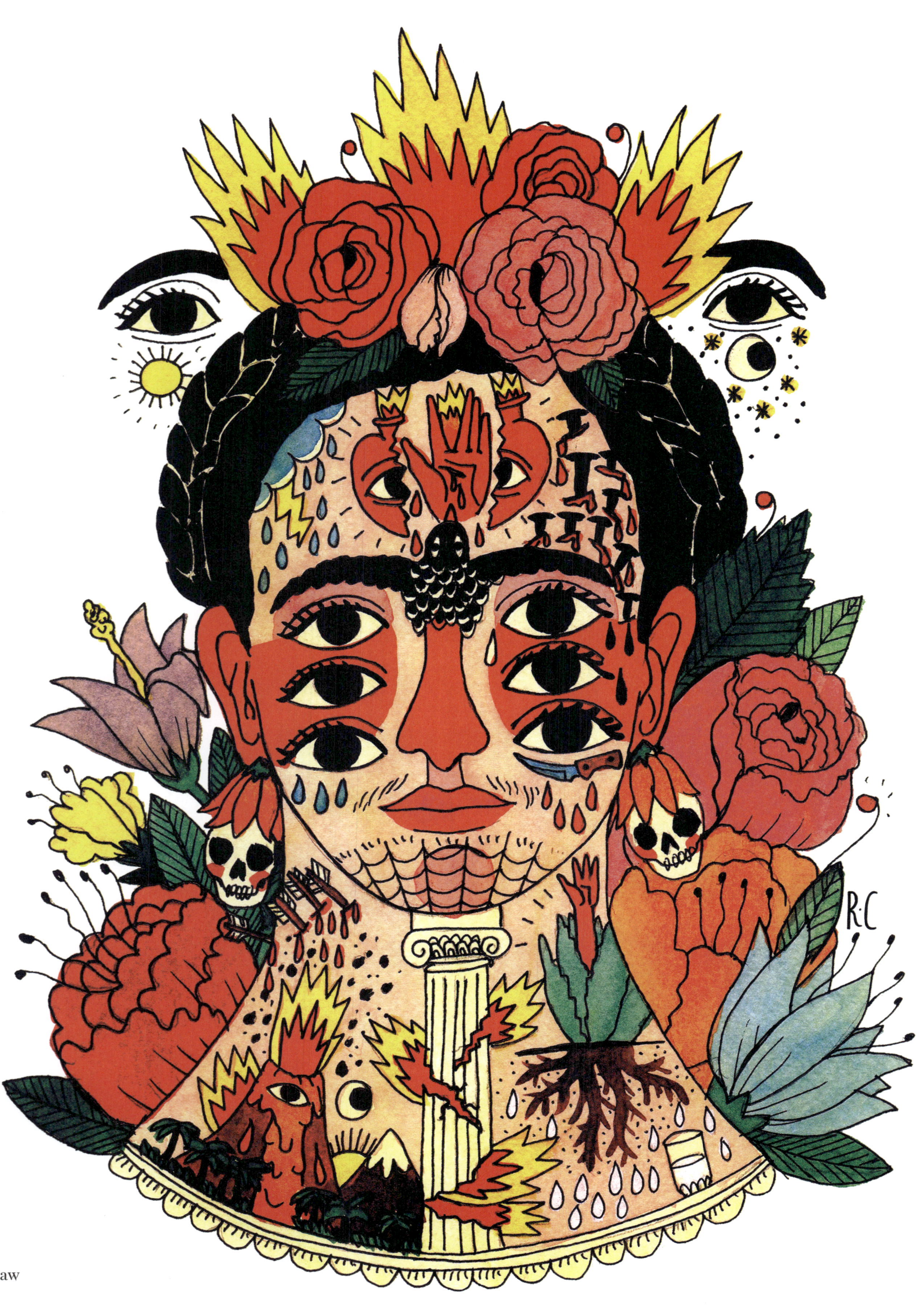

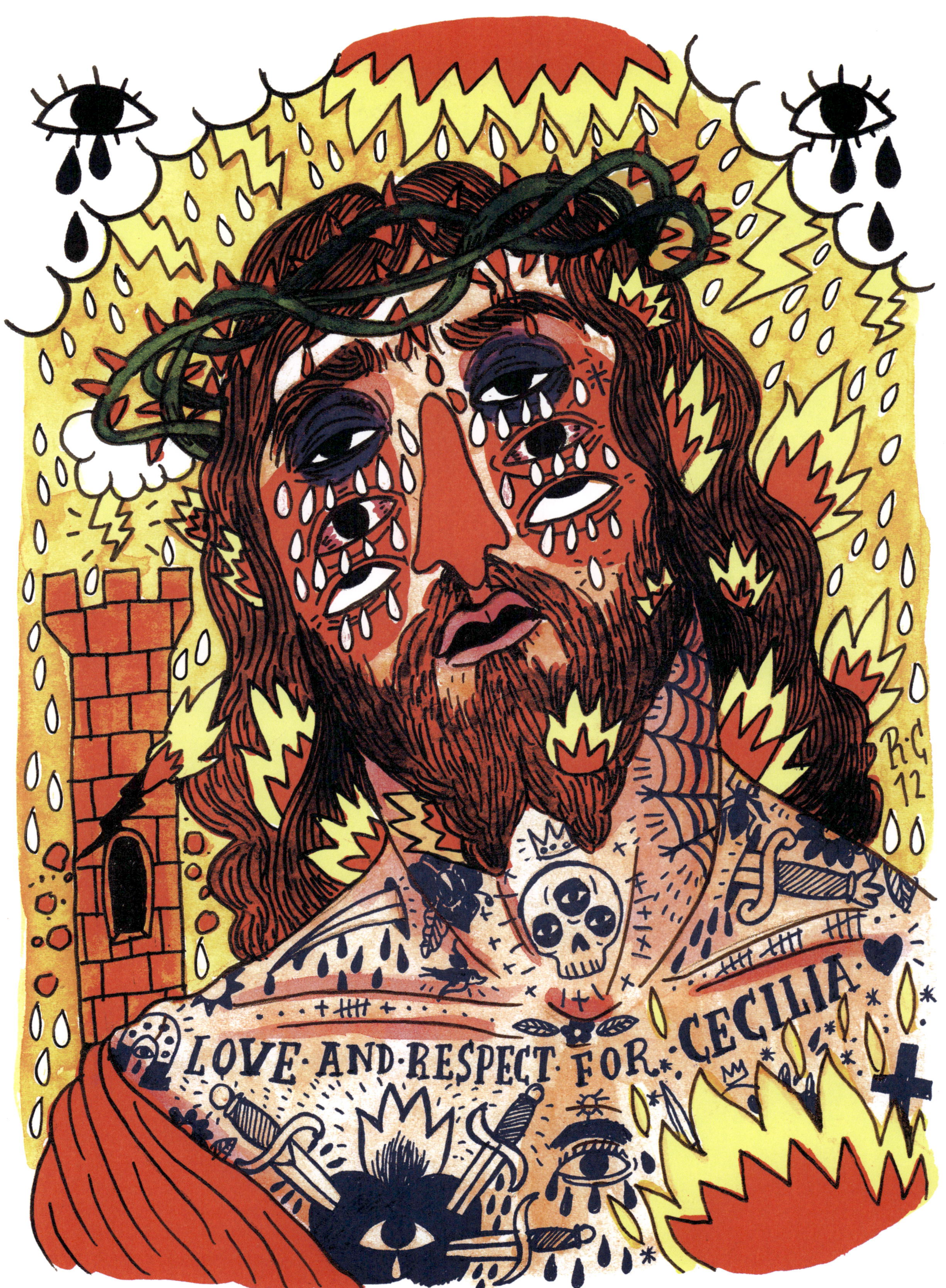

LOVE·AND·RESPECT·FOR·CECILIA
R·C
12

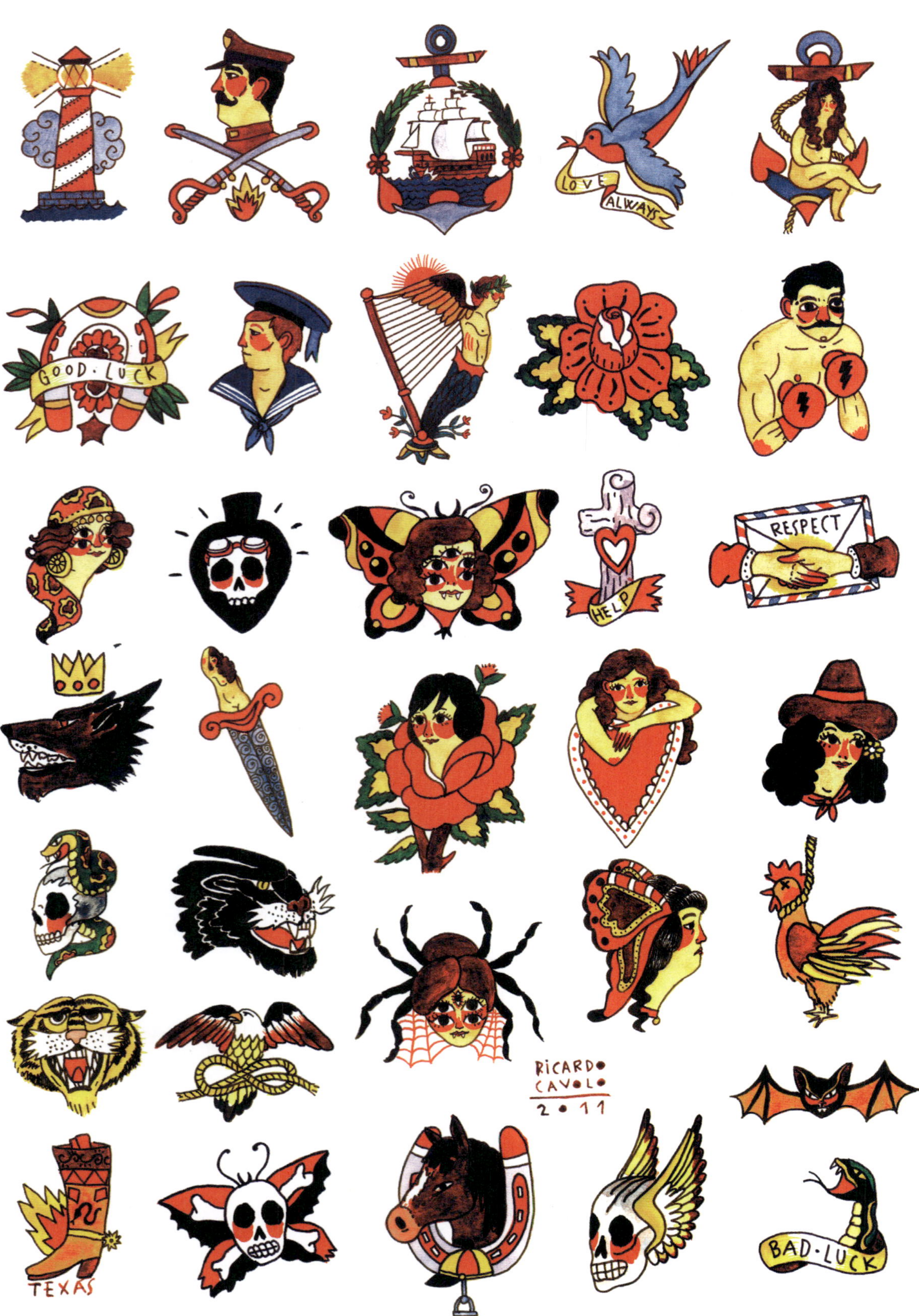

Tattoo Flashes, 2011
Pen and ink on paper
Dimensions unknown

Victoria, 2012
Watercolour and ink on paper
Dimensions unknown

illustrated an ambitious publication, *101 Artists to Listen to Before You Die* (2015), which was a personal journey through the history of music, told via portraits of his musical heroes, from Mozart to Elvis Presley and Kanye West. Full of engaging anecdotes and thoughtful portraits, *101 Artists* is a typical example of Cavolo's painstaking attention to detail and motivation to create work that celebrates his passions, in this case documenting his own wide-ranging musical influences and tastes in the hope that they will be enjoyed and shared by others.

People and the lives they lead fascinate Cavolo, with portraits being an important aspect of his visual repertoire. In these works he seeks to convey the histories of his subjects, not only by means of their facial expressions but also through the symbols and tattoos with which they are embellished. Adorned with tattoo designs of his own making, including a flaming eye on the back of each hand, the artist is also a tattoo aficionado. Of this art form it is its biographical nature to which he is particularly drawn, as he explains: 'Symbols and hidden meanings are the perfect motifs for speaking about a particular subject in my work. It is a pursuit of mine to translate real stories into symbols. I always strive to add narratives to my work, and symbols are the best way to generate this.'

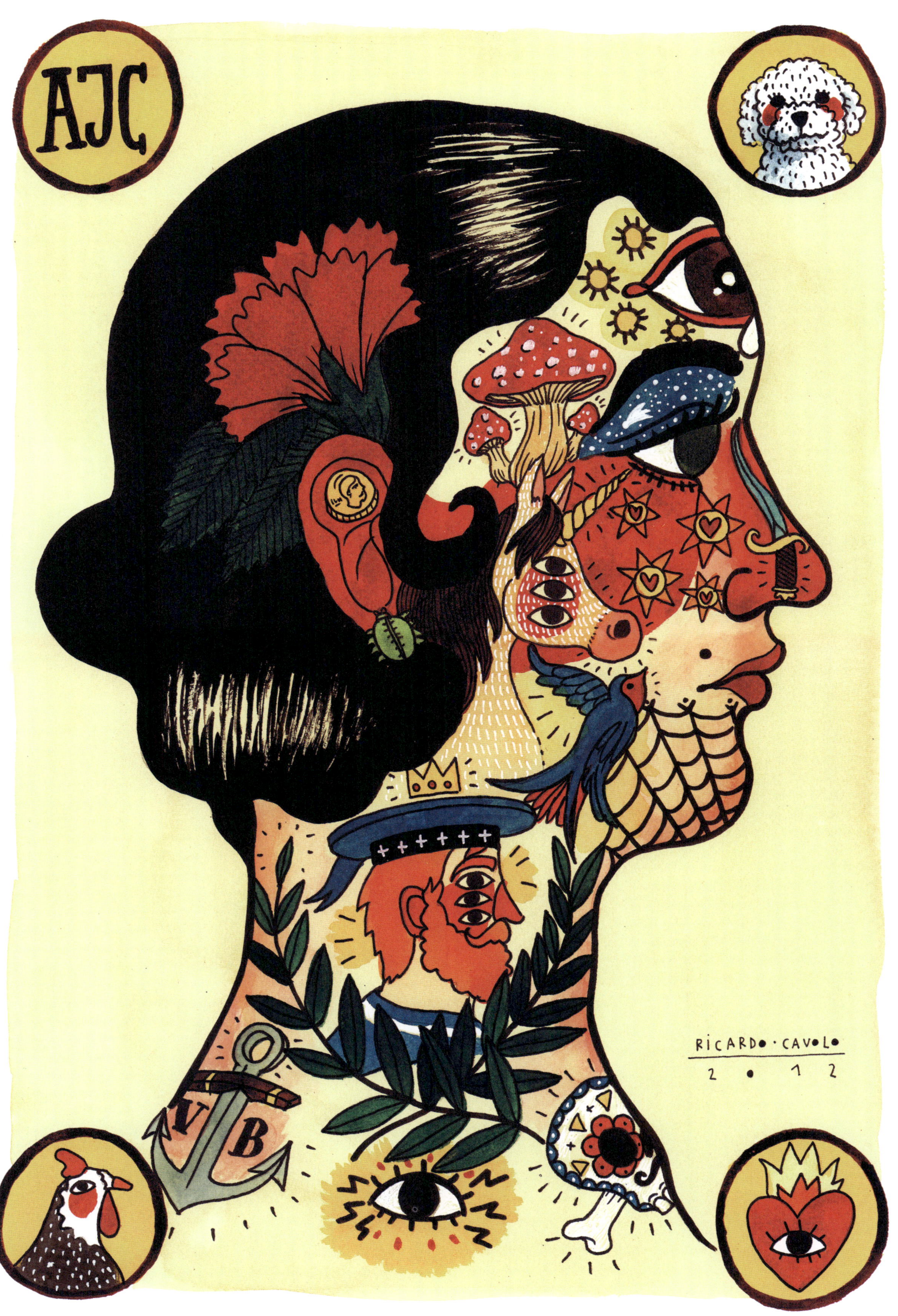
AJÇ
RICARDO·CAVOLO
2 · 1 2

Cern

With his cast of kooky characters, such as playful cats, rainbow-spouting elephants and sunglass-sporting girls,

Brooklyn-based artist Cern conjures up magical
multilayered worlds, both in public settings and on
canvas. As part of his signature style these vivid and
fantastical scenes are often interwoven with energetic
patterns and lush flora and fauna. They reflect life in the
city, its stories and inhabitants and – a thread common
throughout his work – romance and love. As he explains,
'On various levels the work is about regarding love itself
and how that translates through nature, societies and
art-making. A love for what is and what has been lost, a
reverence for what has been destroyed and a respect for
what is most painful in this life.'

Cern became hooked on painting in the public realm
in the early 1990s. Born and raised in Queens, he began
writing graffiti in his neighbourhood at an early age,
an activity that has continued to evolve and guide him
into his current practice. In this location he has found a
freedom of expression and the ability to communicate
to a large audience, both of which he is mindful, seeking

Untitled, c. 2010
Mixed media
Dimensions unknown

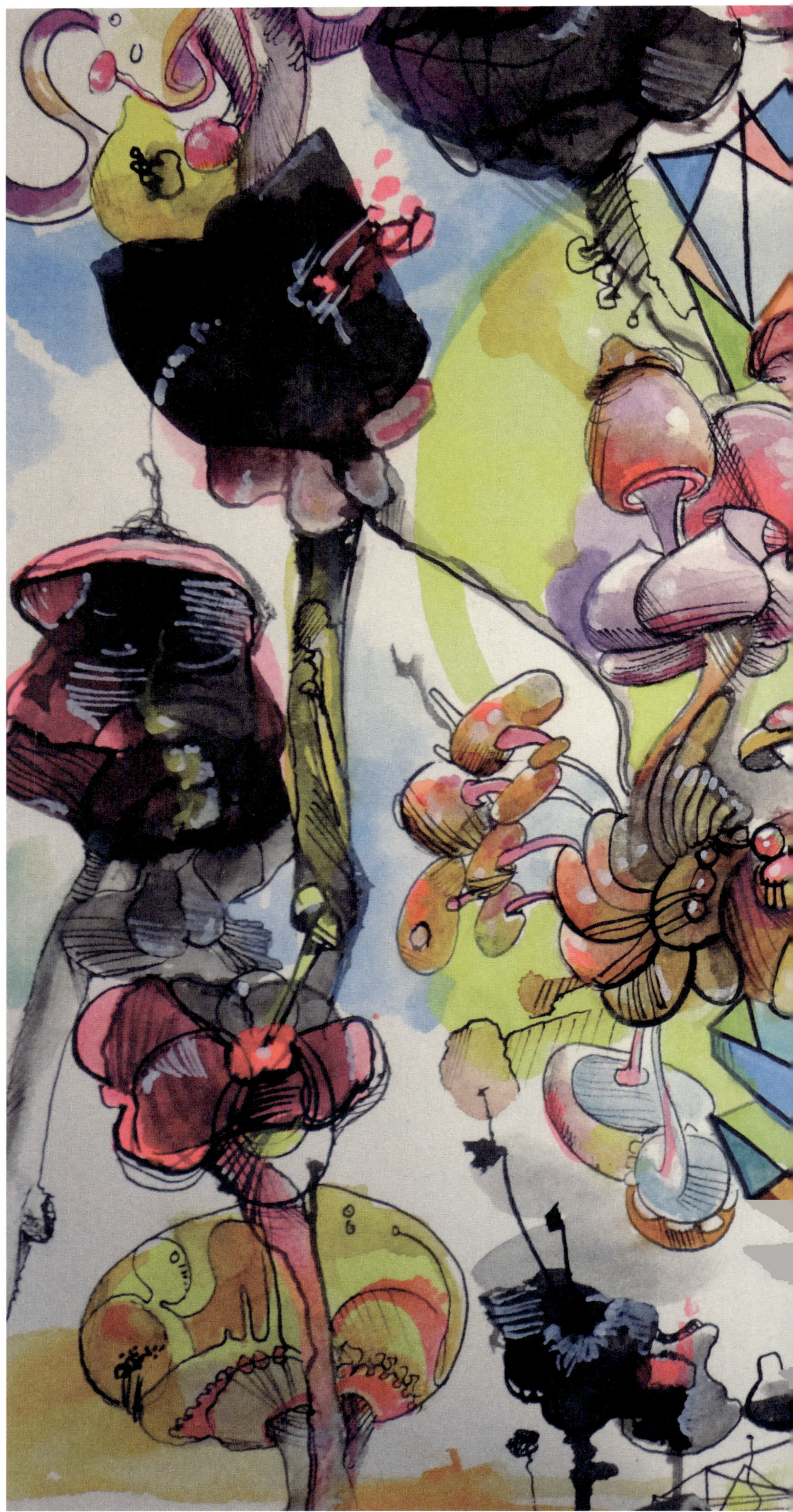

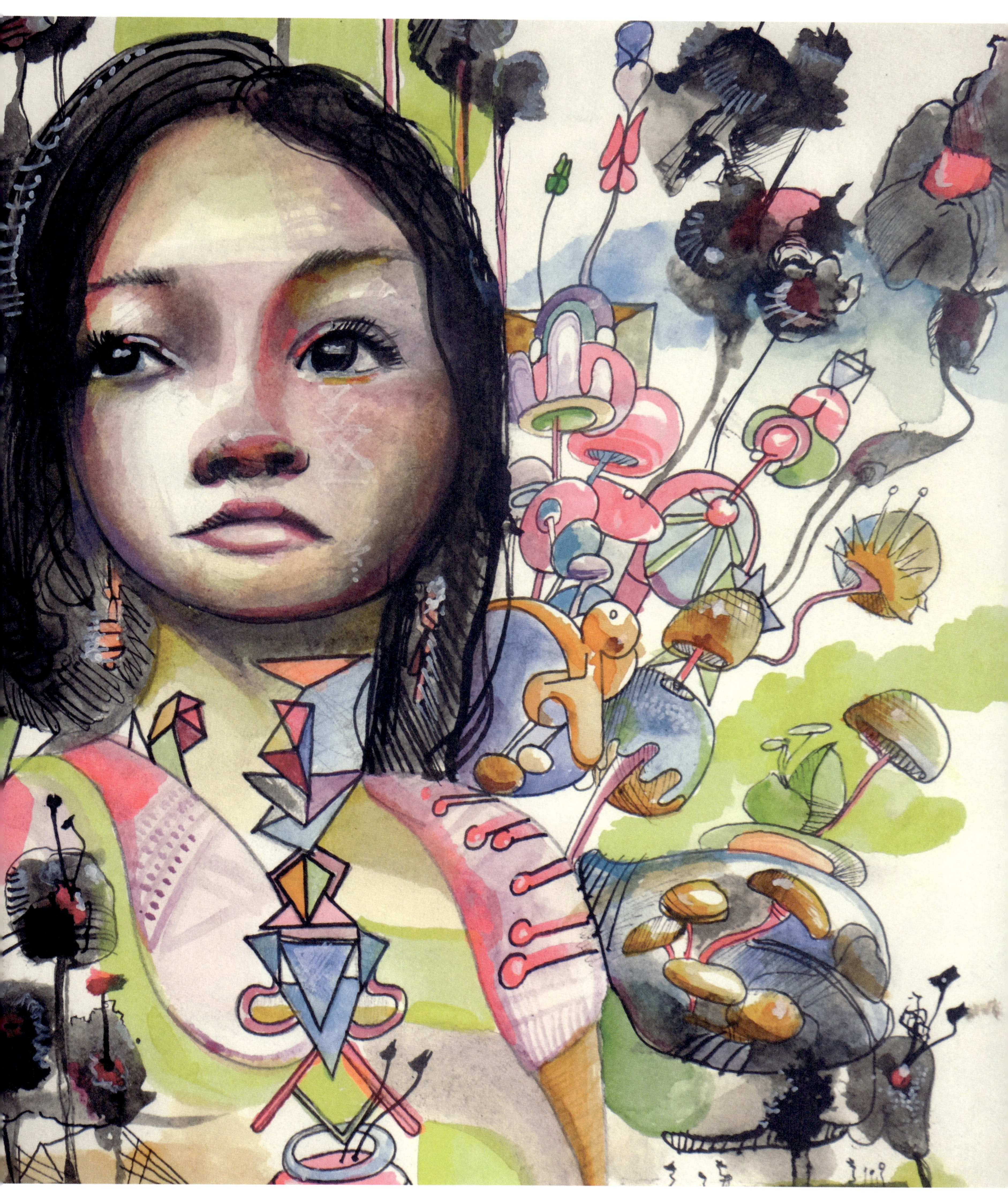

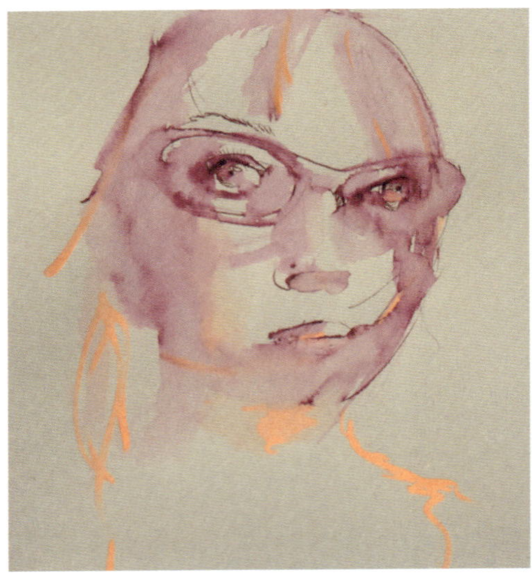

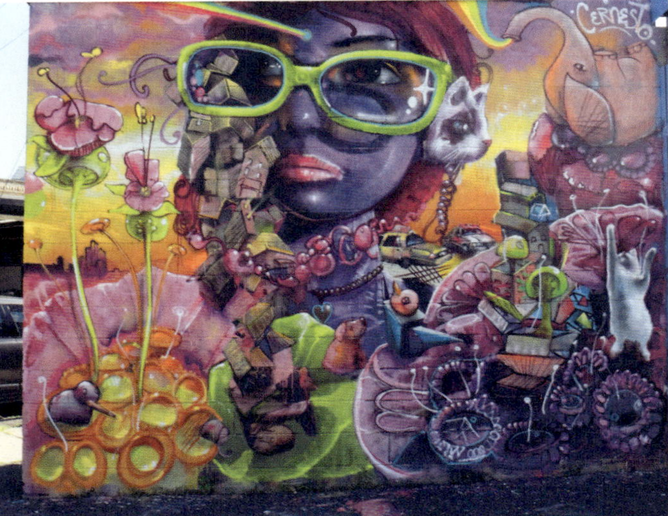

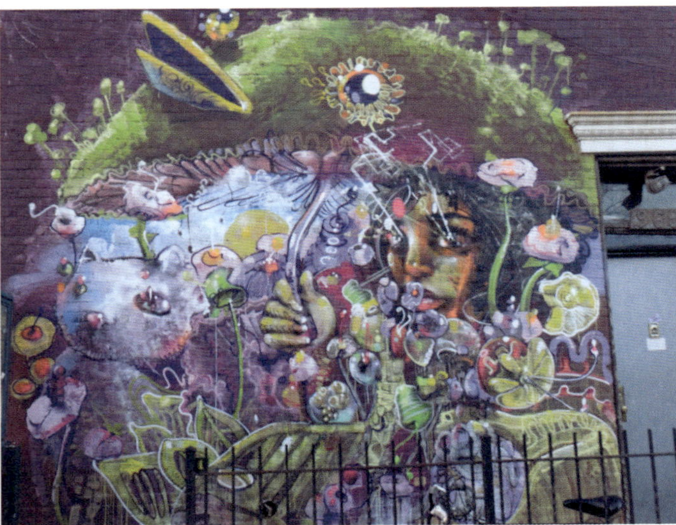

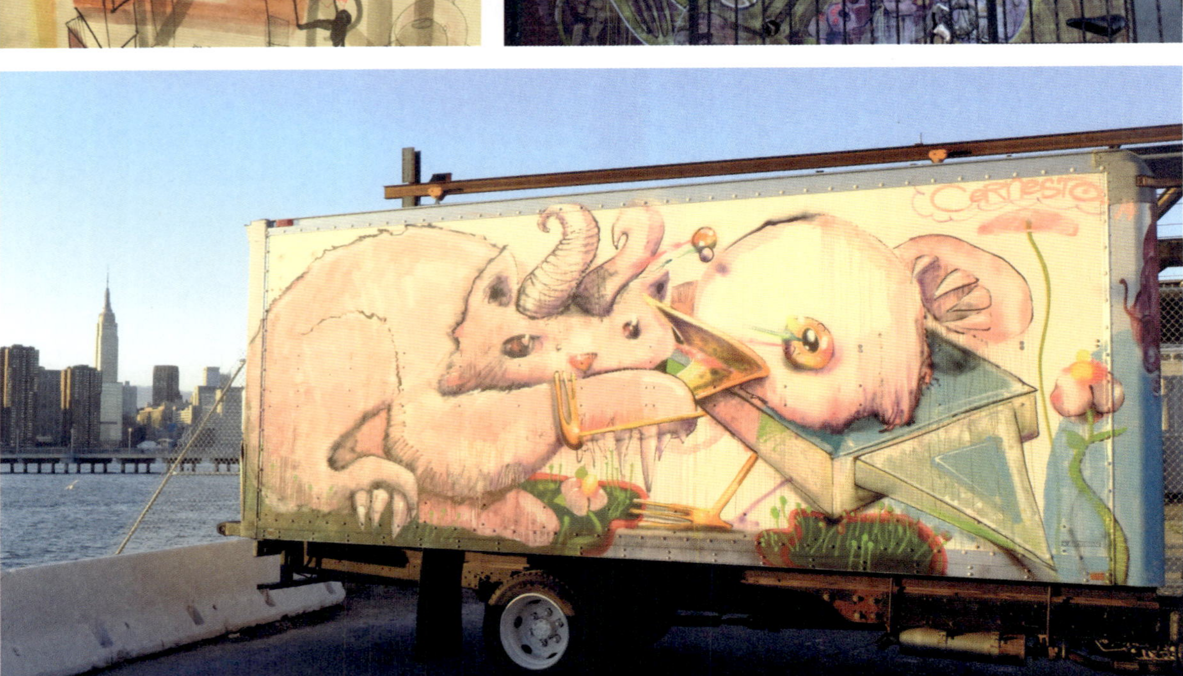

to achieve the right balance between reflecting his own inclinations and the experiences of the local community. As such he has refined his improvisational approach, creating impactful work within the specific restrictions of space, material and time that the city dictates. His studio work, in contrast, tends to be 'more internal with less concern for the viewer'.

The artist's public works and those he makes in the studio evolve together symbiotically; the loose and expressive wall paintings complementing the more time-consuming and detailed techniques applied to canvas, with both feeding into the other. The same is true of the media he deploys – drawing, sculpture and screenprinting – each with its own distinct energy, pace or scale in respect of his output. In his large-scale works he prefers to use acrylic and spray paint combined with water-based house paints, while in smaller compositions he leans towards a more painterly approach, using primarily watercolour and ink.

In whichever media he works, Cern conveys energy and soul in all of his output. He humbly attributes the success of his art to persistence rather than prodigious talent, claiming that it 'demands focus, discipline, persistence and practice and, with all that, sacrifice'.

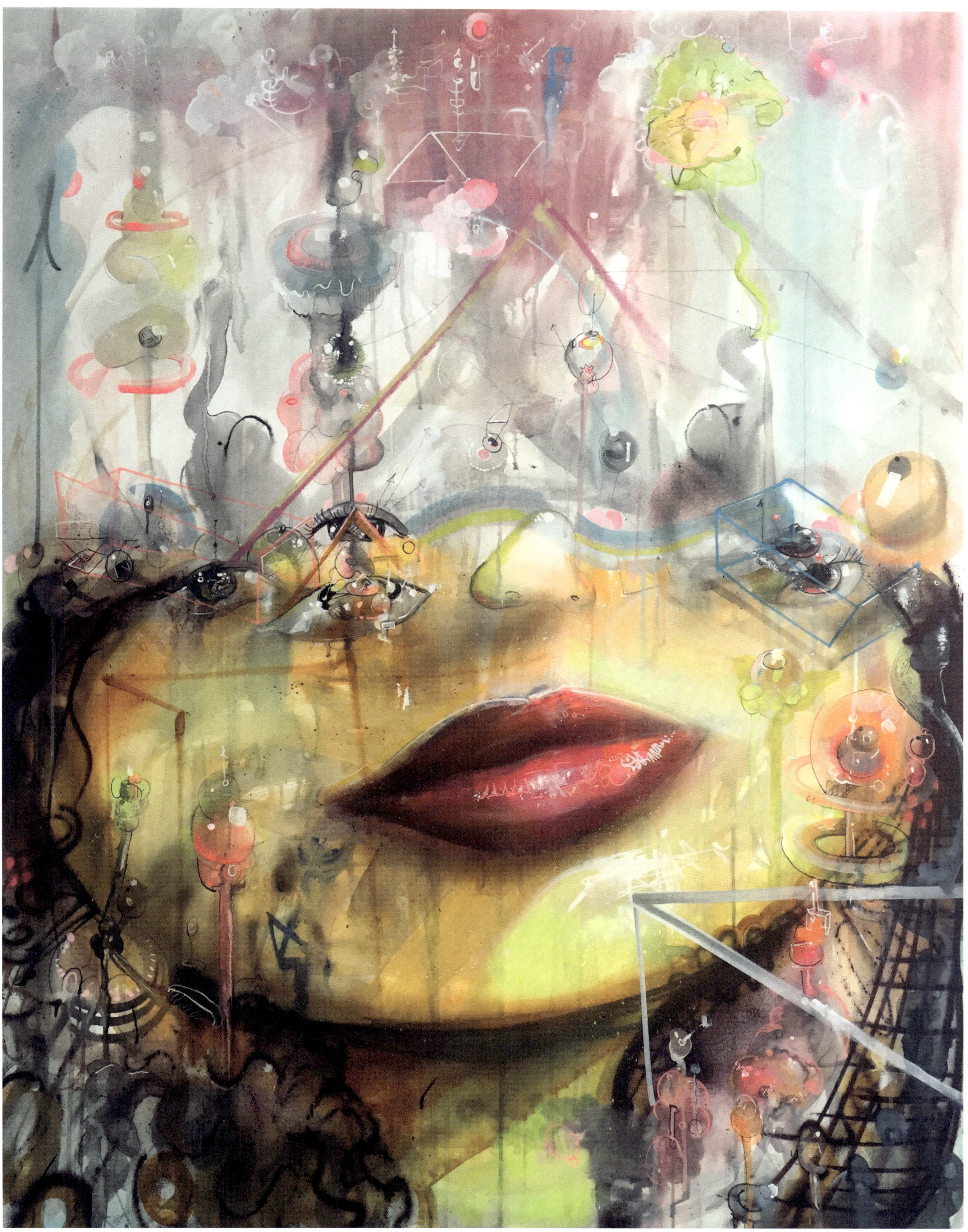

El Curiot

Owing much to his rediscovery of and affinity with the culture and folklore of his home country of Mexico are the paintings of El Curiot (aka Favio Martinez). Born in the region of Michoacán, but raised in Costa Mesa, California, after graduating from high school in the US, El Curiot returned home to study art, which provided him with the foundation he needed to flourish. Here he began to embrace Mexico's rich heritage – its flora and fauna, its colourful art, architecture and handicrafts and its folklore – translating it into his paintings. In filtering these influences he began to create a fictional universe illustrated with mythological creatures, symbols and geometric patterns. These imagined beasts evoke the spirit of ancient times, when folkloric beliefs were centred on natural forces and the cycle of life. With one foot in the past and the other in contemporary aesthetics, the characters expose El Curiot's principal theme – the relationship between man and nature and the significance of the natural world.

Some years after finishing art school and becoming known for both his street art and studio practice, El Curiot moved to Mexico City to make a living, which through hard work he has undoubtedly succeeded in doing. Since then his output has become characterized

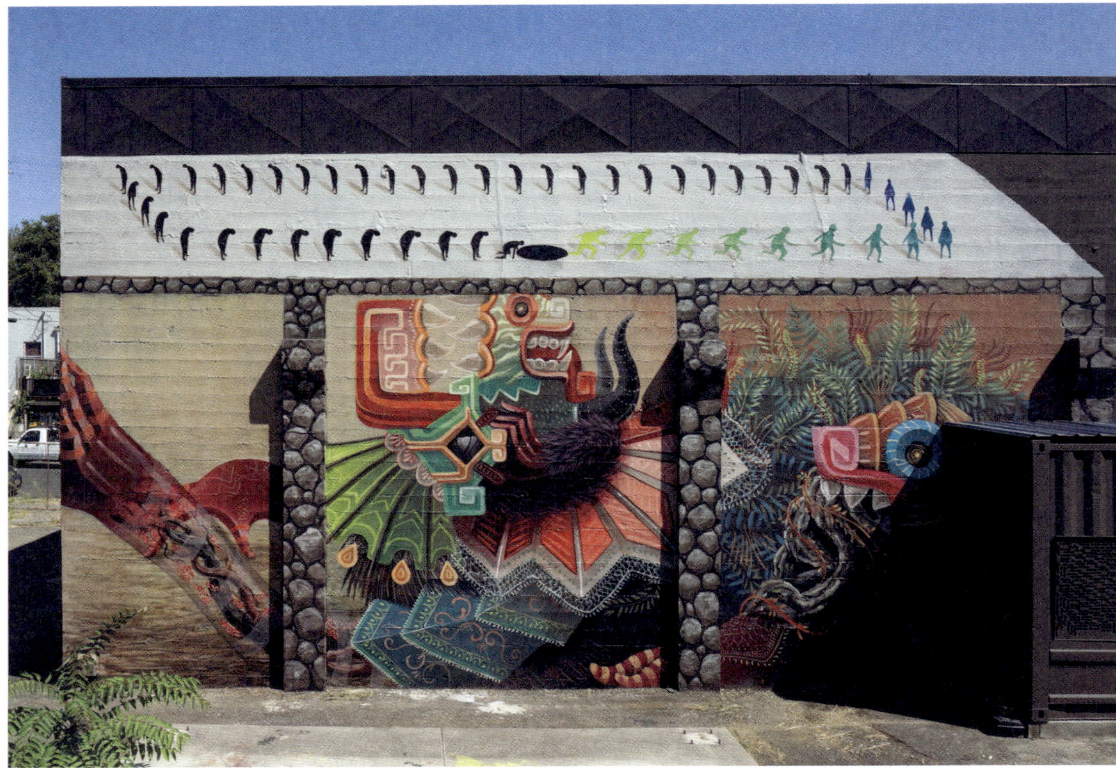

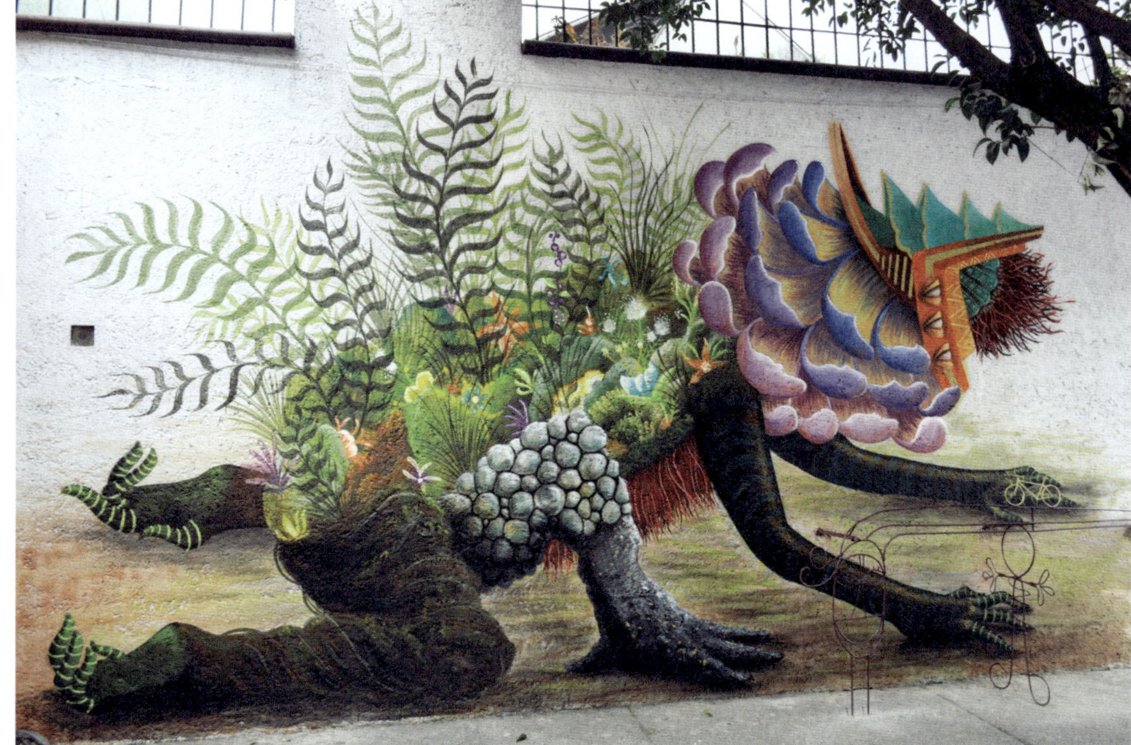

Untitled, mural in Portland, Oregon, 2014
Mixed media
Dimensions unknown

Untitled, mural in Mexico City, 2014
Mixed media
Dimensions unknown

OPPOSITE
First Symptom, 2013
Acrylic on canvas
60 × 50 cm (23⅝ × 19¾ in.)

OVERLEAF LEFT
Sowing Energy, 2013
Acrylic on canvas
100 × 80 cm
(39⅜ × 31½ in.)

OVERLEAF RIGHT
It Left a Sign of Life, 2013
Acrylic on canvas
110 × 80 cm
(40 × 31½ in.)

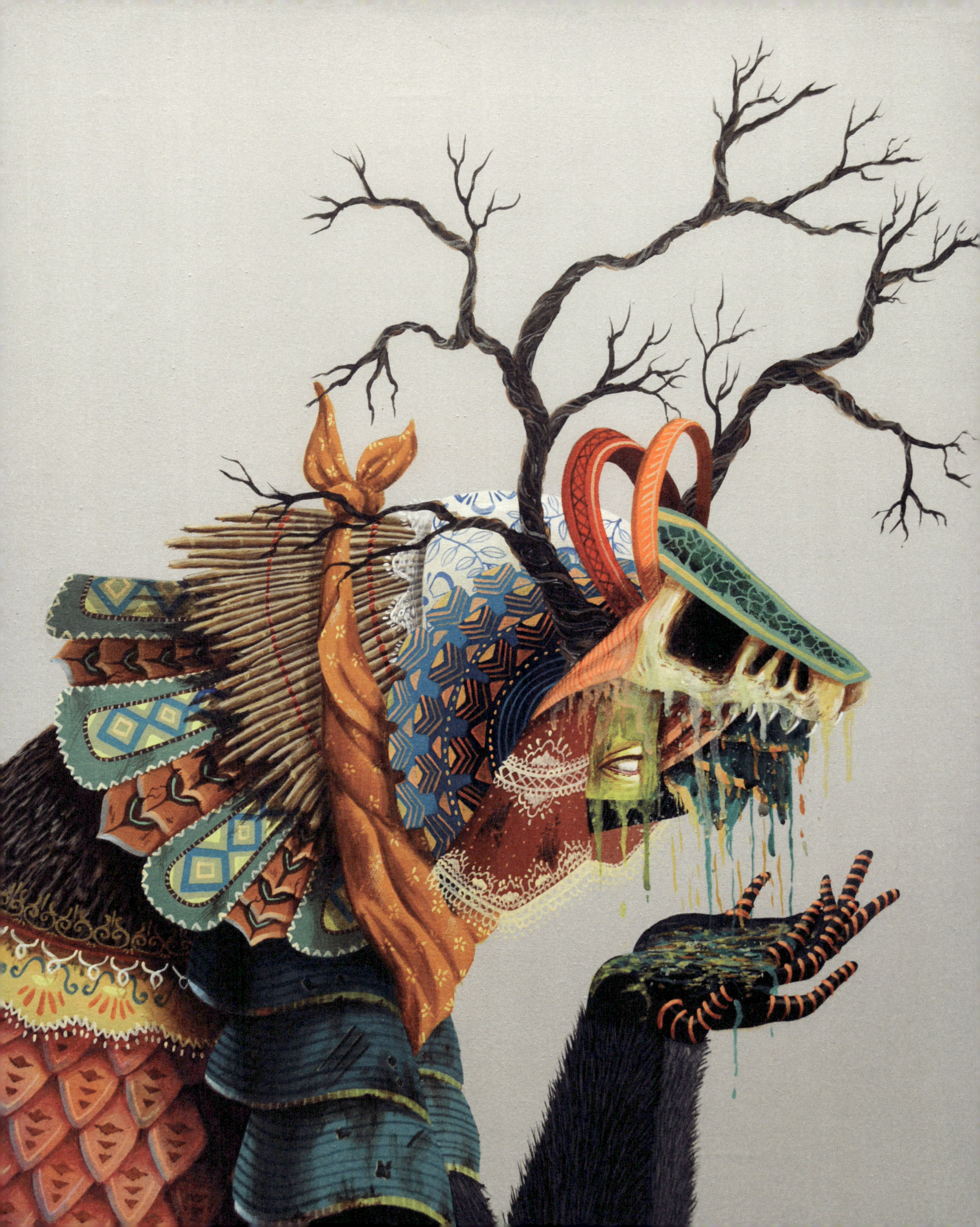

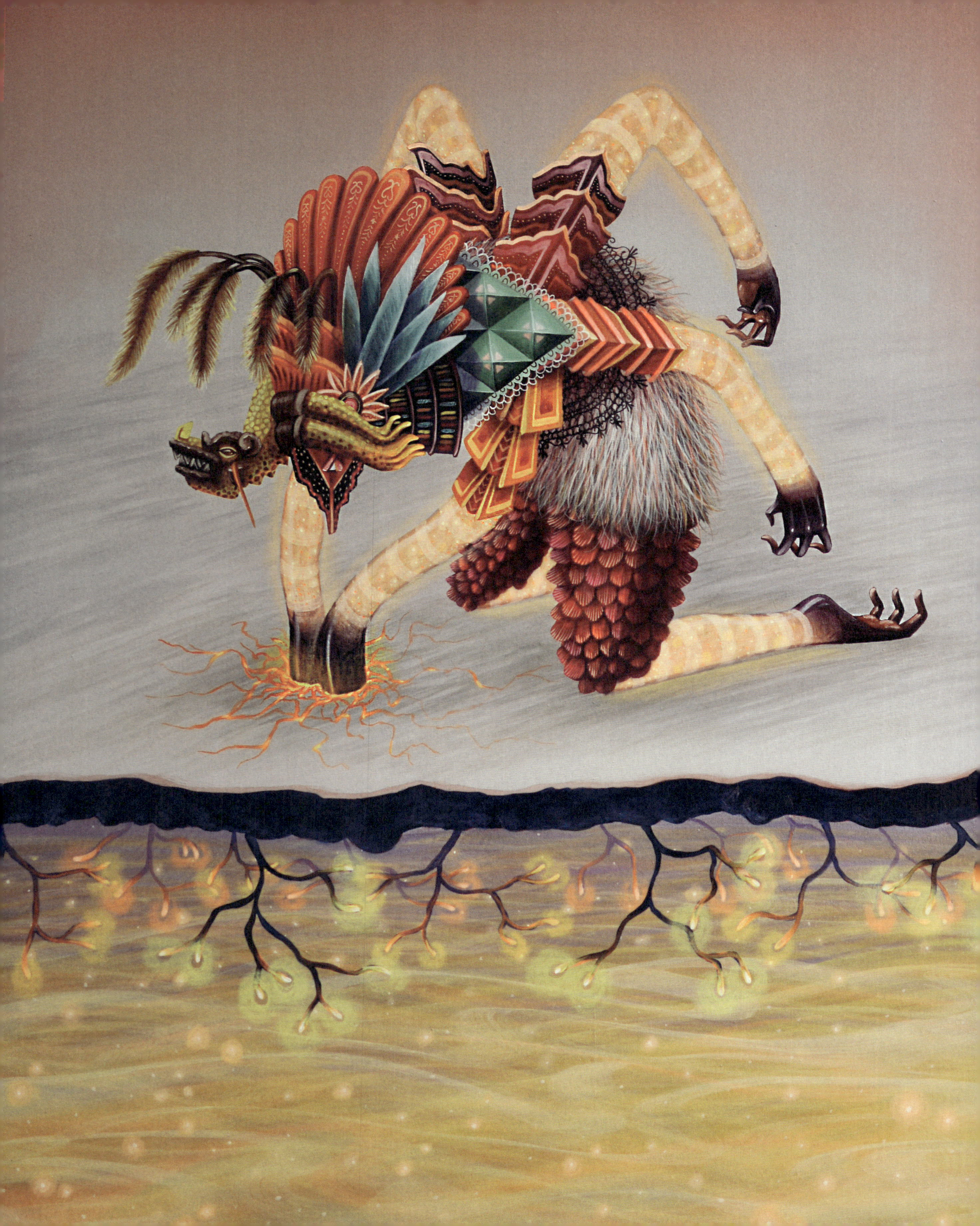

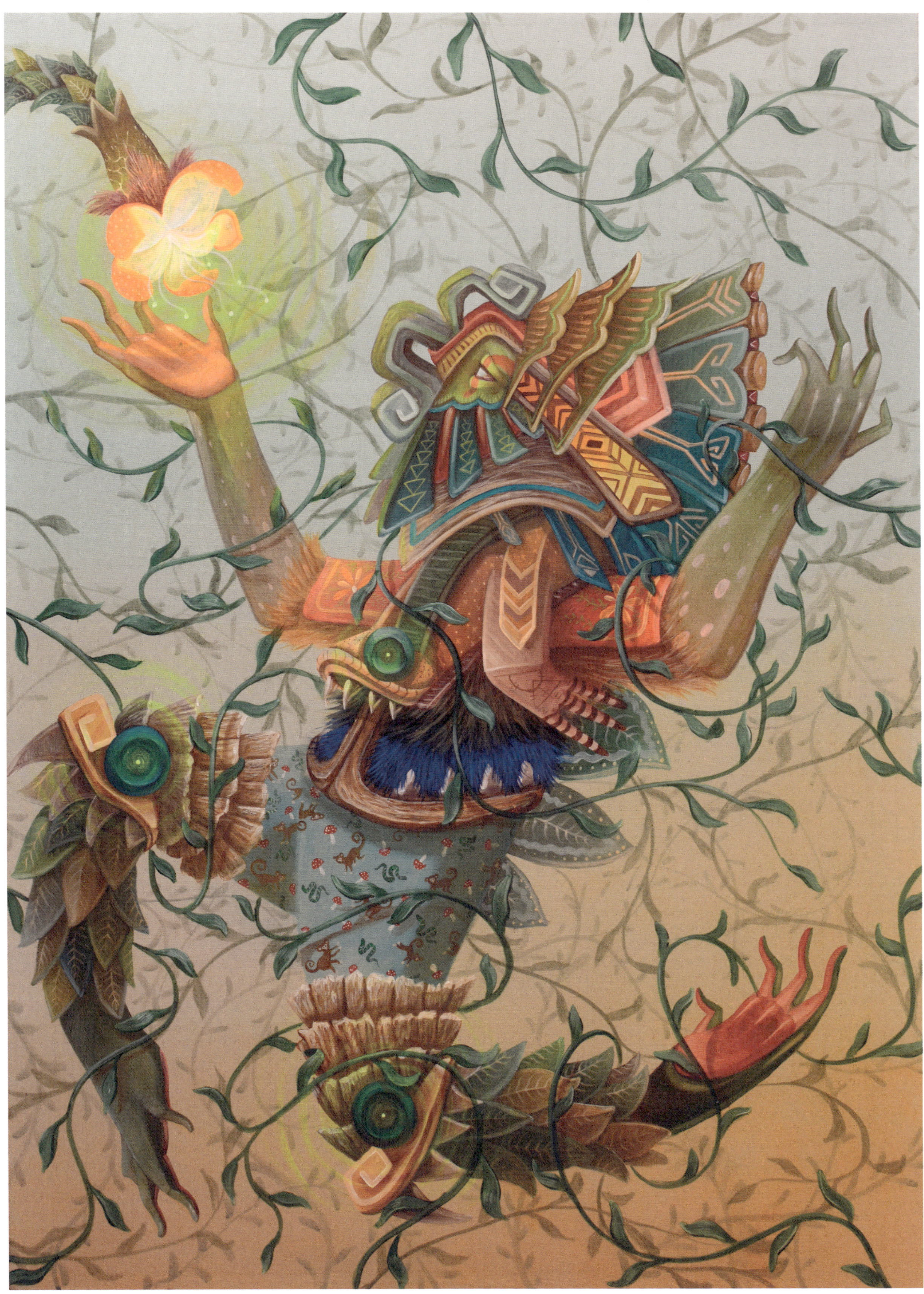

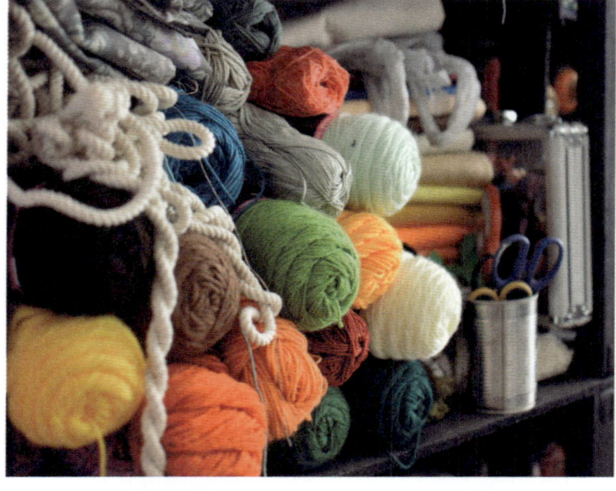
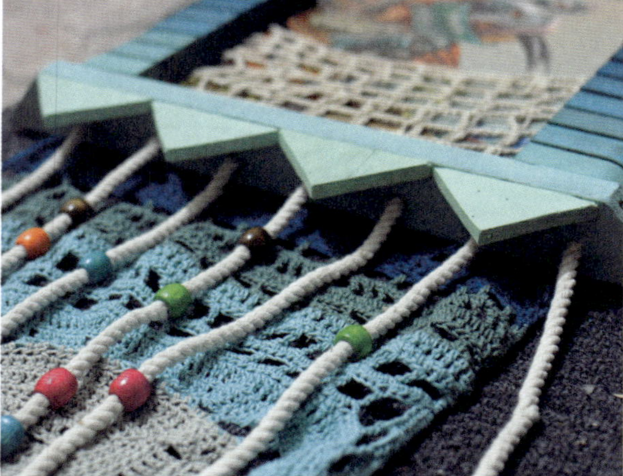

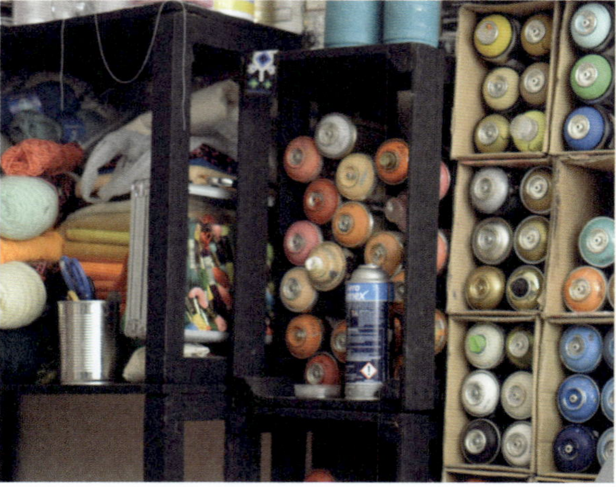
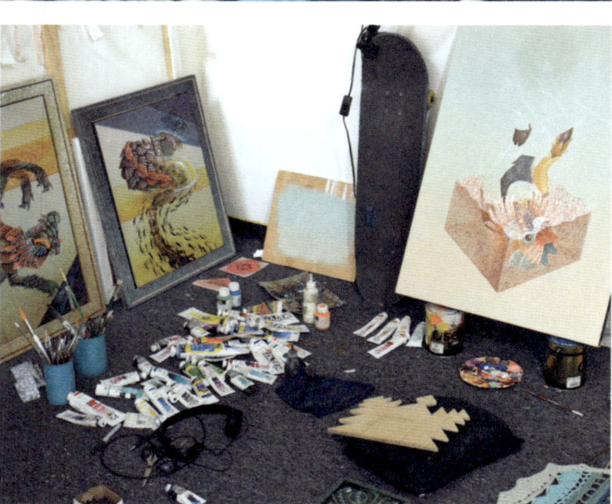

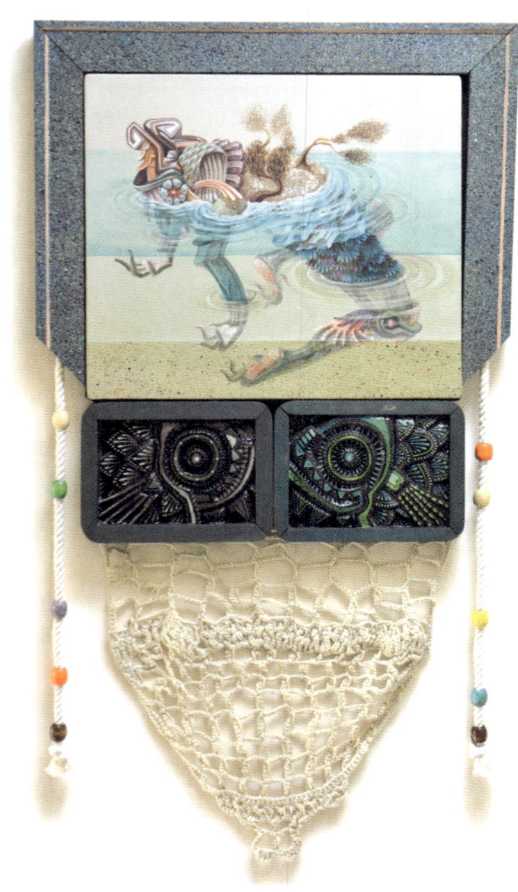

more so by its composition, a refined use of colour and, as is implied by the moniker 'Curiot', its *curioso* (strangeness) in terms of the world and characters depicted. You can expect the unexpected in El Curiot's paintings: creatures take on impossible forms, merging with organic, geometric and metaphysical planes. And his world seems to become richer and more wondrous with each new work, as he explains: 'These creatures began as simple, strange animals and slowly became more complicated and abstract.'

It is in the studio where much of El Curiot's experimentation with texture, colour or subject-matter takes place, which then later finds its way into his murals. Here, and in his wall-based work, he lavishes each piece with detail, filling every segment with different qualities of line and pattern: 'The patterns and colours are my way of incorporating into my work the things I love and that catch my attention as my experience expands.'

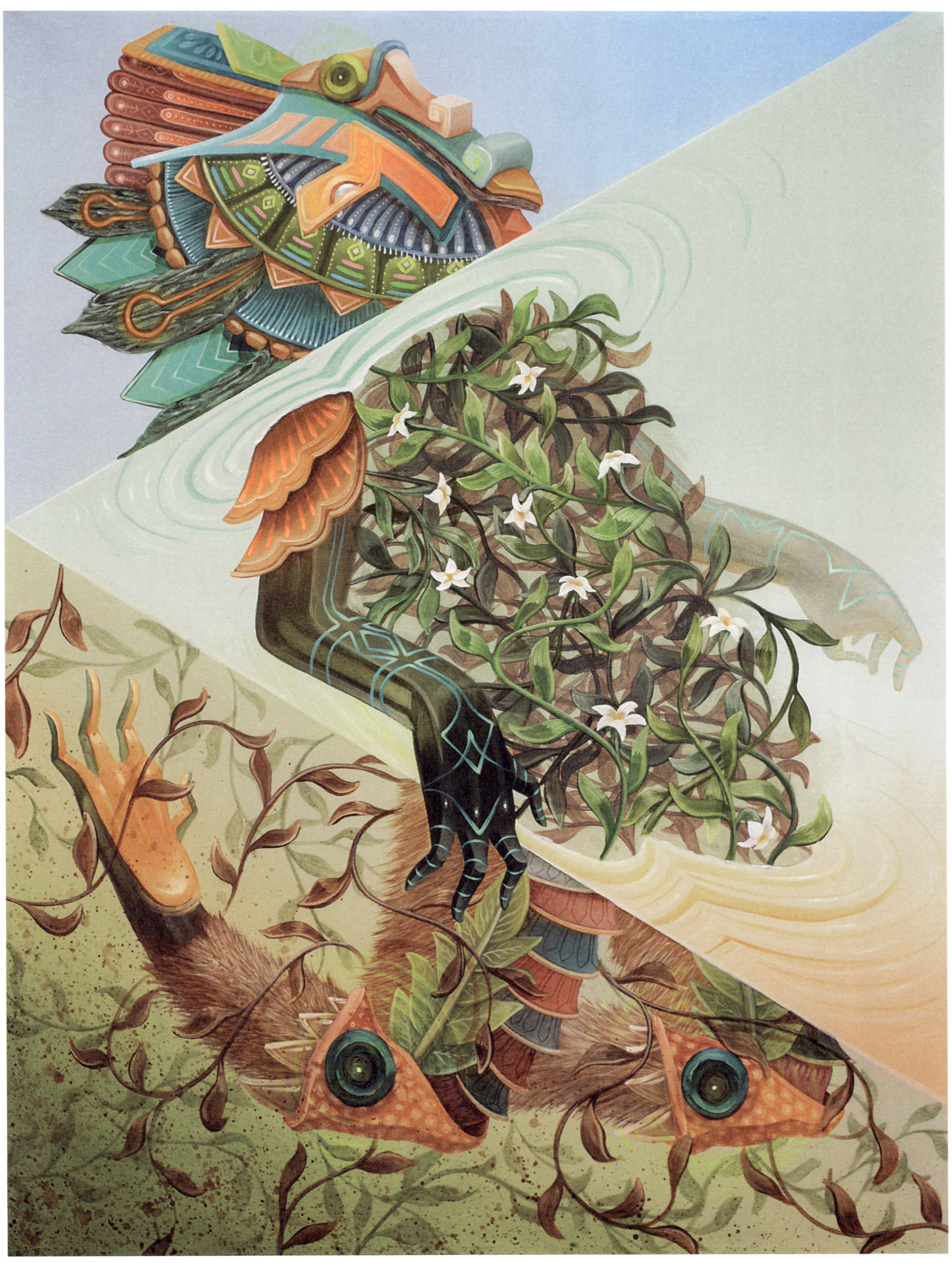

Marat Danilyan

With its roots in graffiti and a radical fusion of abstraction, realism, typography,

Expressionism and Constructivism, along with shades of the work of Gustav Klimt (1862–1918) and Amedeo Modigliani (1884–1920), is the art of Marat Danilyan, who hails from Novosibirsk in Siberia.

Until only recently Russia had been a distant outpost of graffiti culture. However, as groundbreaking urban art exhibitions such as 'Casus Pacis', held at the Street Art Museum in St Petersburg in 2014, show it is fast evolving into a country of daring and cutting-edge street artists, of which Danilyan is a prime example.

Having initially studied philology and economics at the Novosibirsk State University, Danilyan's artistic career took some time to take off. When finally he did discover graffiti he was immediately entranced, and soon began experimenting with spray paint, initially lettering, referring to artists such as Poesia – the Graffuturism blogger, whose work spans from experimental WildStyle (a form of graffiti defined by its complex, interlocking and often indecipherable letters) to Abstract Graffiti – for inspiration.

Under the moniker 'Morik', Danilyan's work has progressed from simple lettering to abstract and figurative compositions. Most distinctively – particularly in his works on canvas – he fractures or fragments his figures, imposing an overall 'flat surface' even when

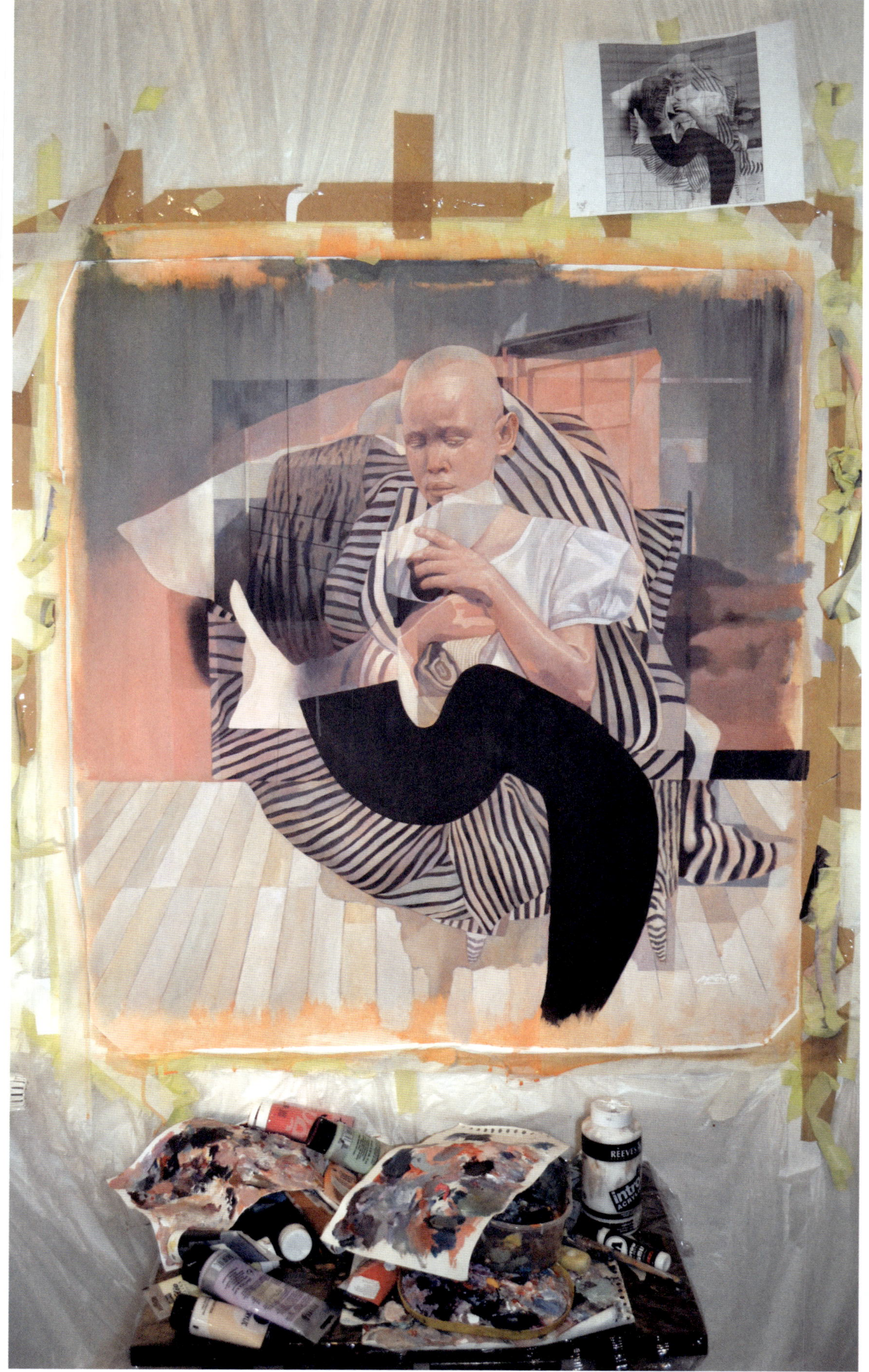

Albino World: Amulet, 2015
Acrylic on canvas
90 × 90 cm (35½ × 35½ in.)

OPPOSITE
The Wonder, mural in the
Longhushan Mountain area,
China, 2015
Mixed media
Dimensions unknown

Community, mural in
Sherbrooke, Quebec,
Canada, 2015
Mixed media
Dimensions unknown

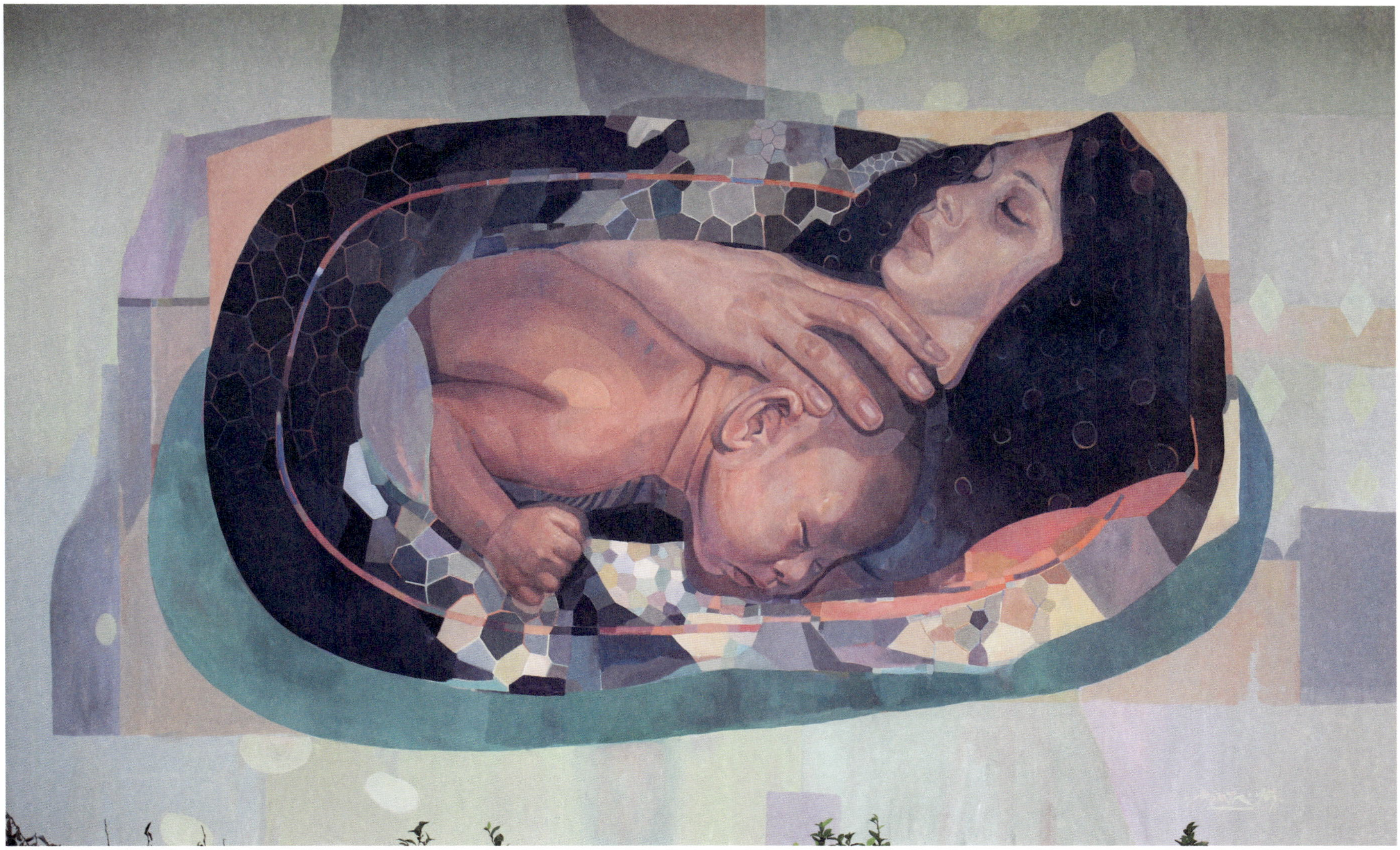

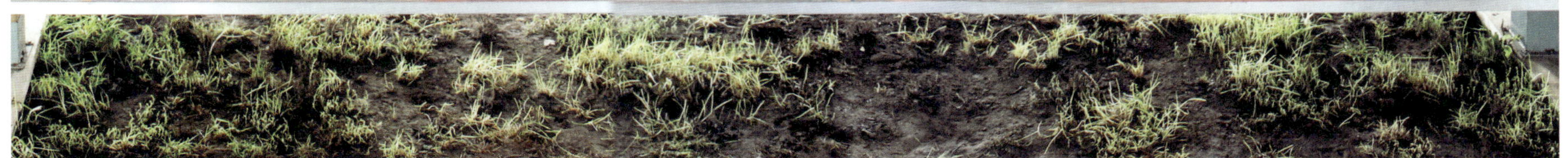

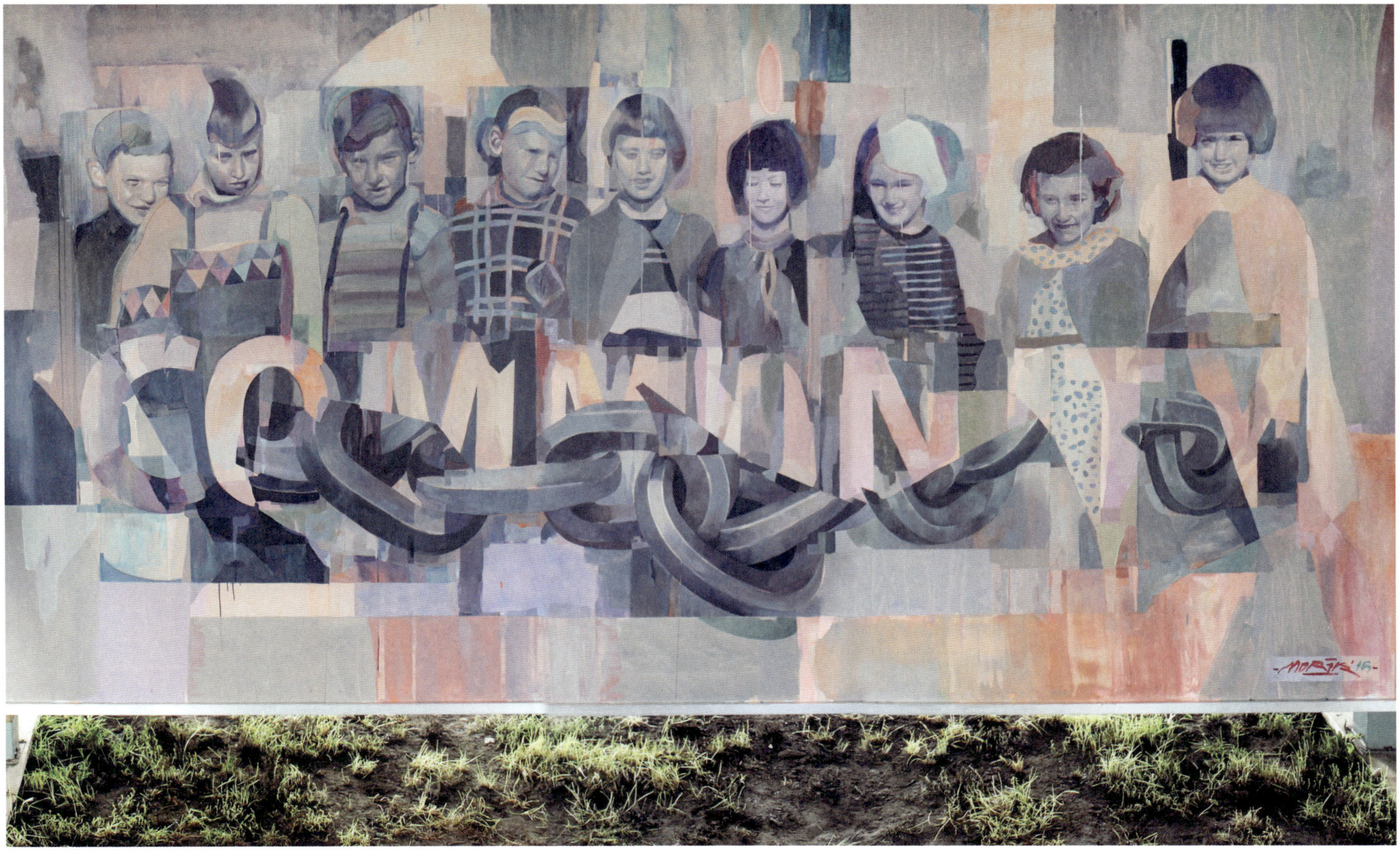

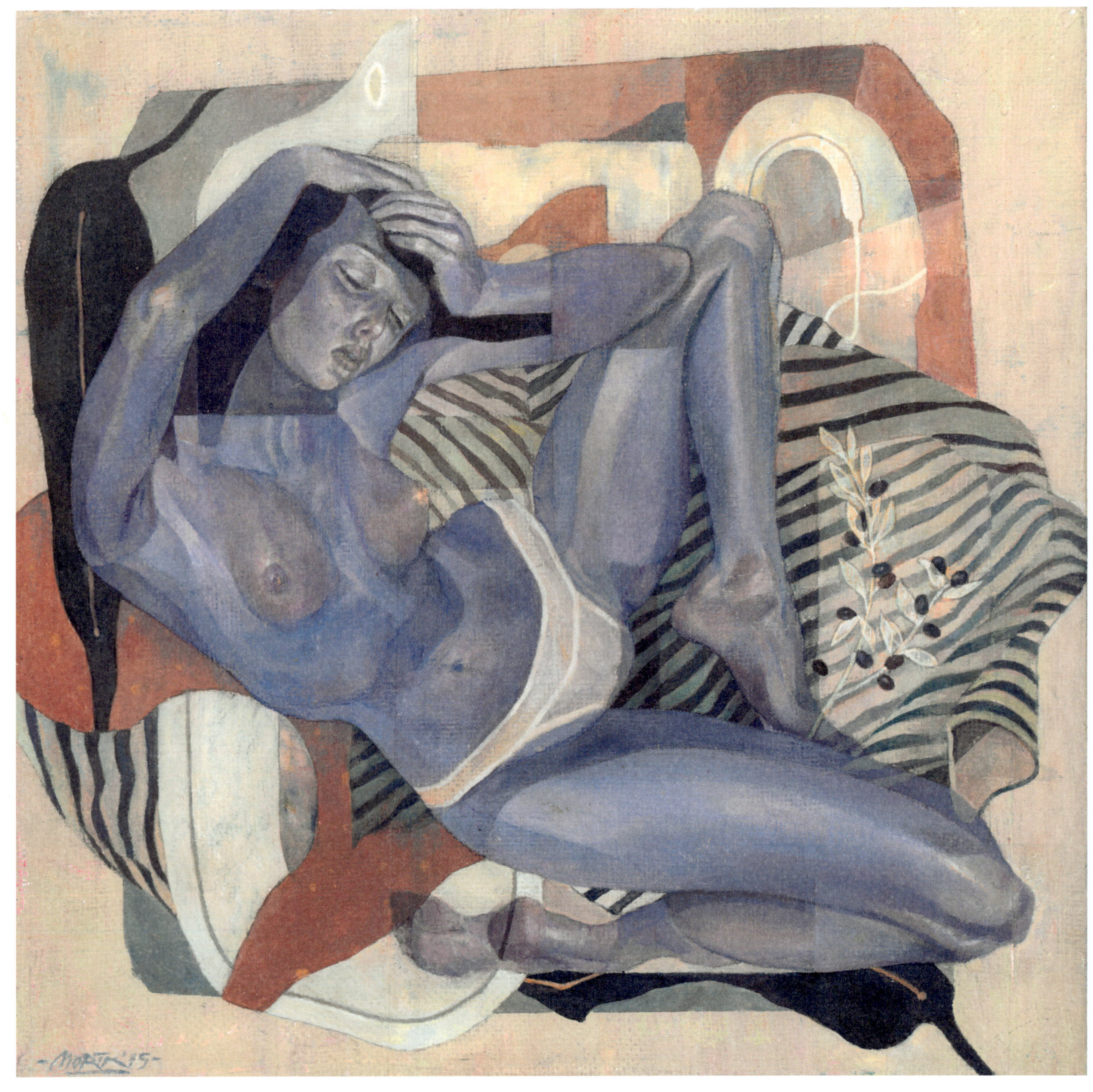

Olivia, 2015
Acrylic on canvas
90 × 90 cm (35½ × 35½ in.)

OPPOSITE
Untitled, c. 2015
Acrylic on canvas
90 × 90 cm (35½ × 35½ in.)

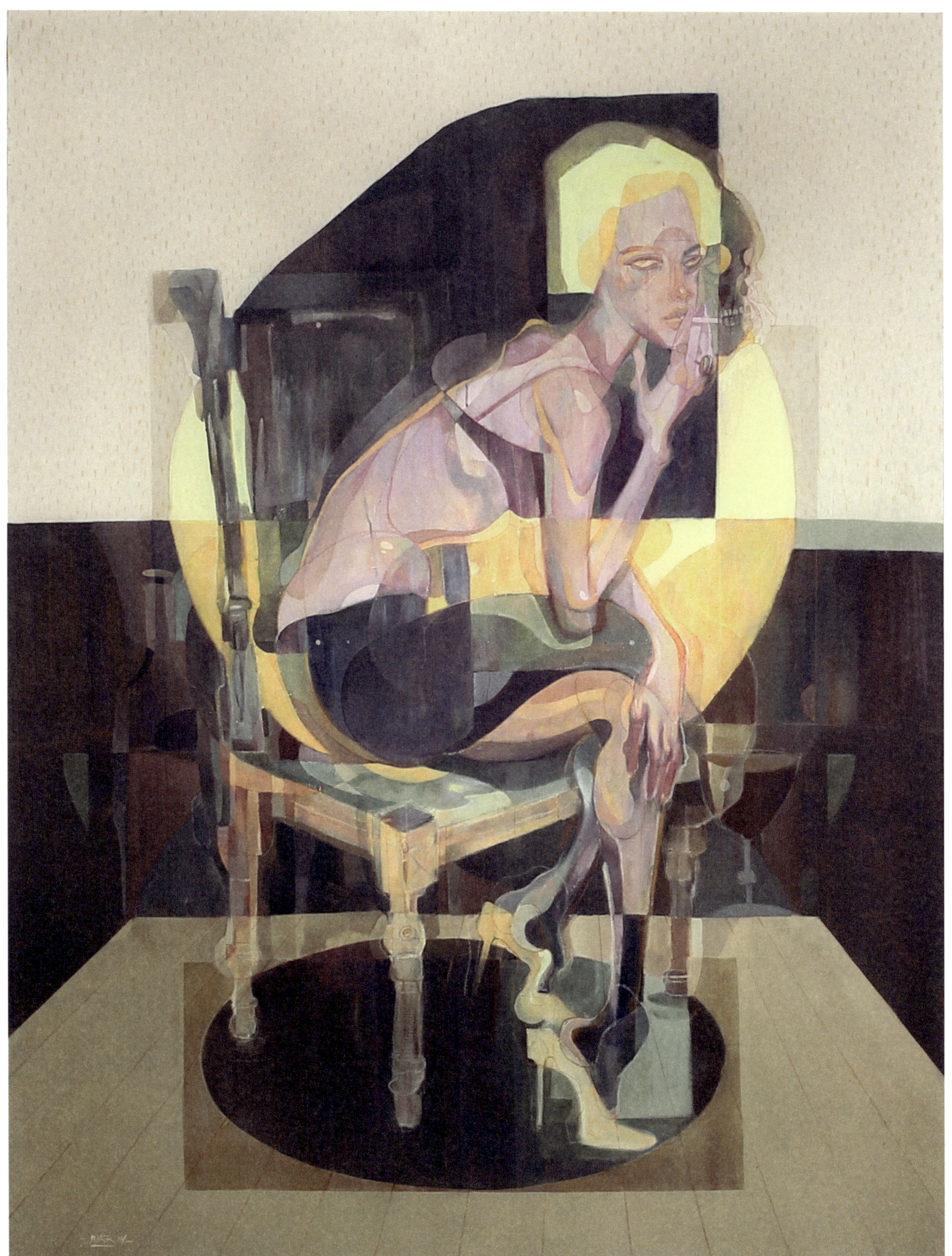

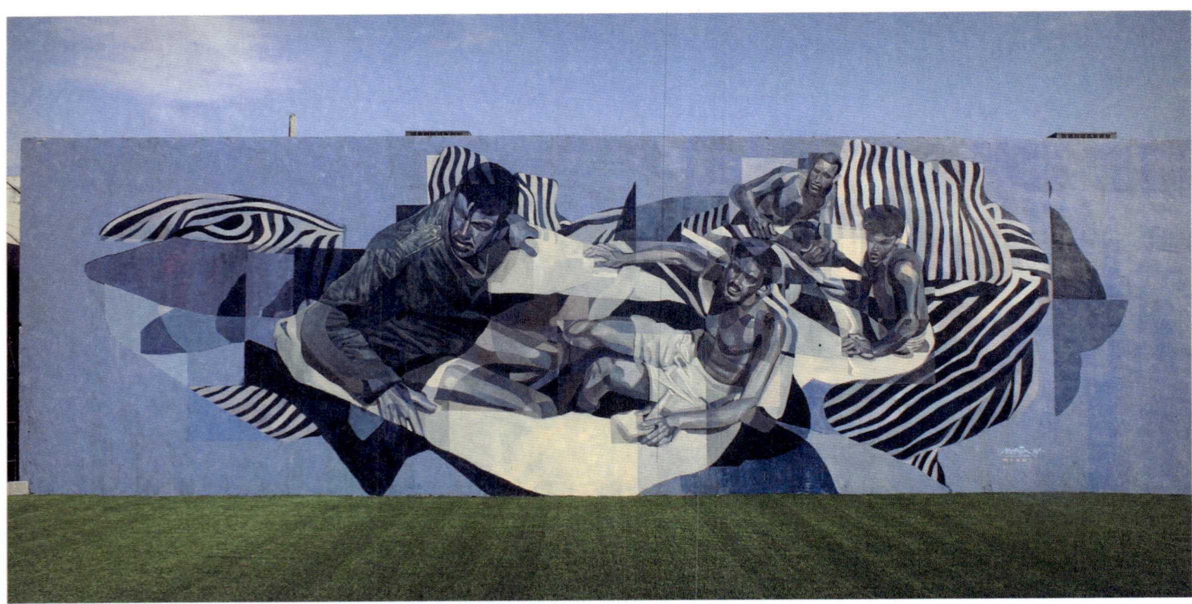

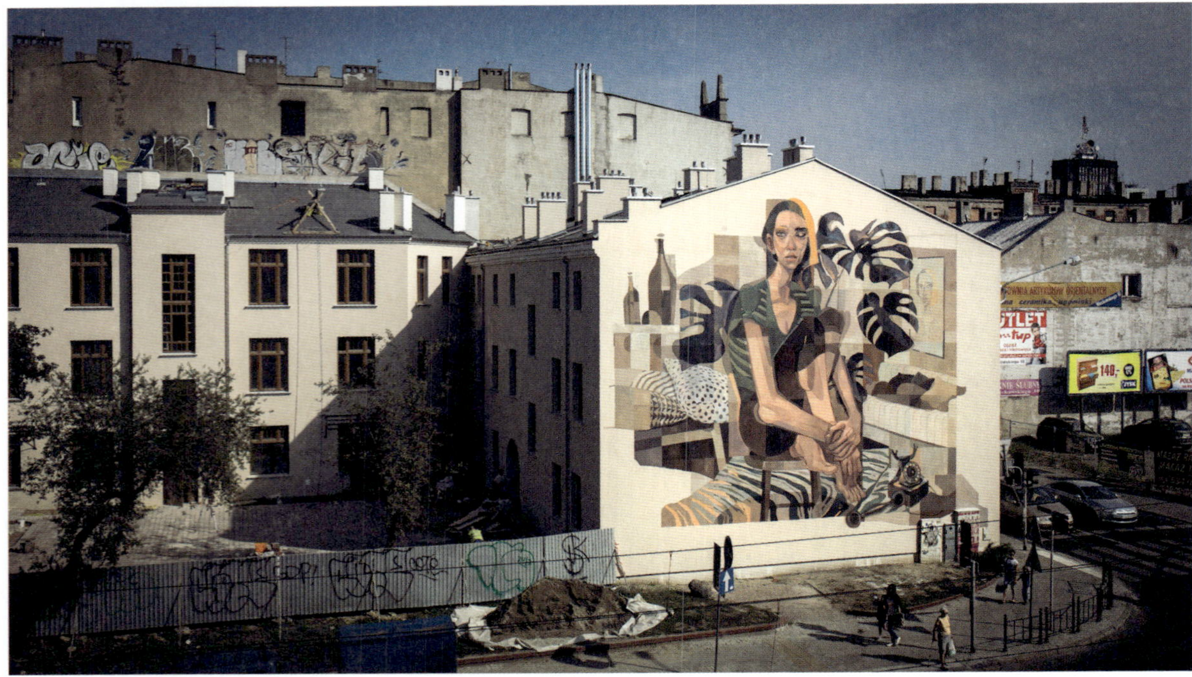

Untitled, mural
commissioned by Miami Ad
School, 2014
Mixed media
Dimensions unknown

Untitled, mural
commissioned by the Urban
Forms Foundation, Lodz,
Poland, 2014
Mixed media
Dimensions unknown

OPPOSITE
Untitled, 2014
Spray paint, acrylic and
watercolour pencil on paper
Dimensions unknown

Untitled, 2014
Spray paint, acrylic and
watercolour pencil on paper
Dimensions unknown

perspectival or realist elements are involved. As he explains, 'I don't want the wall or canvas to be an illusion of a mirror to another world. So the easiest way to make, for example, a realistic portrait look flat is to paint a line over the face and background or to cut a piece from it. That is one of the reasons I love Klimt and Modigliani so much: their paintings look flat to me.' Other painters of significance are those he discovered in his mother's art books as a child – Salvador Dalí (1904–1989), M.C. Escher (1898–1972) and Boris Kustodiev (1878–1927), who was renowned for his voluptuous female sitters.

At the core of Danilyan's compositions is his colour palette of muted pastels and the way that he visually deconstructs his diverse range of subject-matter – be it boxers, samurai, Japanese wrestlers, robotic dogs, nude figures, men at work or prostitutes – into distinct elements. While he notes that the eclecticism of the themes in his work might damage his artistic career he claims that he just can't resist pouncing on countless topics, moods and spirits.

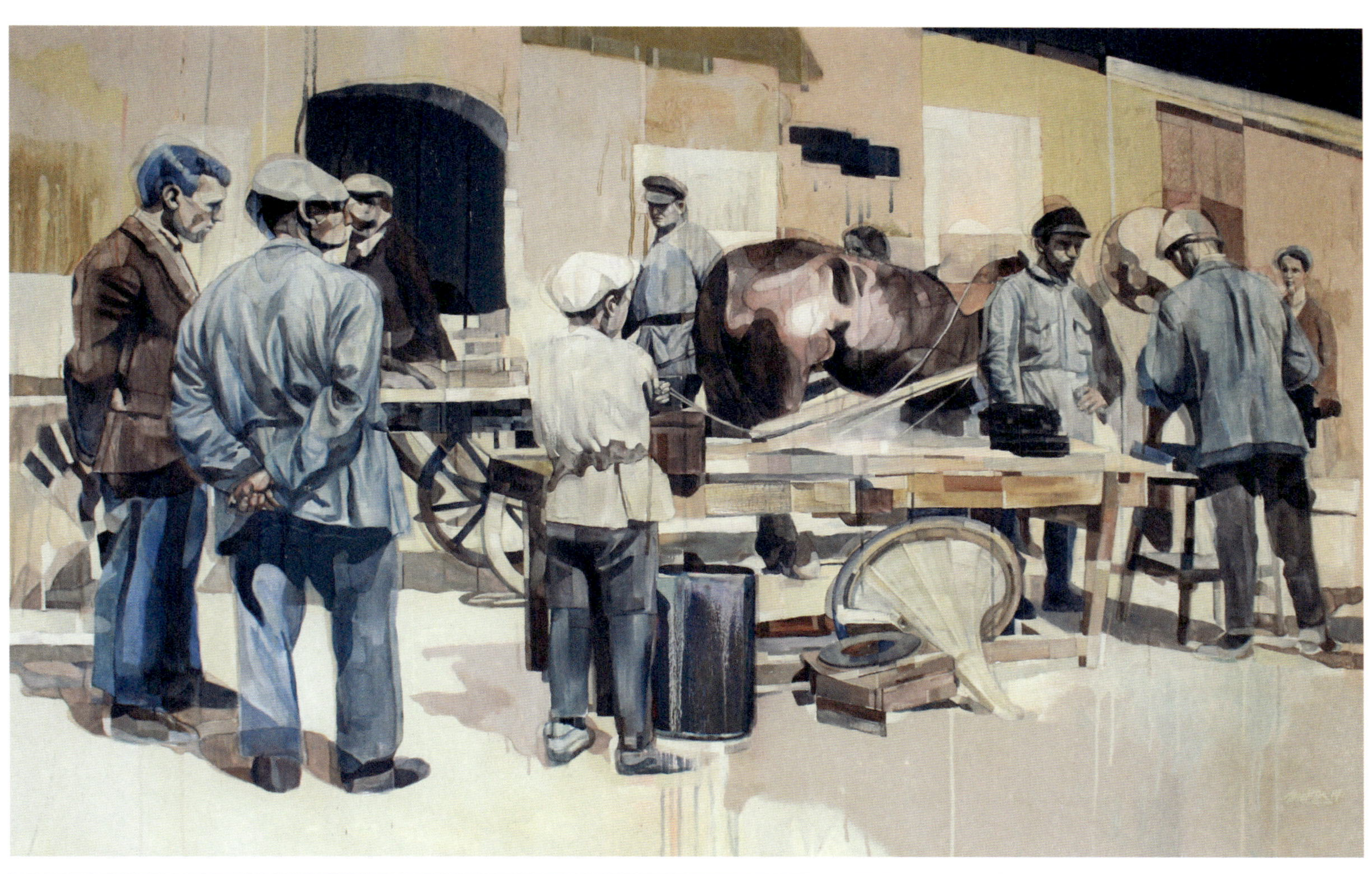

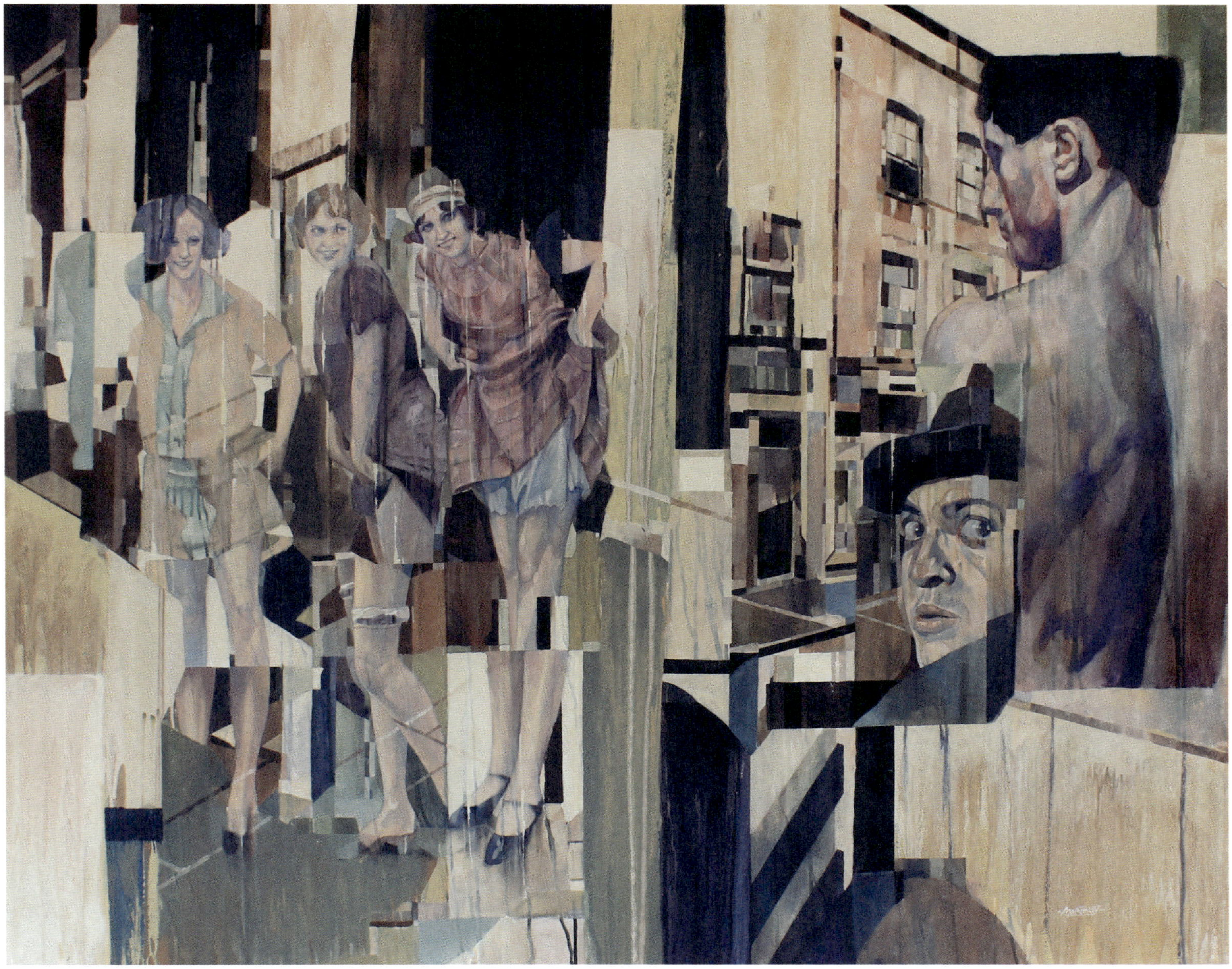

Carlos Donjuán

Having long been aware of his cultural heritage and immigrant status, Mexico-born artist Carlos

Donjuán's experience of being a Mexican living in America has not always been easy. As a child he would hear the term 'illegal alien' frequently, without ever fully understanding its meaning. 'I always wondered,' he says, 'what everyone was talking about, imagining weird creatures in my head…. I wanted to meet one and to know what they looked like.' He interprets such childhood memories within his imagery, creating masked figures, hybrid identities and strange beasts. In so doing he documents his own history, while also questioning the notion of identity, as he says, 'in my case, am I a Mexican, American, Mexican American or just a human like everyone else in the world?'

Donjuán discovered graffiti as a teenager and, having spent more than a decade as a graffiti writer, it has remained a driving force behind his work, complemented by his degree in fine art from the University of Texas, San Antonio. Whether working on the street or in the studio, he likes his work to be accessible; either by making it public, as he does with the murals he paints in his home city of Dallas, or by opening up his studio to visitors and creating affordable books and prints that cater to art collectors even with the smallest budgets.

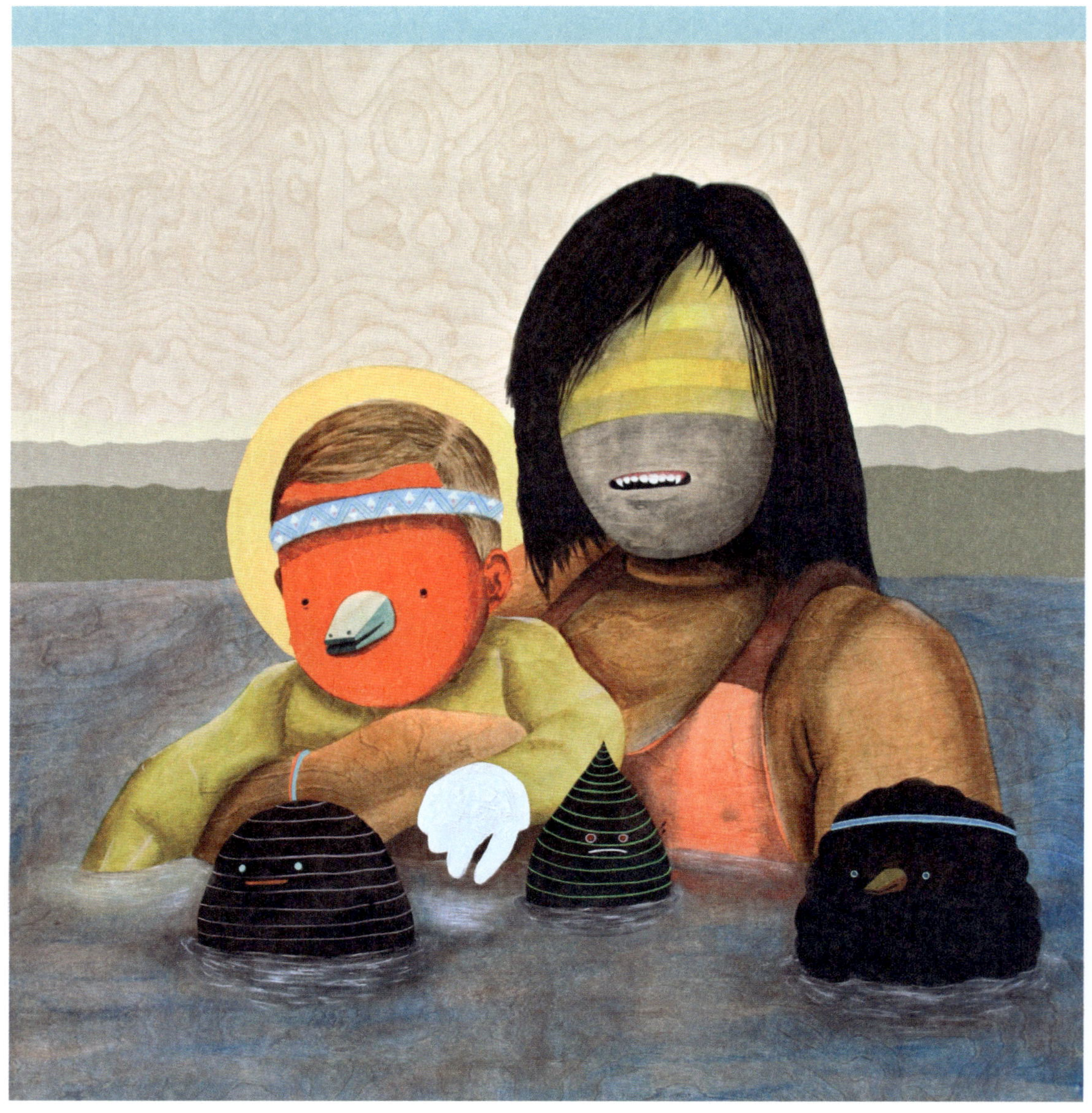

Dreamers, 2013
Mixed media on birch
122 × 122 cm
(48⅞ × 48⅞ in.)

OPPOSITE
Untitled, from the 'Sour Grapes' series, 2012
Giclée print
50 × 40 cm (20 × 16 in.)

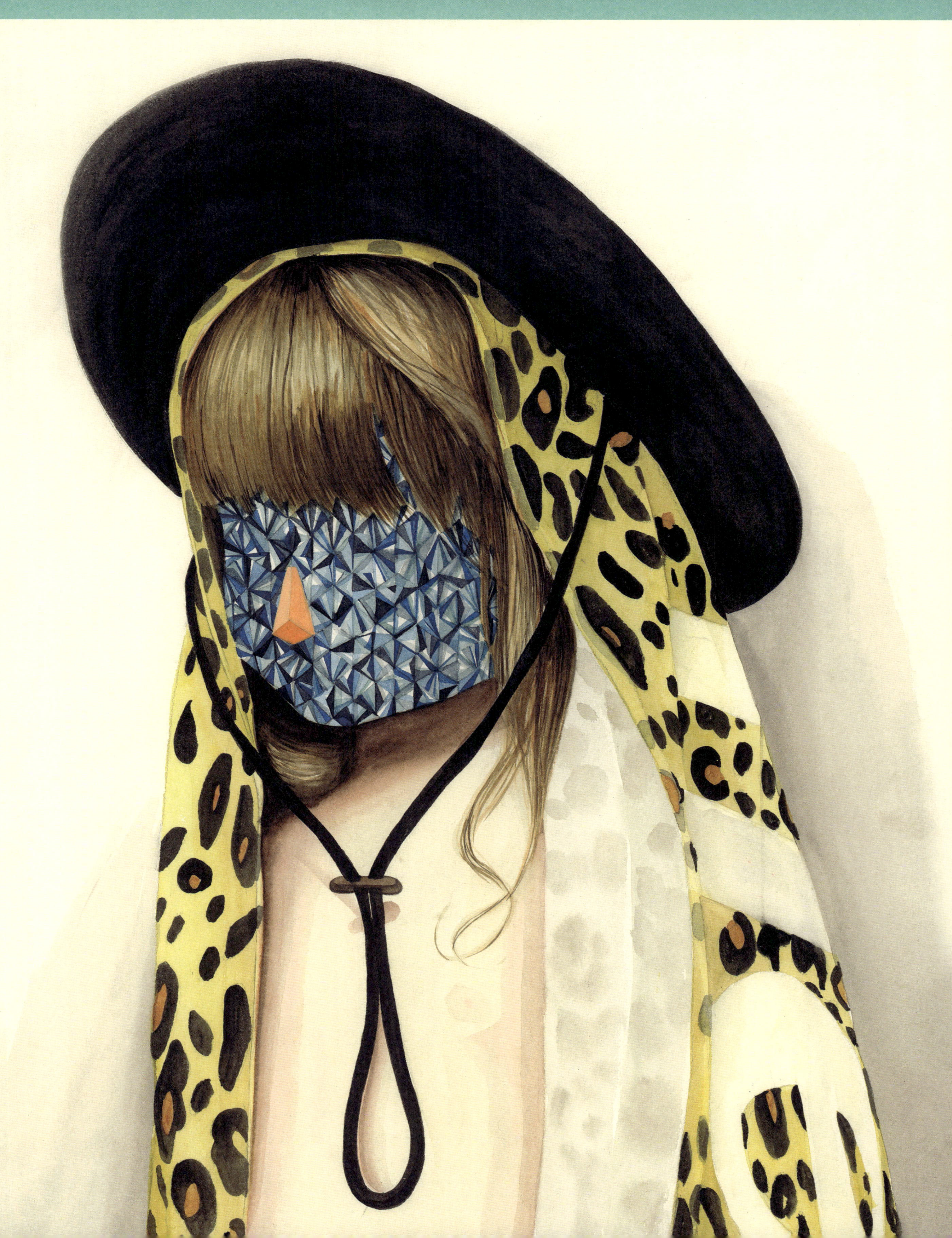

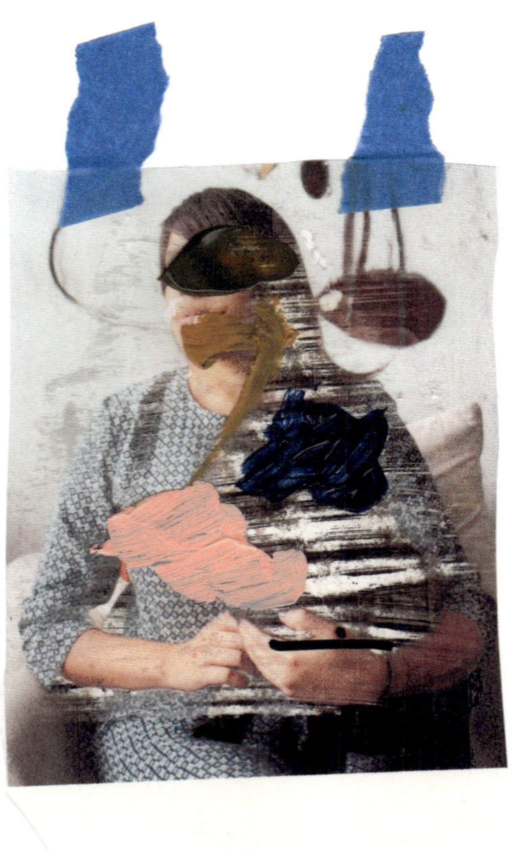

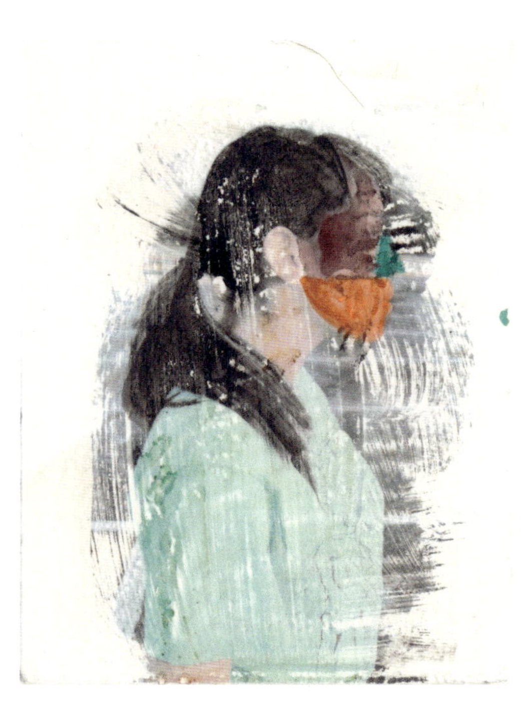

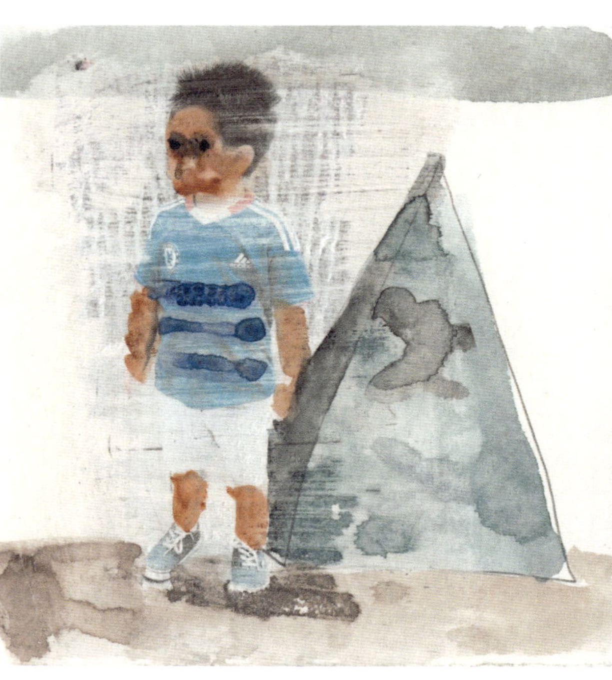

Donjuán's work deals with a combination of several subcultures, such as street fashion, skateboarding and underground music. He sees these scenes as rich and diverse subjects, which he attempts to interpret and, to some extent, glorify. Against this backdrop he adds elements of personal influences such as Native American and Pre-Colombian art, Catholicism, Mexico, Oak Cliff (a notorious predominantly Mexican district in Dallas), illegal immigration, politics and family into his subject-matter. Similarly, his approach to composition is to mix things up, to allow disparate elements – a Renaissance-inspired painting, Frida Kahlo's (1907–1954) colour palette, the animations of Hayao Miyazaki or Hopi Katsina dolls – to coexist. In so doing the resultant works are consistently original and fresh.

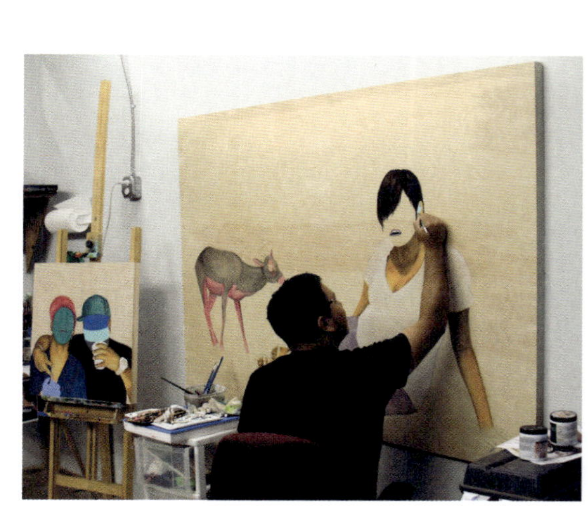

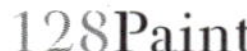

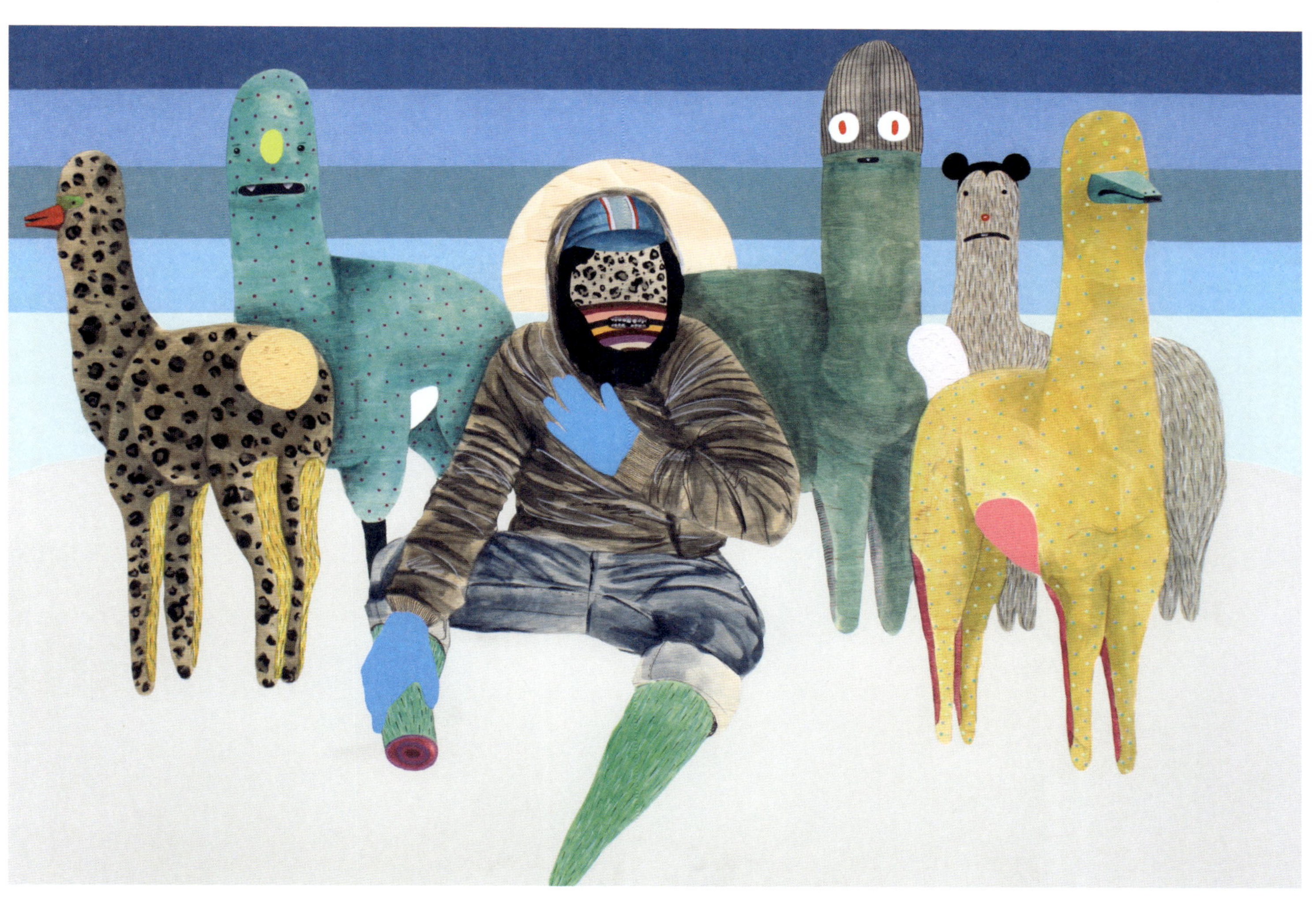

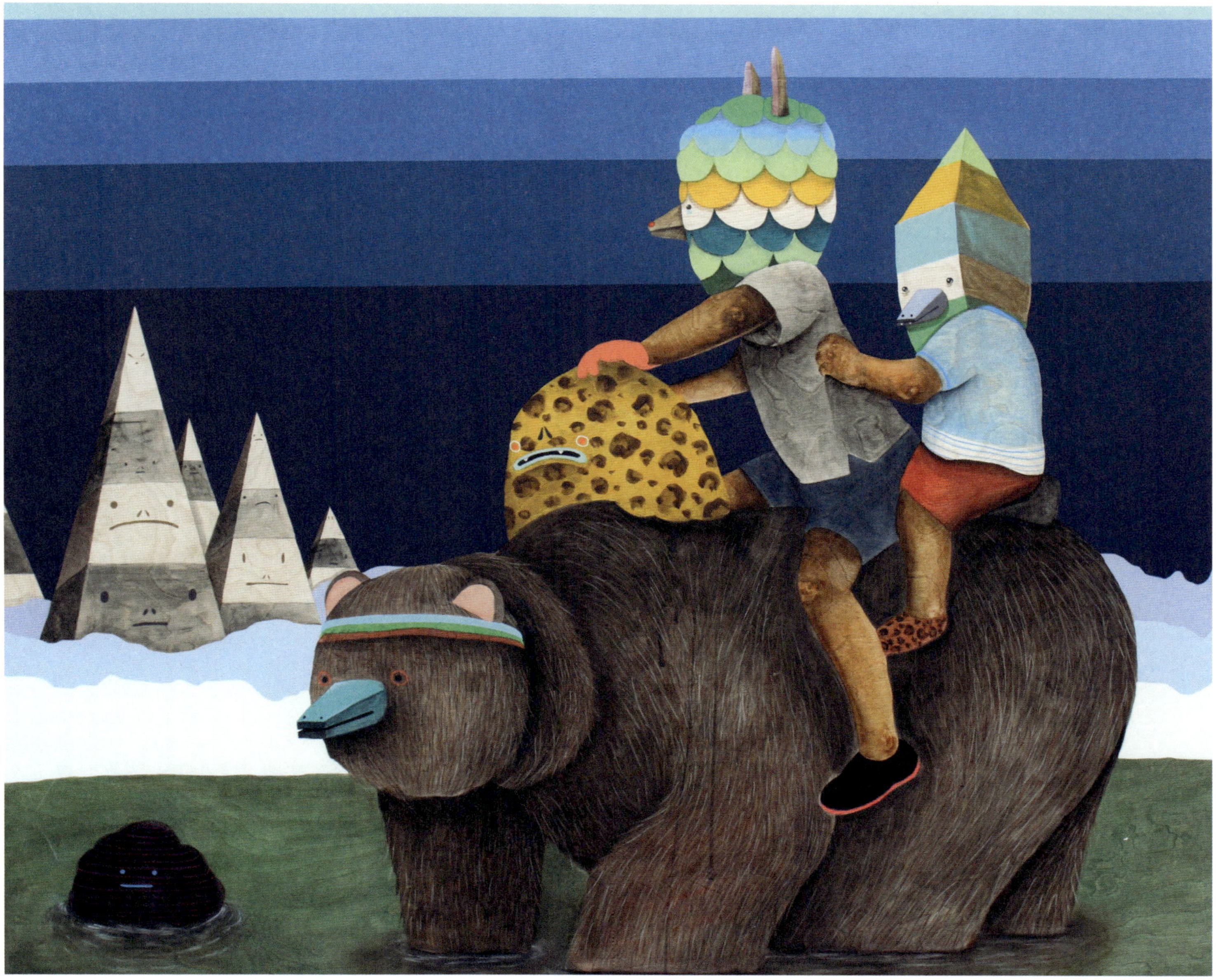

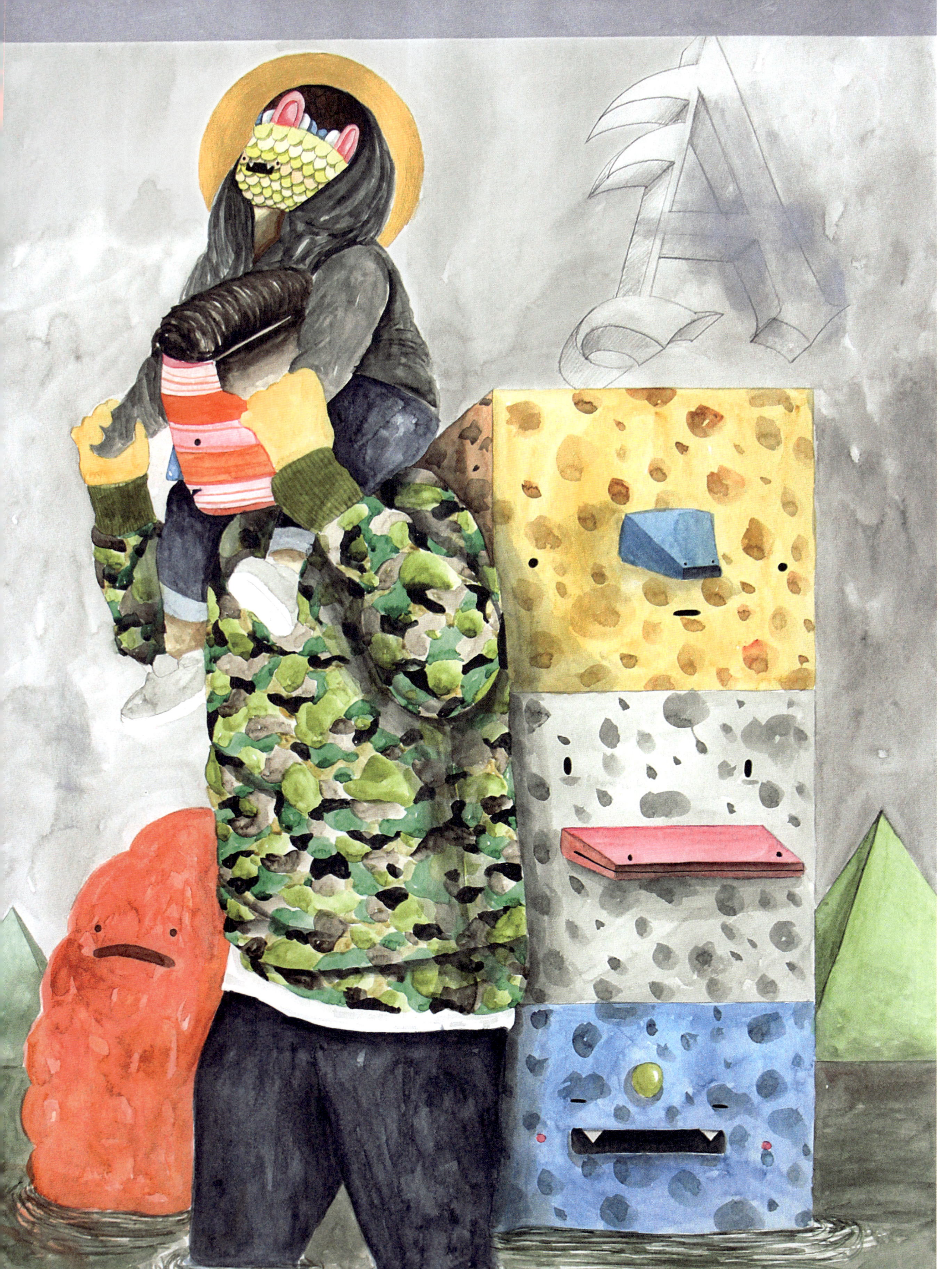

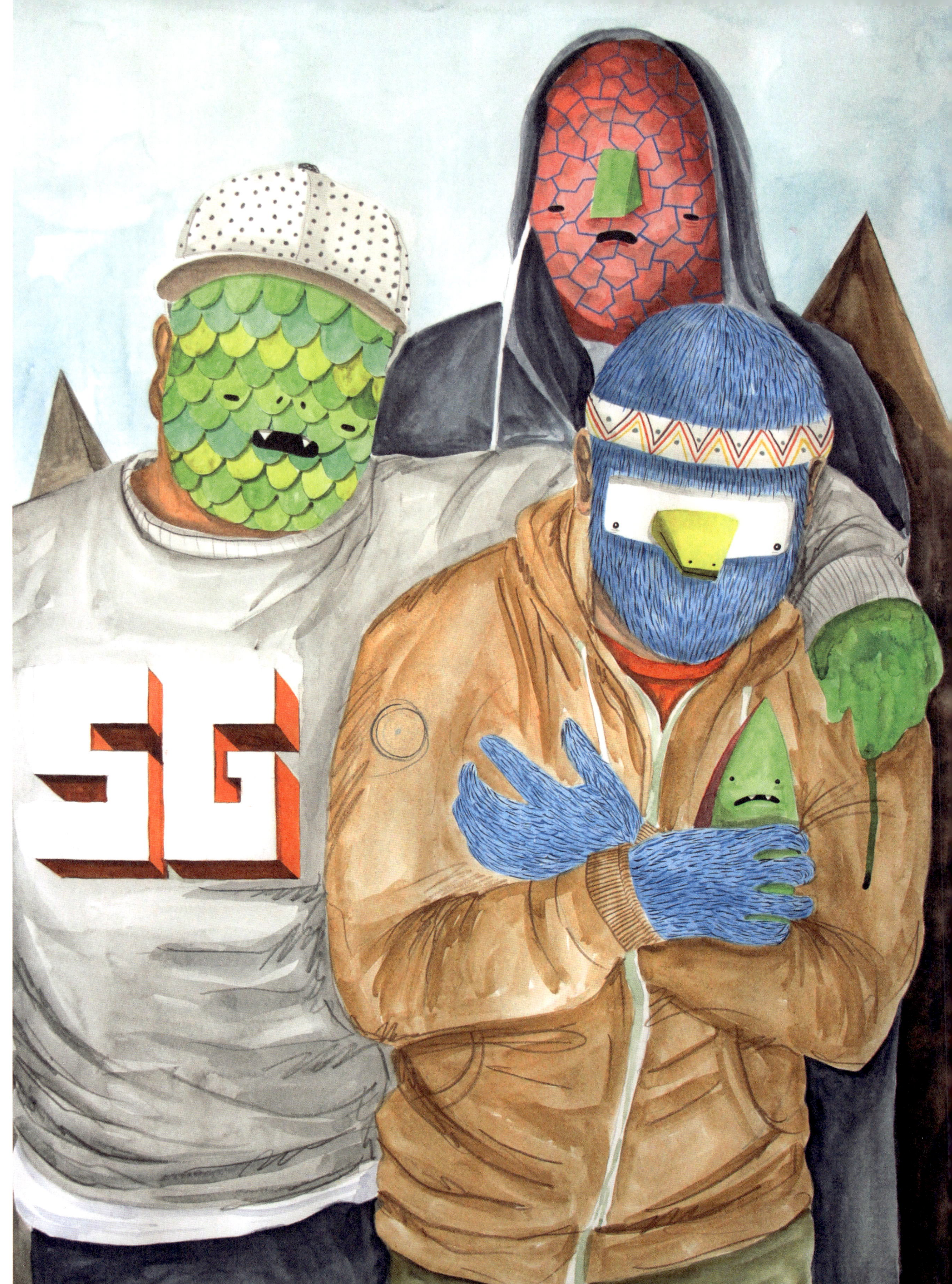
SG

Danny Fox

An emerging British artist who makes large-scale self-referential paintings, Danny

Fox's world is a mixture of fact, fiction and historical reference, ranging from the sublime to the mundane; from famous figures, to reinterpretations of well-known paintings to supermarket façades, gas works and motel signs. Where real life and imagination meet isn't always clear but his compositions are, without exception, a remarkable riot of colour and imagery, both graphic and gritty. His work is a reflection not only of a life lived to the full but also a love of the language of painting.

Born and raised in St Ives in Cornwall, Fox was influenced by his local arts scene, including the work of the acclaimed Cornish naive painter Alfred Wallis (1855–1942). Fox's journey into art has been similarly self-led. He did not go to art school, instead finding his own way into painting, a process of which he says: 'I couldn't have made any of these paintings before the time I made them because I hadn't lived the story yet.' Without the ties of a background in formal education his practice takes on an almost accidental quality, which is coupled with a boundless energy. Today he is based in London, where his work is finding recognition, culminating in solo exhibitions at spaces such as the Cock'n'Bull Gallery, and also residencies in LA and St Ives.

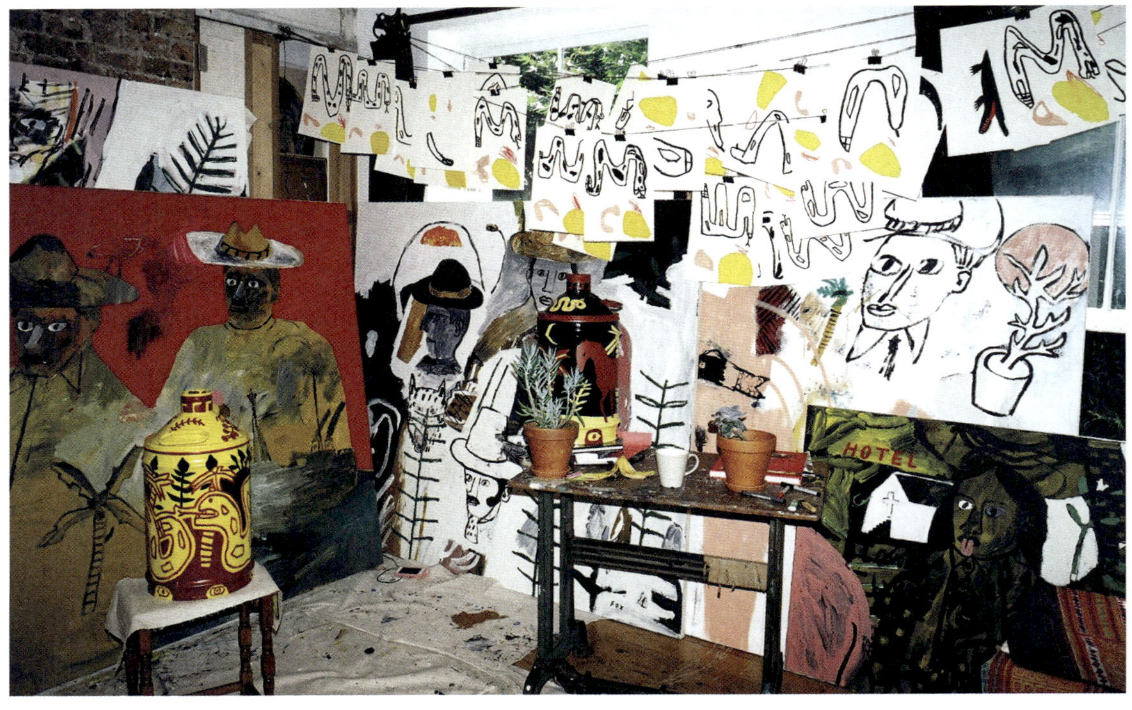

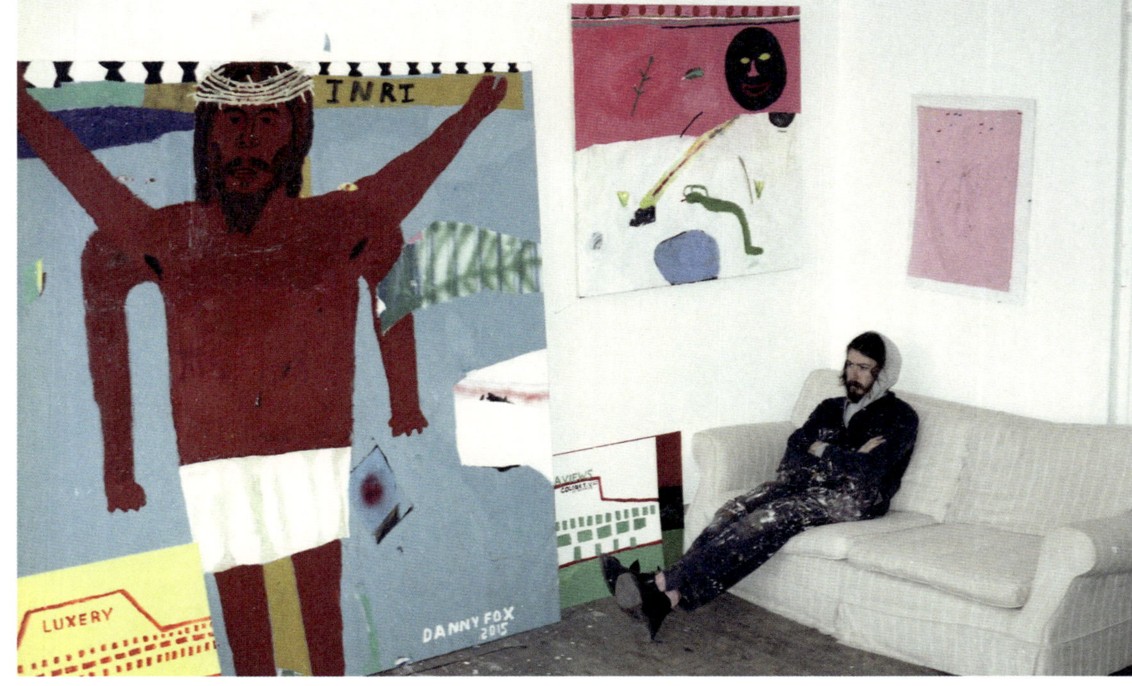

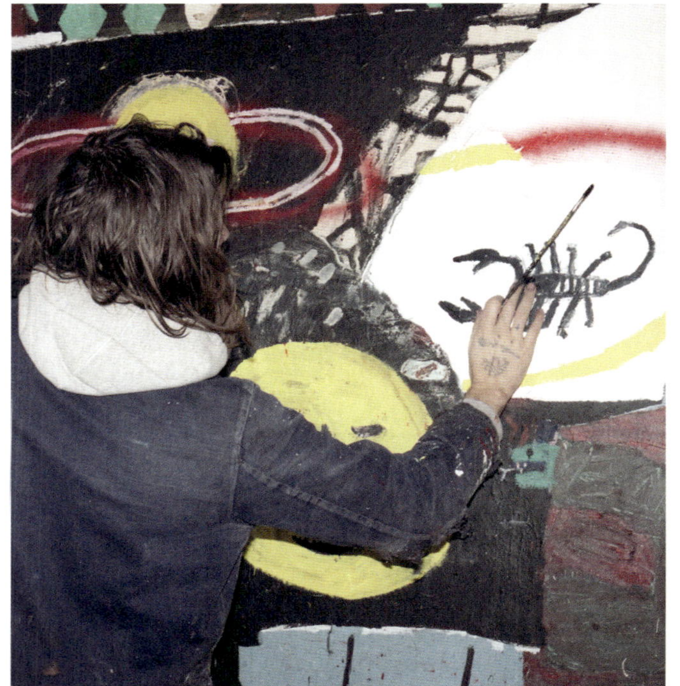

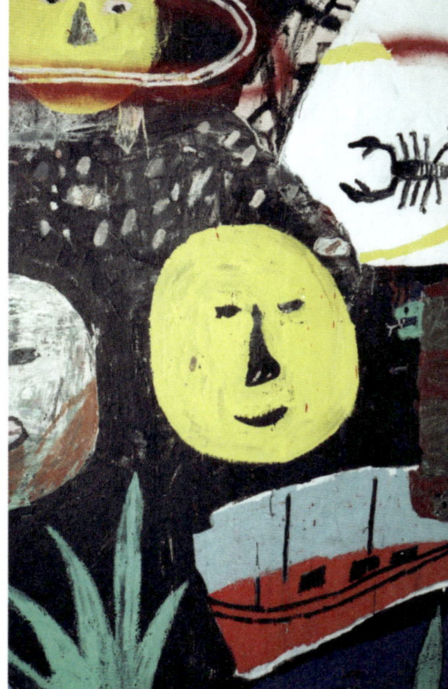

The artist's studio and works in progress, 2015

OPPOSITE
Untitled, 2014
Oil and acrylic on canvas
180 × 200 cm (71 × 79 in.)

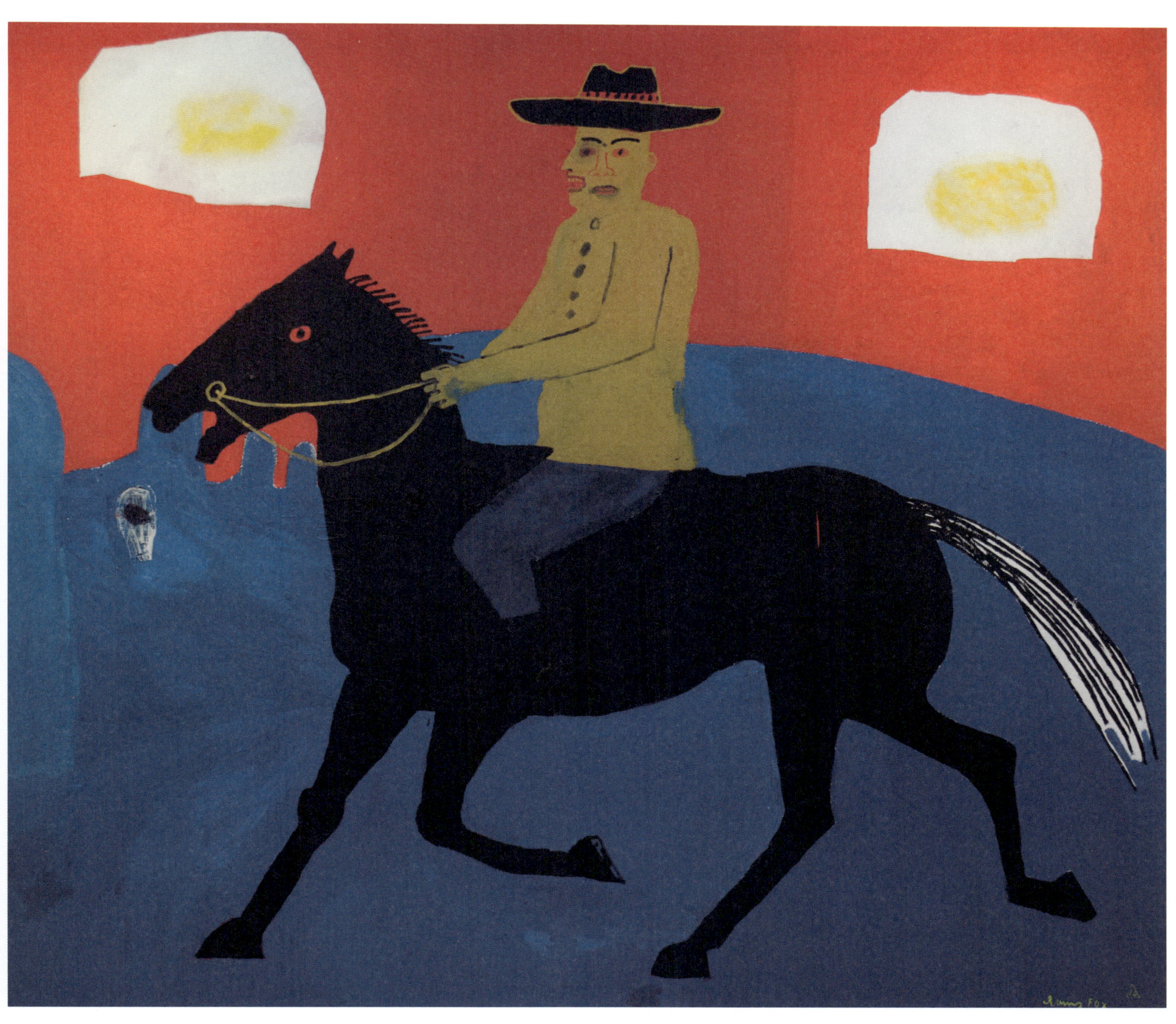

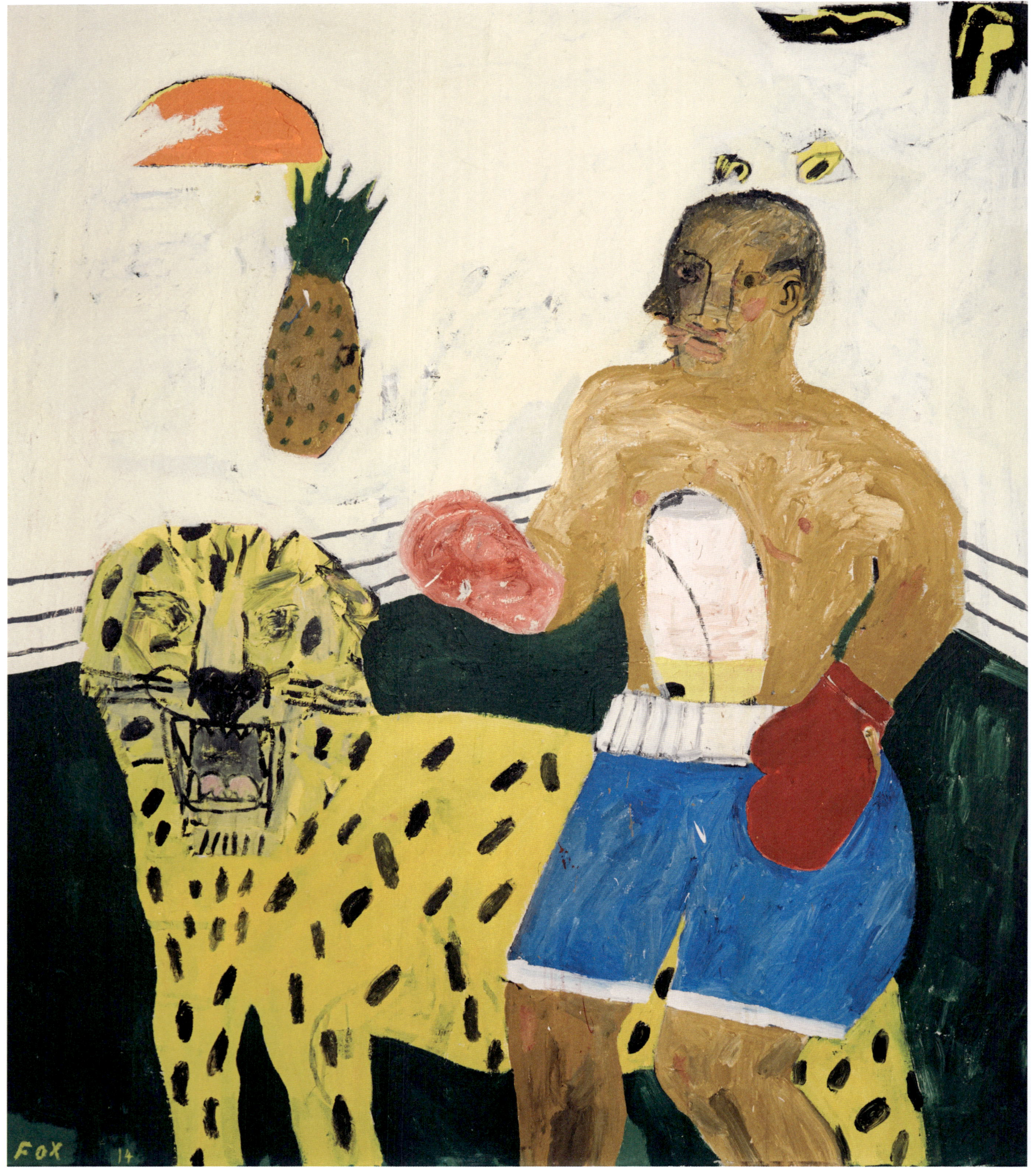

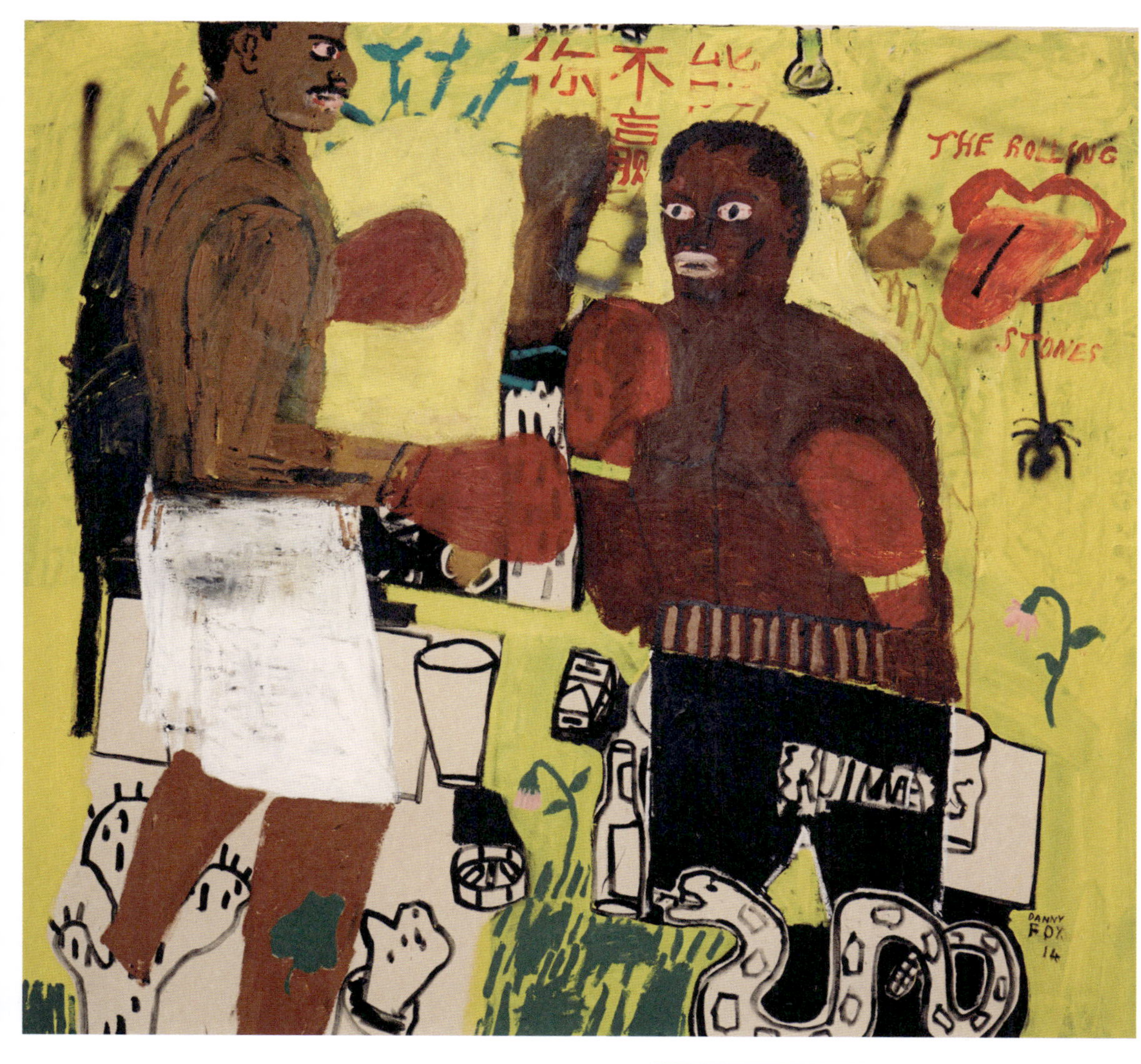

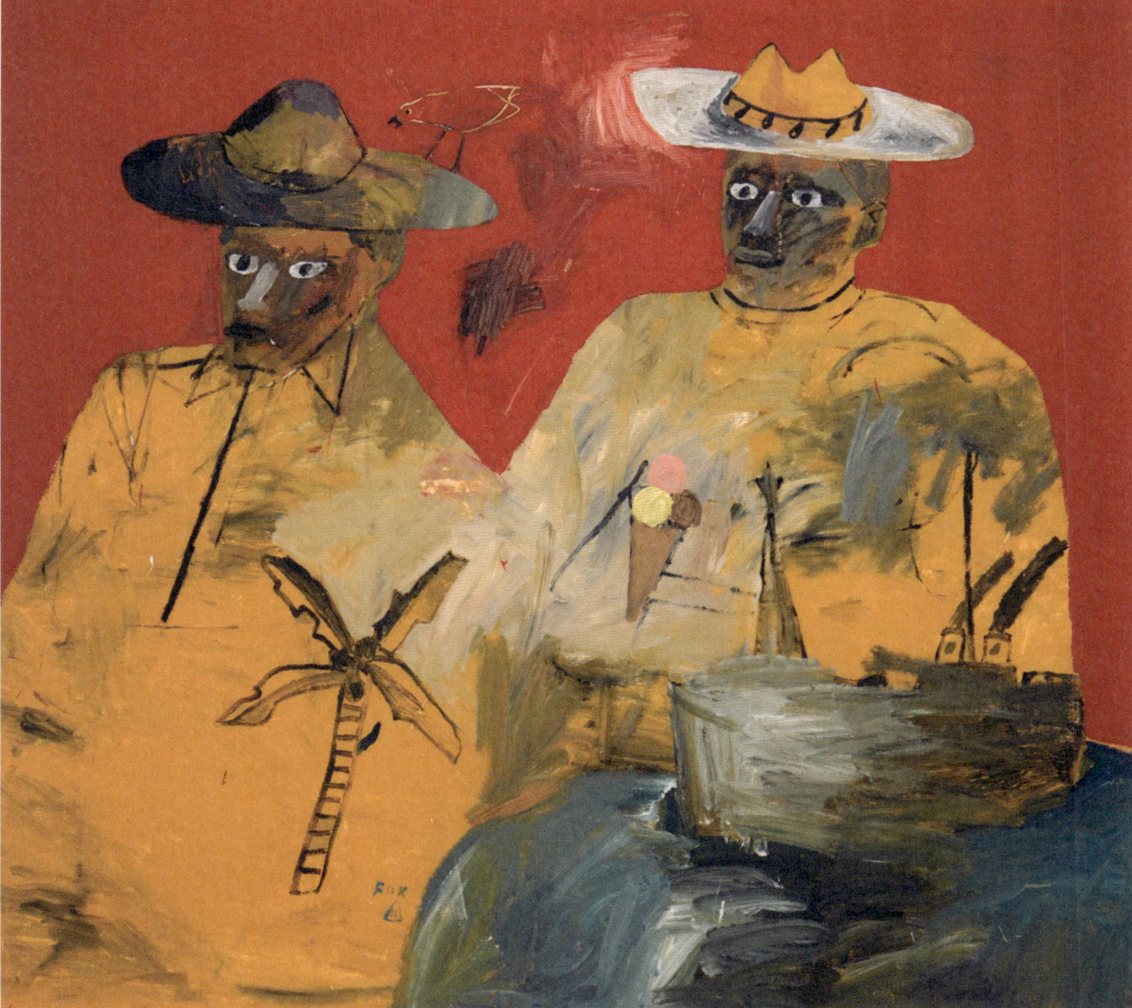

OPPOS TE
Untitled, 2014
Oil and acrylic on canvas
200 × 180 cm (79 × 71 in.)

THIS PAGE
The Winter after the
Summer of Love, 2014
Oil and acrylic on canvas
180 × 200 cm (71 × 79 in.)

What are Cornish Boys to
Do?, 2014
Acrylic on canvas
180 × 200 cm (71 × 79 in.)

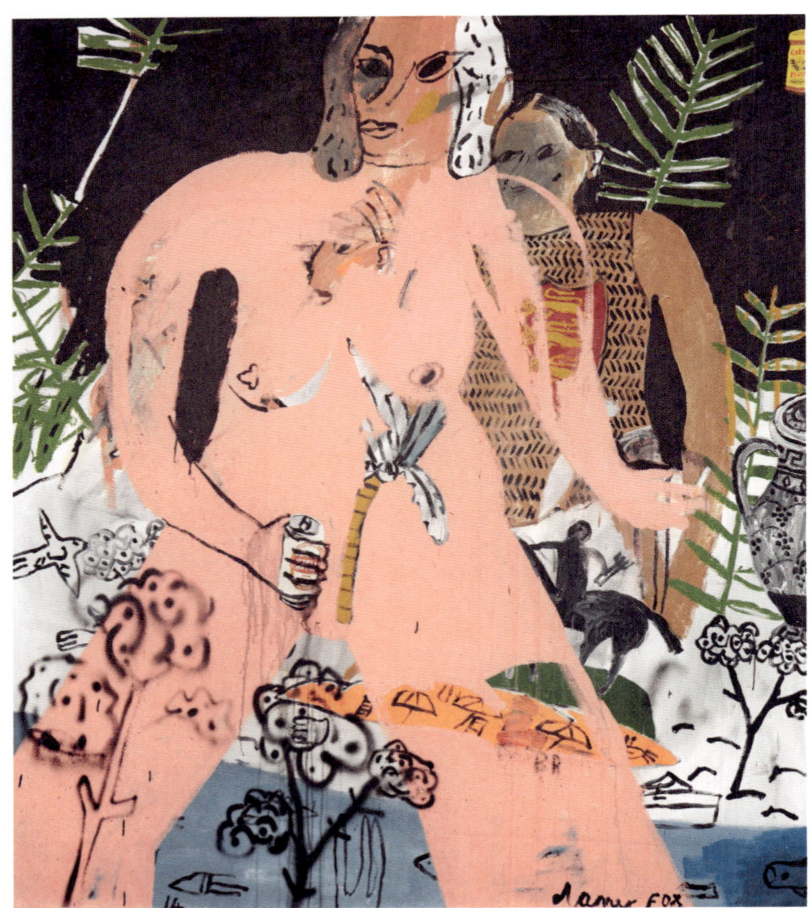

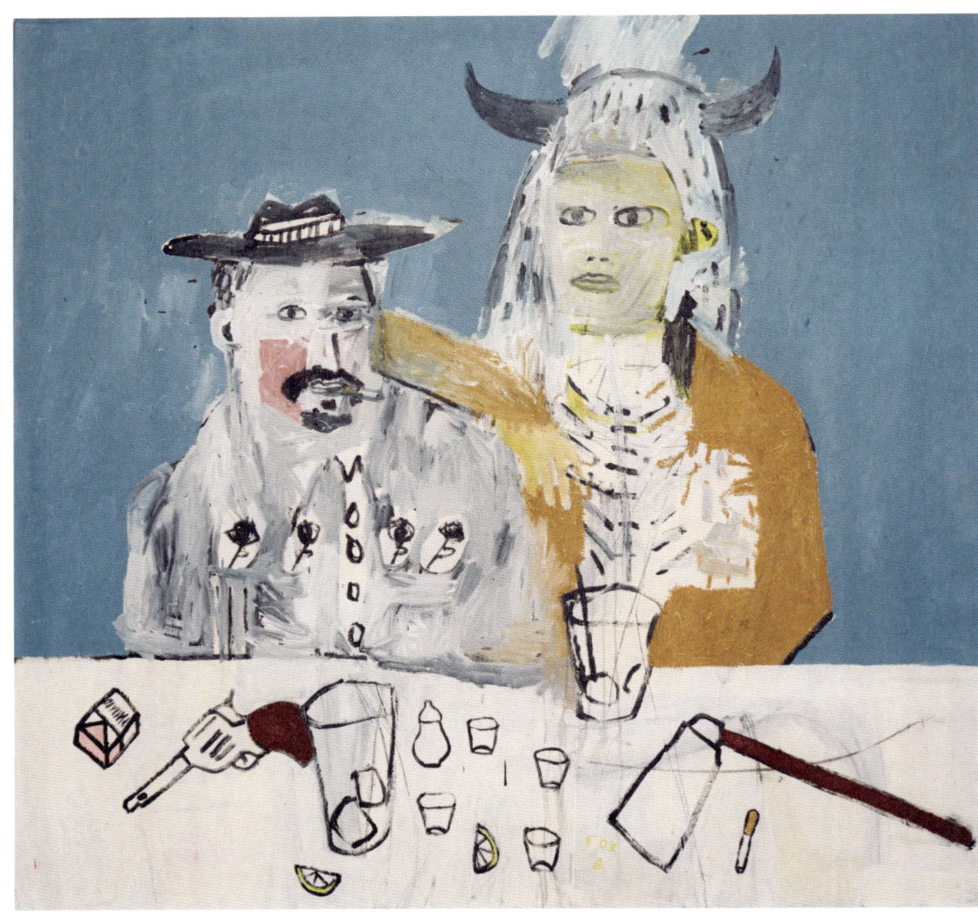

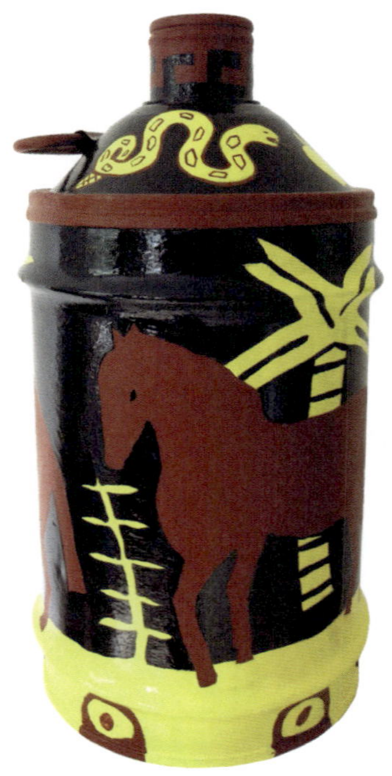

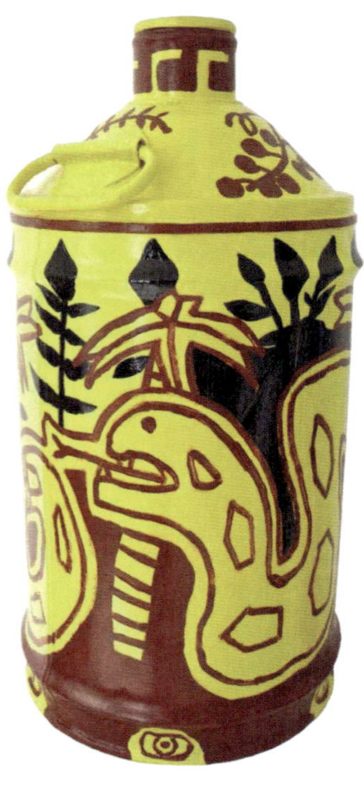

London's tattoo, strip club and party scenes have been a catalyst for the artist's creativity, and are brought to life in his work, which has been aptly described as 'a tasty mixture of sophistication and sleaze'. Sitting alongside this are stylistic nods to and motifs from Classicism, the work of Henri Matisse (1869–1954) Pablo Picasso (1881–1973) and the ingenuous energy of Philip Guston (1913–1980).

Of his influences he says, 'With artists like Picasso or Matisse you can't get anything near it in your painting, but I think it's obvious that I look at those artists'. He adds, 'I'm the most critical person ever; if something looks too much like something else, it goes.' Of his practice overall he explains: 'I've always liked the idea of leaving my mark in this life, I think artists are attracted to the notion that their work will be here after they're dead and gone. As a species even.... I think that it's in our genetics to build monuments that last for centuries and to stick flags into the ground, on this planet and where ever else we can get to. There is no message in my work other than that I'm here now, that I'm alive and when the reaper comes all that will be left of me is my art, so my paintings carry that same ideal.'

CLOCKWISE FROM TOP LEFT
Untitled, 2014
Oil and acrylic on canvas
200 × 180 cm (79 × 71 in.)

Tequila, 2014
Oil and acrylic on canvas
180 × 200 cm (71 × 79 in.)

Untitled works, 2014
Enamel on gas bottle
Dimensions variable

OPPOSITE
Untitled, 2014
Oil and acrylic on canvas
180 × 200 cm (71 × 79 in.)

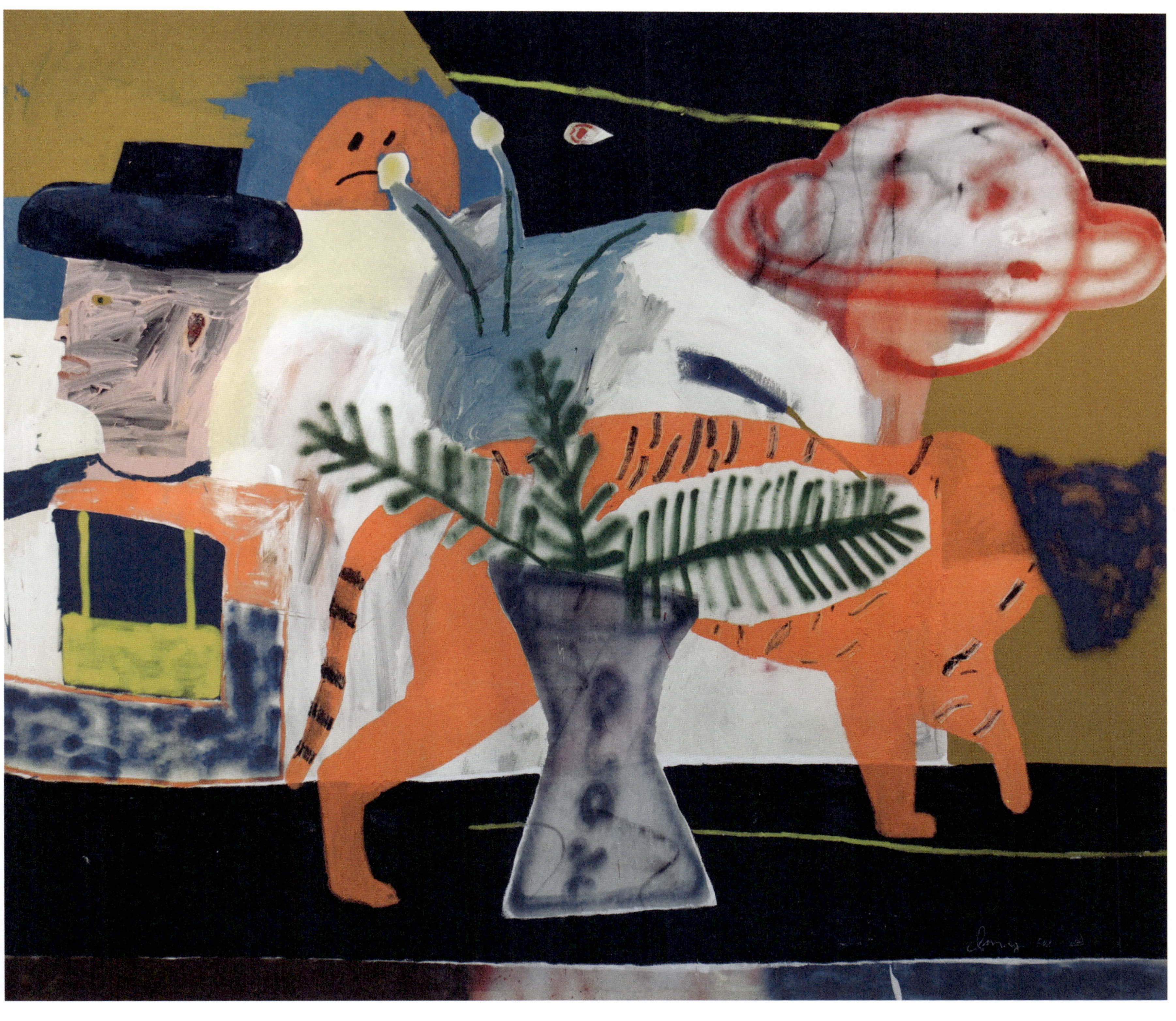

Harold Hollingsworth

Best known for his dynamic mixed-media work on canvas and panel that embraces a whole host of influences, such as graphic art, Pop Art and Abstract art, Harold Hollingsworth's compositions often blend imagery, such as found typography, street photography and signage from disparate sources, which he then reconfigures into abstract forms. The resultant works are often aged and weathered in appearance, with blocks of muted colour evocative of the vintage hues of Bakelite or old magazines permeating the many layers of under- and over-painting.

Hollingsworth cites popular culture as a big influence in his work. Adopting a philosophy not dissimilar to his Pop artist forebears, he maintains that his practice involves 'finding things we see every day and reconstructing them in a subtle and potent work of art'. These 'things' range from ripped posters to found graphics and ornamentation, which he repurposes within his painting and is part of the process of participating in a 'multigenerational conversation…. It's my way of talking with artists both past and future, a note inside the art bottle if you will, floating through our world.' Such a statement is the artist's nod not only to the ubiquity of Pop Art but also to how we all contribute to the wider world of popular culture.

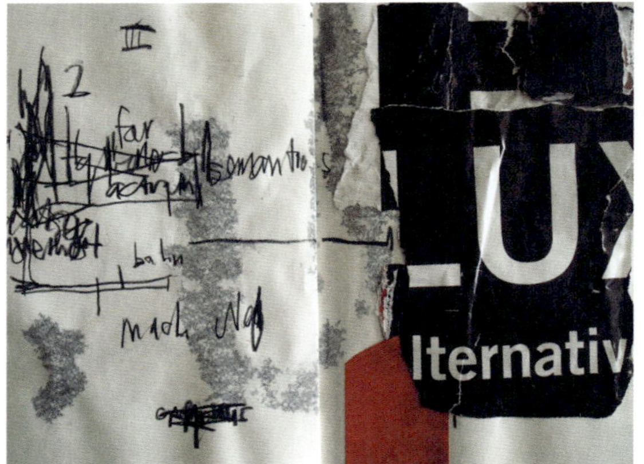
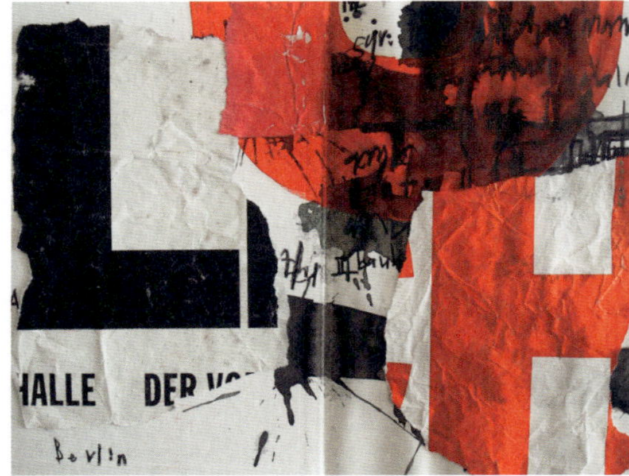
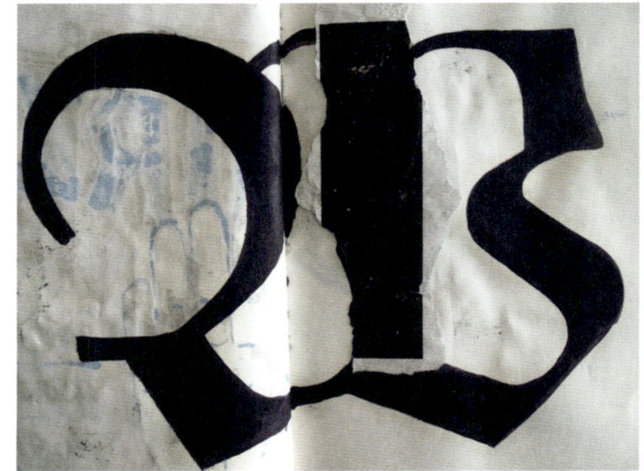
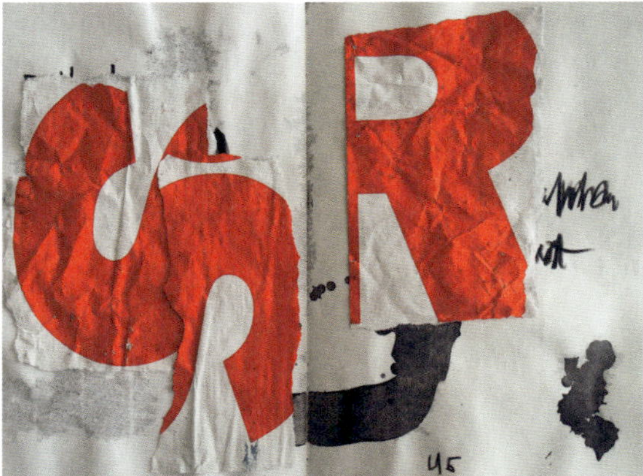
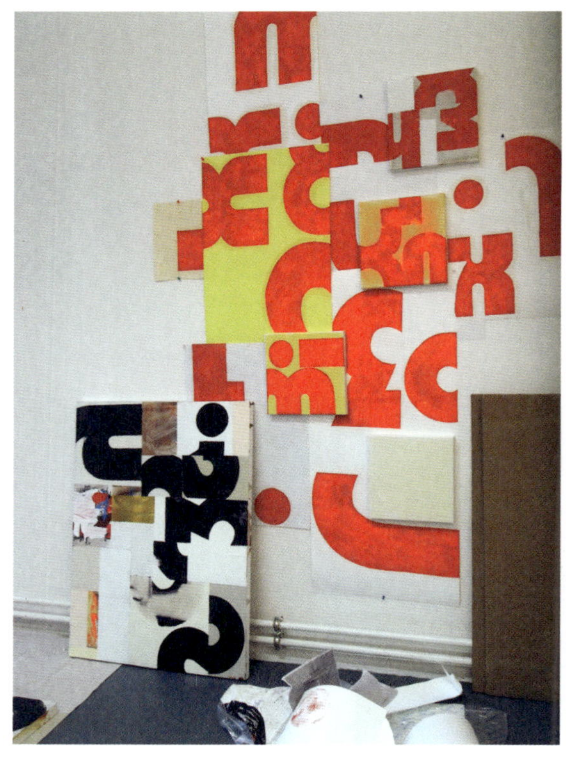
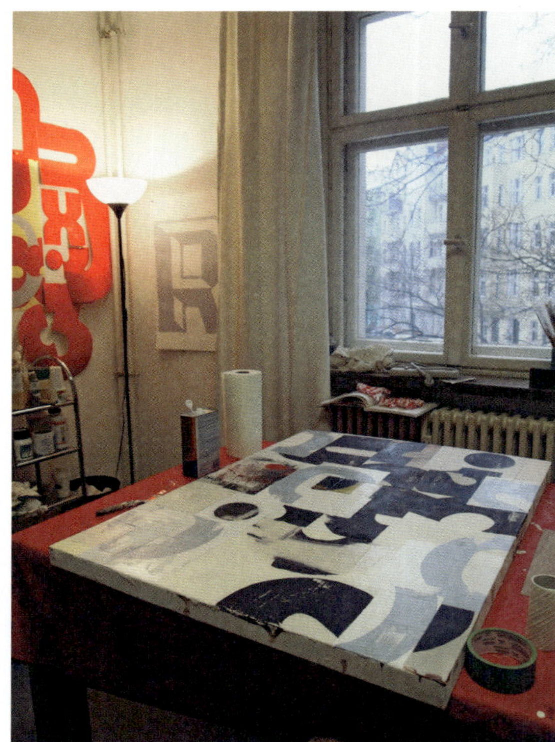

Pages from the artist's sketchbook, 2015, and the artist's Berlin studio.

Untitled, c. 2014
Mixed media on canvas
152 × 122 cm (60 × 48 in.)

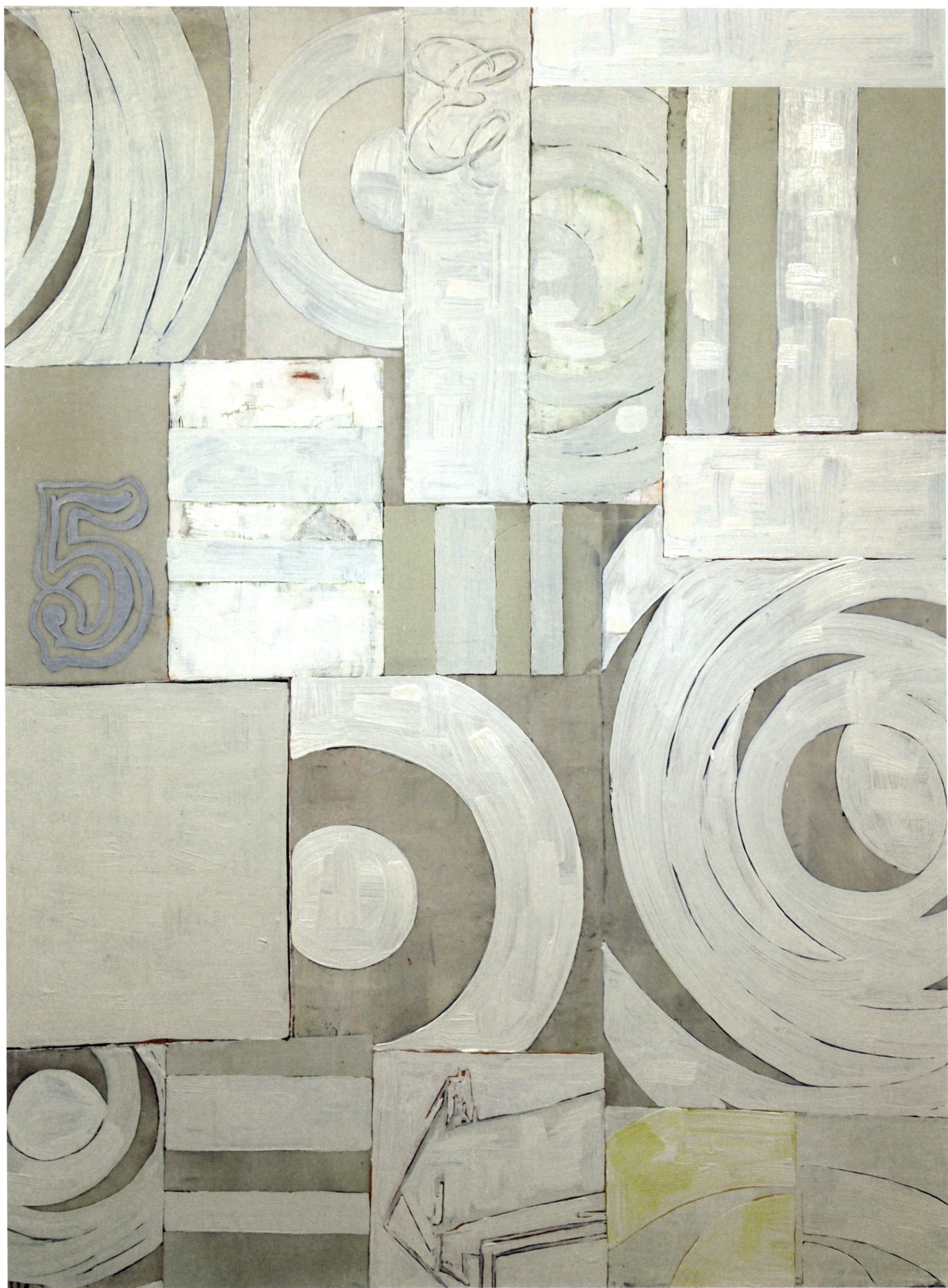

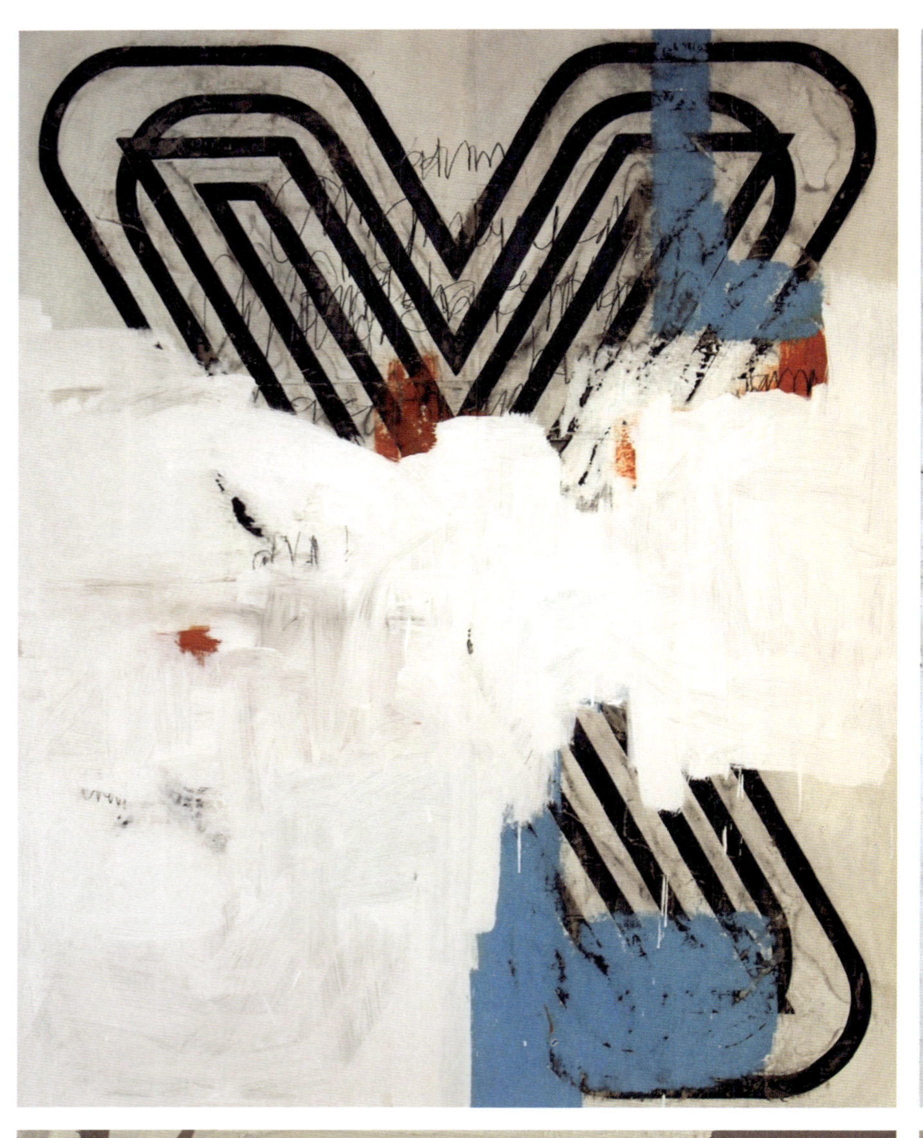
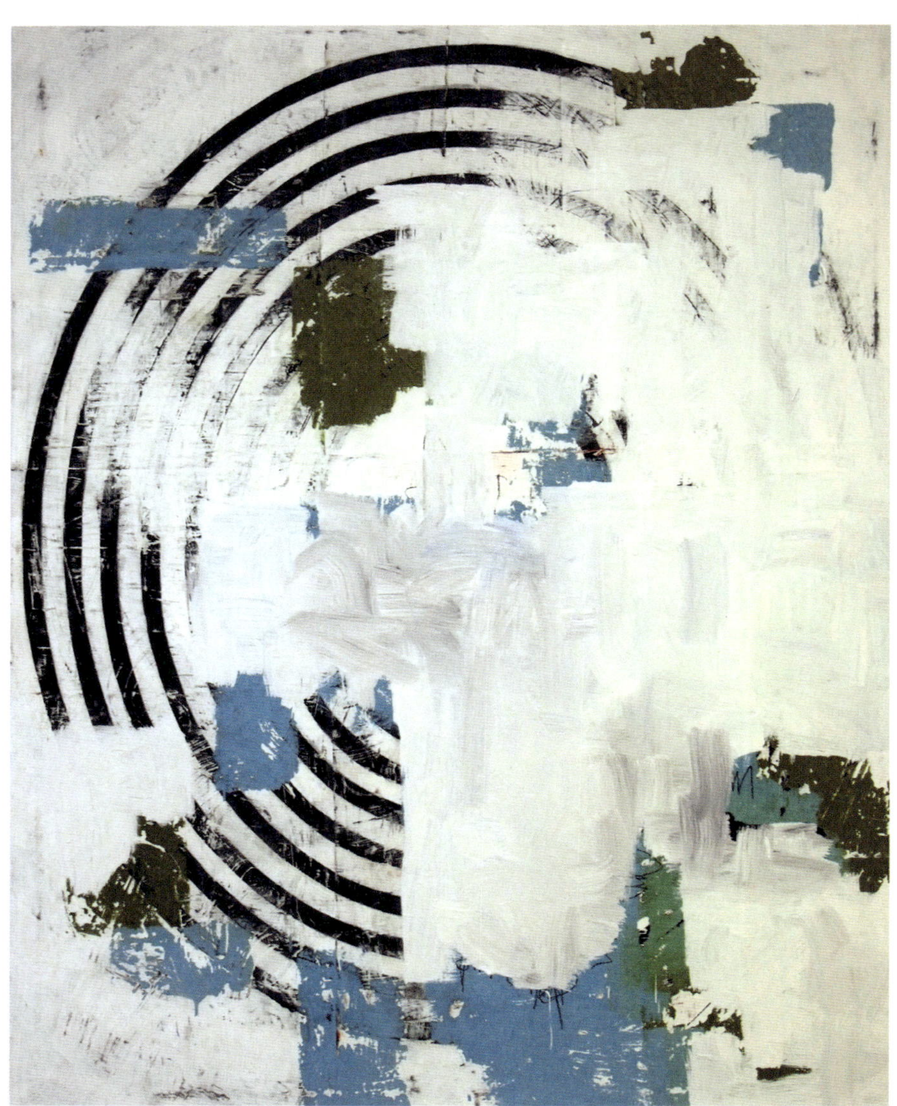
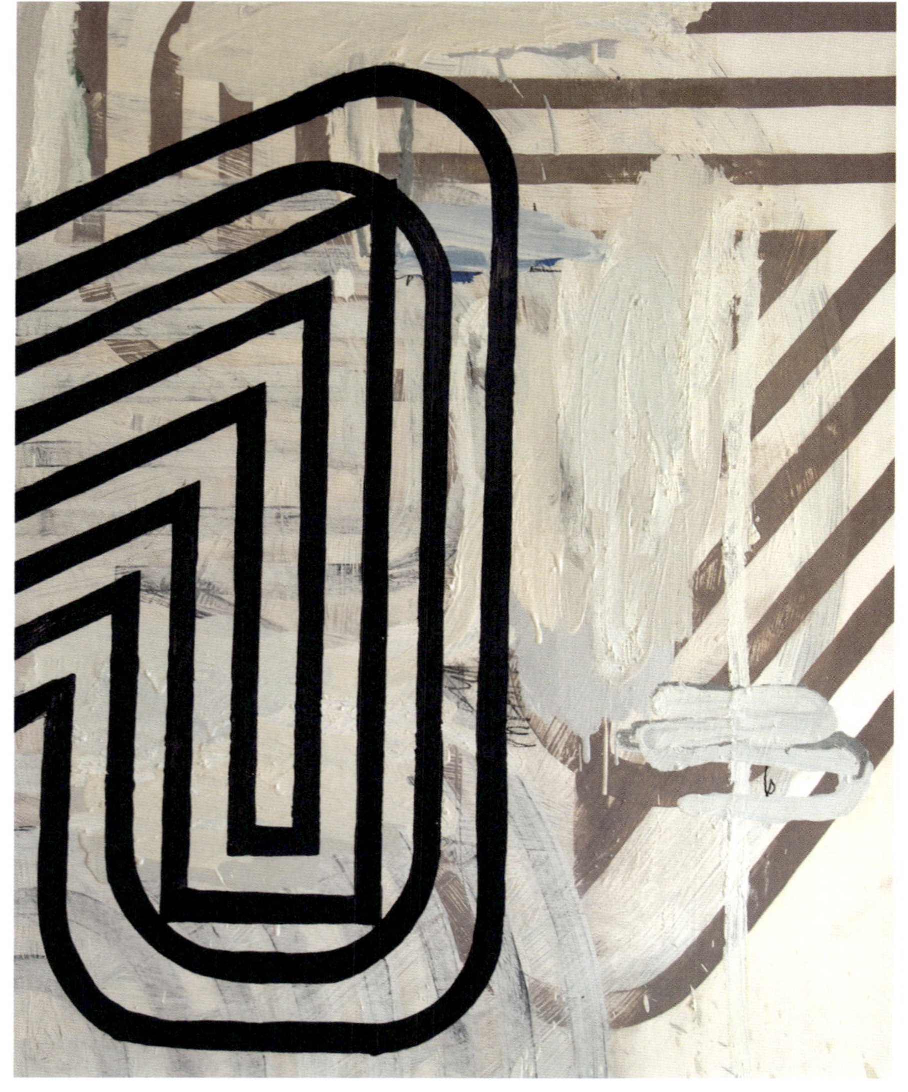
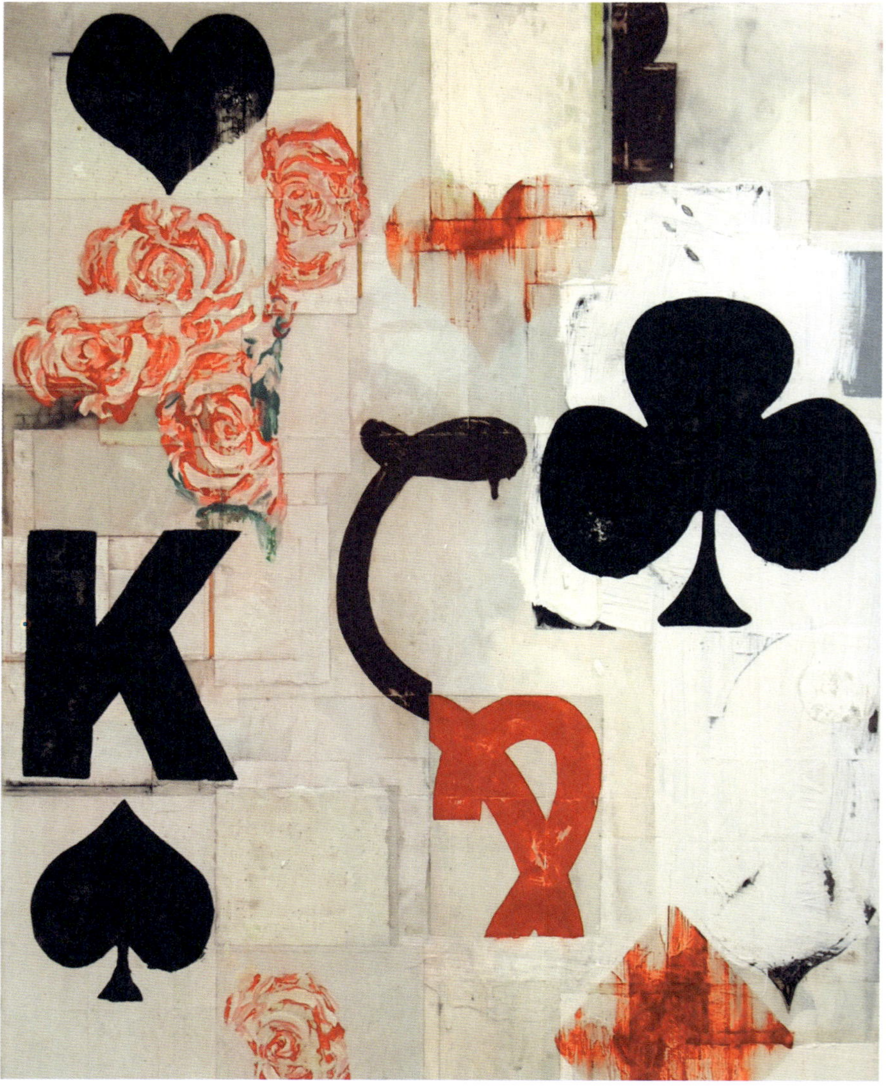

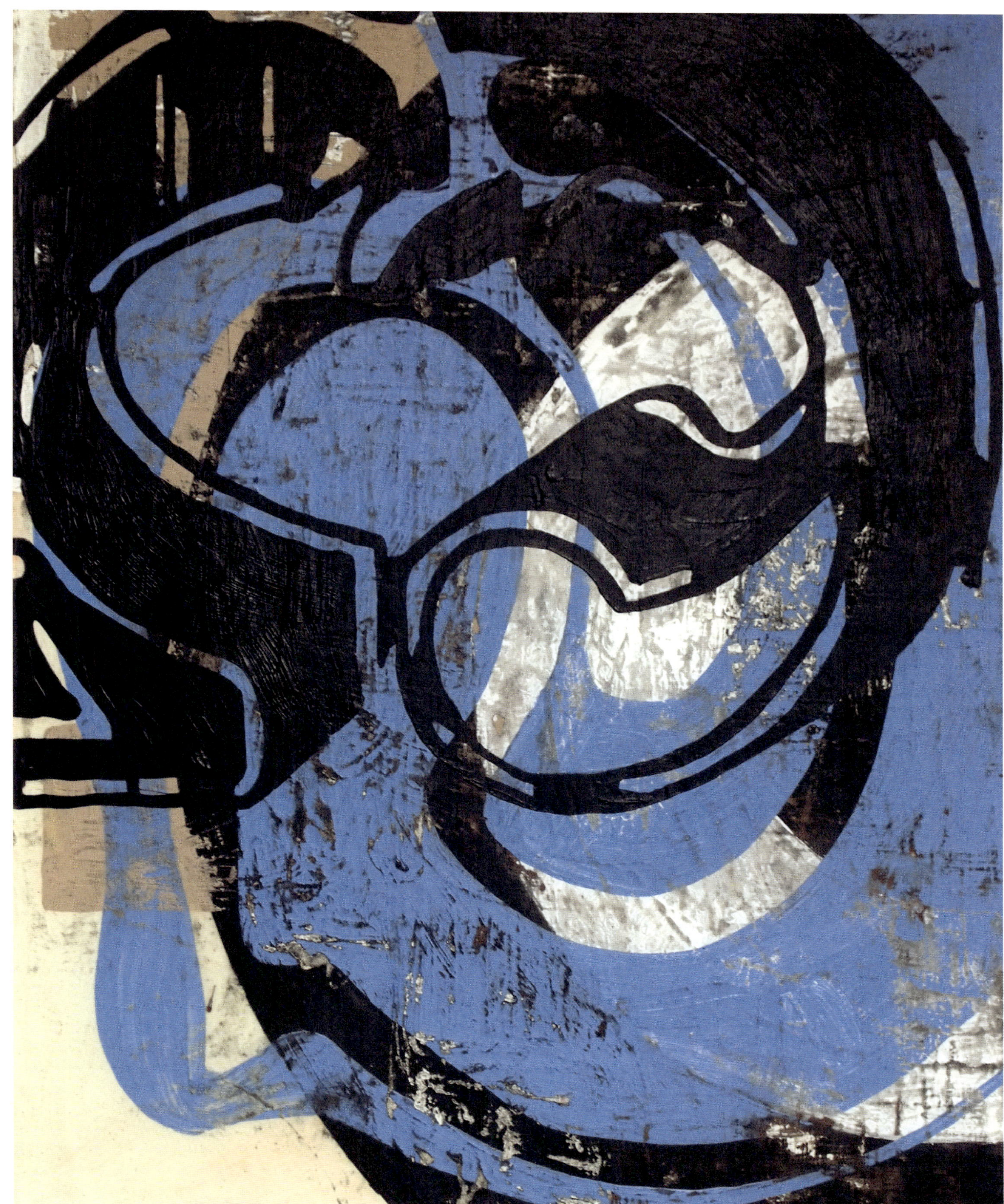

Double Rocker, 2014
Mixed media on canvas
152 × 122 cm (60 × 48 in.)

Untitled, c. 2010
Mixed media on canvas
Dimensions unknown

Untitled, 2012
Mixed media on canvas
152 × 122 cm (60 × 48 in.)

Untitled, c. 2010
Mixed media on canvas
Dimensions unknown

Untitled, c. 2011
Mixed media on canvas
152 × 122 cm (60 × 48 in.)

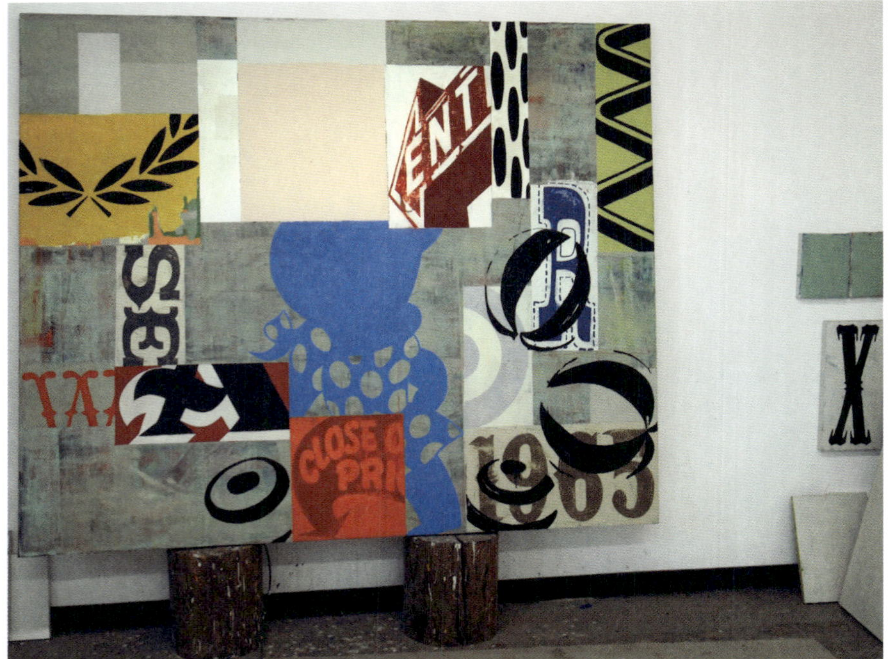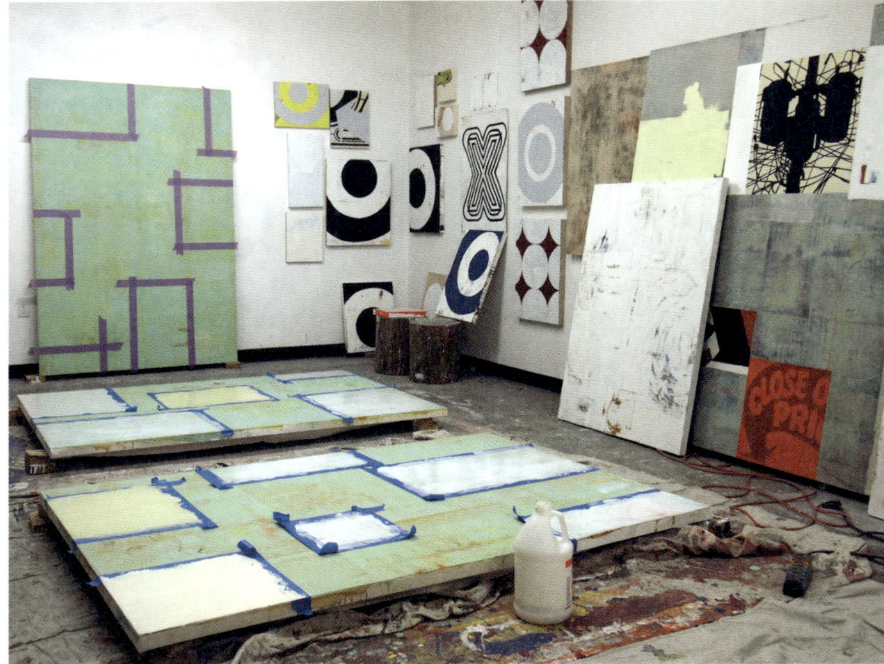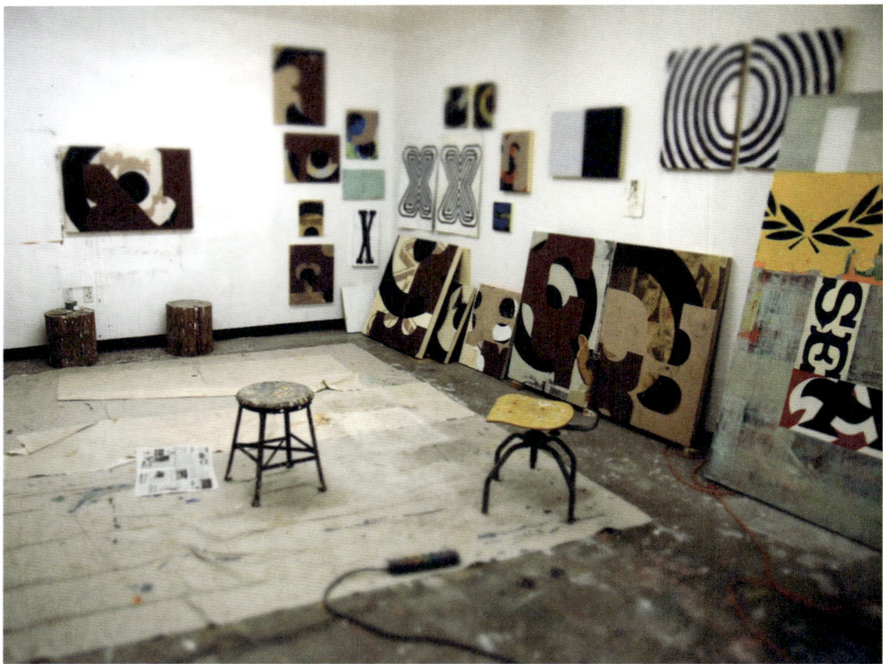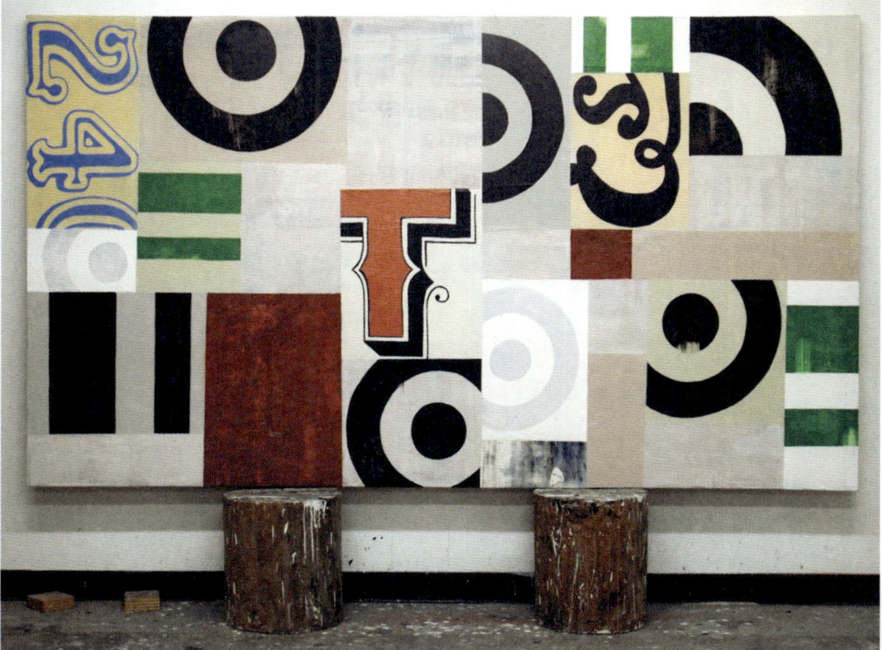

Hollingsworth refers to his visual *mélanges* as a 'call-and-response…. I make a move on the painting and then wait to see how it responds, since I can't always anticipate the way that it will play out on the canvas'. Technically the means justify the end, and the artwork can be assembled in many different ways, for example, by applying paper collage, overlaying it with oil paint and then removing it, in a fluid process of collage, décollage and painting. Often there comes a point at which it is no longer clear how the painting came to reveal itself, with the technique being less important than the overall feel of the surface and the final composition.

Hollingsworth has participated in numerous solo and group shows around the world. His work is collected by both private collectors and corporate firms. He also recently took up residency at TAKT in Berlin.

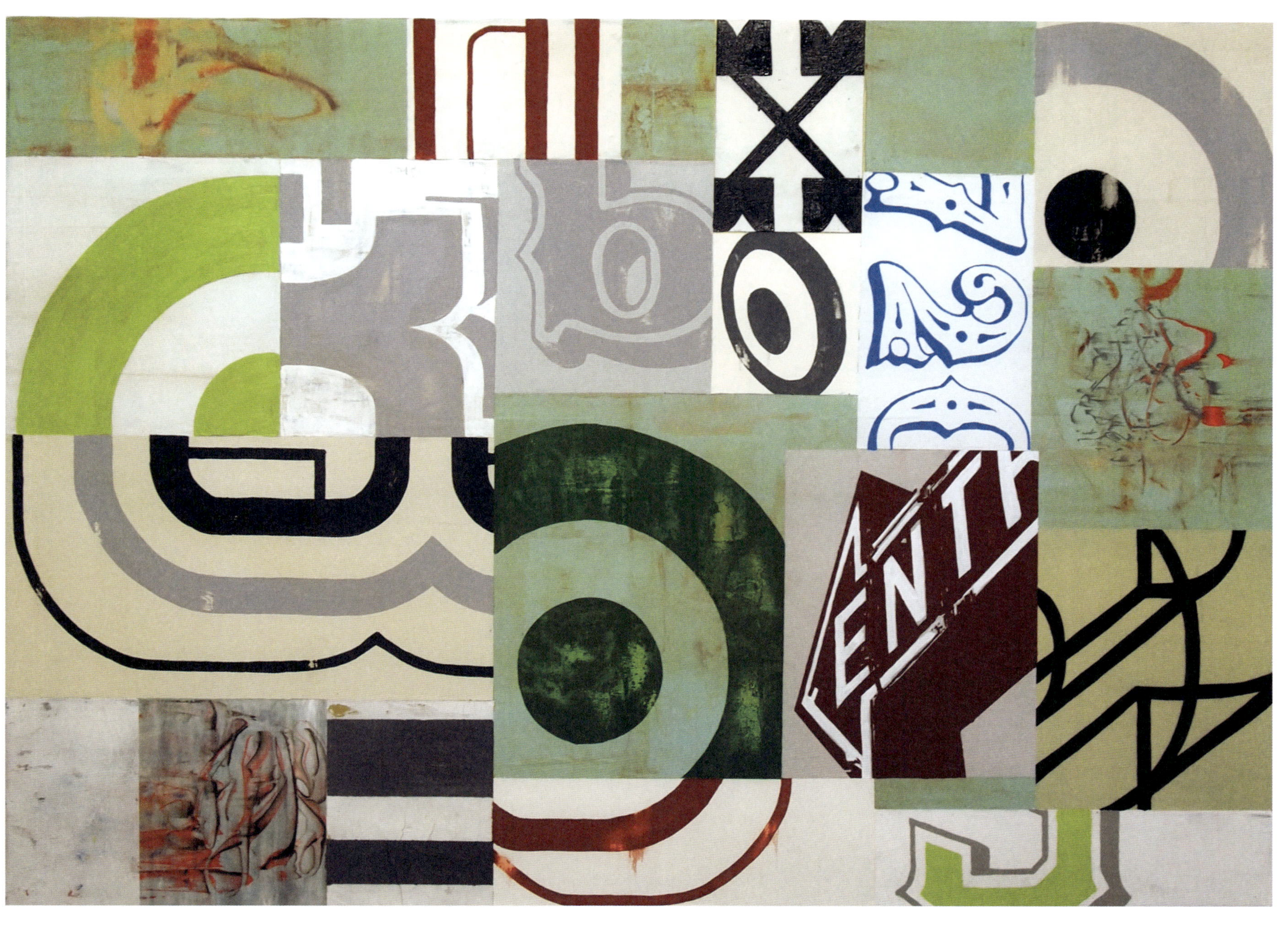

ENT

Agostino Iacurci

Internationally renowned for his large-scale, idiosyncratic murals,

which are painted in bold, flat colours and in a childlike visual language, and comprise figures, curvilinear shapes, and a strong sense of composition, Rome-based Agostino Iacurci's work is exceptionally striking.

In some ways Iacurci's paintings echo the streamlined forms of the French modernist painter Fernand Léger (1881–1955) or Italian Art Deco, while also being influenced by contemporary illustration. His work has a welcoming appeal; it is full of visual humour and resonating colours, drawing the viewer in and inviting them to contemplate the intriguing scenarios within. Of his methods Iacurci explains: 'You can use a childlike language to narrate light images as well as catastrophic ones. Personally, I have a cynical vision of reality; I'm very critical and sometimes pessimistic, so making art becomes a cathartic process, a space in which to stage a drama and at the same time sublimate it, alleviating its power.'

In addition to making murals in Italy, Iacurci has undertaken commissions in countries such as Brazil, Russia and Australia, and made monumental works in others, including his 300-metre-long painting in collaboration with

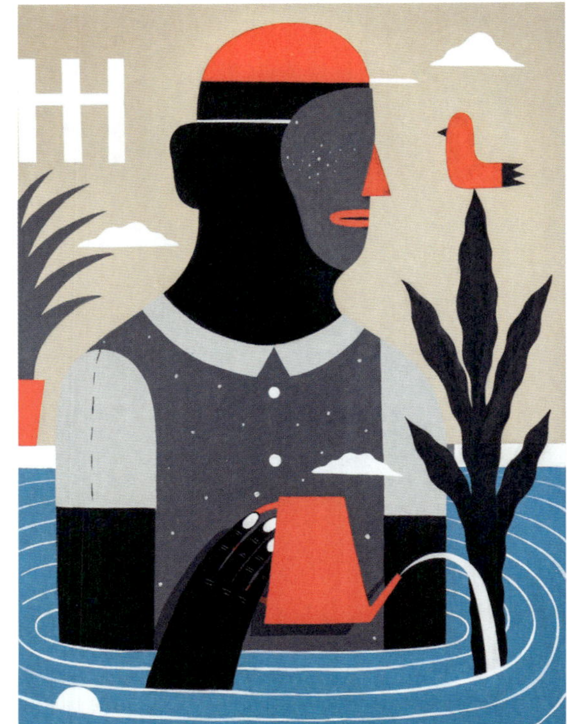
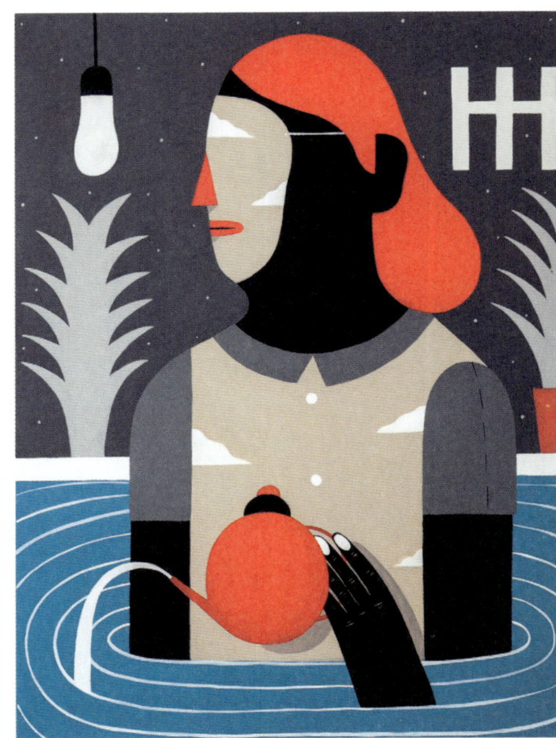
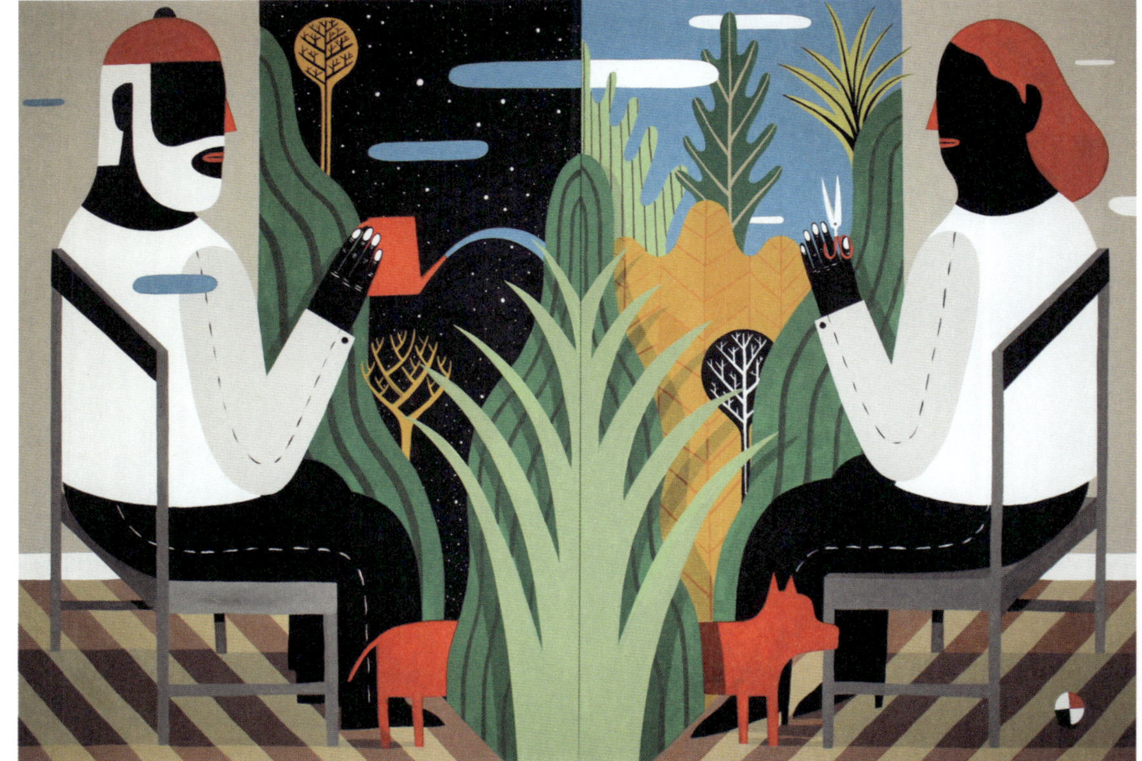

Interiors (diptych), 2015
Acrylic on canvas
130 × 200 cm
(51¼ × 78½ in.) each

Study for the Blind Wall, 2014
Mixed media
Dimensions unknown

Tondo 1–3, 2015
Acrylic on wood
70 cm (27⅝ in.) in
diameter each

One White Bulb, 2015
Acrylic on canvas
92 × 142 cm
(36¼ × 56 in.)

Small Wheel Big Wheel,
c. 2013
Mixed media
Dimensions unknown

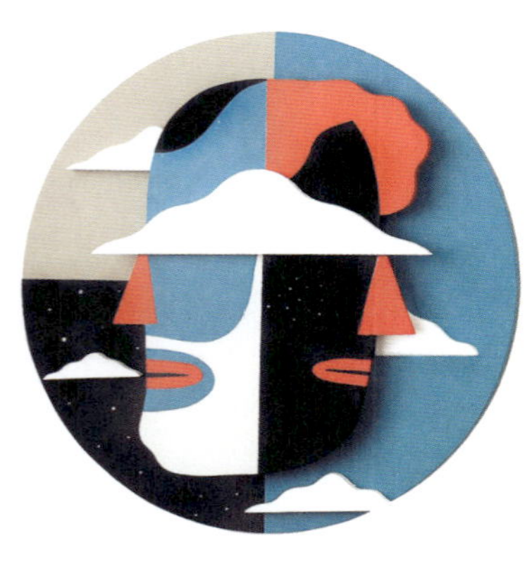
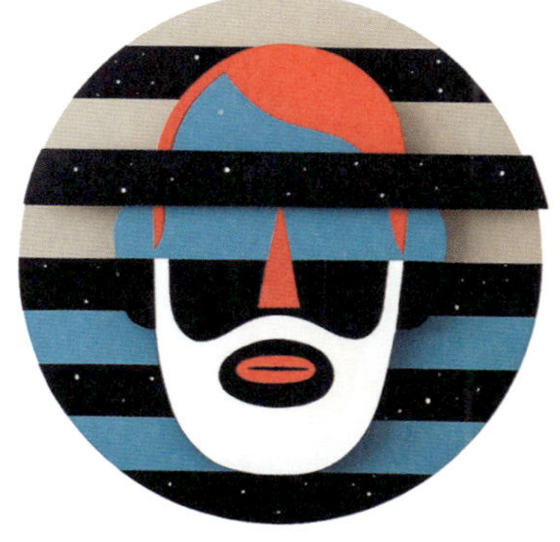
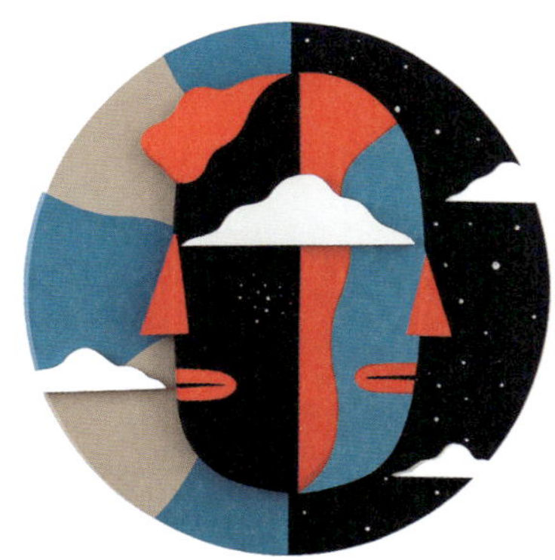

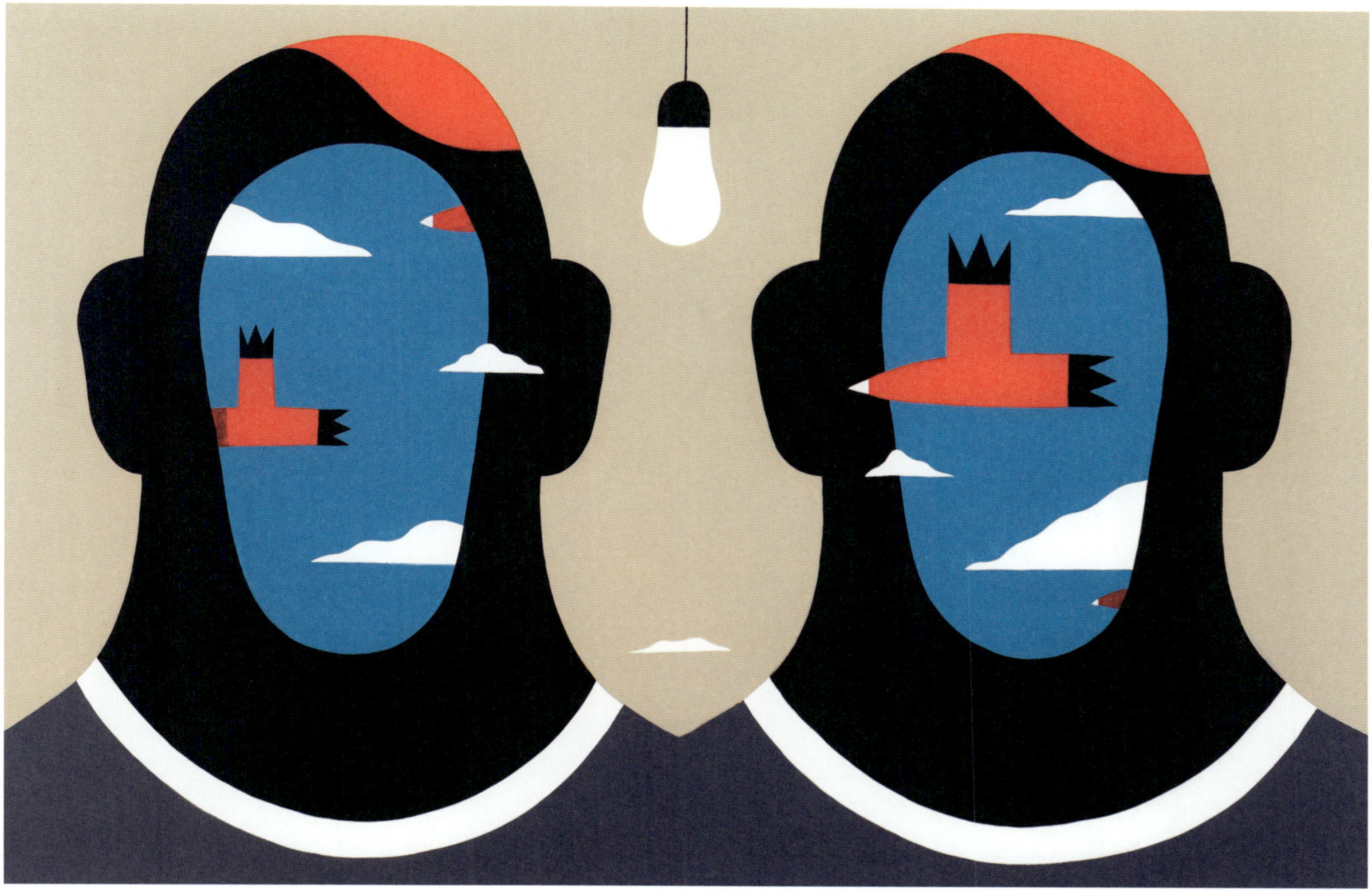

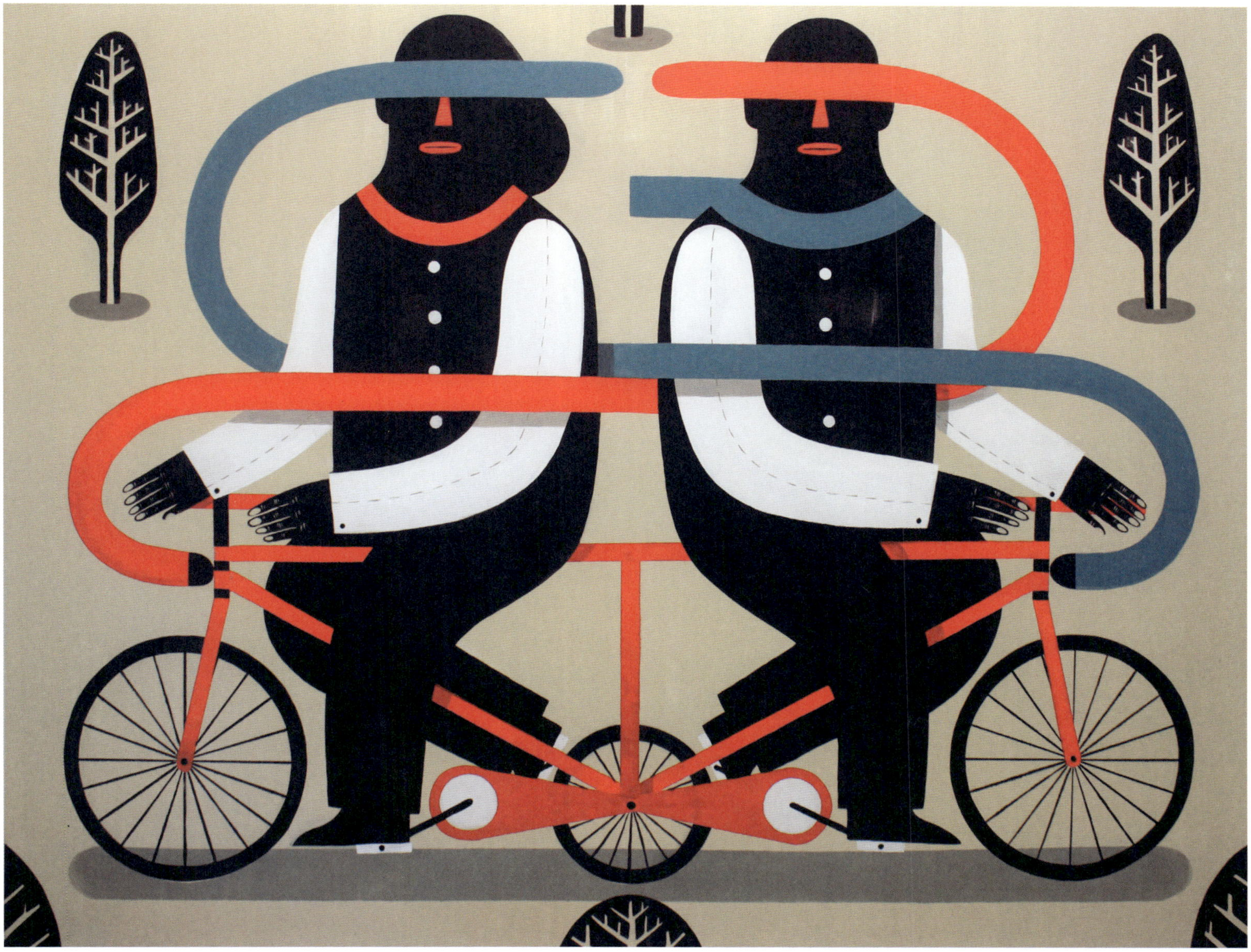

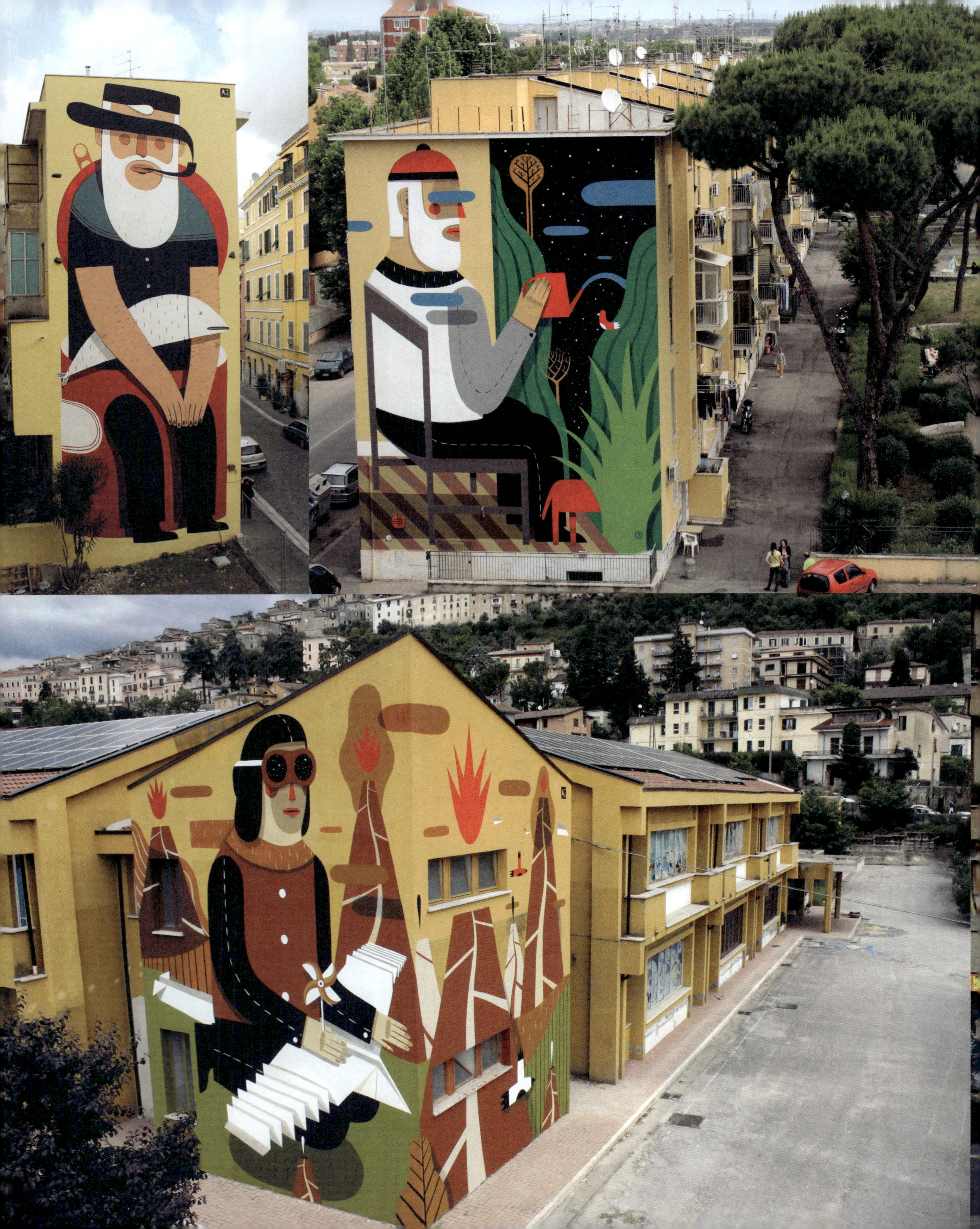

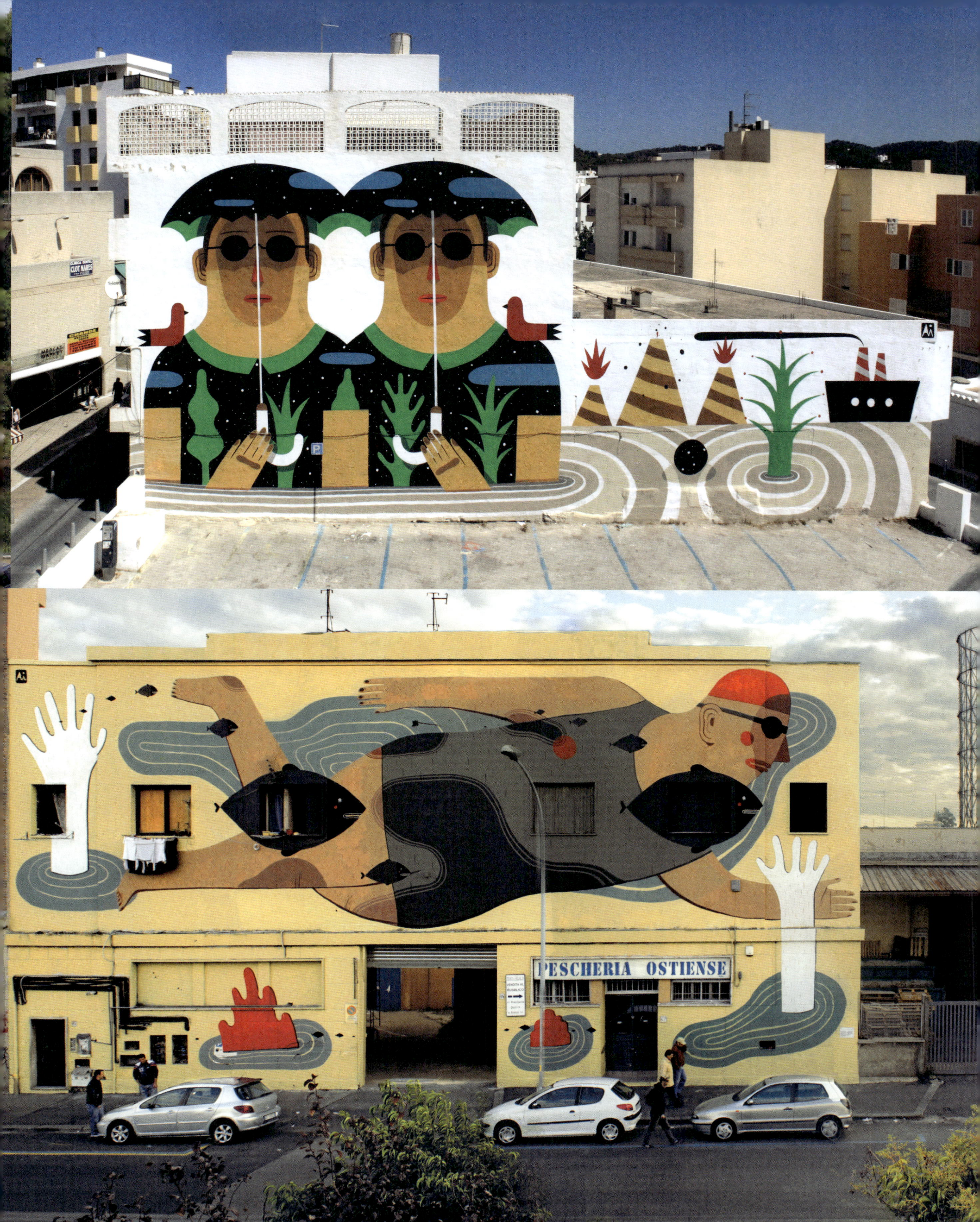

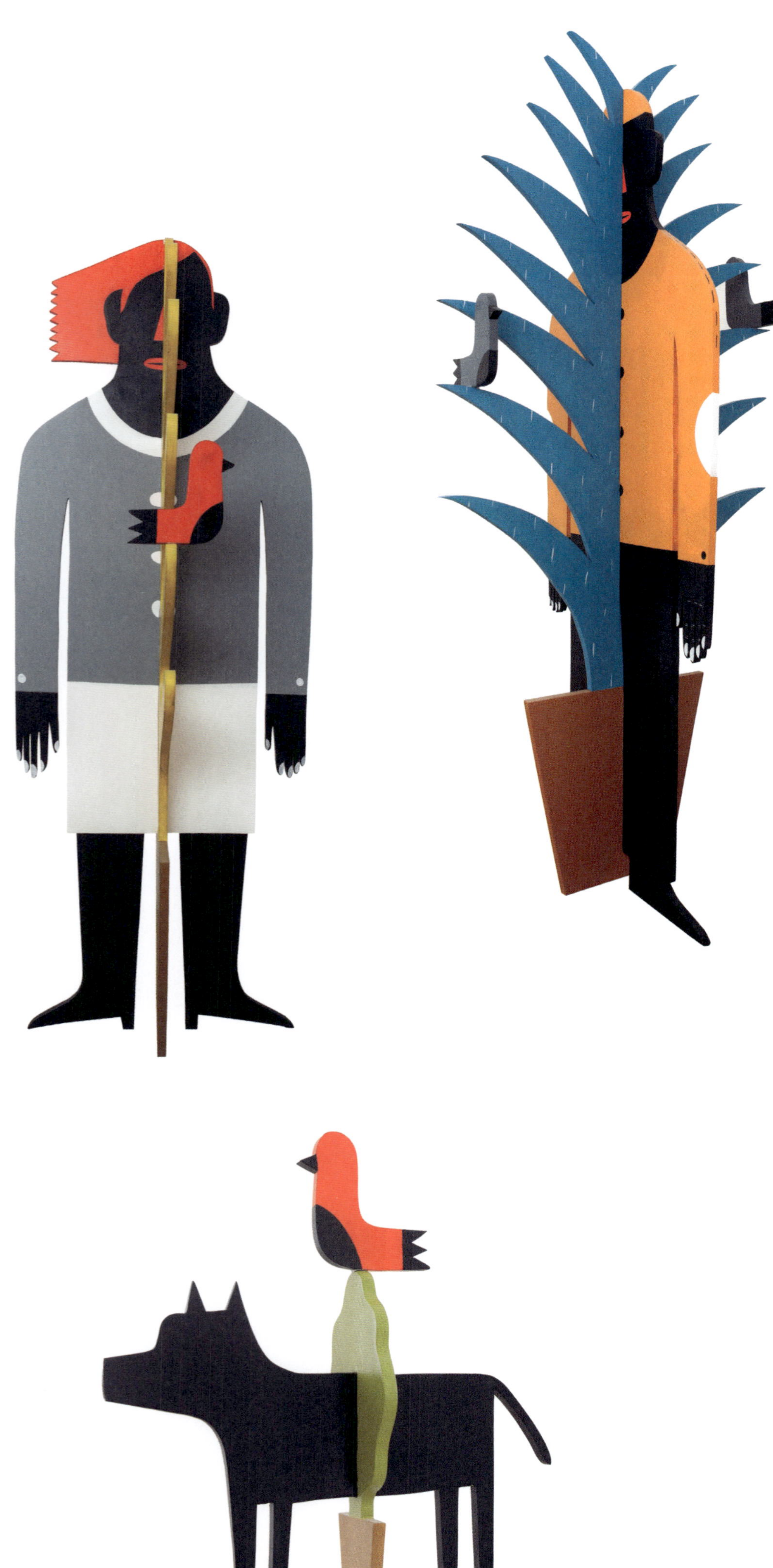

students from the Saba School in Western Sahara in 2009 and a work in a skyscraper twenty-one storeys high for the 'Fubon Art Foundation' in Taipei in 2013.

Iacurci adapts his work to its location, taking into account its local stories and histories in his subject-matter and adjusting his colour palette to the site. He also adopts a collaborative approach, discussing with local people their expectations of his work, and taking this into consideration as he composes each mural. This tactic he extended to his 2011 work *Vanishing Points*, which was part of the project 'Rebibbia on the Wall'. Along with the inmates of a maximum-security prison, he made three large murals for the prison courtyard, in response to the prisoners' desire to improve their immediate surroundings. As Iacurci says, 'To me each work is more than a painting, it is a tangible sign of a complex experience I've been through, since it includes being exposed to people's direct feedback, with all the unexpected consequences this can generate.'

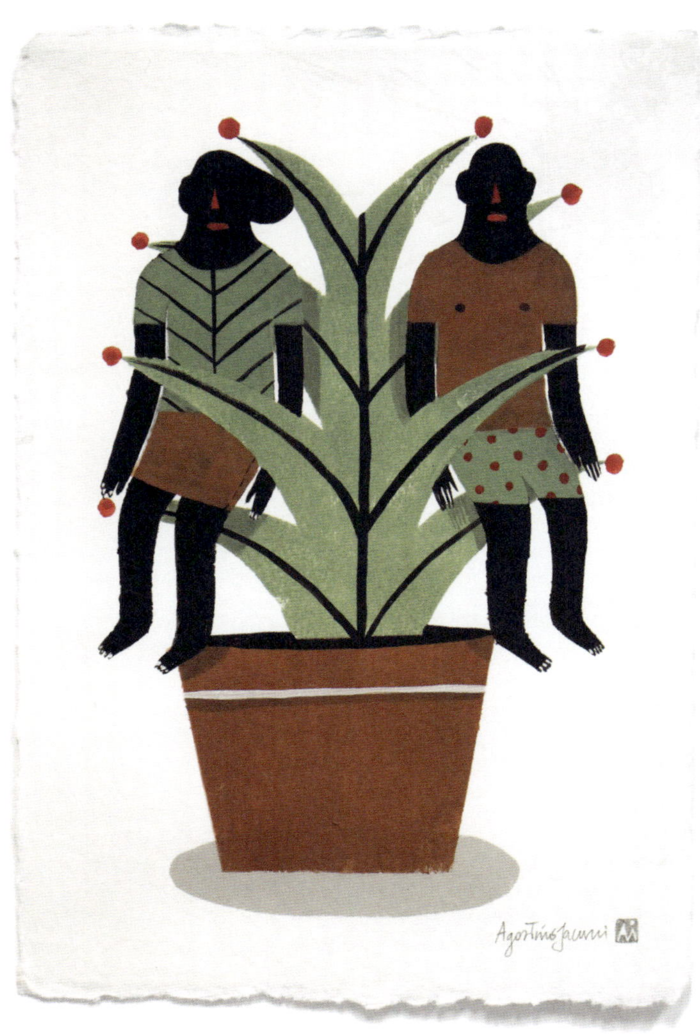
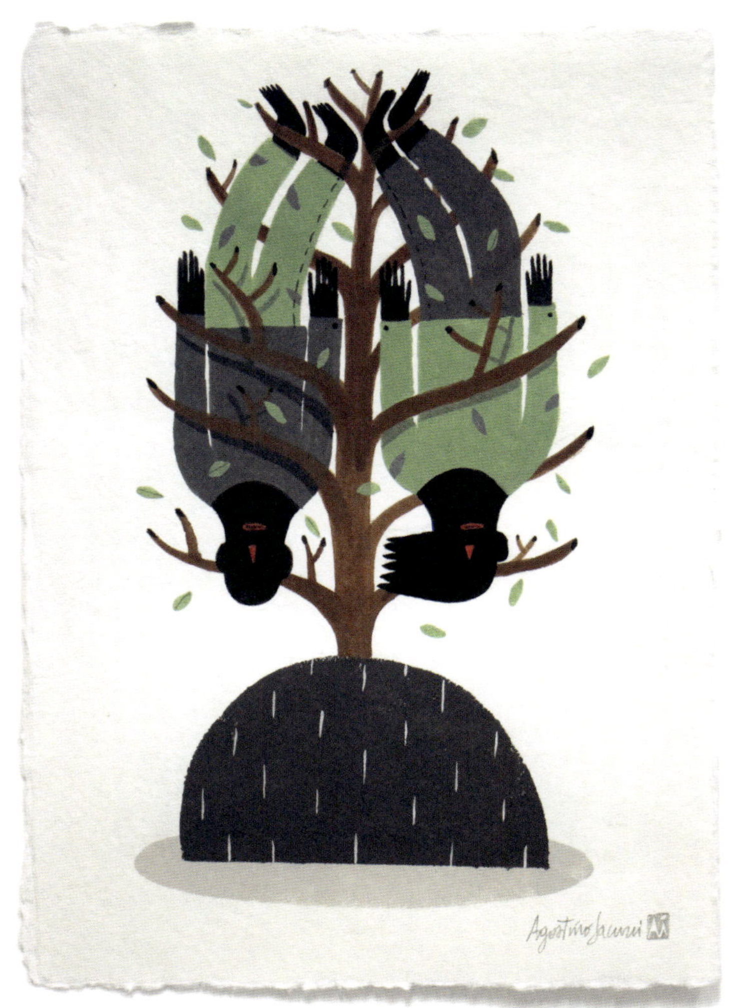
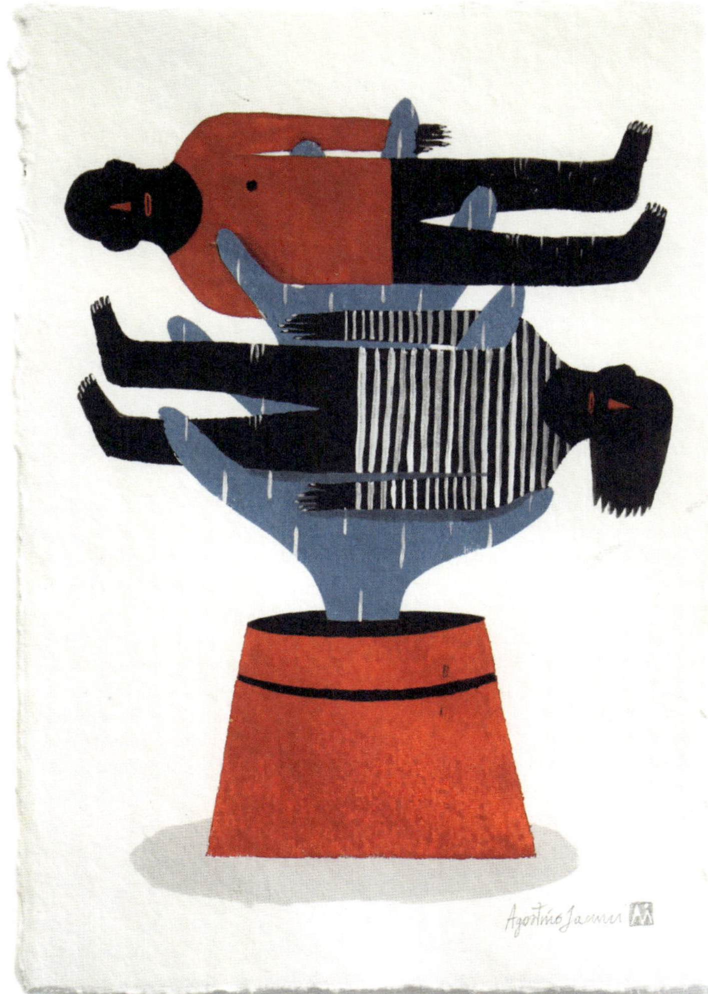
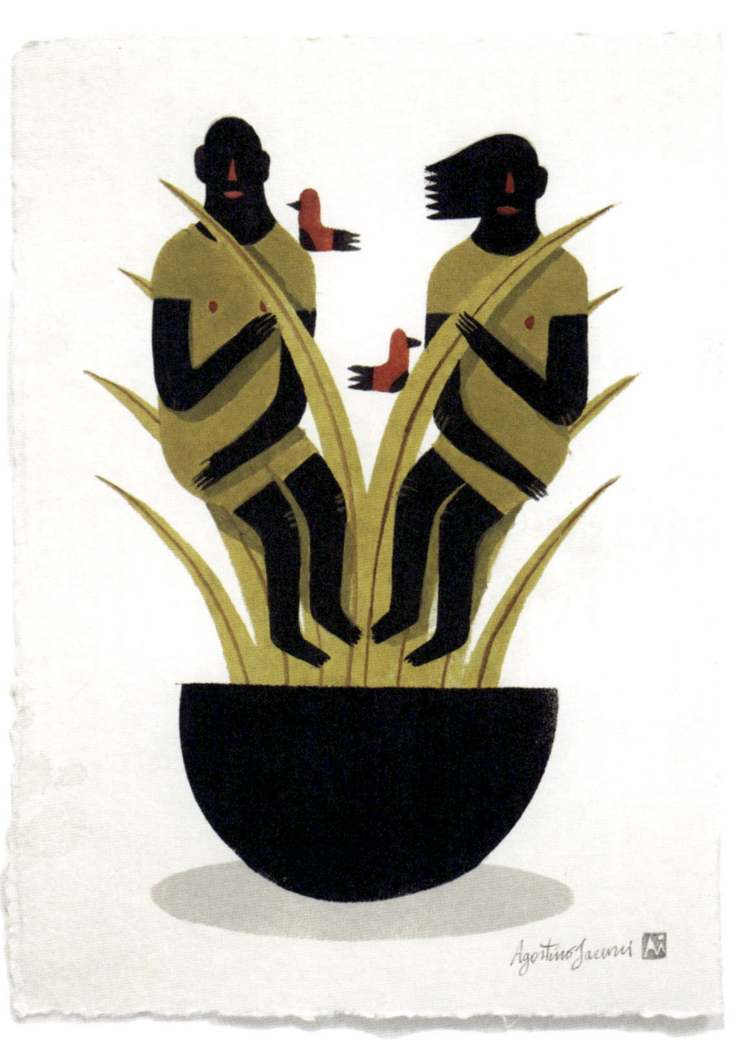

Pastel

Like the pages of a botanist's specimen book writ large – featuring beautifully rendered interpretations of local flora, in a palette that reflects their urban location

— the work of Buenos Aires-based artist/architect Pastel (aka Francisco Diaz) hits you with its scale and intriguing iconography. In his murals he brings together plants, geometric shapes and arrowheads, creating potent symbols of the relationship between man and nature, a subject to which he returns time and again. Rather than being incidental, the location of these works is integral to their meaning, and a reflection upon the connection between nature and architecture. This dialogue between art and the city and the human and the natural world is something that continually fascinates the artist.

Pastel's first foray into painting was through graffiti, and he has been working with this form since 2001. After studying architecture at the University of Buenos Aires (UBA), rather than starting up his own architectural practice, he turned to painting, and in taking up this art form began to see himself as a maker of 'urban acupuncture' – producing pieces that might change how the places in which they are located are perceived. As he explains, 'Modern cities are full of "non-places" because of irregular and non-inclusive master-planning, so painting walls can bring attention to those areas, recovering empty spaces of the city, rather than building over and over.'

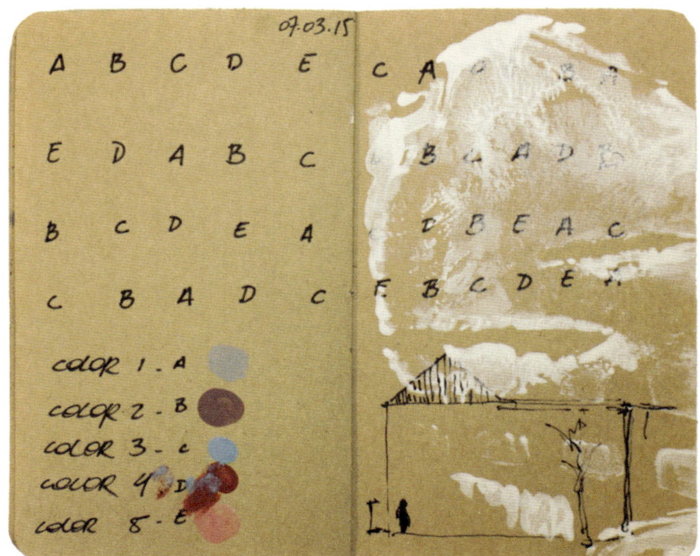

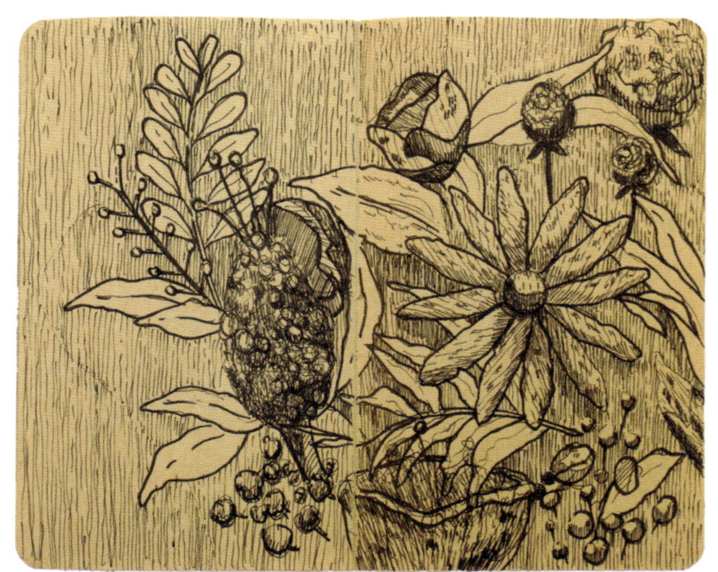

Pages from the artist's sketchbook.

OPPOSITE
Funeral Rib 04, 2014
Ink and gouache on paper
90 × 90 cm (35½ × 35½ in.)

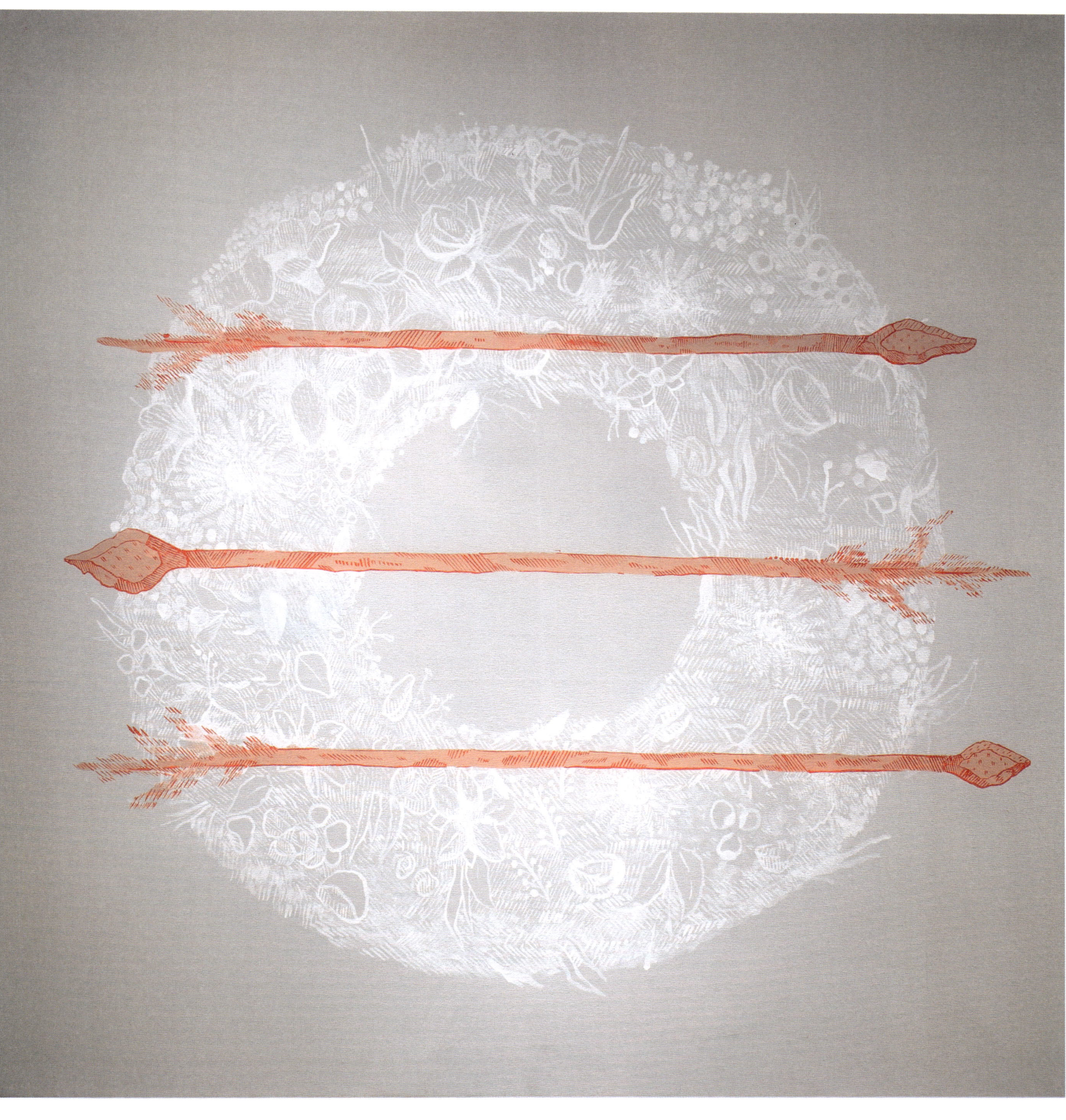

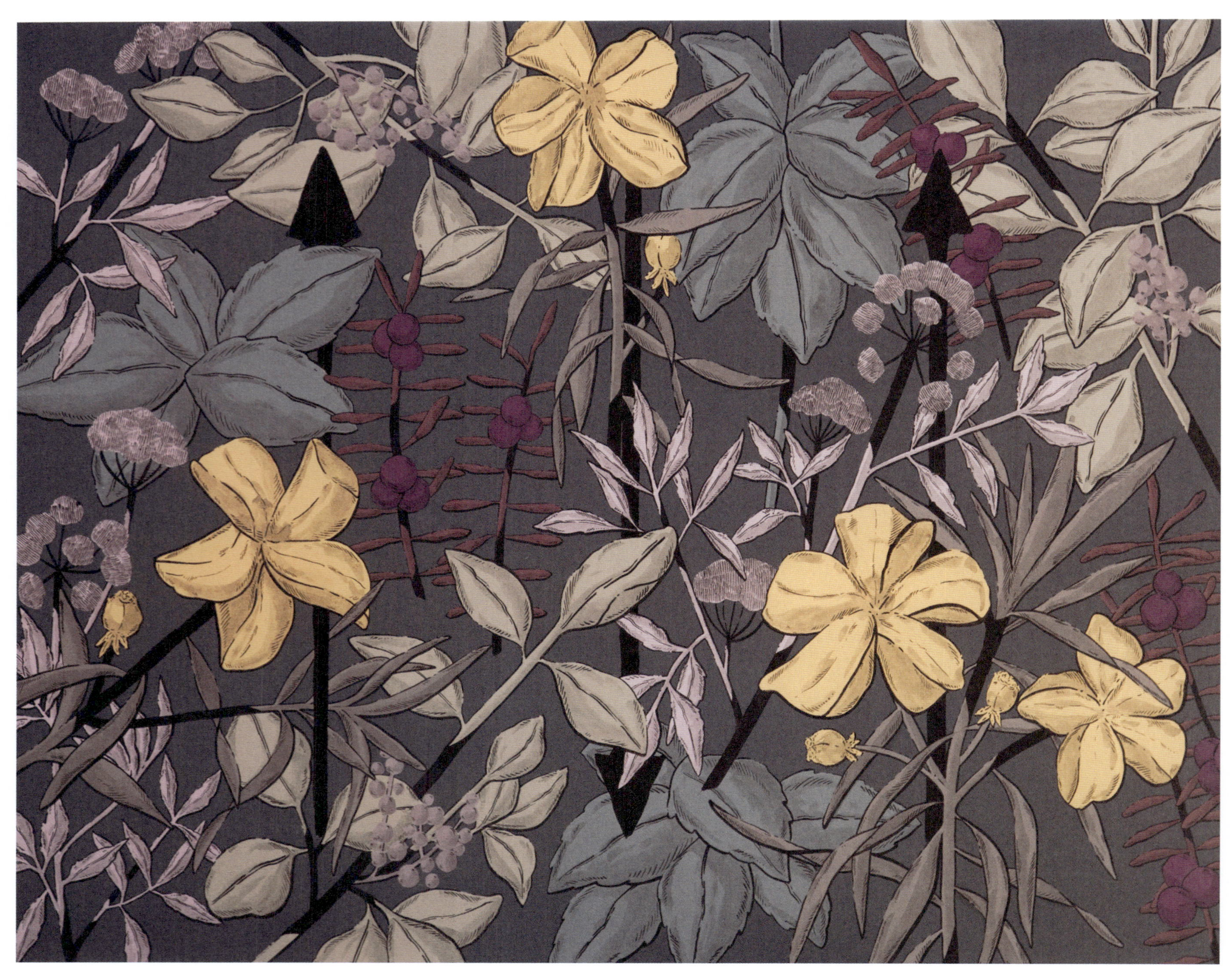

ABOVE AND OPPOSITE
Untitled, from the series
'Lethal Flora', 2015
Acrylic on canvas
70 × 90 cm
(27⅝ × 35½ in.) each

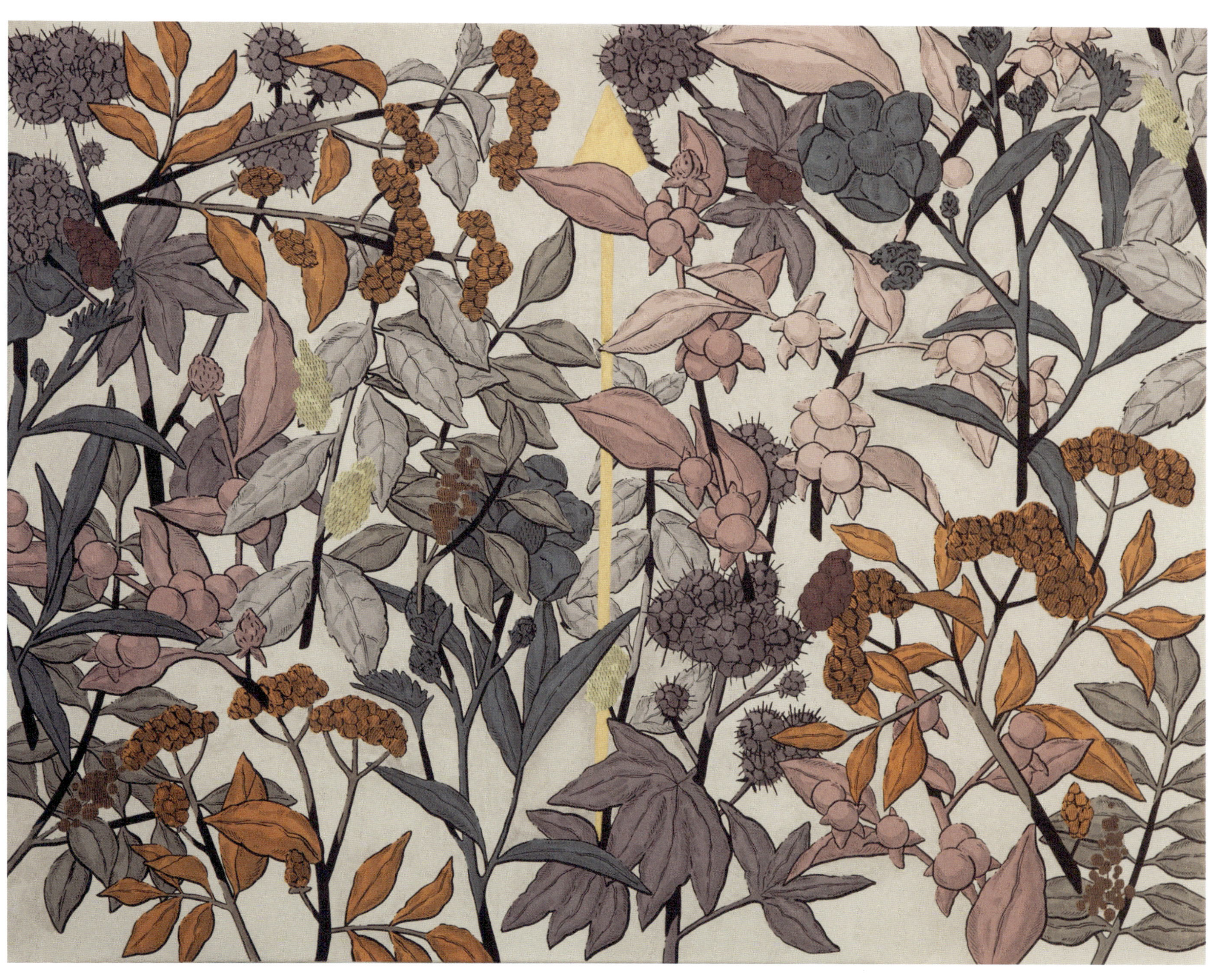

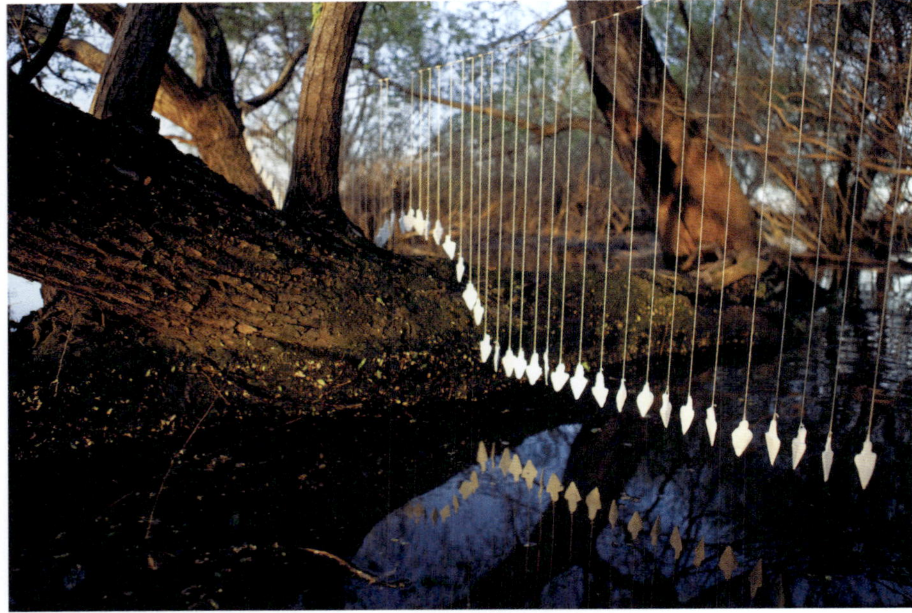

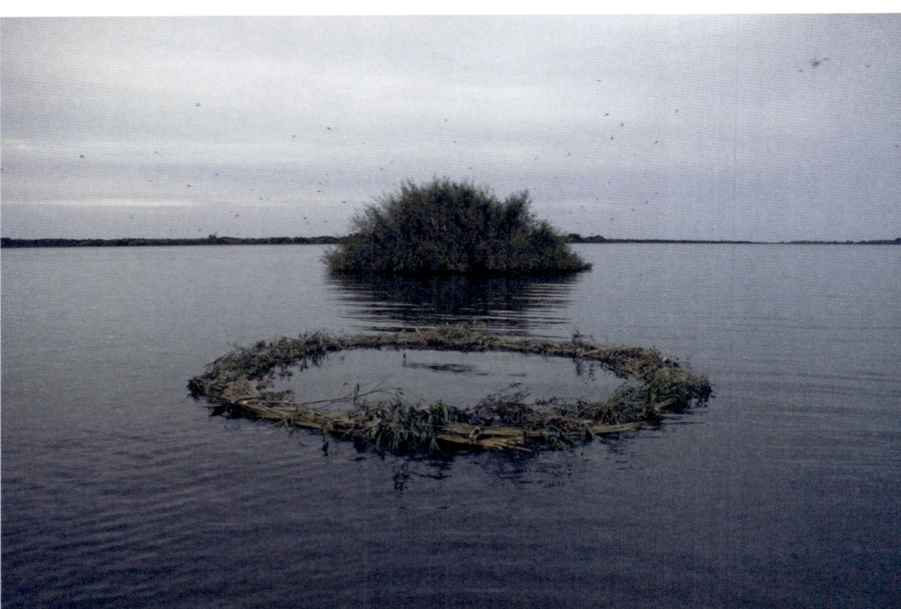

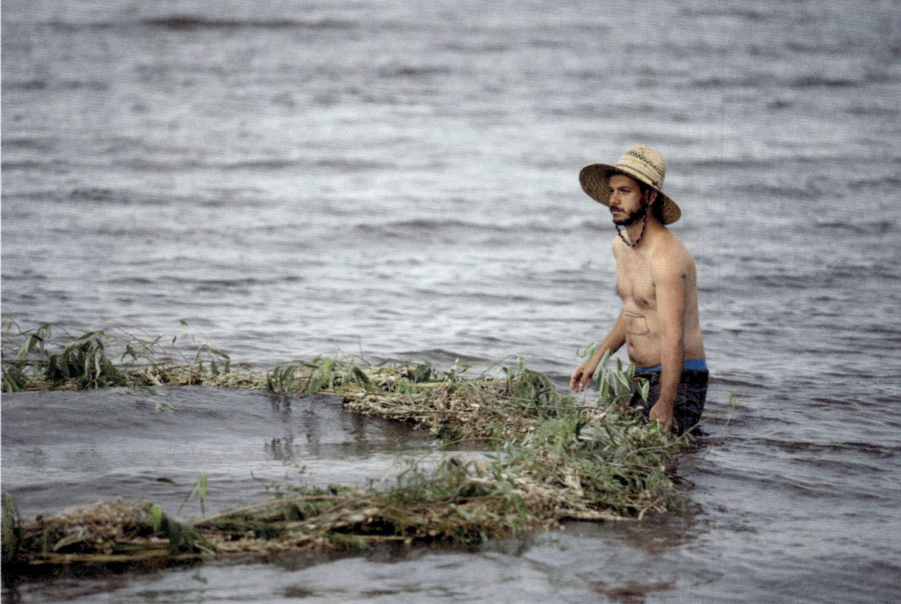

Untitled, site-specific
work commissioned by the
Ka'aguy Retã Project in Villa
Soriano, Uruguay, 2014
Mixed media
Dimensions variable

Eternal Over Ephemeral,
site-specific work in Villa
Soriano, Uruguay, 2015
Mixed media
Dimensions variable

Eternal Over Ephemeral
in progress.

OPPOSITE, CLOCKWISE FROM
TOP LEFT
Untitled, mural
commissioned by the
Festival de Murales de
La Escocesa, Barcelona,
Spain, 2014
Mixed media
Dimensions variable

*Idealism of Aboriginal
Ngarluma*, mural
commissioned by the
PUBLIC festival, Perth, 2015
Mixed media
Dimensions unknown

Untitled, mural
commissioned by the
Residencia Vatelón cultural
centre, as part of the
Ka'aguy Retã Project
Mixed media
Dimensions variable

Not Now, mural in Memorie
Urbane, Gaeta, Italy, 2015
Mixed media
Dimensions variable

Caoba Maguá, mural in
Rio San Juan, Dominican
Republic, 2014
Mixed media
Dimensions variable

Pastel's public art, which can be found the world
over, including Spain, Italy, Poland, Australia and
Argentina, may be specific to its location but the
symbolism embedded within is global in its reach.
So, while the flora he paints may be indigenous to the
location of the work, or there may be other references
to local histories or geographies, the overarching
message is that architecture should not impose order
upon or limit the environment in which it is located,
but rather that it should enable social patterns of
behaviour to develop naturally, as organic forms might.
Pastel hopes to change our perceptions of urban
life, wherever we might be: 'There is no difference
between nature and human nature. There is only one
history, and our chaos is based on humans trying to
differentiate those terms. Working with nature and
stone-age tools to glorify humanity's strength without
referencing a specific culture is my way of drawing
attention to it.'

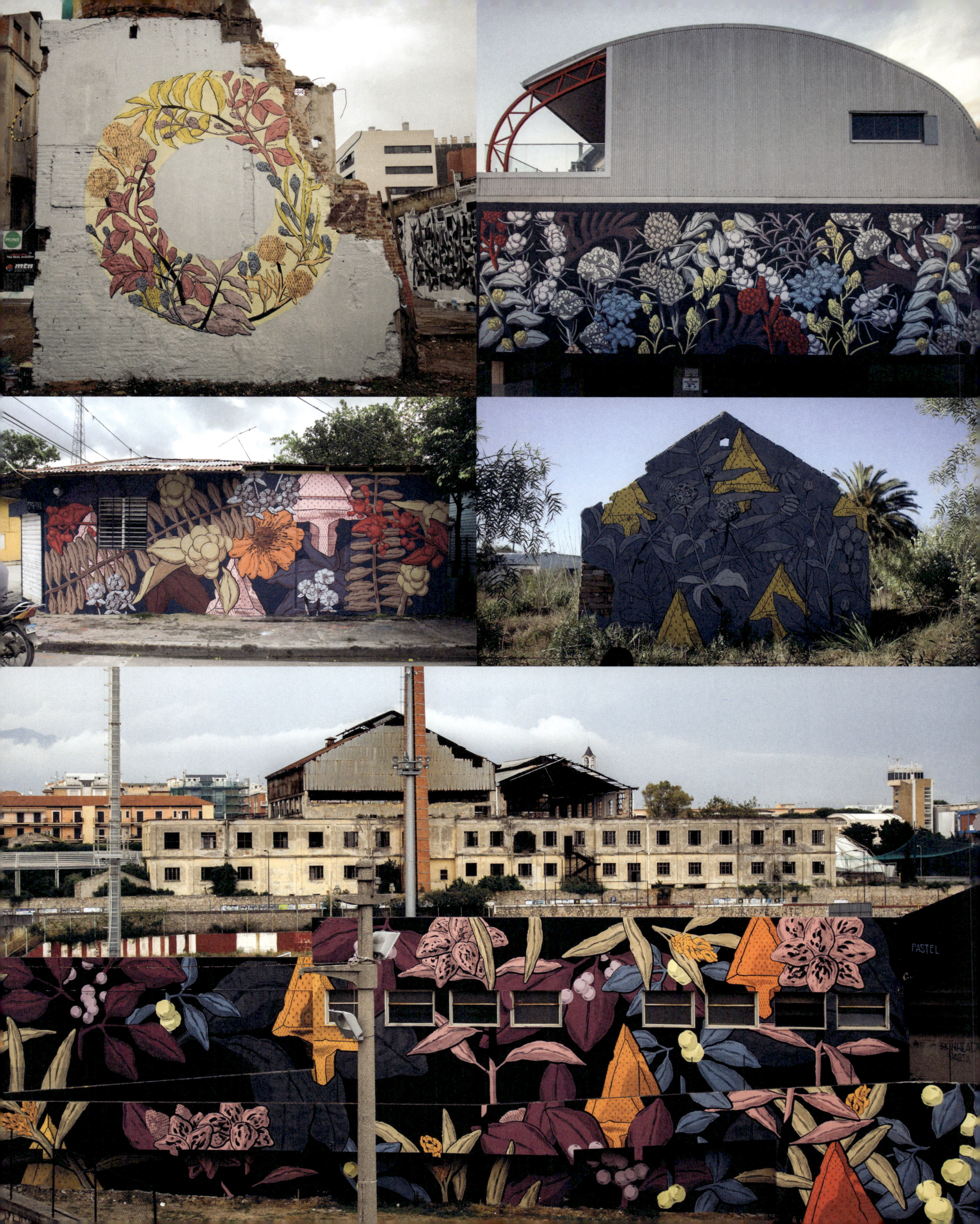

Pejac
Tackling the hard truths of subjects such as extinction and the degradation of the planet

without being radical or 'preachy', the subtle and imaginative work of the Spanish artist Pejac manages to distil a critical vision of the world in powerful and thought-provoking ways. Employing a monochromatic palette and deceptively simple concepts, he cuts to the bone of often heartbreaking issues. In the elegant watercolour *Gulliver* (see page 8), for example, he depicts a single wilted rose, standing like a flag at half mast, staked out with ropes as if by Lilliputians – a sadly pertinent metaphor for the human race's penchant for enchaining nature.

In his murals, which can be found in London, Paris, Milan, Istanbul and Moscow, and in his studio work, Pejac deals with seemingly straightforward subject-matter – landscape, nature, people and animals – but subtly changes its form through illusion and inconceivable juxtapositions. In his studio work he professes to be meticulous and obsessive in his approach, creating pieces that often draw on personal experiences and dreams. His street works show similarly exacting standards, hand painted in a wonderfully convincing *trompe l'oeil* style. These are the result of very particular

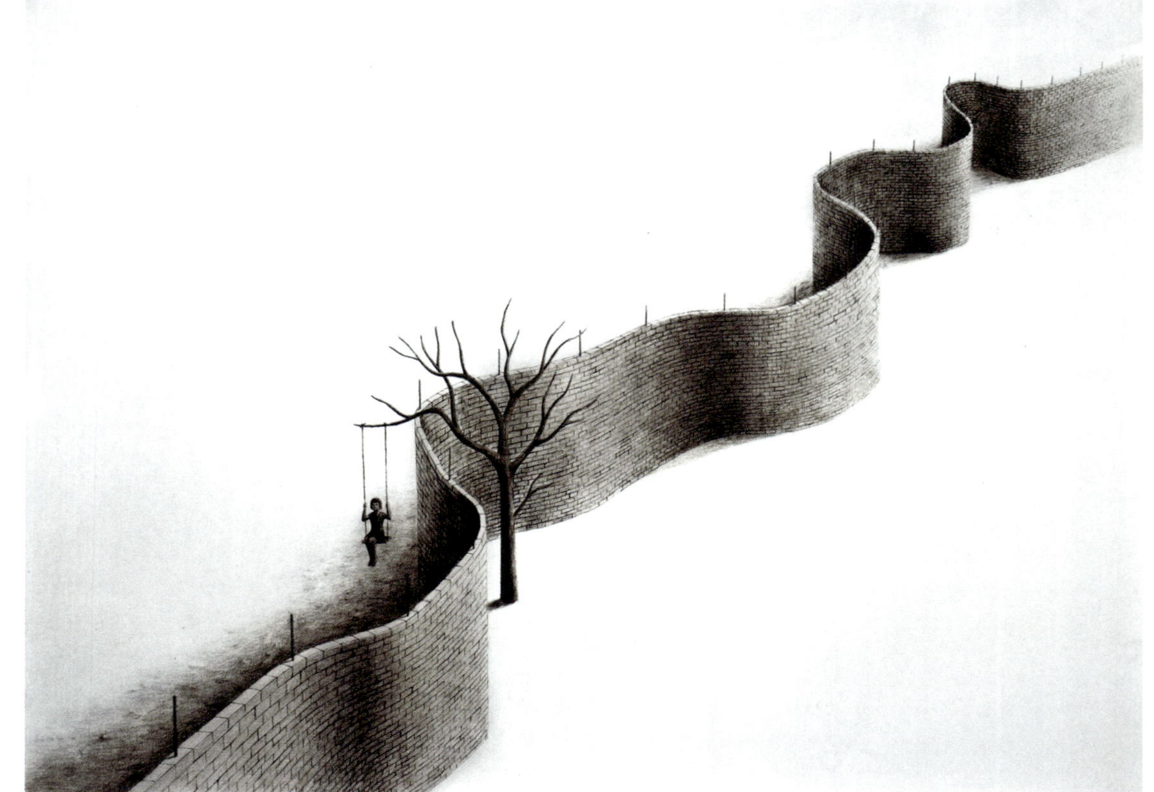

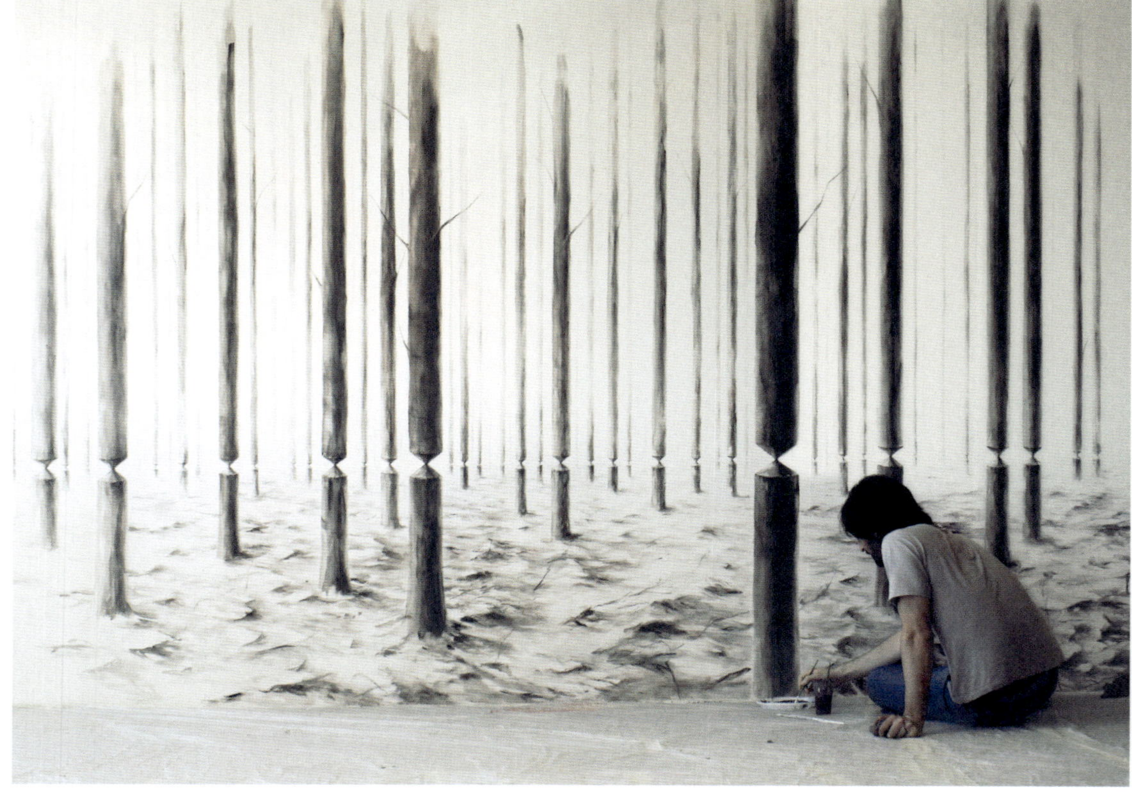

Icarus, wall-based work in Seoul, South Korea, 2015
Mixed media
Dimensions variable

Extramuros, 2012
Charcoal and pencil
on paper
Dimensions unknown

My Only Flag, 2013
Watercolour on paper
70 × 100 cm
(27⅝ × 39⅜ in.)

New Order, wall-based
work in El Astillero,
Spain, *c.* 2013
Mixed media
Dimensions variable

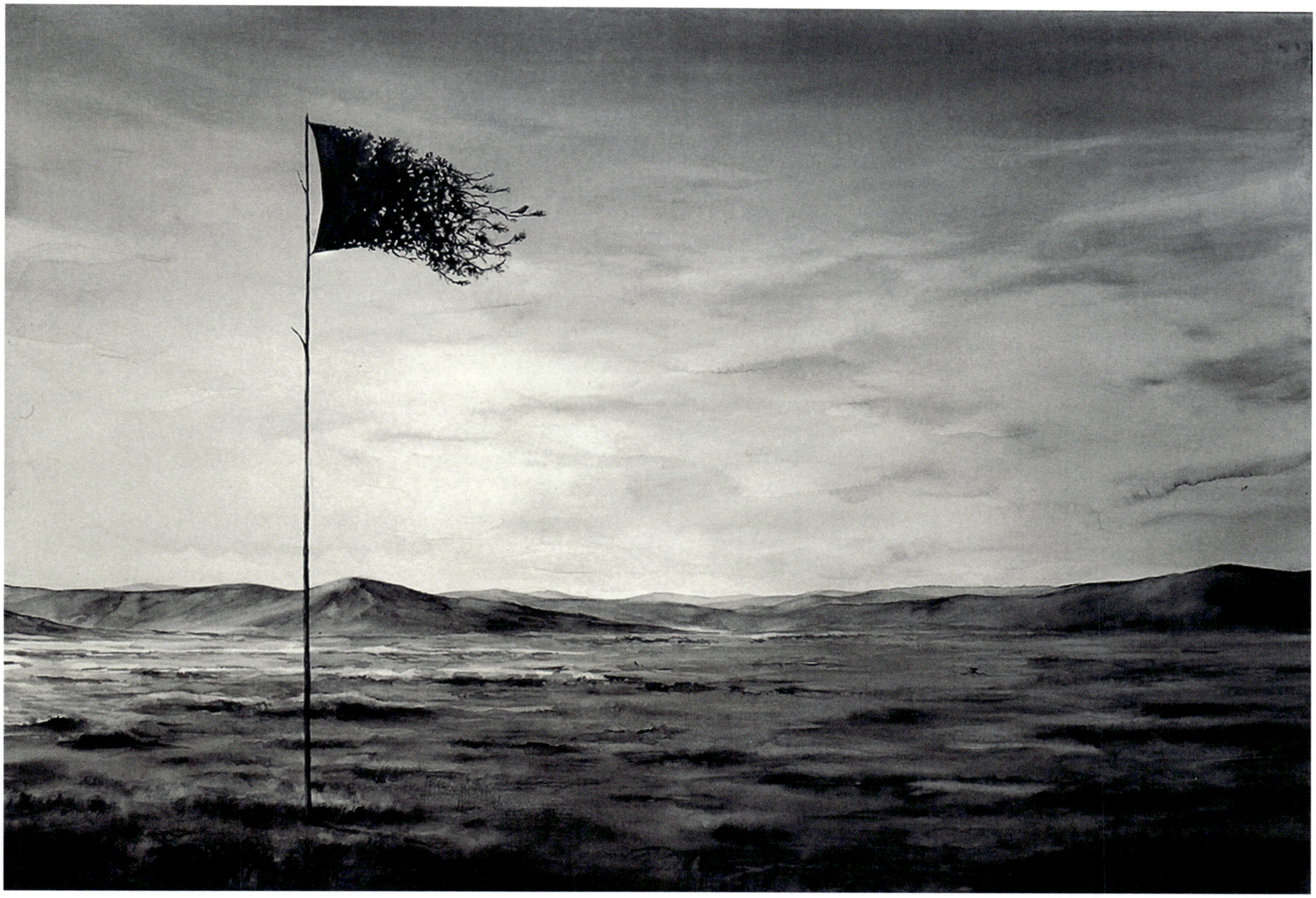

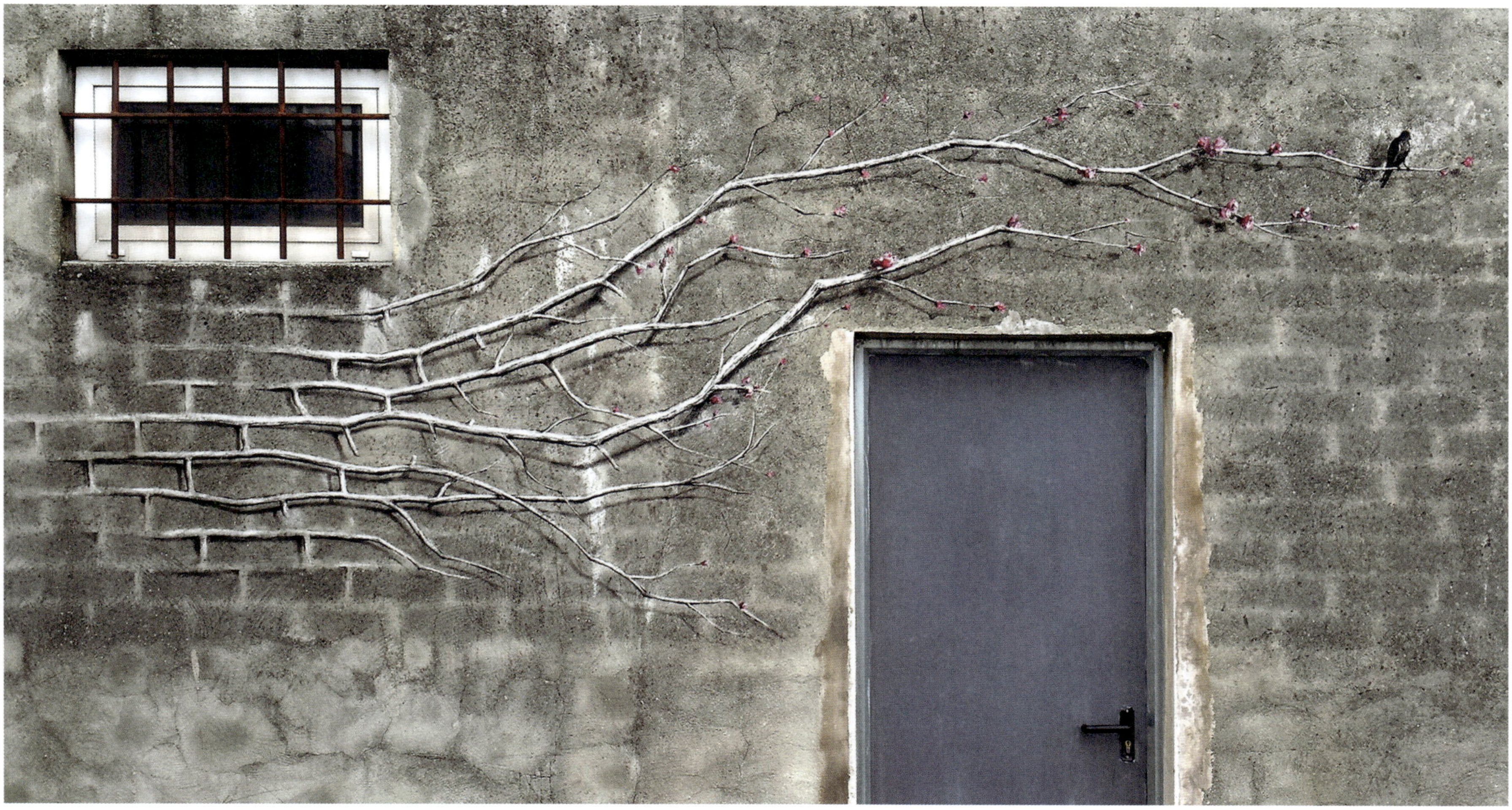

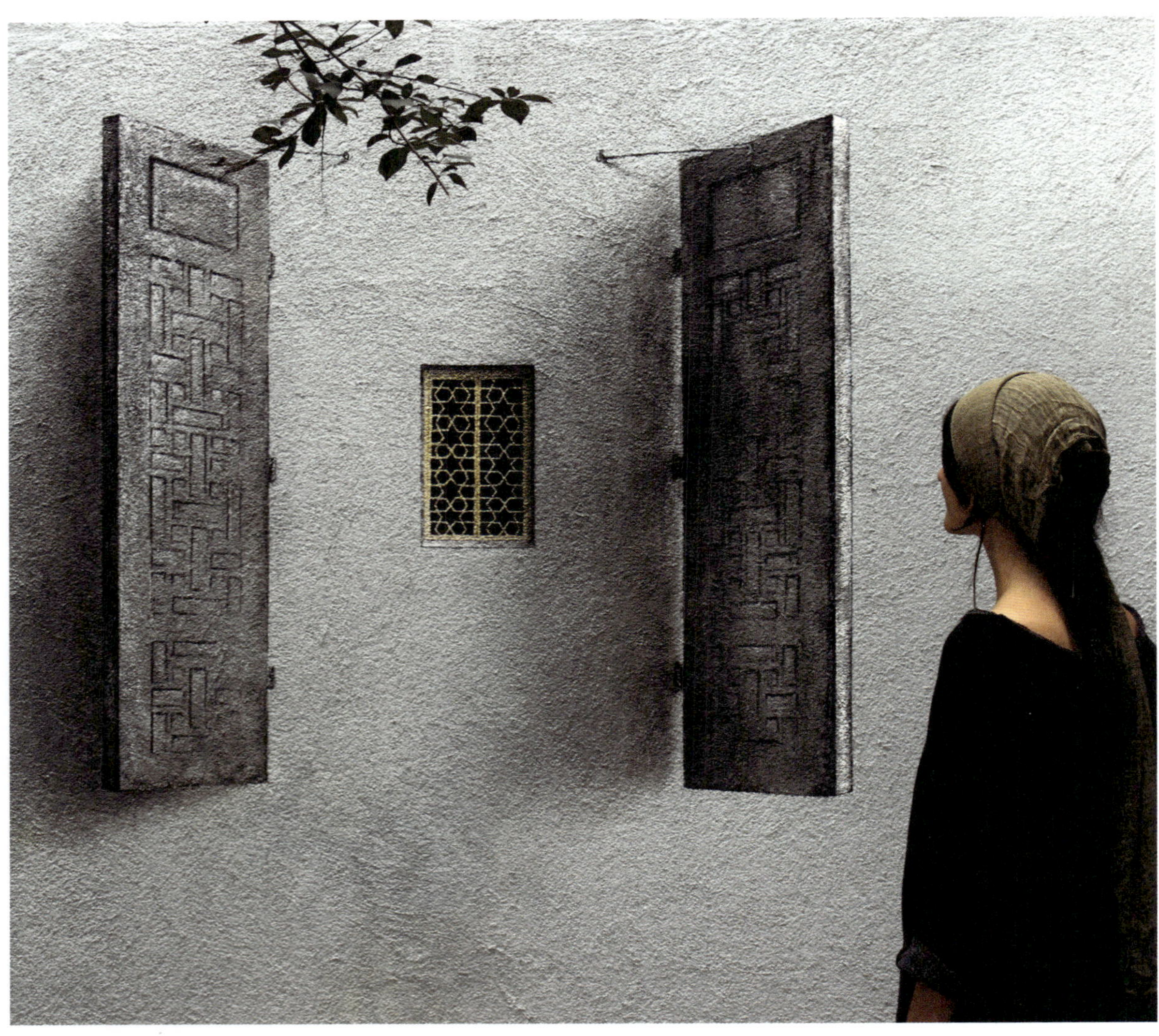

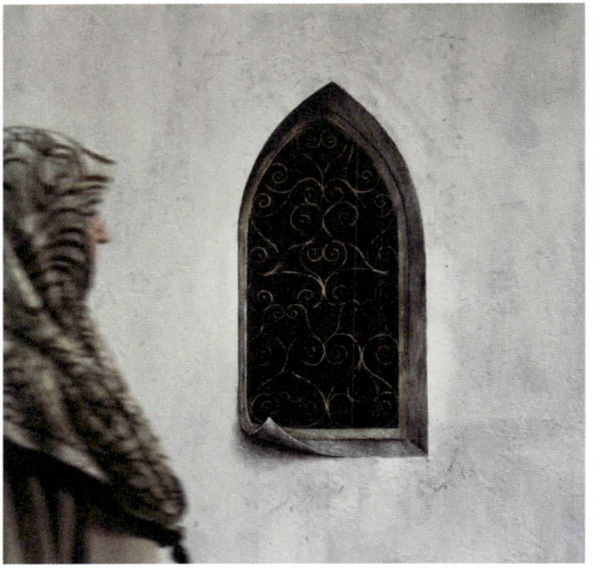

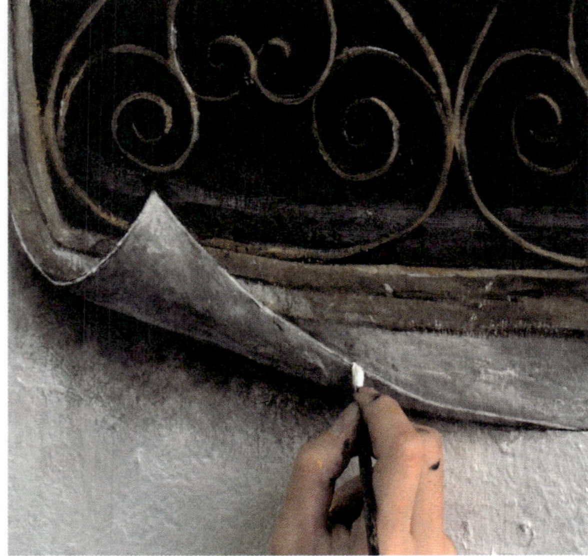

CLOCKWISE FROM TOP
Shutters, wall-based work
in Üsküdar, Istanbul, 2014
Mixed media
Dimensions variable

Poster, and detail, wall-based
work in Istanbul, *c.* 2014
Mixed media
Dimensions variable

OPPOSITE, TOP
Mainmast, site-specific work in
Seoul, South Korea, 2015
Acrylic on glass
Dimensions variable

OPPOSITE, CENTRE
Tagger, wall-based work in Sheung
Wan, Hong Kong, 2015
Mixed media
Dimensions variable

OPPOSITE, BOTTOM
Everyone is an Artist, and detail,
wall-based work in Tokyo, 2015
Mixed media
Dimensions variable

research and planning in relation to their context, as the artist stresses: 'A wall is not a canvas, it's a place with its own identity and moreover surrounded by living history. When I travel to other countries to paint in the streets, I try to inform myself the best I can about their past and present. Once there, when I live among the people and get the feel of their culture, the ideas I came with very often no longer make sense and I have to design new pieces better suited to the reality of the area.'

One of the artist's motivations is to recreate the magic that drawing held for him as a child, while also taking a critical stance in his choice of subject-matter. He is not concerned so much with style or coherence, and while his work is distinctive and identifiable, he attempts not to let this dictate his output or affect his experimental approach. Summing up the driving force behind his creations he says, 'I enjoy thinking that my works would make somebody feel and reflect at once. It would be quite an achievement for me.'

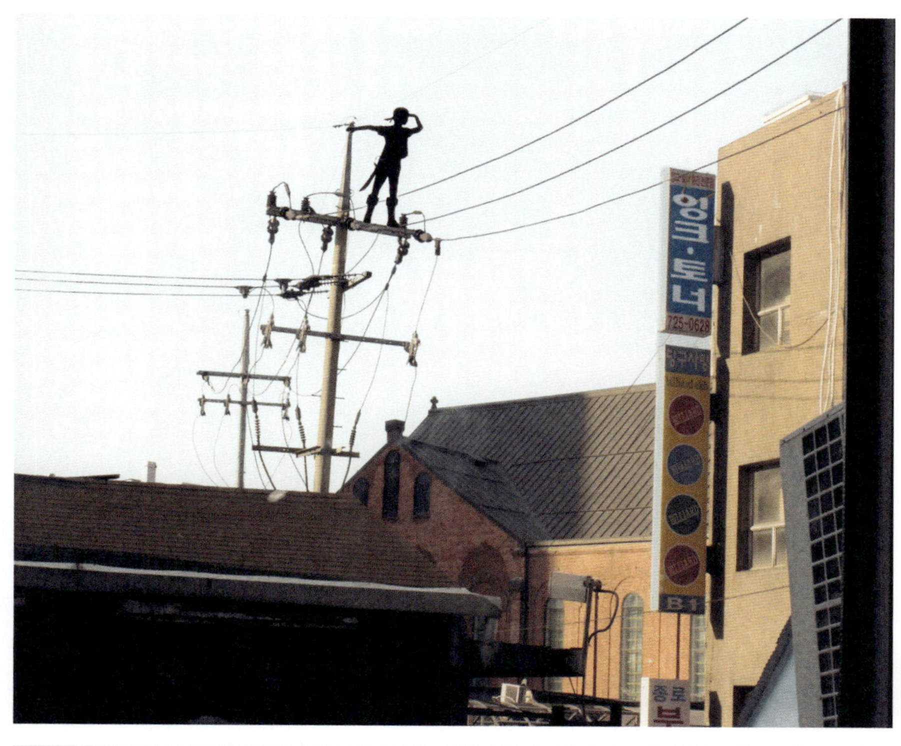
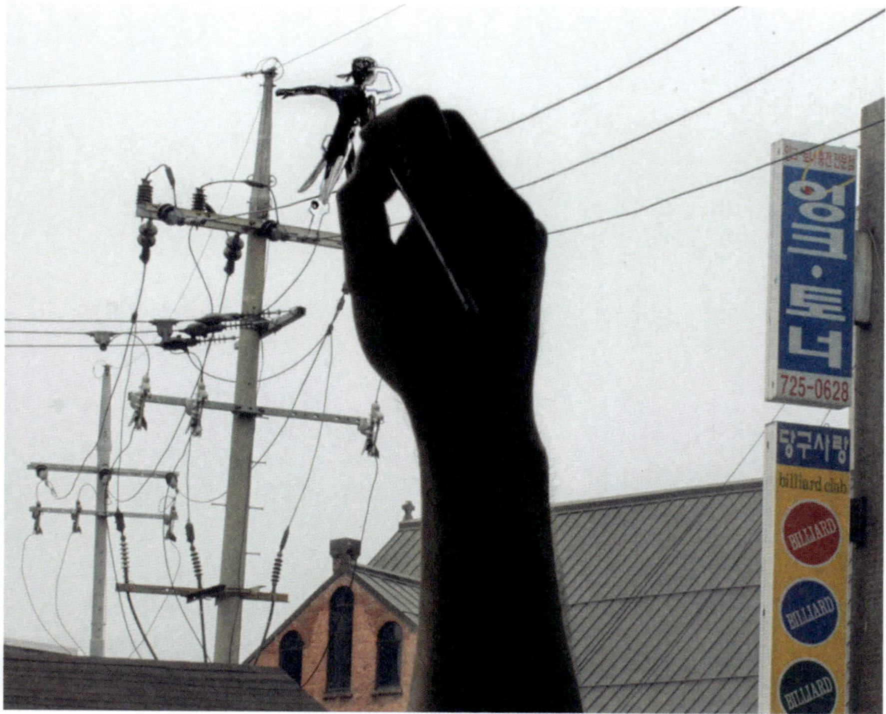
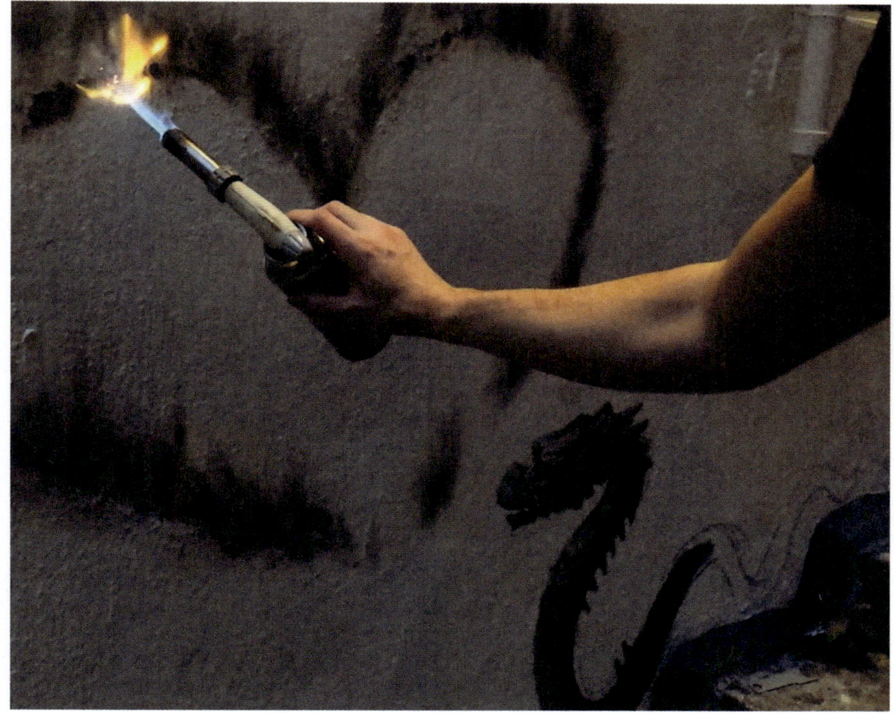
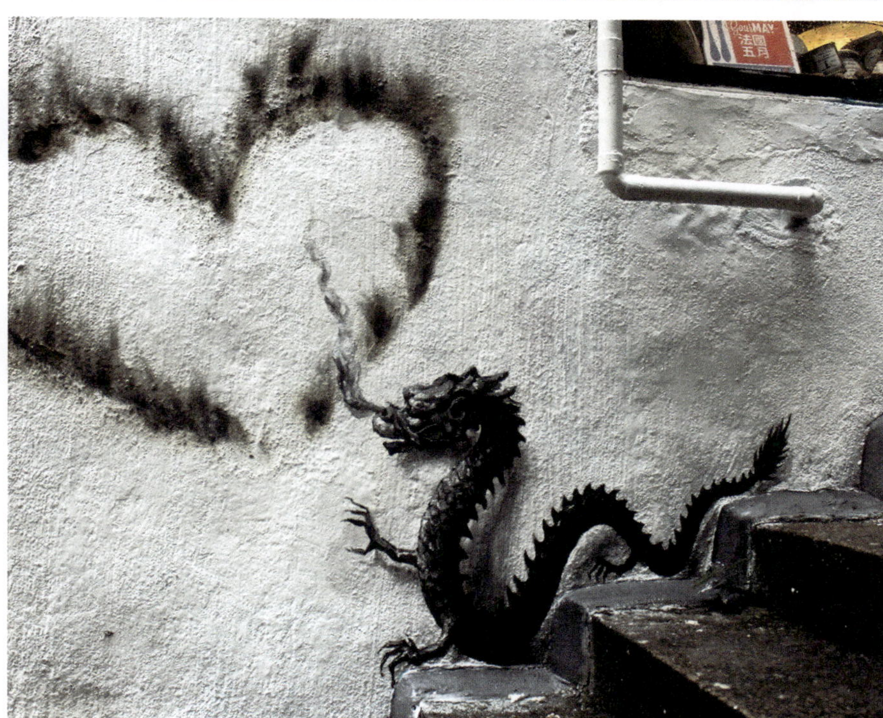
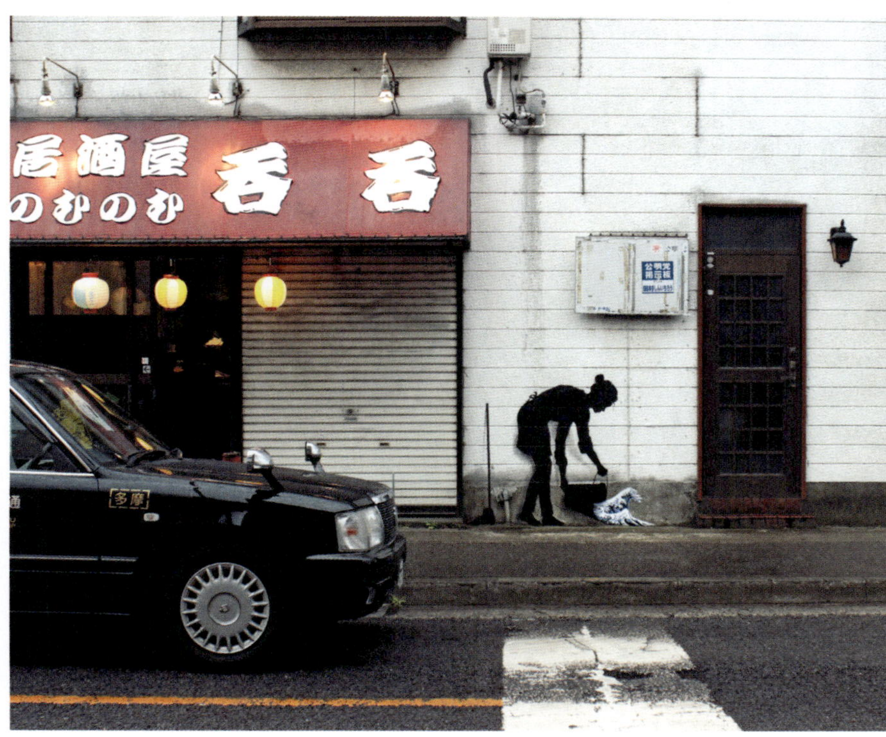
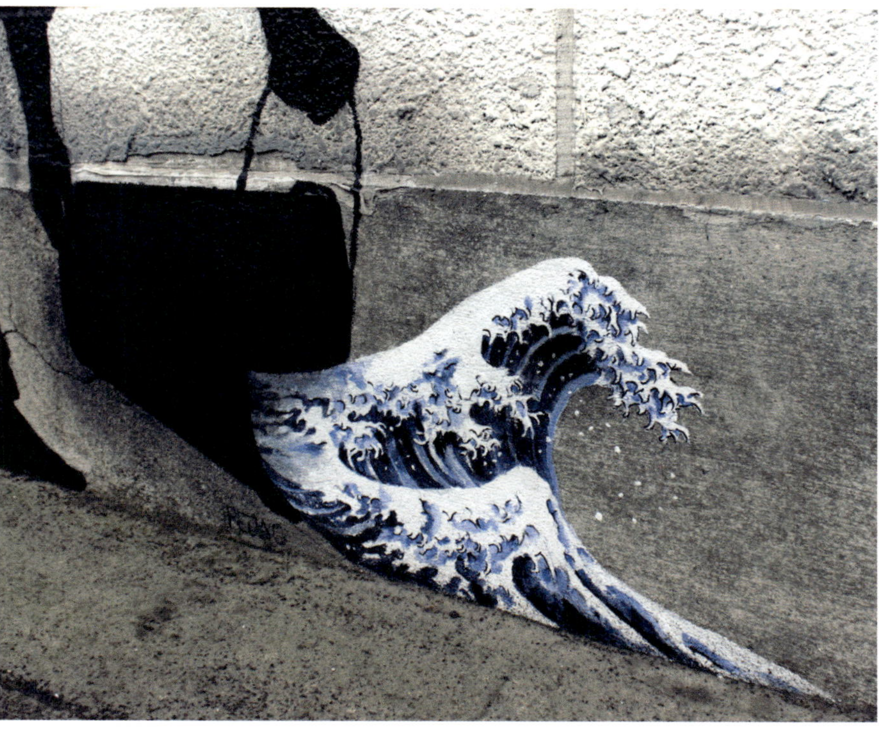

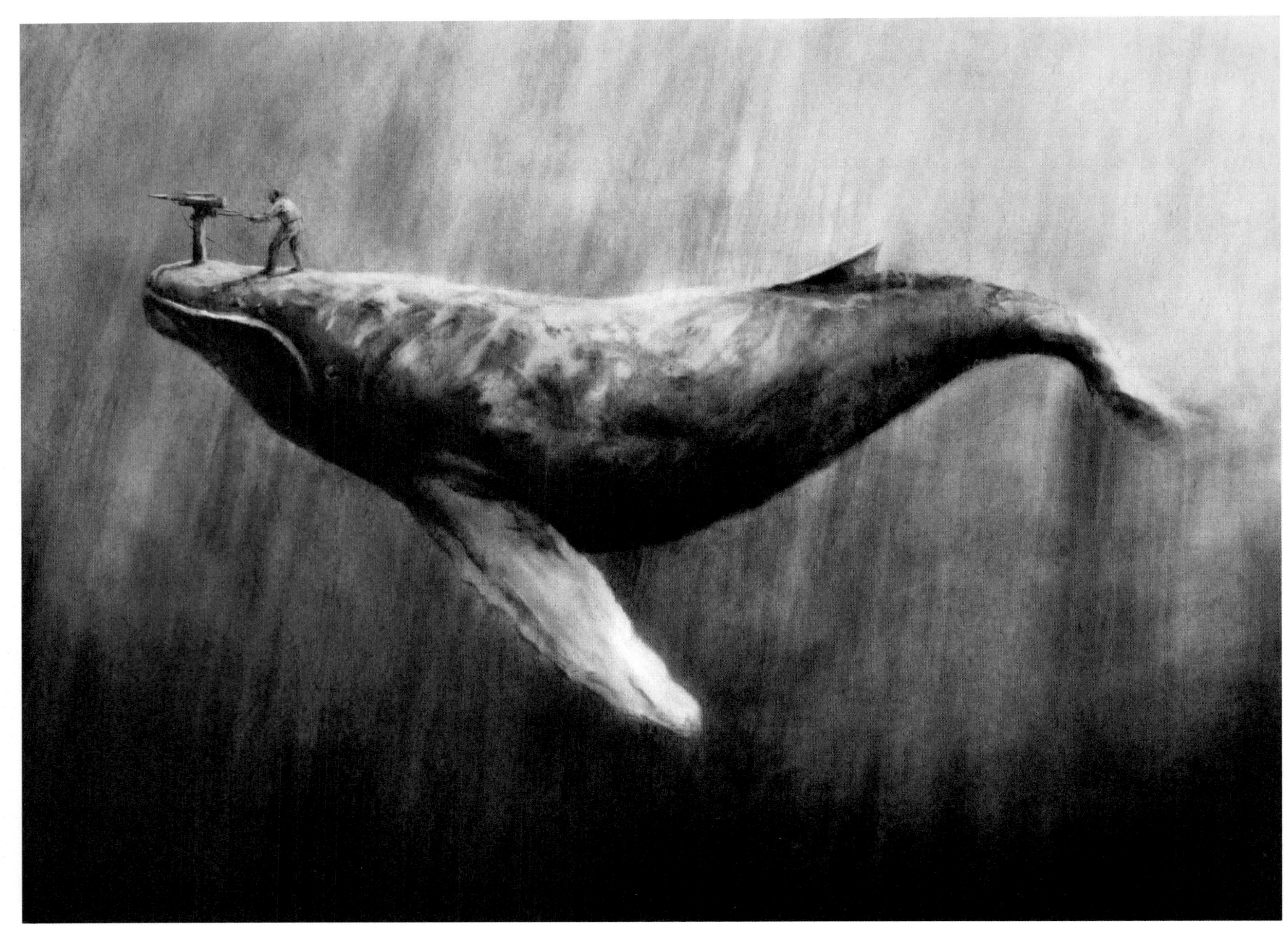

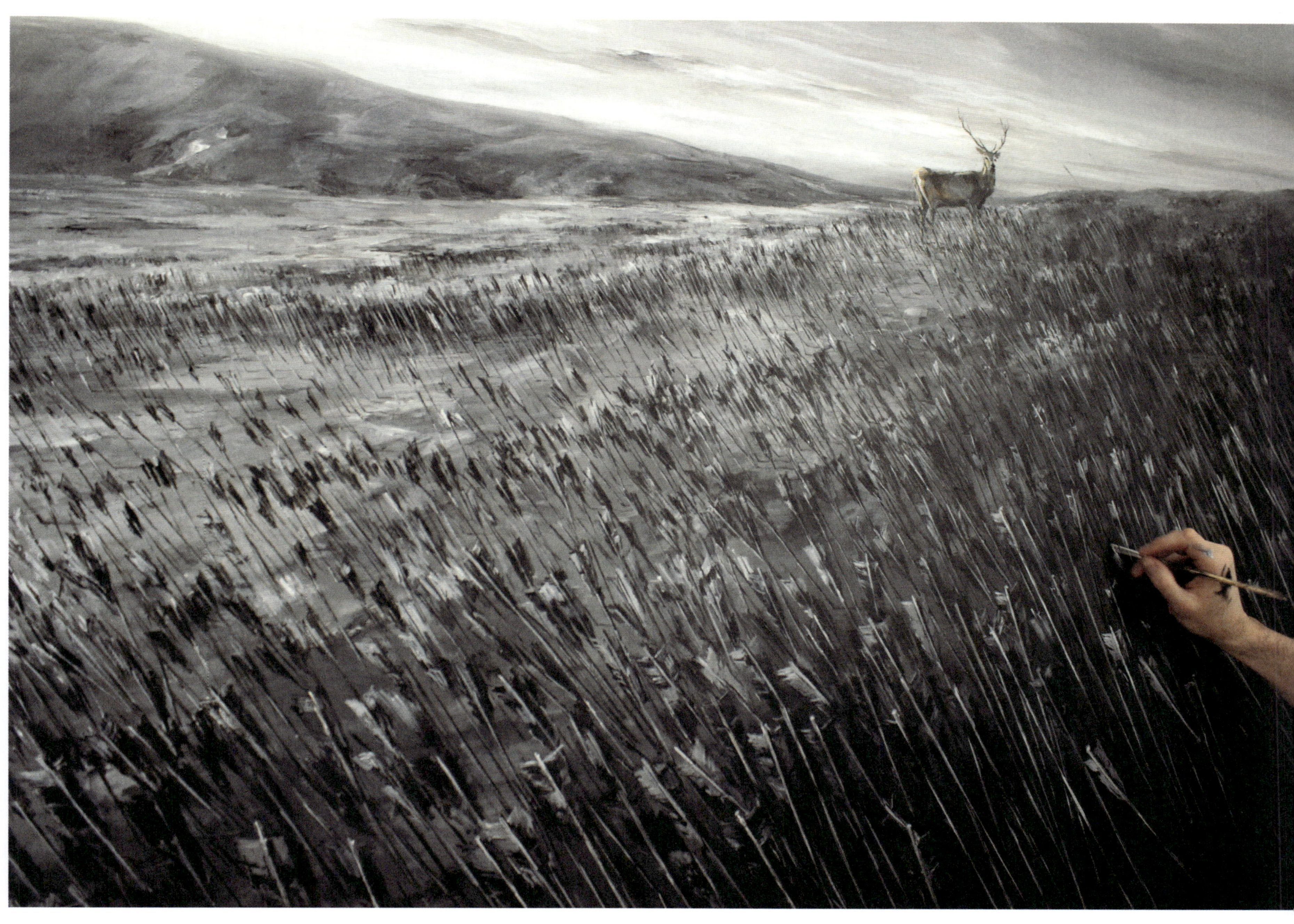

João Ruas

Creating ethereal works that seem to transcend time and place,

São Paulo-based artist João Ruas's work is reminiscent perhaps of the chalk drawings of Leonardo da Vinci (1452–1519) or the watercolour and ink illustrations of the Victorian book illustrator Arthur Rackham (1867–1939), in terms of its subtle colour palette. His paintings and drawings conjure up dreamscapes that are both Neoclassical and fantastically futuristic in style. In his work he fuses together real and imagined histories, as well as Eastern and Western mythologies, motifs and symbols, to create a timeless and universal history of his own.

Ruas has been interested in drawing since he was a child, due to his exposure to countless comic books, one example of which was *Turma da Monica* ('Monica's Gang'), a popular Brazilian series that has run since the 1960s. It was the personalities and power of imagination that this art form conveyed to which he was most attracted. Later, on discovering Spiderman, he became addicted to the genre.

Having trained as a designer he has worked in many studios, including a three-year stint in London, producing all manner of projects, from comic books to films and advertising campaigns, however, today he

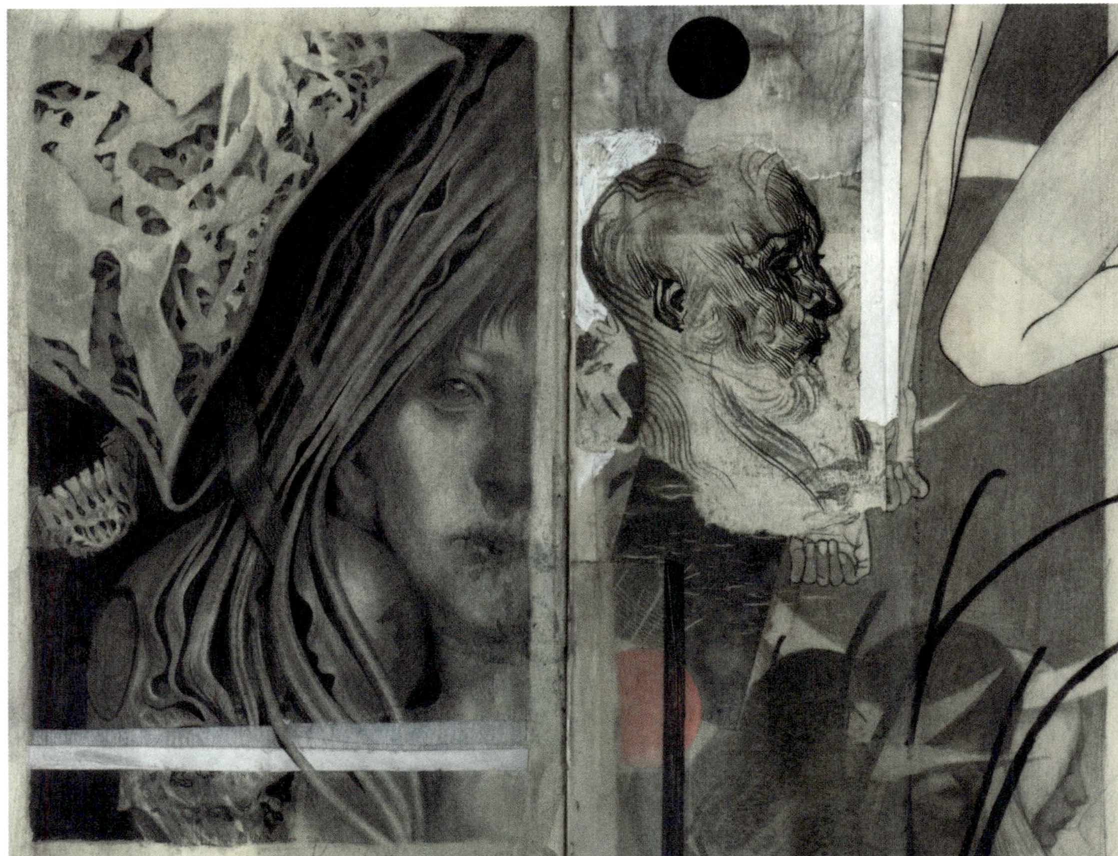

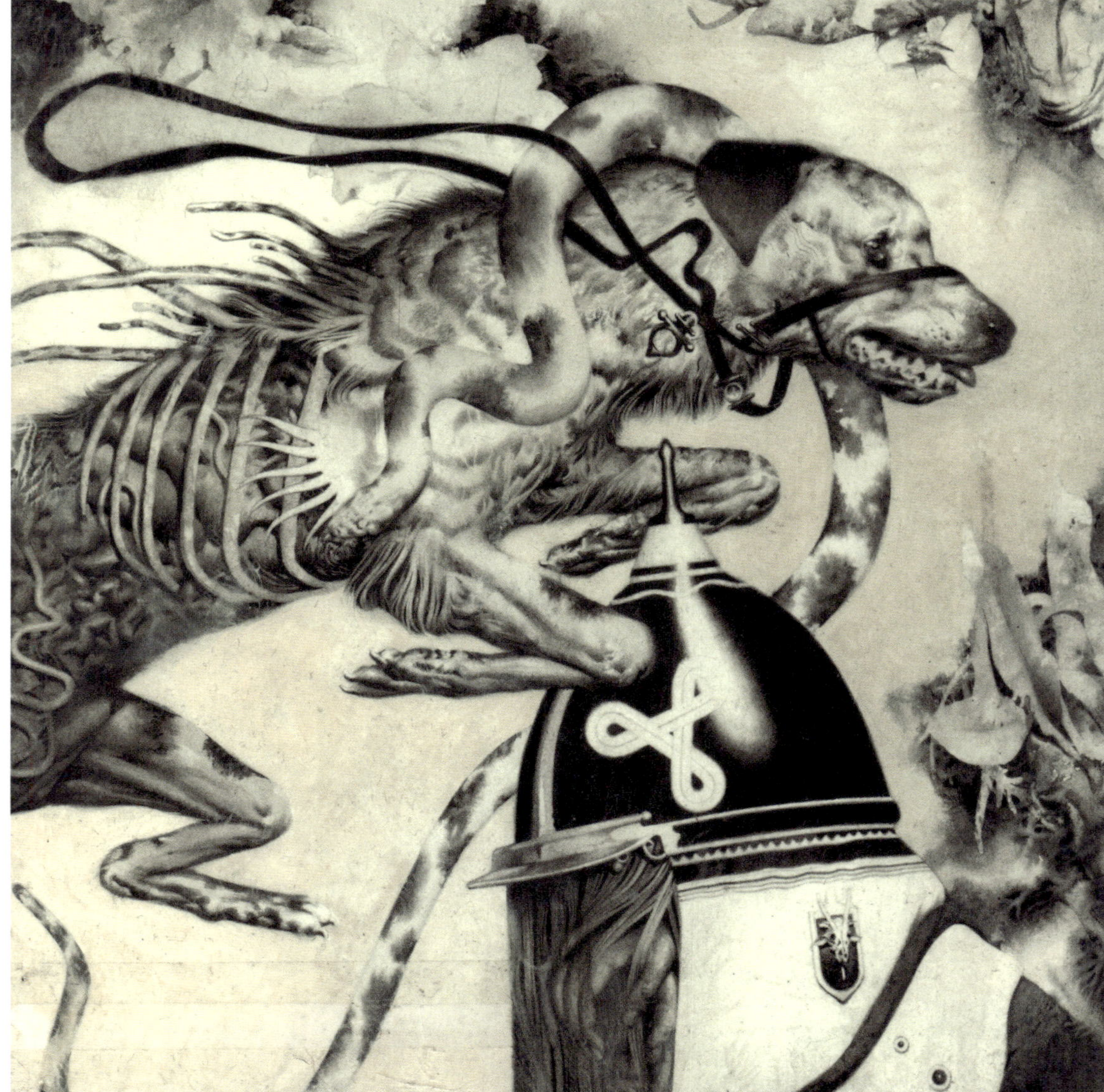

Untitled, c. 2013
Acrylic on Fabriano
and wood
Dimensions unknown

Running Dog, 2015
Acrylic on Fabriano
and wood
31 × 31 cm
(12¼ × 12¼ in.)

OPPOSITE
Harakiri, 2013
Acrylic on Fabriano
and board
53 × 42 cm
(20⅞ × 16⅝ in.)

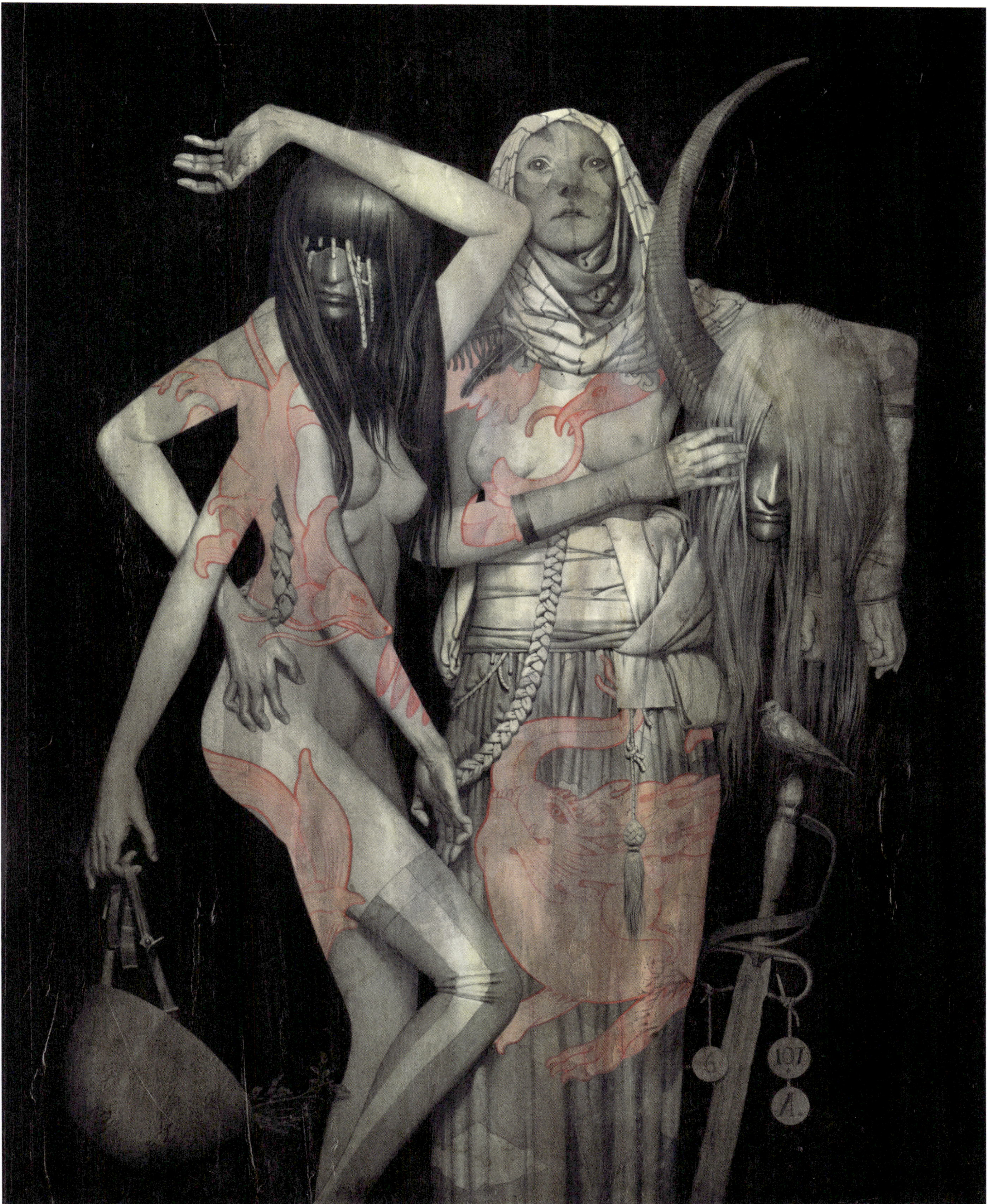

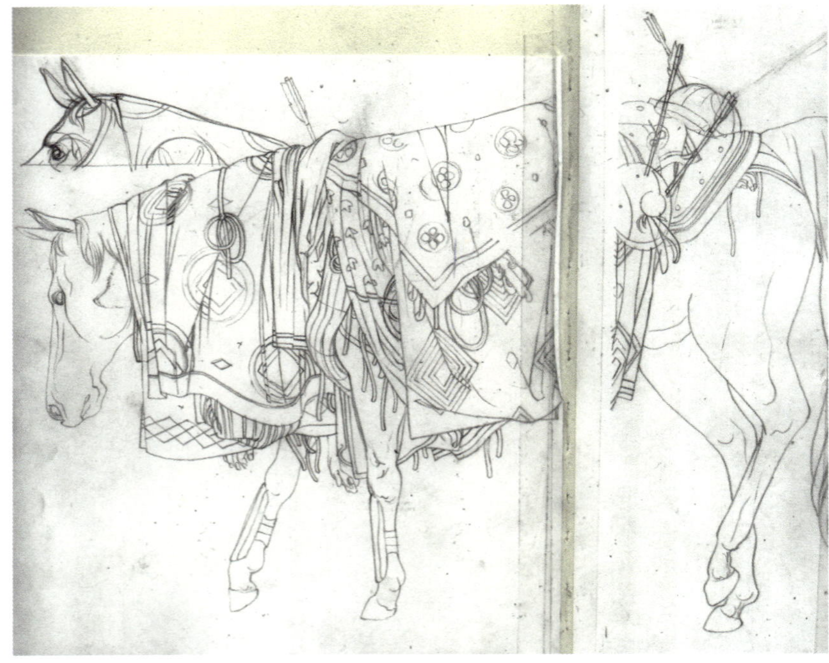

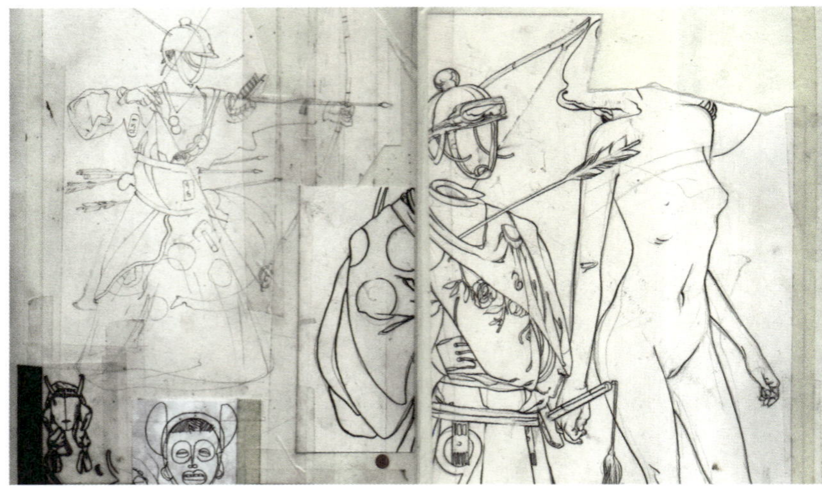

primarily makes artworks, which he exhibits in locations across the globe, including Germany, Italy, Spain, the US and China. As his style has developed he has become an intense consumer of images of all kinds, from Japanese woodblock prints to the work of European comic artists such as Moebius (1838–2012).

Of the techniques he deploys in his art – building up the colour in his compositions from light to dark with water-based media – he says, it is 'a really unforgiving process, and sometimes tense, but I do love that feeling of always being next to the cliff because it gives a fragile quality to the work that I couldn't find doing anything else. I am also really fond of using different pieces of paper or drawings on the same work, I like how it breaks the composition and feels a bit like sampling myself.'

Study for Godiva, 2013
Pencil on paper
Dimensions unknown

Pages from the artist's
sketchbook, *c.* 2013
Pencil on paper
Dimensions unknown

OPPOSITE
Godiva, 2013
Acrylic on Fabriano
and wood
64 × 74 cm
(25¼ × 29⅛ in.)

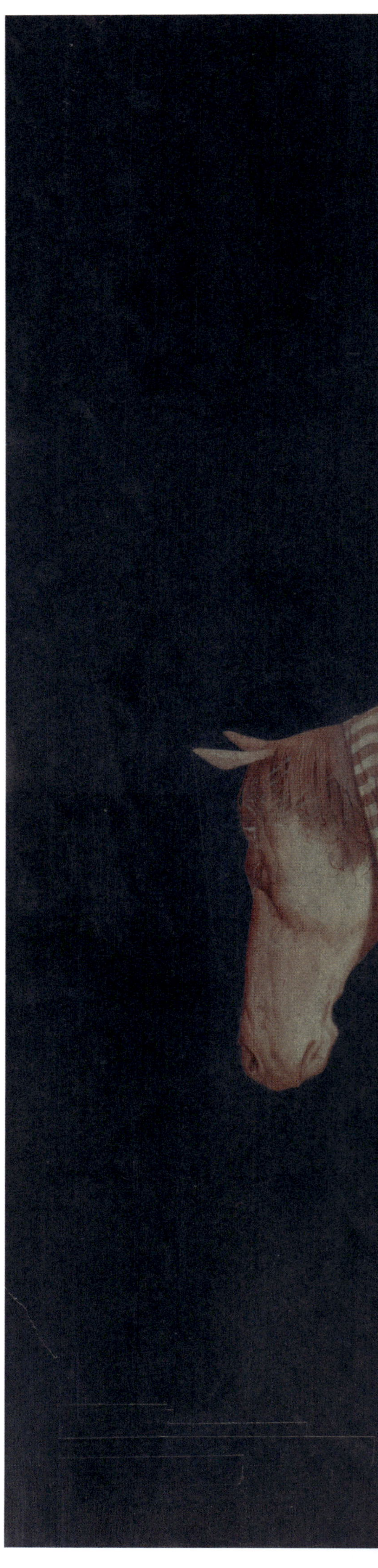

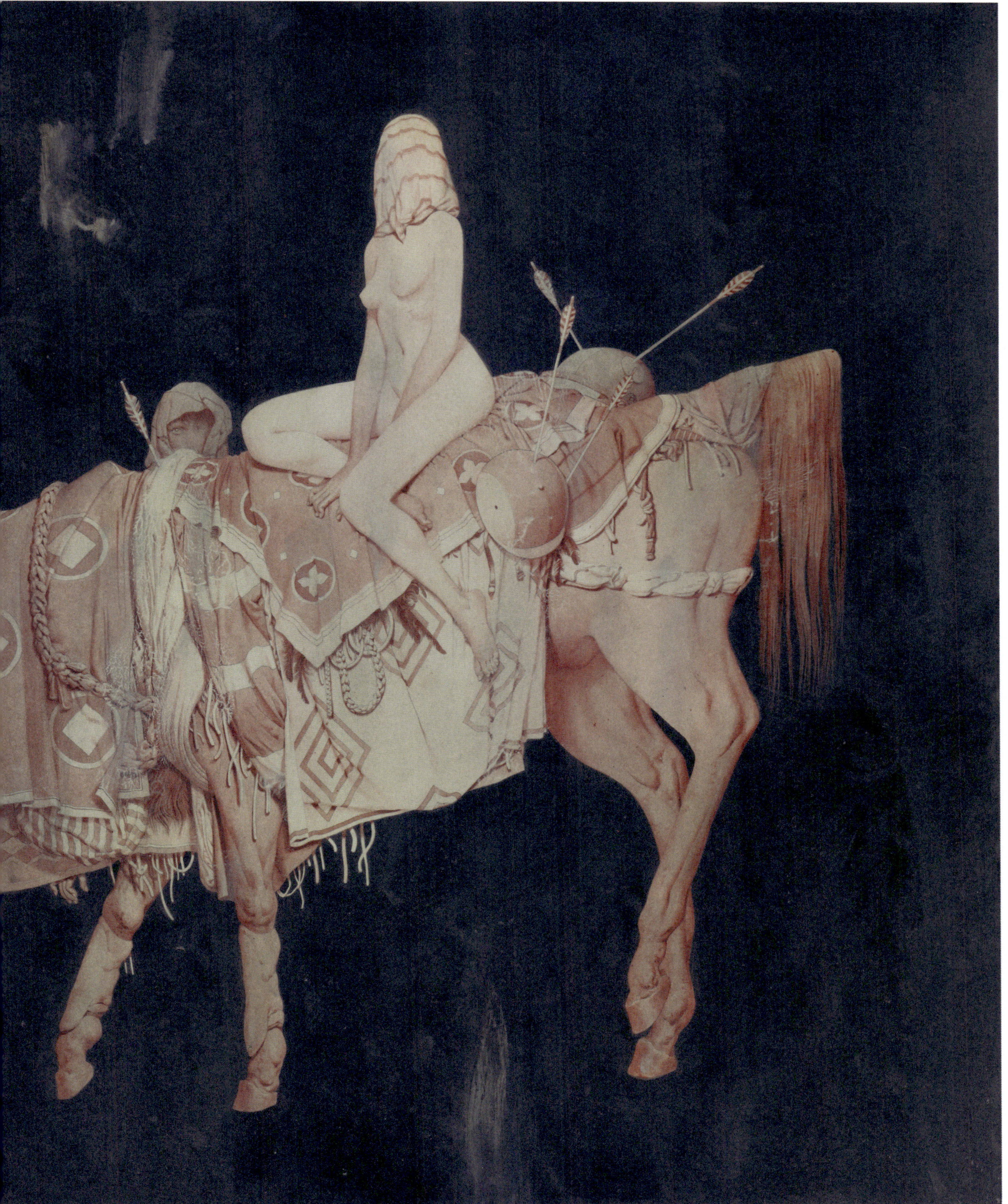

Rob Sato

Best known for his stunning illustrations and paintings in watercolour,

produced either in massive scale or as tiny paper sculptures, Rob Sato's narratives are allegorical and loaded with colour, texture and detail. In them he pushes watercolour – both in terms of technique and subject-matter – to its limits, exploiting the perceived 'lightness' of the medium to pursue ideas about war, death and decay.

Sato began using watercolour in his work for purely practical reasons. He had been producing hand-painted comics and illustrations and needed a medium over which he could easily draw. However, somewhere in the process of experimentation he became entranced: 'I rediscovered the playfulness of paint. Up until that point I had been a line-drawing fiend…. I've gradually pursued a path toward letting the paint and marks retain their freshness and avoiding a fussy, overly rendered quality…. The difficulty in controlling watercolour was somehow harmonious with my tendency to try to control too much; it forced me to improvise and leave

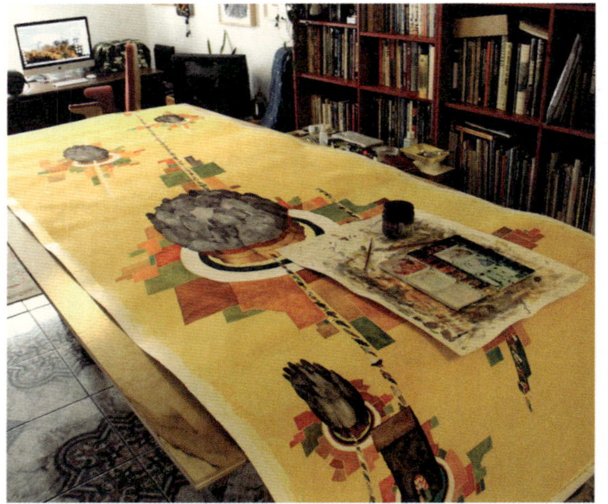

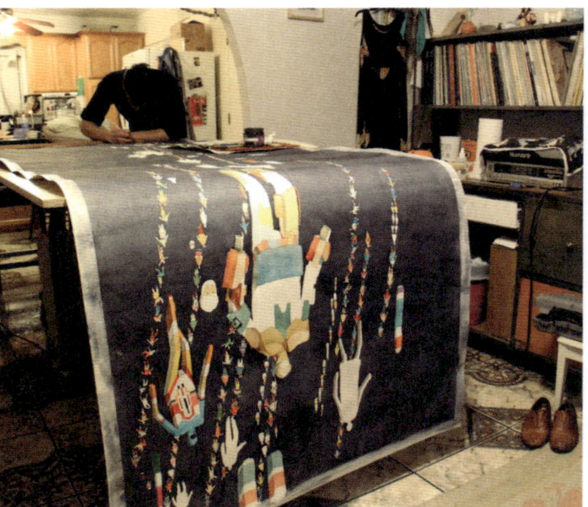

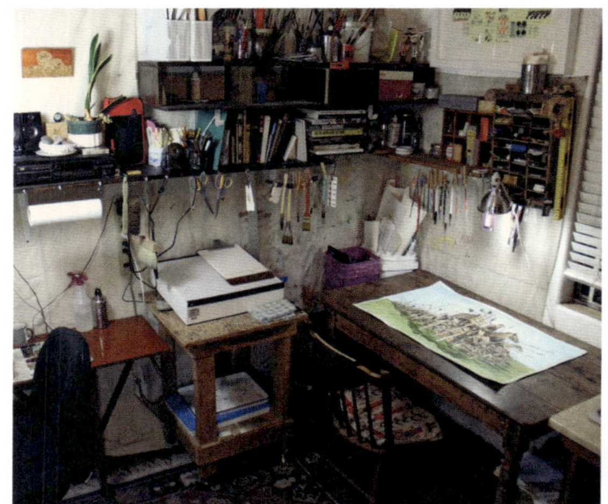

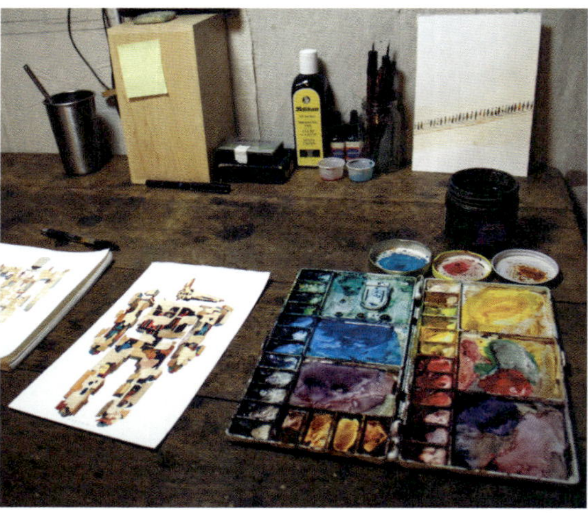

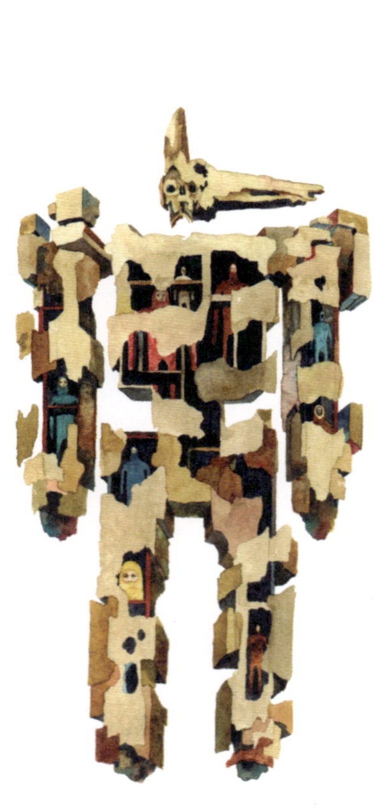

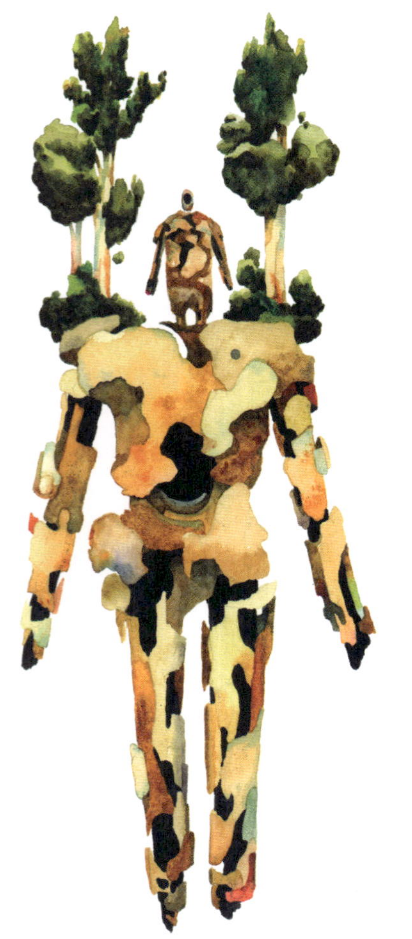

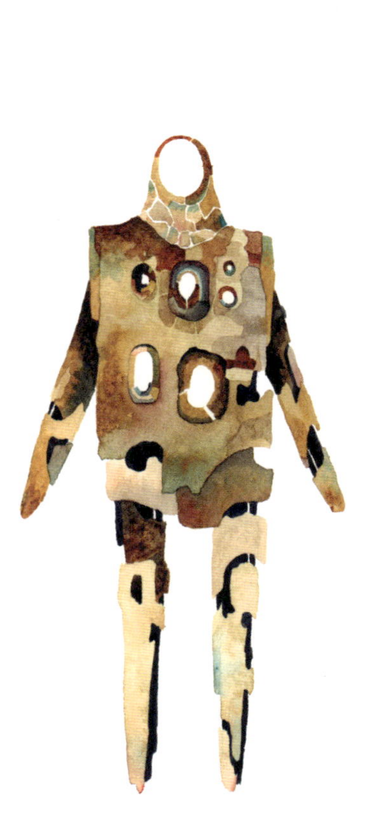

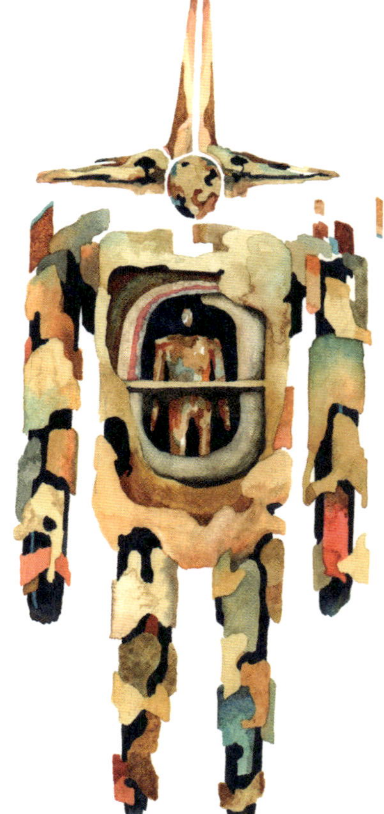

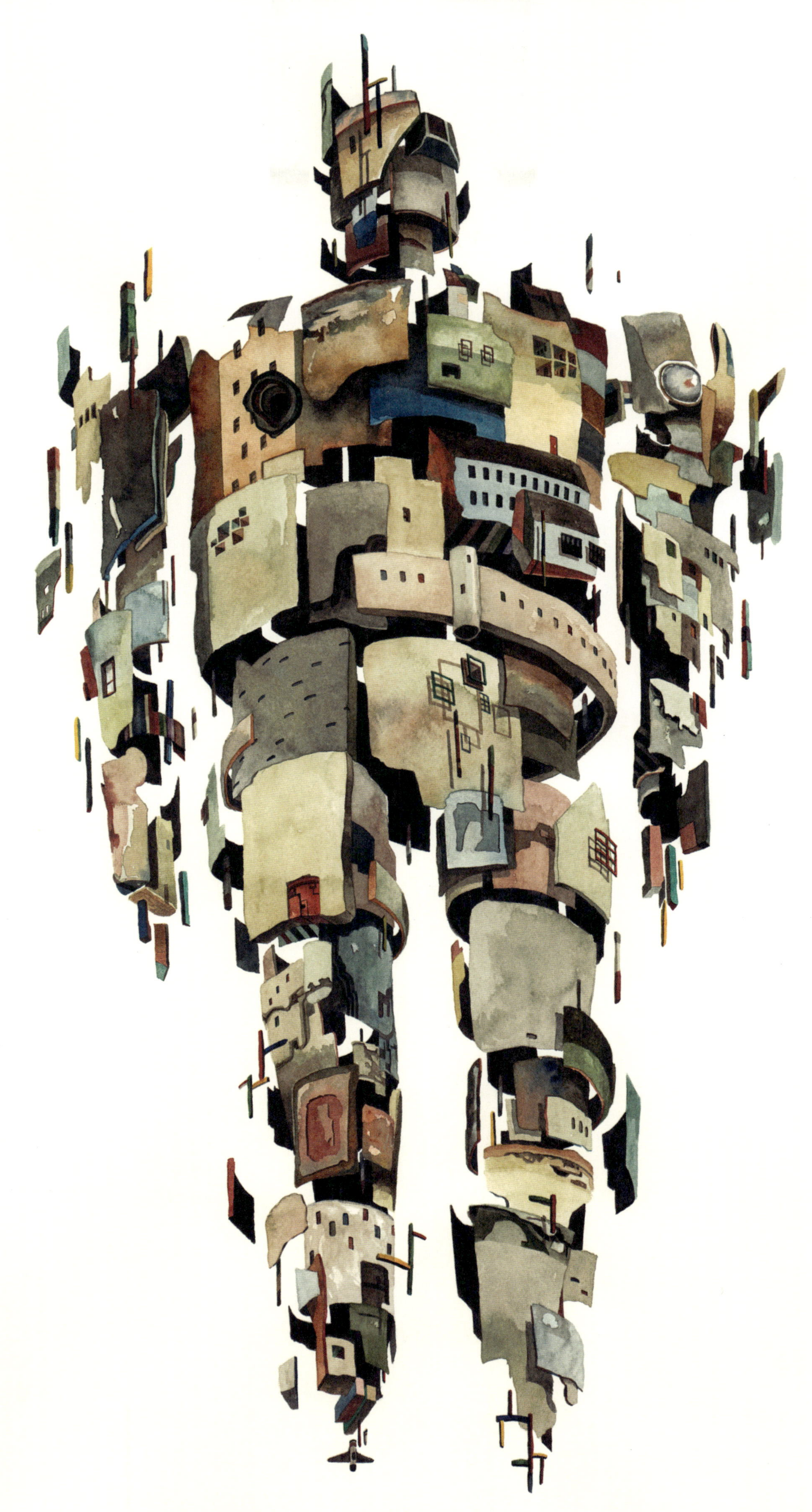

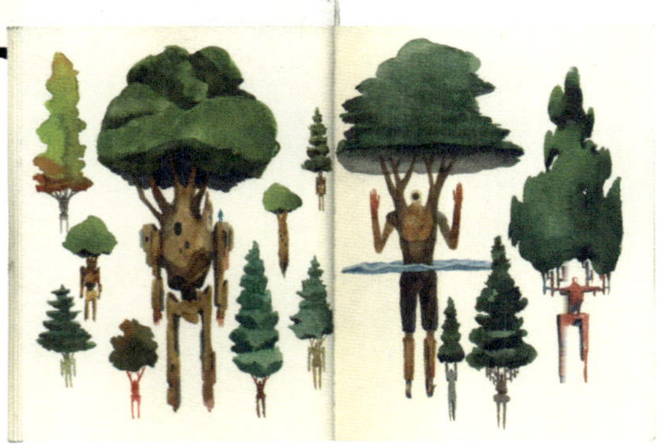

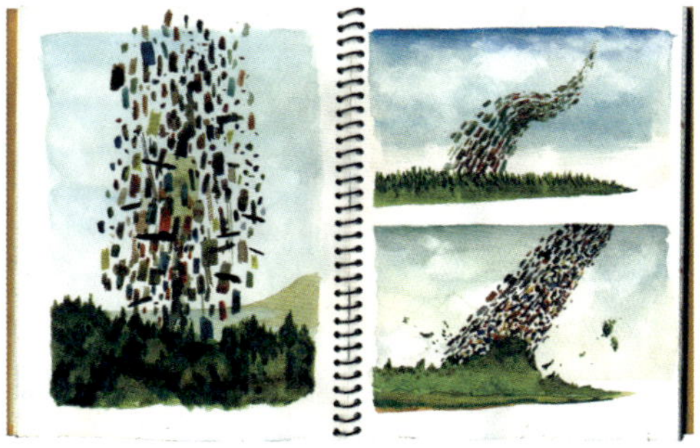

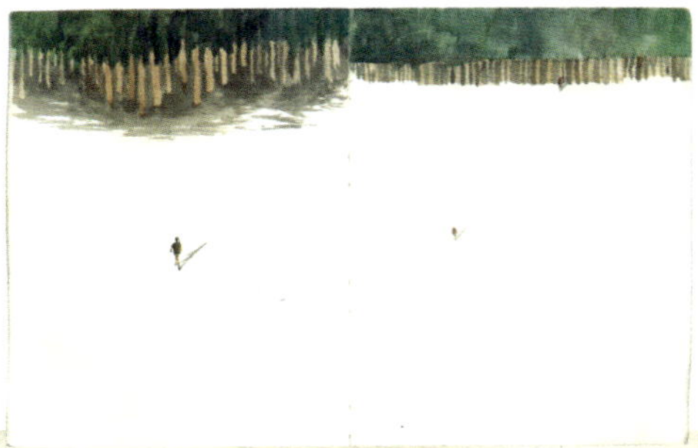

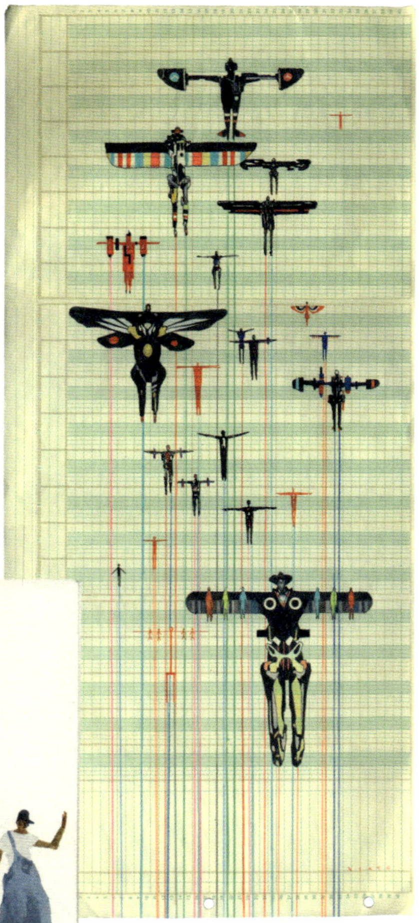

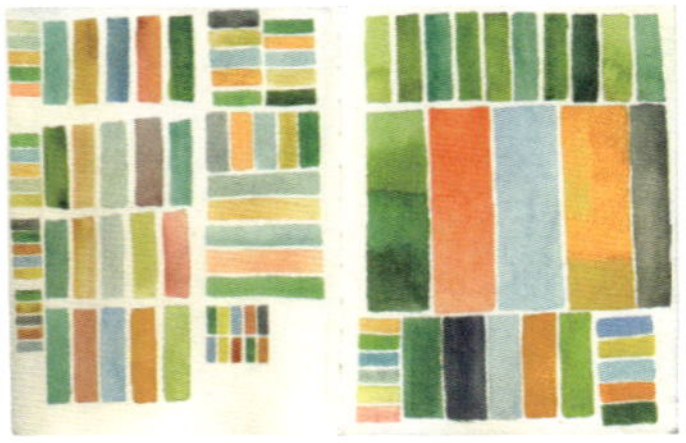

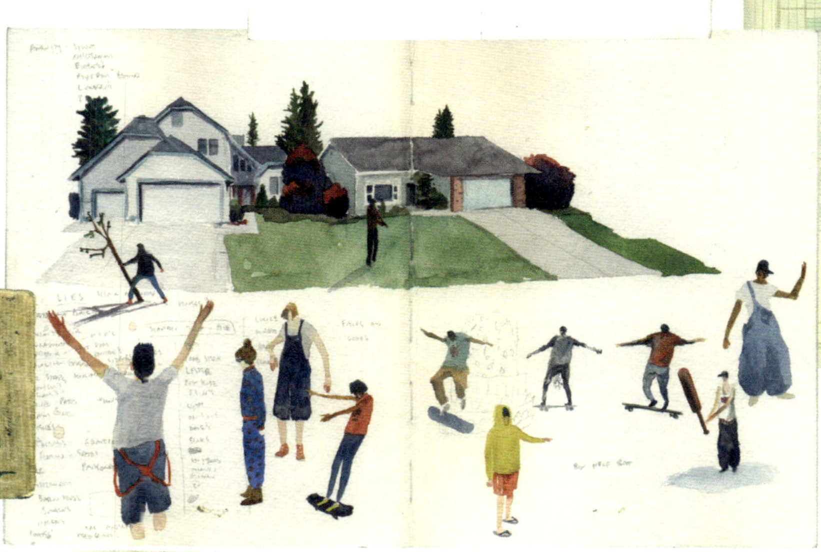

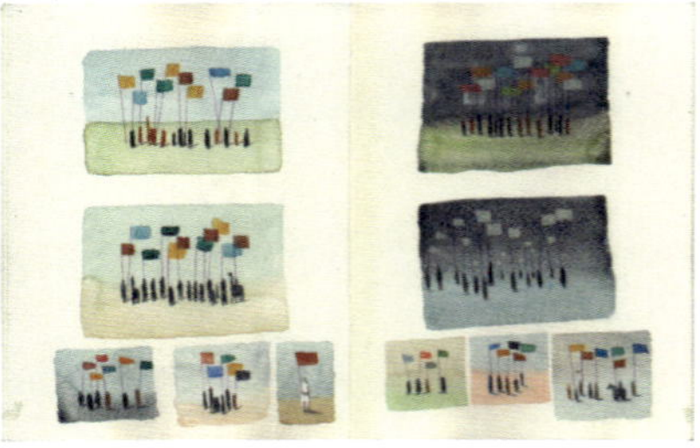

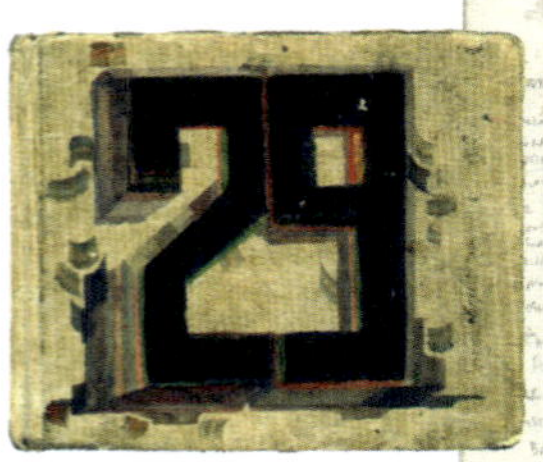

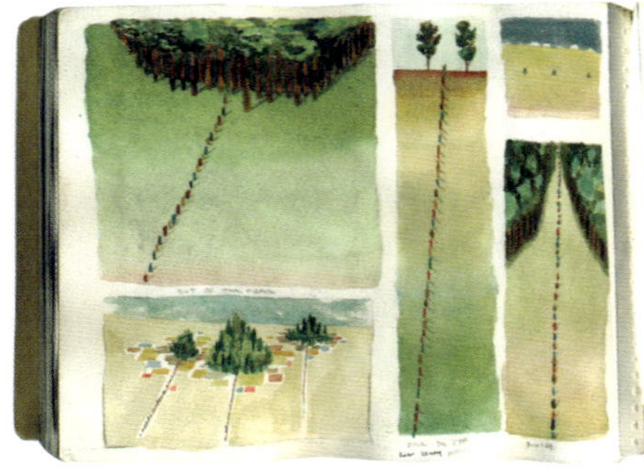
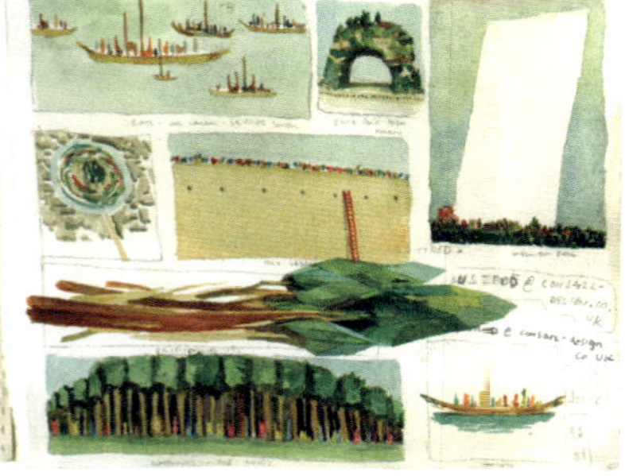
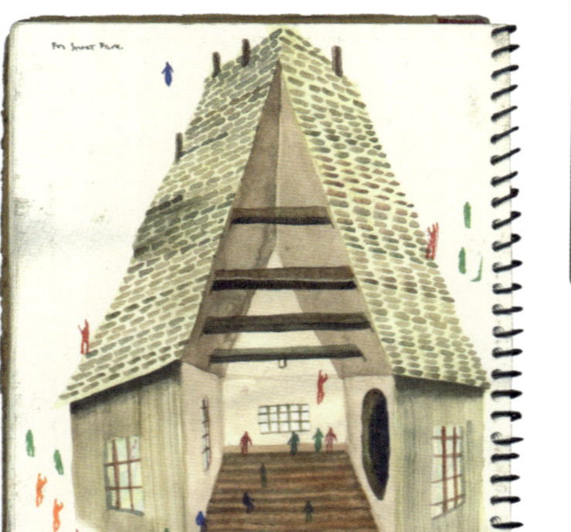
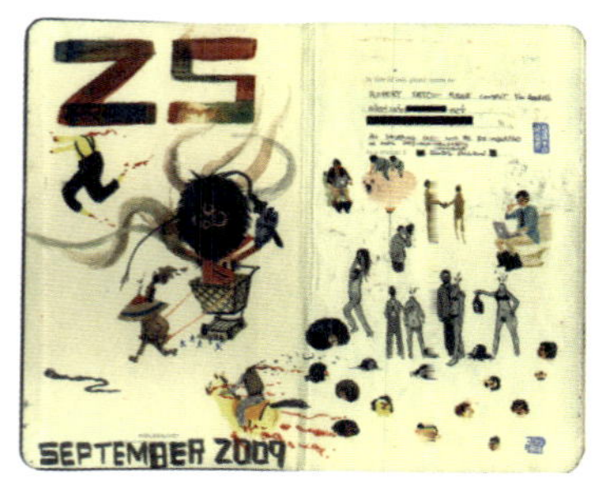
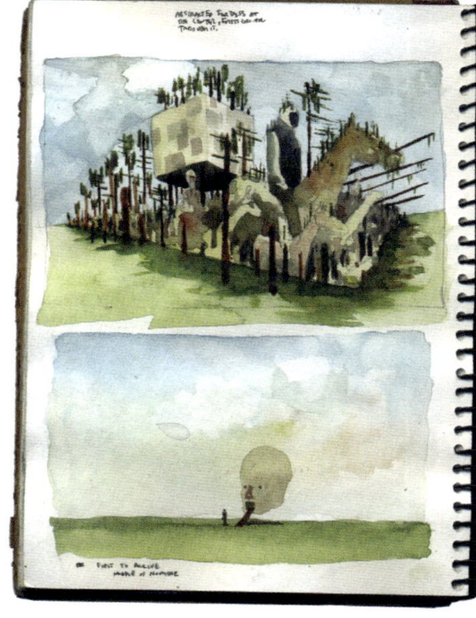
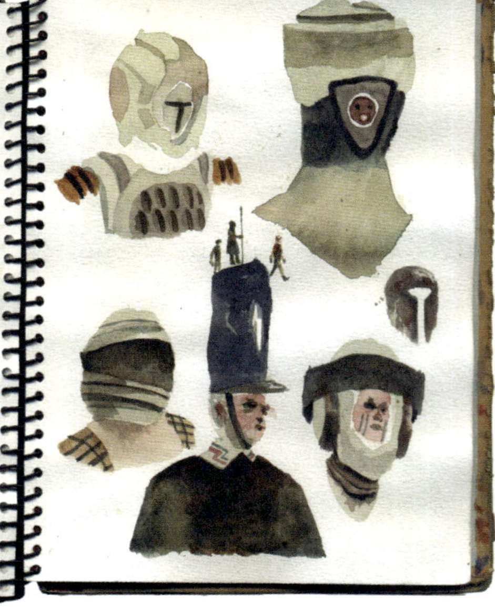
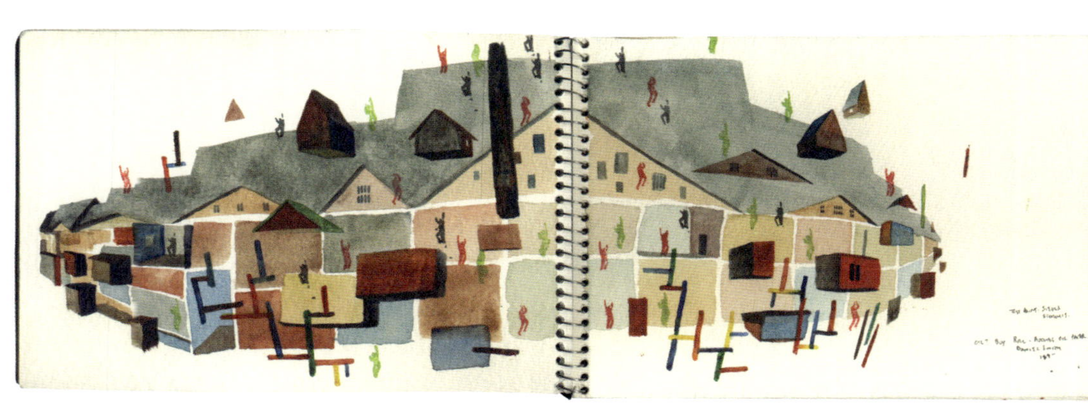

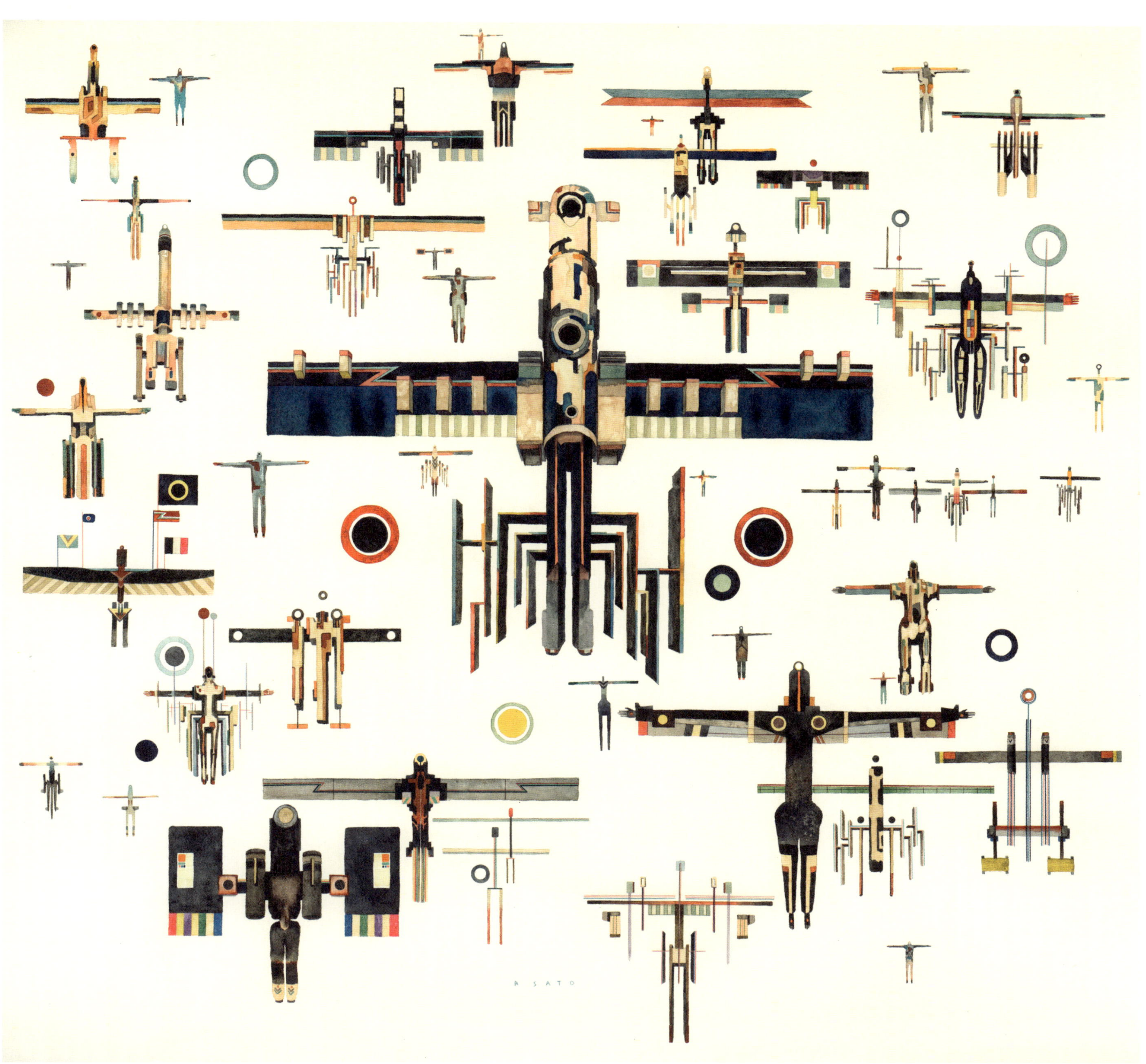

OPPOSITE
A selection of the
artist's sketchbooks.

ABOVE
Squaring the Sun, 2014
Watercolour on paper
101 × 109 cm (40 × 43 in.)

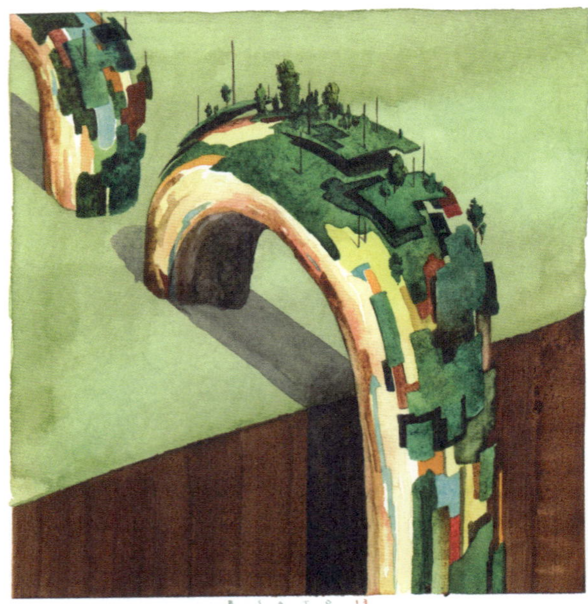
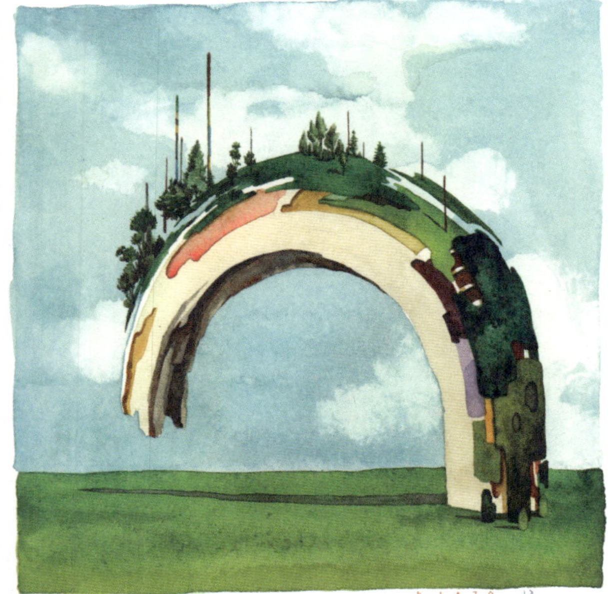
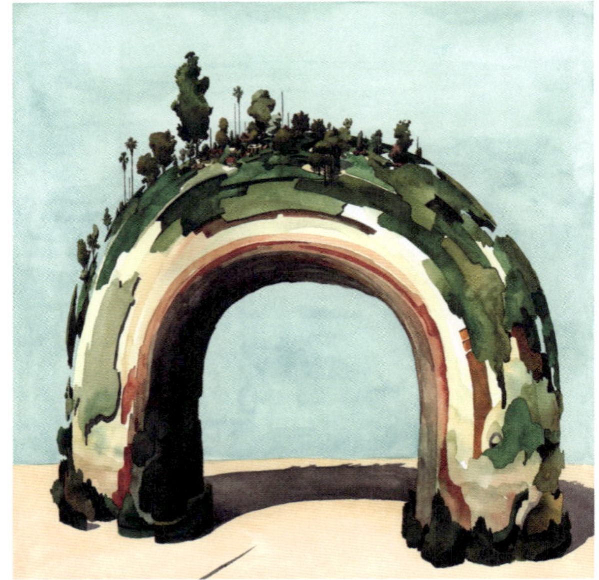
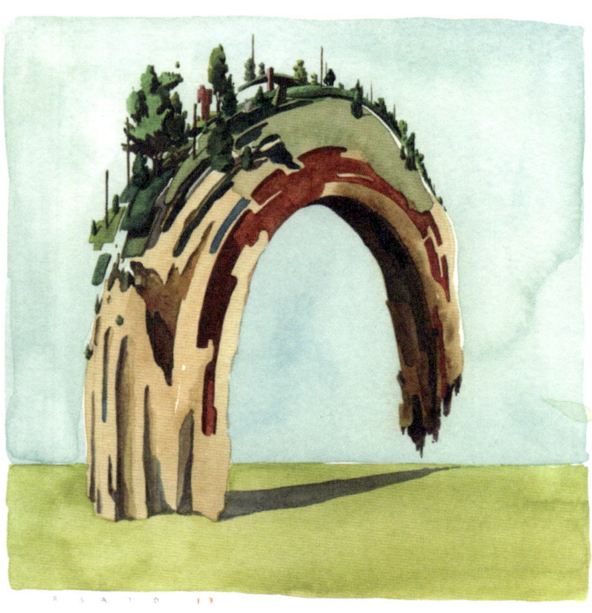

the paint alone. Watercolour cannot be "corrected" or reworked much, if at all. Once the mark is made, it can't be taken back.'

Since graduating from the California College of Arts and Crafts in 1999, Sato self-published his graphic novel, *Burying Sandwiches* (2005), and has been the subject of many solo and group exhibitions, in which he has been able to showcase a huge range of works. Of particular note was a display of fifteen years' worth of his wonderfully packed sketchbooks at the Giant Robot Biennale 3 in Los Angeles in 2013. Within these sketchbooks, he claims, are concealed 'secrets, lies, origins, false starts, raw bleeding honesty, pretentious self absorption, stabs in the dark, rage, love, grocery lists, long lost friends, hopes, fears and petty grievances'.

Without setting out to make fantasy or Surrealist art, Sato understands how much of his work might be interpreted as such: 'I tend to set narratives in environments I find appealing and enjoy matching subjects to imagery that I feel supports or enhances the themes being explored. Still, beneath it all, I feel that most of my work is very rooted to the here and now, and more specifically to me.... A lot of my work is concerned with elevated mundanity. I love the everyday. Without it, nothing would be fantastic. The everyday is where the weirdness lives.'

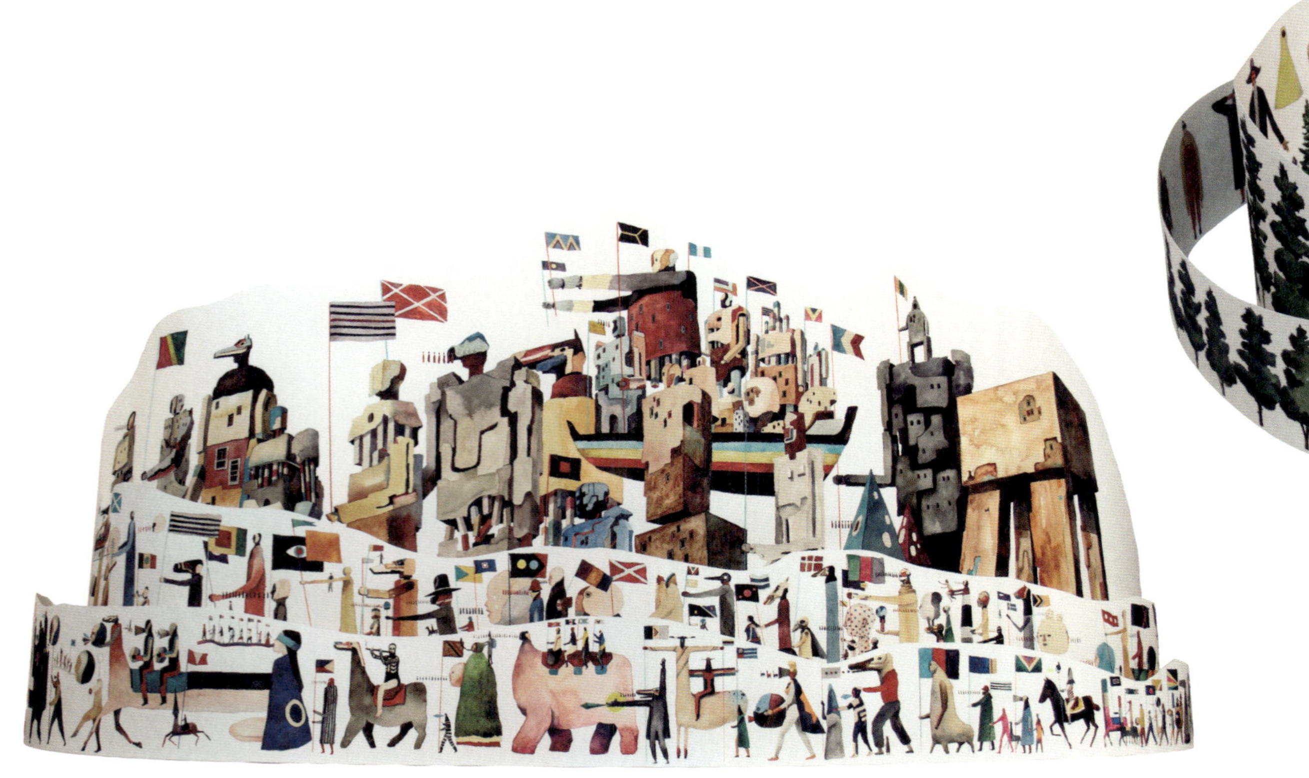

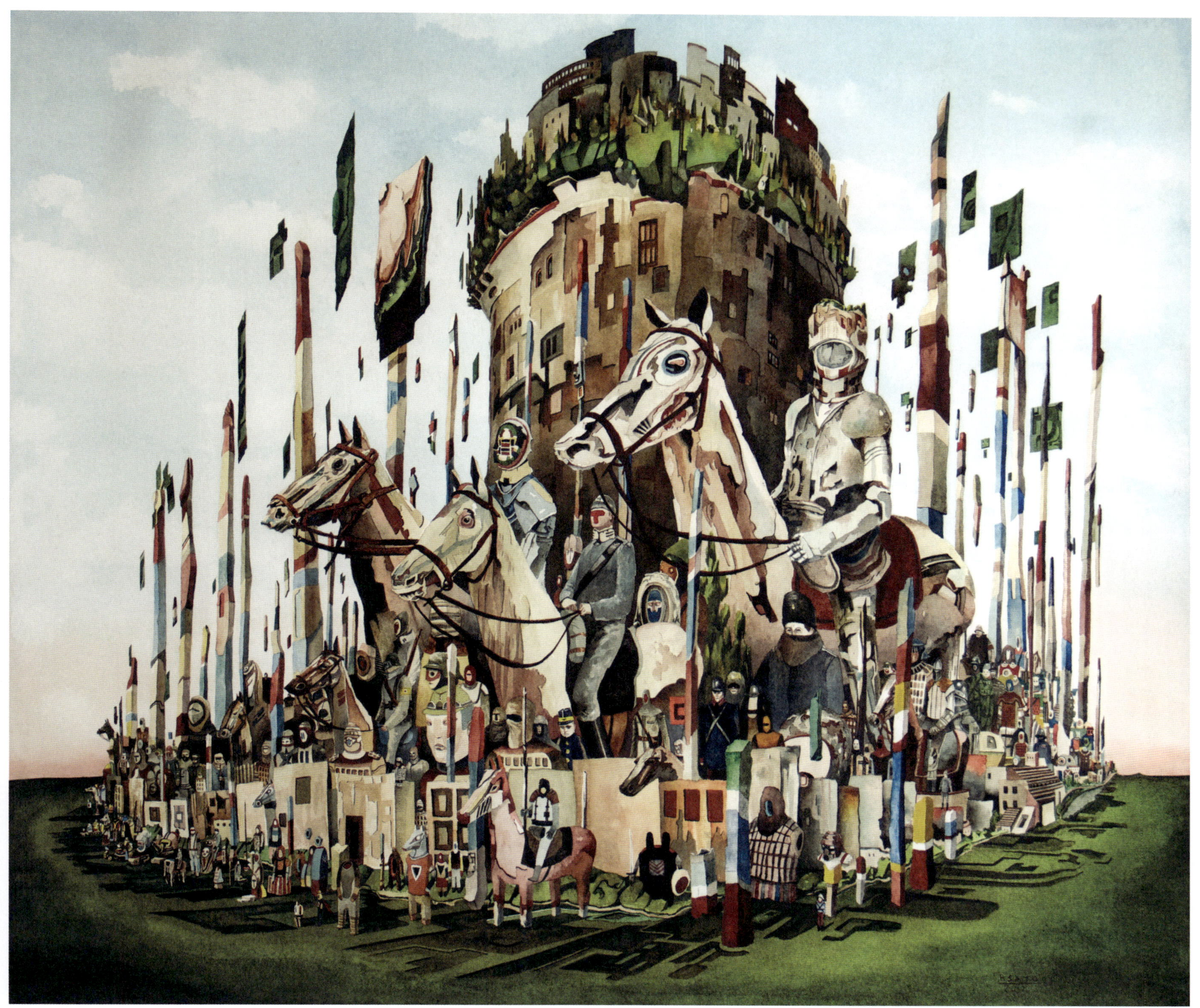

OPPOSITE, TOP LEFT, TOP RIGHT AND CENTRE LEFT
Details from *Four Arches*, 2013
Watercolour on paper
Dimensions unknown

OPPOSITE, CENTRE
LA Arch, 2013
Watercolour on paper
Dimensions unknown

OPPOSITE, BOTTOM LEFT
Seance II: Jericho Rebuilt, 2014
Watercolour on paper
77.4 × 76.2 × 213 cm
(30½ × 30 × 84 in.)

OPPOSITE, BOTTOM RIGHT
Seance I: Watchers in the Woods,
inside detail, 2014
Watercolour on paper
Dimensions variable

ABOVE
The Mad Guard, 2012
Watercolour on
Arches paper
50.8 × 61 cm (20 × 24 in.)

Ricardo Solís

Reimagining both the divine and evolutionary theories of the origins of life

through meticulous drawings and oil paintings, Ricardo Solís conjures up playful scenes that envisage an army of Lilliputian figures building, sculpting and painting animals in celebration of their particular characteristics or qualities. Solís began painting at the age of fourteen, later studying at the School of Visual Arts in his home city of Guadalajara and, after graduating, worked as a studio assistant for the artists Omar Centeno and David Villasenor. It is only relatively recently that he has been able to support himself through his own art.

Solís's work takes on many themes, and he develops numerous series before eventually transitioning to new subjects. The topic of animals, however, has been an endless source of fascination. Citing Hieronymus Bosch (*c.* 1450–1516) and Salvador Dalí as being among his influences the fantastical and Surrealist works of these artists are very much alive in his compositions. Solís strives for a flawless technique, using texture and glazes to bring his work to life. But he also likes them to be playful and humorous: 'I love to play, it's part of my character, but I am also a serious and committed person. I think that my work shows that I take very seriously its technical development. I demand of myself quality in my craft and at the same time I enjoy experimenting. I let myself surpass the limits of what is possible and what is expected of a work of art.'

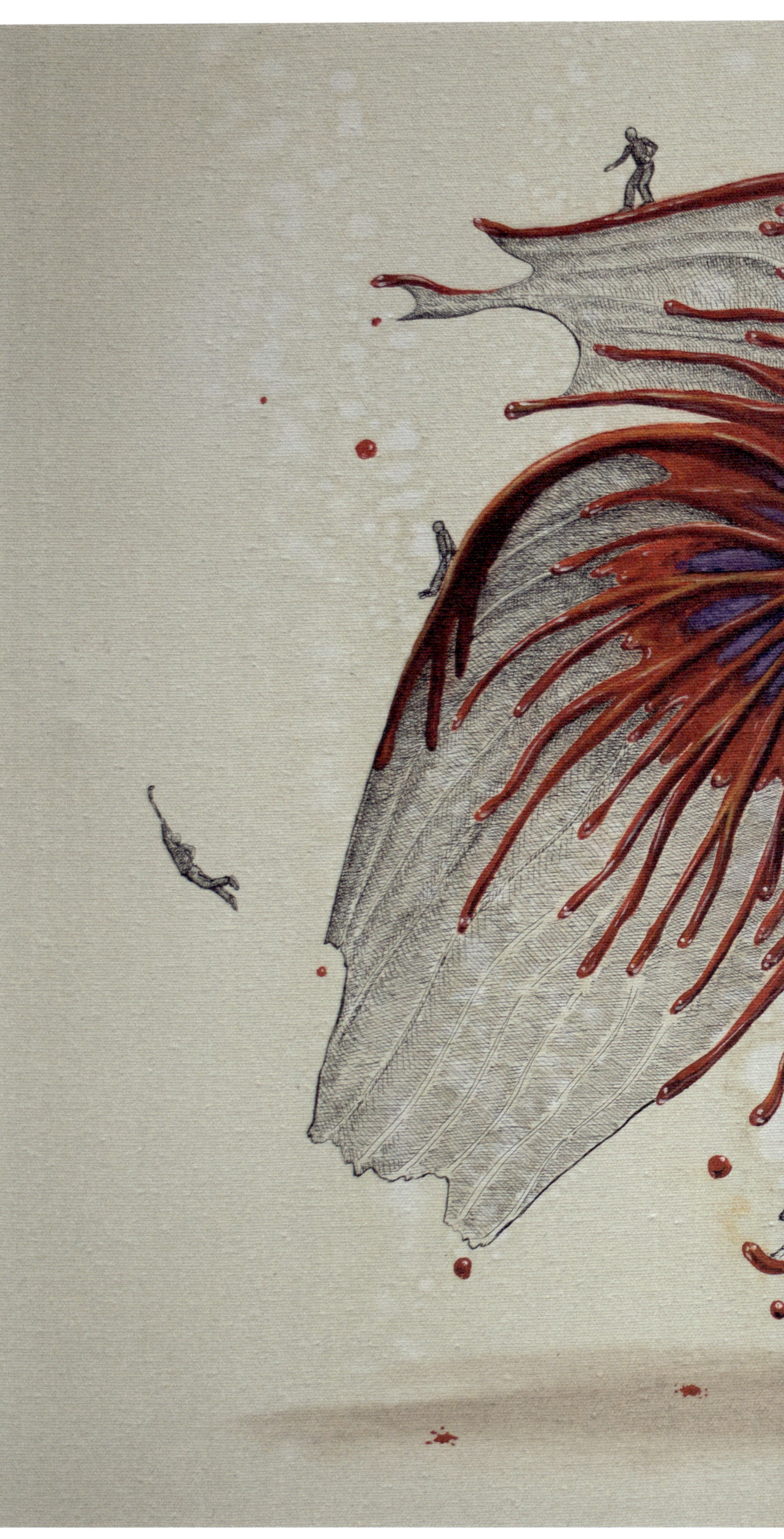

Betta Fish, 2014
Oil and Indian ink on canvas
50.8 × 71.2 cm (20 × 28 in.)

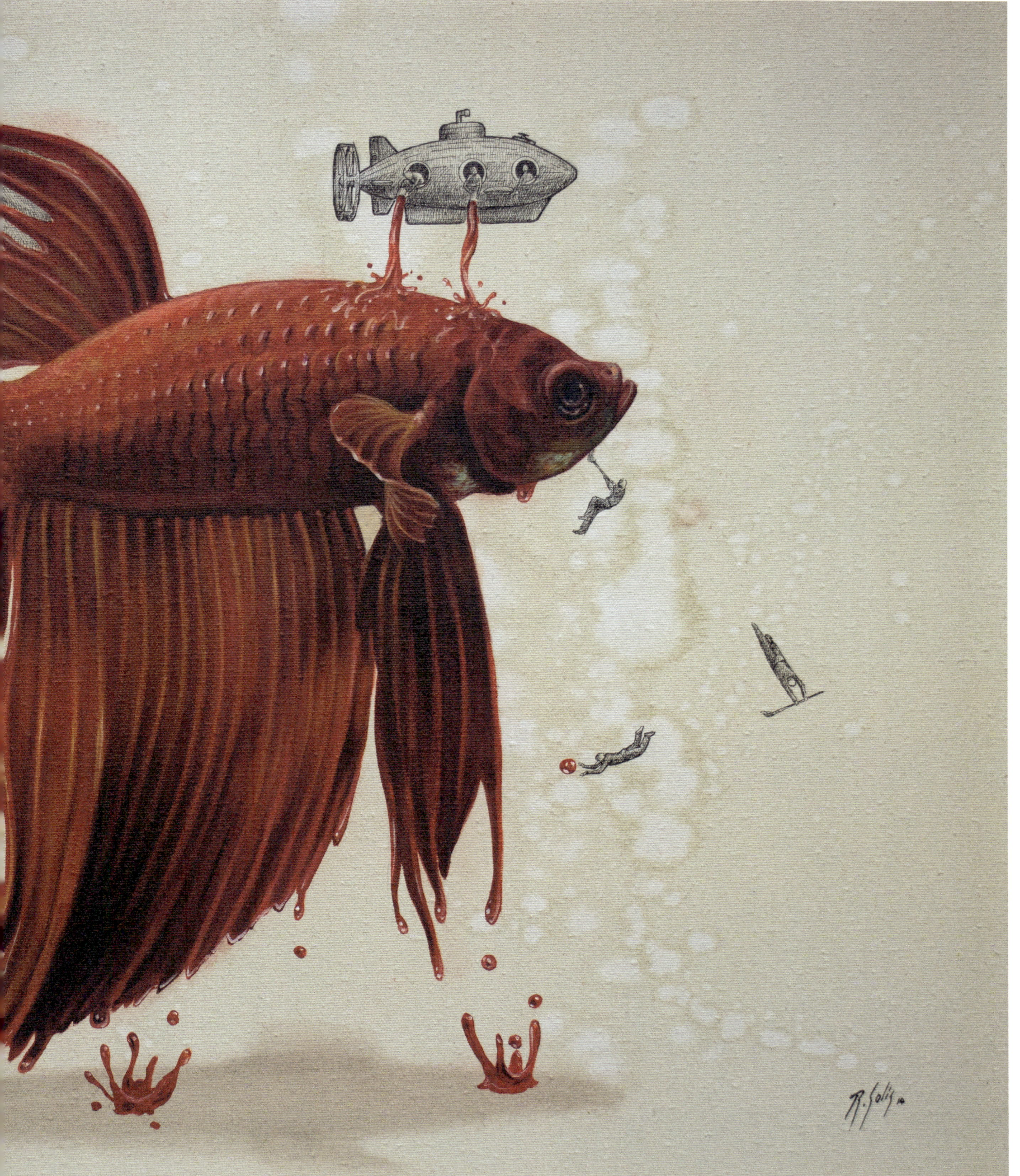

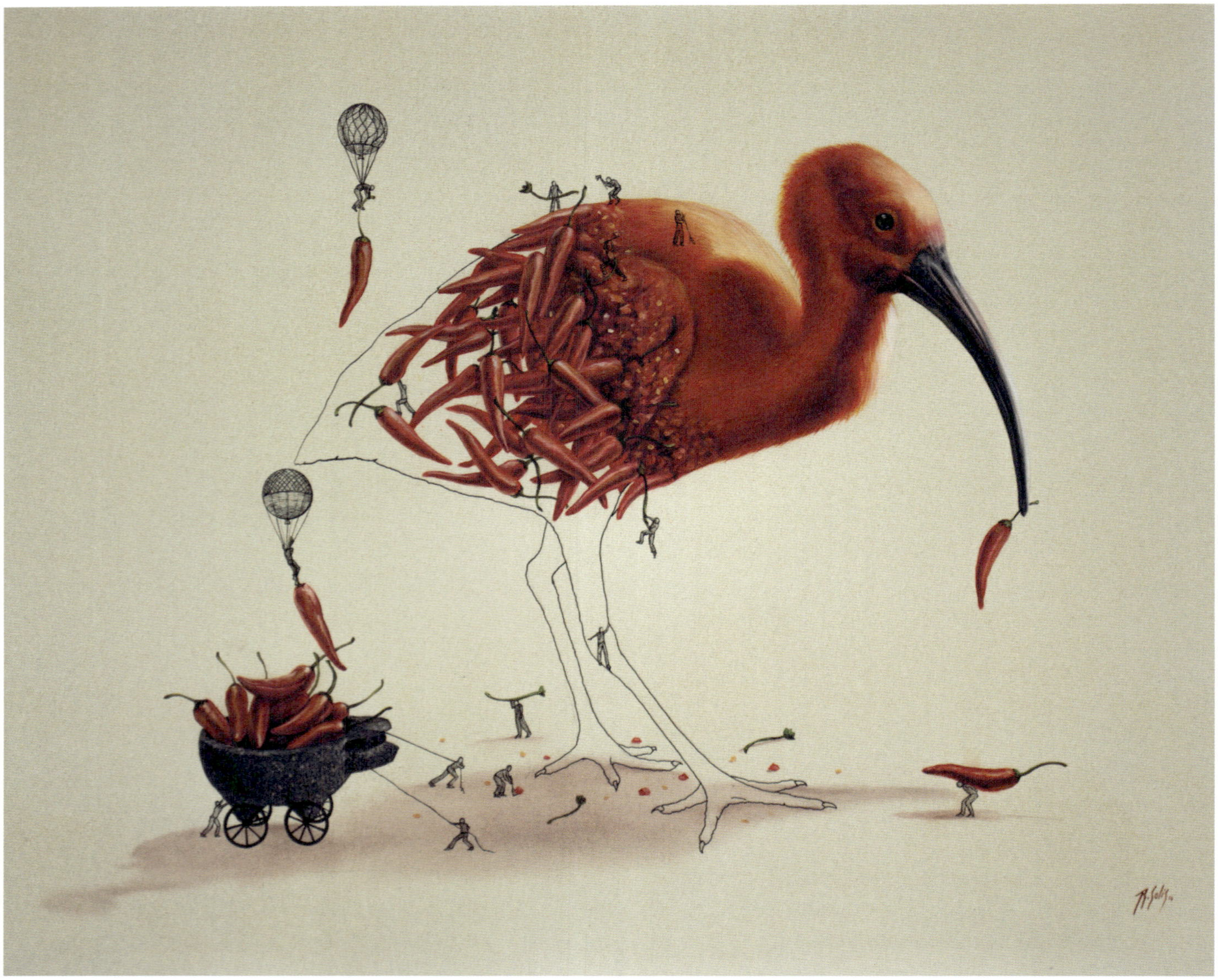

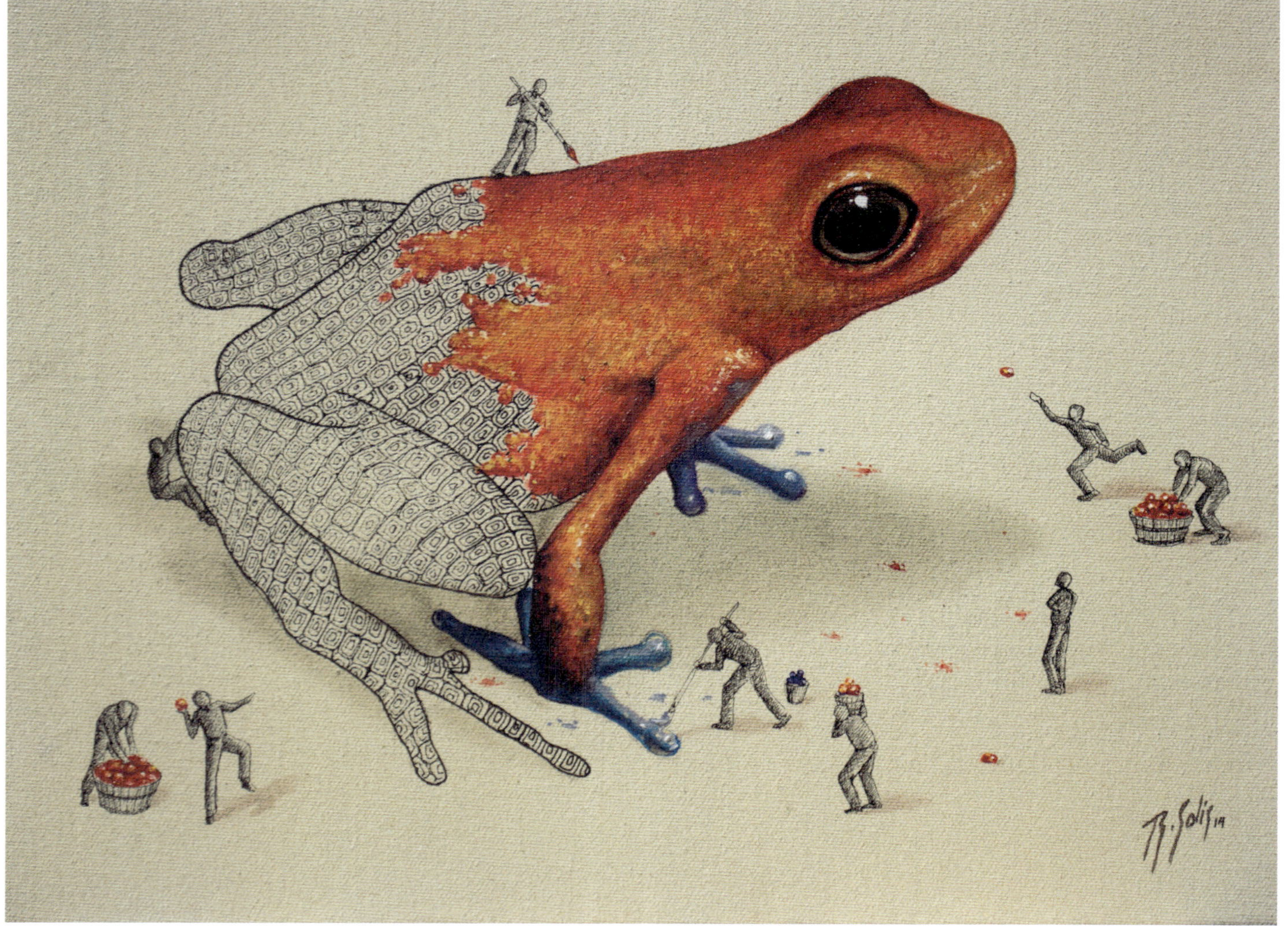

Red Hot Chili Bird, 2014
Oil and Chinese ink
on canvas
69.8 × 92.8 cm
(27½ × 36½ in.)

Poisonous Color, c. 2014
Oil and Chinese ink on canvas
28 × 40.7 cm (11 × 16 in.)

Preliminary sketches, c. 2014
Pencil on paper
22.9 × 28 cm (9 × 11 in.)

Aumentando la resolución,
2014
Oil and ink on canvas
28 × 40.7 cm (11 × 16 in.)

Solís's paintings are suggestive of antique zoological prints and illustrations, possessing an illusion of scientific authenticity that makes them all the more charming. At the same time his work supports themes of science and ecology – the preservation of the natural world and the 'designs' that can be found within. Solís believes in an intelligent creator, who, he says, 'Made everything according to his character and elevated purpose; this is why I enjoy painting nature. Although we are becoming more and more separate from the natural world…we still long for the Garden of Eden, a place where we once strolled among animals in perfect communion. I think that this is the reason for the success of this series. We all identify with or admire a certain animal for its characteristics or qualities, they also remind us that we have a divine origin.'

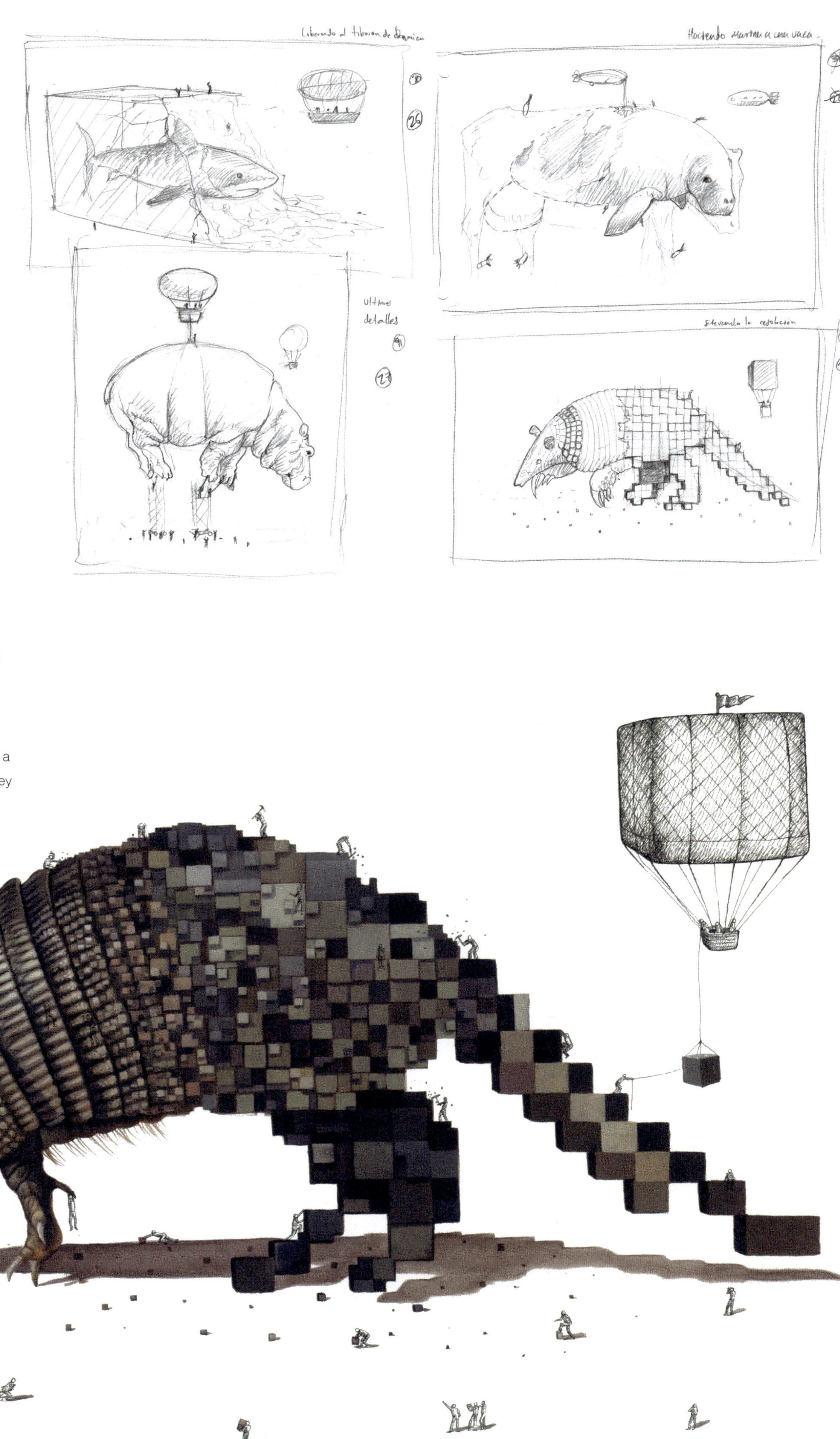

Le Super Demon

Inspired by theories relating to chaos, infinity and the cosmos, as well as the rich mural tradition of the city in which he lives, the work of Le Super Demon (the Mexico-based artist and designer Raúl Sisniega) is invariably characterized by colourful geometric forms and mythical or archetypal beasts, painted either at large scale in murals or on canvas. Le Super Demon's route to wall painting has been a circuitous one; having initially studied graphic design, he was a commercial photographer for several years. In 2009 he stumbled upon the works of two highly regarded street artists, the Belgian ROA and the Italian Blu, both of whom had worked in Mexico. Excited by this discovery he began to develop his own drawings and paintings. Since then murals have been integral to his practice, but he also works as an illustrator and designer, undertaking commissions for clients such as local skate brands and educational institutions. In his work Le Super Demon also nods to the history of the mural art of his country, in particular the

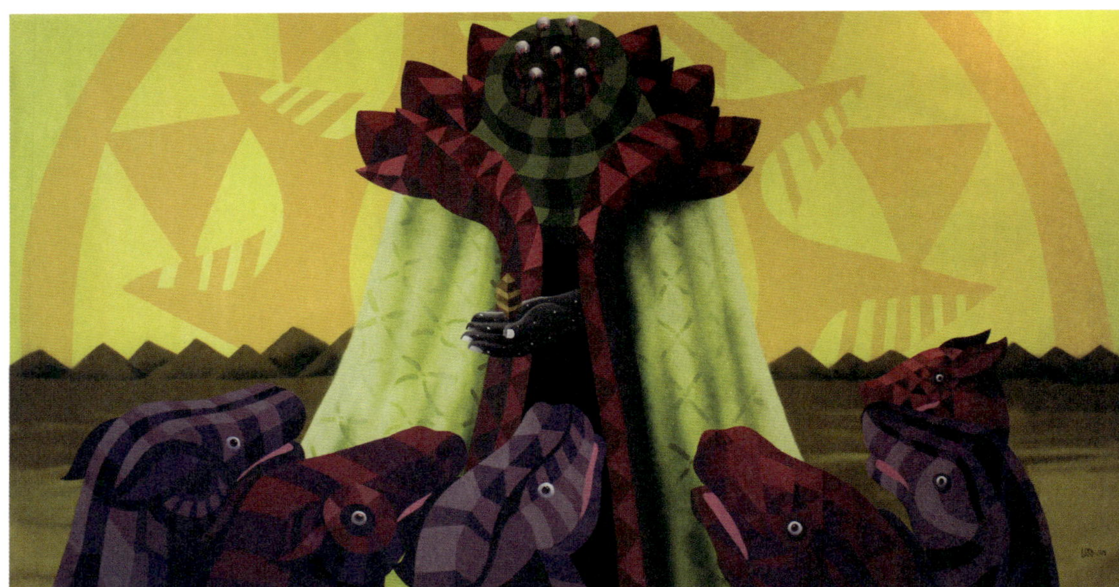

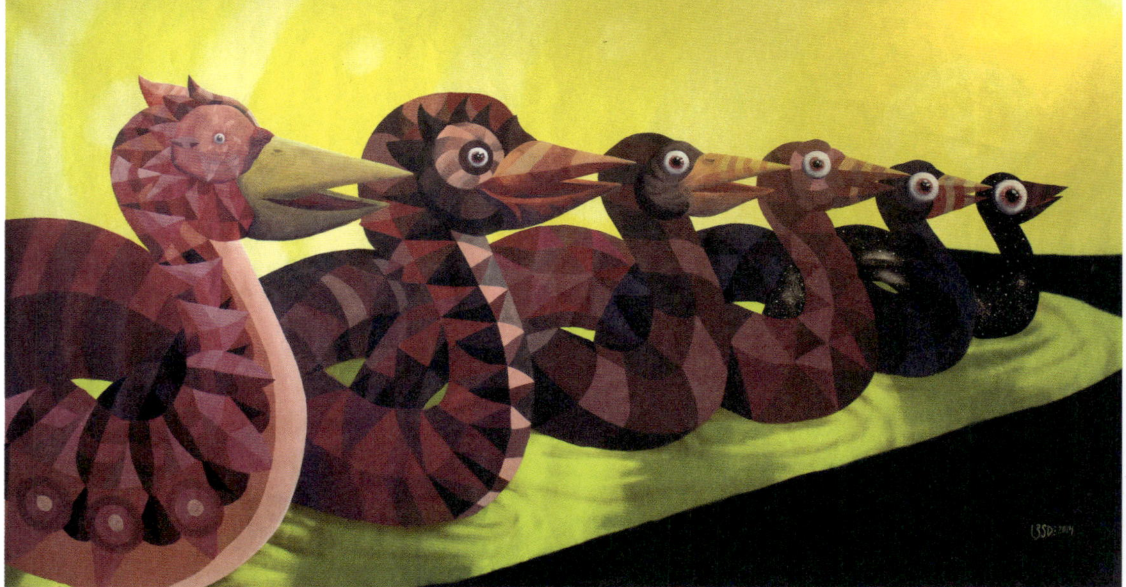

The Shaman, 2015
Acrylic on canvas
180 × 320 cm (70⅞ × 158 in.)

Evol, 2015
Acrylic on canvas
180 × 320 cm (70⅞ × 158 in.)

Study for Community, 2014
Pencil on paper
Dimensions unknown

OPPOSITE
Todo es uno, 2015
Acrylic on canvas
60 × 90 cm (23⅝ × 35½ in.)

Tevatron, 2015
Acrylic on canvas
180 × 320 cm (70⅞ × 158 in.)

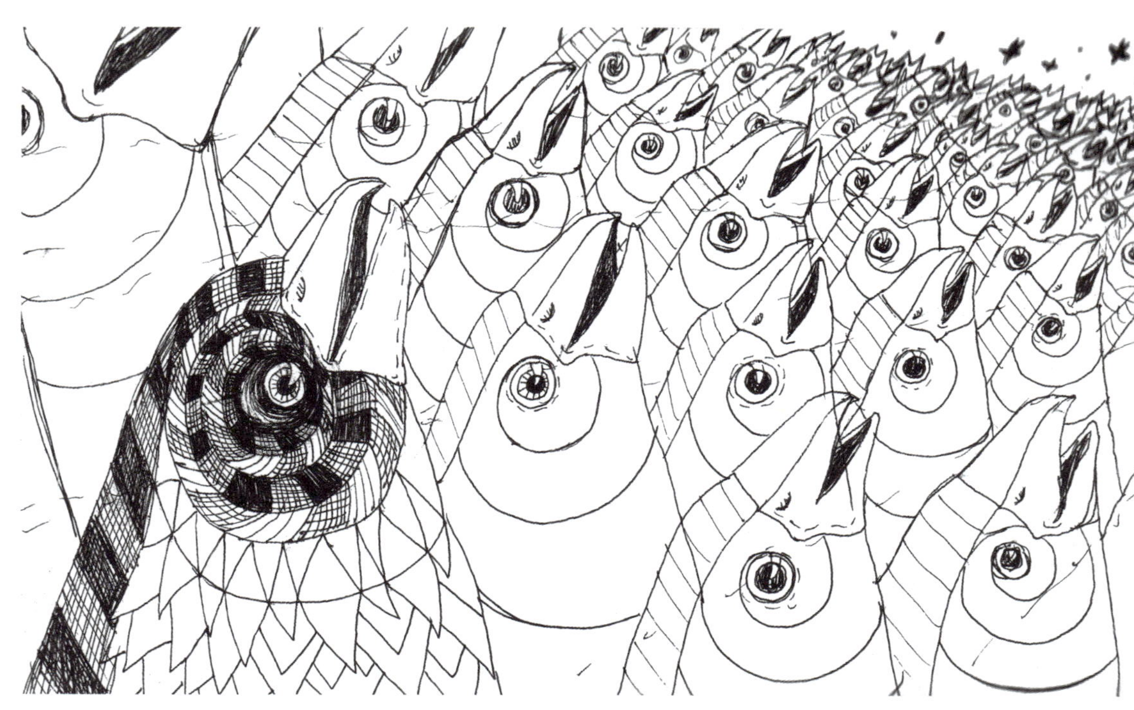

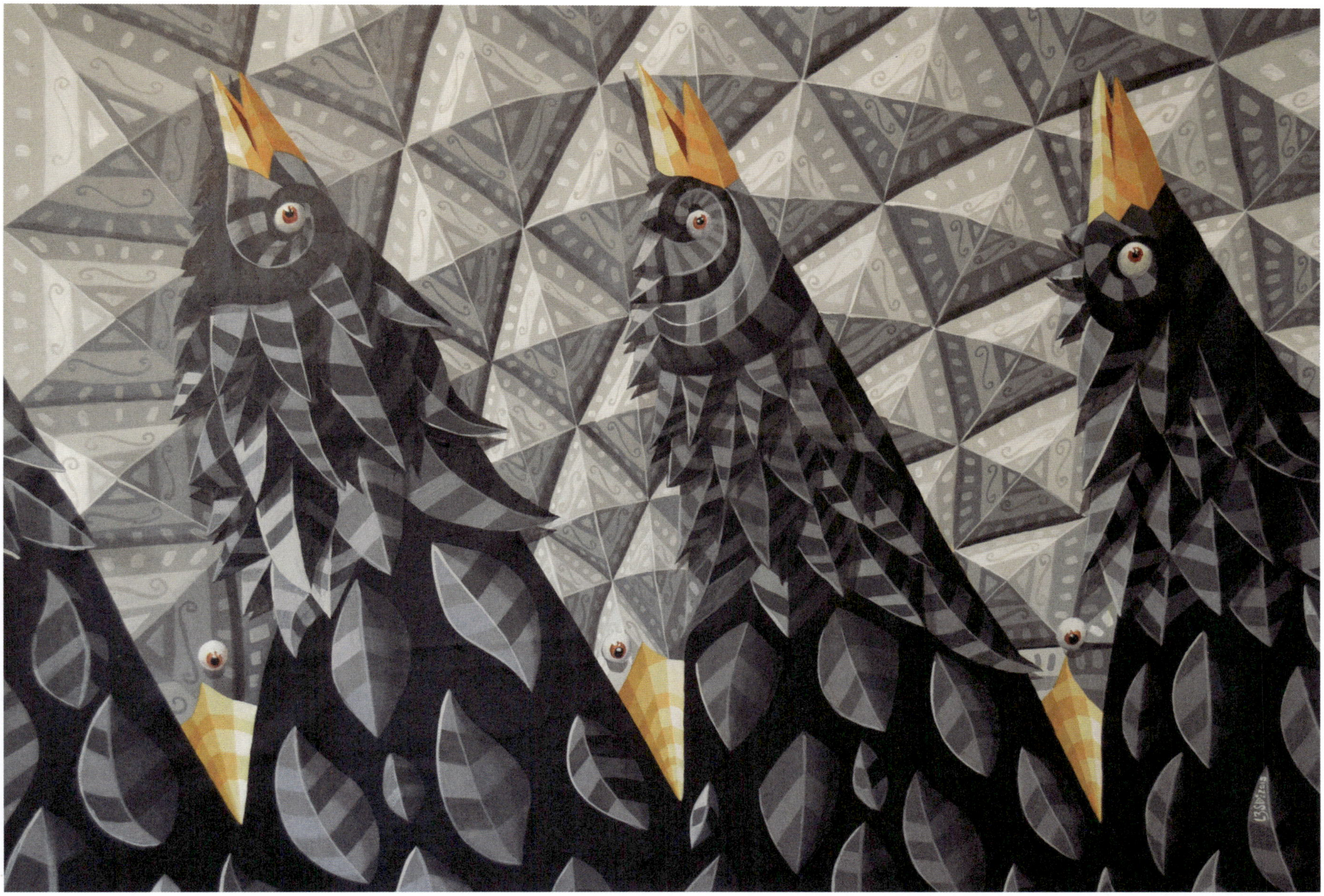

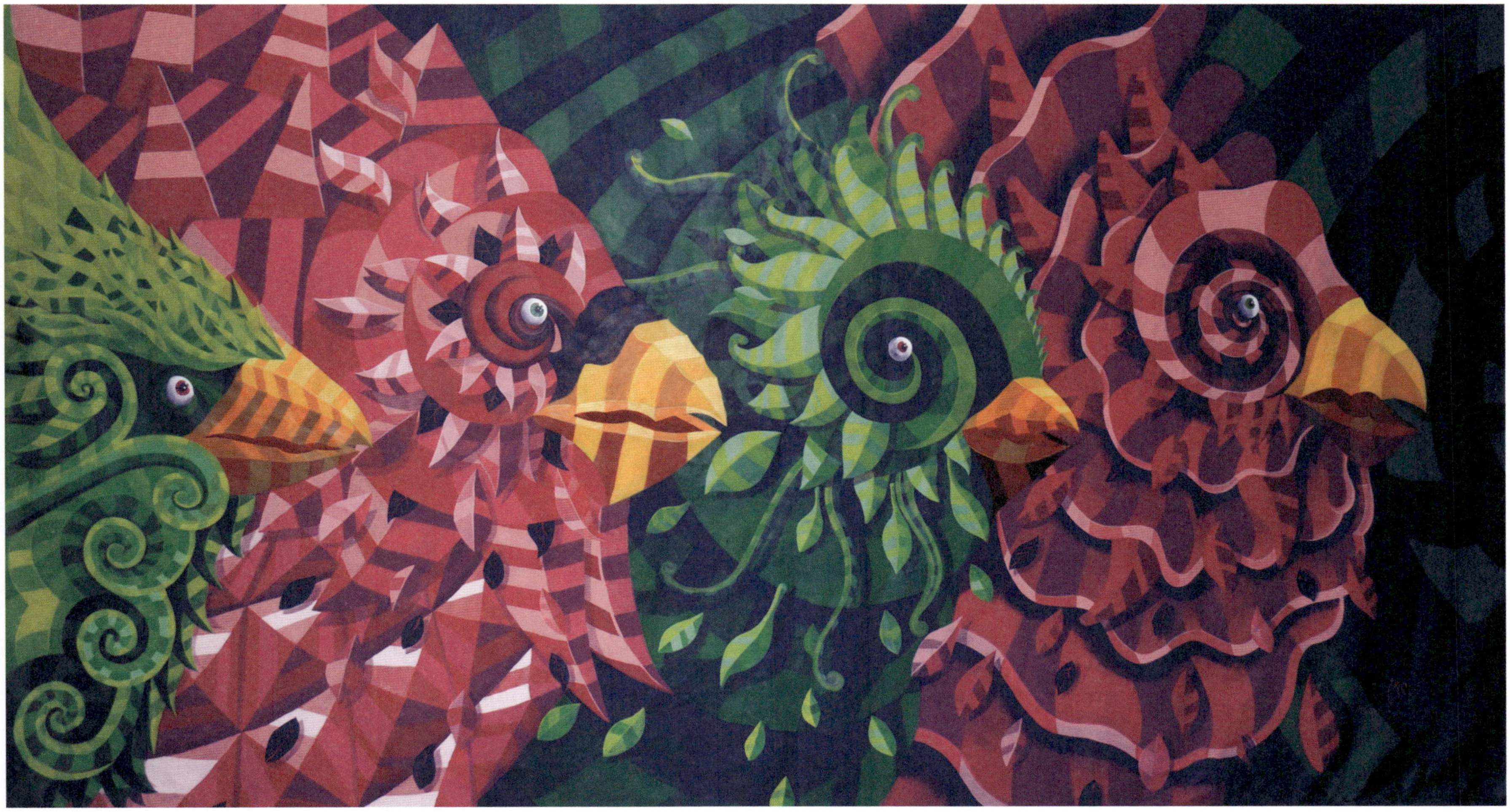

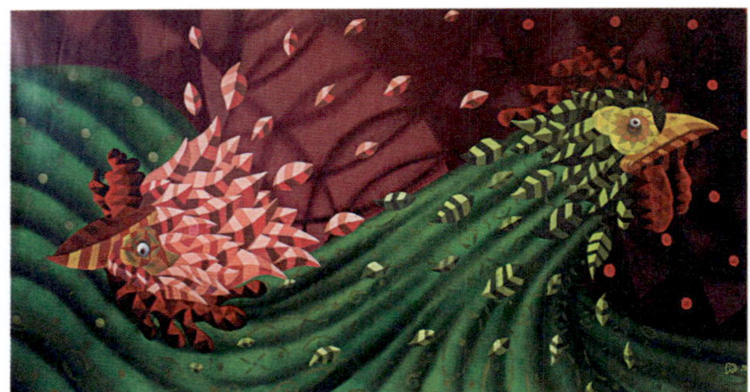

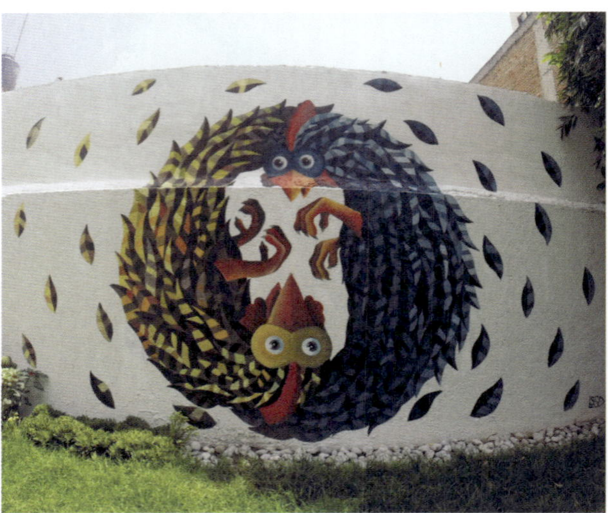

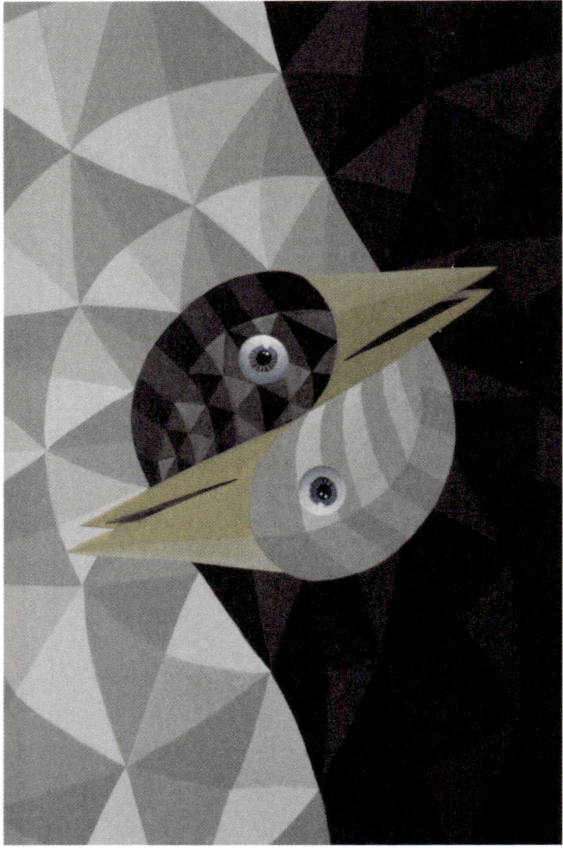

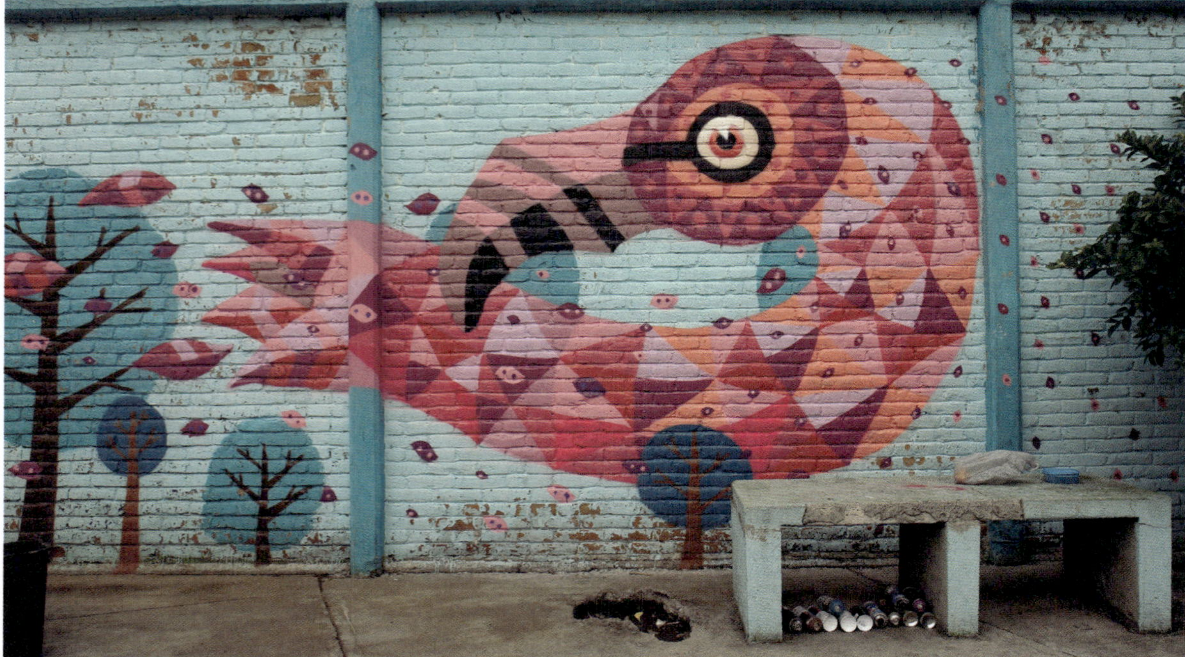

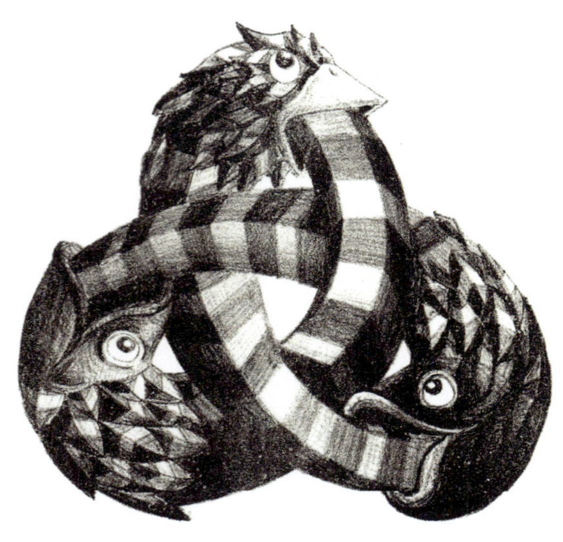

Mexican Mural Movement of the 1920s, of which the Social Realist painter David Alfaro Siqueiros (1896–1974), José Clemente Orozco (1883–1949) and Diego Rivera (1886–1957) were all key proponents.

Restlessly creative, Le Super Demon's sketchbooks are full of doodles, notes and drawings, from which his paintings take shape. Integral to his approach are the geometric patterns or structures that form the skeleton of the artwork, on to which he adds the 'flesh' – colour and texture – which itself, he feels, has 'an overwhelming power to transmit feelings and to create atmosphere'. In his street art Le Super Demon's preferred material is spray paint, since it allows him to work quickly and be daring in his use of colour. In the studio he is more introspective, producing works that focus more so on fine detail.

Le Super Demon's output is both rational and playful. His ingenious designs recall the work of M.C. Escher (1898–1972), particularly his use of pattern and structure. In his compositions creatures are often divided into blocks visually demarcated by colour, but all the while retain a sense of 'wholeness' and continuity. As the artist explains, 'The same infinity pattern applies to greater and smaller organisms: microcosmos and macrocosmos, it doesn't matter, we all come from the same nucleus.' This theme – the celebration of life and the natural world – is one to which Le Super Demon is endlessly drawn.

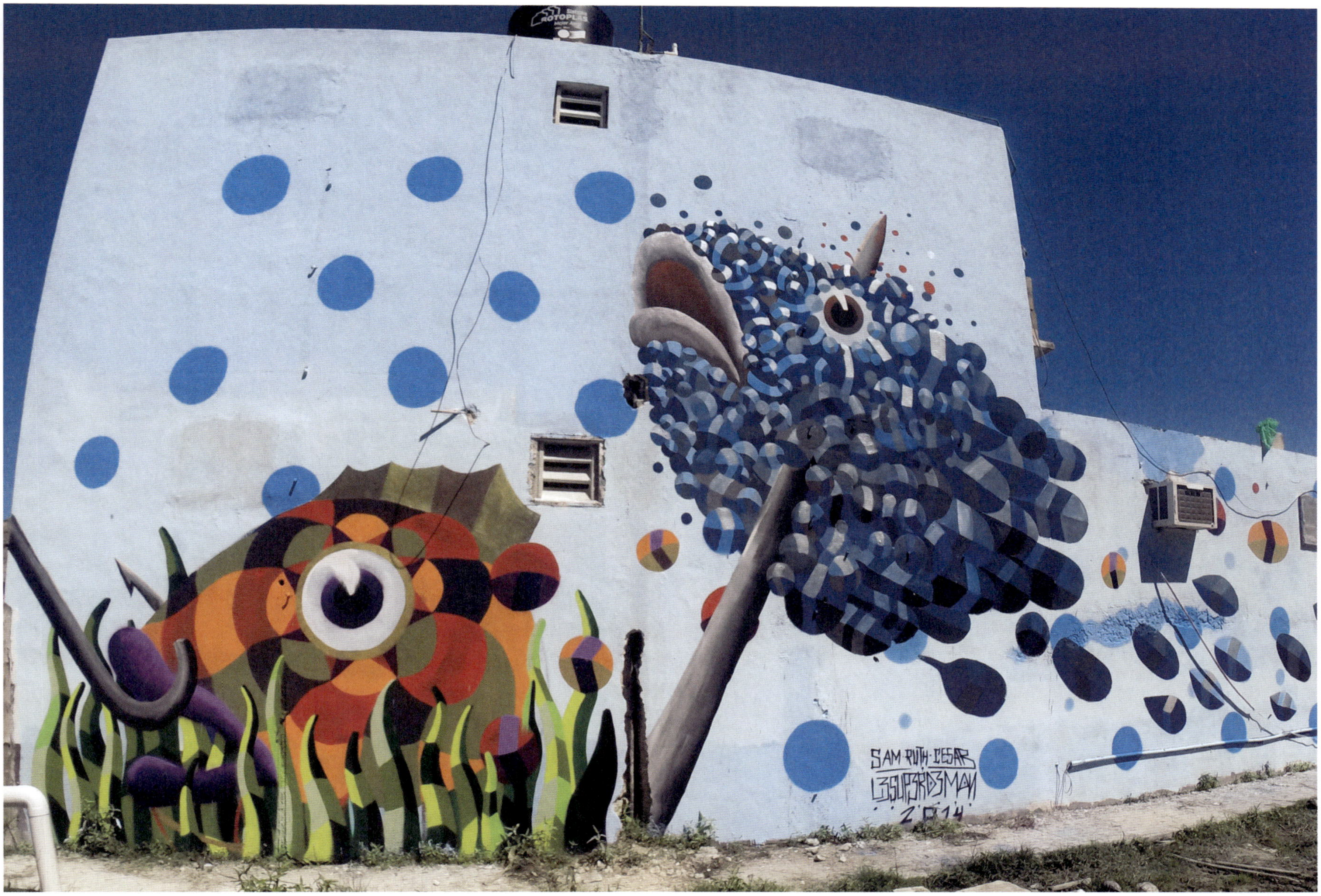

SAM·RUTH·CESAR
L3SUP3RD3MAN
2014

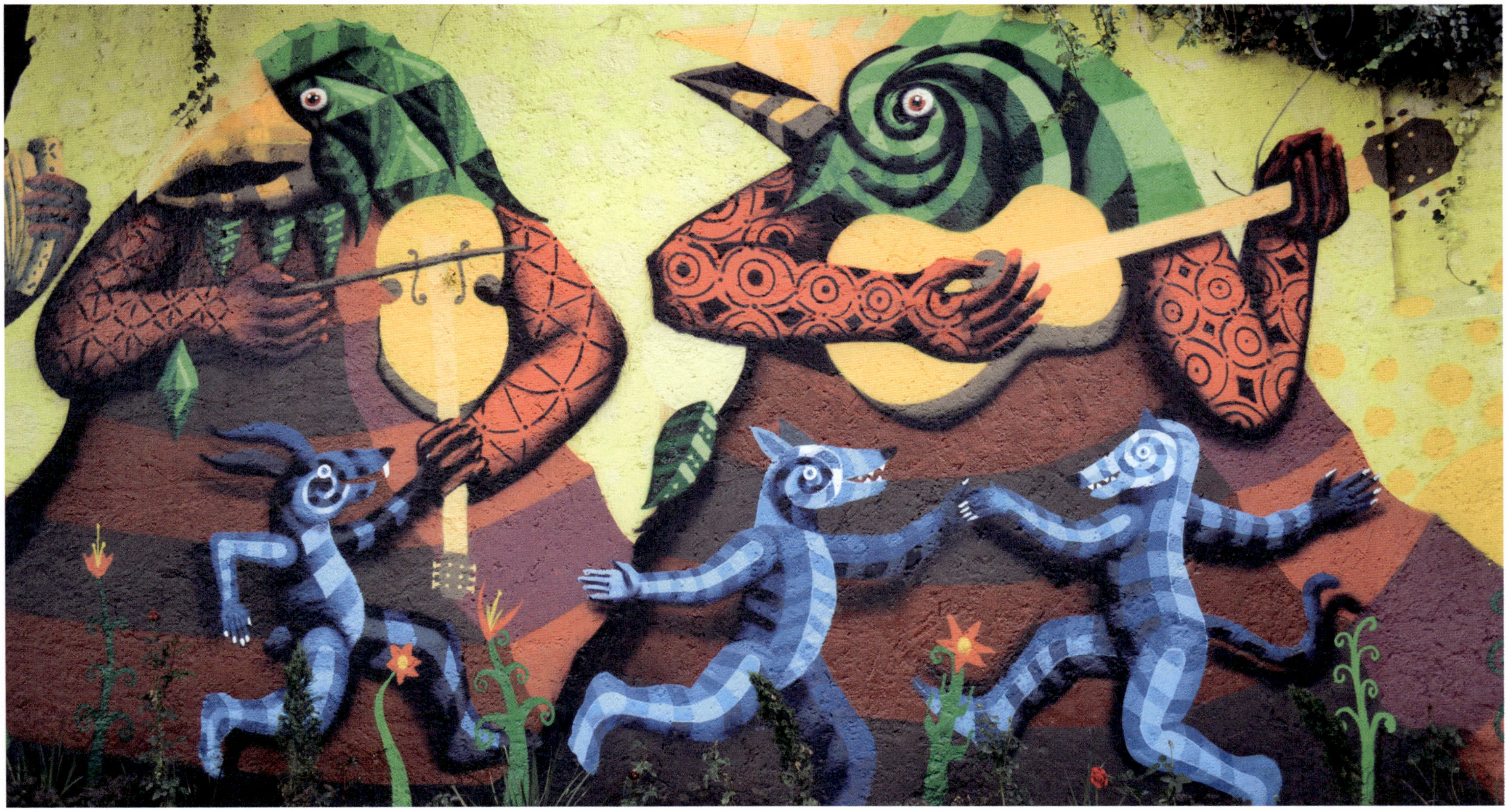

Fuco Ueda

Suggestive of daydreams, the subconscious, and the metaphorical,

the compositions of Japanese artist Fuco Ueda are radiant, enigmatic, meticulously crafted and, above all, captivating. You can lose yourself in the detail of her paintings, such as the curling fronds of a delicate chrysanthemum, or become absorbed in the symbolism of her dreamlike narratives. The central characters she depicts are usually young girls, who inhabit strange worlds, often surrounded by exquisitely portrayed flora and fauna. Of these figures she says, they 'do not exist as specific individuals. They may wake up one morning as deer, or turn into birds and fly away.'

Graduating from the Tokyo Polytechnic University's Graduate School of Arts in 2003, Ueda has been the recipient of many prizes and has exhibited widely in cities across the world, including Tokyo, Hong Kong, Los Angeles and New York. Early and continuing influences include the novels, comic books and movies she grew up with as a child. Her work is both classic and contemporary in feel, alluding to Japanese *manga* as well as traditional art forms such as *nihonga* – paintings that follow particular artistic conventions, and use specific techniques and materials, to expresss an ideal of perfection, a practice which has existed for more than one thousand years – and *ukiyo-e*, the hugely popular genre associated with the prosperous Edo period (1603–1868) of woodblock printing or painting worldly pleasures, such as folklore, landscape, the female form and erotica.

Ueda's art builds on this rich tradition, and embraces many of its principles of composition – her use of colour washes, graduation and outline, for example – as well as its themes, but with a contemporary twist. Many of her materials are also traditional, such as the slender writing brush with which she paints. While her principal medium is acrylic, thinned down to the consistency of watercolour, she also uses powdered mineral pigments on paper, cloth and wood.

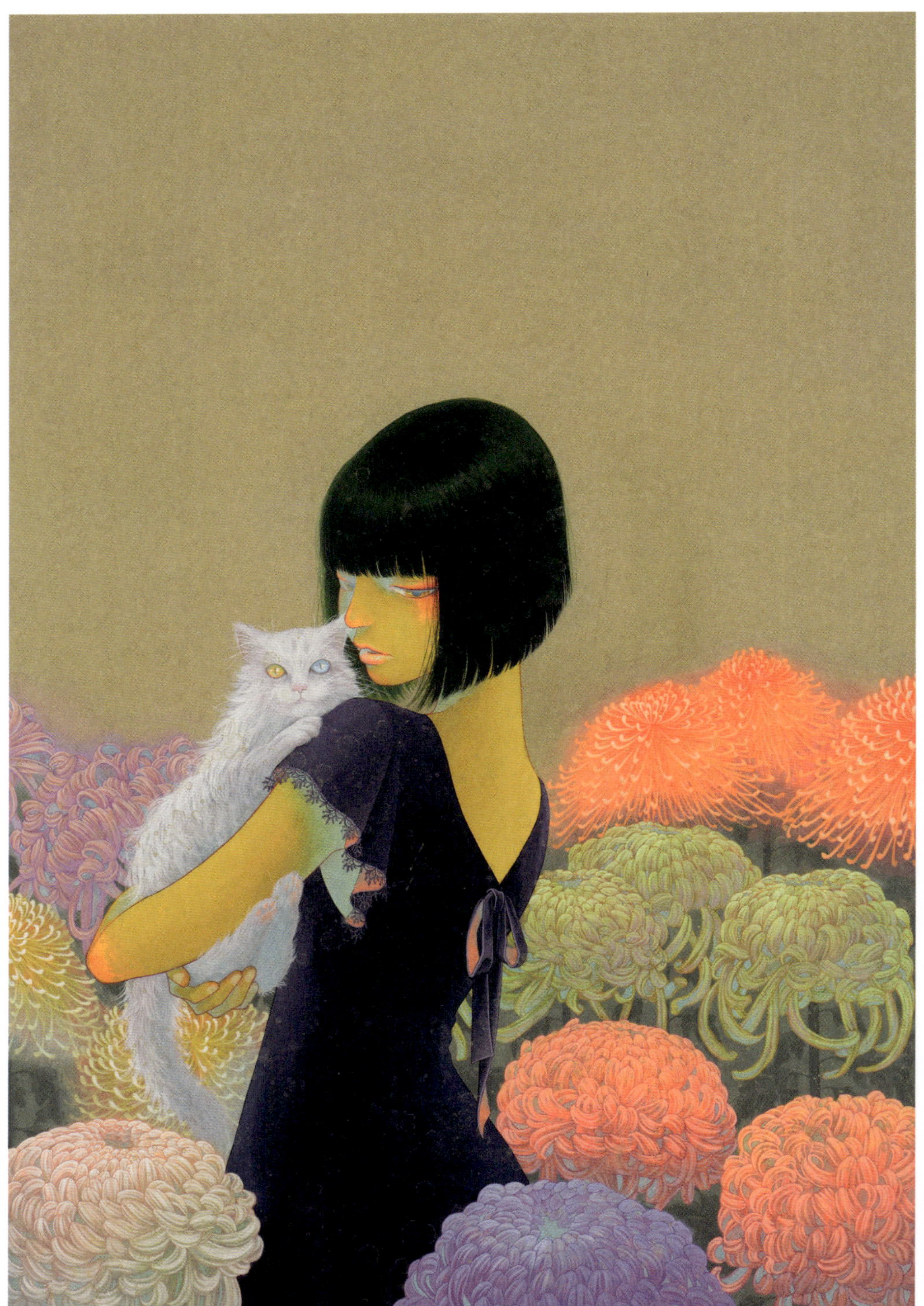

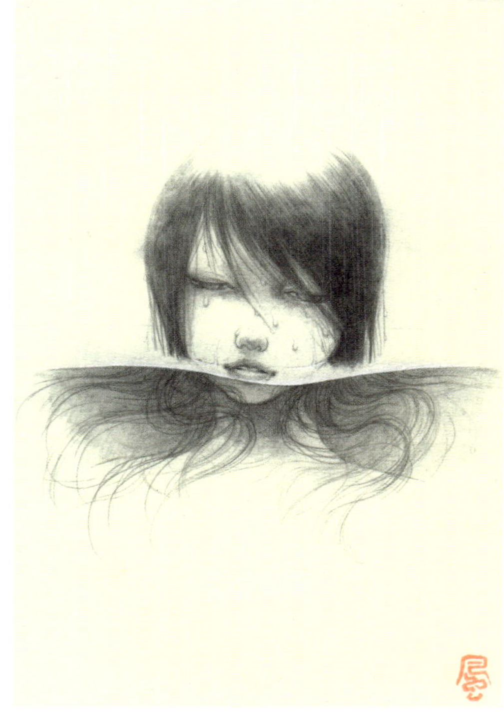

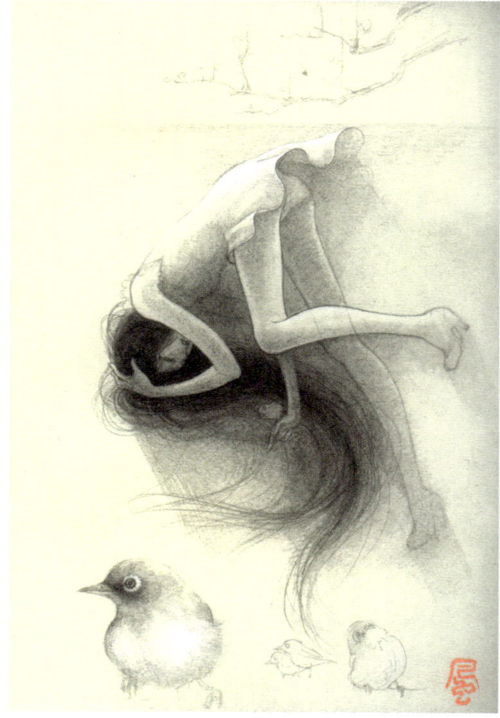

CLOCKWISE FROM TOP
Friend, 2013
Acrylic on canvas
72.7 × 50 cm (28⅝ × 19¾ in.)

Untitled, 2010
Pencil and acrylic on paper
29.5 × 21 cm (11⅝ × 8¼ in.)

Untitled, 2010
Pencil and acrylic on paper
29.5 × 21 cm (11⅝ × 8¼ in.)

OPPOSITE
Flower of Memory (triptych, central panel), 2014
Acrylic on canvas
46 × 35 cm (18 × 13¾ in.) each

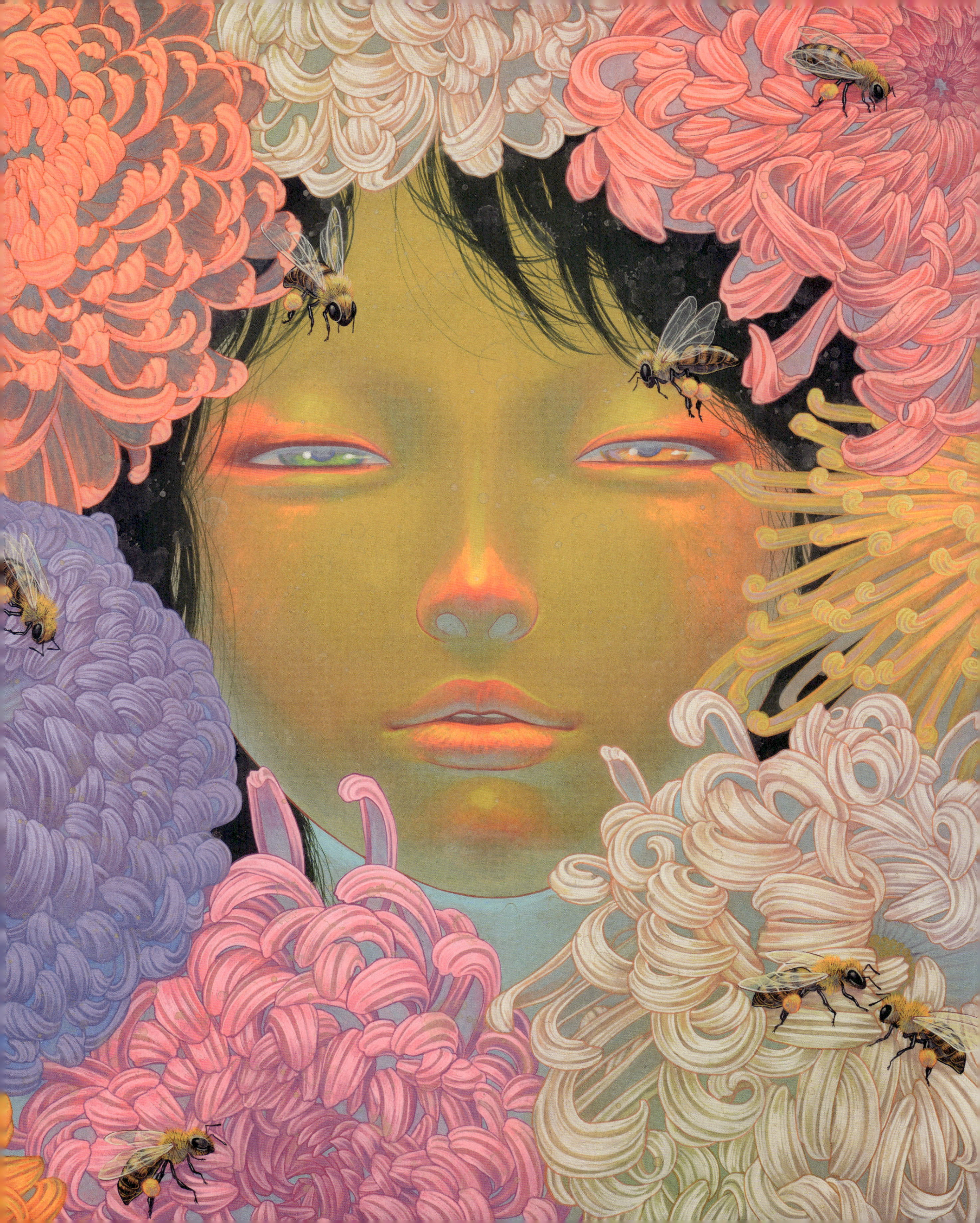

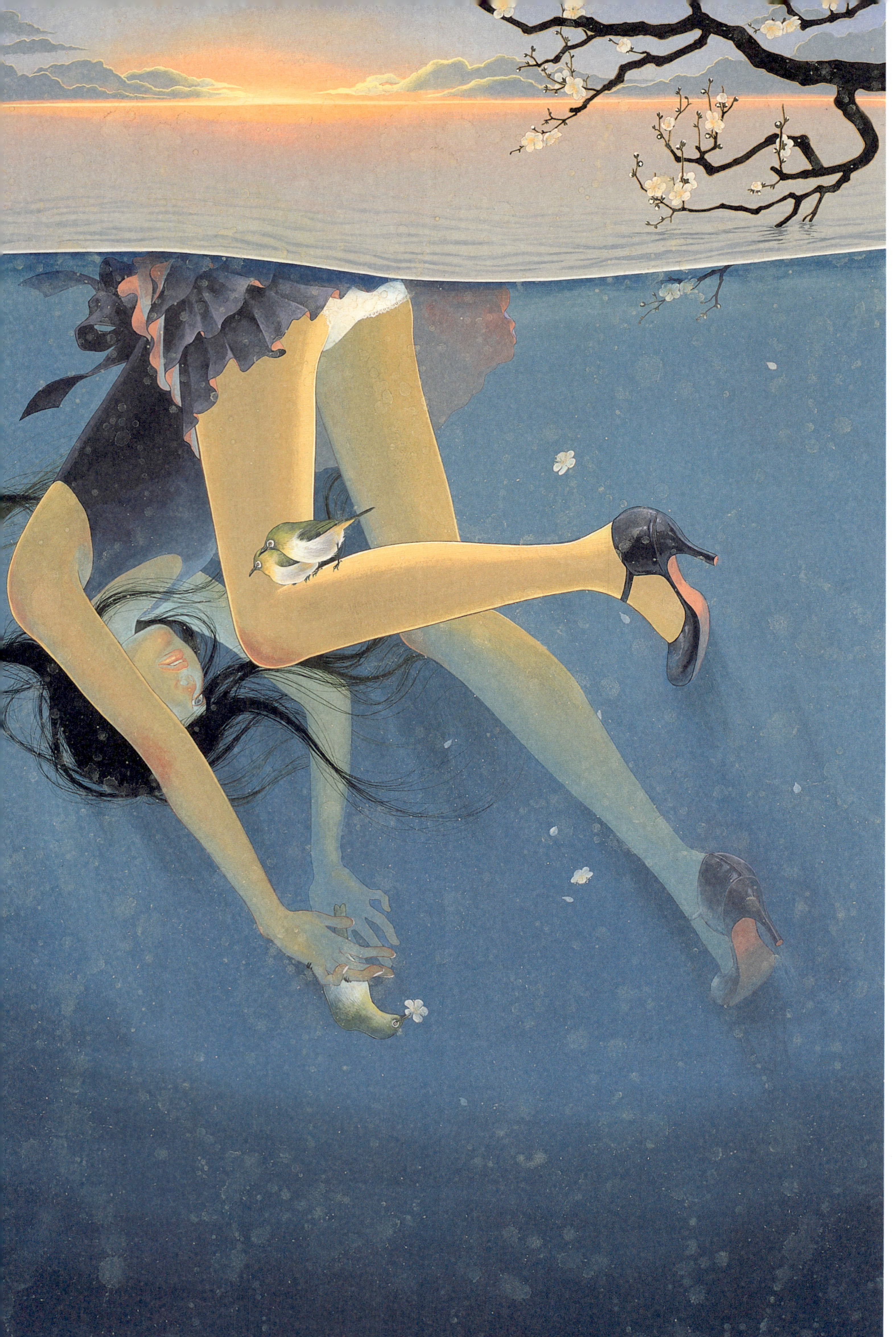

Piece of Spring, 2010
Acrylic on canvas
91 × 61.6 cm
(36 × 24¼ in.)

Inner Garden, 2011
Acrylic on canvas
100 × 80.3 cm
(39⅜ × 31⅝ in.)

Untitled, 2014
Pencil and acrylic
on paper
29.5 × 21 cm
(11⅝ × 8¼ in.)

Spring Rain, 2010
Acrylic on canvas
116.7 × 91 cm
(46⅜ × 36 in.)

*Study for Garden
of Silence*, 2014
Pencil and acrylic
on paper
39.8 × 29.8 cm
(15¾ × 11¾ in.)

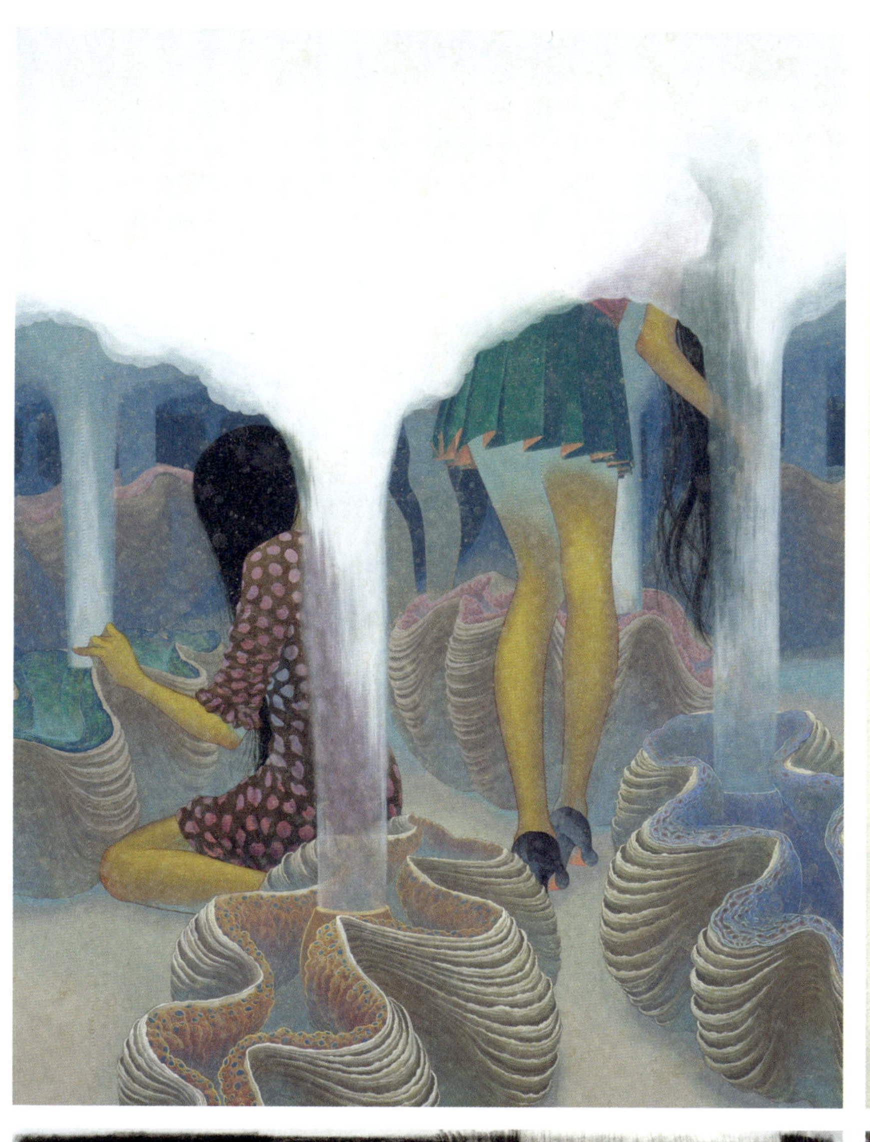
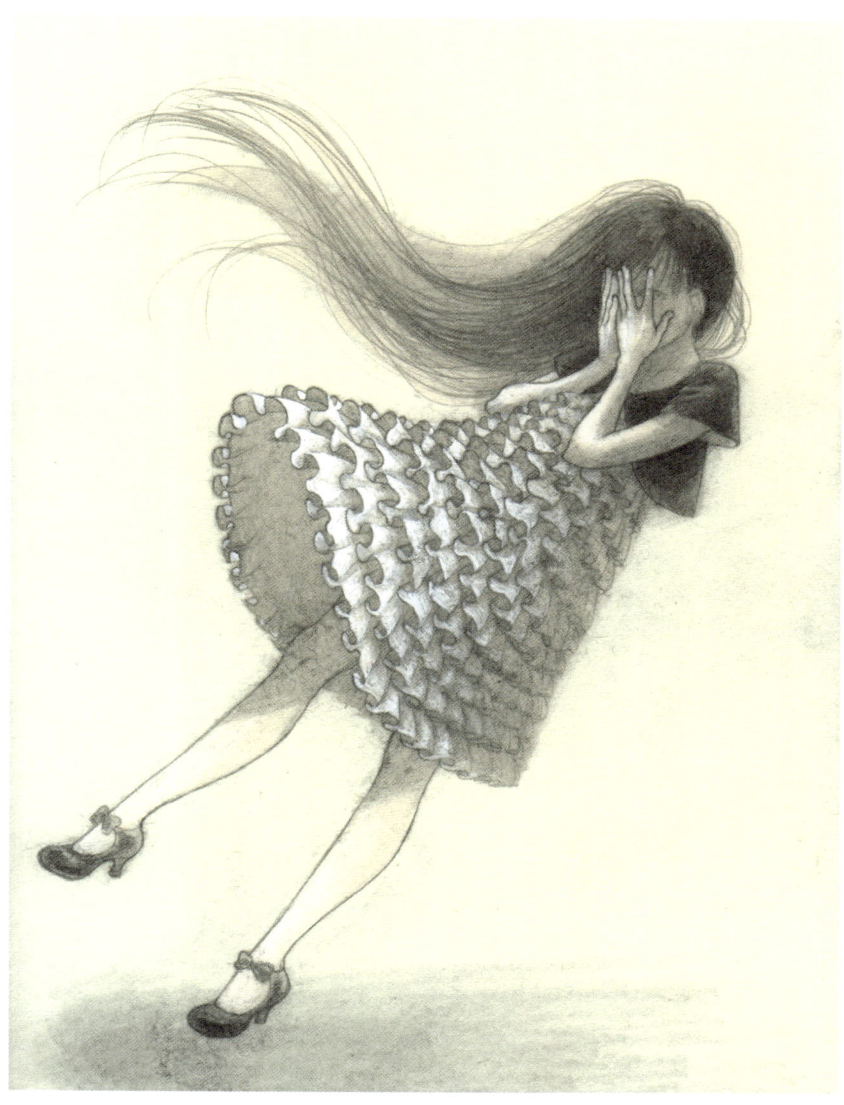
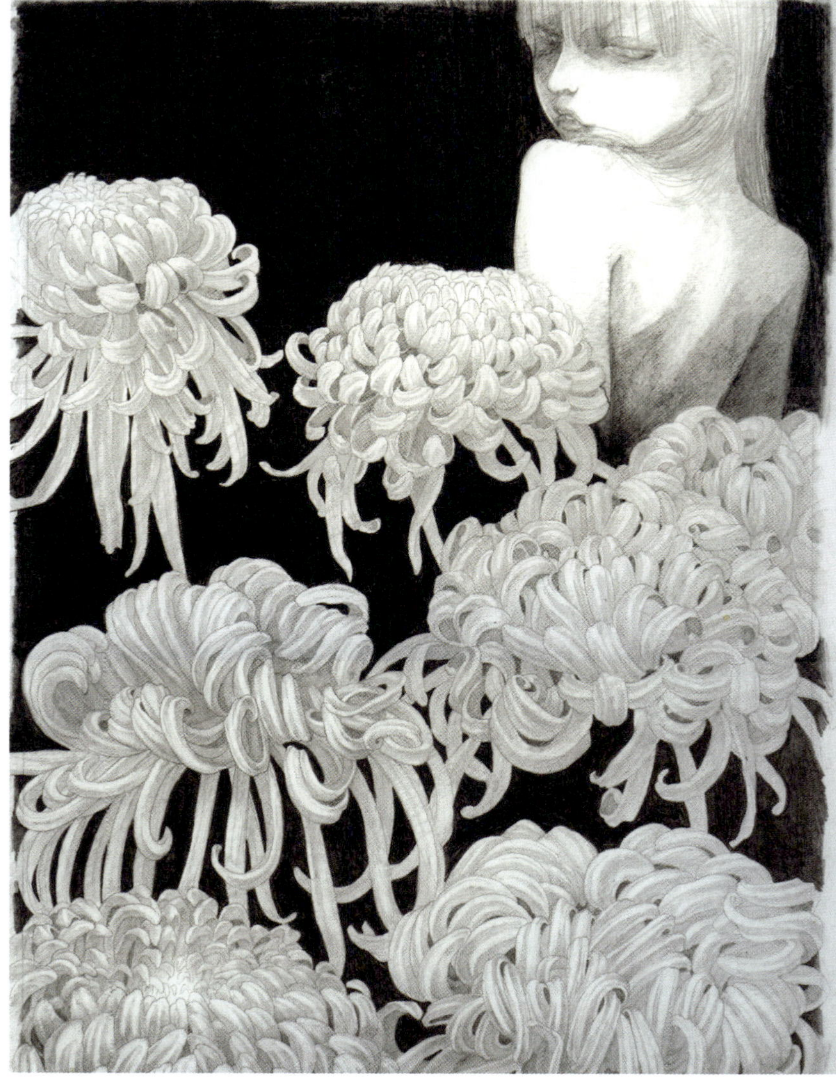
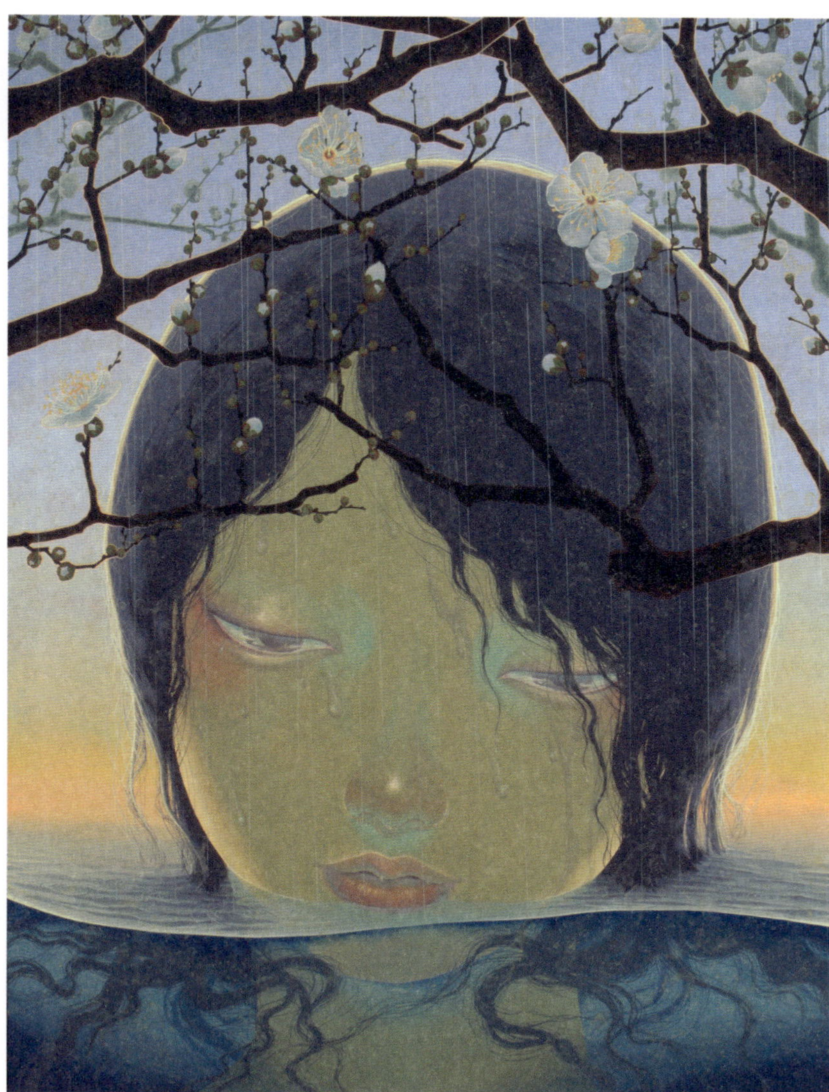

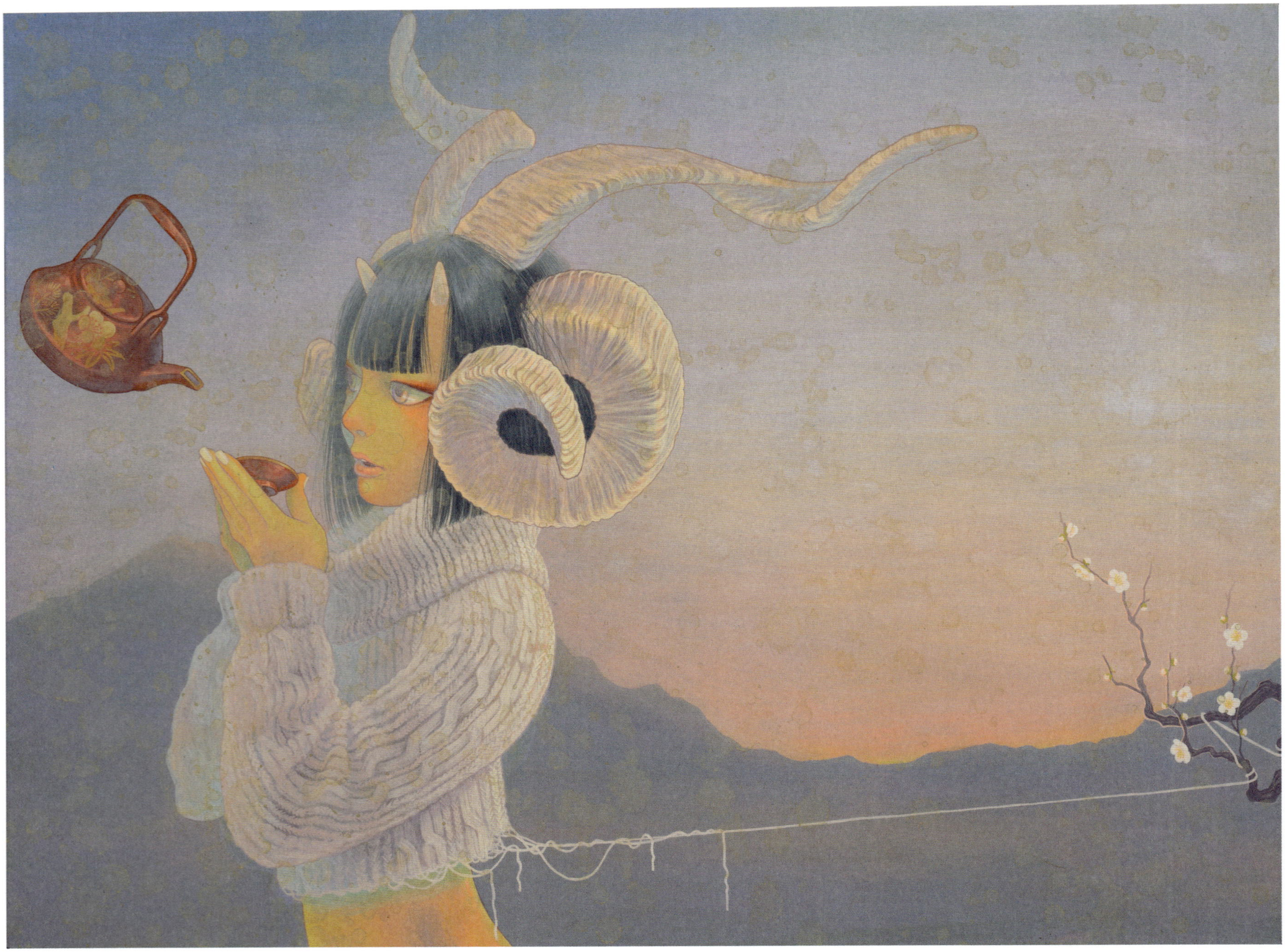

Ueda cites among her Western influences the French symbolist painter Odilon Redon (1840–1916), in particular his use of colour. A visionary artist, Redon was interested in portraying the psyche in his work, by depicting strange beings and ghosts. Similarly, Ueda's paintings open a door on to the invisible, otherworldly places with evocative narratives, a sense that is heightened by their titles, such as *Inner Garden* or *Garden of Silence*.

In these luminous and beguiling worlds often confounding or supernatural elements become manifest: a cat with different-coloured eyes, a snake with two heads or, more disturbing, visions of figures who appear to be drowning. Ueda states of these worlds that they emerge initially as 'visions…that are very clear and vivid' and, with a mastery of paint, she skilfully brings them to life, connecting the past, present and subconscious in one fell swoop.

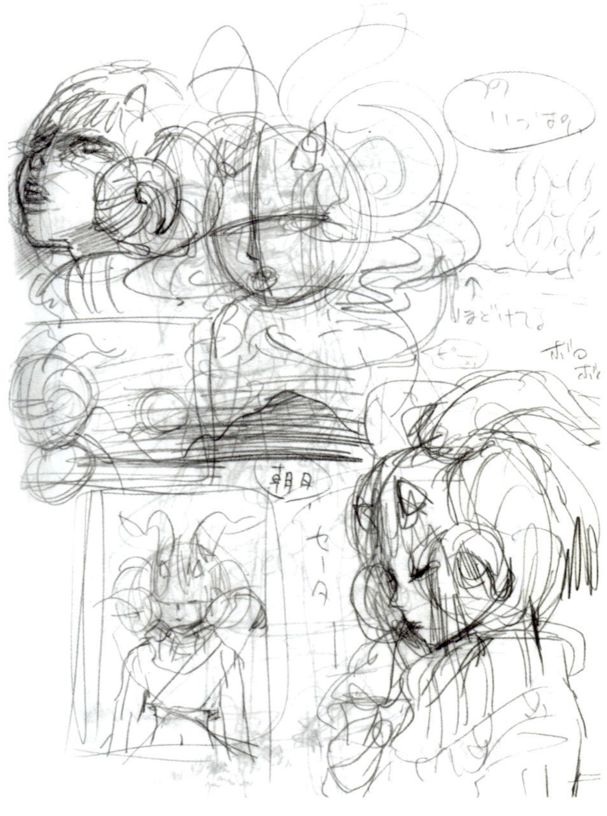

Otoso, 2014
Acrylic on canvas
33.3 × 45.5 cm
(13⅛ × 18 in.)

Preliminary drawings, 2014
Pencil on paper
29.8 × 24 cm (11¾ × 9½ in.)

OPPOSITE
Yabusame, 2014
Acrylic on canvas
46 × 35 cm (18⅛ × 13¾ in.)

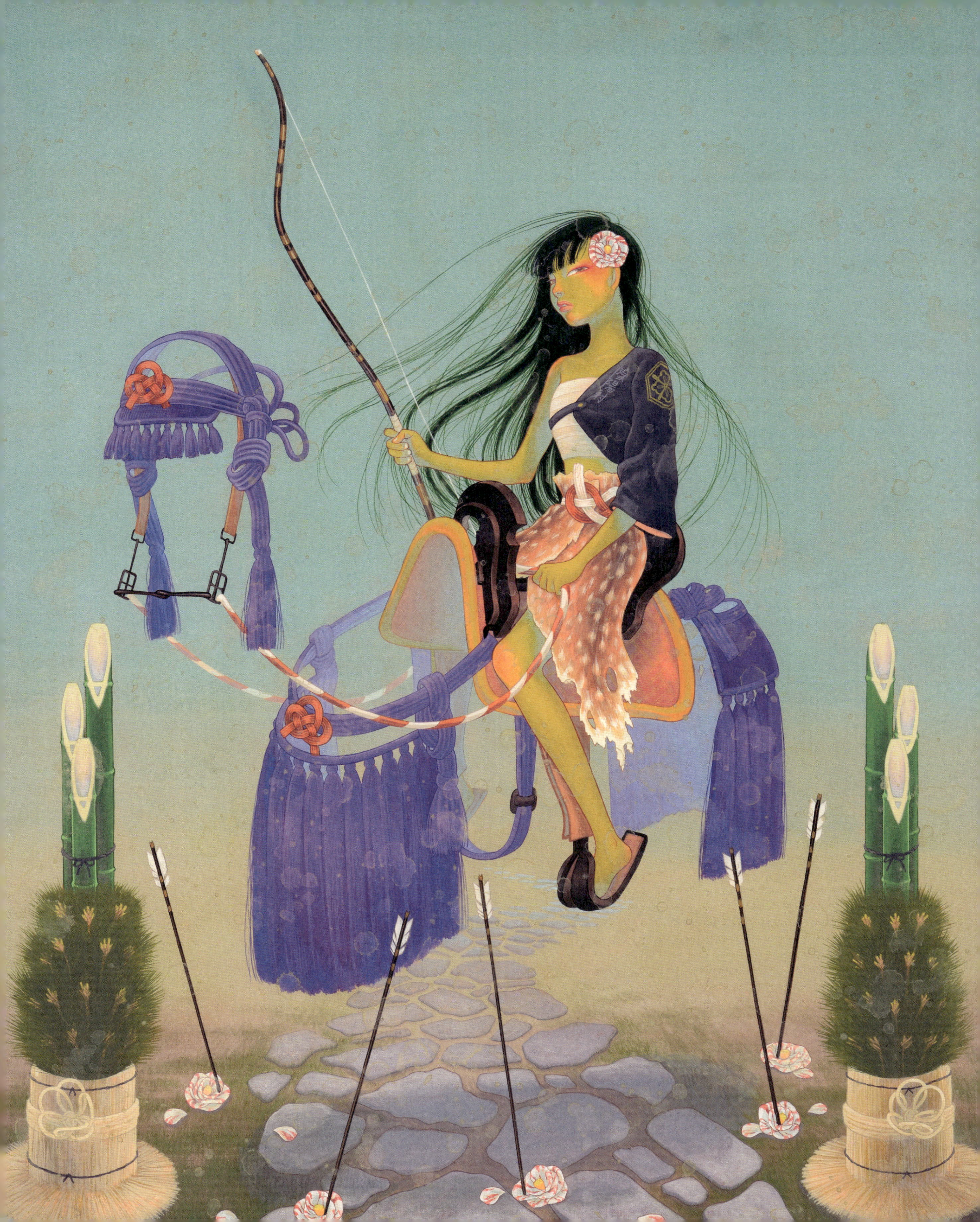

Ernest Zacharevic

With an admirable attention to detail and a delightful playfulness,

the site-specific works of Lithuanian artist Ernest Zacharevic are a visual treat. Zacharevic often combines two- and three-dimensional elements within his work, as in his famous mural in George Town, in Penang, Malaysia, in which two children he has painted on a wall appear to be speeding along on a discarded bicycle that has been left to rest there.

Zacharevic was born and raised in Vilnius, and from an early age expressed an interest in art. He studied at the Vilnius Academy of Art before moving to London in 2006, where he undertook a BA in Fine Art. The city's East End was a great source of stimuli for Zacharevic and he soon became enthusiastic about the graffiti he saw there, particularly the works that were socially and politically motivated. It was at this junction that he began to start making graffiti work.

Soon after he travelled to the city of Penang, where he now lives and works. At the time of his move, there was little evidence of an urban art scene, with locals being curious and unprejudiced in their reactions to the small street-art community that did exist. In this environment Zacharevic felt that there was no pressure to conform or to limit oneself in terms of technique or subject-matter, and so his work thrived.

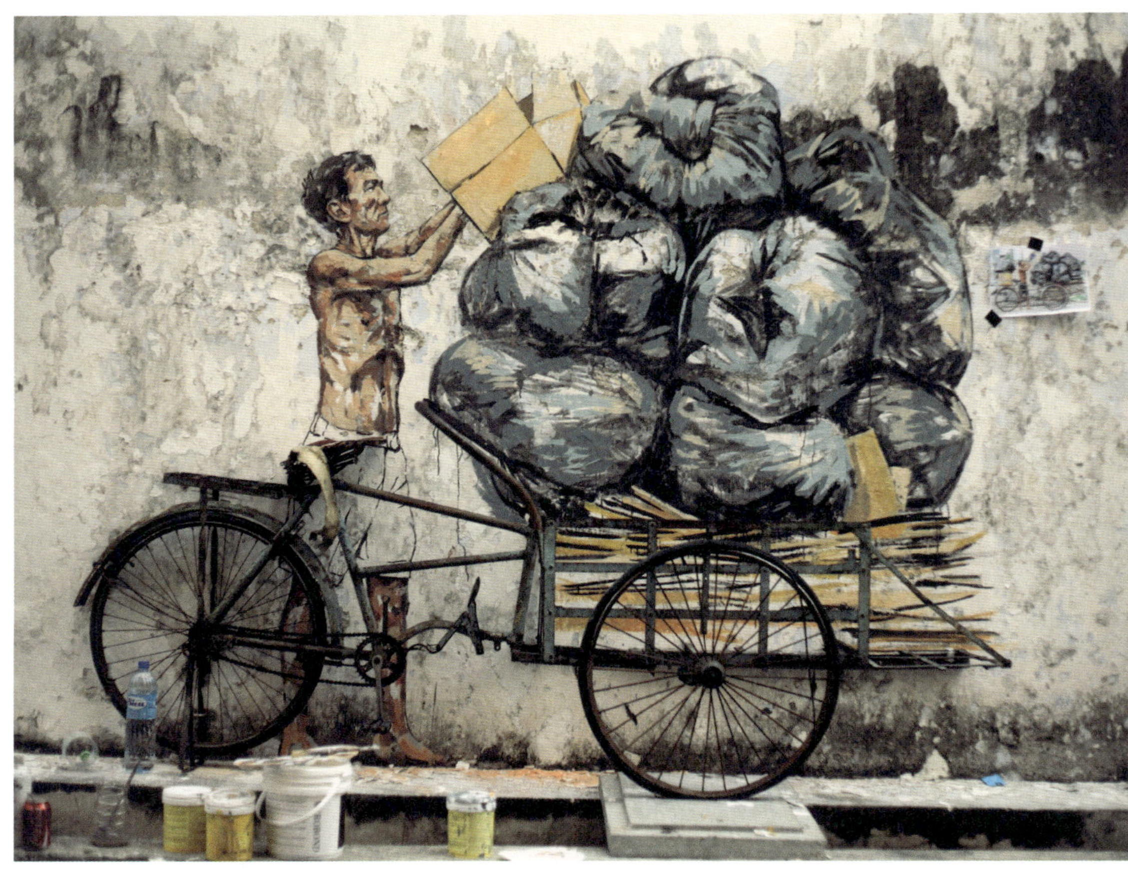

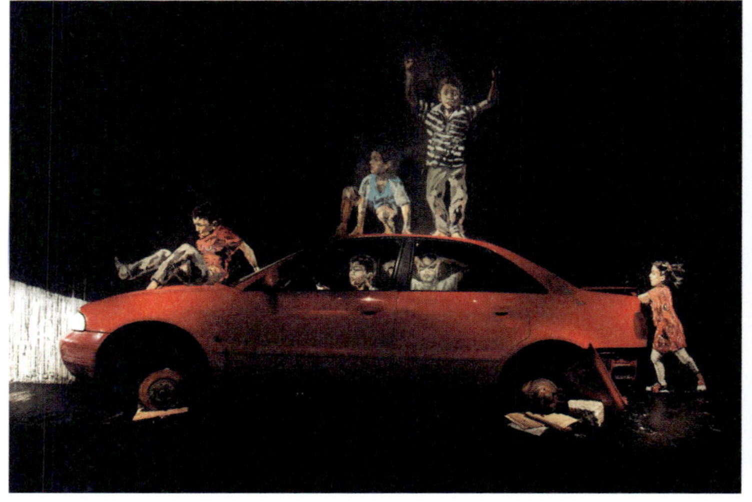

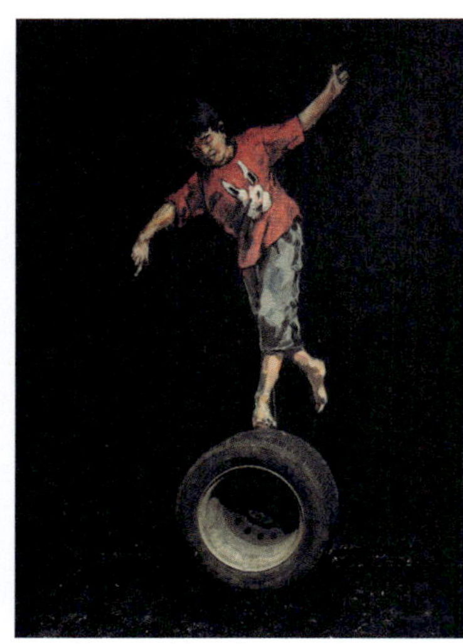

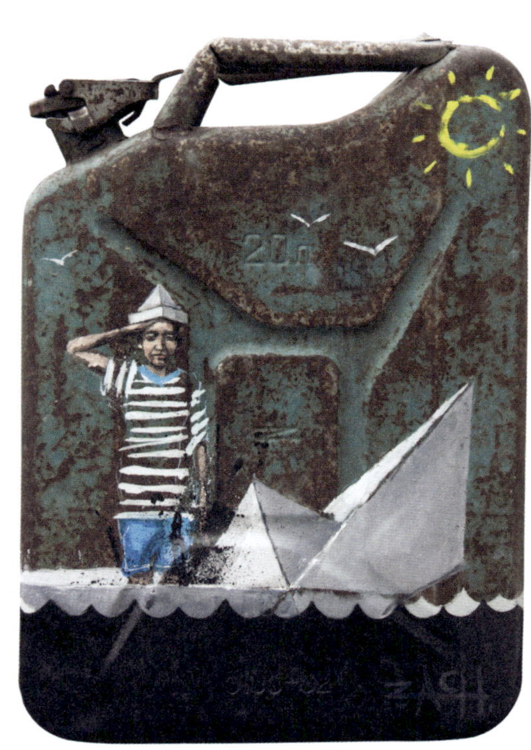

CLOCKWISE FROM TOP
Untitled, from the series
'Art is Rubbish', 2014
Mixed media
Dimensions variable

Untitled, c. 2014
Mixed media
Dimensions variable

The Spill, 2014
Mixed media
Dimensions variable

Untitled, commission by
Nuart Festival, Stavanger,
Norway, 2015
Mixed media
Dimensions variable

OPPOSITE
*Little Children on the
Bicycle*, 2012
Mixed media
Dimensions variable

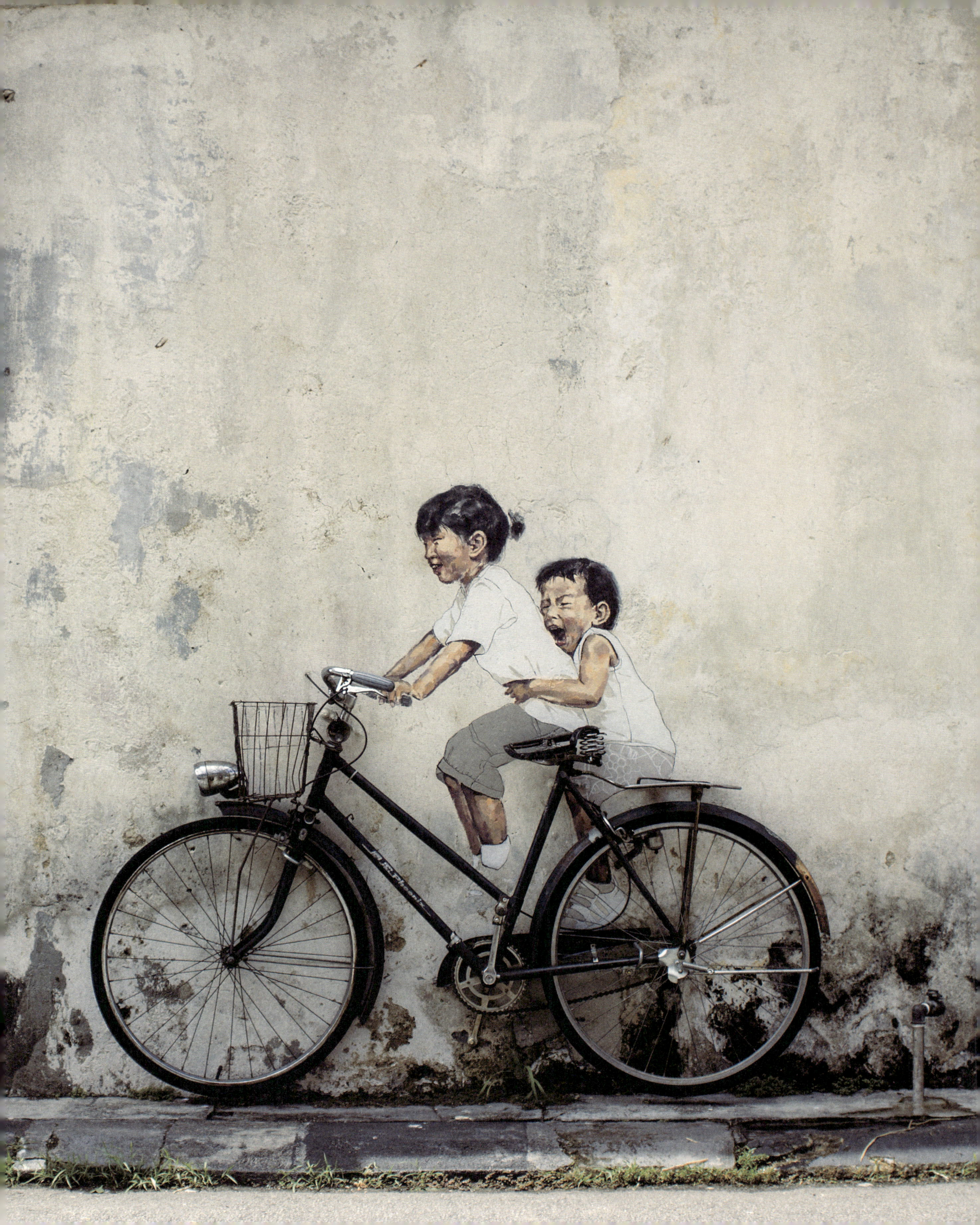

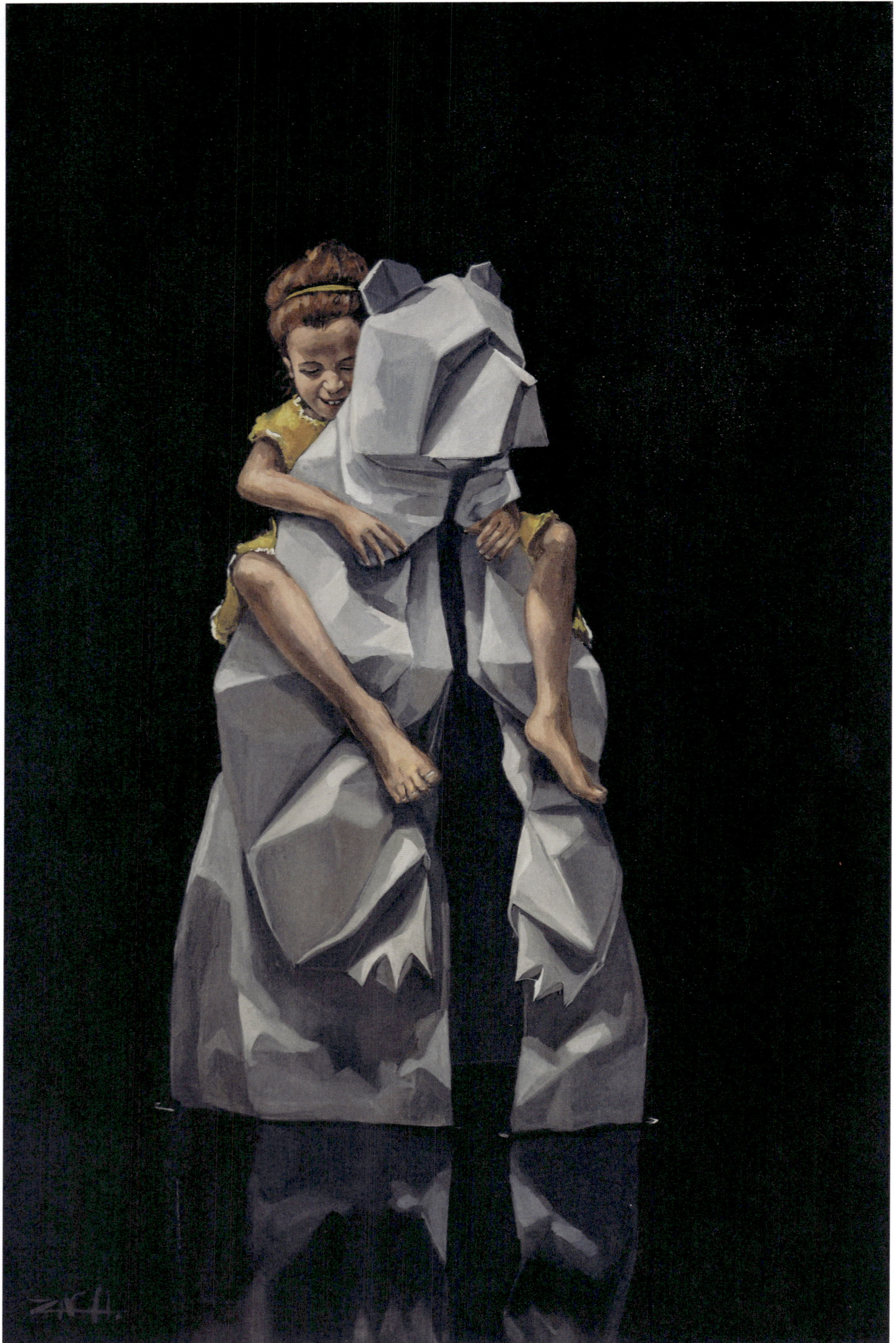

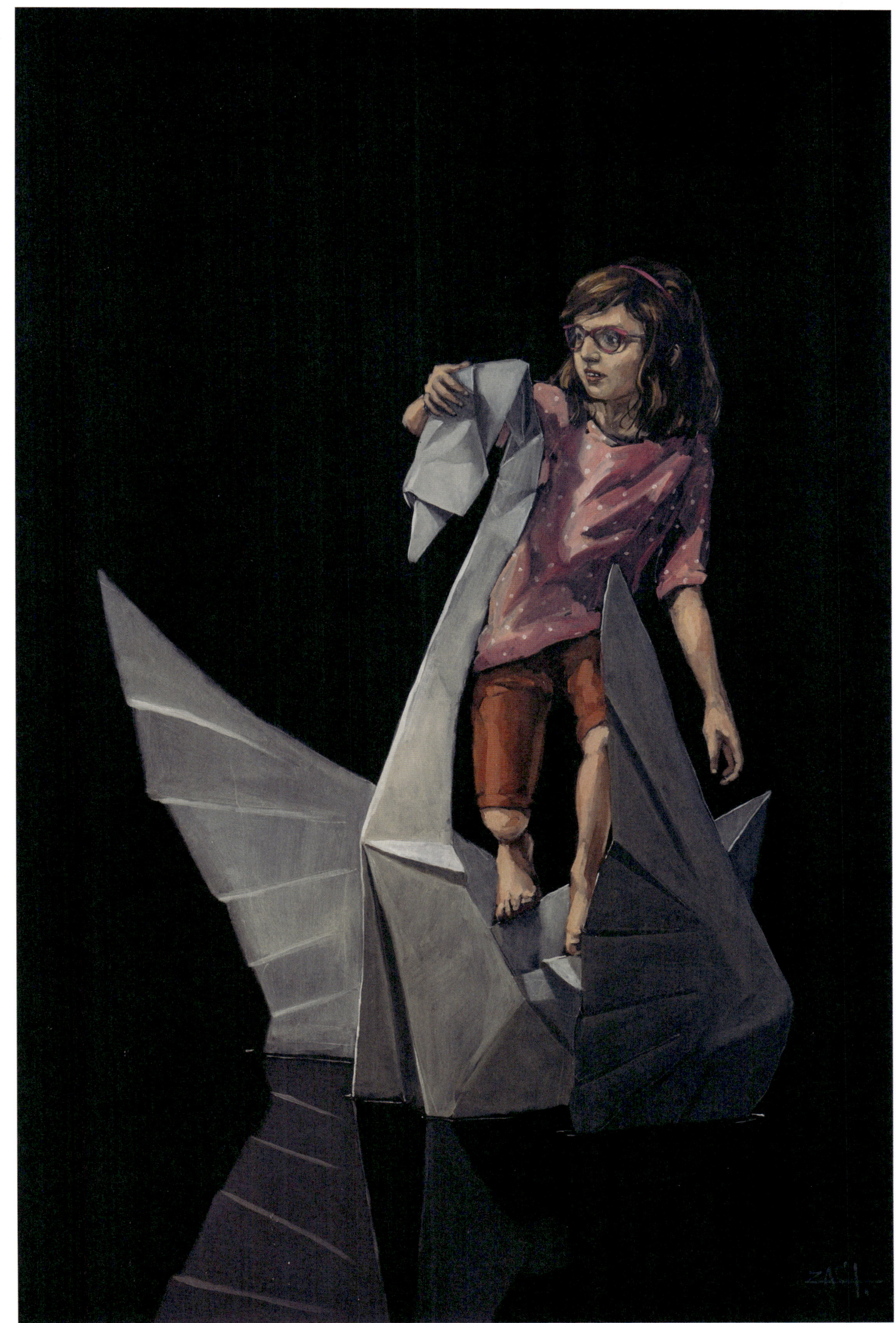

OPPOSITE AND RIGHT
Untitled, both from the
series 'Floor is Lava', 2015
Oil on canvas
Dimensions unknown

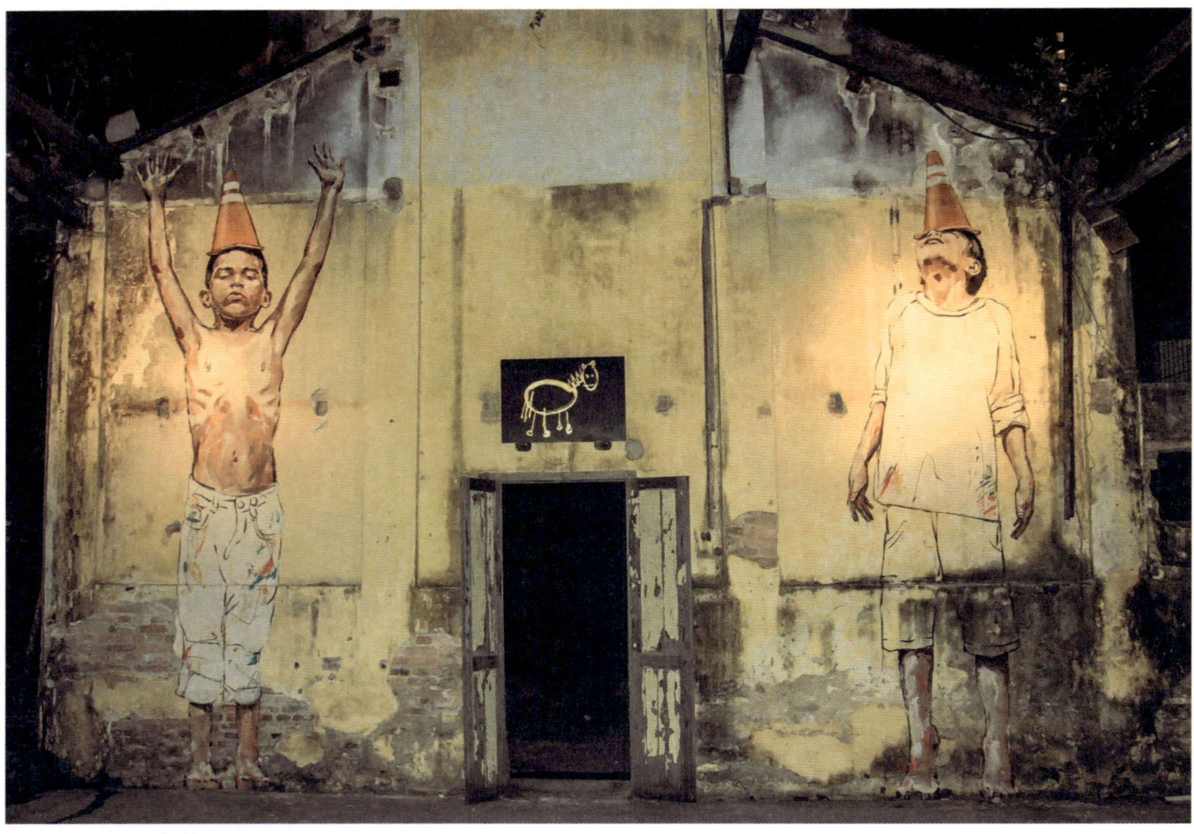

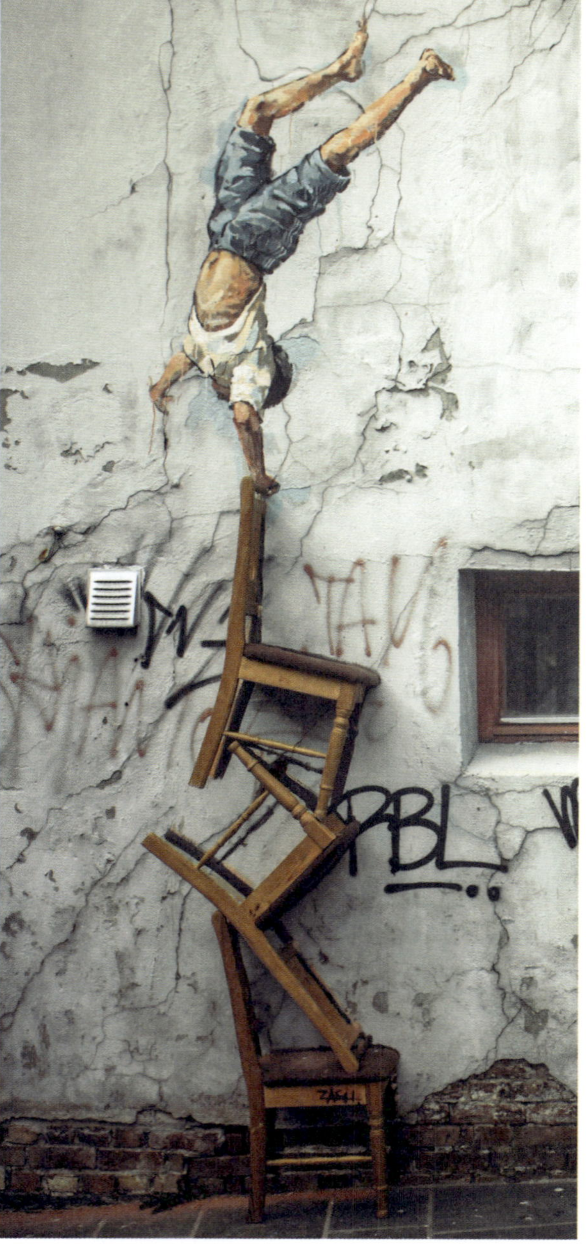

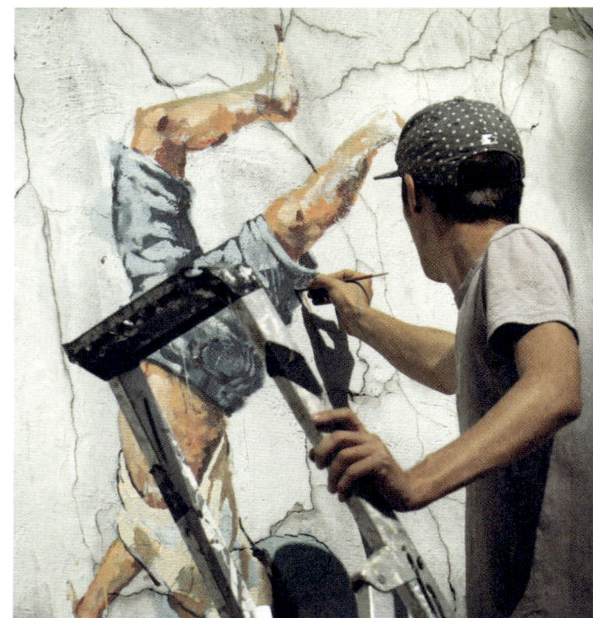

Alongside his street art Zacharevic has a busy studio practice that is focused on painting, into which he often incorporates unusual or found mixed media. Shifting between the street and studio he enjoys the challenge of the varieties of scale and environment that he encounters, and the manner in which the work might be received – from the 'organic' interaction between the viewer and his art in the public realm, to the more structured viewing environment of the gallery – all of which feeds back into his output.

Of his practice Zacharevic says: 'Art is a natural part of my life, with everything I do affecting everything else. I enjoy many different hobbies and pastimes: listening to music, socializing, learning new languages. The activities I engage with blend, inspire and enhance other areas of my life. That transference of skills is what makes you different and stand out.'

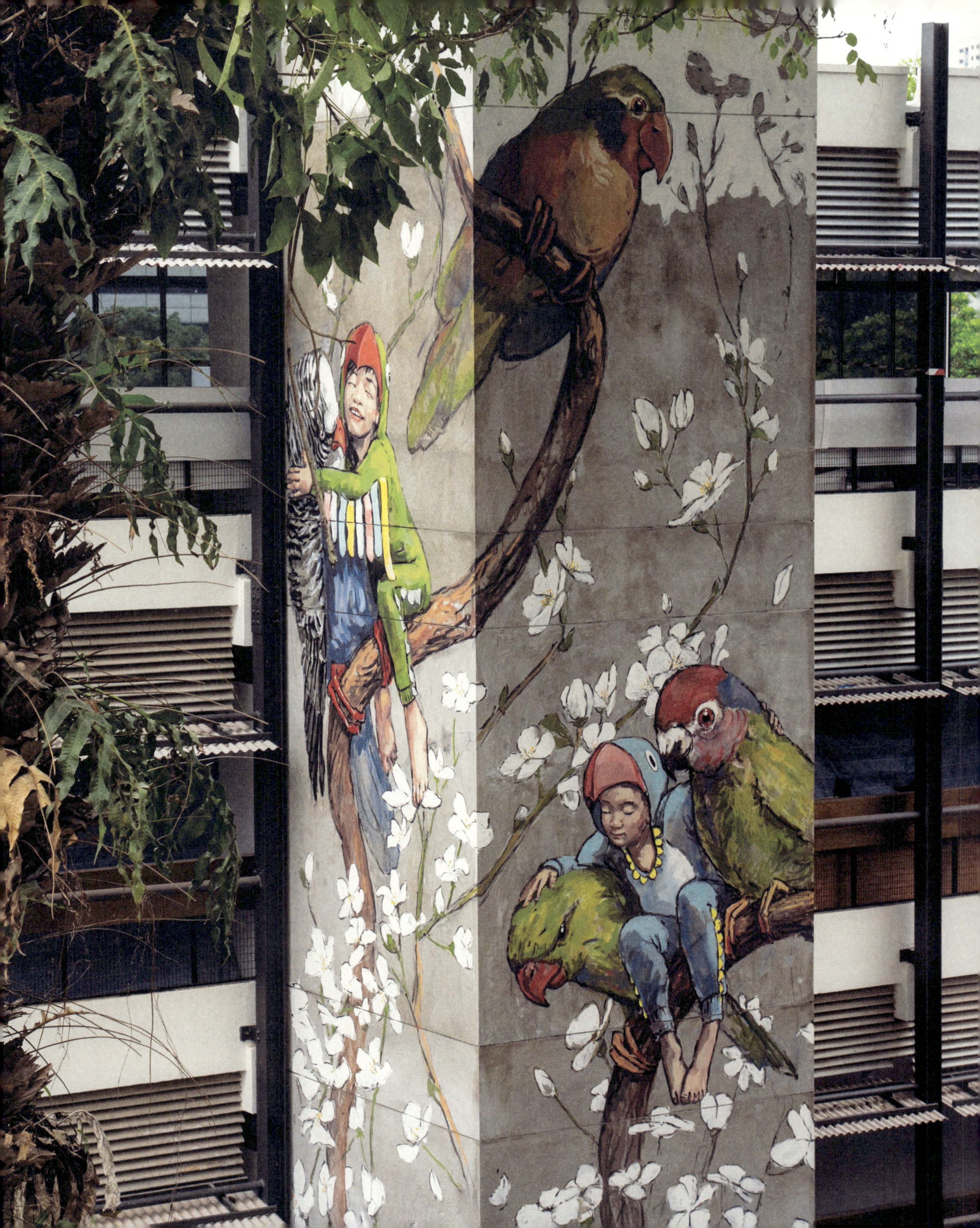

Zio Ziegler

Internationally recognized for his bold and intricately patterned large-scale murals and dynamic works on canvas,

the young American artist Zio Ziegler is energetic, entrepreneurial and prolific. He purportedly creates up to one thousand paintings and sketches a year, while his home city of San Francisco boasts forty of his murals across its neighbourhoods. There are numerous others in locations around the world. Even at this level of production he has found time to design clothing and shoe collections for Vans and founded his own clothing label Arte Sempre, which produces textiles incorporating the patterns he depicts in his paintings.

Both on the street and in the studio Ziegler approaches the art of painting with an all-embracing raw energy and joyful unselfconsciousness, which is intoxicating to behold. This vigour is particularly apparent in his murals, which are produced at a furious pace, almost always rendered in black and white with spray paint, using designs that are improvised in situ. Populated with primitive-style figures, flora and fauna and mythological symbols, his compositions seemingly contort themselves to fill the spaces to which they have been assigned. These free-flowing characters have an almost sculptural quality to them, comprising strong, silhouetted forms inscribed with sinewy graphic patterns, which highlight not only their muscles and their mechanics but also their internal energy. As these forms interact with one another, these interlocking graphic shapes add to the dynamism of their distorted poses.

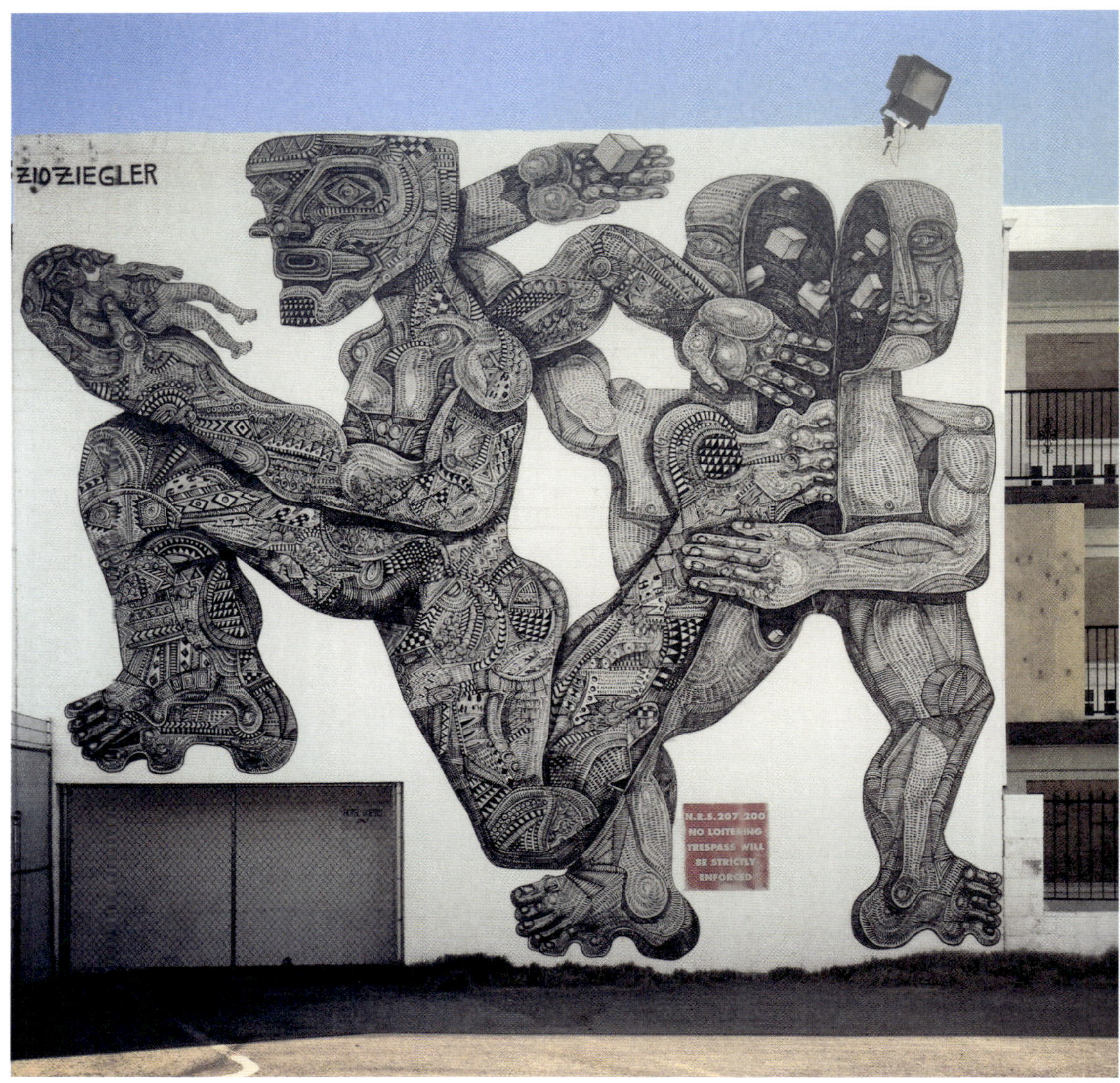

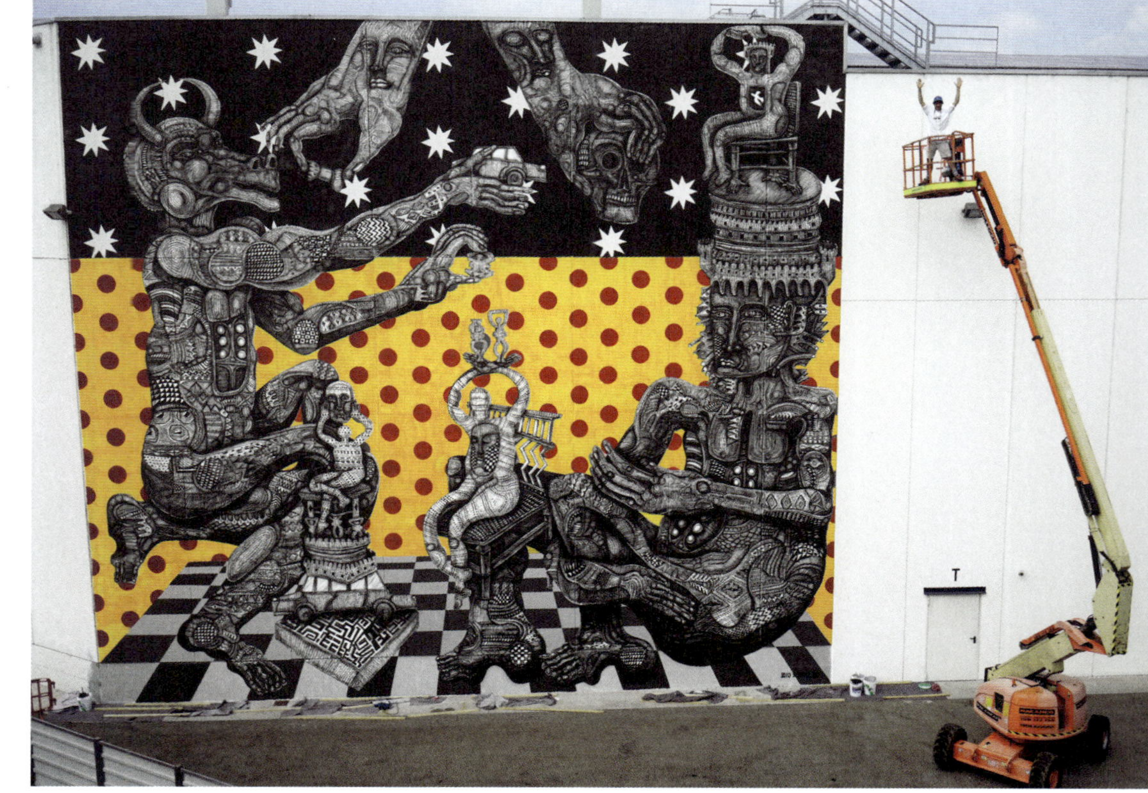

Untitled, c. 2015
Mixed media
Dimensions variable

The Metamorphosis of Self,
c. 2015
Mixed media
Dimensions unknown

OPPOSITE, CLOCKWISE FROM
TOP LEFT
Self Portrait Study, 2014
Mixed media on board
61 × 46 cm (24 × 18⅛ in.)

The Spill, 2014
Mixed media
Dimensions unknown

Untitled, c. 2015
Mixed media
Dimensions unknown

Untitled, c. 2015
Mixed media
Dimensions unknown

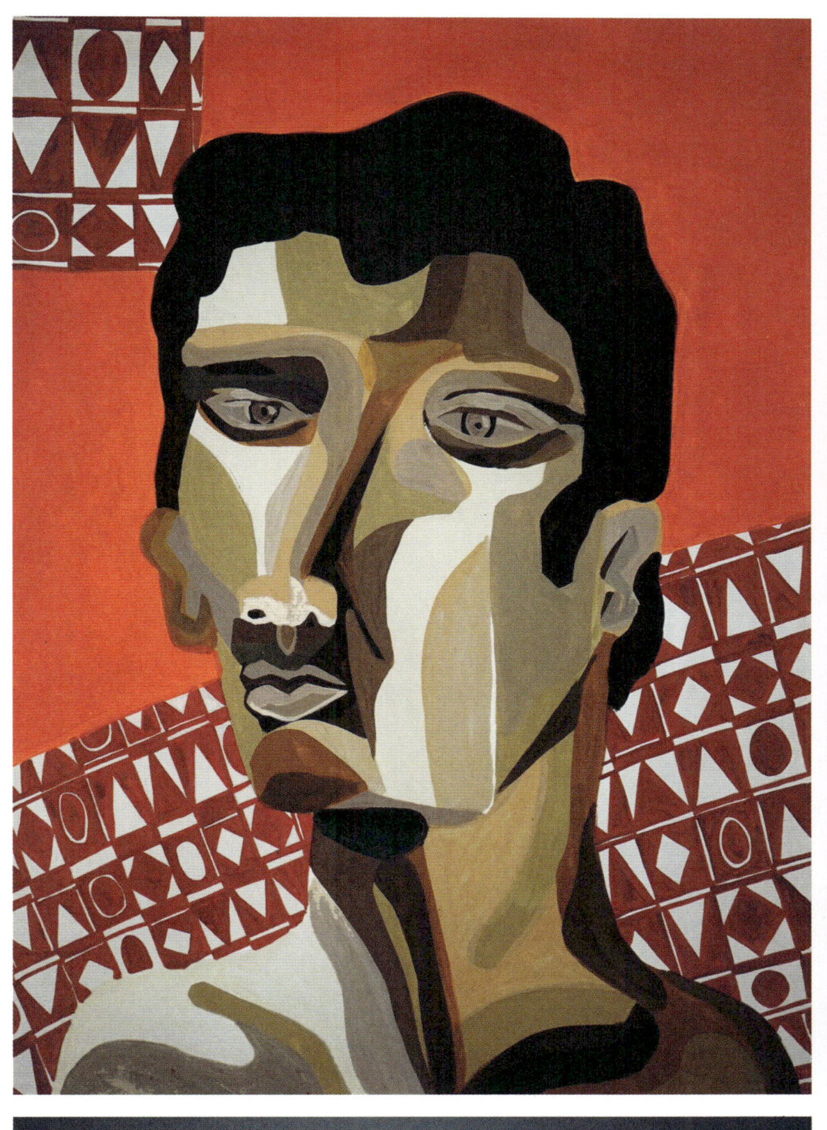
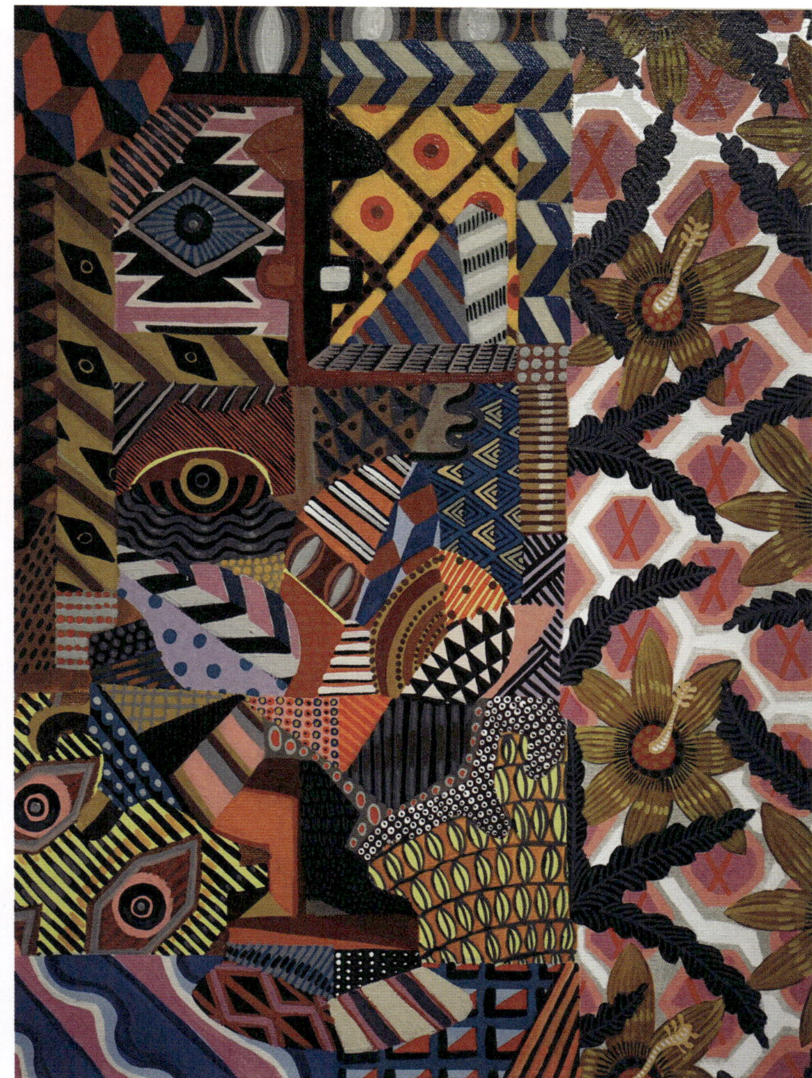
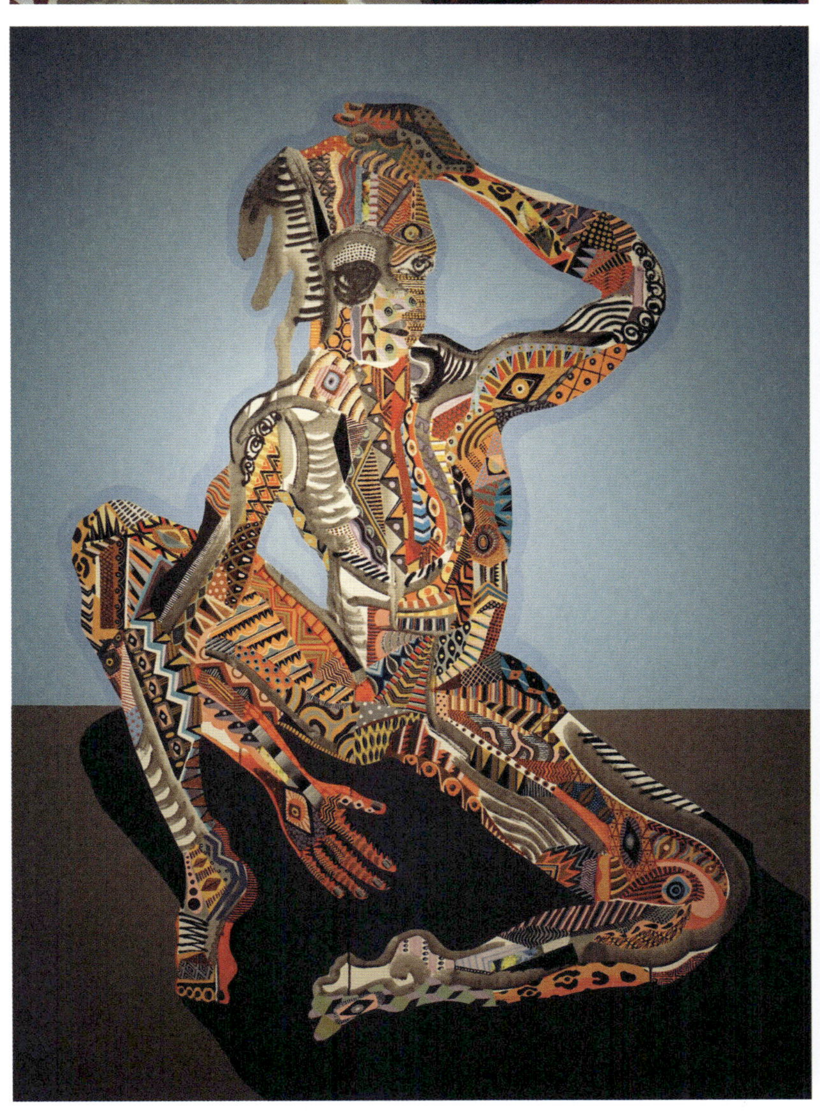
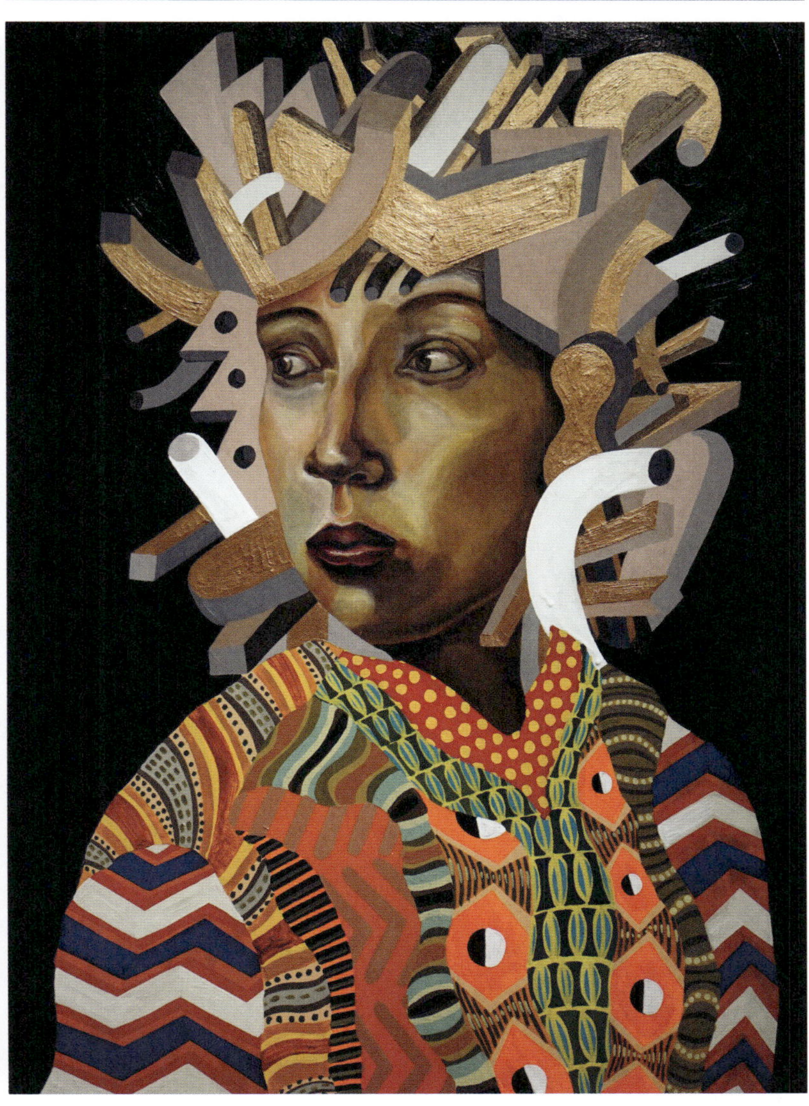

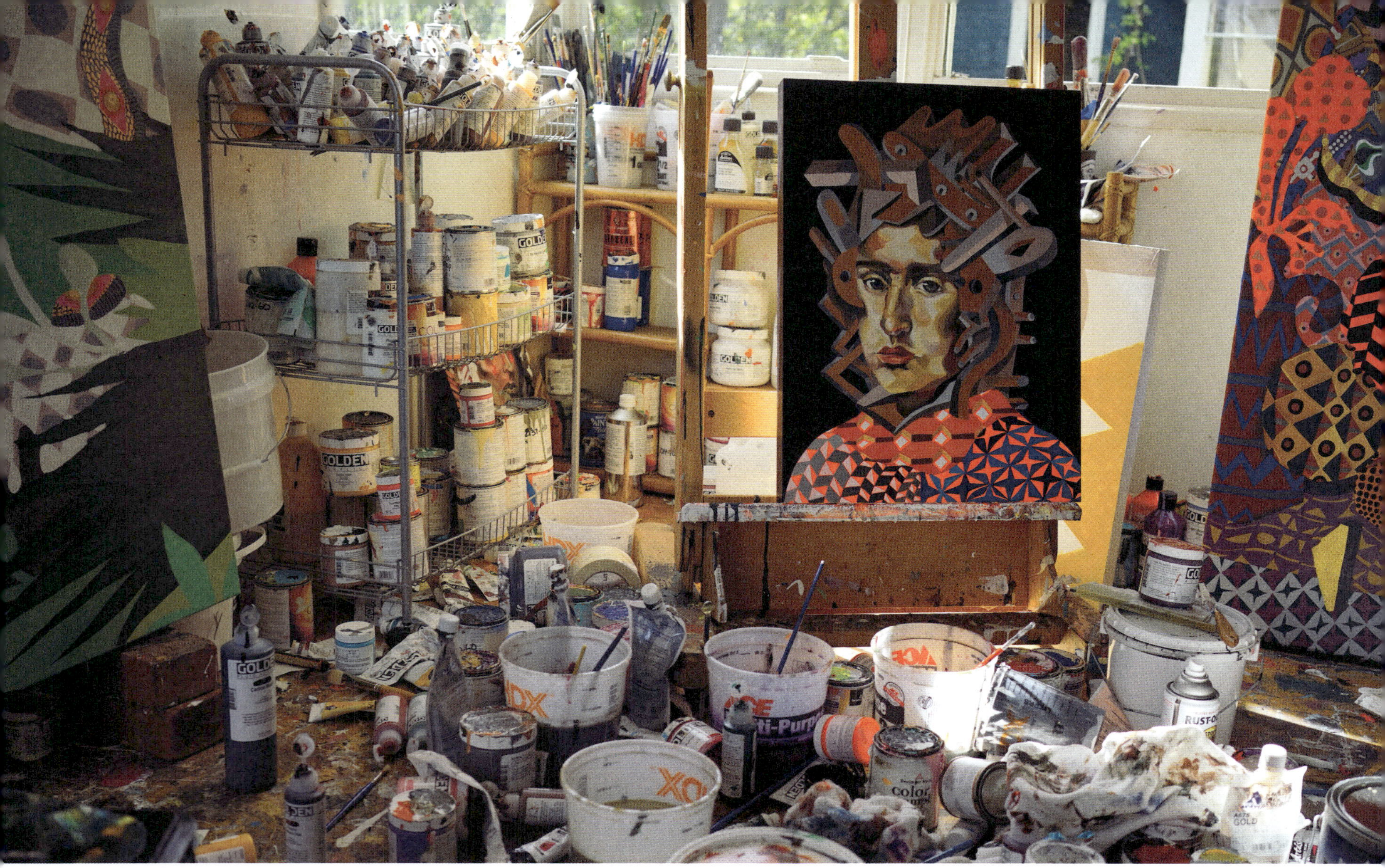

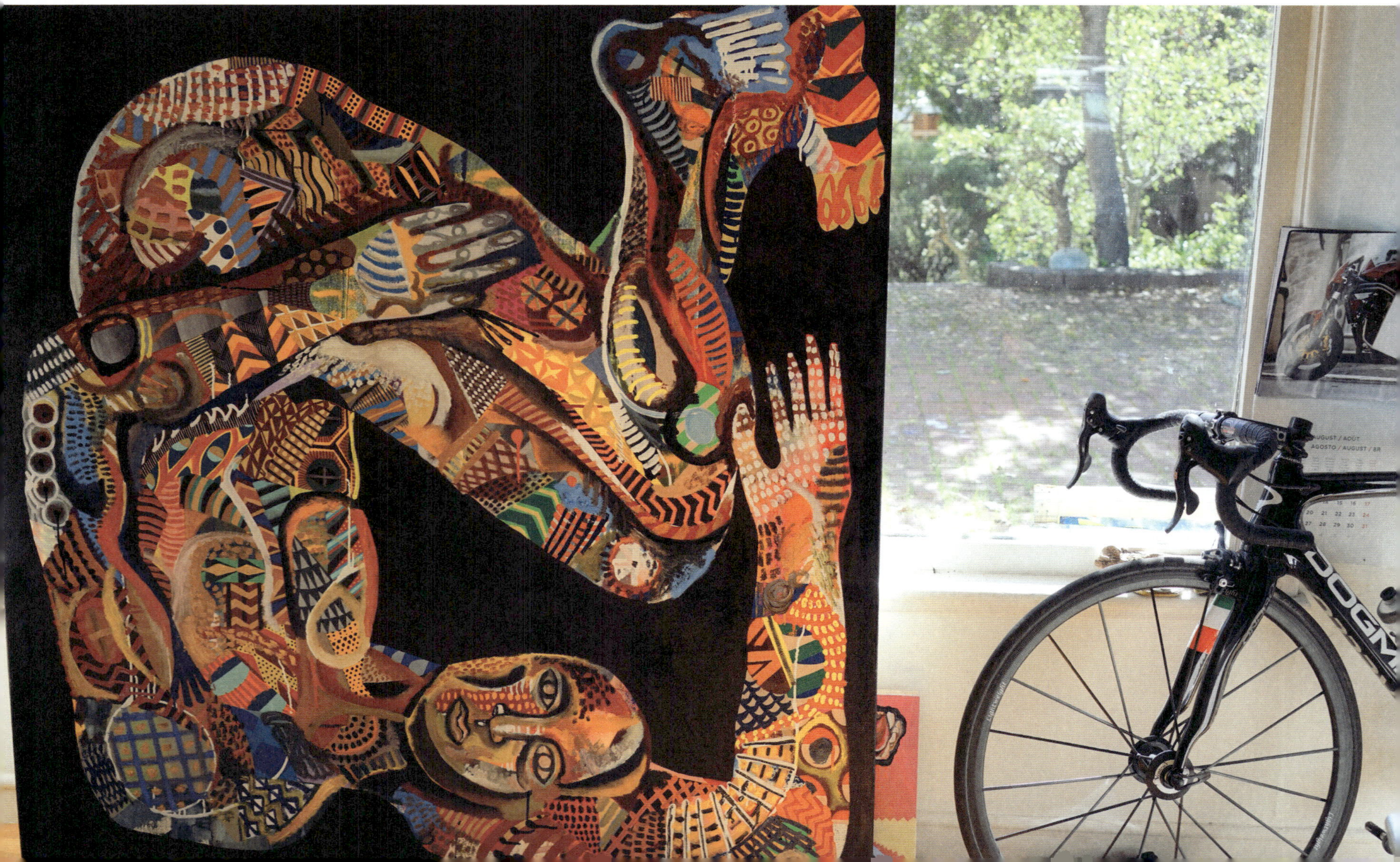

As the art critic Ivan Quaroni summarizes of
Ziegler's work, 'For him, the practice of painting is a
form of personal investigation and, at the same time,
a spiritual discipline that is expressed in the form
of an erratic path through the winding bends of the
individual and collective unconscious.' In a paint-strewn
studio away from the city Ziegler is unceasingly active,
producing a great body of work in which the visual ideas
underpinning one piece will feed into the next. Working
primarily on canvas or linen he uses a mix of oil and
acrylic and sometimes enamel, crayon and pigment to
build up his complex surfaces. Of the intuitive paths he
takes – his choice of colour, materials and pattern – to
create his work, he explains: 'I paint how I feel, not how
I see…. My work is not about a final product, rather the
process that helps me solve a problem.'

Equally instinctive are Ziegler's diverse artistic
influences, which include late medieval and
quattrocento painting, aboriginal, African and naive
art, and the European graffiti movement. Often it is
a fusion or clash of different genres, with numerous
stylistic elements from the history of painting – such
as Classicism, Cubism, Primitivism – juxtaposed with
contemporary graphic forms that defines his style.
His choice of visual inspiration is also linked to the
expansive themes within his work; with a universal
language he looks at concepts such as the balance
between nature and artifice, instinct and civilization.

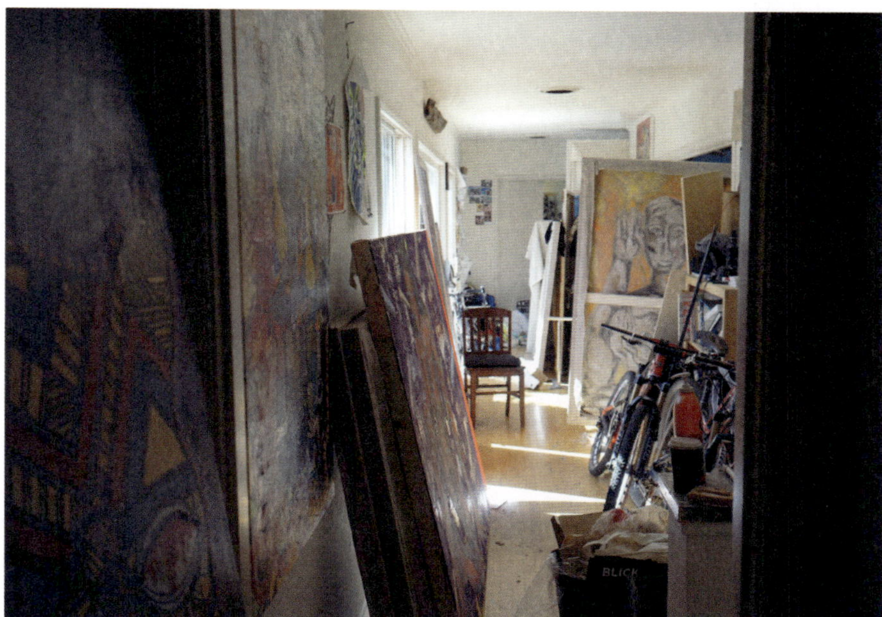

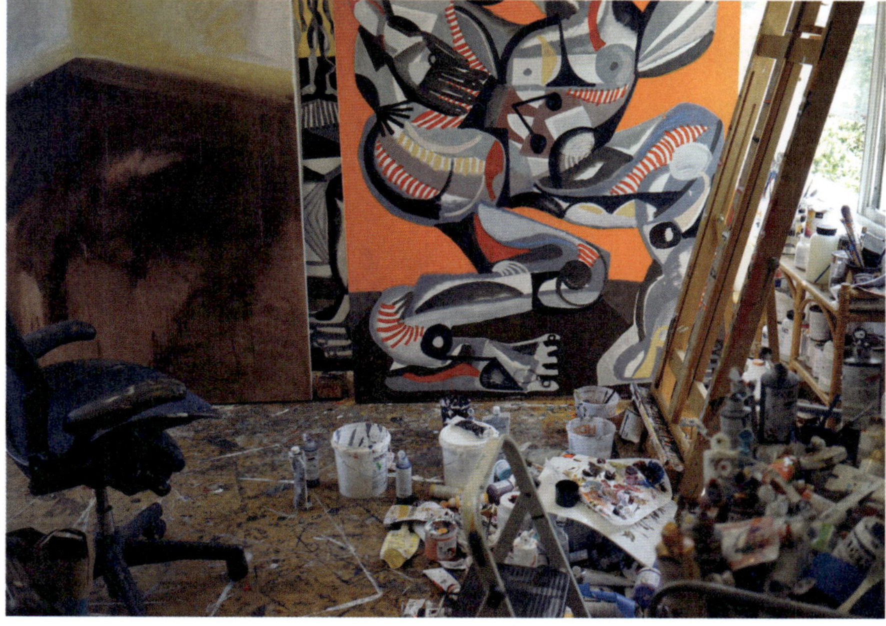

**Works in the artist's
studio, *c.* 2014**

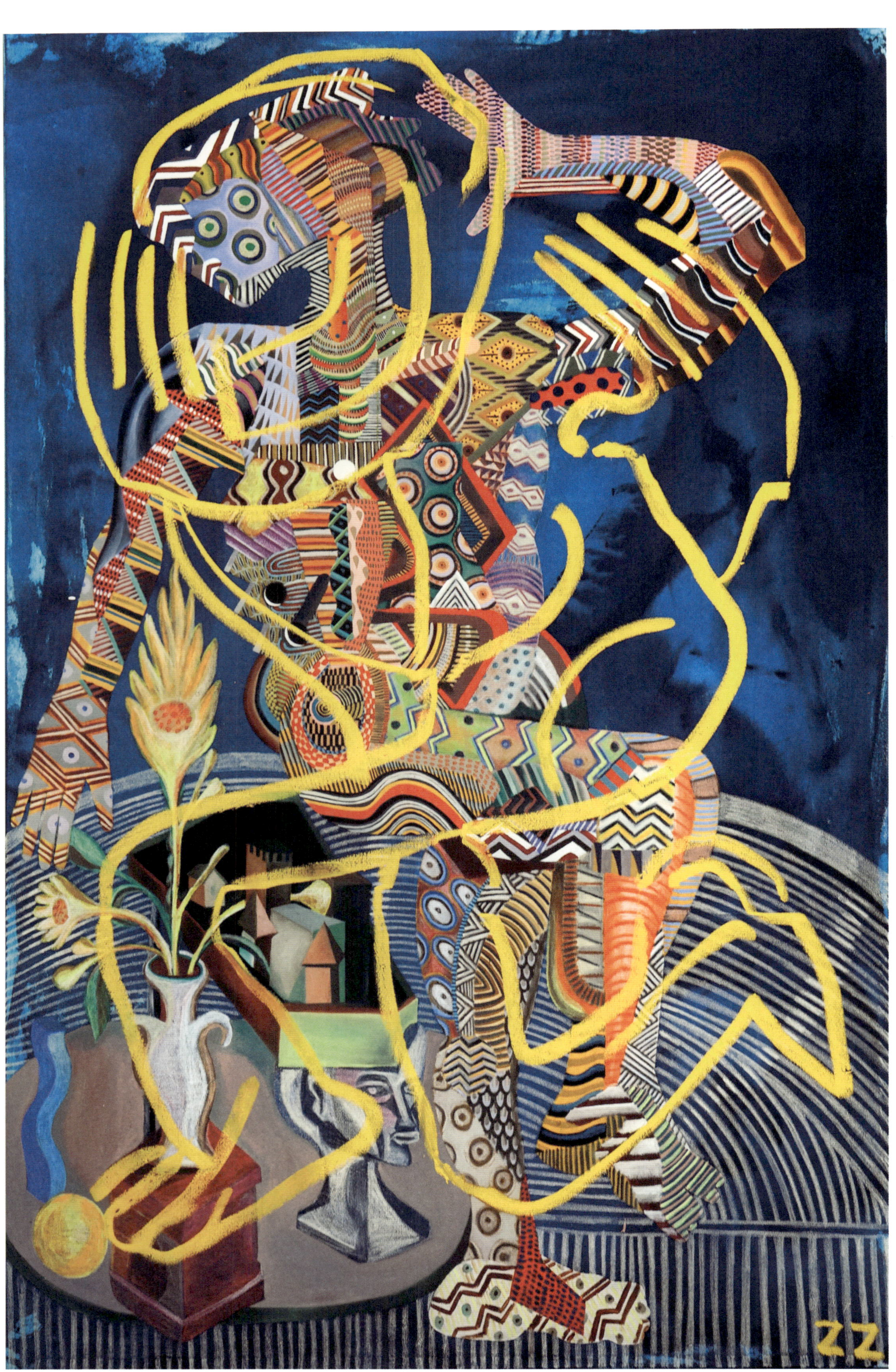

How You Are and Who You Want to Be, 2014
Oil, acrylic, enamel, crayon and pigment on canvas
279.6 × 182.9 cm (96 × 72 in.)

OPPOSITE
The Path and Goal, 2014
Oil, acrylic, mixed media on canvas
279.6 × 182.9 cm (96 × 72 in.)

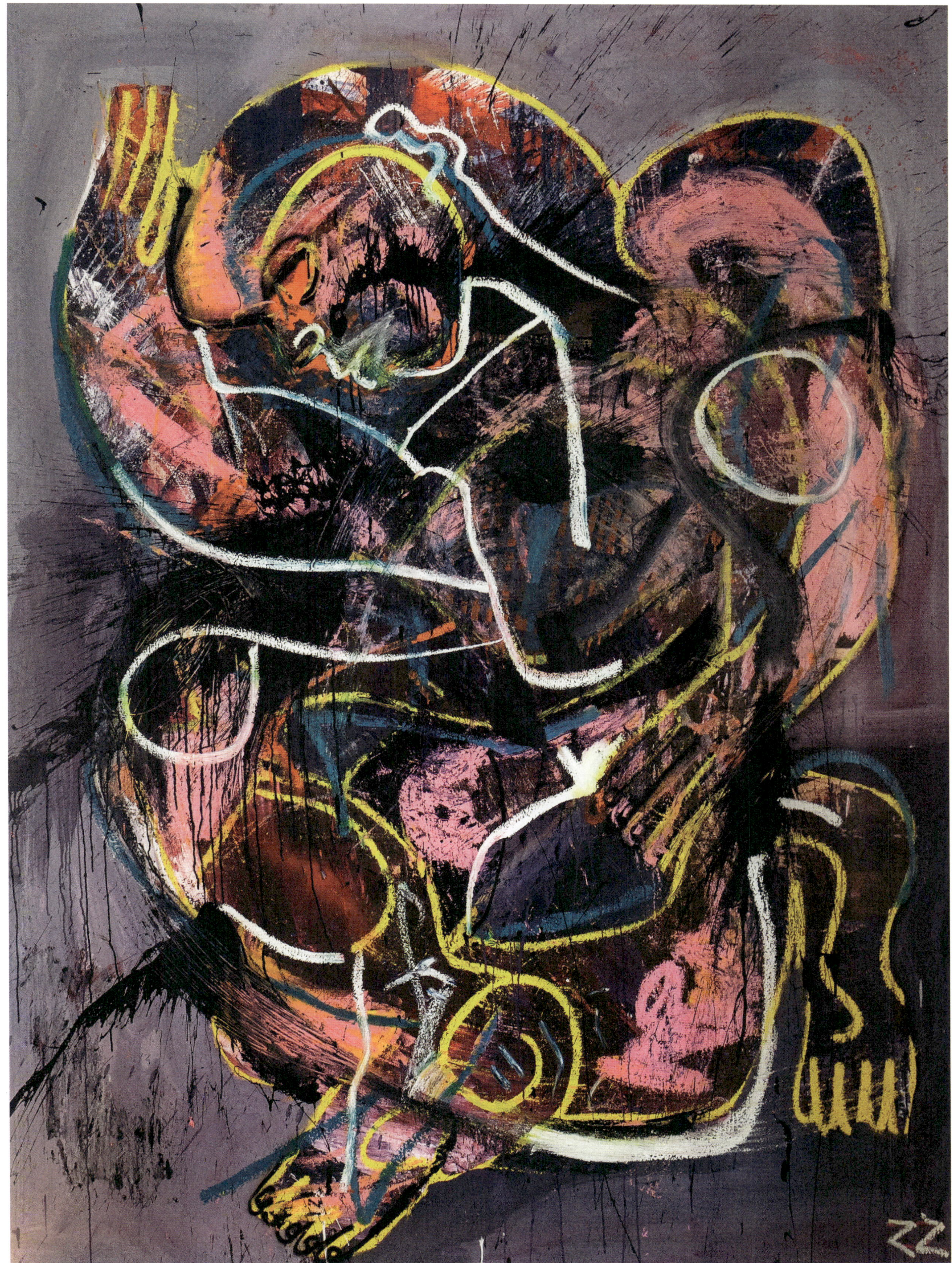

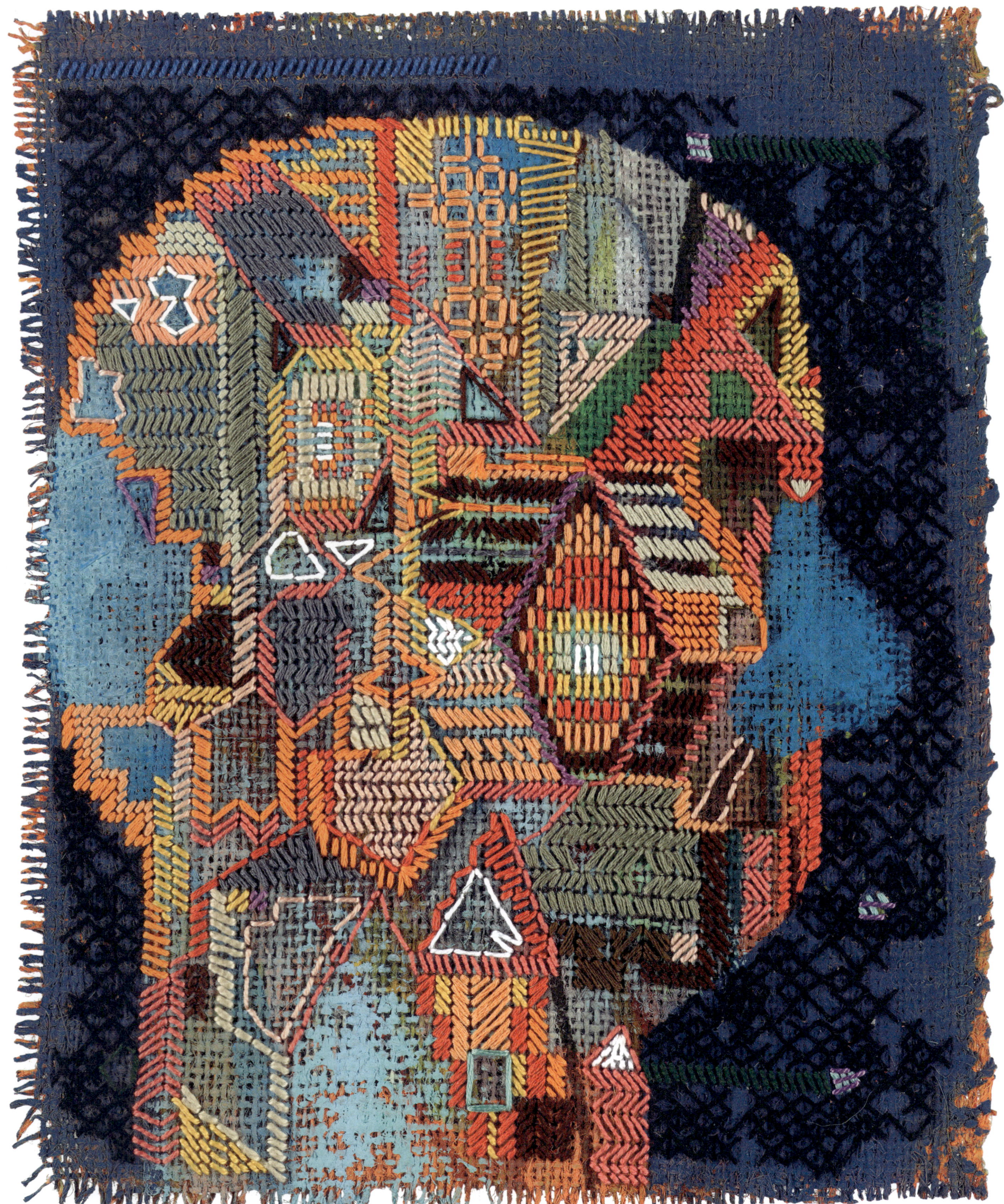

Make

Our final chapter celebrates artists who employ a raft of methods and materials, which not only complement but go beyond the realms of drawing and painting. From small models to sculptures, installations, public art and mixed-media pieces, investigated here are three-dimensional and textural artworks made from materials such as ceramics, paper and textiles, as well as a whole range of found objects. In terms of technique, there is an emphasis on the handmade and handcrafted – sewing, collage, décollage and construction – which is often applied by the artists in unusual ways or interesting contexts that confound our expectations. A significant example that encompasses all of the above is the work of the American artist Ben Venom, who turns the tradition of quilt-making on its head by applying heavy-metal iconography to what is essentially a decorative medium – patchworking together sections of his heavy metal T-shirts and biker jackets and reconceptualizing and contrasting the dark and Gothic imagery found in these textiles within soft fabrics.

Many of the artists we see here making, sculpting and creating worked initially in two dimensions. However, having been invariably drawn towards a particular material or concept because of its ability to invigorate their practice, they have turned into accidental sculptors, collagists or ceramists. Many have a background in painting, for instance the Argentinian muralist Franco Fasoli, who until recently had developed a reputation for his works realized in paint and petrol, but who has since exchanged brushes for scissors, to create the collages that are illustrated here. The shapes and lines he makes in his paper works are vibrant and dynamic, and thus his whole approach to image making has been revitalized.

In a similar way Canadian painter Jason Botkin has been to-ing and fro-ing between making two- and three-dimensional pieces with some regularity since the early 1990s, turning to the use of plywood as a support structure on which to base his paintings and to give them a more object-like appearance. Drawing and painting as processes are still integral to the work of the artists here, which they mix with other media to invent new combinations of surface, process, line and texture. Such an approach is exemplified by American artist Robert Hardgrave, who has invented a particular method of making large-scale Xerox transfers that encompasses drawing, paper cutting, collage, printmaking and sculpting all in one practice. Comparably, the work of Egyptian artist Ibrahim Ahmed III involves his own particular take on décollage. Using culturally resonant textiles such as *khayamaia* cloth, which combines the iconography of Islamic art, ancient Egyptian motifs and Coptic Christian crosses, he constructs canvases from layers of cloth and paint, which he then tears and deconstructs. The artists' choice of media is in part conceptually driven by the emotive qualities that working with a certain combination of materials can evoke. An example is Spanish artist Borondo, who includes stacks of hay bales in his repertoire of materials, onto which he applies spray paint, to produce groups of sombre and eerie-looking protagonists. The result is partly sculptural, with the charcoal-like effect of the paint being suggestive of the application of fire. This technique – displayed in works both in and outside of the gallery – recalls the elemental relationship we have with nature, cultivation and the seasonal cycles of life. In other examples the artist utilizes a method whereby he paints and scratches figures, faces and other forms into framed glass windows, revealing an etching of sorts that exposes its shadows in negative as light passes through. While in this chapter there is a focus on the materiality of the works, mark making is still evident in the output of the artists here – wood is painted, paper is cut and cloth is sewn, physical actions that mark and mould with the same compositional rules found in two-dimensional work. However, the artists also engage with the thoughts, sensations and memories often evoked by specific materials, and how this enhances the viewer's experience. Street art is one influence that provides an extra dimension of physicality, with the artists who work on different surfaces and in a multitude of contexts outside finding a similar sensibility manifesting itself in their studio pieces and gallery exhibitions. One remarkable example is Diogo Machado, a young Portuguese artist who has adopted the ubiquitous *Azulejo* – the traditional mosaic tiles that adorn the façades of many buildings in Portugal – as his chosen medium. Rather than imposing traditional ornamentation he uses contemporary and mischievous iconography in the tiles, which he makes by hand, and also in his large-scale *trompe l'oeil*-style murals created with the use of stencils.

Many of the artists featured in this chapter display an exceptional creativity, a drive to explore anything and everything and an infectious exuberance to bring art to all places. One example is the output of art duo 44flavours, whose works span painting, sculpture, murals and graphic design: they seem to find a way to smuggle art into everything they do, even into commercial branding. From lectures, to public art commissions or poster-making workshops, these artists bounce between projects buoyed by each new experience, keen to use as many different media as possible. Although they recognize that having a coherent style may be more marketable, they prefer to function like a lab in which unconventional approaches might bear fruit. With time and budget often being limiting factors, they tend to veer towards affordable and found materials, which they collect and store in their studio, and later recycle into their art. In the work of 44flavours there is integrity and a purposeful experimentation but also a positivity and sense of humour. We see this also in the work of artists such as David Méndez Alonso, in whose exuberant pieces, it seems, just about anything might happen. Ranging from large three-dimensional collages to clothing and tapestries, his is an energetic output where ideas bounce between one media and another. And one cannot help but be charmed by the wonderful paper birds produced by Colombian artist Diana Beltrán Herrera. Her creations are a perfect marriage of medium and subject-matter – a metaphoric celebration of the science and beauty of nature. Also using paper to create colourful mixed-media collage is the work of Argentinian artist Gustavo Ortiz, whose art is equally meticulous, with each tiny piece of his intricate designs being hand-cut and painstakingly composed. Within his symbolic forms, creatures and explorations of abstraction and pattern are encapsulated.

The artists in this chapter, and indeed the book as a whole, have all achieved a good measure of success through exhibitions, commissions and awards and rising acclaim despite of, or indeed because of, their following of unconventional and personal paths. They continue to find an honesty and truth in working with materials by hand in ever new and inspiring ways.

Ben Venom with works made during an artist residency at Kimball Art Museum, Fort Worth, Texas, in 2015

David Méndez Alonso
Untitled, 2014
Mixed media
150 × 150 cm (59⅛ × 59⅛ in.)

Franco Fasoli
Untitled, 2015
Collage
Dimensions unknown

44flavours
Untitled, c. 2014
Mixed media
Dimensions variable

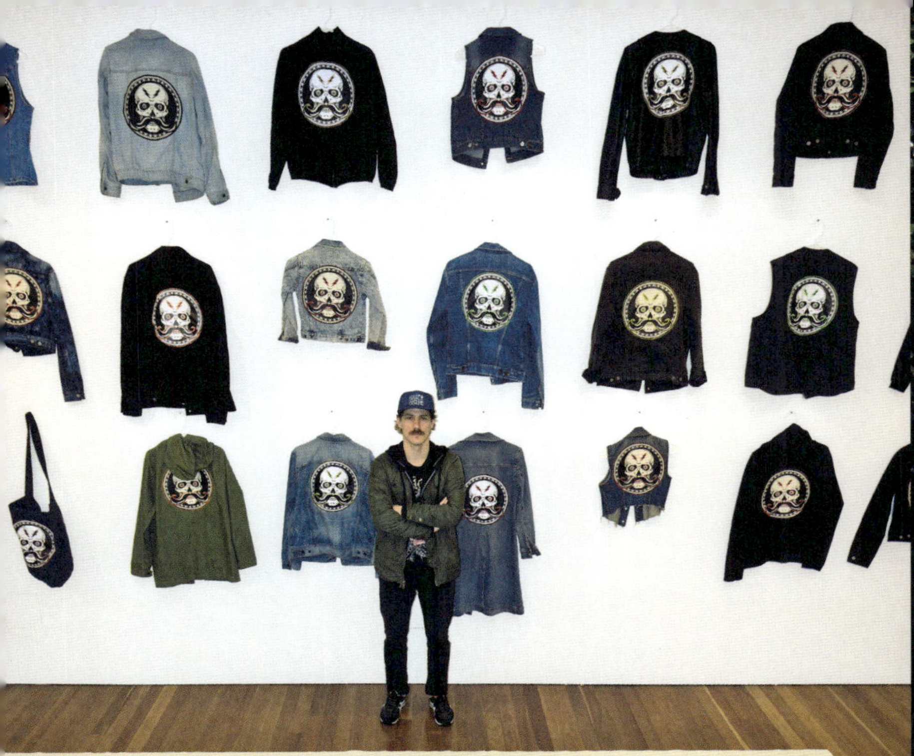

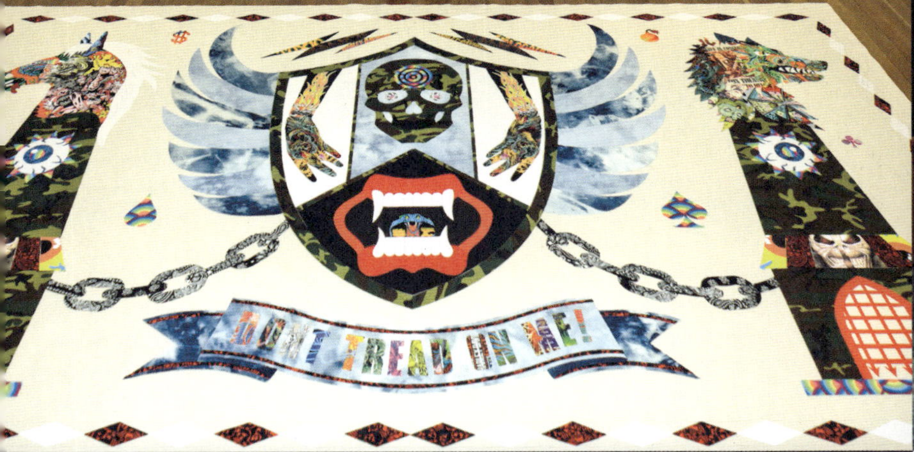

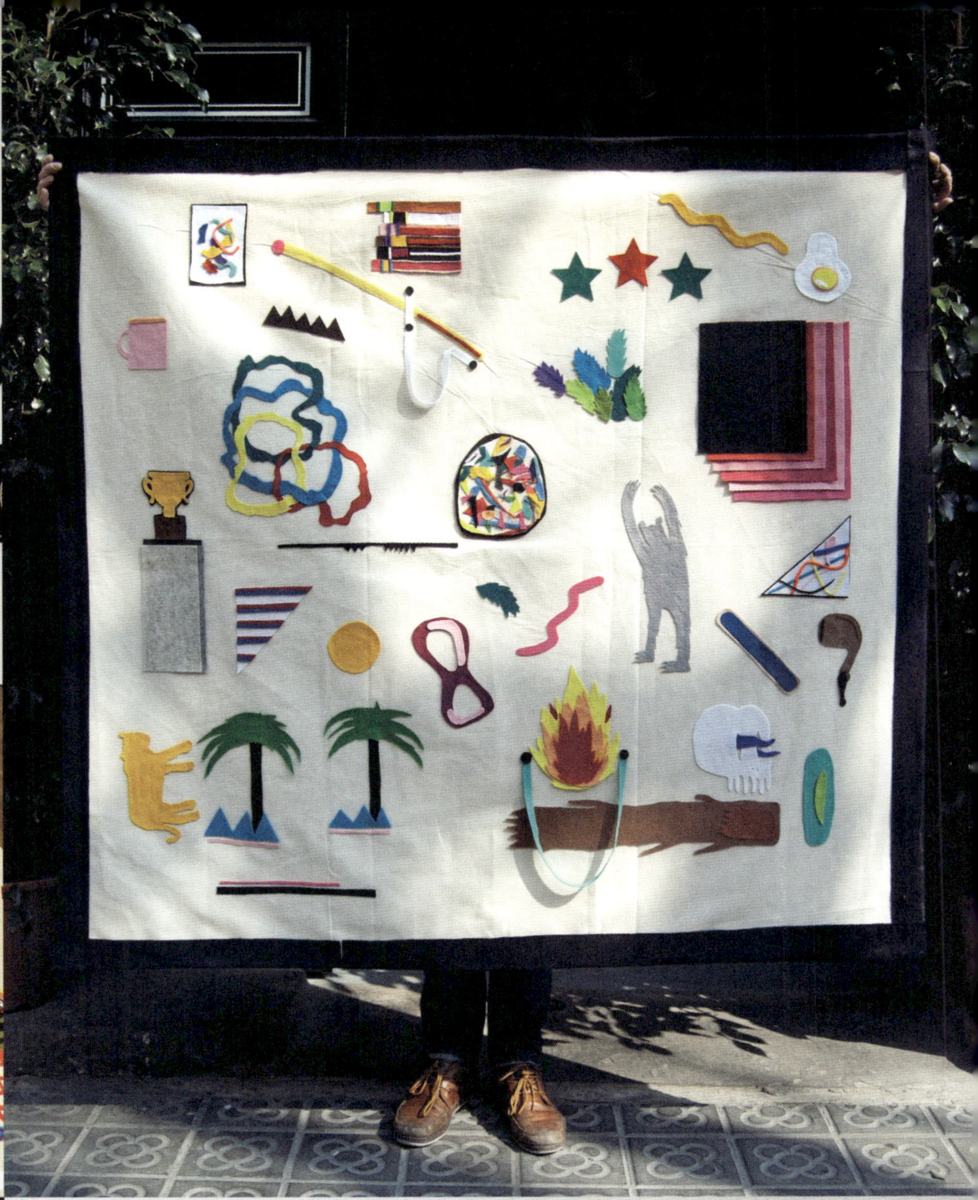

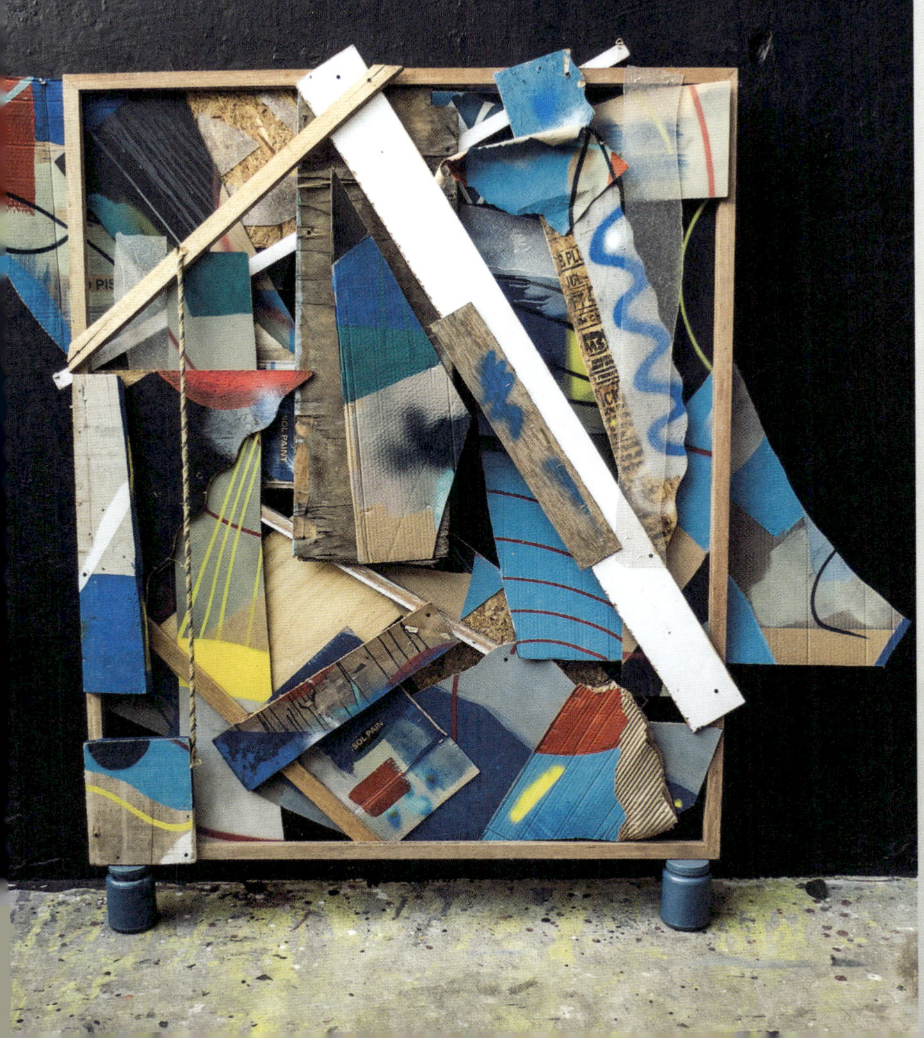
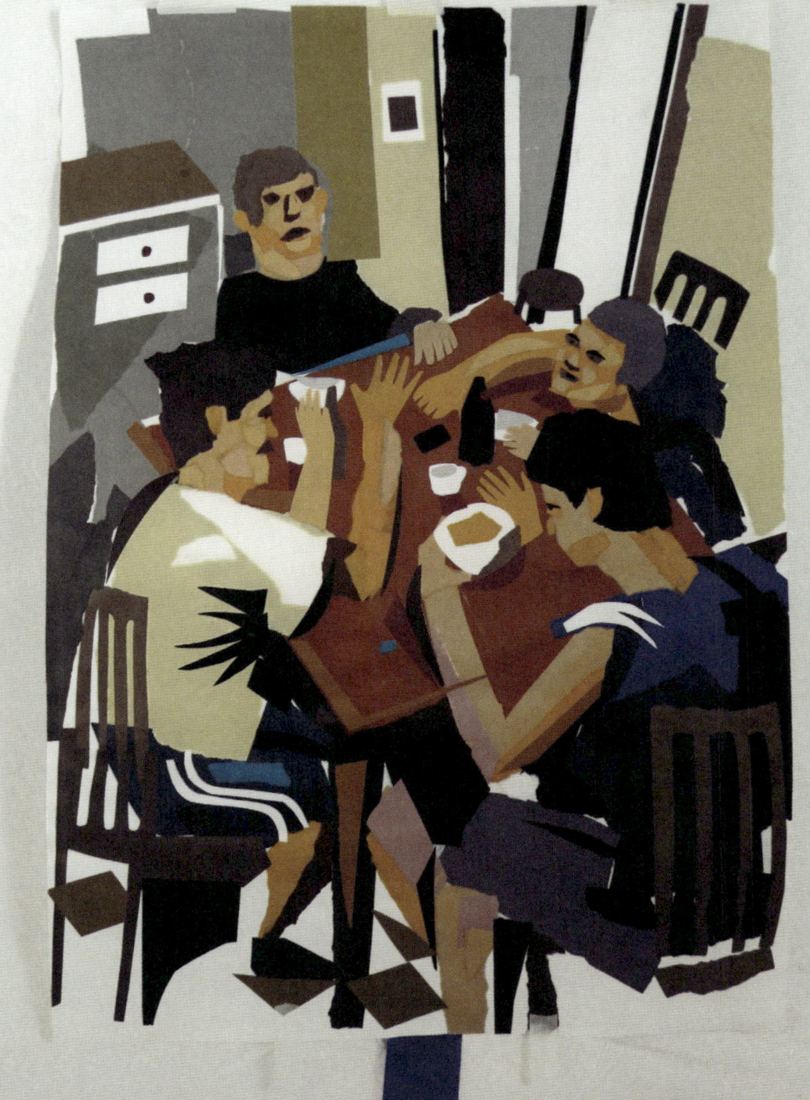

44flavours

Their exuberant work comprising all kinds of media, from murals to posters, and painting to sculpture, 44flavours seem to effortlessly straddle the worlds of art and design. Otherwise known as Sebastian Bagge and Julio Rölle, the two friends have collaborated since they were students in 2003 and have not looked back since, with a combination of teamwork and creative chaos being part of their enduring success.

Diversity is part of their ethos, the name '44flavours' coming to them after they stumbled across an old illustration of an American ice cream van on which the words were scrawled. It also sums up their eclectic approach and sense of fun. Part of the duo's distinctive style is the recurrence of handwritten type, which stems from a shared interest in typography. Bagge has always been inspired by graphic design, while Rölle has a background in graffiti, which informs his lettering. Whether designing a poster or creating an art installation, inventive letterforms, messages and

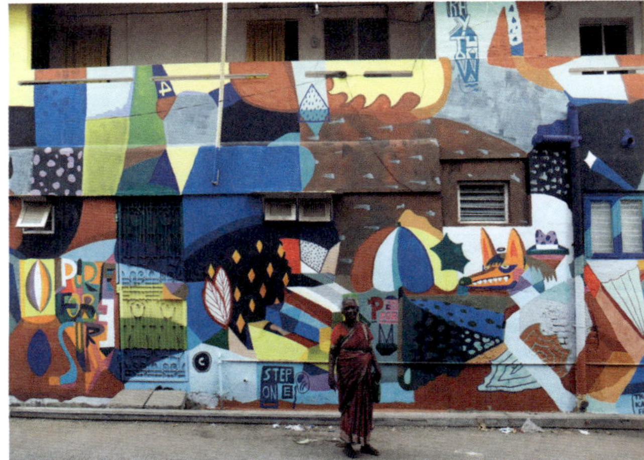

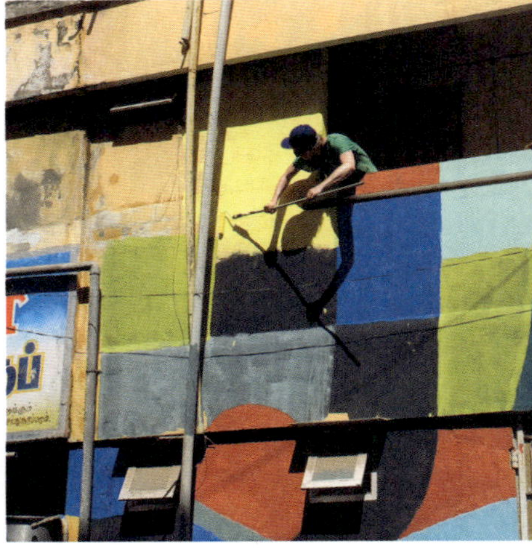

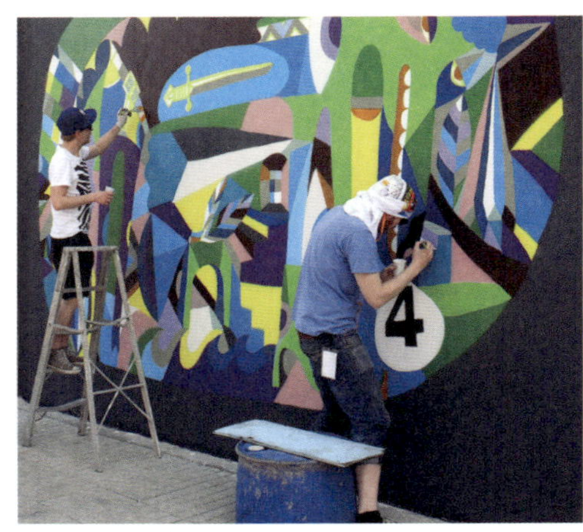

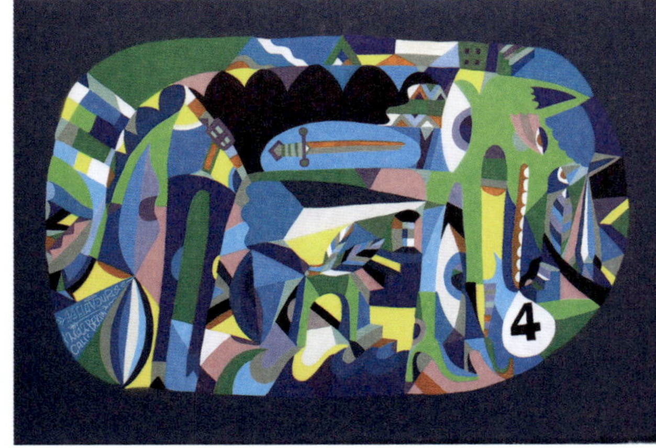

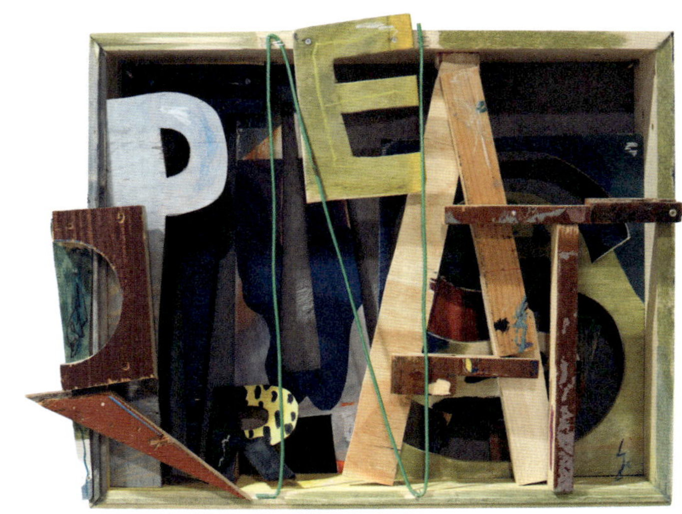

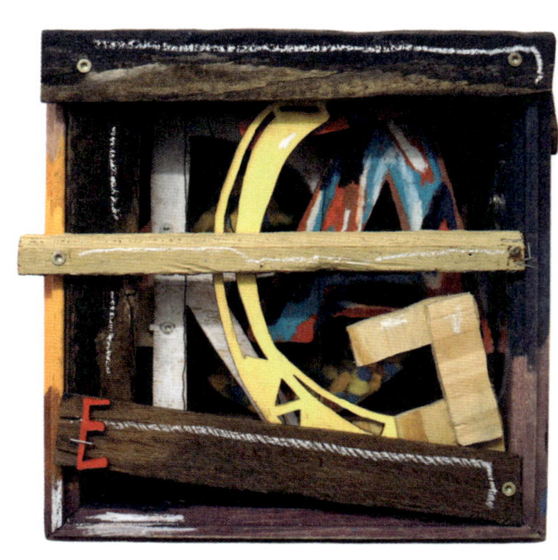

TOP
Untitled, and detail, from the project 'Each One Teach One', Pondicherry, India, 2103
Mixed media
Dimensions variable

CENTRE
Untitled, and detail, mural commissioned by the International Biennal of Muralism, Cali, Colombia, *c.* 2014
Mixed media
Dimensions variable

RIGHT
Untitled works, *c.* 2014
Mixed media
Dimensions variable

OPPOSITE, CLOCKWISE FROM TOP LEFT
Jumping Jack Bear, 2014
Mixed media
Dimensions variable

Untitled, *c.* 2014
Mixed media
Dimensions variable

Untitled, 2011
Mixed media
Dimensions variable

Rollerboard, 2012
Mixed media
Dimensions variable

OVERLEAF, LEFT TO RIGHT
Untitled works, 2014
Mixed media
Dimensions variable

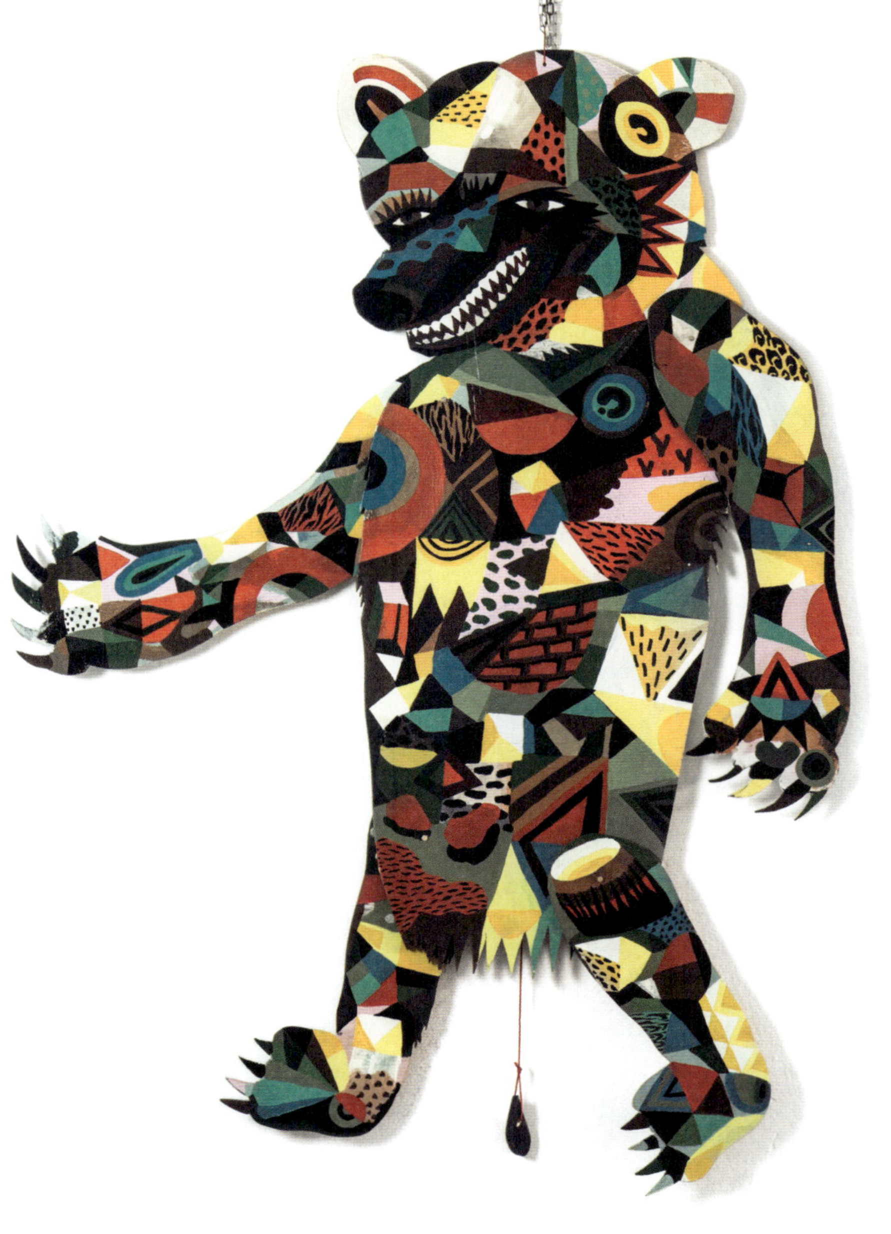
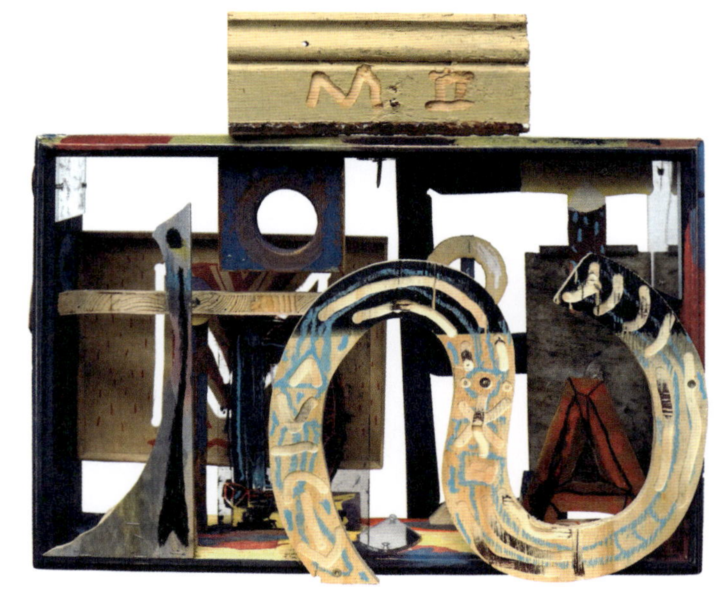
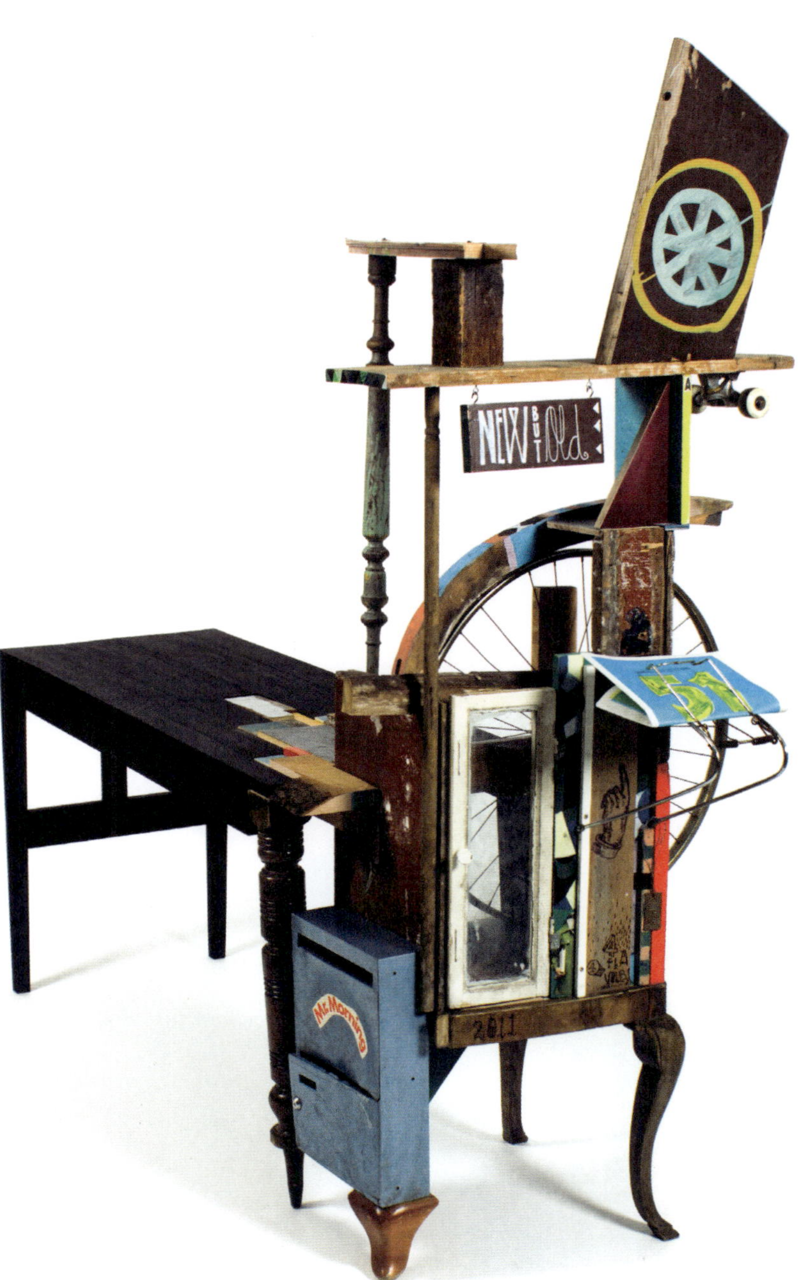
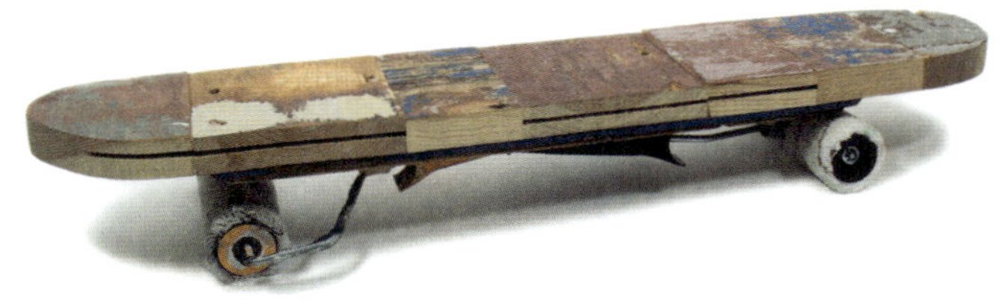

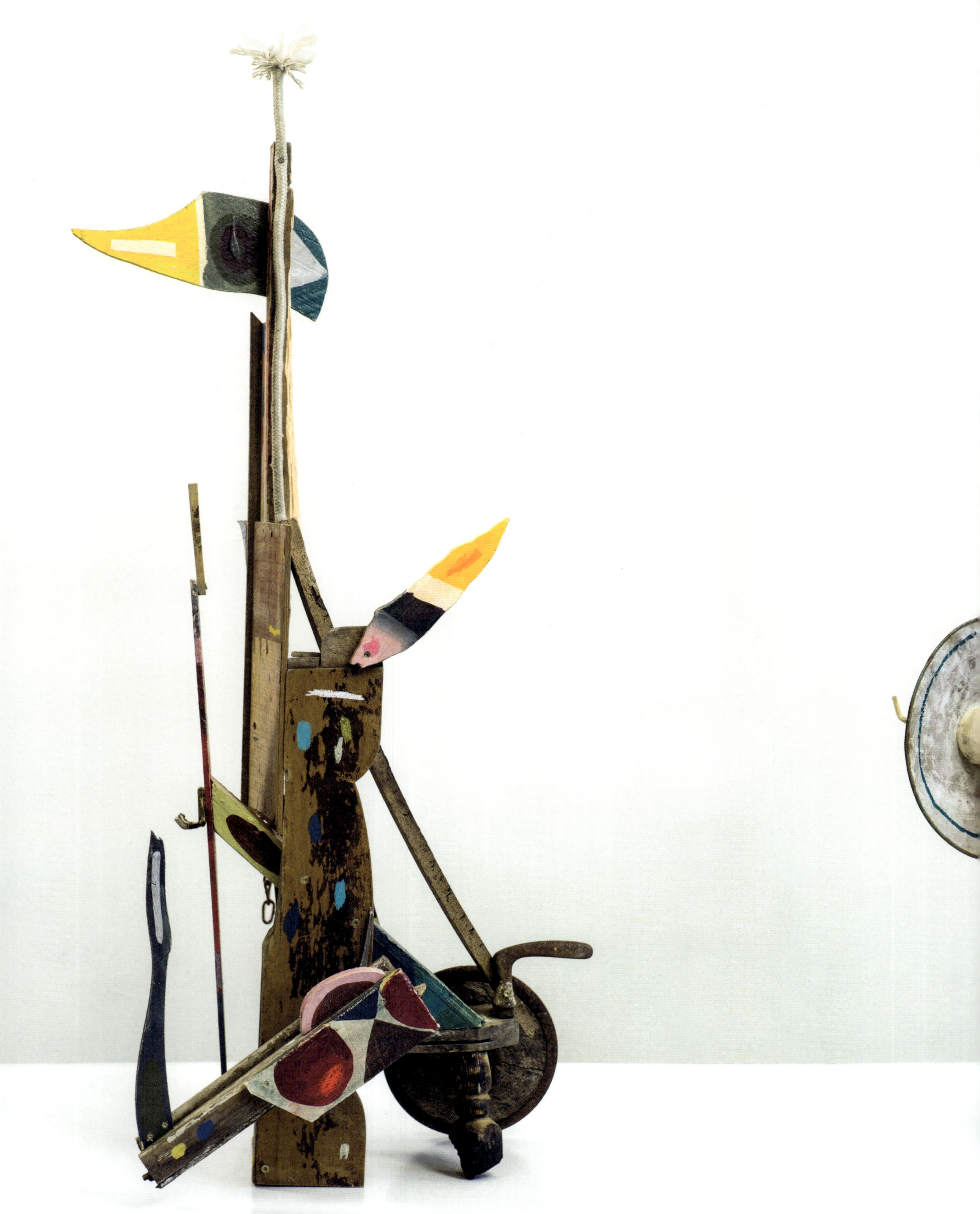

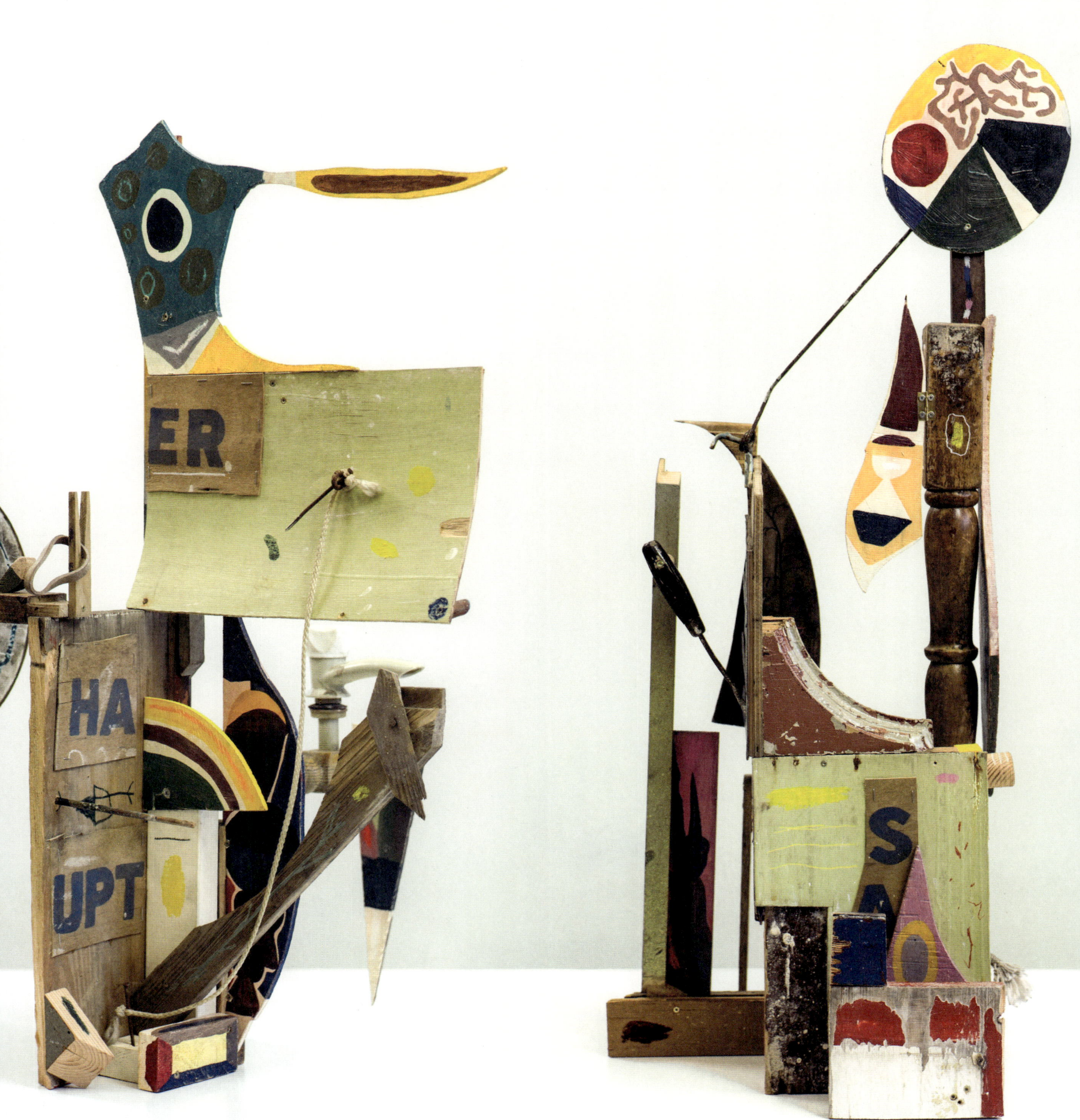
ER
HA
UPT
S

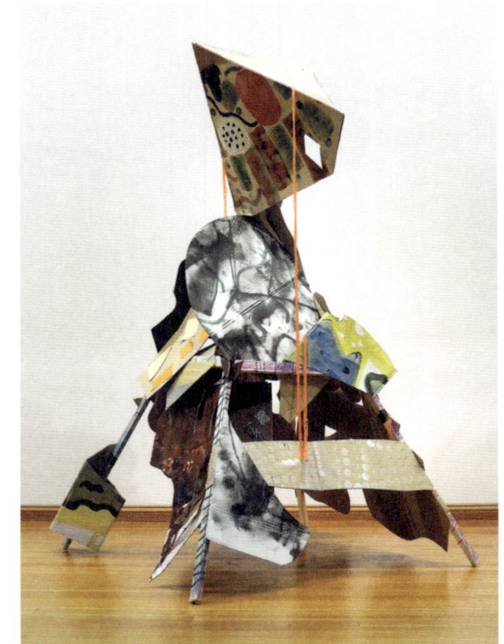
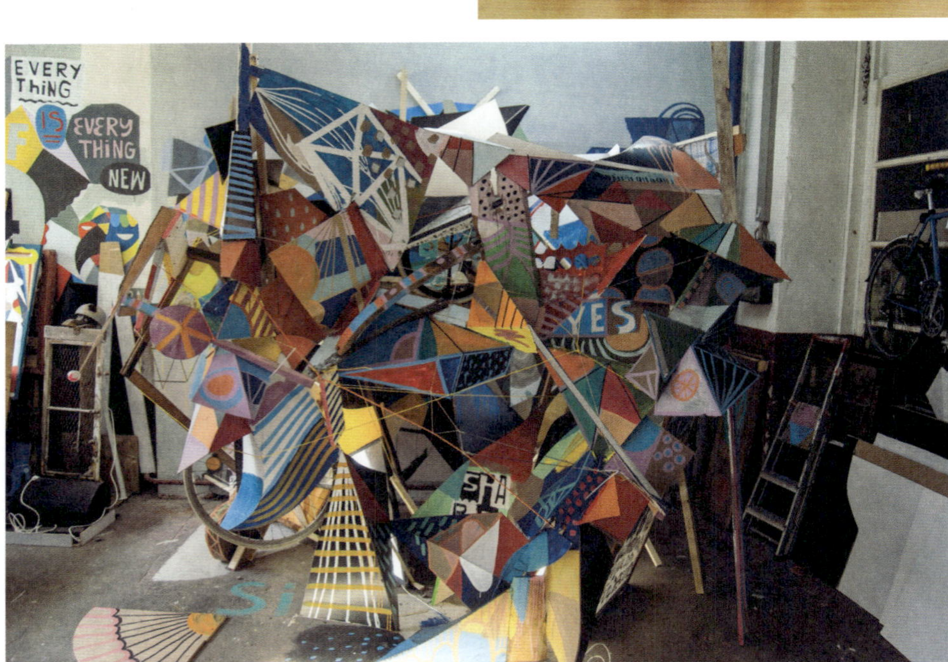
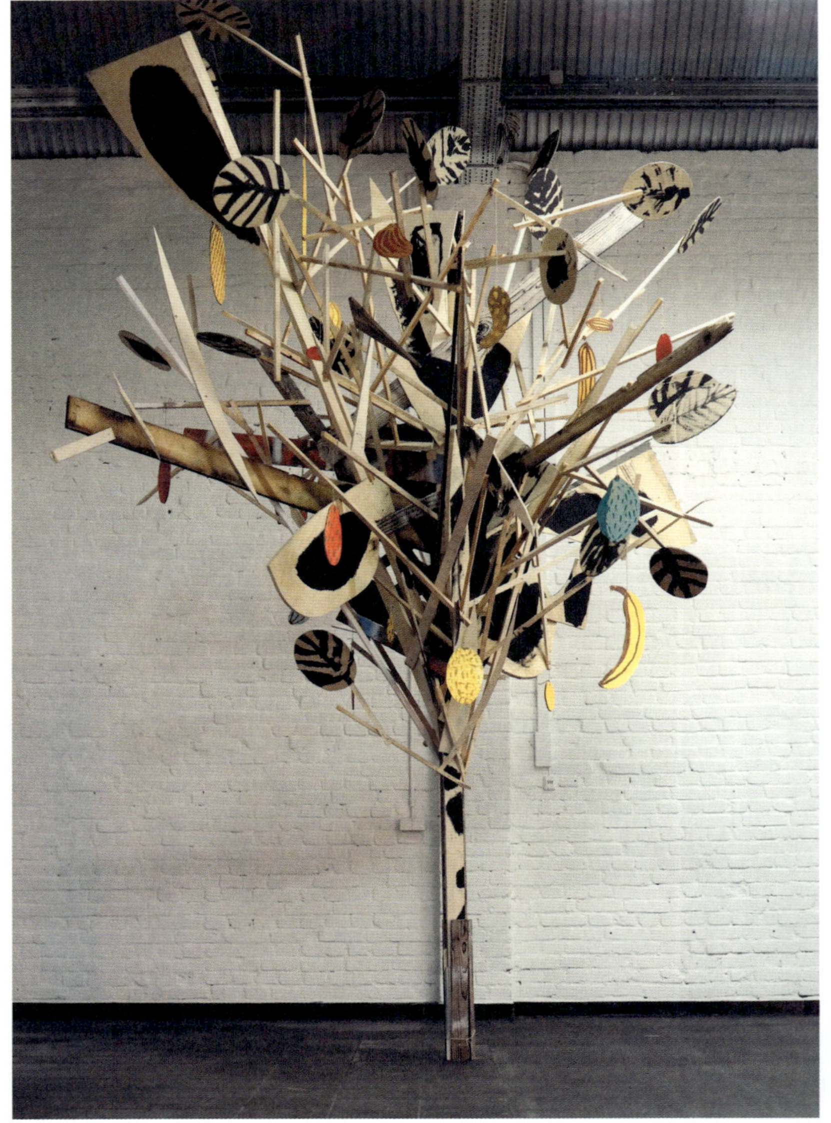
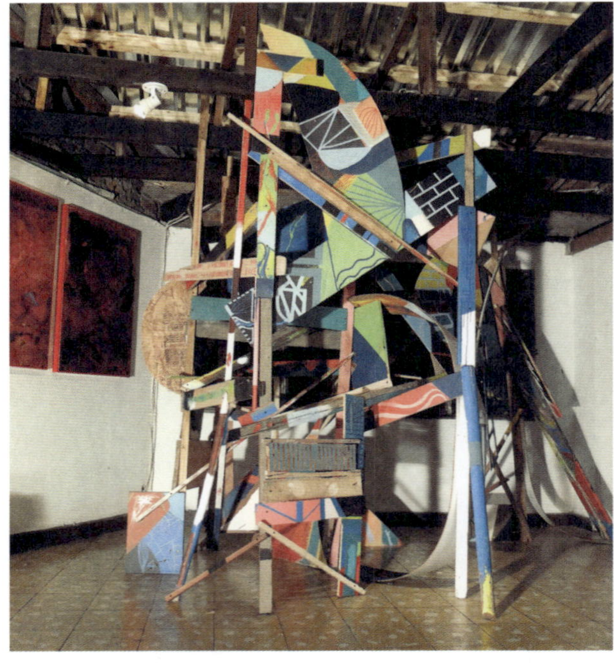
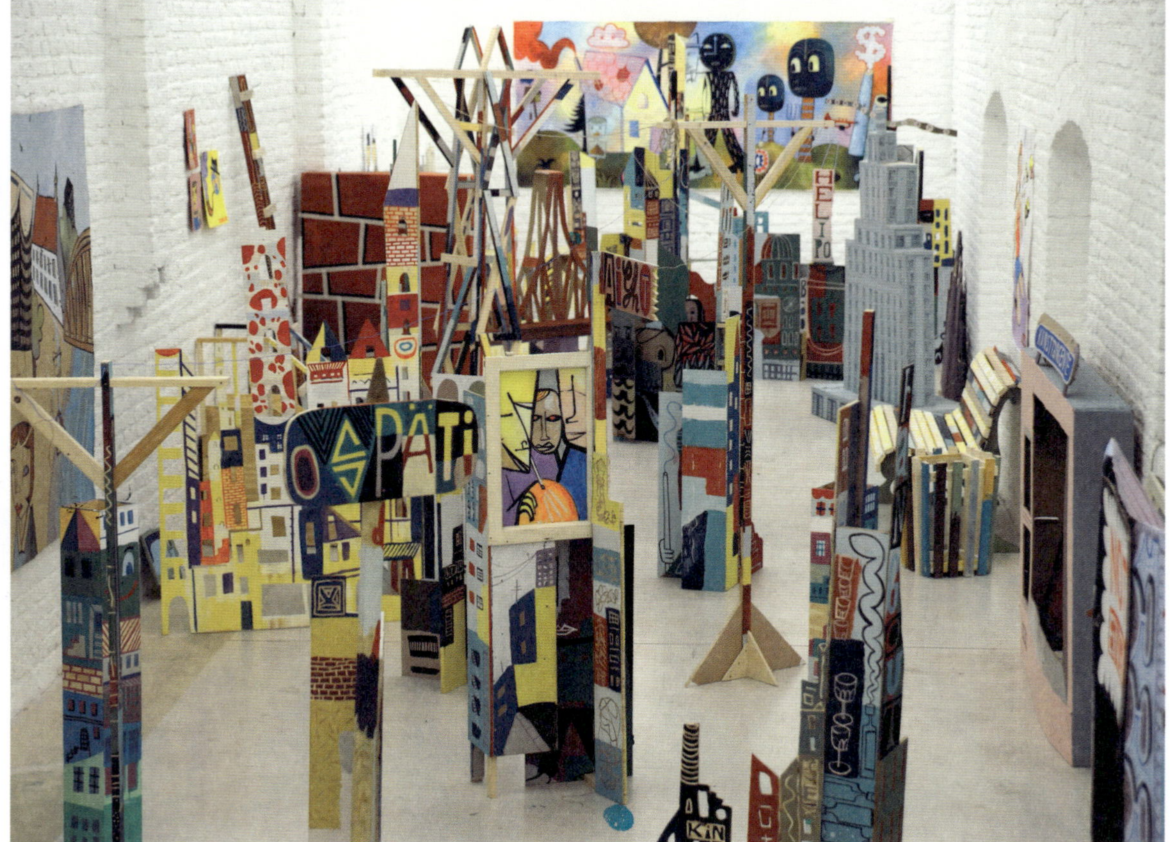

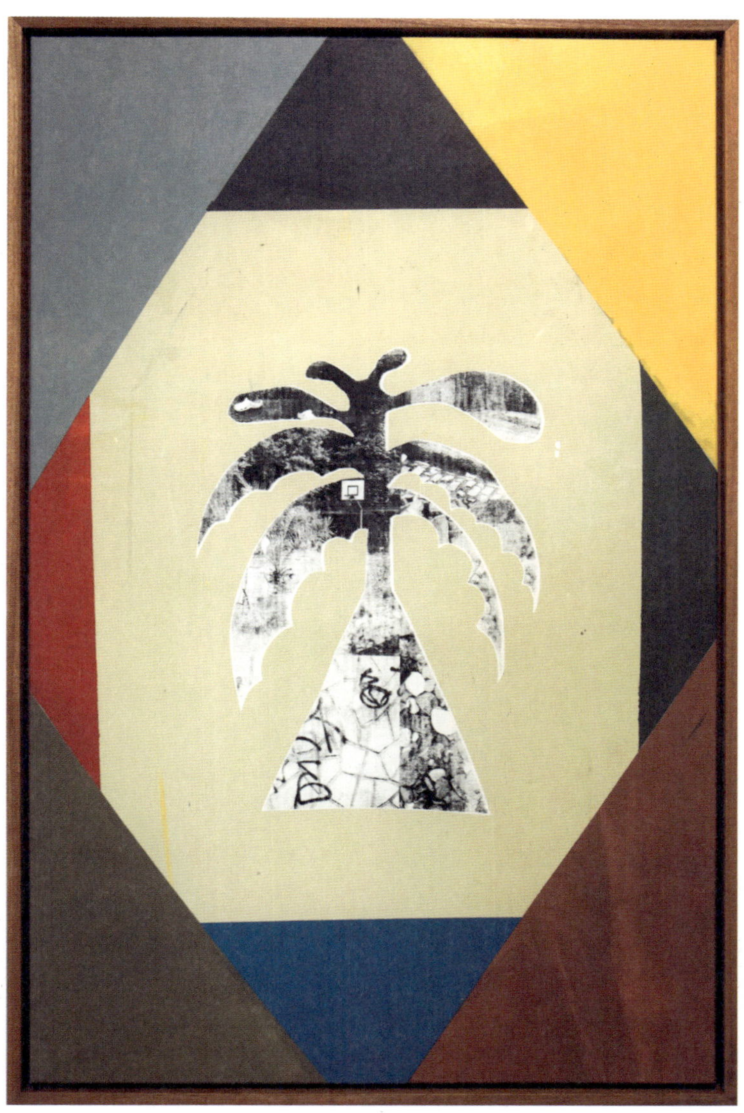

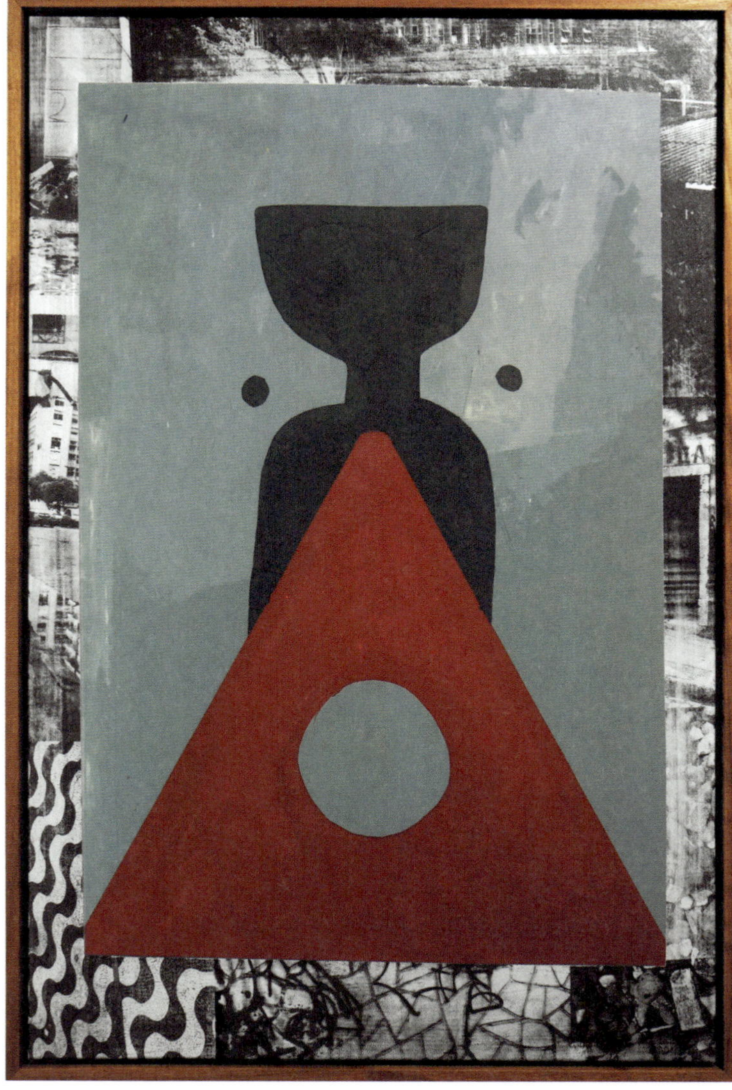

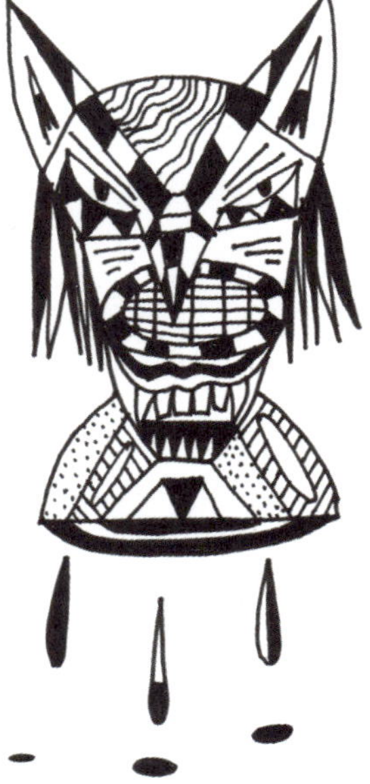

Kunstherbst, 2013
Mixed media
Dimensions variable

Tree, *c.* 2014
Mixed media
Dimensions variable

44flavours and Jim Avignon
Untitled, 2013
Mixed media
Dimensions variable

Untitled, sculpture commissioned
by the International Biennal of
Muralism, Cali, Colombia, *c.* 2014
Mixed media
Dimensions variable

Untitled, 2014
Mixed media
Dimensions variable

Untitled, 2014
Mixed media
Dimensions unknown

Untitled, 2014
Mixed media
Dimensions unknown

Maske Pano-social, *c.* 2012
Pen on paper
Dimensions unknown

phrases often find their way into their work, breaking down the barriers between art and design.

44flavours use colour in abstract motifs in a considered and playful way that somewhat echoes, in contemporised form, the work of Modern Masters such as Henri Matisse (1869–1954) and Alexander Calder (1898–1976). Their energy and inventiveness becomes magnified as they apply these traits to their three-dimensional assemblage sculptures and installations. In the tradition of the Cubist constructions of Pablo Picasso (1881–1973), the duo take materials such as offcuts and waste matter and transform them into precariously balanced compositions, painted and incised with unusual patterns. The textures of the surfaces and shapes of the found objects all add to the weathered and vintage feel of these curious flotsam artefacts.

The duo have taken part in cultural exchanges across the world, from Glasgow to São Paulo, Pondicherry to Istanbul. From Indian auto-rickshaws to Second World War bunkers in Brittany, the artists have been drawn to all kinds of surfaces and projects. Above all 44flavours have an enviable confidence in what they do, valuing honesty, spontaneity and the courage to experiment and be different.

Ibrahim Ahmed III

An Egyptian artist whose work is concerned with identity and immigration,

Ibrahim Ahmed III was born to Egyptian parents living in Kuwait, moving with his family between Bahrain and Egypt before finally settling in the US when he was thirteen. It was while pursuing a major in English at Rutgers University in New Jersey that Ahmed started to make art. Since then he has become known for his work in both traditional and non-traditional media, creating sculptures and installations that have been celebrated in numerous solo shows in the US and Egypt.

Despite being embraced by the art world in both Cairo and New York, a driving force in Ahmed's output is the idea of 'otherness', a result of growing up on both sides of the Atlantic and feeling that he has been perceived as not quite belonging. This is expressed in the recent series 'There is No Clash', in which fabric sourced from around the world forms the foundation for a group of paintings, all of which explore the history of cultural exchange. The title itself is a visual retort to *The Clash of Civilizations and the Remaking of World Order* (1996), a well-known book by Samuel P. Huntington that examines the global politics that challenge Western dominance.

'There is No Clash' first began to germinate as an idea during a visit to Egypt in 2006, during which Ahmed attended his grandmother's funeral. At the ceremony

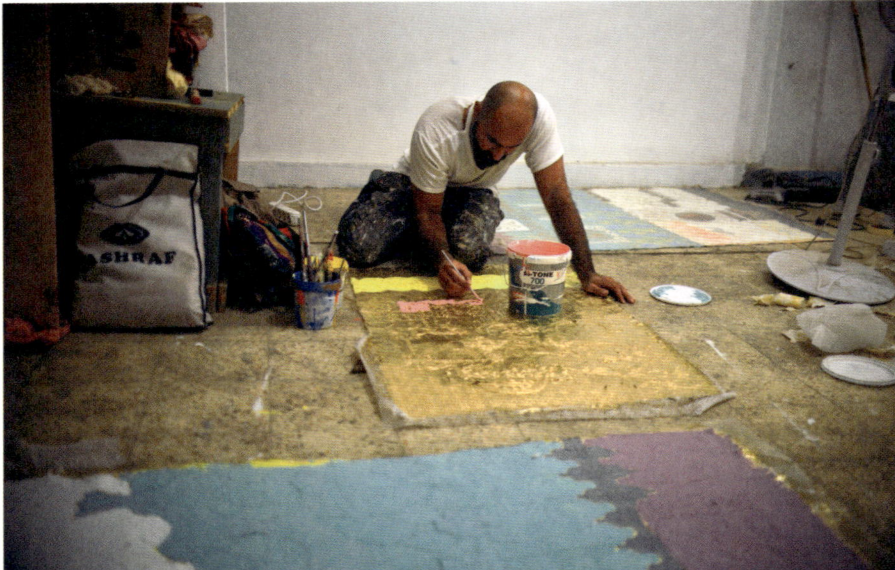

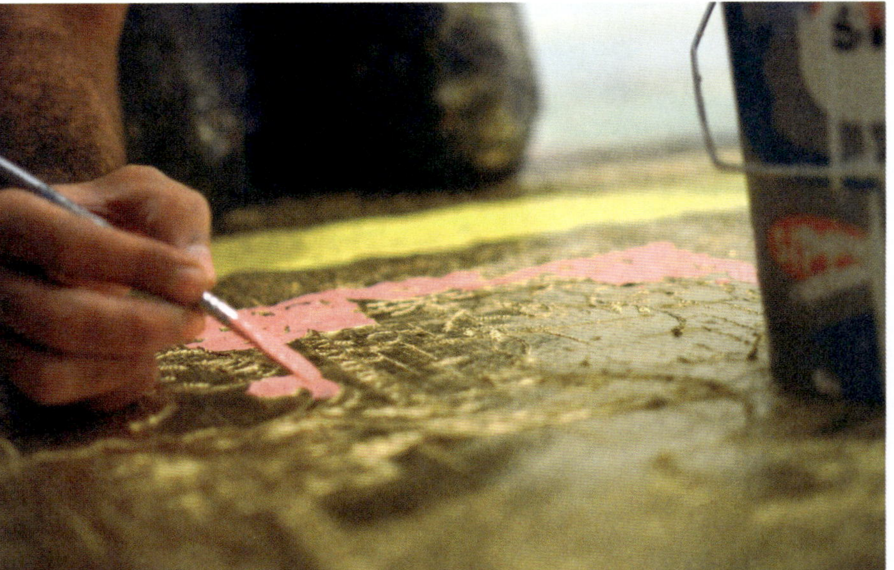

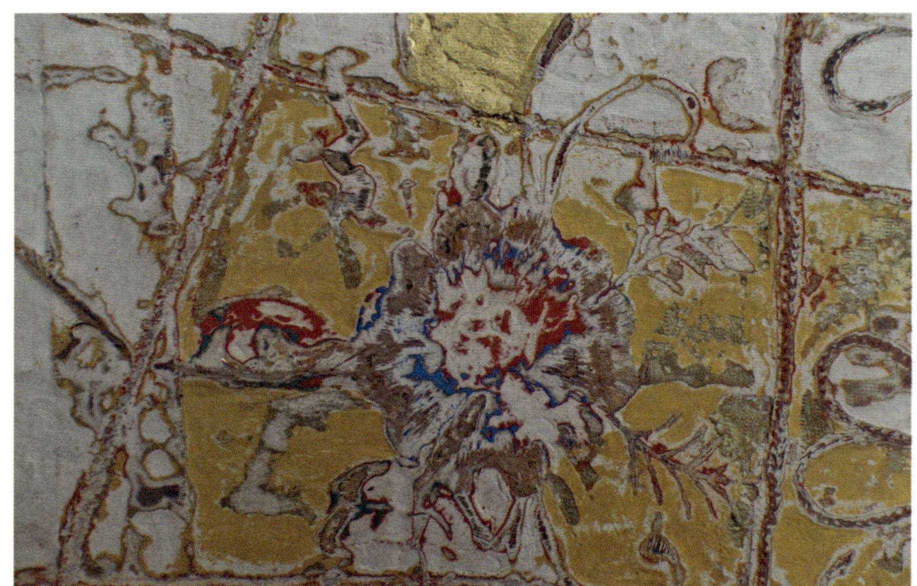

The artist at work on a painting from the series, 'There is No Clash', and detail, 2015

OPPOSITE
Untitled, from the series 'There is No Clash', 2014
Mixed media on canvas
120 × 120 cm
(47¼ × 47¼ in.)

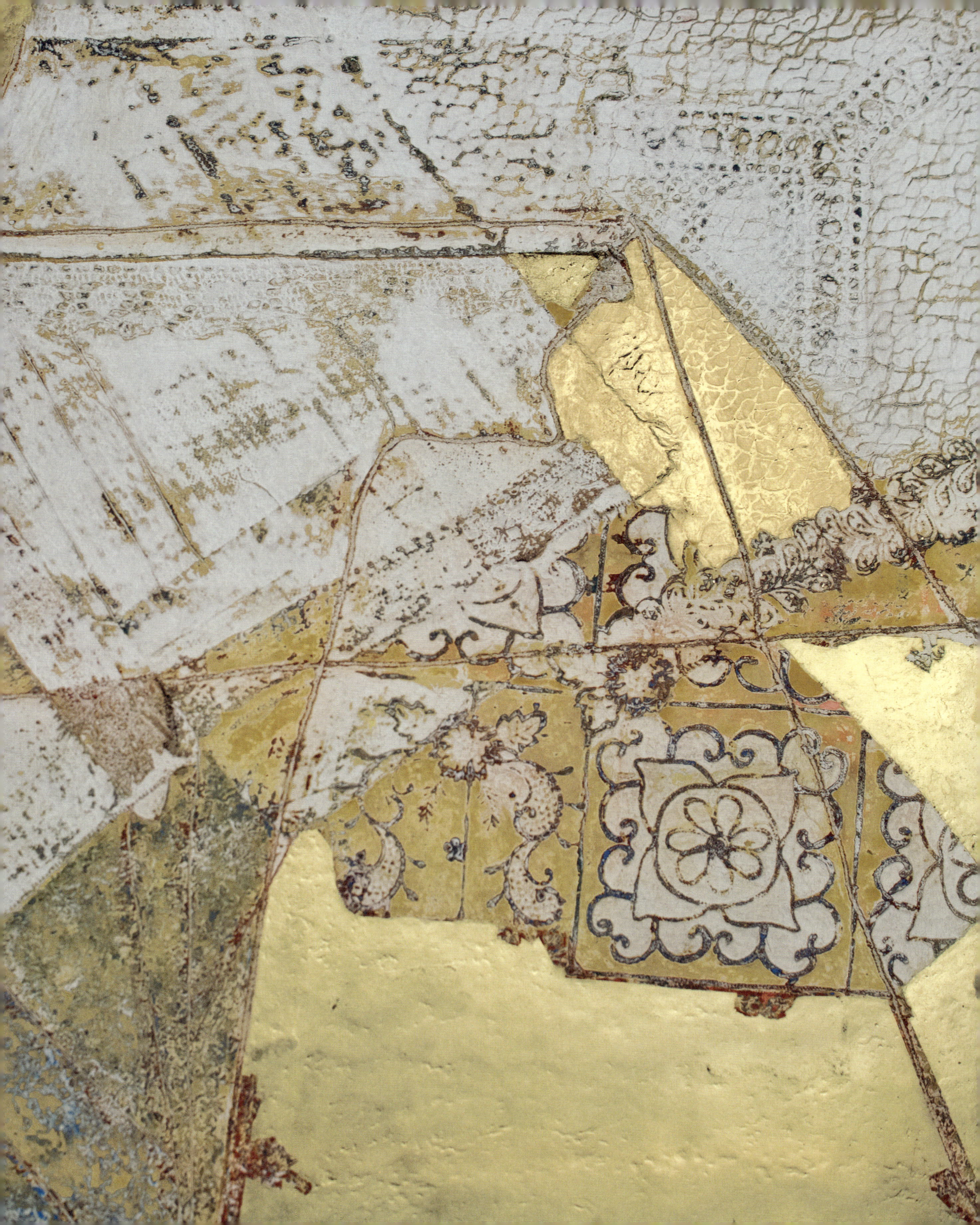

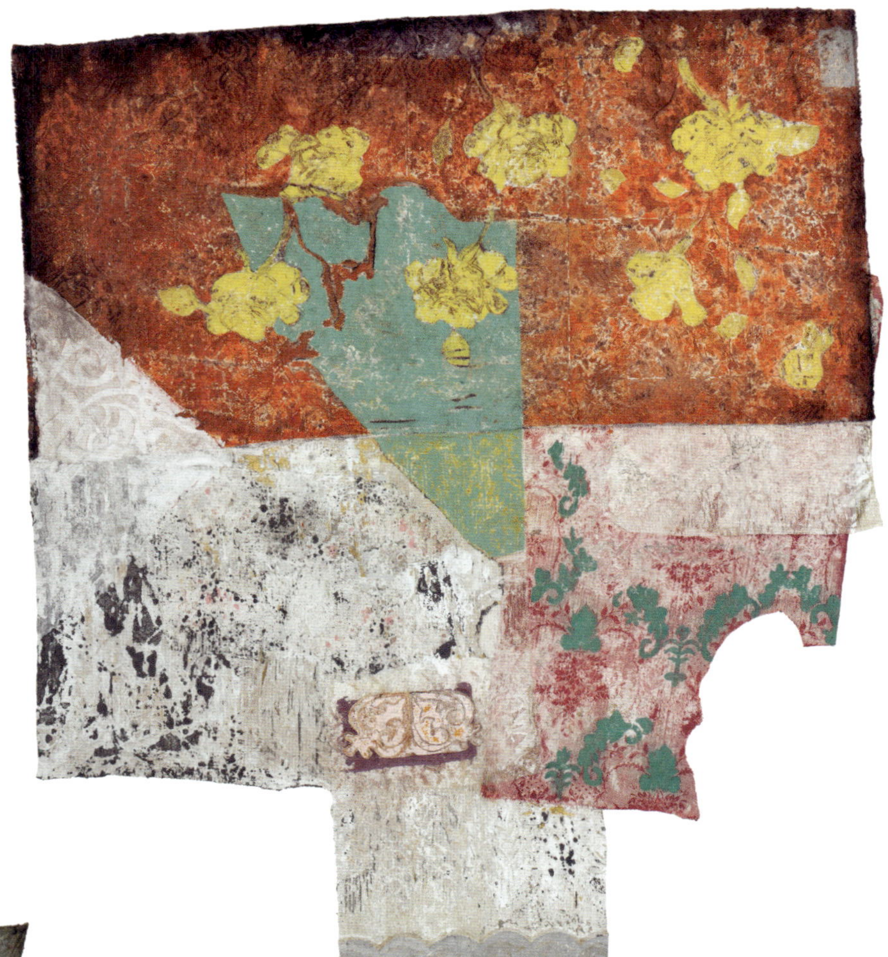

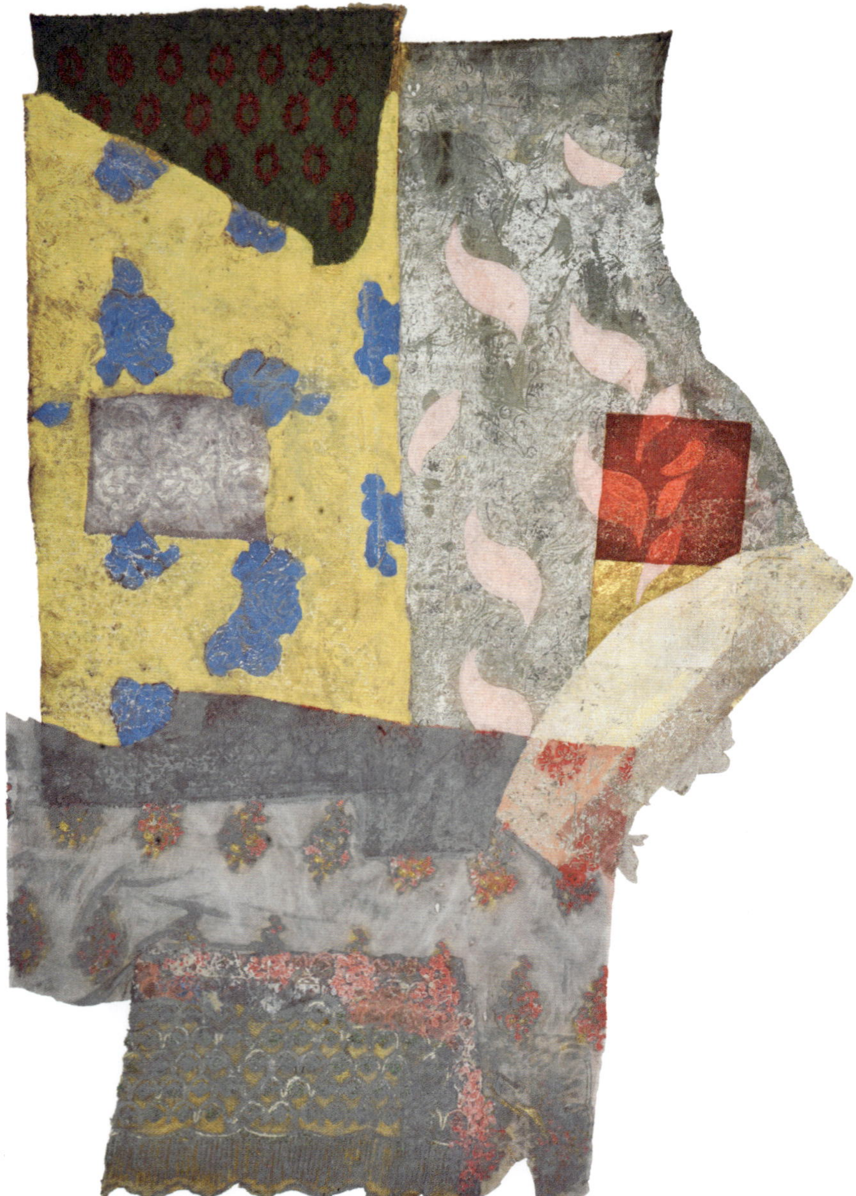

he took note of the *khayameya* cloth – a fabric that incorporates Islamic iconography with ancient Egyptian symbols and Coptic Christian crosses – that was on display. It struck the artist that the history of the enmeshing of cultures symbolized by the cloth was symptomatic of a larger global narrative concerning the complex intertwining – rather than the 'clashing', itself being too simple a description – of cultures over centuries.

The series began with the *khayameya* but has evolved to take on a global perspective in terms of the materials it encompasses. Using sailcloth as a canvas, Ahmed builds up each work with layers of patterned cloth that he has unearthed from markets across the world. Multiple coats of paint are then applied and sanded down, with the artist in a sense excavating and meshing together the materials to reiterate that we are all connected through history, culture and commerce. As a result of this process the detail can become lost, with a 'whole' emerging that makes visual reference to the palette and textures of ancient Egyptian ruins. These works he perceives as 'maps' that represent an all-inclusive 'nation', which 'acknowledges the intertwined history of the human experience, which can be neither compartmentalized nor separated'.

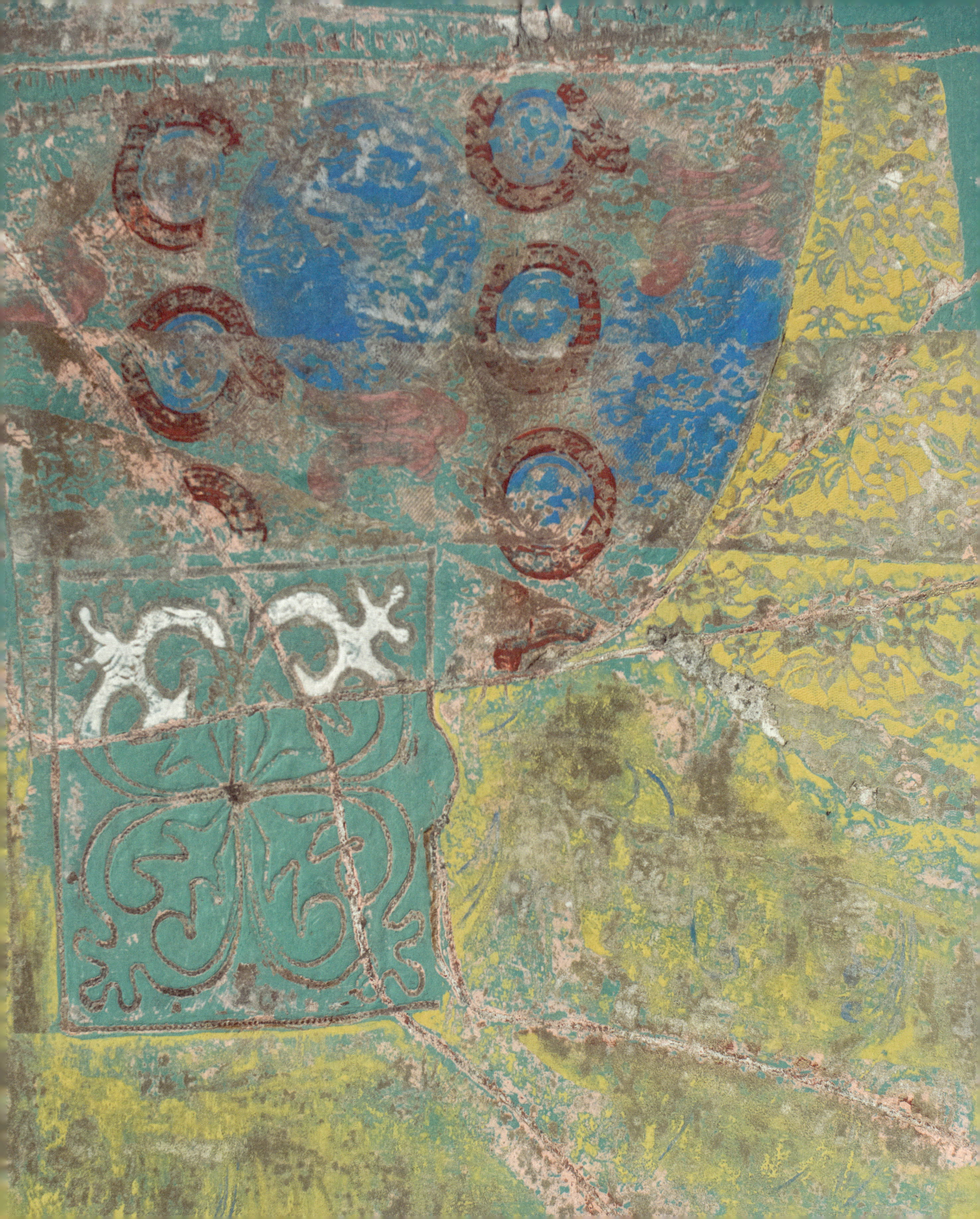

Diana Beltrán Herrera

Celebrated the world over for her exquisitely detailed bird sculptures, which she lovingly constructs from paper,

through patient application Colombian artist and designer Diana Beltrán Herrera transforms this humble material into works that are full of life, well observed and incredibly realistic. Herrera has participated in solo and group exhibitions in Colombia, Europe, Asia and the US, as well as being highly sought after for commissions by individuals and organizations such as The Cornell Fine Arts Museum in Florida and Longwood Gardens in Pennsylvania.

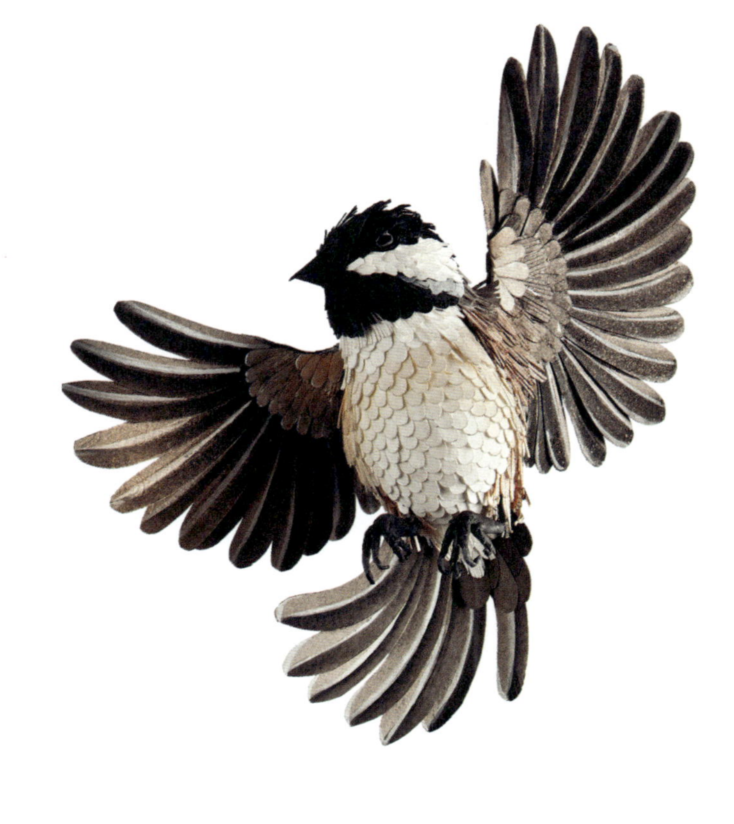

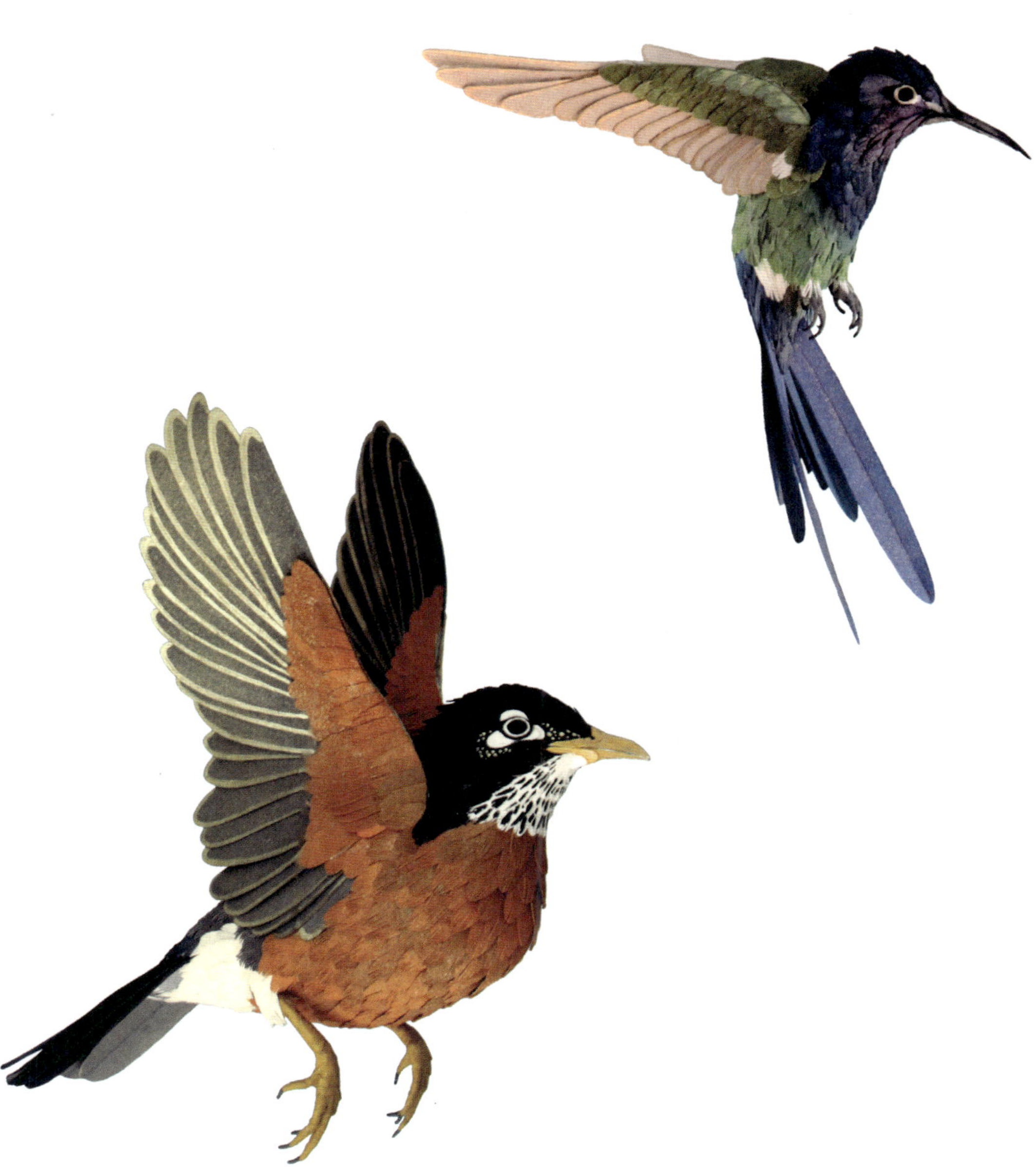

Coal Tit, c. 2013
Paper sculpture
Dimensions variable

Collared Inca Hummingbird, 2014
Paper sculpture
Dimensions variable

American Robin, 2014
Paper sculpture
Dimensions variable

OPPOSITE, CLOCKWISE FROM TOP LEFT
Inca Collared Hummingbird, 2014
Paper sculpture
Dimensions variable

Sun Bird, 2013
Paper sculpture
Dimensions variable

European Bee Eater, 2013
Paper sculpture
Dimensions variable

Hoopoe, 2014
Paper sculpture
Dimensions variable

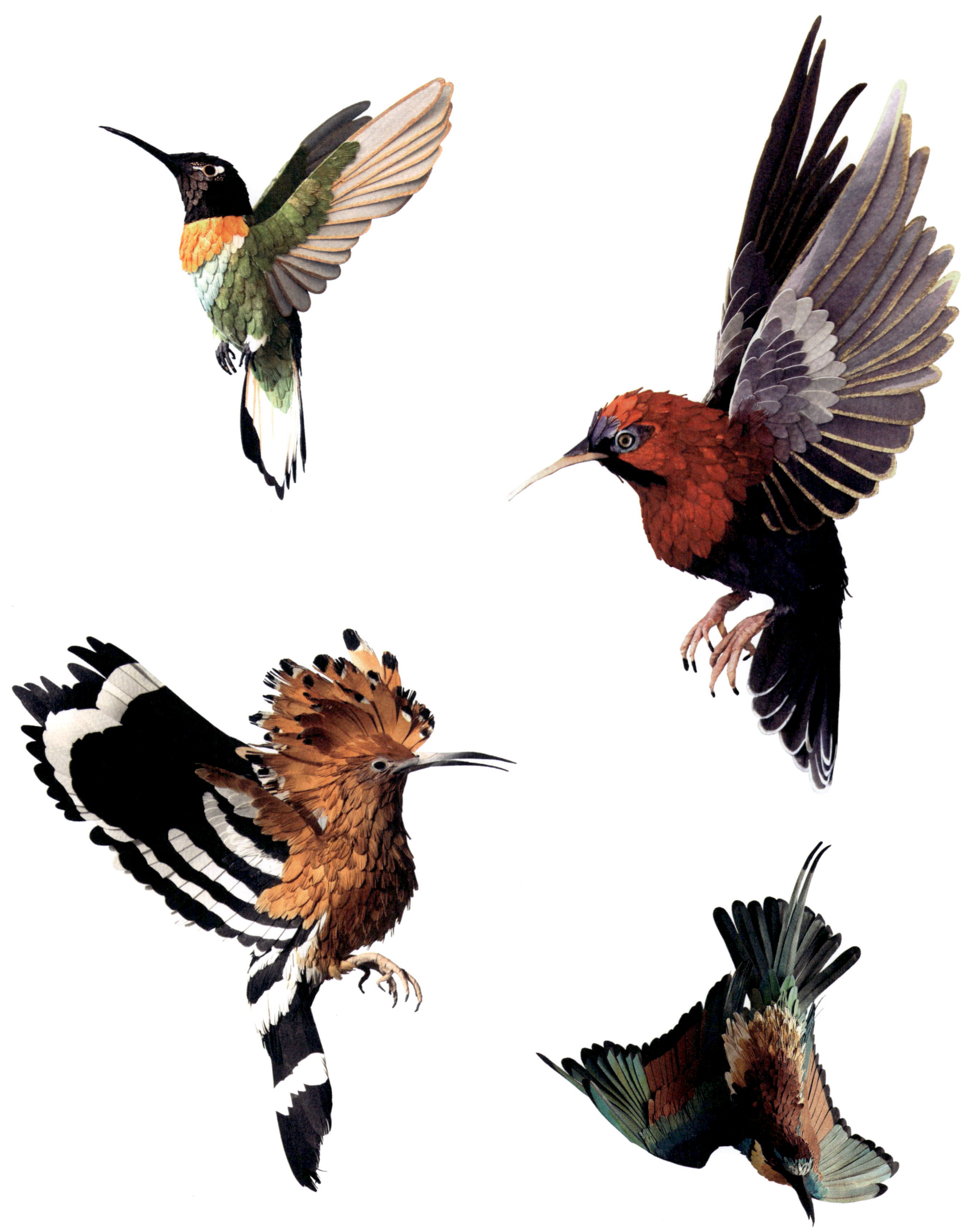

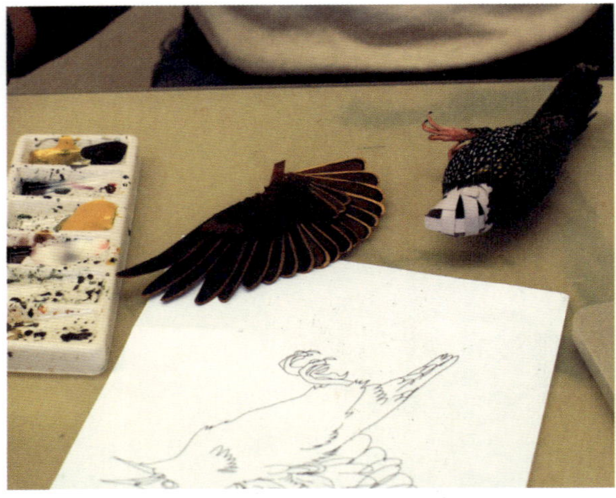
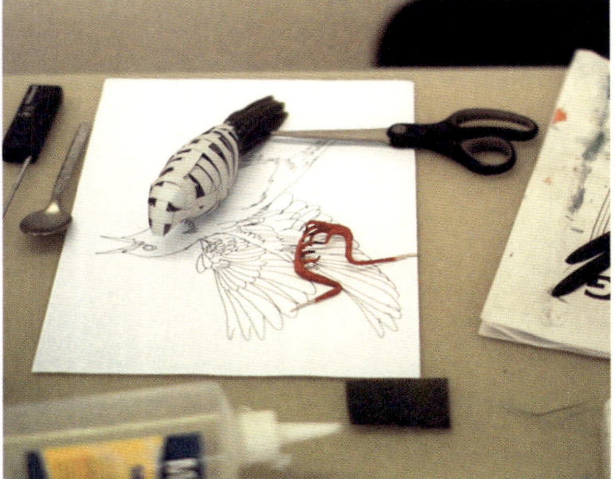
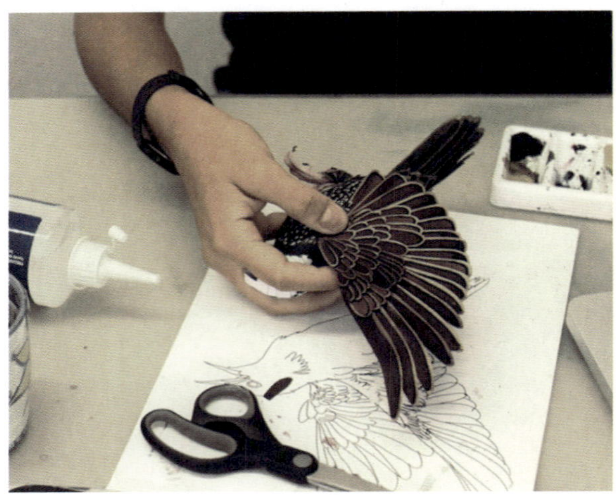
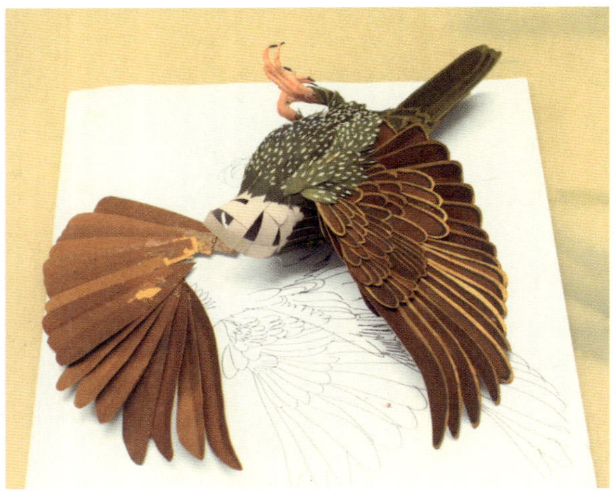

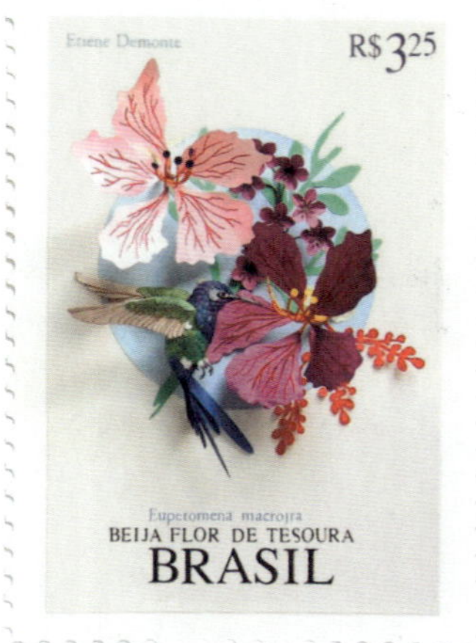

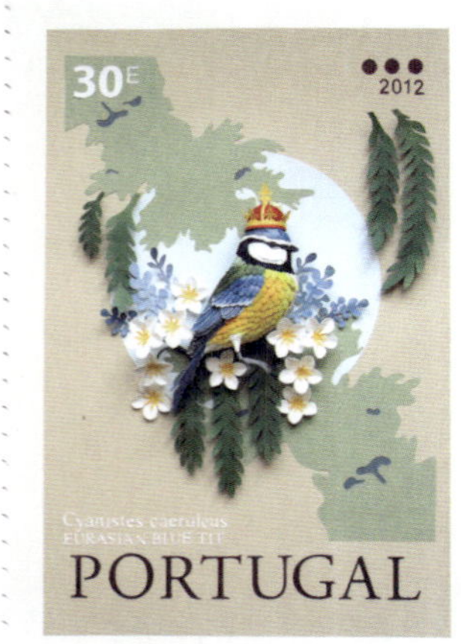

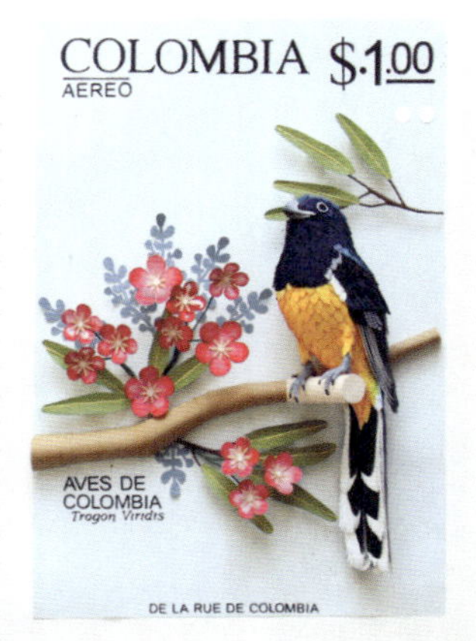

Although Herrera has become synonymous with her extensive work in paper, the sculptures have been developed over a long period of time and are the result of cumulative studies and other factors. After graduating with a BA in Industrial Design at the Jorge Tadeo Lozano University in Bogotá in 2010, Herrera came to realize that she wasn't interested in pursuing a design practice, instead becoming more focused on a 'purer' arts-based route. This took her initially to Finland, where she studied ceramic sculpture, and subsequently to the UK, where she undertook an MA in Fine Art at the University of the West of England in Bristol. Early on at these institutions Herrera began to develop work in paper in three-dimensions, but quite soon abandoned them to make sculpture in wood. It was only when she began to explore the theme of animals that paper as a material came back into play.

The colour and extraordinary forms of birds fascinate Herrera. In making her sculptures life-size they have a simple and immediate appeal, something for which the artist strives. Creating these extraordinary sculptures is a very complex and time-consuming process, from the step-by-step planning of the construction to the choice of colour. However, the malleability of paper, and its ability to hold both its form and colour makes it a practical and accessible choice, as the artist explains, 'I am interested in producing work with materials that are available to me, and which don't have a huge value or meaning…. I enjoy using whatever I find to create shapes, to develop forms. This comes from my design practice in which immediate materials are constantly transformed to test ideas, such as balsa wood, glue, paper, cardboard, acetate, and so on, all those materials are very appealing to me'.

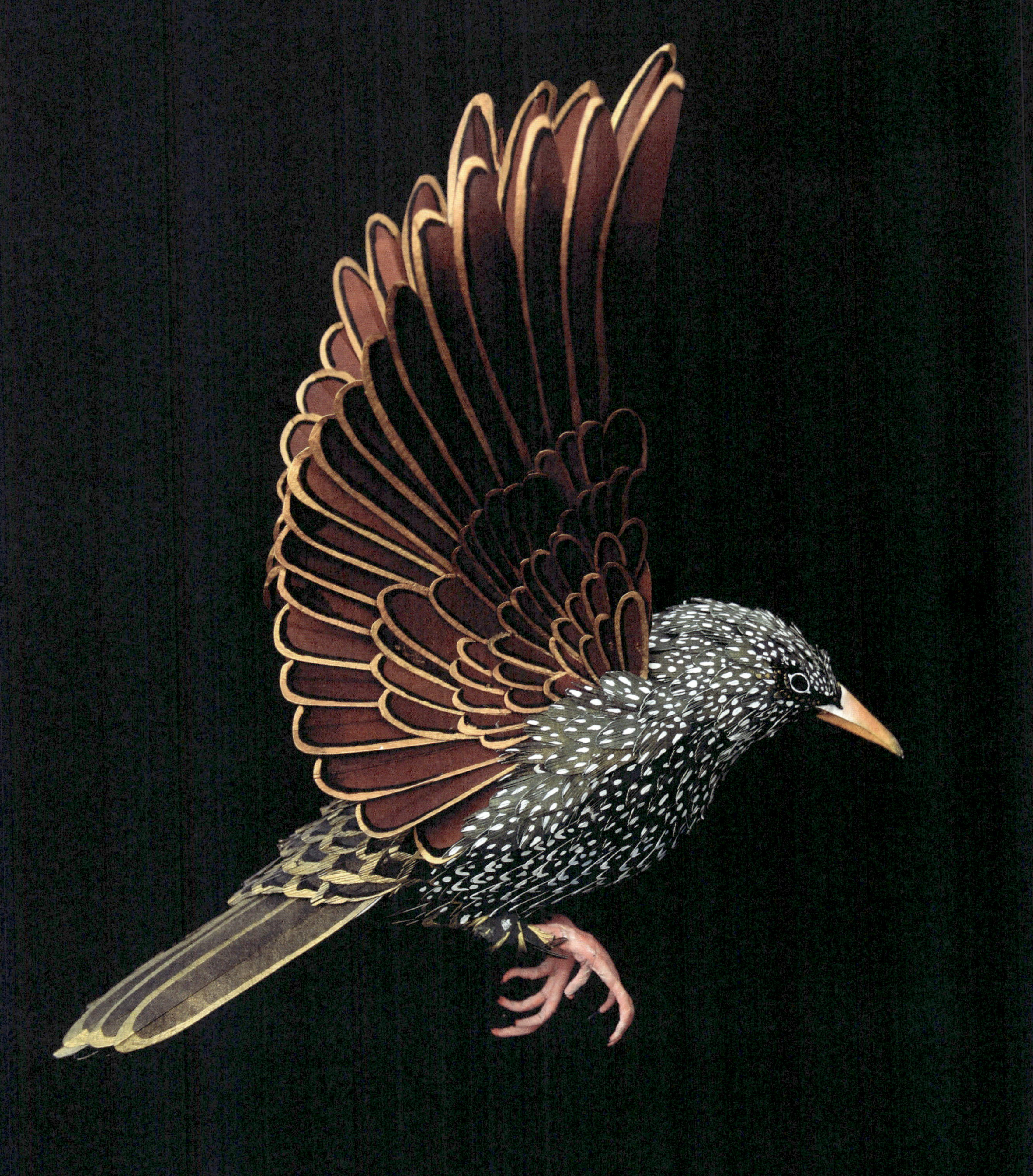

Borondo

Having gained a worldwide reputation for his innovative approach to art both in the street and the studio,

what makes the work of Spanish artist Borondo so appealing is that it seems to lie somewhere between the Classical and the cutting-edge – he is skilled in traditional painting techniques but also often wilfully deconstructs and re-evaluates the conventional methods of this medium. Another facet of his innovation is his use of a variety of materials, such as wood, glass or wire mesh, which come to coalesce in an output that ranges from animation to sculptural installation.

On becoming acquainted with the breadth of Borondo's work, the impression is of an artist working at a passionate fever pitch to realize a myriad of concepts, but belying this ferocious pace each work is enduringly reflective and well considered. Borondo grew up in the city of Segovia under the influence of his mother, who let him paint the walls inside his house, and his father, who was an art restorer. Upon moving to Madrid in 2003, his already growing interest in graffiti was ignited, while some years later he found a path to art, regularly

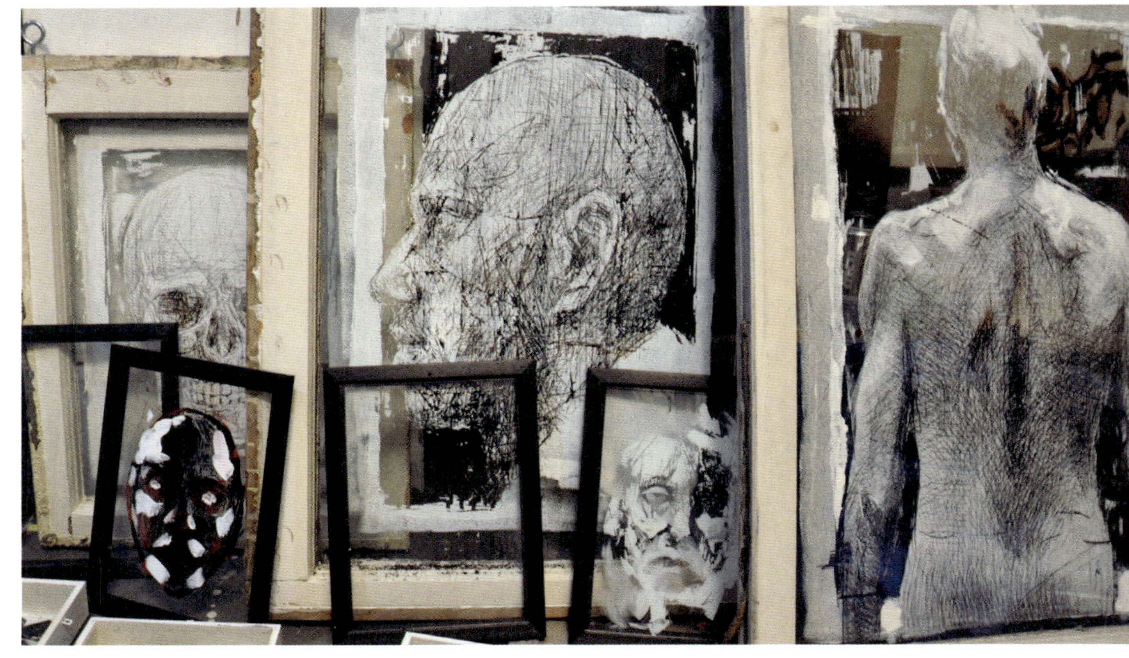

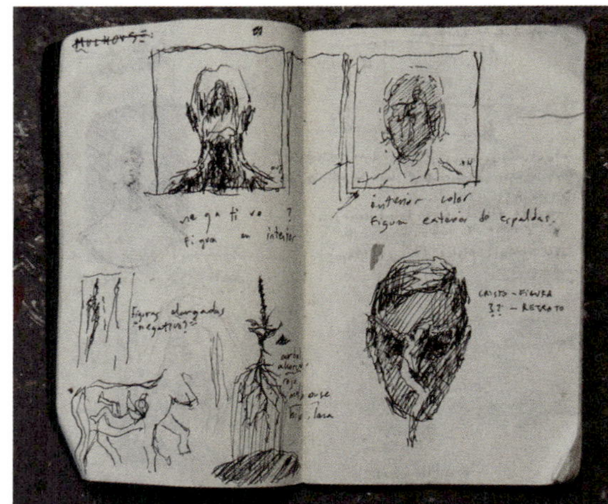

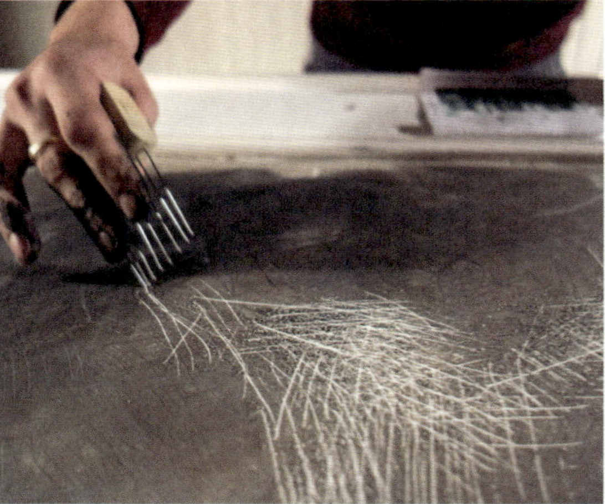

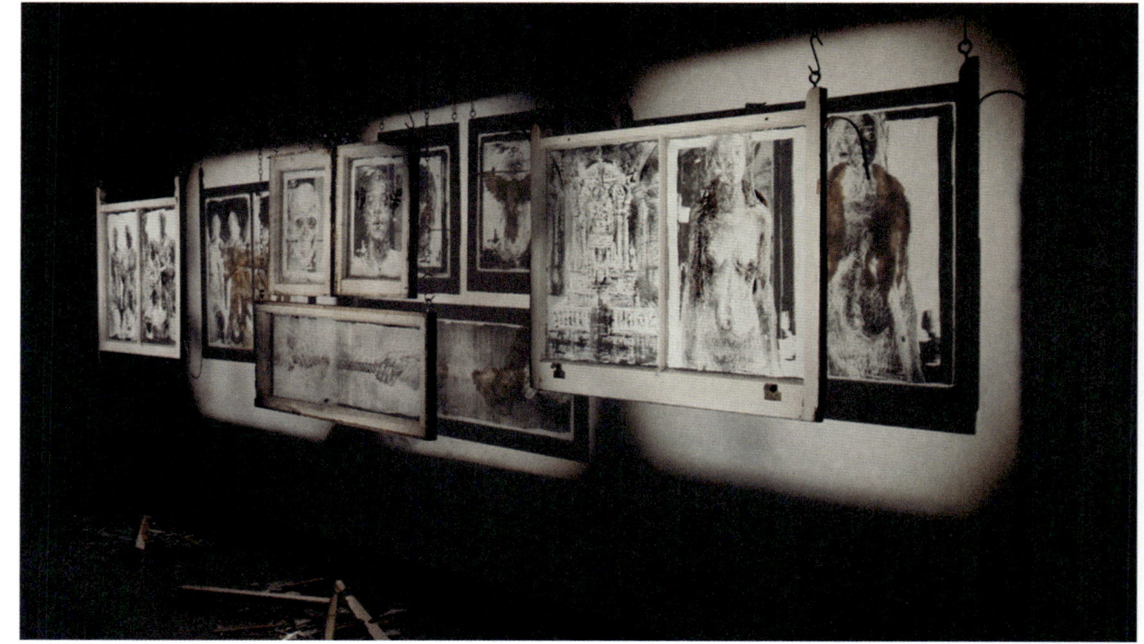

CLOCKWISE FROM TOP LEFT
Borondo's studio in
London, 2015

The artist working on
Animal, 2014

Works from the 'Entranas'
series, 2015
Mixed media
Dimensions variable

Pages from the artist's
sketchbook.

OPPOSITE AND OVERLEAF
Limbo, 2015
Acrylic on Plexiglass
Dimensions variable

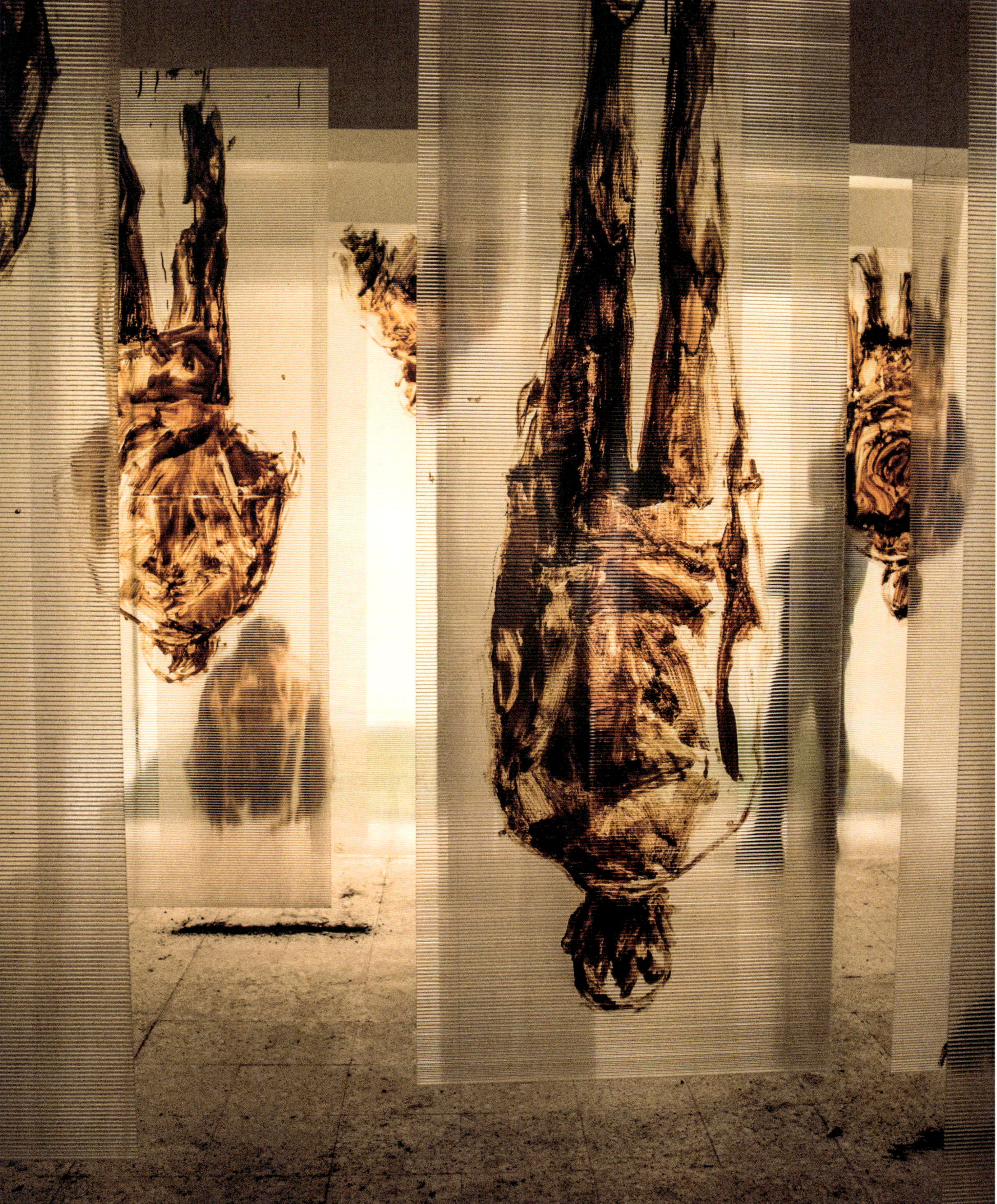

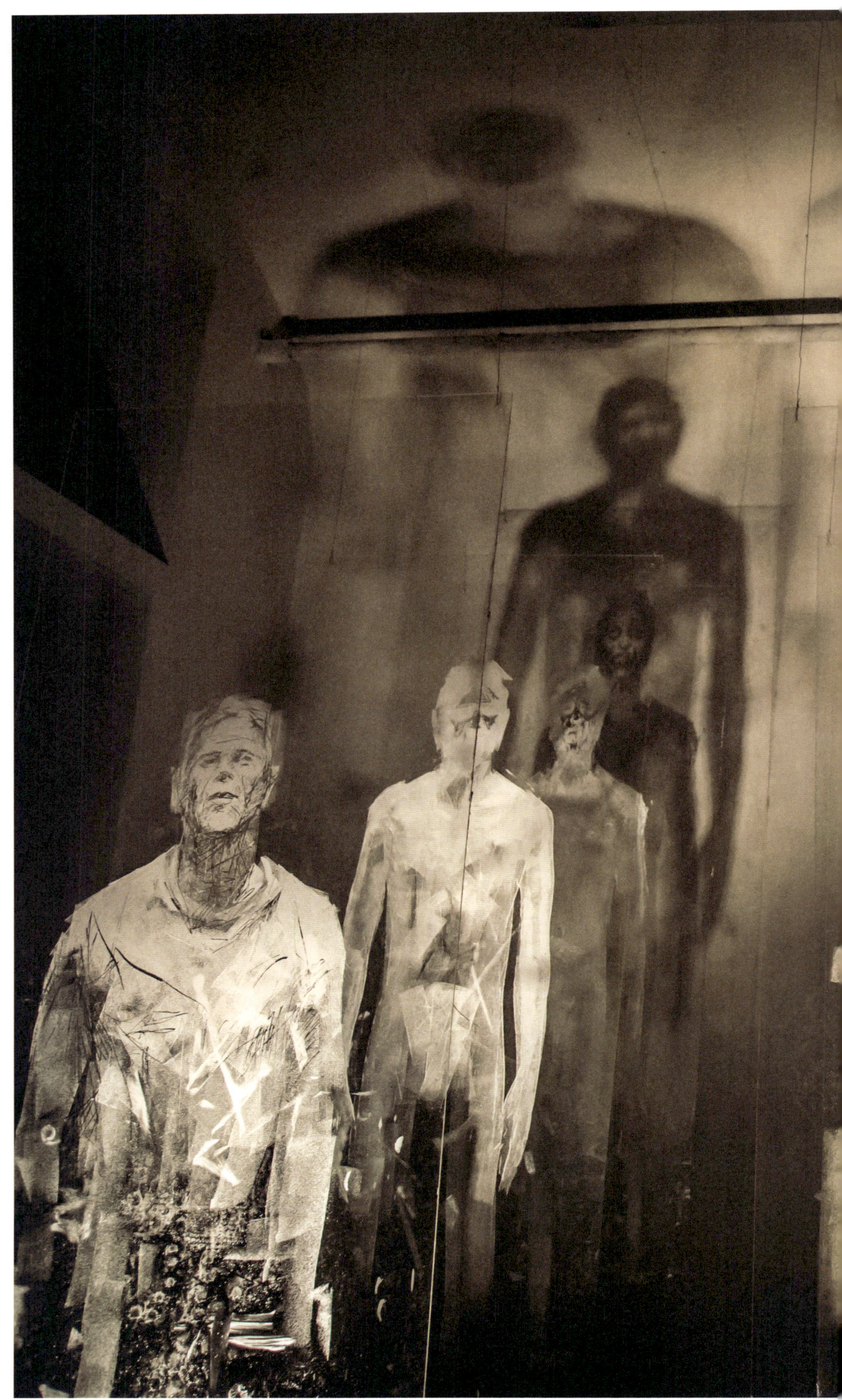

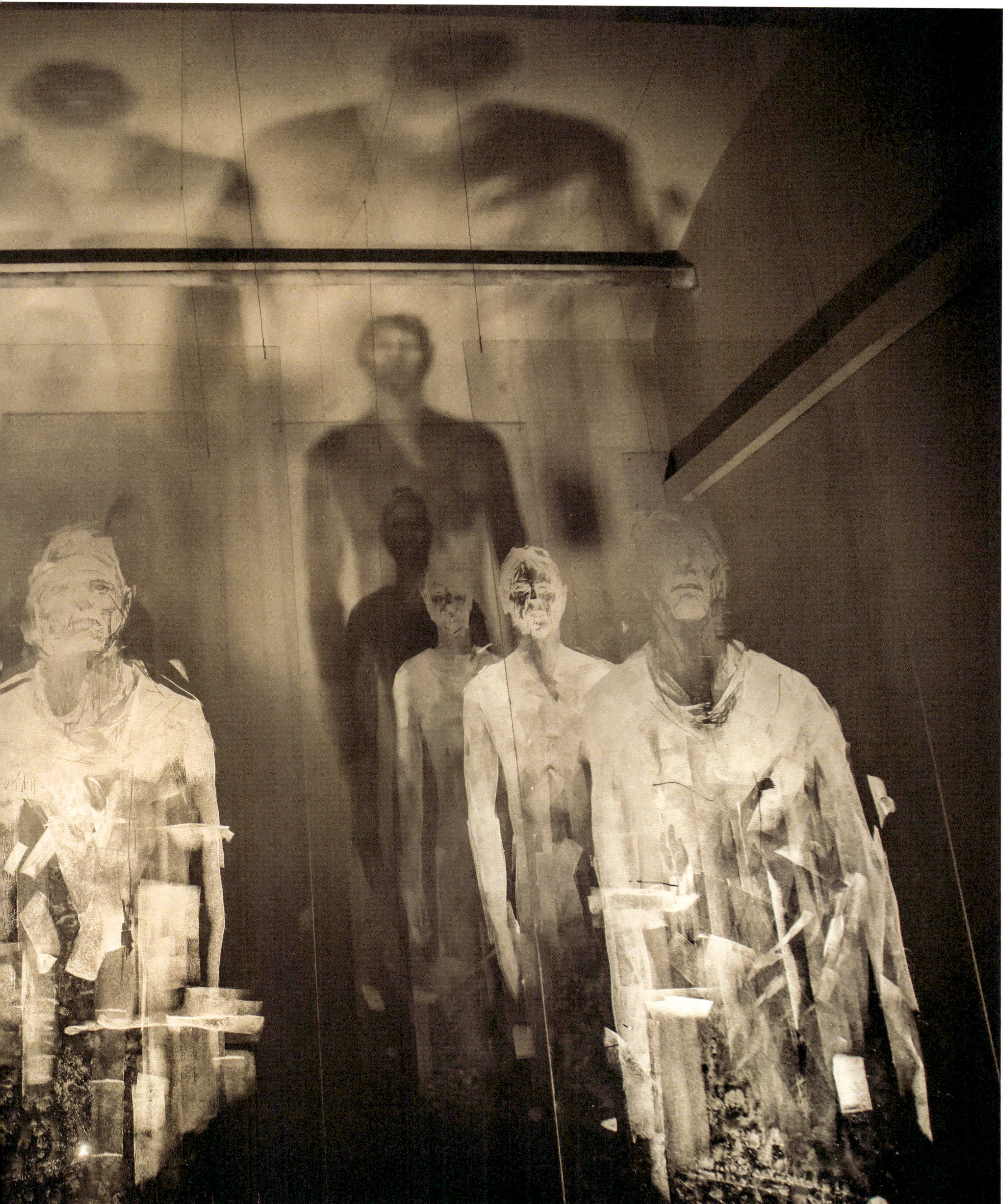

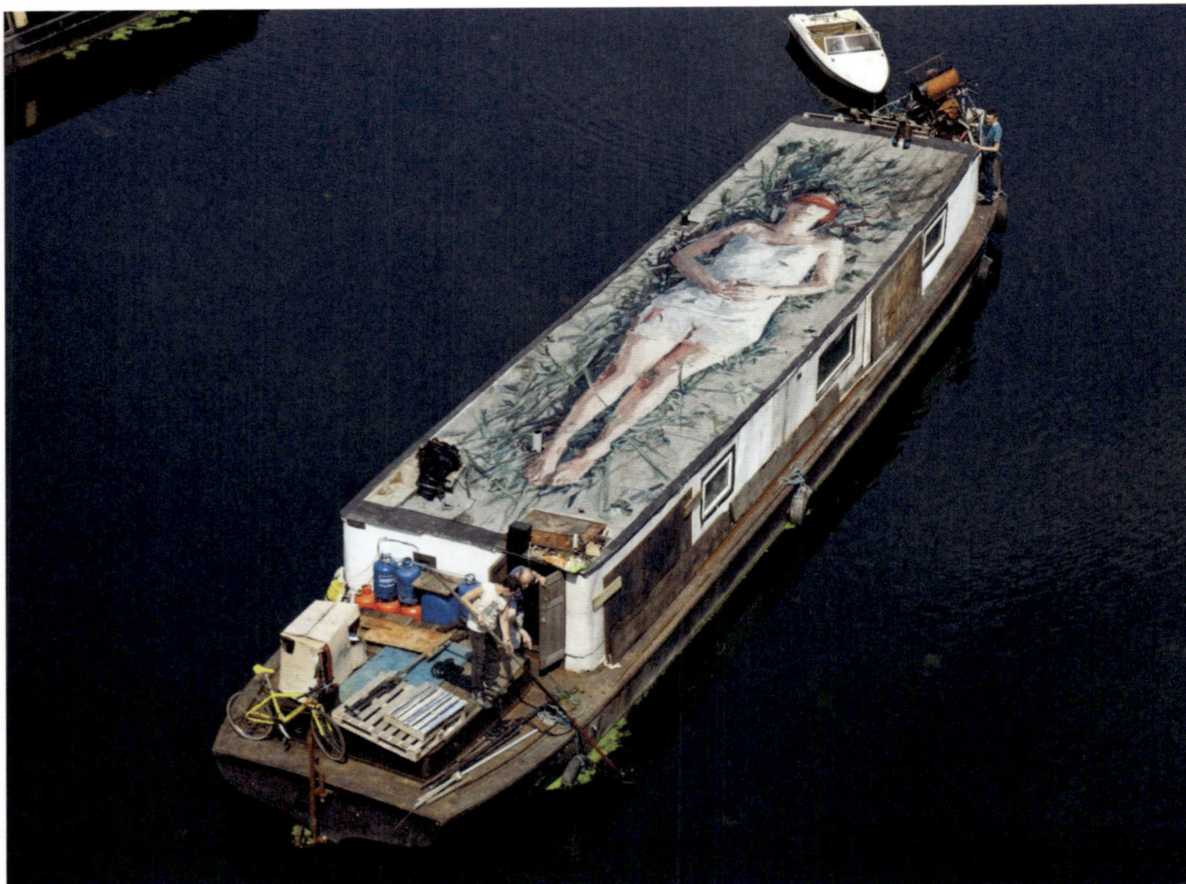

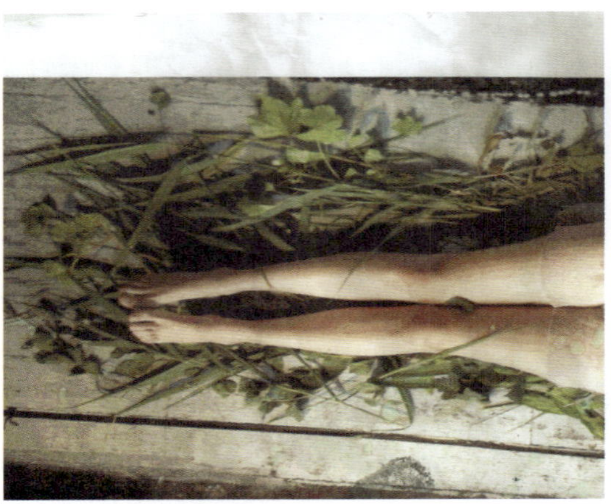

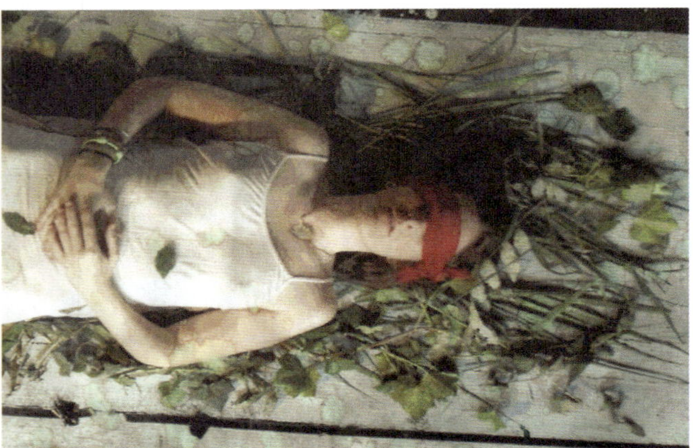

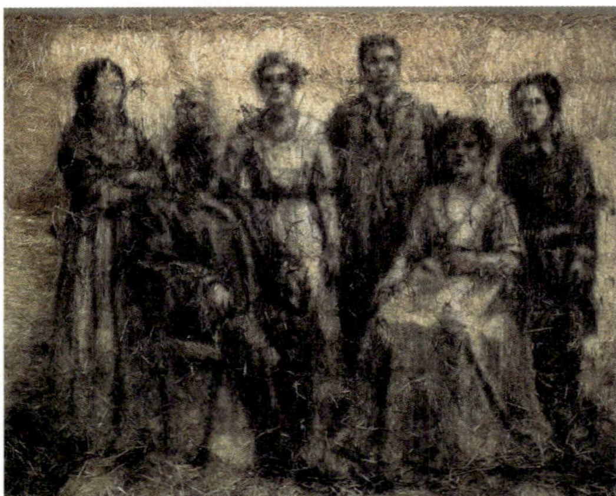

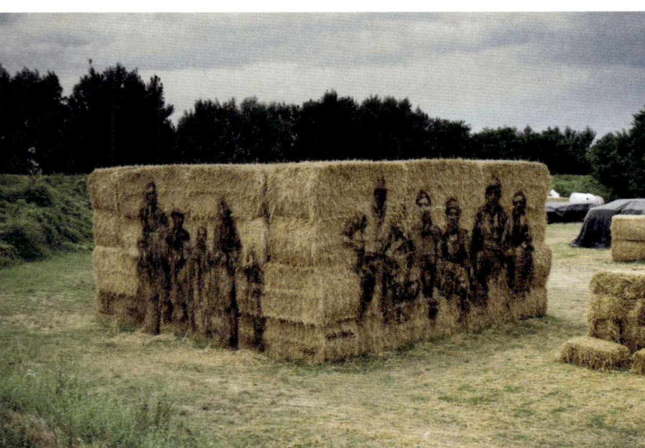

visiting the studio of his soon-to-be-mentor, the artist José García Herranz. A friendship and informal apprenticeship evolved, which stirred in him a love for the work of the Old Masters, such as Francisco Goya (1746–1828). Later he studied fine art in the cities of Madrid and Rome, but without graduating. By that time he had already embarked upon his own path, exhibiting pieces in solo shows in Rome, Madrid and Paris, while creating art in public spaces across the world.

Street art has been an activating force in Borondo's career, shaping his outlook and *modus operandi*, with the great outdoors being his preferred 'gallery' space. For him, 'It is really important for a street artist to be part of the context, to be able to adapt…. I focus on the public space, the environment and the reality. It is there, outside, not here on the canvas or in the gallery.' This approach can be seen in works such as his portraits of farmworkers produced in Cotignola in Italy in 2013, in which he applied spray paint directly onto bales of hay, or *Ophelia*, which he painted directly on the roof of a canal boat on the River Lea in east London, in collaboration with the artist Carmen Maín. In this latter piece he took the iconic Shakespearean character made well-known pictorially by the Pre-Raphaelite John Everett Millais (1829–1896), but reimagined in modern attire and with the addition of a blindfold.

In a multitude of ways Borondo's work requires us to look again, to contemplate our surroundings, our fellow citizens and eternal themes such as life and death. His images are challenging, unexpected and contain multiple layers of texture and meaning, all of which oblige the viewer to pause and listen.

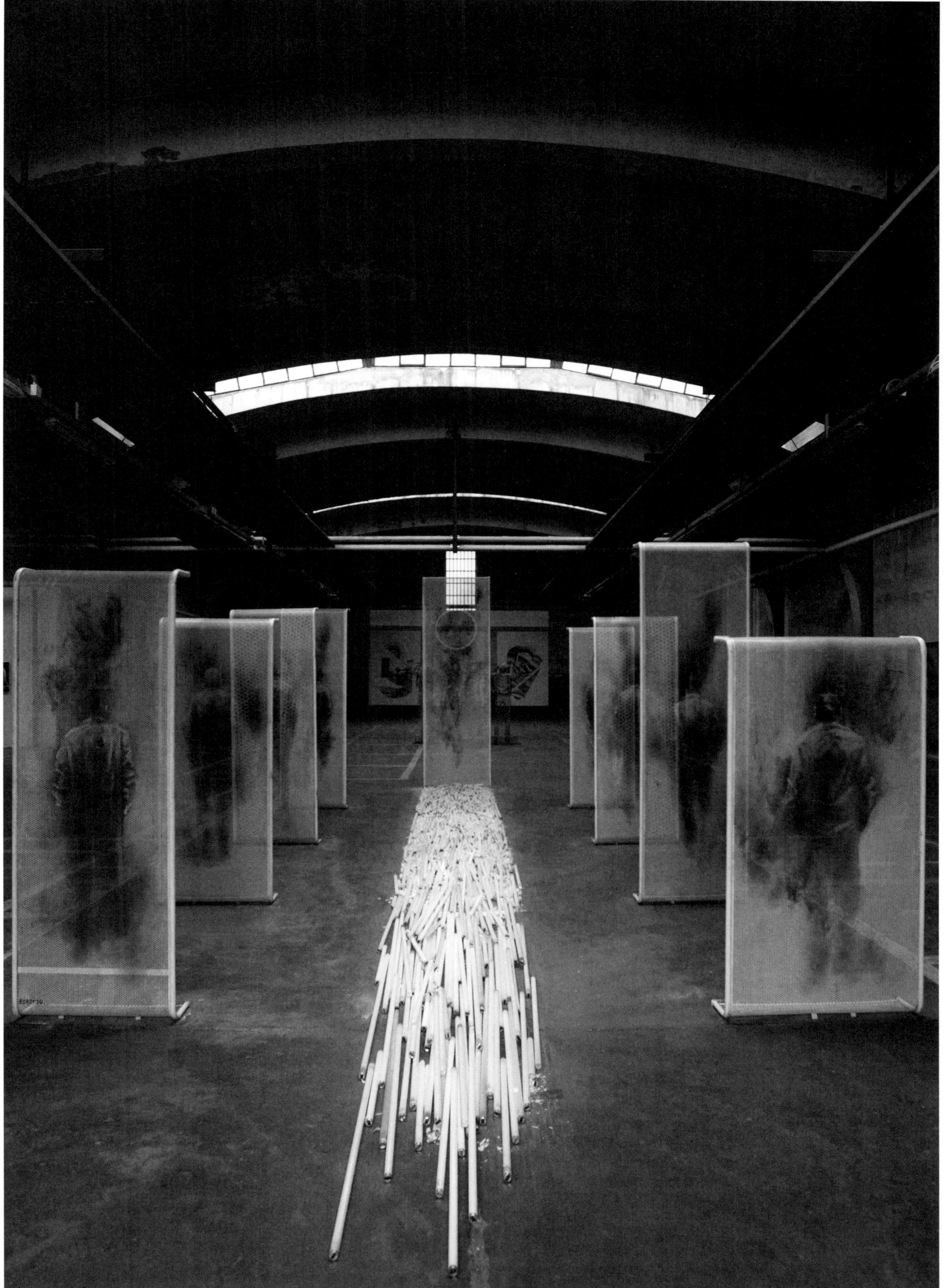

Jason Botkin

Known for his vibrant paintings and sculptures, as well as his collaborative approach to making art,

Jason Botkin is a Québécois artist based in Montreal. He is a co-founder of 'En Masse', an artist collective famed for its huge black-and-white murals that have laid claim to large swathes of urban space in Montreal, and which boasts more than 250 contributors. Formed in 2009 to 'touch, blend, balance, fuse and reconcile different worlds through communication', En Masse has restored Botkin's 'love of intuitive experimentation and play, surrounded by a community of artists that offer incredible support, interest and critical feedback'.

The influences of En Masse can be seen in Botkin's own work in numerous ways. In keeping with the collective's overarching theme of connectedness his subject-matter seems to embrace the idea of a communal human spirit, exploring the many sides of humanity and society through a cast of exaggerated characters that are either painted or sculpted. These figures, often masked or totemic in style, seem to

Allkin Lndmrk, 2013
Mixed media on plywood
Dimensions variable

OPPOSITE, CLOCKWISE FROM TOP LEFT
Untitled, mural commissioned
by the Festival Internacional de
Arte Público, Cancun, 2015
Mixed media
Dimensions variable

Untitled, mural commissioned
by the Festival Internacional de
Arte Público, 2015
Mixed media
Dimensions variable

Blue Face, c. 2015
Mixed media on plywood
Dimensions variable

Untitled, mural commissioned
by the Festival Internacional de
Arte Público, 2015
Mixed media
Dimensions variable

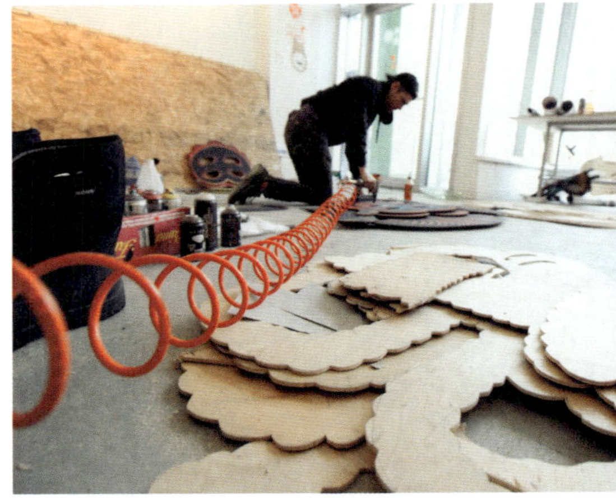
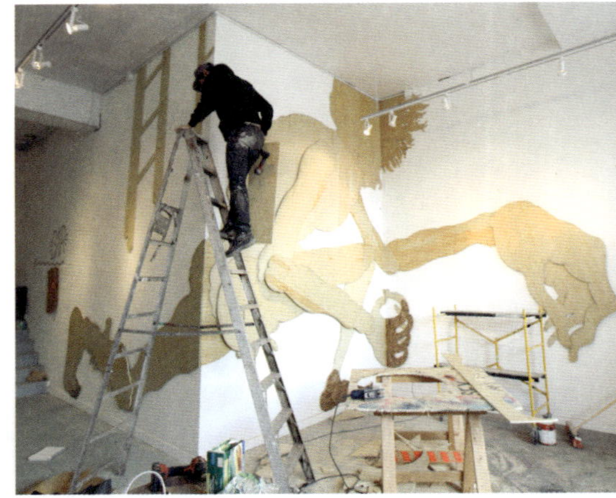
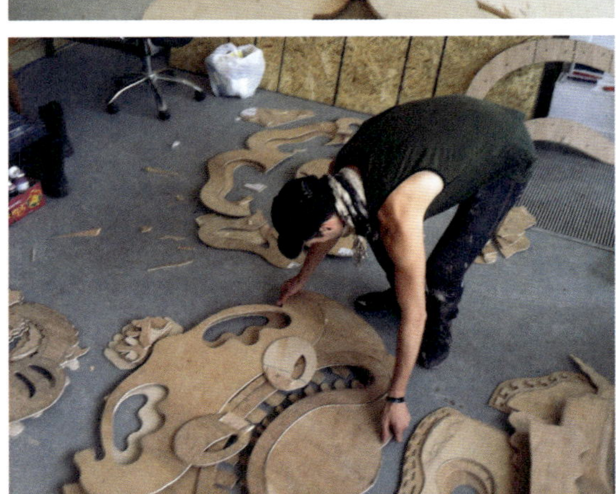
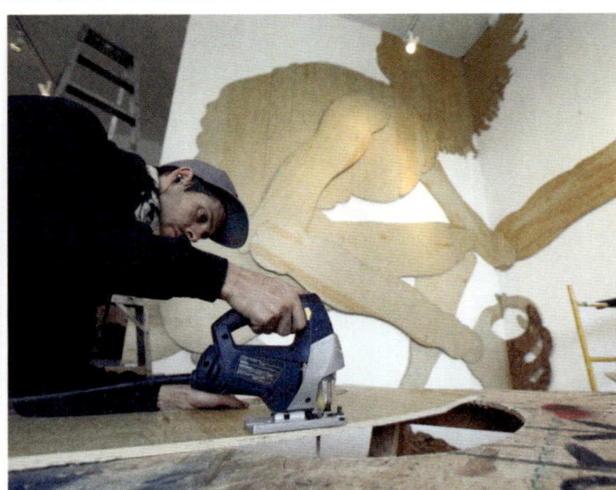
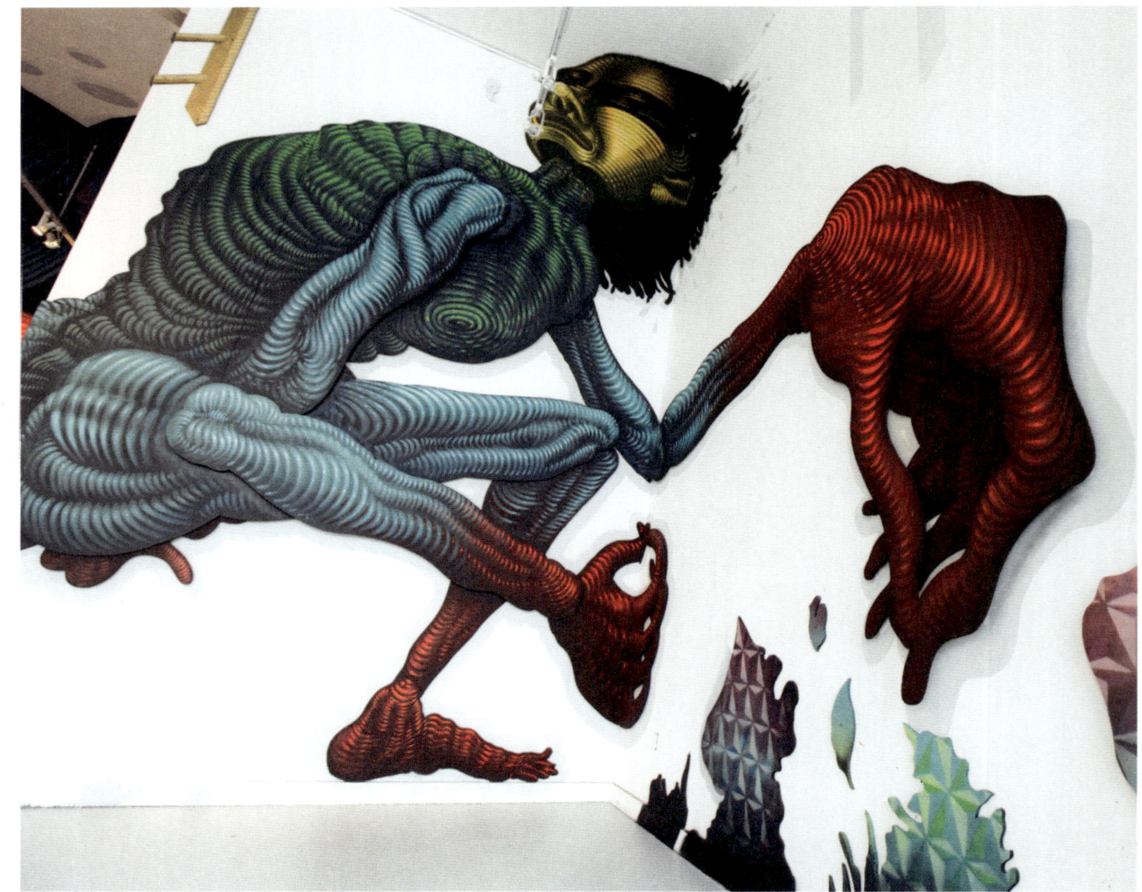

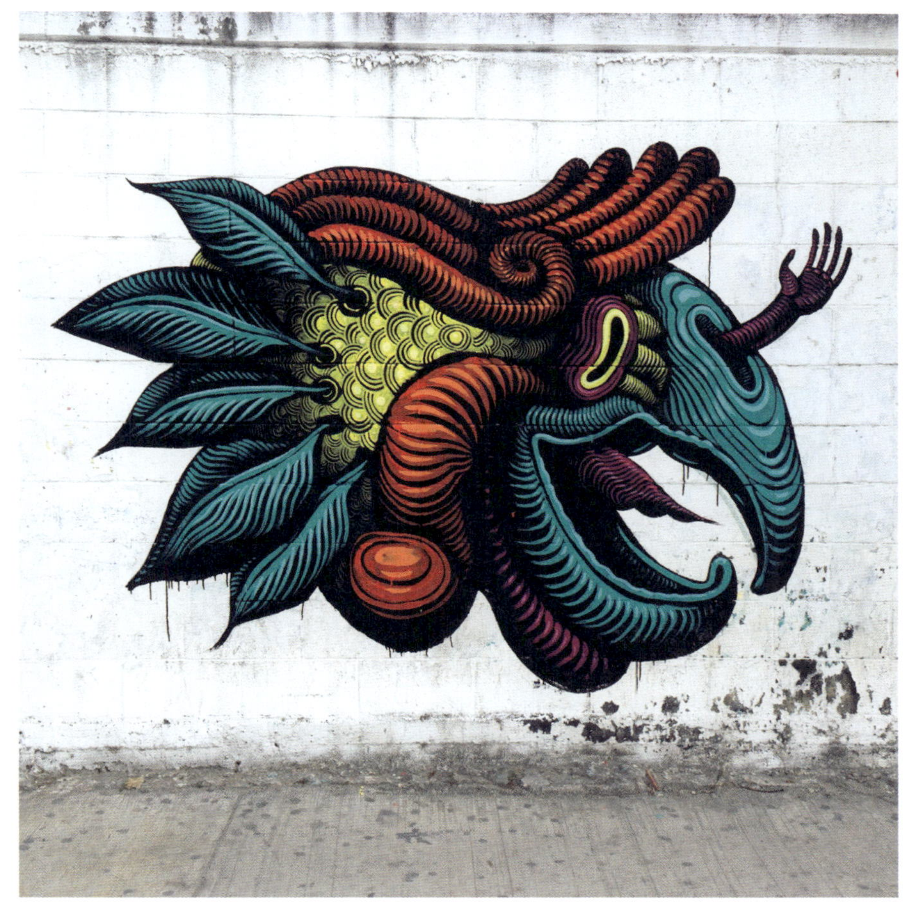 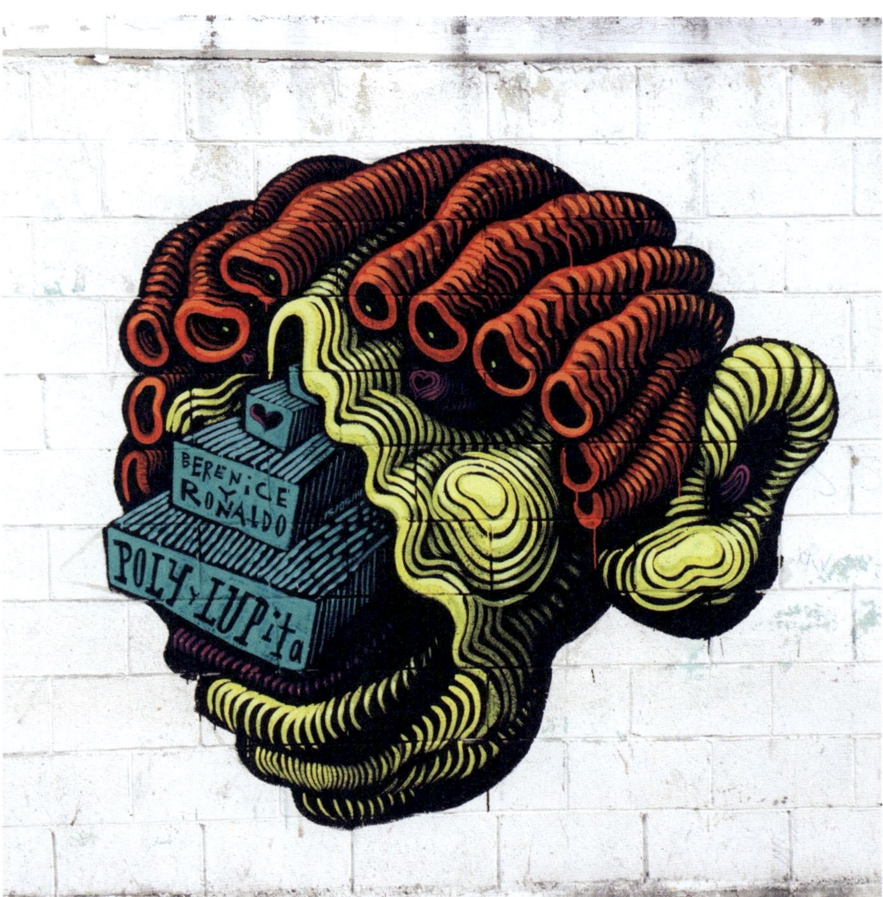

BERENICE
RONALDO
POLY+LUPita

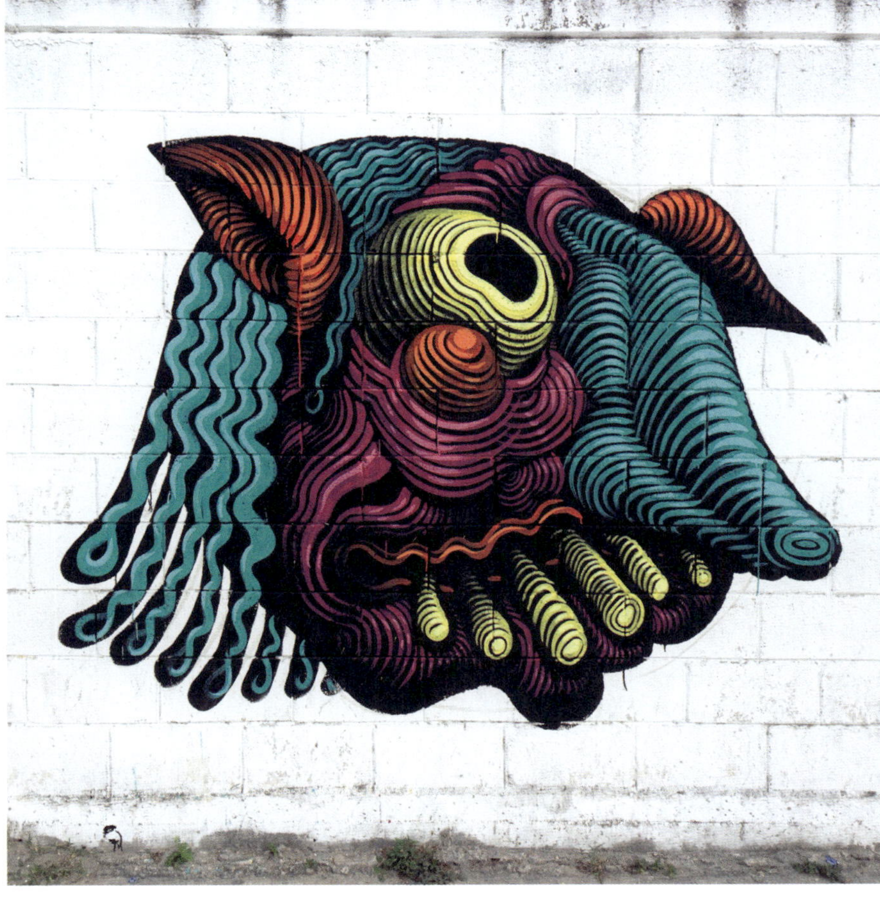 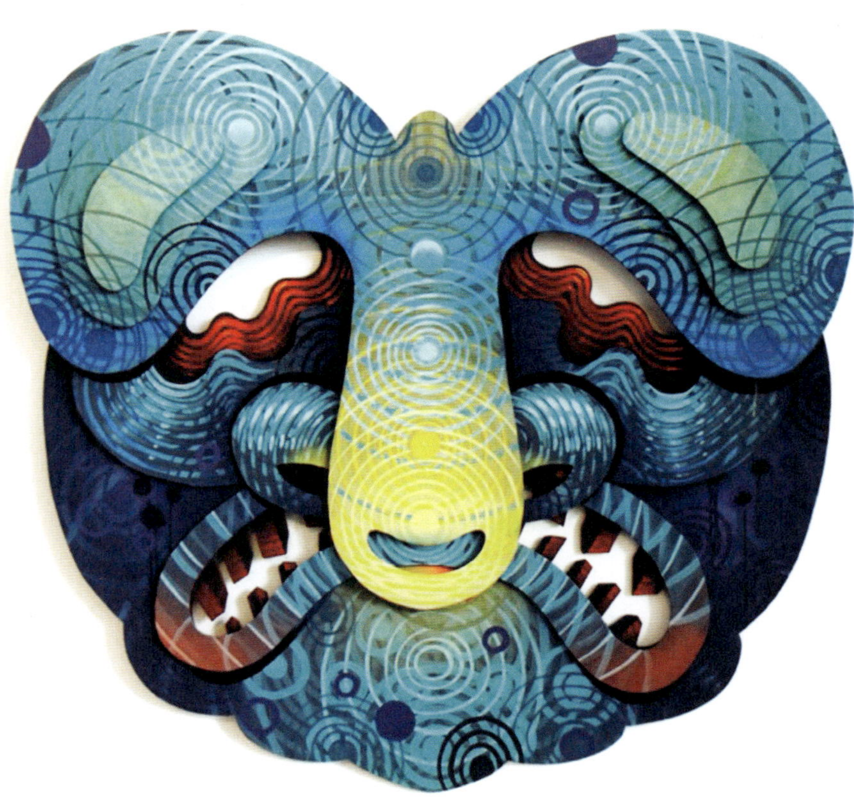

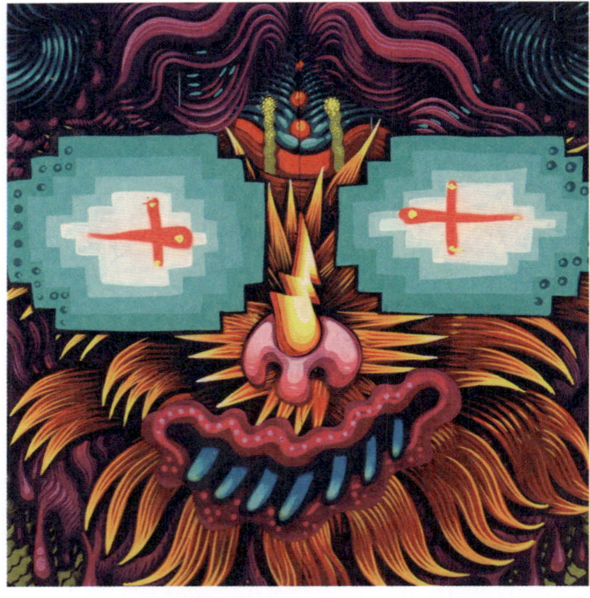
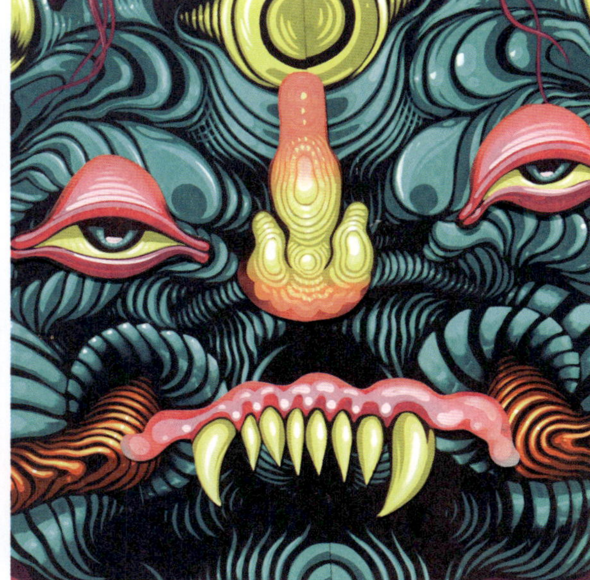
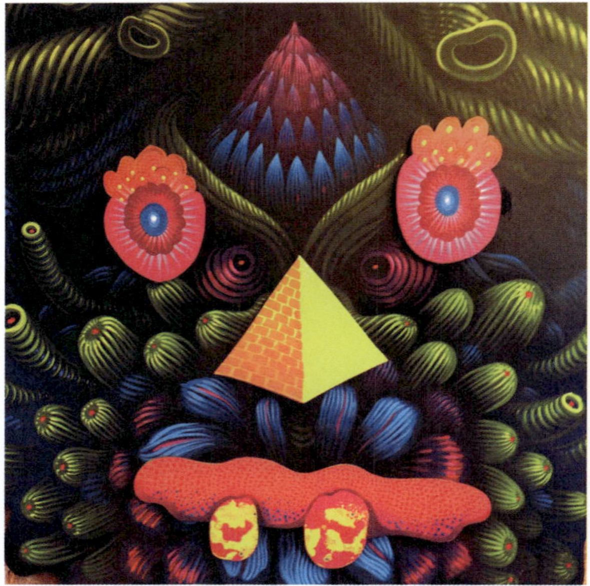
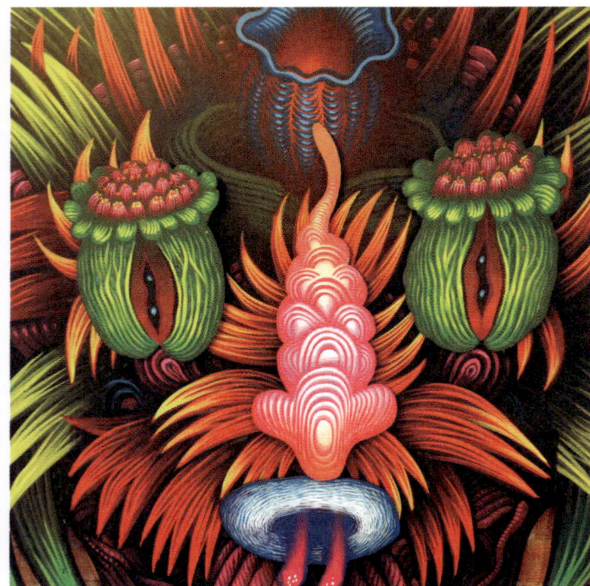

represent archetypes or puppets. His use of distinctive dark or black sinewy lines against bright and bold colours also has tribalistic or ritualistic intimations. Botkin describes himself as a restless artist, one who is curious to explore new techniques and media and who is also constantly on the move, participating in a myriad of projects both at home and across the globe, and tirelessly working with a 'constantly changing landscape of personal creativity and craft'.

Sculpture is a medium to which Botkin continually returns in between periods of painting. Since the early 1990s he has been making plywood structures on to which he paints shapes and identities. The attraction of this material to him is that it is cheap, strong and easy to manipulate. 'From early on,' he explains, 'it was important for me to break out of the square/rectangle of the canvas. Giant figures cut from wood like paper dolls forces the wall that supports it to act as canvas… a space that directly impinges on the viewer as an installation…. Working in this way is very physically direct…it satisfies me enormously, even if it *rarely* sells.' Sculptural elements such as this accentuate many of the philosophies found in his painting and in particular emphasize the mask-like quality of the works. As Botkin explains, 'they allow me to address identity through the vehicle of the "face", a subject-matter I'm endlessly captivated by. I love how these "second skins" act as tools that enable us to change identities and assume new personalities; underlining a deeply ingrained need to transform ourselves and the environment around us.'

Potato Head Robotkins, 2015
Acrylic on board
Dimensions unknown

Potato Head, 2015
Mixed media
Dimensions variable

Mr Potato Head Mural for FIAP2015, 2015

Potato Heads, 2015
Acrylic on board
Dimensions variable

The artist at work, 2015

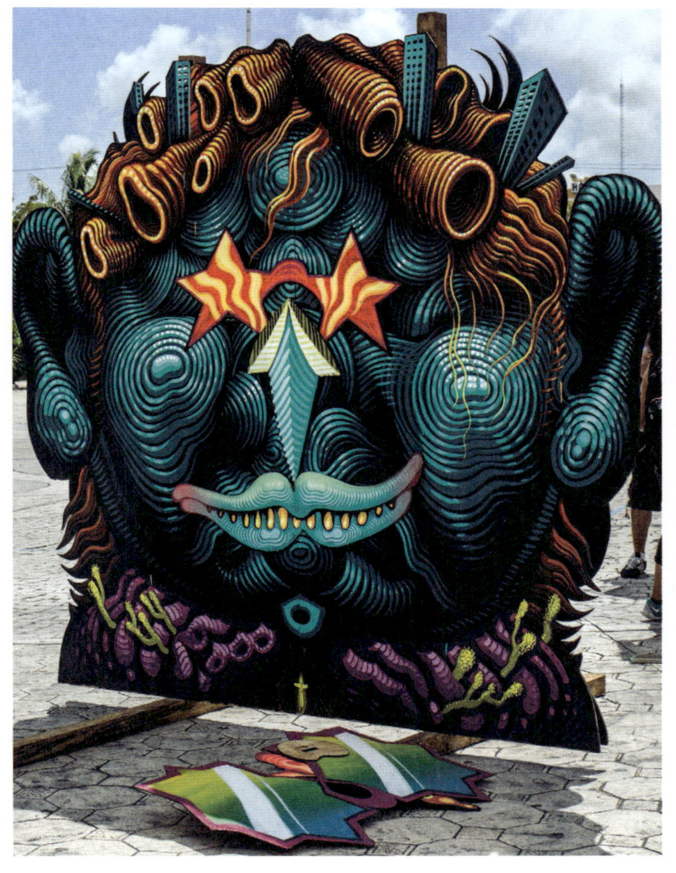
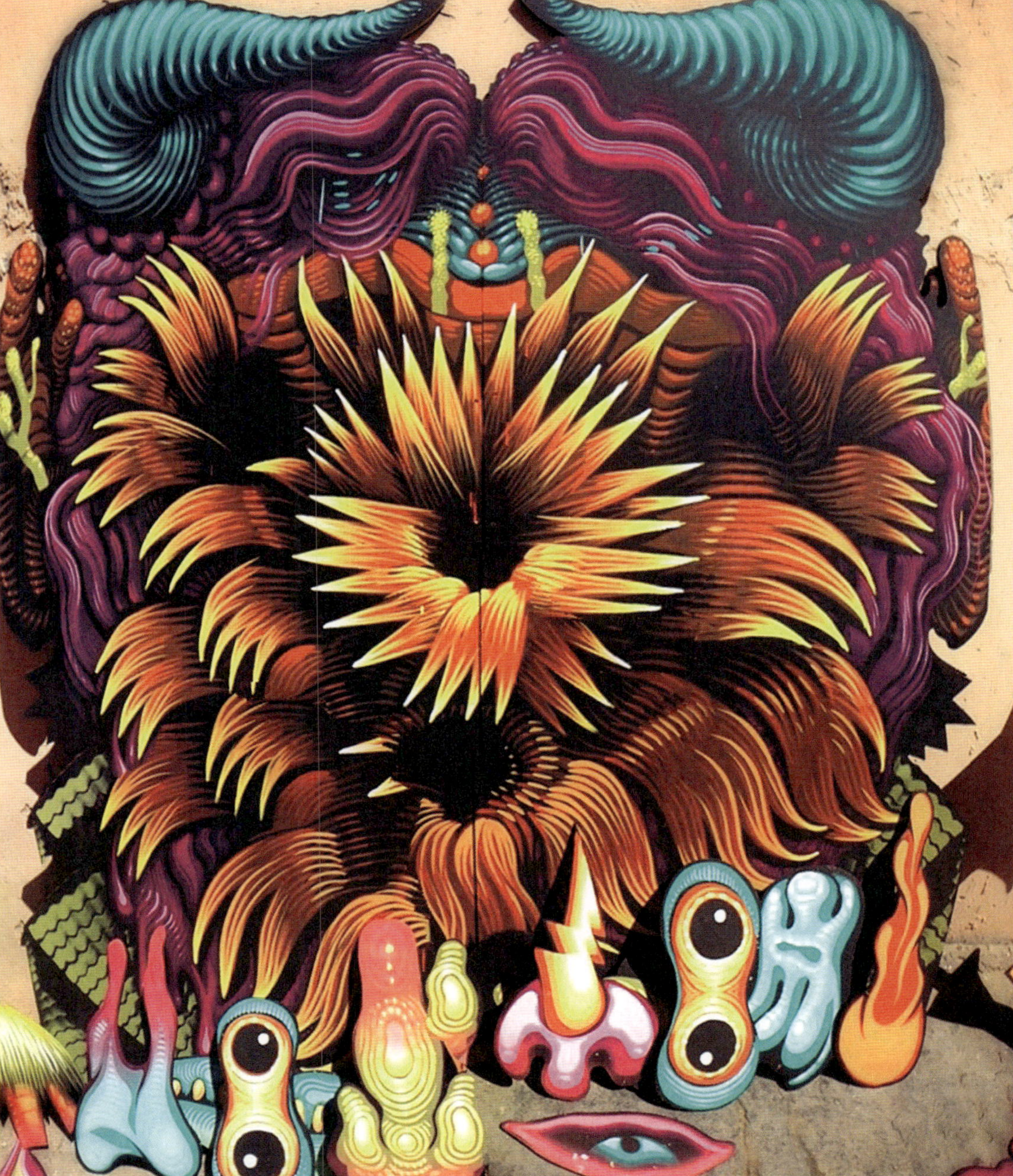
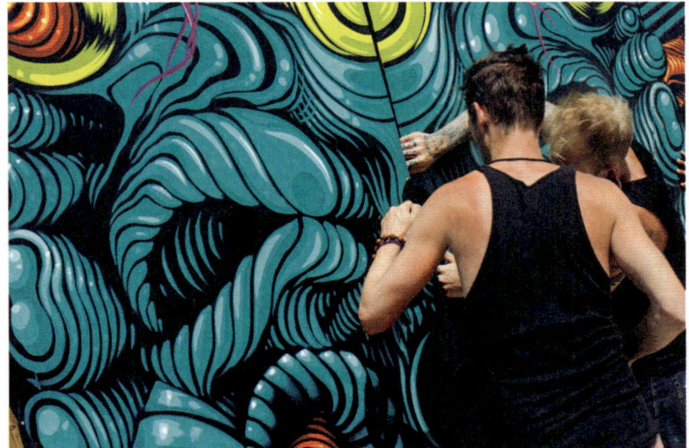
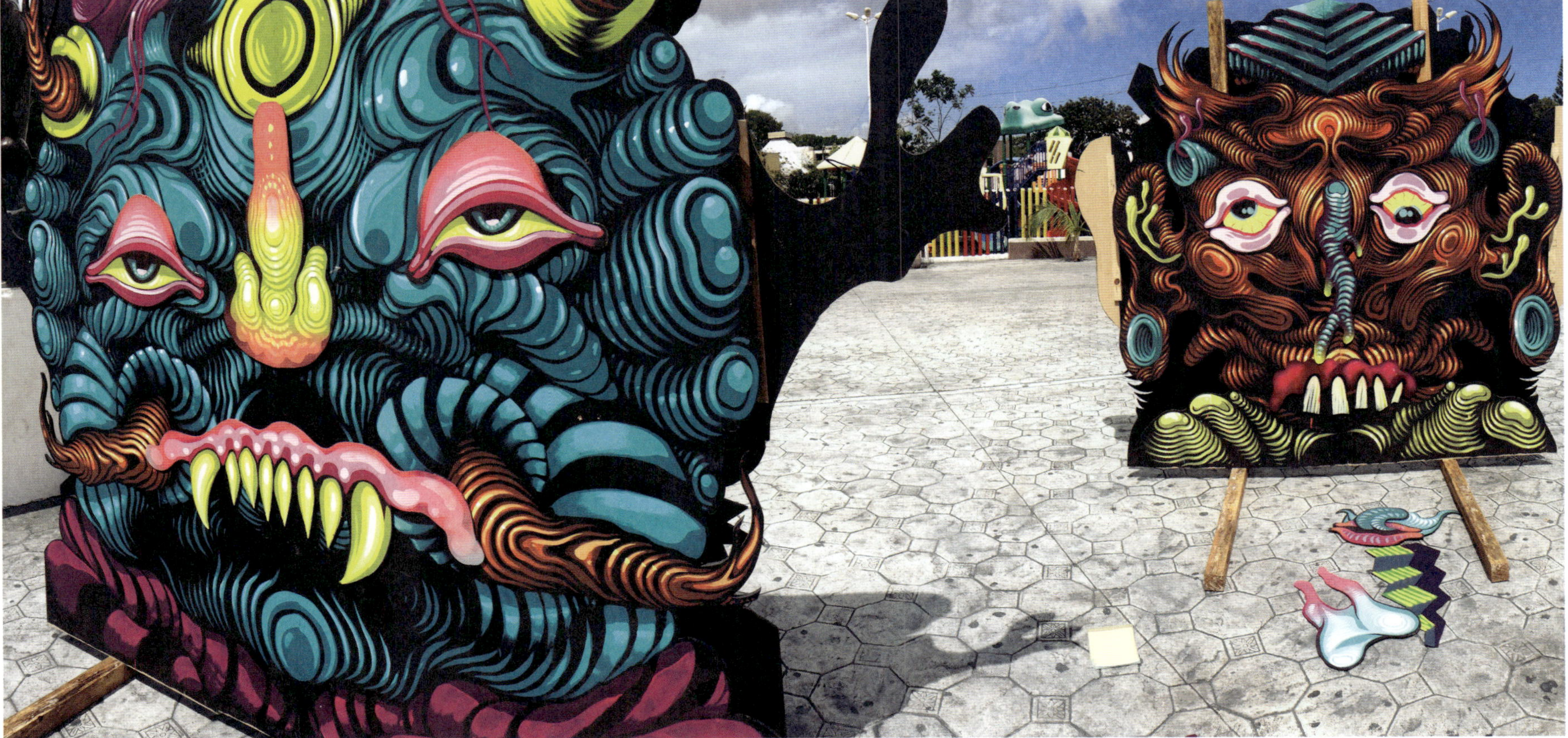

Franco Fasoli

A leading proponent in Argentina's flourishing street and graffiti art scene,

Franco Fasoli (otherwise known as Jaz) has been painting in his home city of Buenos Aires since 1999. He belongs to a new generation of artists who have been creating a homegrown style of Latin American, and more specifically Argentinian, mural art, which references local culture and concerns rather than the imported styles of generic American or European graffiti. Most recently he has become known for his use of colourful paper cuts, which he has adopted as a technique both in his street art and on the canvases that he exhibits in galleries, a process that Henri Matisse, the originator of the cut-out technique, famously described as 'carving into colour'.

Using different techniques and materials has always been a fundamental factor in Fasoli's work as it has evolved stylistically and thematically. At first his street art comprised graffiti lettering inspired by the particular *fileteado porteño* ornamental style of commercial hand-painted signwriting native to Buenos Aires. This approach was driven by his desire to meld together the traditionalism of the genre with a more contemporary expression, something that continues to be an underlying aspect of his work. By 2005 his focus shifted to figurative art, which he renders at a huge scale in a technique involving unconventional materials such as asphalt paint and petrol, in wash effects that resemble watercolour.

Coming from a background of set design, ceramics and painting, for more than a decade Fasoli worked in theatre, television and advertising concurrent to his mural painting. However, in the last few years having found himself in a rapidly expanding urban art circuit, he has been able to devote himself entirely to his own art, through exhibitions, festivals and site-specific projects.

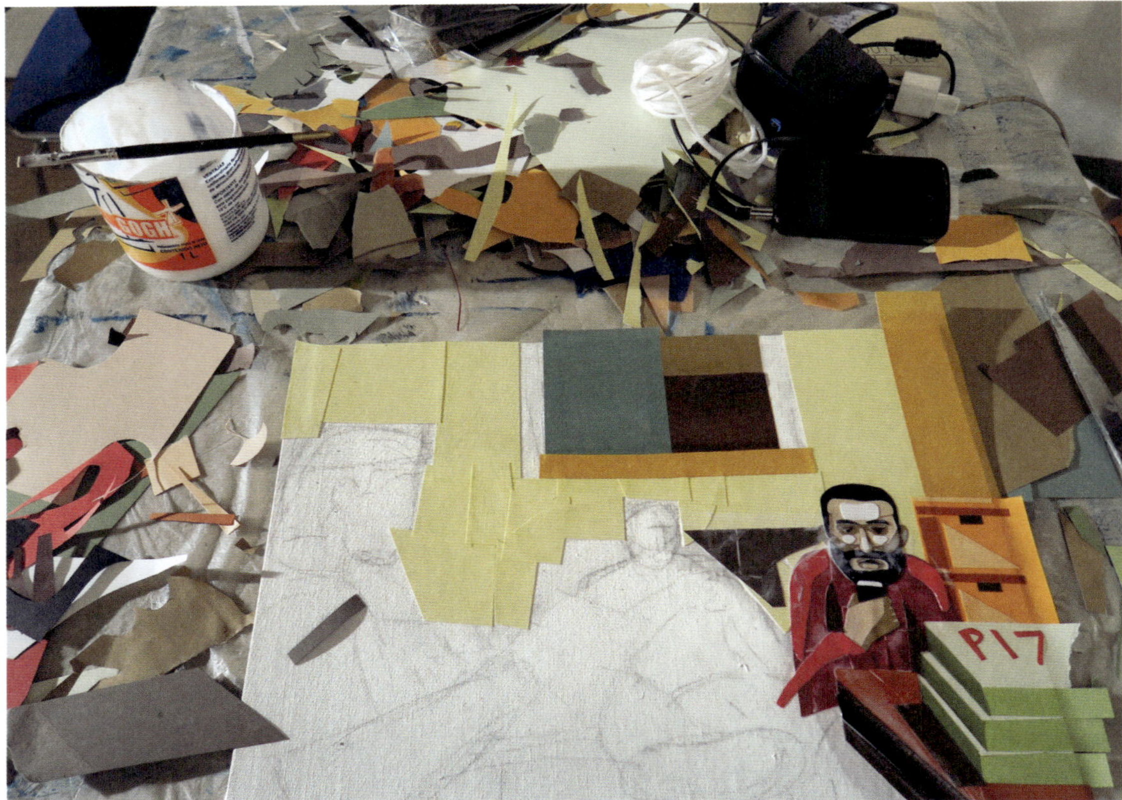

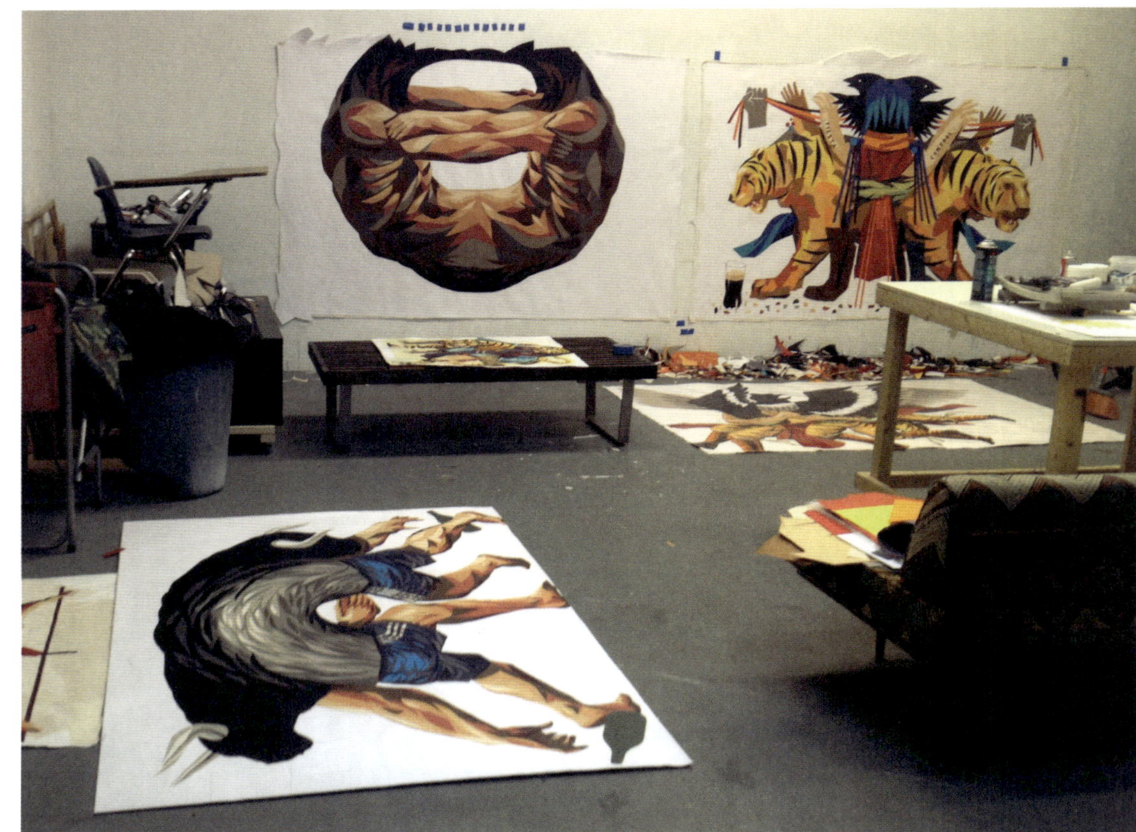

Works in progress in the
artist's studio, 2015

OPPOSITE
Naturaleza, 2015
Collage on canvas
90 × 70 cm (35½ × 27⅝ in.)

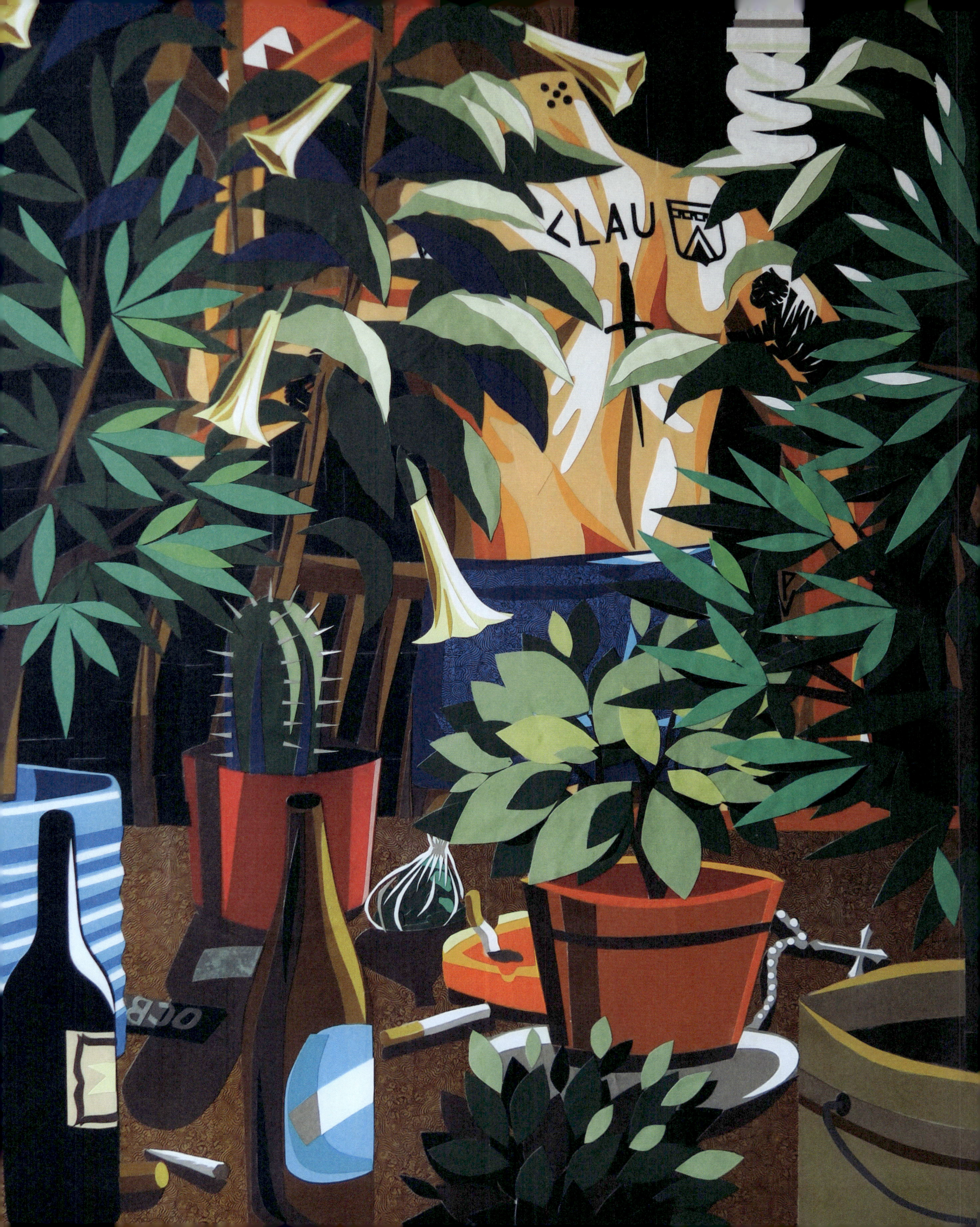

CLAU
OCB

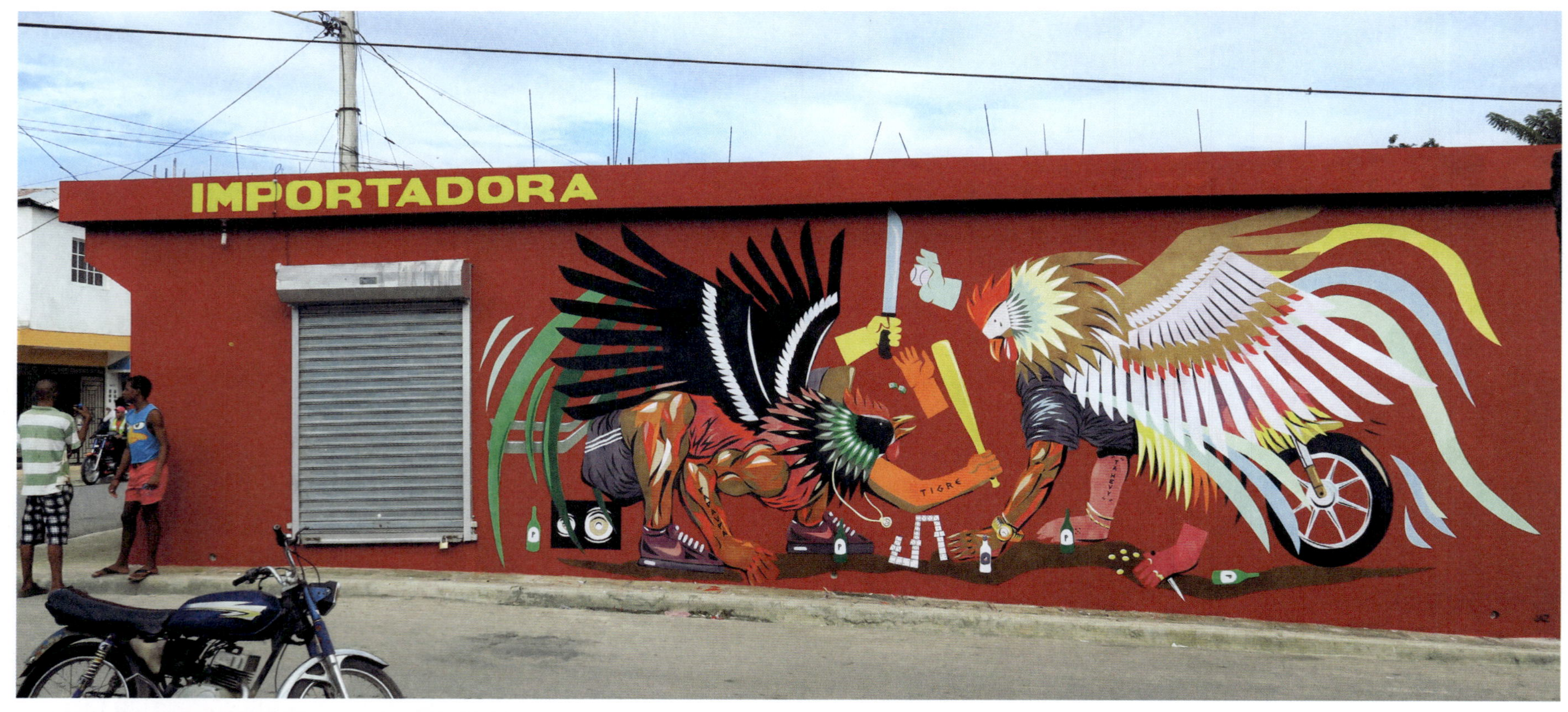

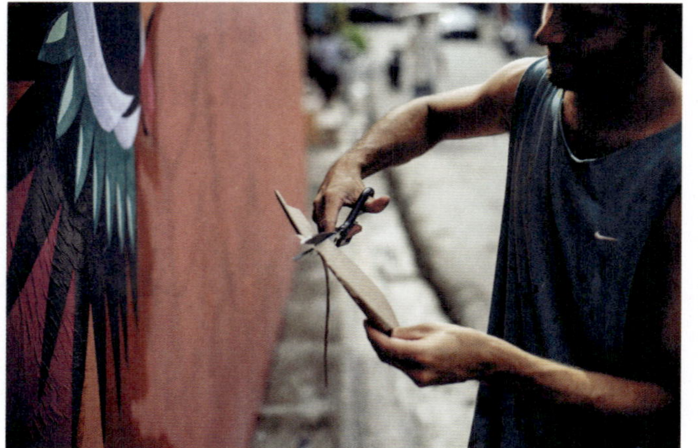

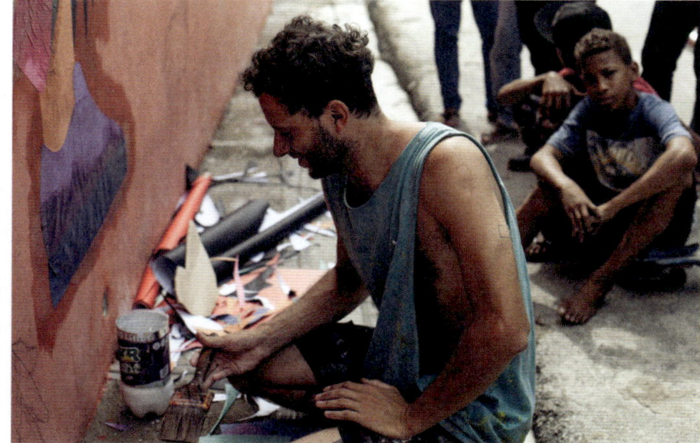

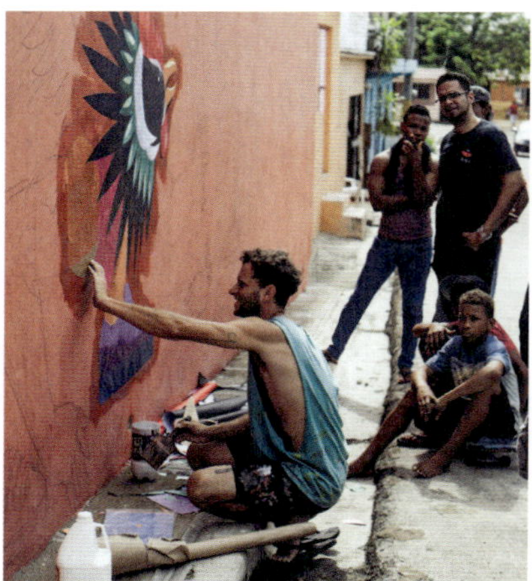

Untitled, and the work
in progress, 2015
Collage on wall
Dimensions variable

OPPOSITE
Madre, 2015
Collage on canvas
120 × 80 cm (46⅝ × 31½ in.)

In terms of his thematic concerns, Fasoli has long
been interested in violence and confrontation as
a means of searching for a shared Latin American
identity, looking at different traditions from
throughout the continent and seeking to find a thread
that connects Latin America's diverse indigenous
and colonial influences. Topics include football
hooliganism, Mexican wrestling or metaphorical
struggles between man and beast; very often he uses
symmetry in his work to signify the tension between
opposing forces.

The strong forms and colours of his paper cuts
complement these powerful themes, elements that he
sometimes incorporates with materials that he finds
at the sites of his murals, such as earth, bricks and
coal. To Fasoli it is this course of making that is just
as important as the end product: 'It's this process, the
dialogue it creates between people and the history of
a place, that gives the mark I make a meaning.'

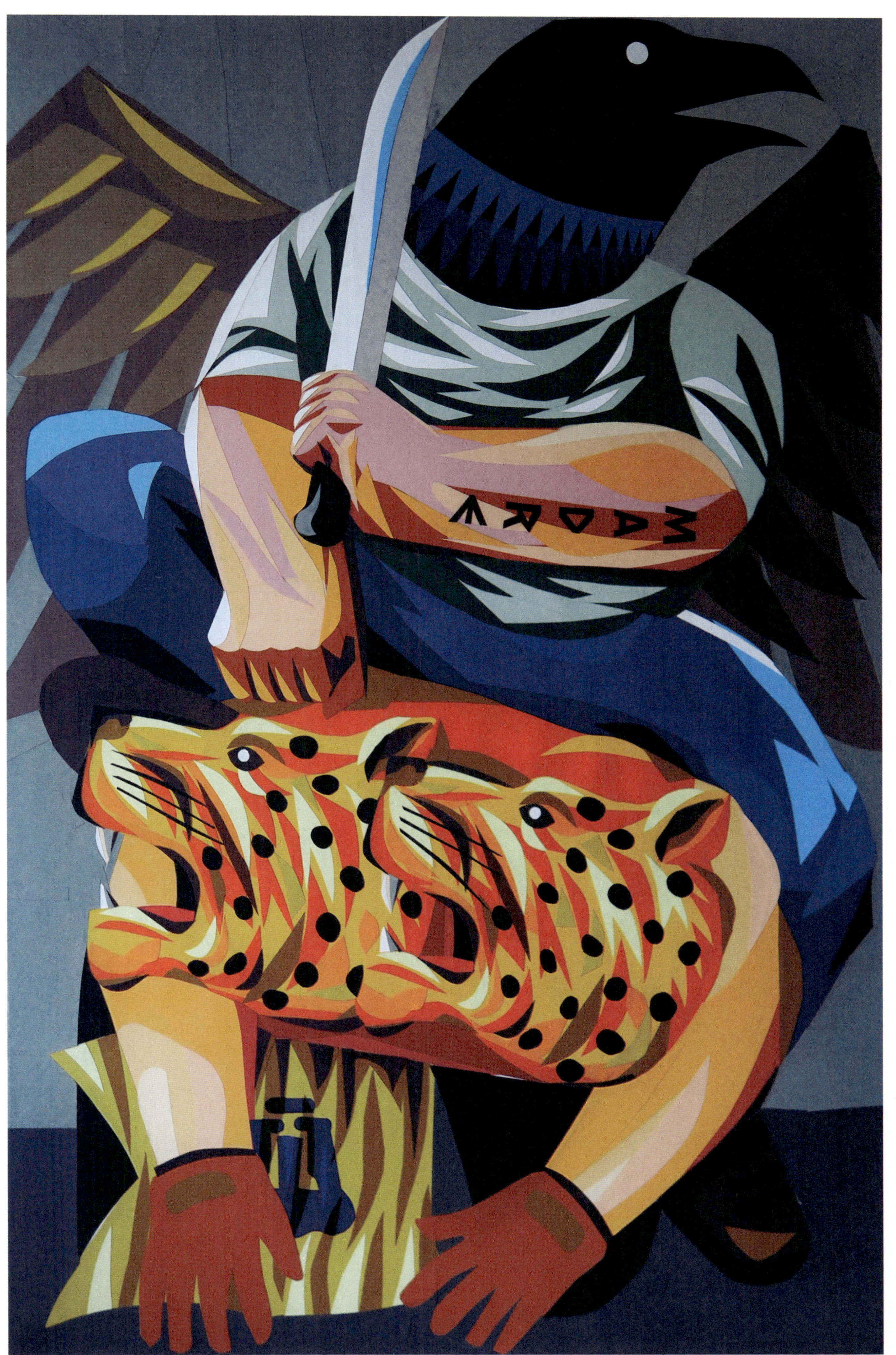

Robert Hardgrave

Describing his practice as finding its basis in the traditions of drawing and painting,

media such as printmaking, collage, textiles and more recently an arcane method of Xerox transfer also find their way into the output of Seattle-based Robert Hardgrave. Energetic, experimental and improvisational, Hardgrave always seems to break new ground with each body of work, attracting more and more followers, particularly in Europe and America. As a result his pieces have been the subject of many group and solo shows worldwide, featured in numerous publications, nominated for awards and celebrated in a monograph titled *Magic Beans* (2008).

Hardgrave's approach and aesthetic is vintage in feel, recalling perhaps early Surrealist collage, primitivism or the Cubist works of Eduardo Paolozzi (1924–2005), but at the same time there are innovations that appear to be more futuristic. Part of the attraction of his work is that he uses traditional techniques such as drawing but in refreshingly contemporary ways, creating a distinctive language of line and form. His is a process and expression that is entirely personal, which is possibly a reflection of the artist's unique and partly accidental journey into art. Having initially studied graphic art at Seattle Central Collage he became focused on drawing during a period of recovery in hospital. His endless doodling led to painting via more or less self-discovered

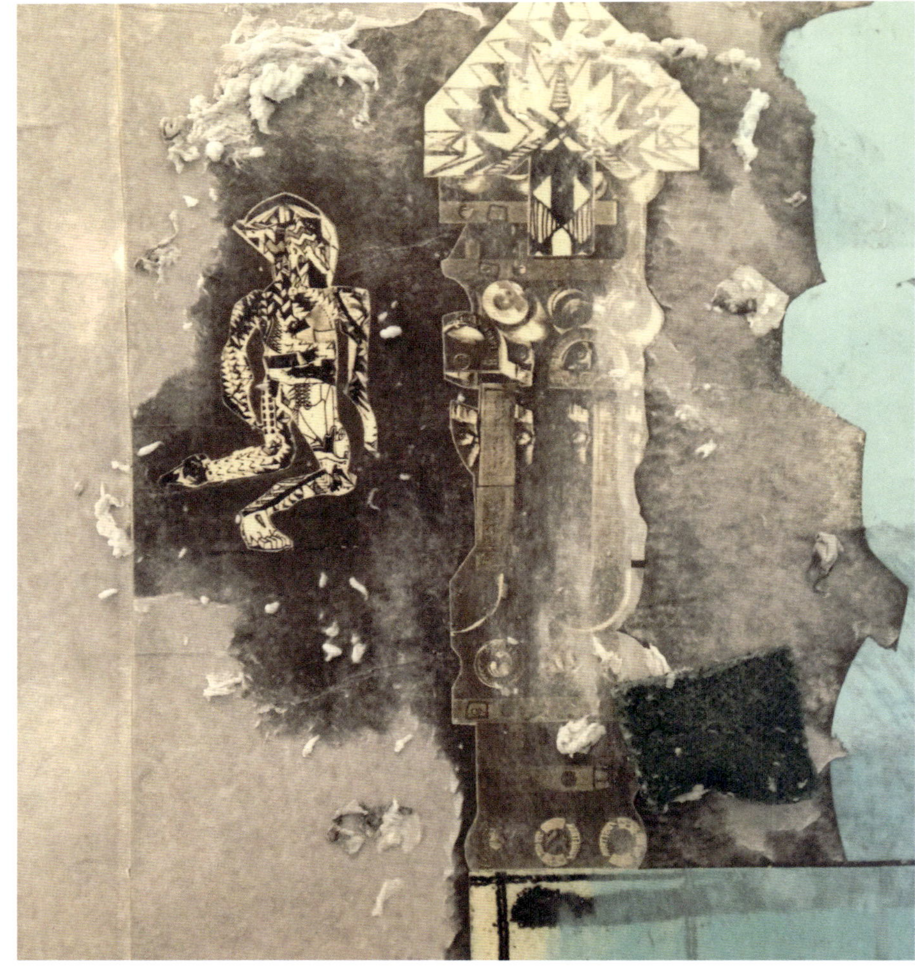

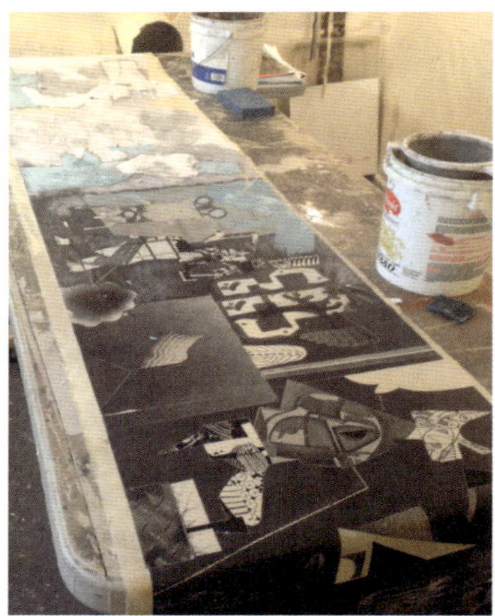

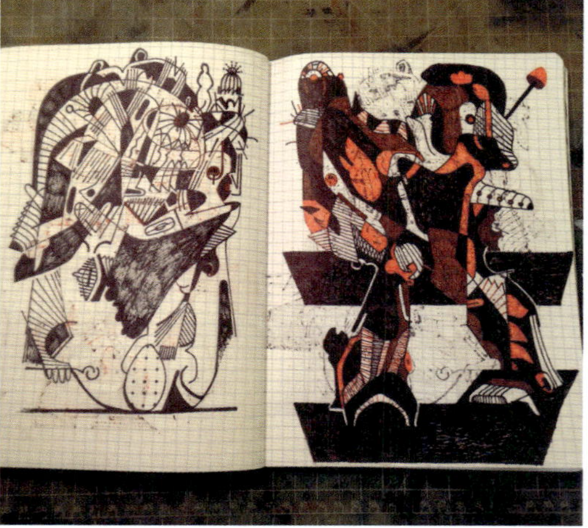

TOP, RIGHT AND BELOW
To Be Determined,
2015
Collage, toner
transfer on
Mulberry paper
61 × 1.46 m
(24 × 576 in.)

FAR RIGHT
Pages from the
artist's sketchbook.

OPPOSITE
Retirement Fund,
2014
Collage, toner
transfer on
Mulberry paper
182.9 × 182.9 cm
(72 × 72 in.)

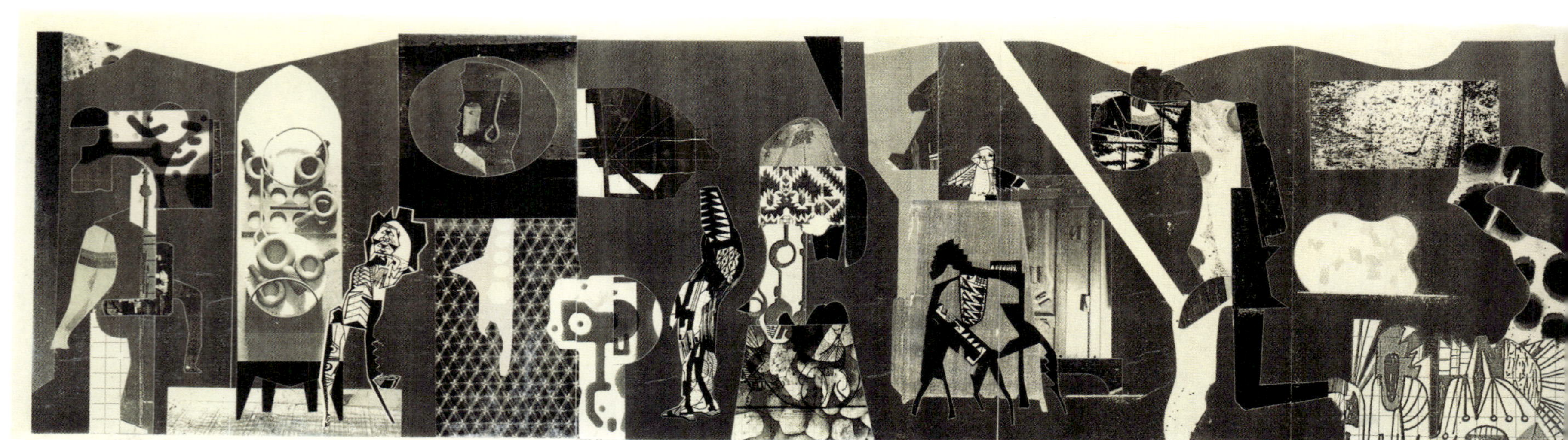

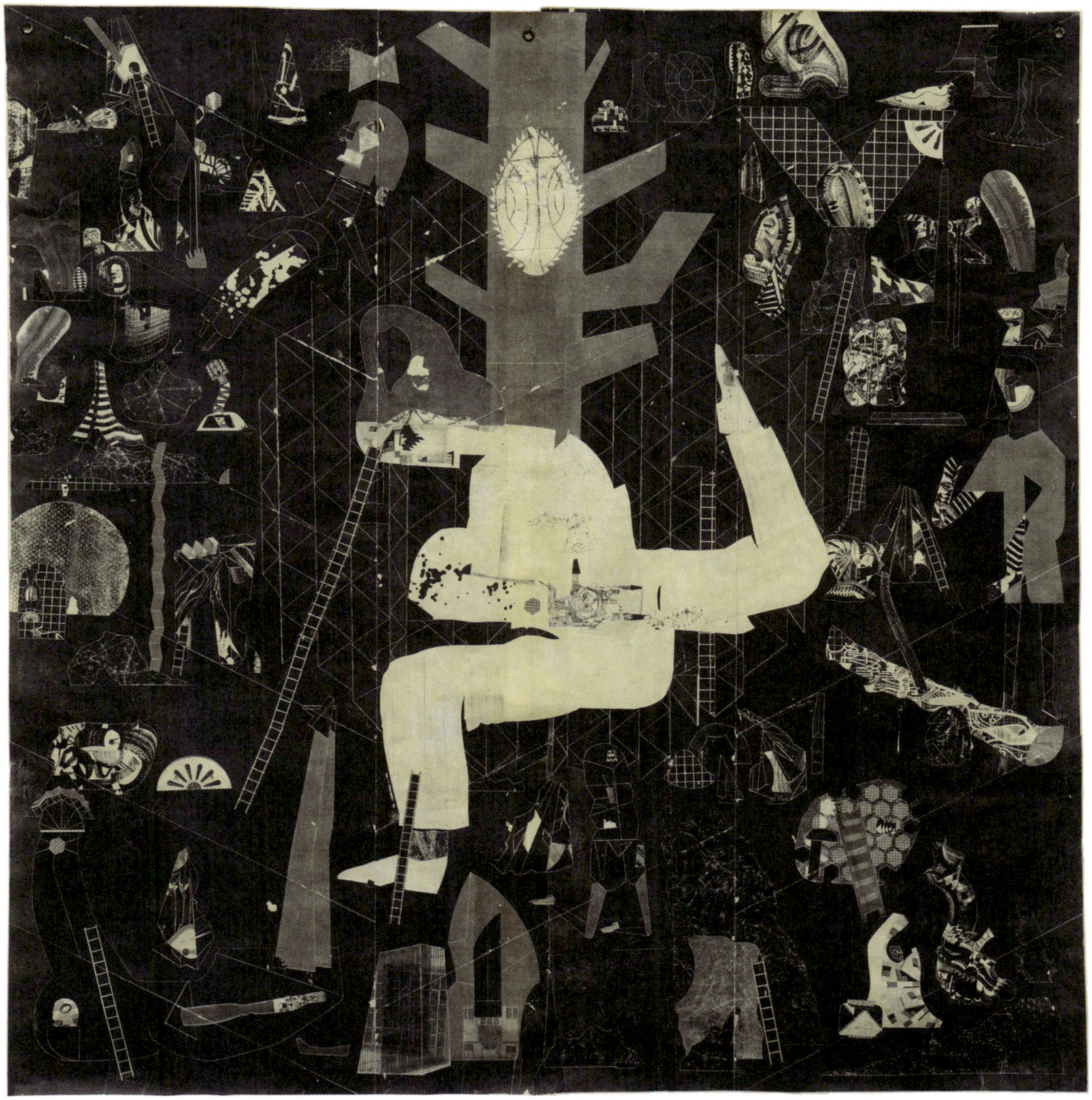

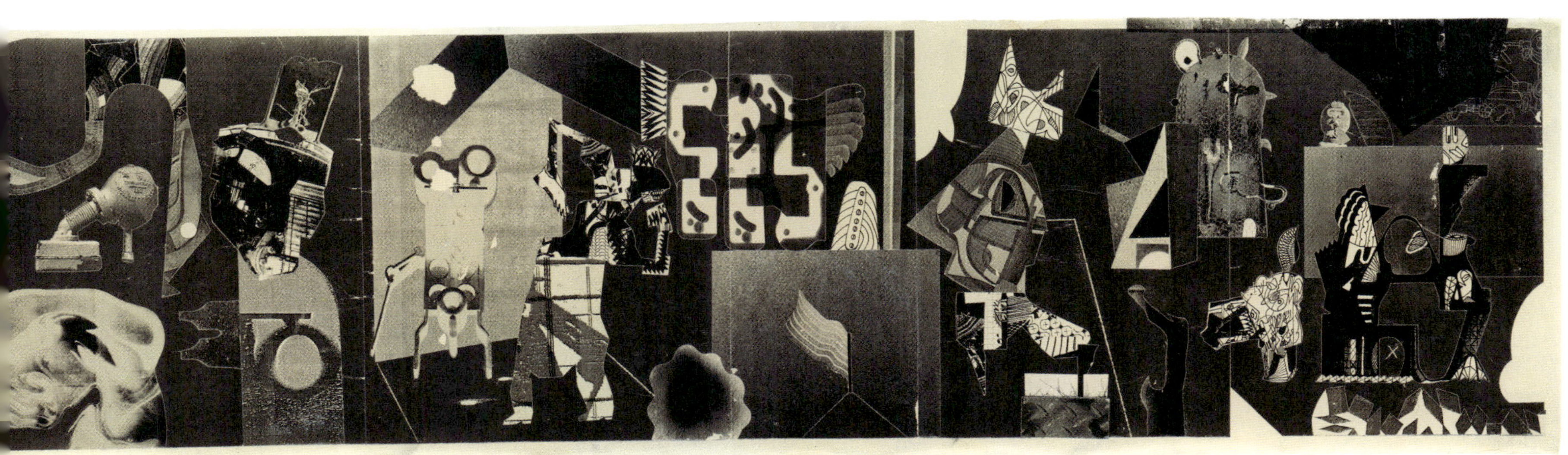

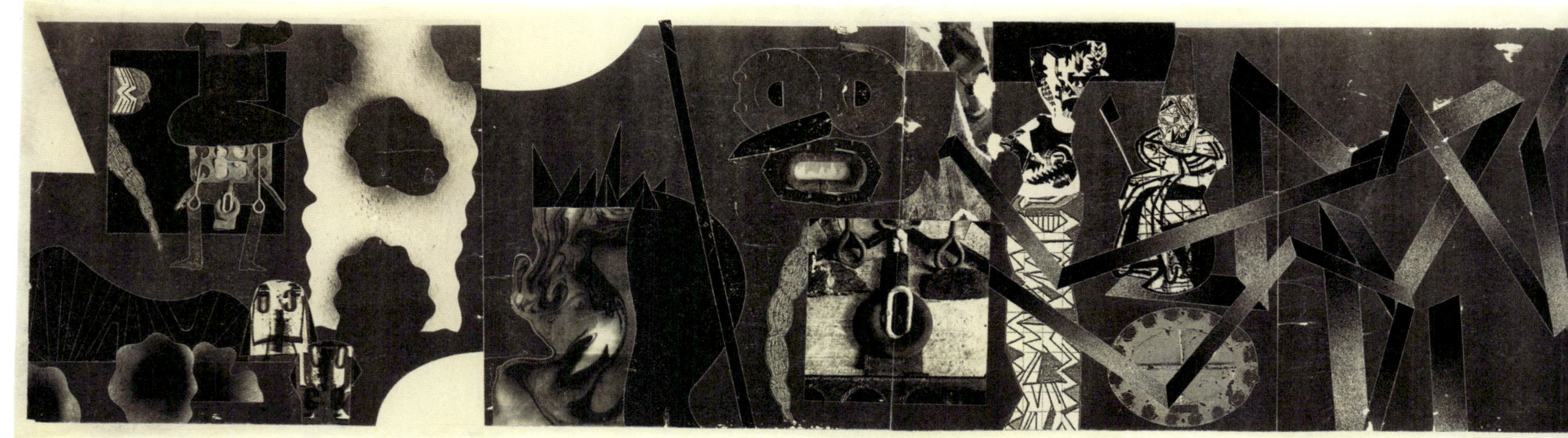

methods. His primary influence was comic books but through the Internet he began to discover other young practitioners and a wider world of art. By 2005, he had built up an online following for his work, which eventually led to his first solo show.

Hardgrave has recently developed a method of transfer printing that seems to combine many of the techniques he enjoys. The results are vast monochromatic prints on paper filled with layers of intriguing multi-processed textures. In describing this evolution he says, 'I get these large sheets of toner-covered paper from the copy shop to build collages. I then make copies of drawings, prints and photos to build the images. I can enlarge or reduce things to make them intricate or more gestural. The image you see in the final print is the reverse of the collage. It still looks like a collage but has been reduced down to one layer of toner on the surface.' The final stage is essentially an excavation whereby he soaks the paper with water and slowly works the original paper away from the collage to free the image, proceeding slowly until it is entirely clear.

Although largely abstract, figures and faces are suggested within his compositions, his aim being to 'build work that encompasses figuration, object and place all at one time'. He also intends for the materials to guide the work towards its final outcome, while retaining a consistent aesthetic throughout: 'I believe that, by allowing only a few variables to exist, the materials are forced to reveal their nuances. This permits my vocabulary to be louder, conducing cross-pollination between media, where ideas, discovery and surprise reign supreme.'

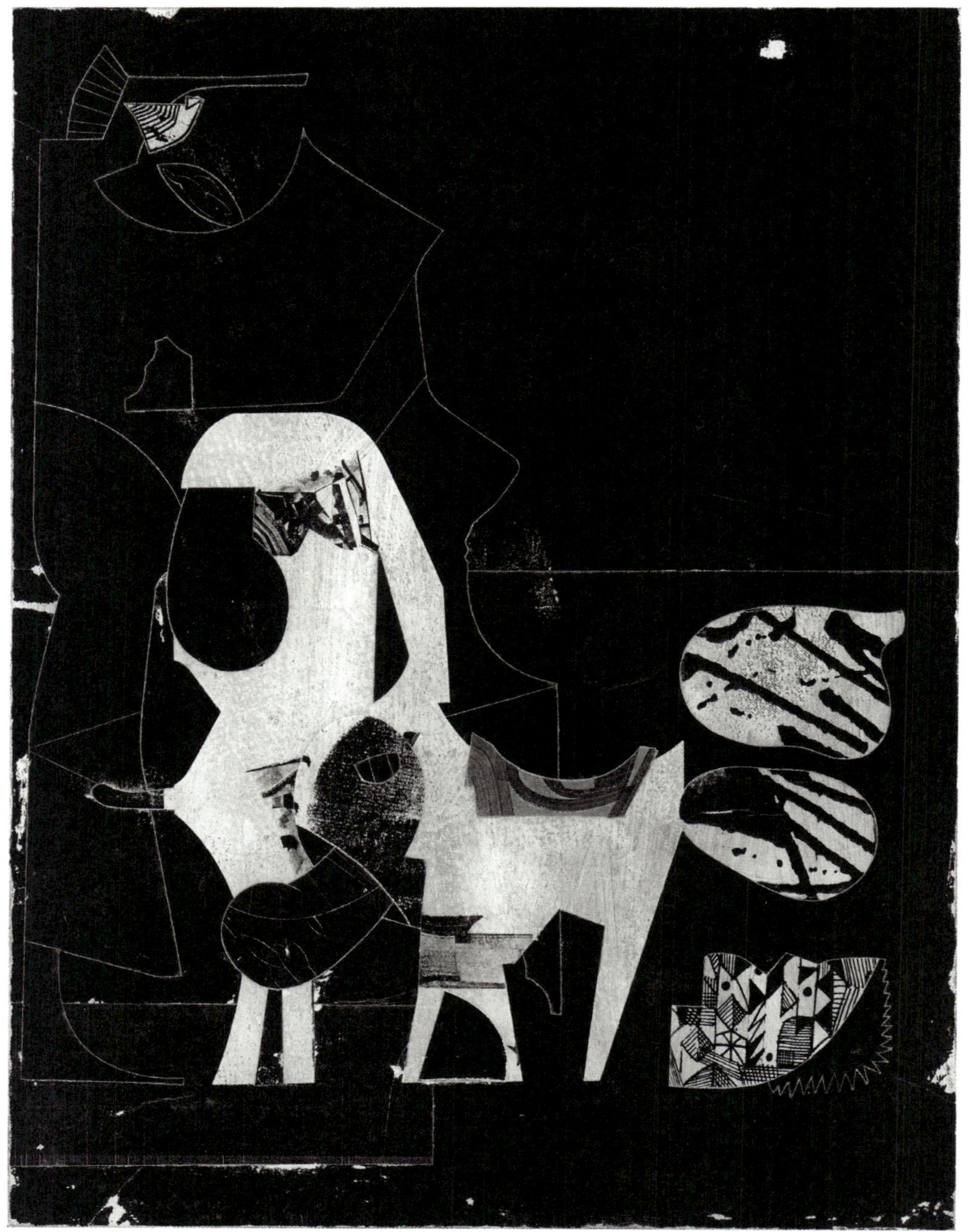

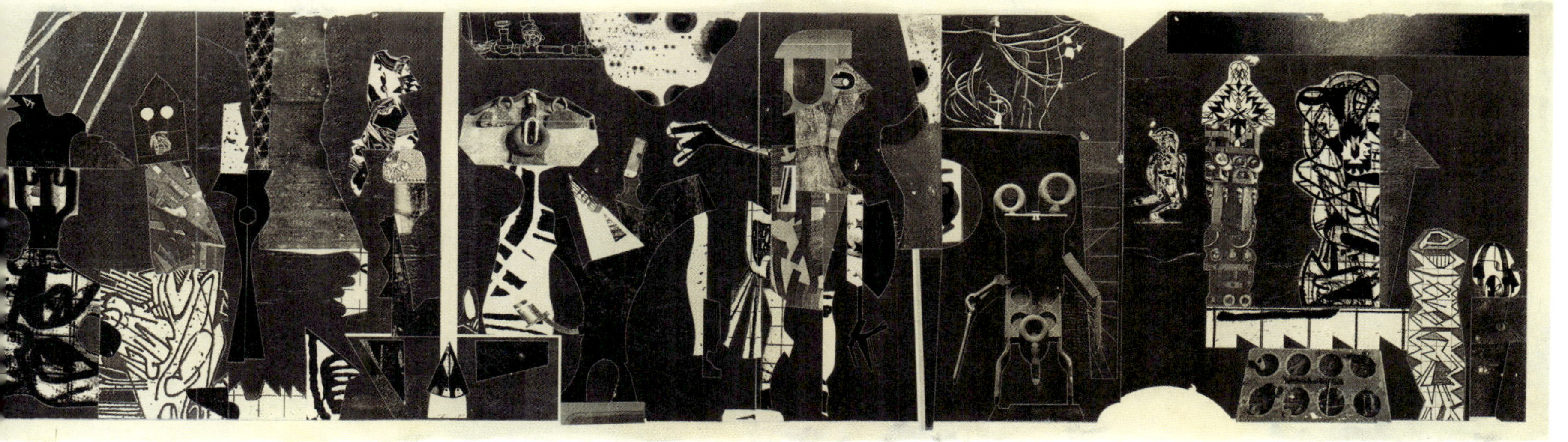

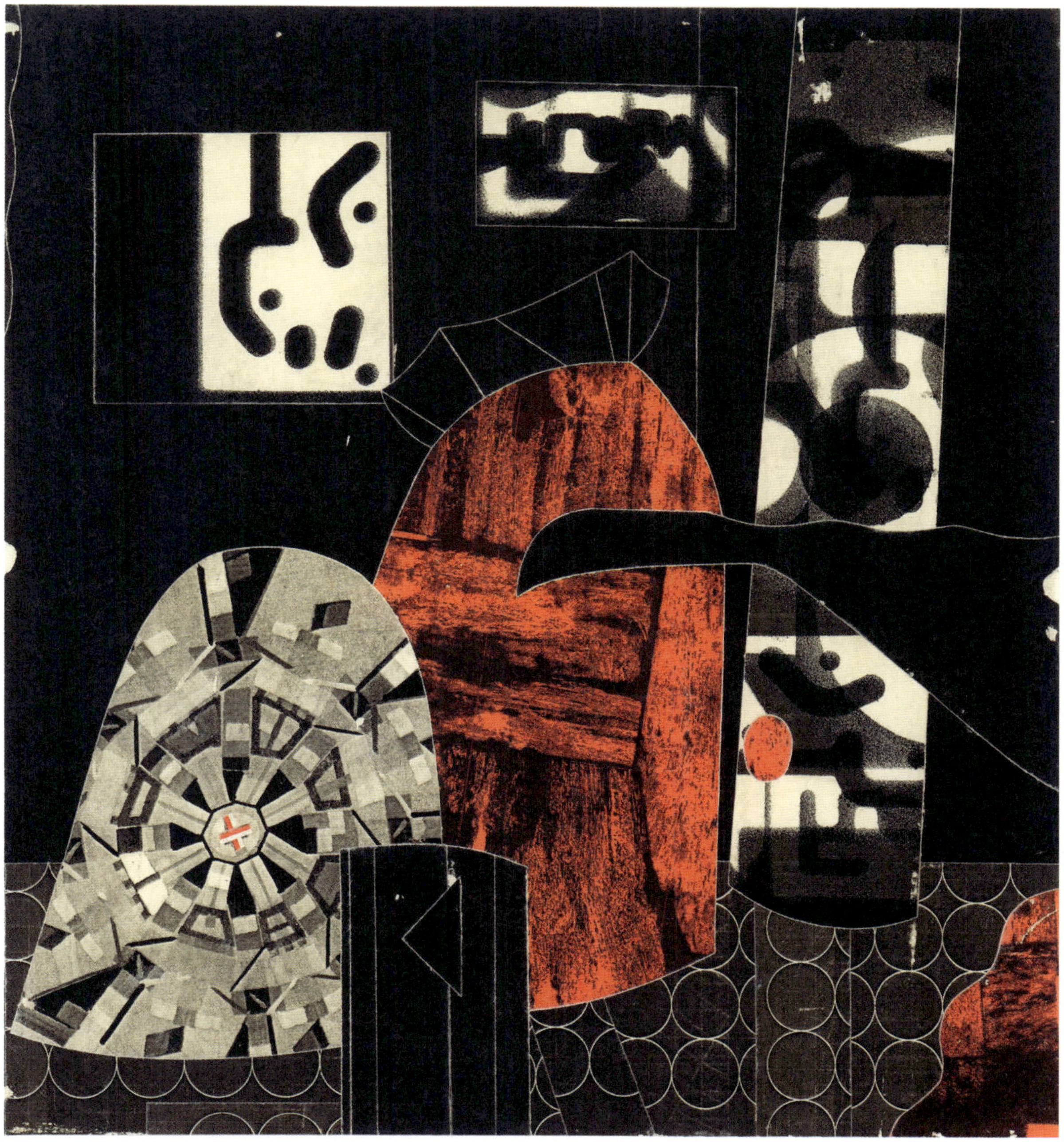

Robert Hardgrave233

Diogo Machado

Concerned with double vision, a kind of *trompe l'oeil* effect

that reads in one way at a distance and then, in close-up, is revealed as being full of detail and hidden meaning, are the striking works of Portuguese artist and illustrator Diogo Machado. Working under the moniker 'Add Fuel' his art fuses the past and present, referencing such contemporary forms as comic art, graffiti, graphic design and *azulejo* – traditional, glazed Portuguese mosaic tiles – in equal measure. More than being purely decorative, *azulejo* have been a platform for artistic expression for more than five centuries, with many public buildings, churches and even railways boasting huge friezes – depicting religious scenes or monumental narratives – in this material. The *azulejo* tradition has continued into this century but in his work Machado has updated it further still to include contemporary subject-matter, and techniques such as stencil graffiti.

Machado's background is in graphic design and illustration, but he has also long been an active element in Lisbon's street-art scene. His illustrative prowess comes to the fore in his public doodles and cartoon vector drawings, which are full of detail and humour. The idea of adopting the style of *azulejo* was one he first explored in 2008, when he was invited to cover a building with a giant printed canvas for the Cascais ArtSpace festival in Portugal. As a resident of this city it made

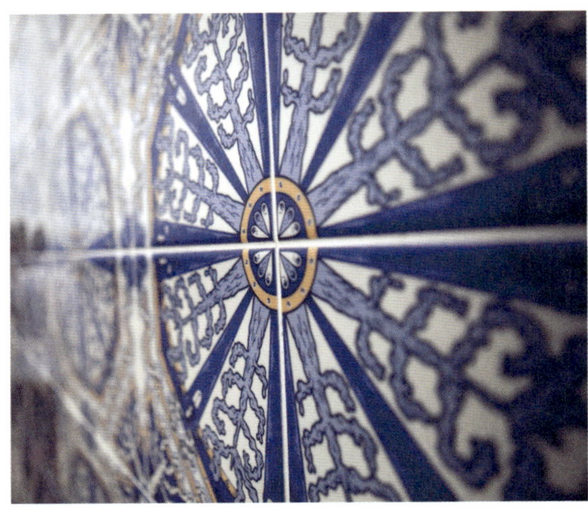

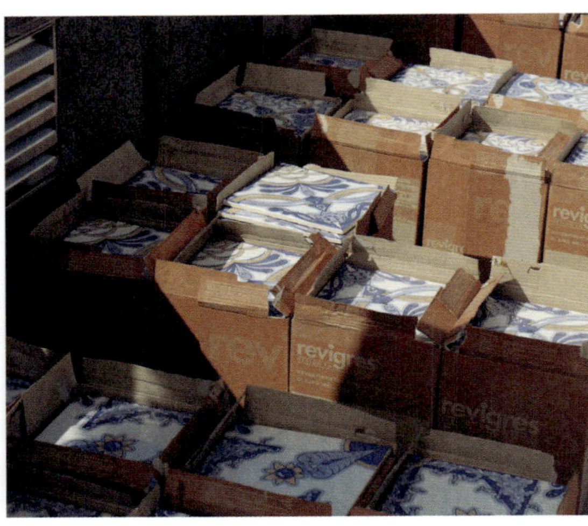

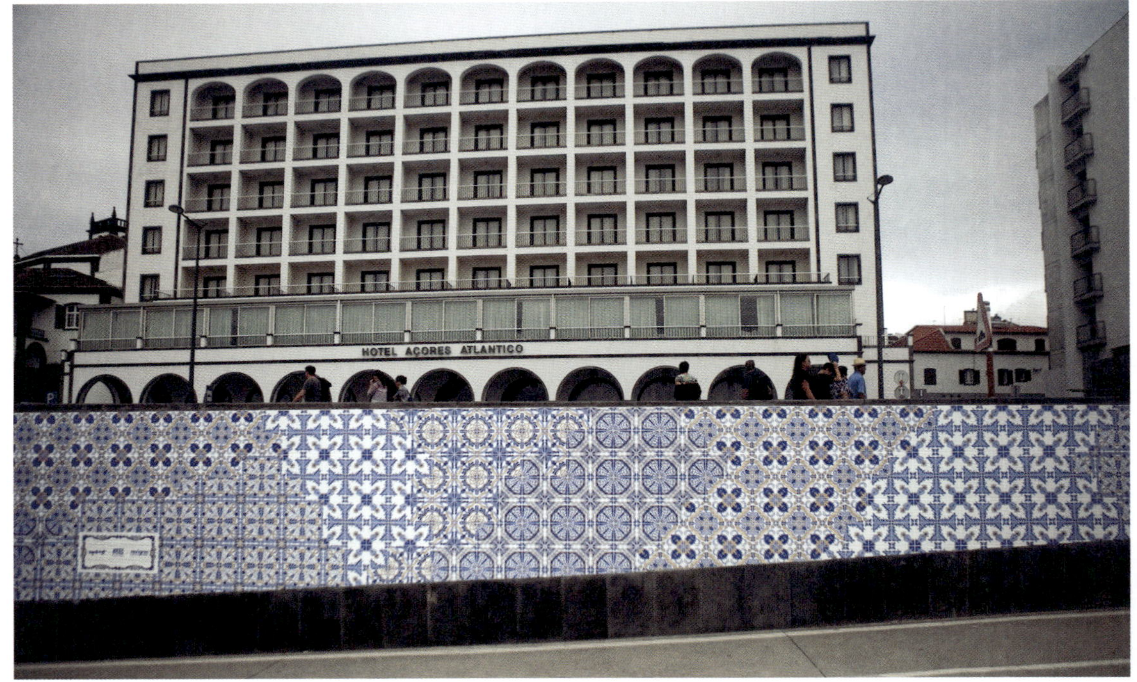

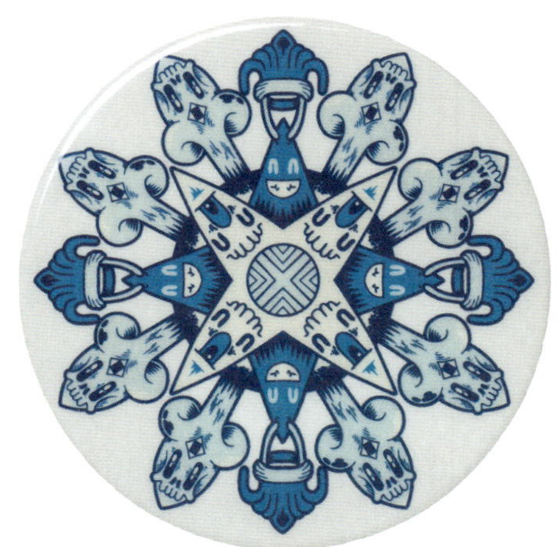

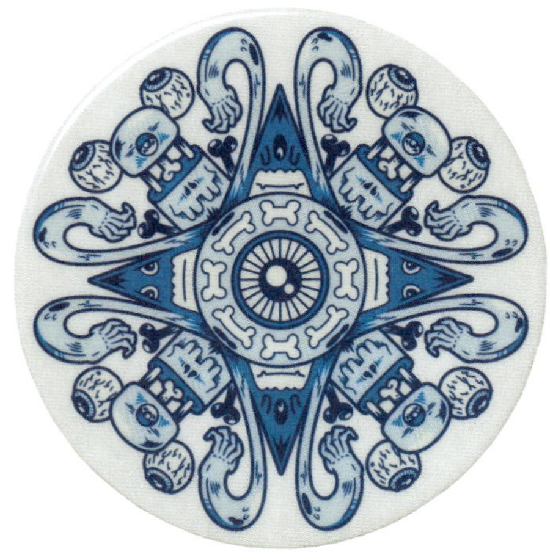

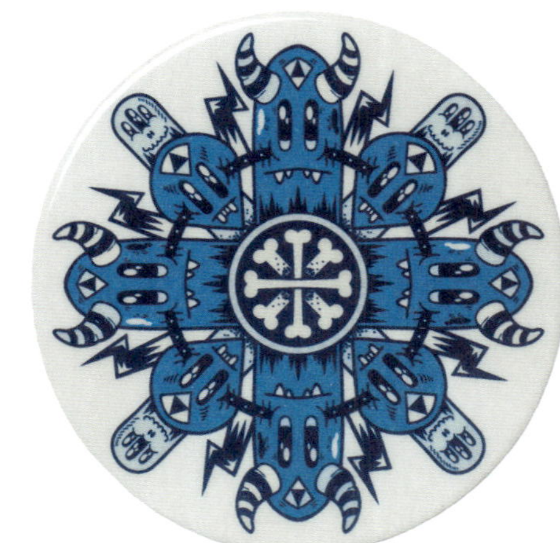

TOP LEFT AND CENTRE
Untitled, and detail, from the series 'Morphing', mural commissioned by the Walk&Talk Public Art Festival, Azores, Portugal, 2012
Azulejo ceramic tiles
Dimensions variable

TOP RIGHT
Tiles used in *Untitled*, from the series 'Morphing', 2012

RIGHT
Three *azulejo* ceramic tiles, c. 2015
15 × 15 cm (5⅞ × 5⅞ in.) in diameter each

OPPOSITE
AZ102, c. 2015
Azulejo ceramic tiles
40 × 40 cm (15¾ × 15¾ in.)

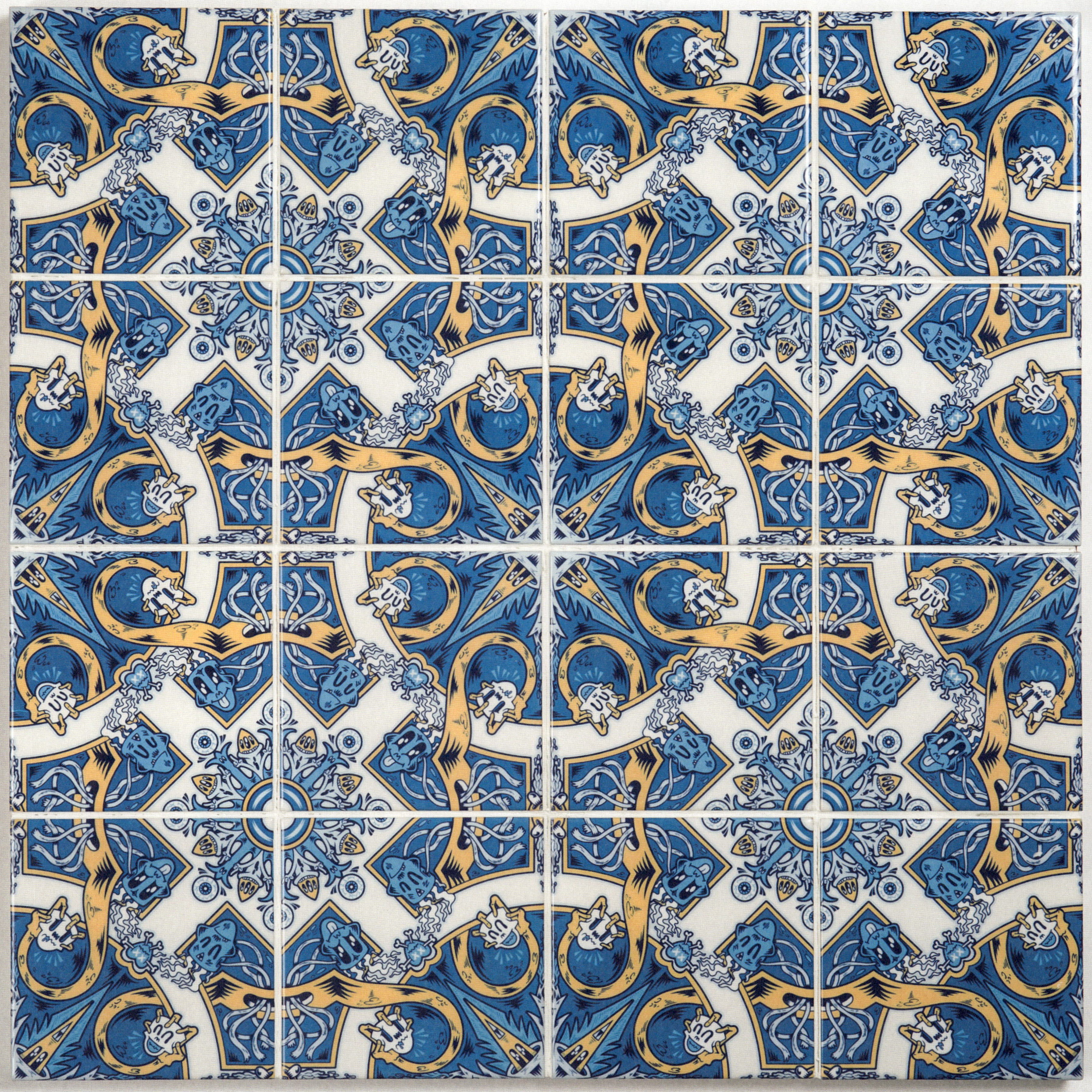

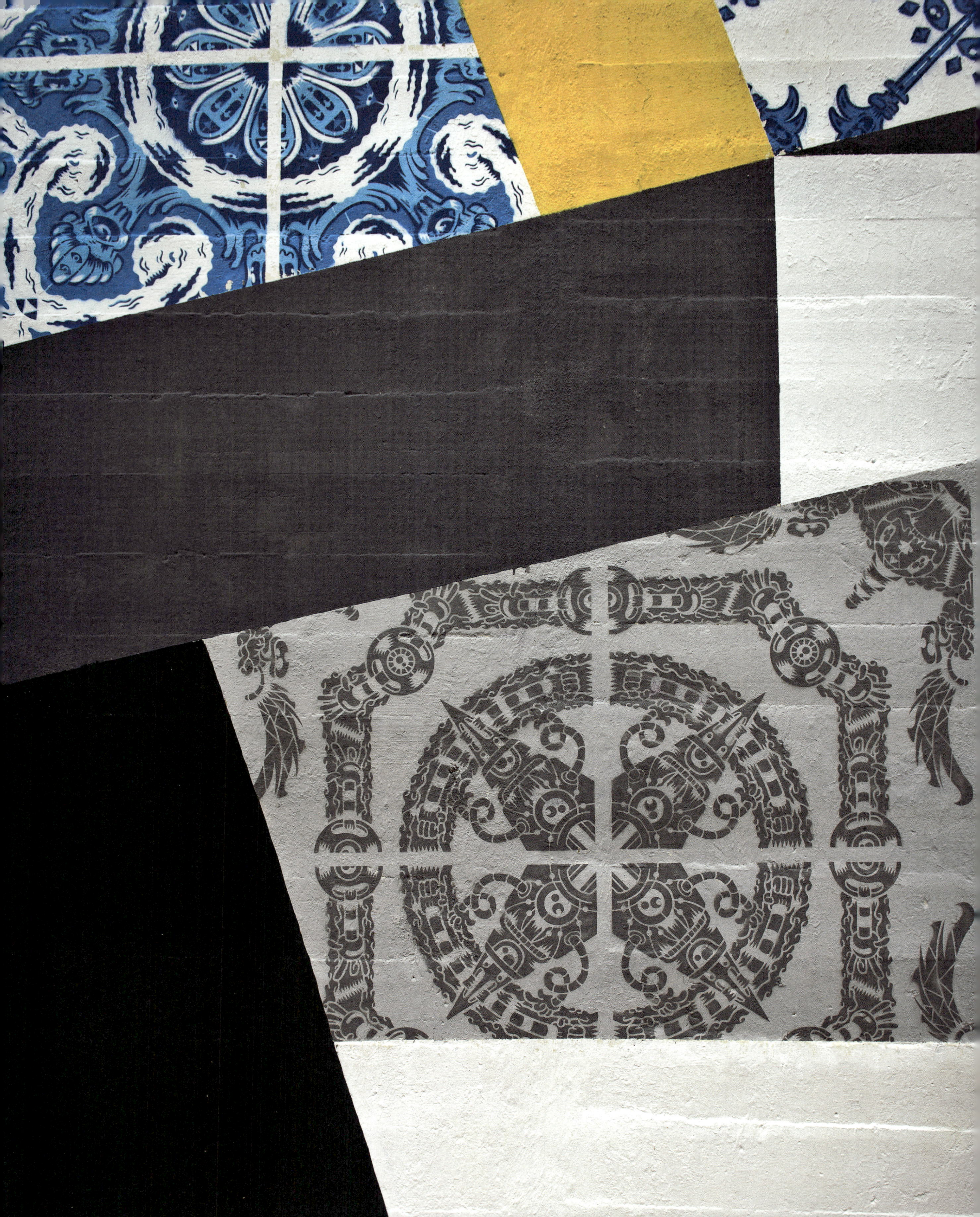

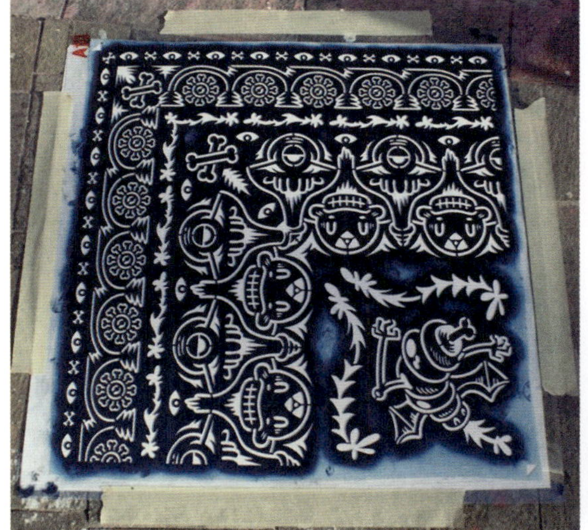

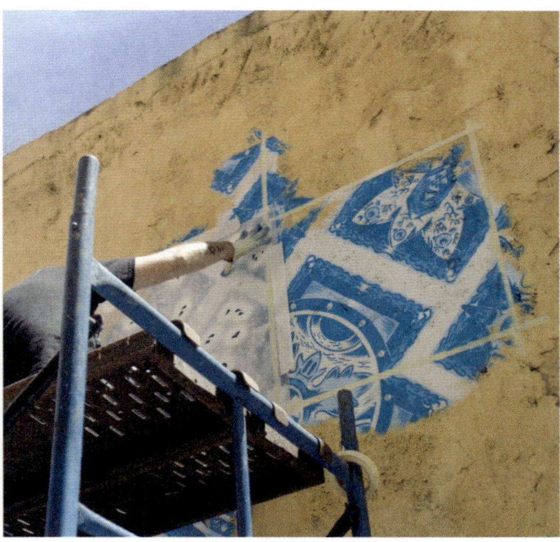

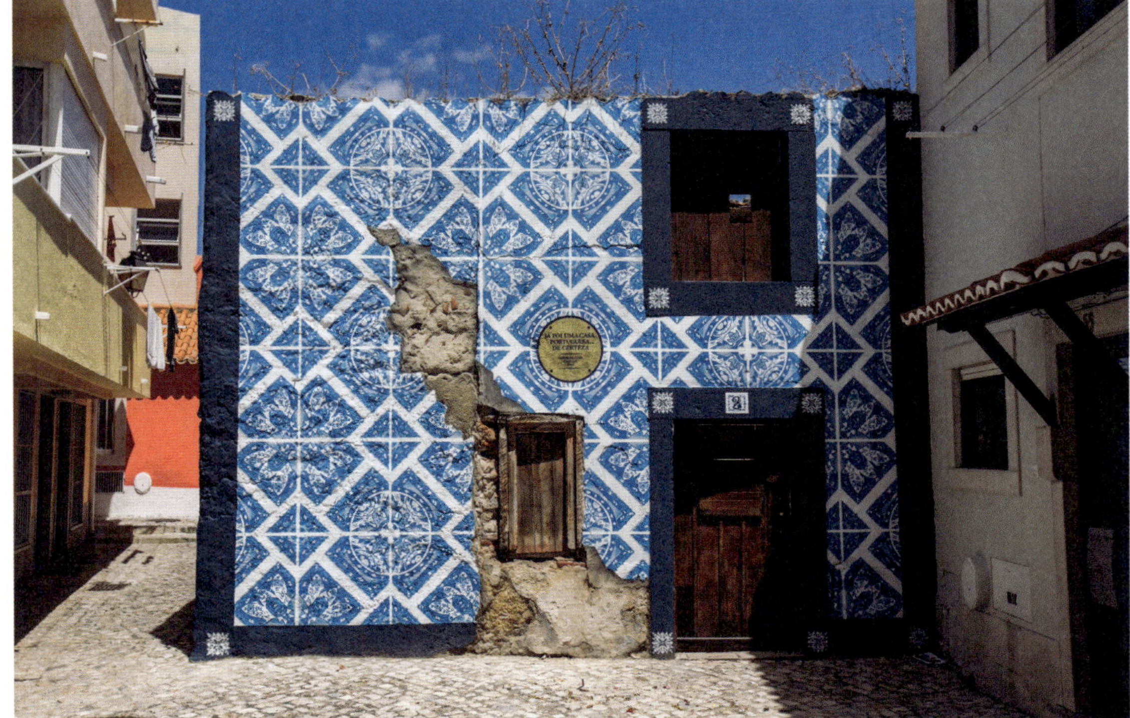

sense for him to take inspiration from his surroundings, to investigate local traditions, and the aesthetic style of *azulejo* seemed to be one that complemented his illustrative work perfectly. He began to study ceramic techniques and return the *azulejo* to the streets in a new guise, as an 'urban intervention'.

These interventions take on different forms. Sometimes they encompass only a single ceramic tile cemented to a wall, which at first glance appears to be traditional *azulejo*, but on closer inspection is exposed as the artist's rendering. For his large-scale murals Machado also creates the illusion of the *azulejo* by using stencils, since making works at this size in ceramics is prohibitively expensive. The concepts that he explores, such as life and death, become manifest in the form of skulls and guts, motifs that are presented so decoratively that the viewer can initially confront them more easily. In summation of this approach Machado says, 'I like to use mystical elements in subverted ways, so that they might lose their meaning or gain a new one. I like to play with people's minds and make them feel quite the opposite of what they were expecting.' In many ways Machado's work can be seen as renewing a tradition and, by utilizing a material that potentially will last for centuries to come, ensuring longevity for many of his pieces.

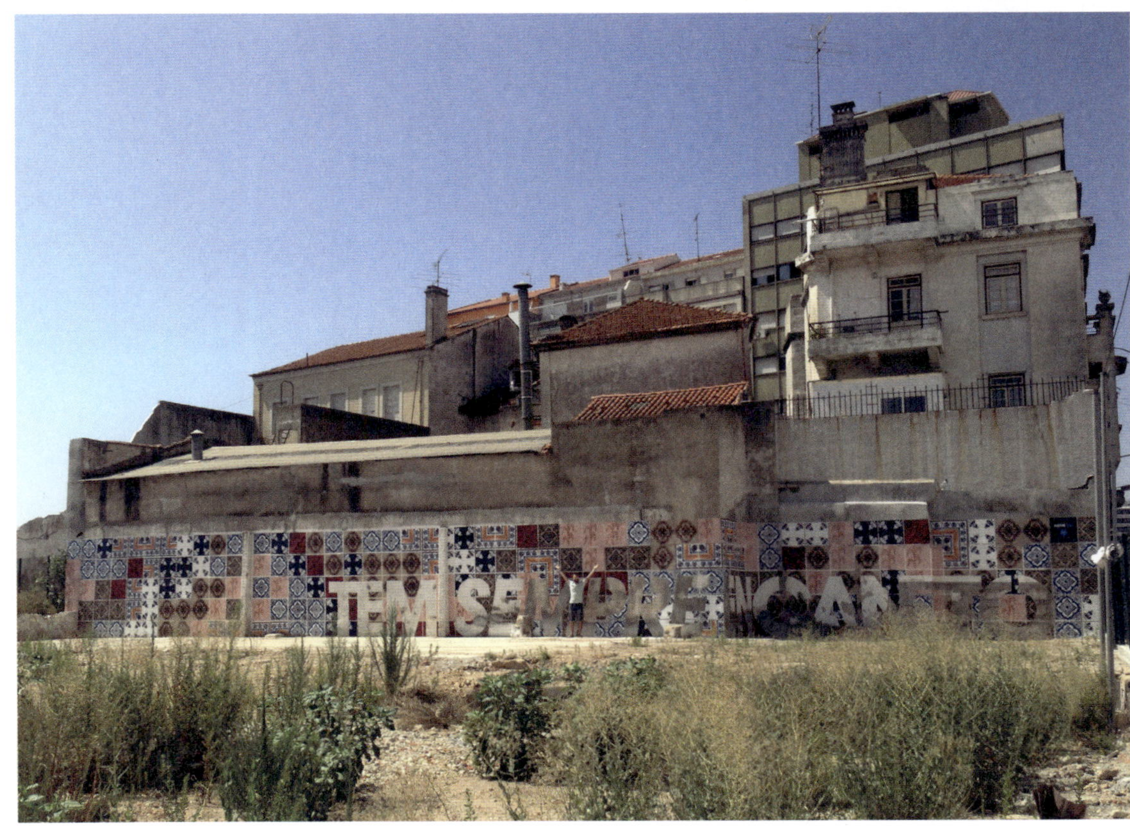

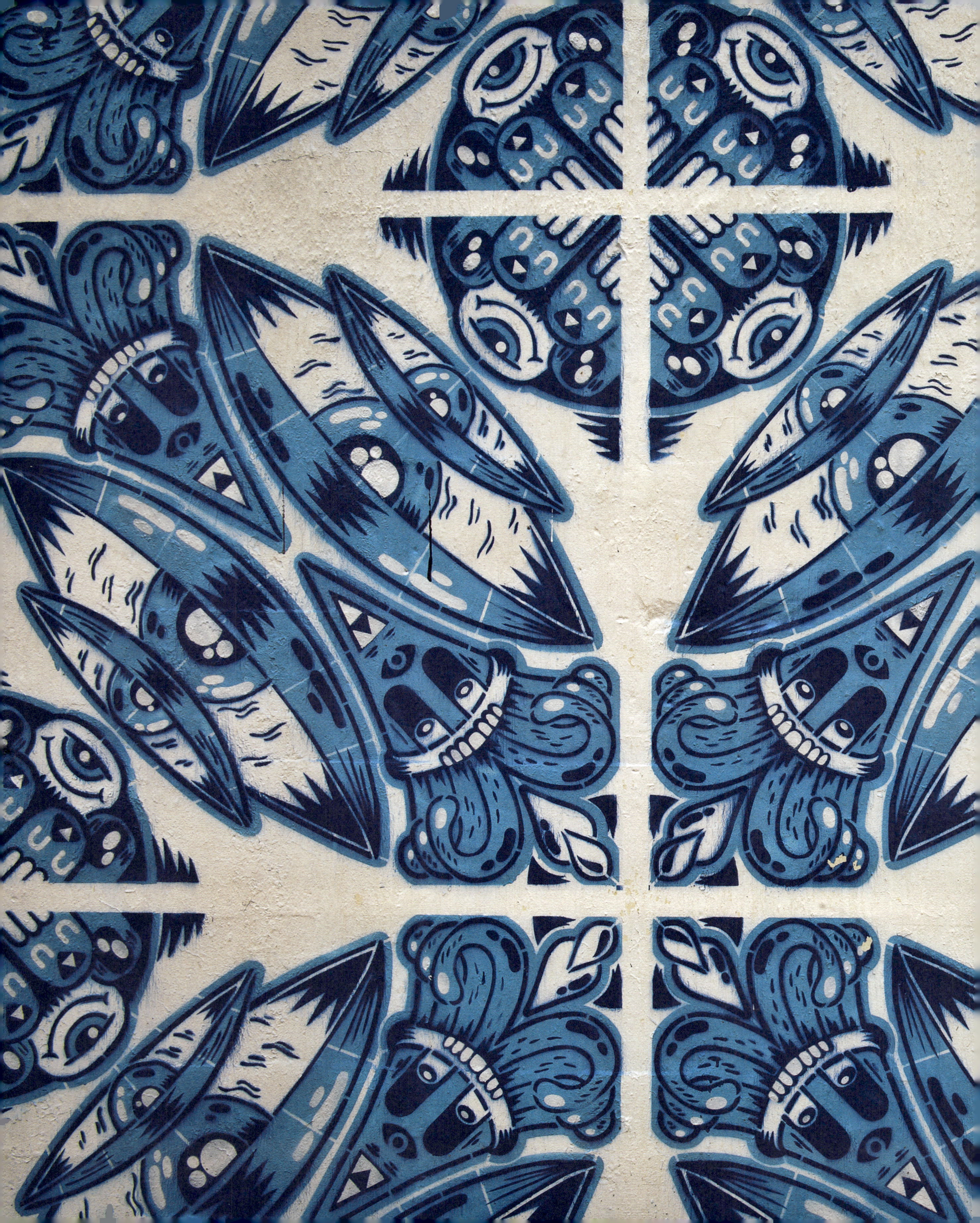

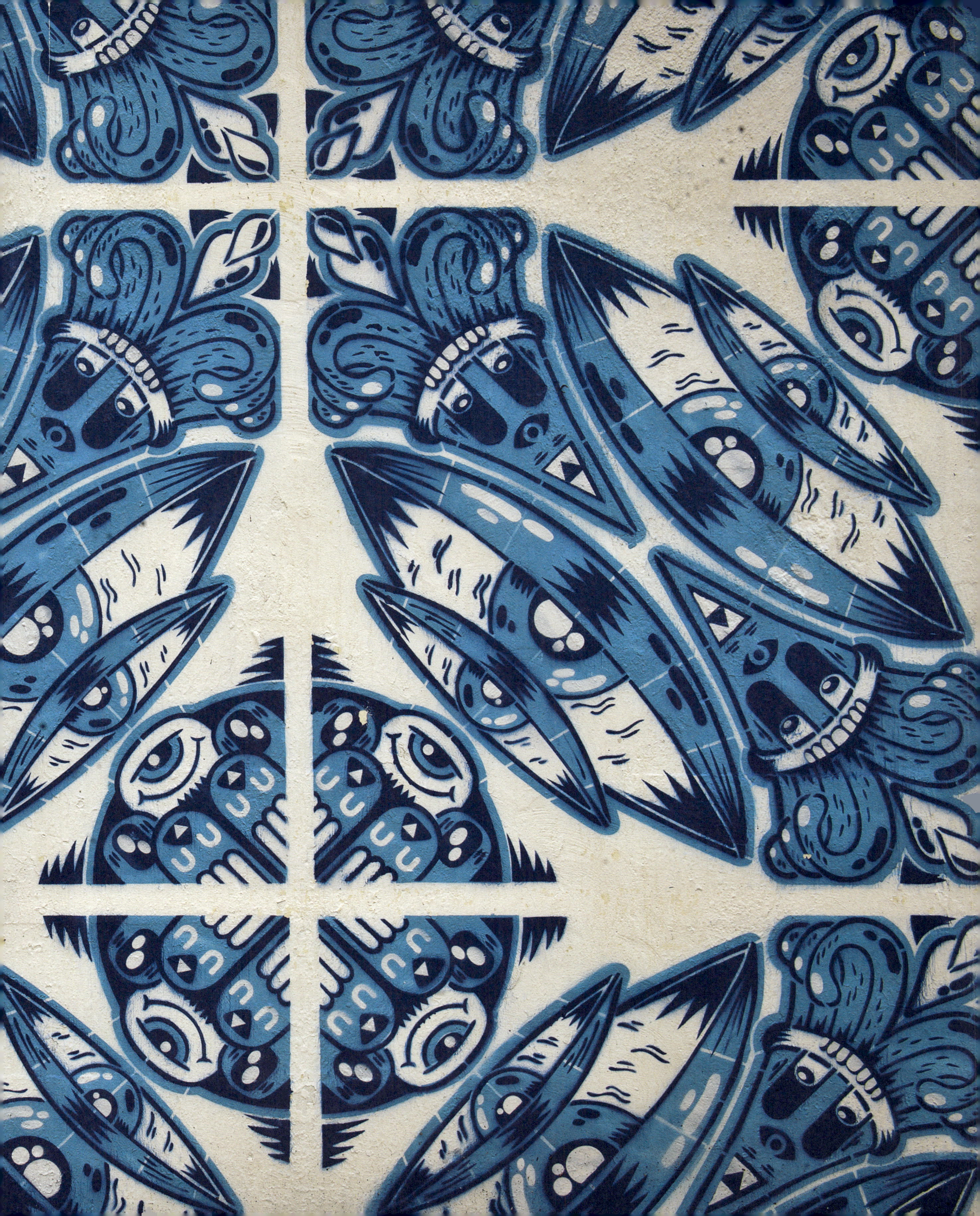

David Méndez Alonso

A painter, illustrator and art director, who works with a multitude of media, including ceramics, textiles and sculpture,

artist David Méndez Alonso is a man of many talents. His playful creations sit somewhere between fine and graphic art and seem to embrace every which way that they are displayed. Méndez Alonso's eclectic approach may be traced to his varied academic training, having studied painting, communication strategies and, most recently, art direction and design. As a backdrop to this is the culturally vibrant city of Barcelona, in which he has studied and now works, the Catalan spirit of which seemingly pervades all that he makes.

Méndez Alonso's work has a great openness, and appears to be unrestricted by a prescribed format or formula. In it he embraces Pop Art, naive art, comic books, figurative and abstract forms, along with inspirations that come, variously, he says, 'from everyday life situations, grandparents, Morrissey, Joseph Beuys, Matisse and the colour yellow'. His candidness has also

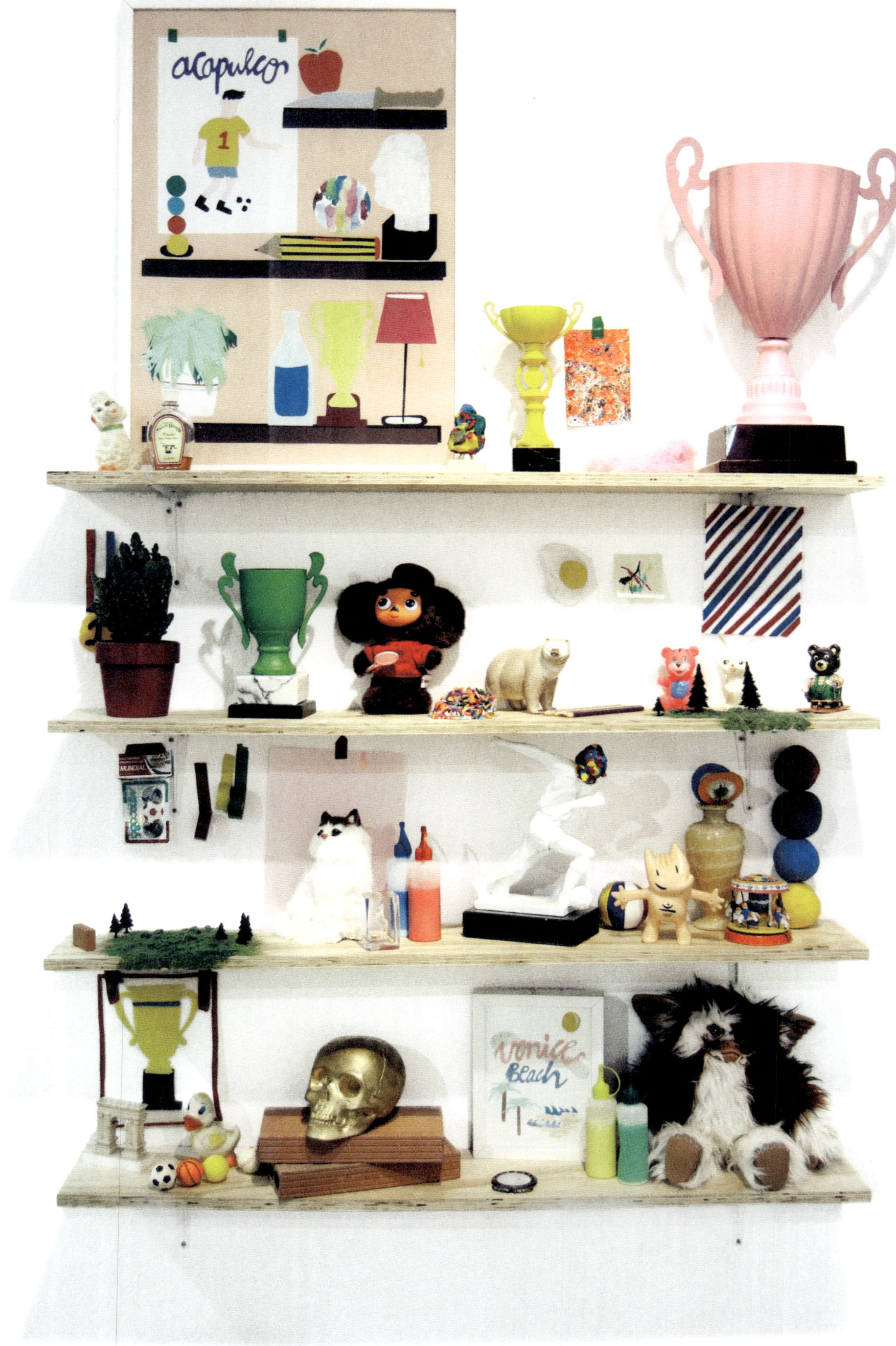

Untitled, c. 2013
Mixed media
Dimensions variable

OPPOSITE, FROM TOP
Untitled (series of 12), 2014
Watercolour on paper
30 × 30 cm
(11¾ × 11¾ in.) each

Grids (diptych), 2014
Mixed media
200 × 140 cm
(78¾ × 55⅛ in.)

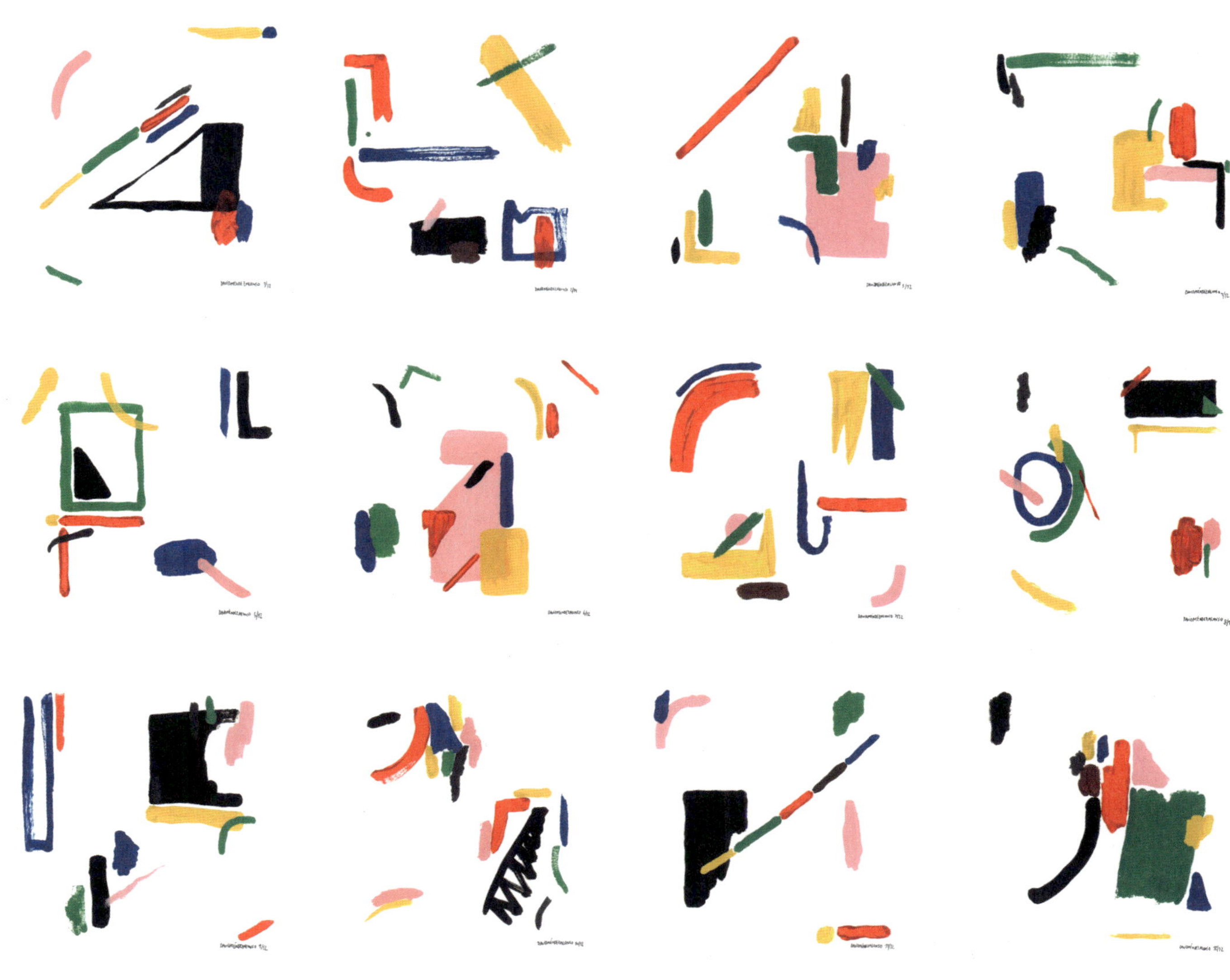

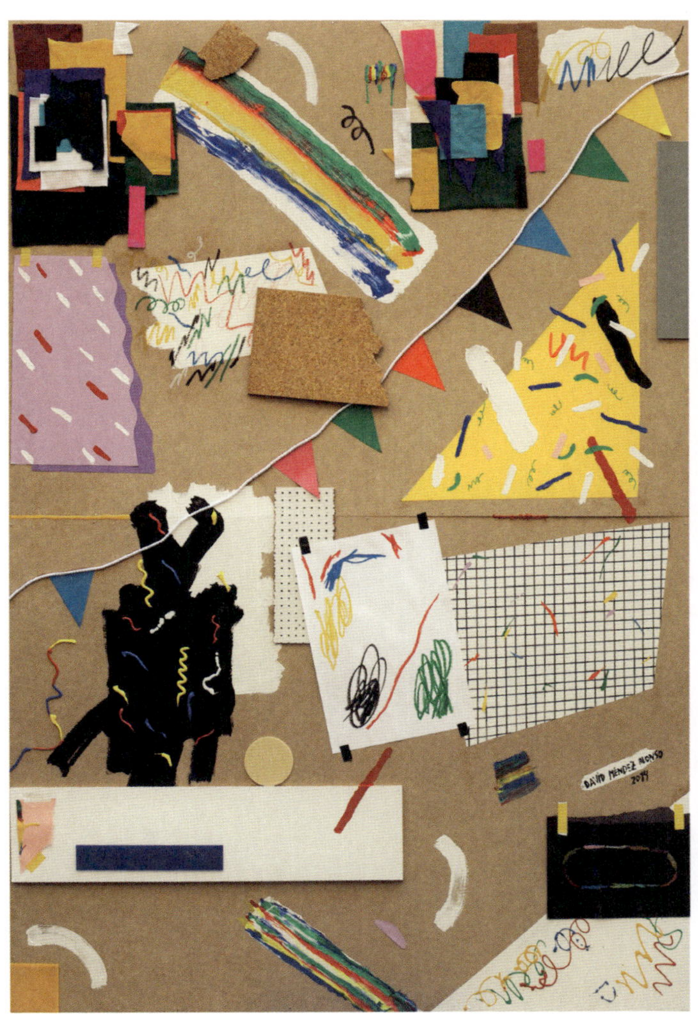

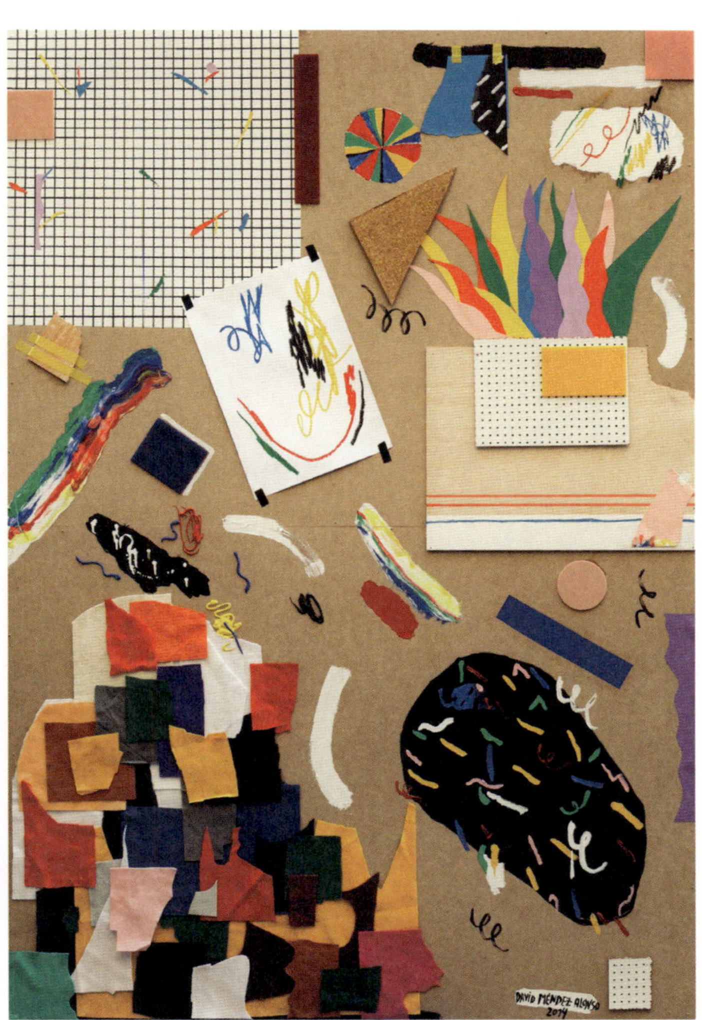

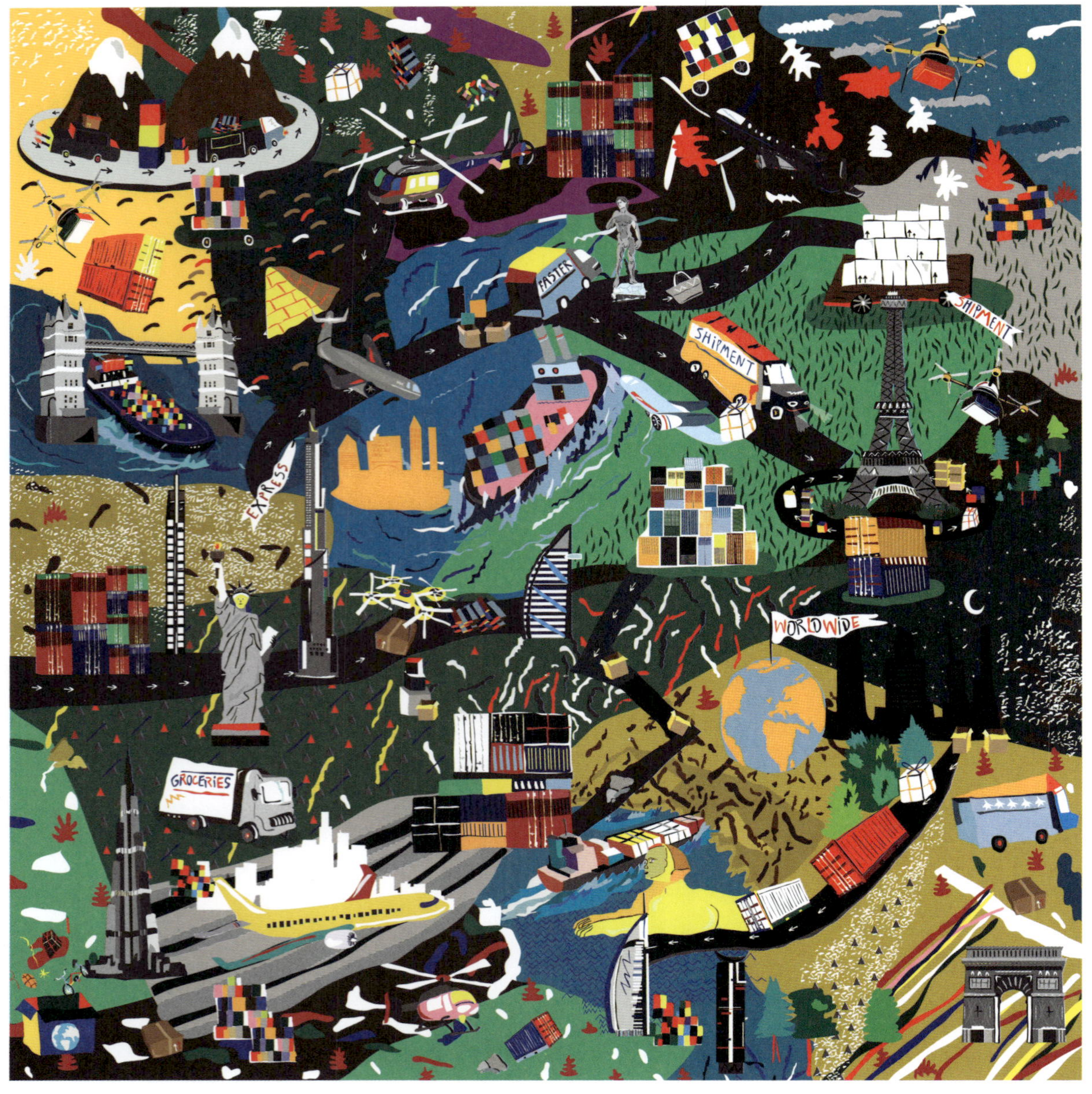

extended to collaborations with fashion designers, for example, the label Outsiders Division. In addition, under the guise of his graffiti moniker 'Mister the Freak' he has joined forces with many of Barcelona's progressive street artists. His attitude is perhaps representative of a new generation of Barcelona artists, whose work intersects fine art, comic art and design, and recalls the Bauhaus style and Memphis Group in its approach to colourful abstraction.

However one discerns these multiple influences, Méndez Alonso seems to approach each work with a clean slate. For every new commission – for clients ranging from Adidas to Pull & Bear and Warner Music – or exhibition, the format will likely be different and vary greatly in scale and form, to which his stage sets, tapestries, masks and collages are all testament. Throughout the work there is a handmade methodology, a process of which he notes: 'In an age when Photoshop is becoming obsolete I think it is very interesting to return to the handmade in the creative process. Reconnecting with our bodies and bringing that to a digital surface…generates new interpretations, languages and styles.'

Even while some of his output is digital, the predominant use of mixed media is what makes his work so charming, humorous and accessible. Not only are the materials unusual but they also seem to transcend their limitations when grouped together by the artist within his installations. Thoughtful and exuberant, Méndez Alonso's work reminds us of the value of play and of what can be achieved creatively through physical exploration.

Goods, digital illustration commissioned by the 'Dubai Expo 2020', 2015

The Operation Table, 2014
Mixed media
160 × 70 × 100 cm
(63 × 27⅝ × 39⅜ in.)

OPPOSITE
Untitled, 2014
Mixed media
180 × 140 × 9 cm
(70⅞ × 55⅛ × 3⅝ in.)

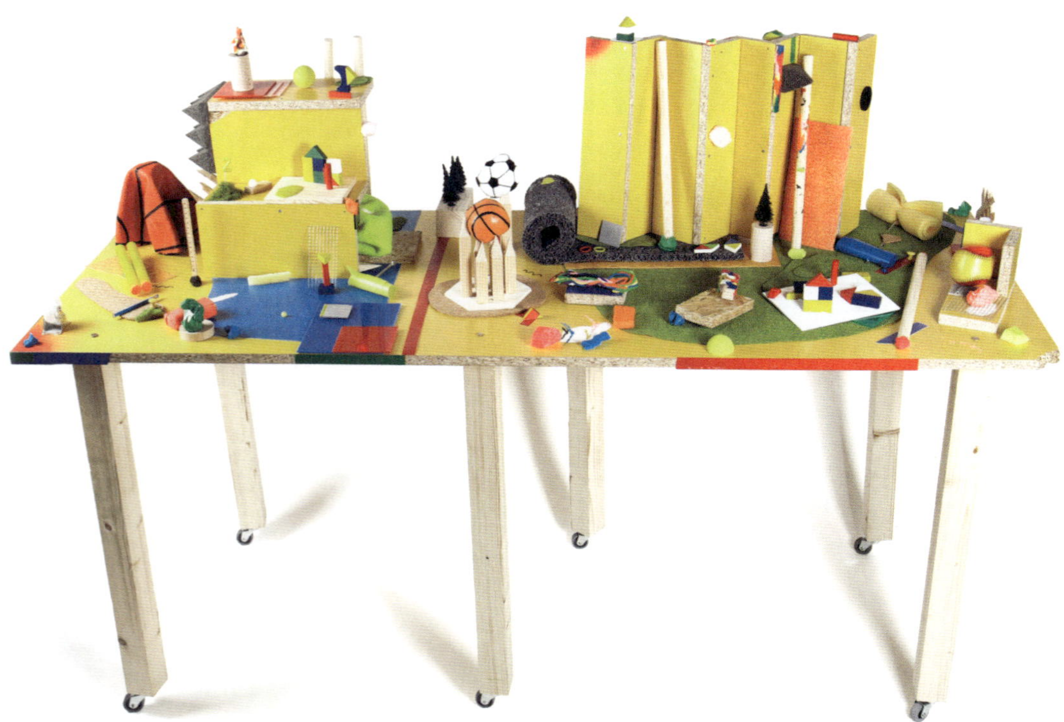

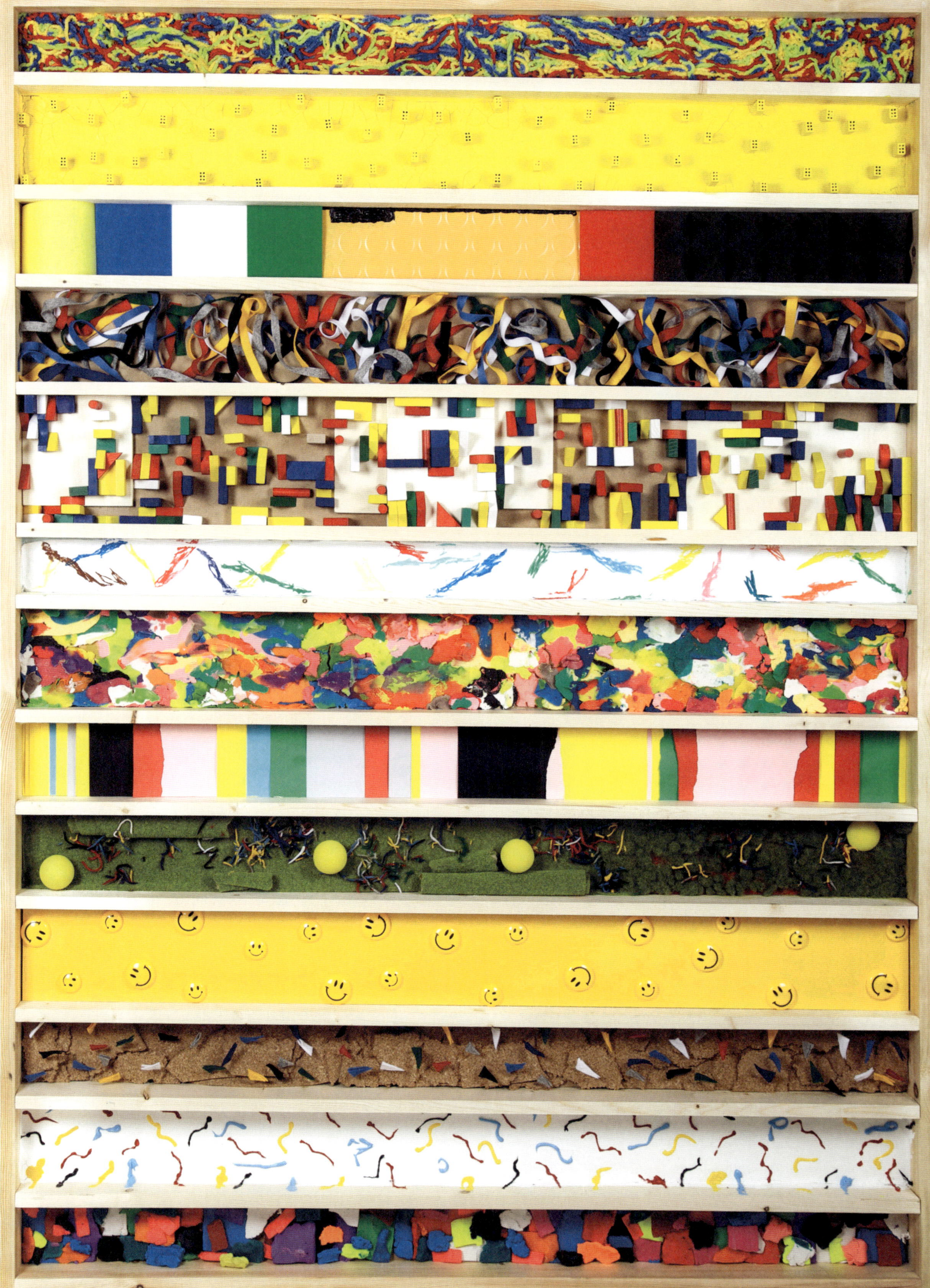

Gustavo Ortiz

A hybrid mix of influences both Latin American and European, from colonial art to indigenous artistic practices,

become manifest in the collages of Argentinian artist Gustavo Ortiz. Raised in the small rural town of Realicó, in the central Pampas region, but now living and working in London, each of his series varies in subject-matter, although certain themes – animals, human figures and landscape – frequently recur. These elements are often symbolically arranged in emblematic compositions, mostly in a square format, which recall the language and feel of Russian icon paintings, Medieval art and Latin American legends. The tactility and texture of the work adds to this ambience, for example his use of gold

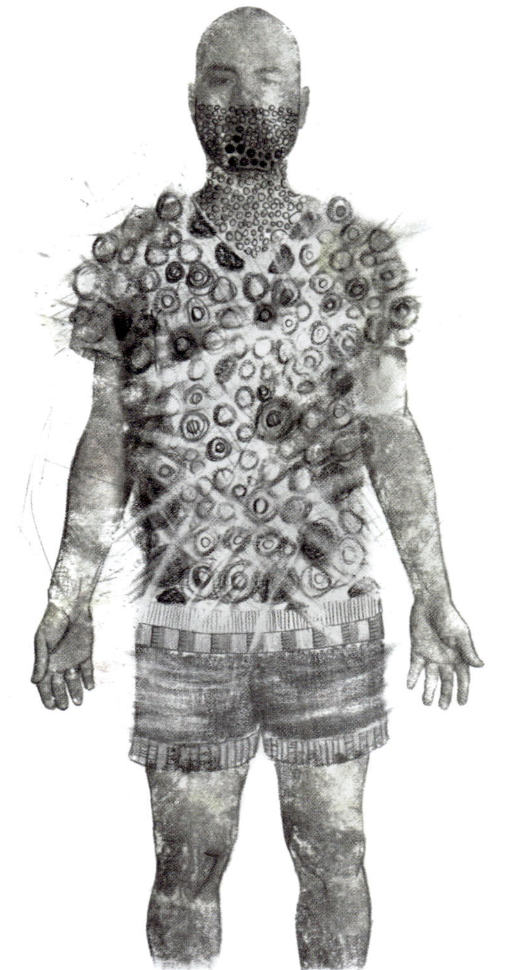

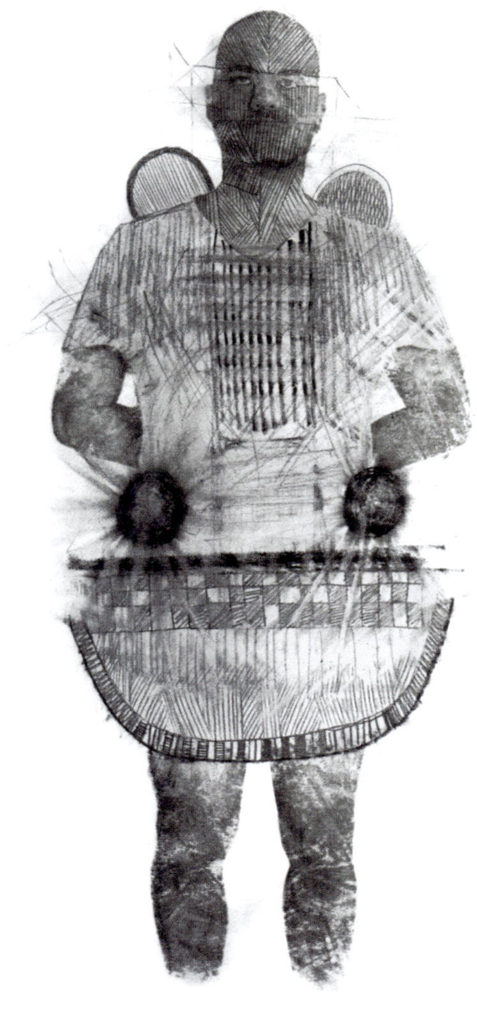

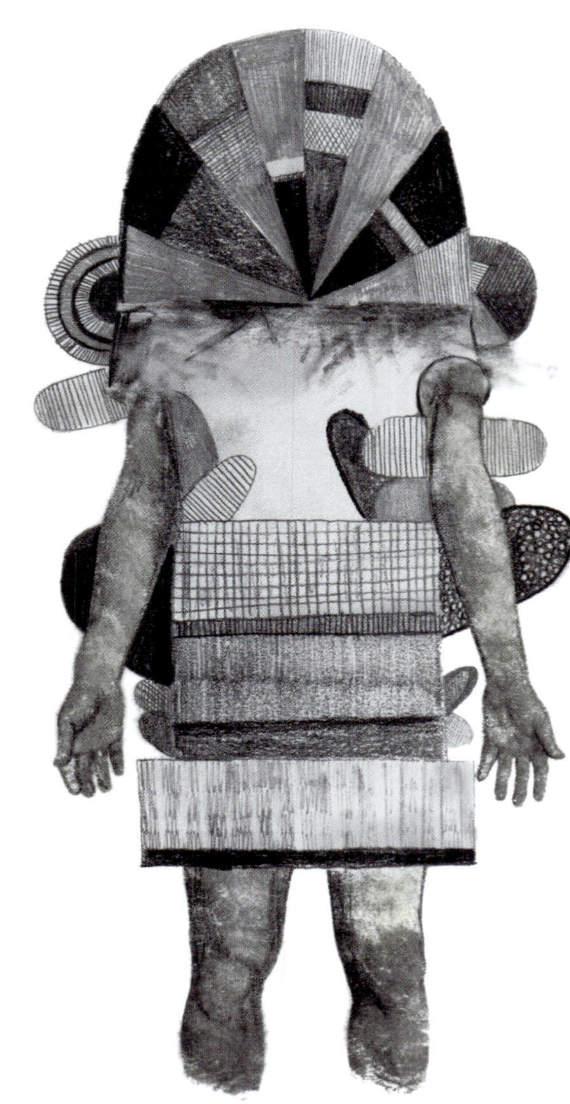

Untitled works, 2012–13
Pencil on paper
21 × 14.8 cm (8¼ × 5⅞ in.)

OPPOSITE, CLOCKWISE FROM
TOP LEFT
Gold Self-portrait III, 2014
Paper collage and wax
on canvas
35 × 25 cm (13¾ × 9⅞ in.)

Self-portrait with Mask II,
2015
Paper collage and wax
on canvas
35 × 25 cm (13¾ × 9 ⅞ in.)

Self-portrait with Mask III,
2015
Paper collage and wax
on canvas
35 × 25 cm (13¾ × 9⅞ in.)

Self-portrait with Mask I,
2015
Paper collage and wax
on canvas
35 × 25 cm (13¾ × 9⅞ in.)

OVERLEAF LEFT
Psychedelic Calf I, 2013
Paper collage and wax
on canvas
50 × 50 cm (19¾ × 19¾ in.)

OVERLEAF RIGHT
Psychedelic Calf II, 2013
Paper collage and wax
on canvas
50 × 50 cm (19¾ × 19¾ in.)

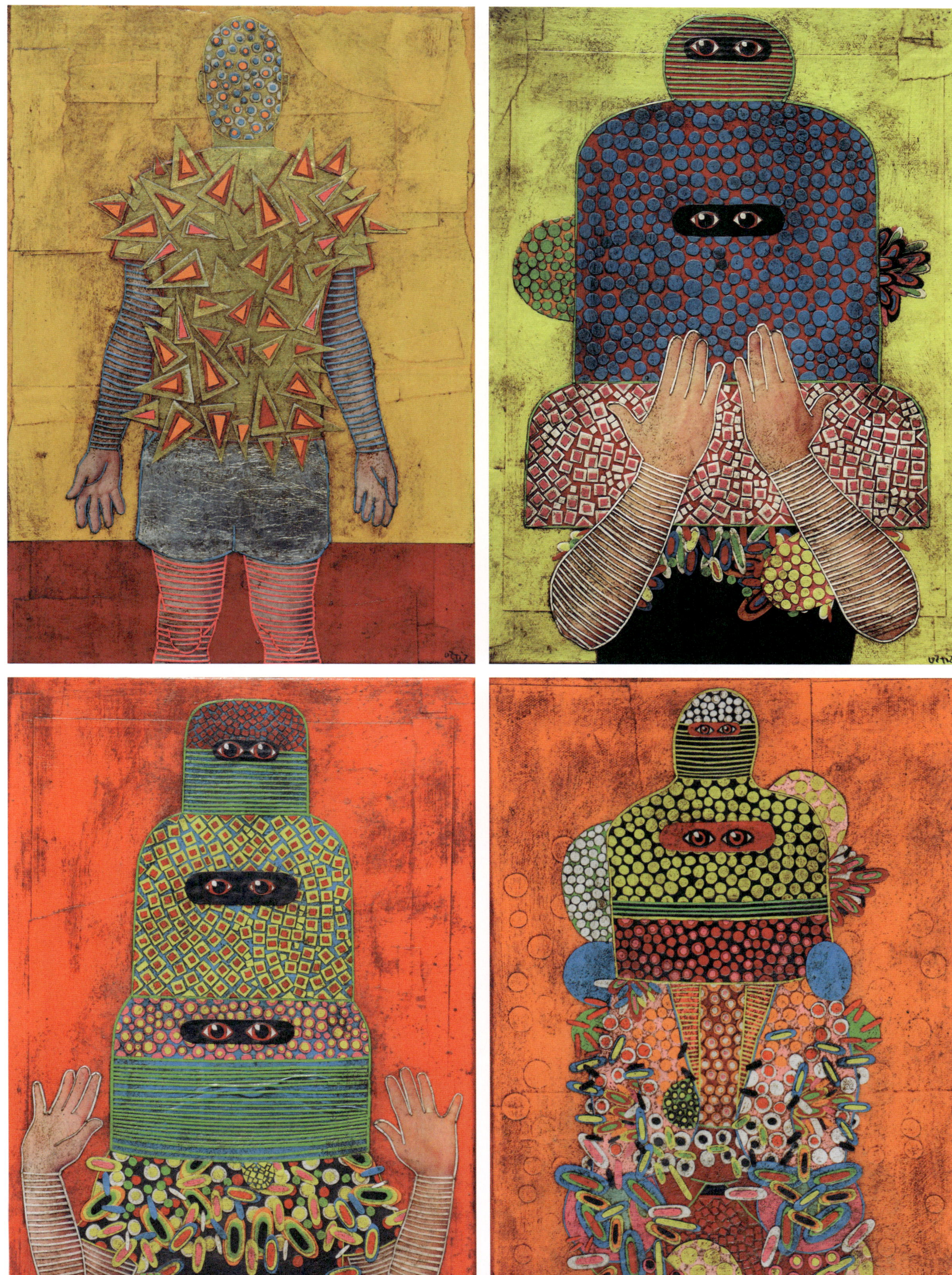

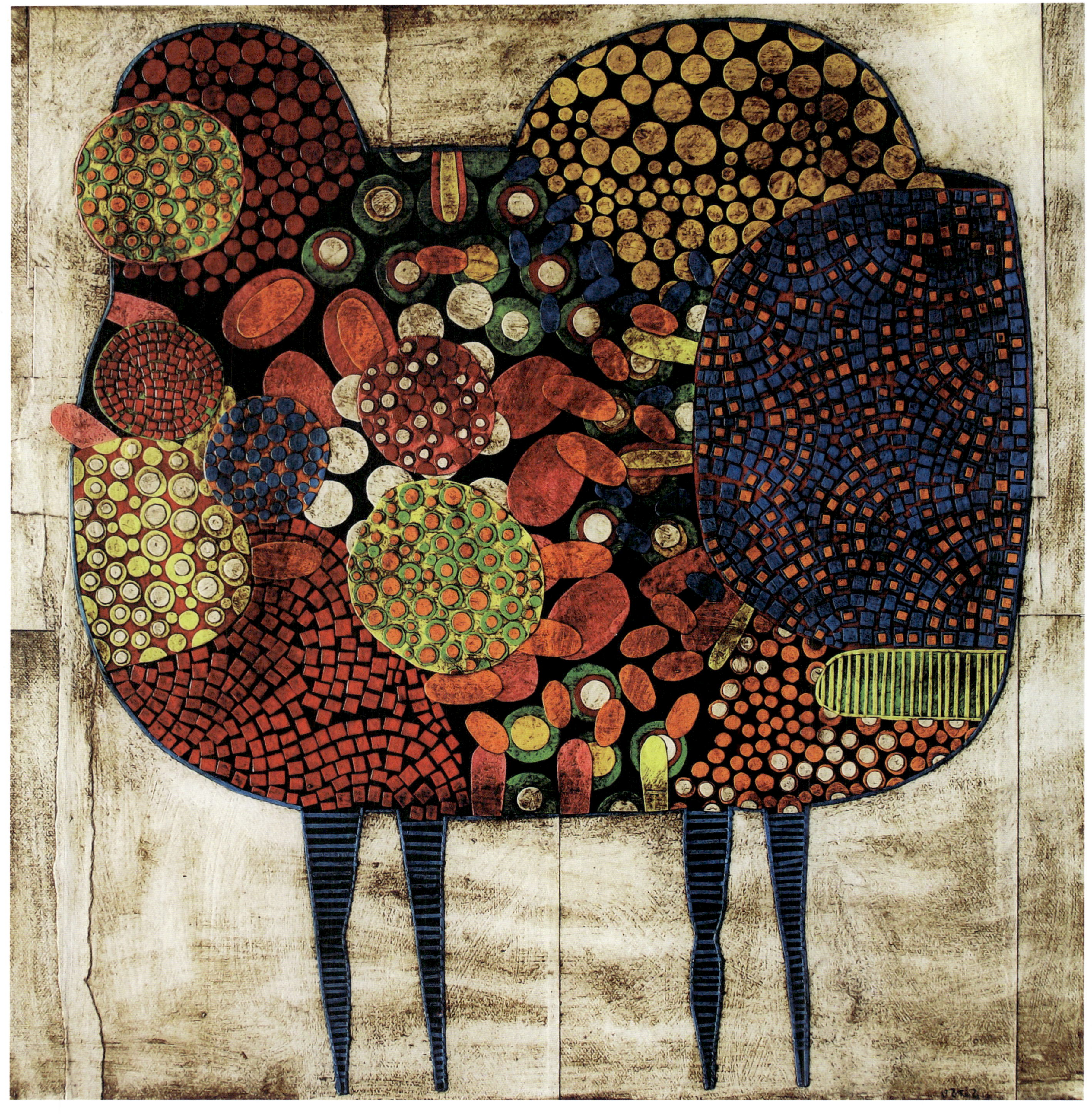

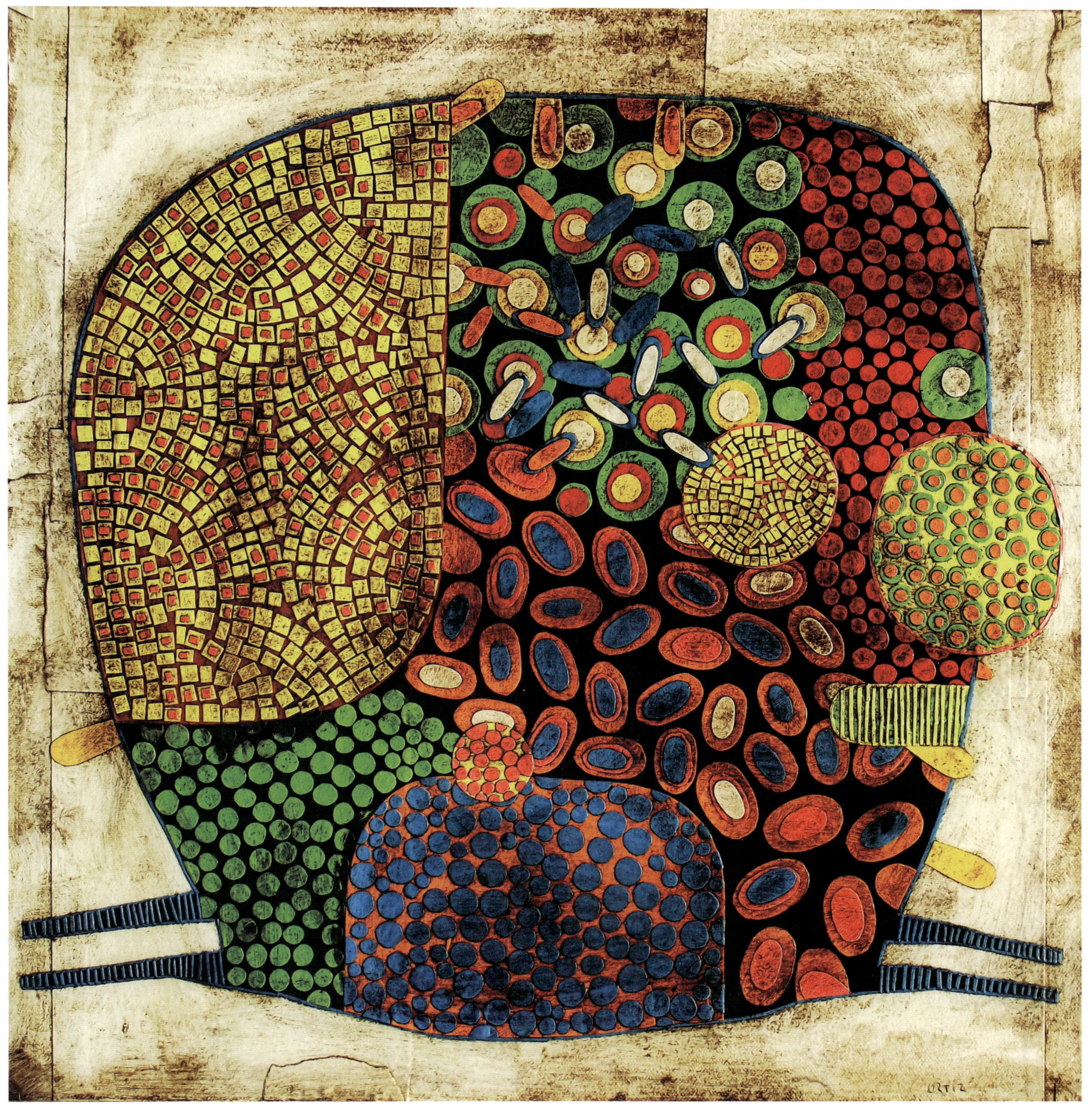

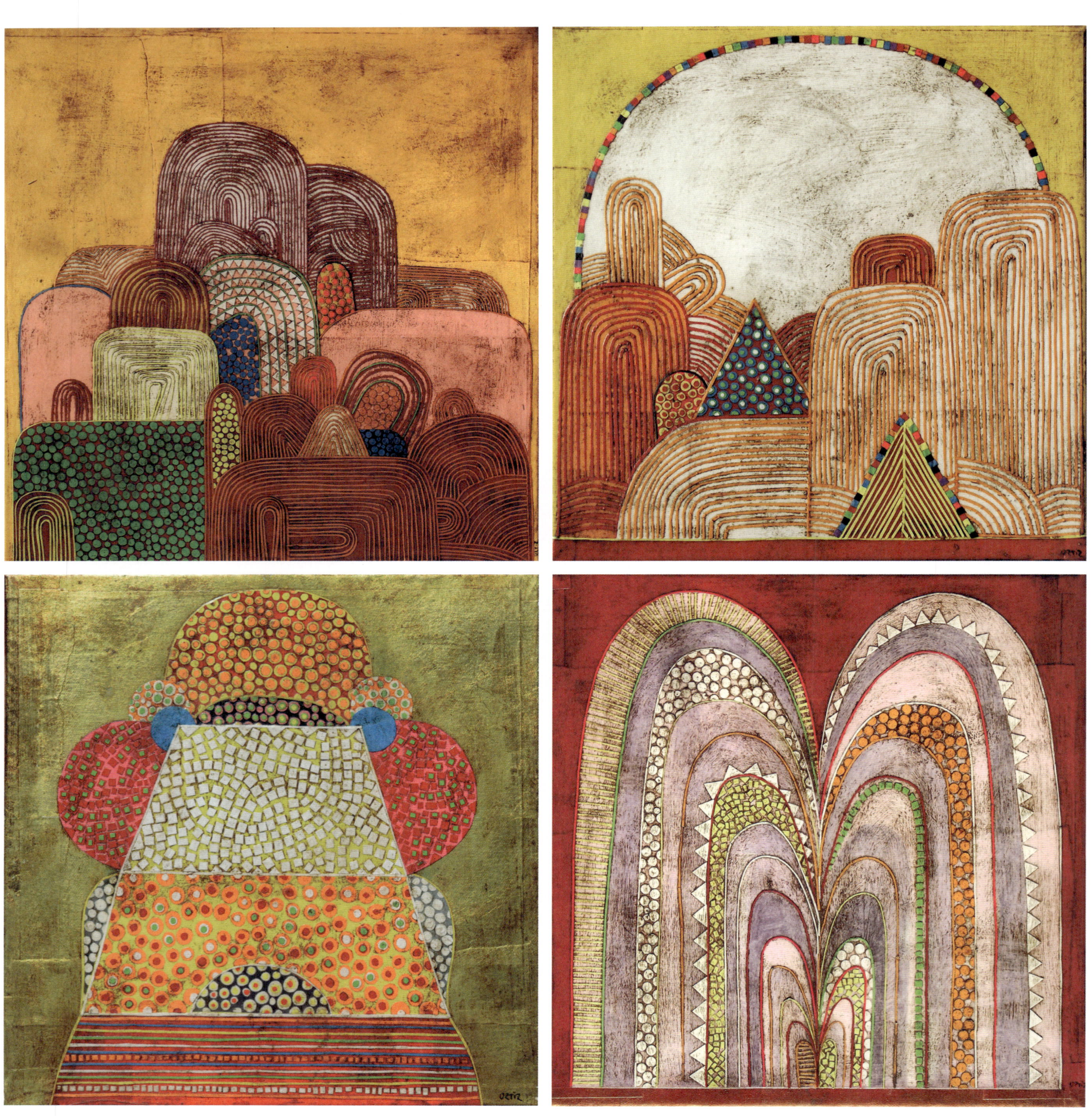

leaf recalls icon painting, and his strong colour palette and striking use of pattern suggests the decorative and ceremonial qualities of native art and craft.

At the heart of Ortiz's work is his exploration of personal identity. Armed with a sketchbook, or 'the big book of minimalism' as he calls it, he explores initial ideas through the use of material left over from earlier collages, allowing new combinations of colour and texture to evolve before developing them into series. It is as a result of this process that works such as his 'silhouettes' were born, or indeed his 'mythological stories', some of which relate to his family, and contain cryptic messages or in-jokes known only to them. While some compositions have a strong narrative element, there are others in which the story remains a mystery or is still developing, an approach deployed by the artist to create 'a situation where the spectator is more active in the conceptual process', with their interpretation of the work becoming integral to its meaning.

Many of his collages have titles that are culturally and personally significant. For example, figures such as his *Machi* relate to the dominance of the matriarch in Argentinian culture; whereas the *Chemamüll*, which in the language of the Mapuche people means 'wooden people', refers to the stylized, totem-like figures, usually two metres or more in height, that this group use as headstones. Ortiz's work seeks to preserve elements of ancient culture such as this, somehow saving them from extinction while also proliferating new interpretations.

Living in London has also exposed the artist to a melting pot of cultures and art scenes. Once a week he takes a day out from his East End studio to visit various museums or to soak up the street art in the area, so that new influences are always being drawn into his practice. Like his choice of materials, then, his work can be seen as a collage of influences – ancient and modern, surreal and abstract – from across the globe, all of which unite in expressing the wonder and enchantment of the human experience.

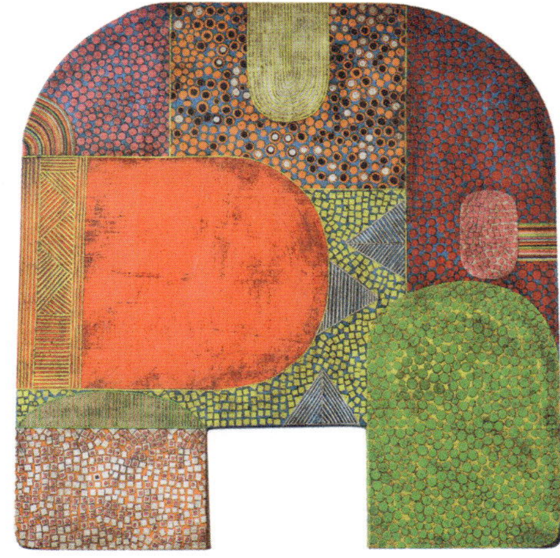
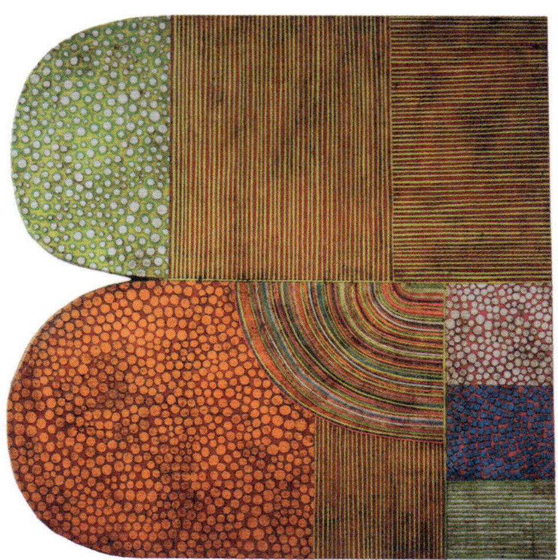
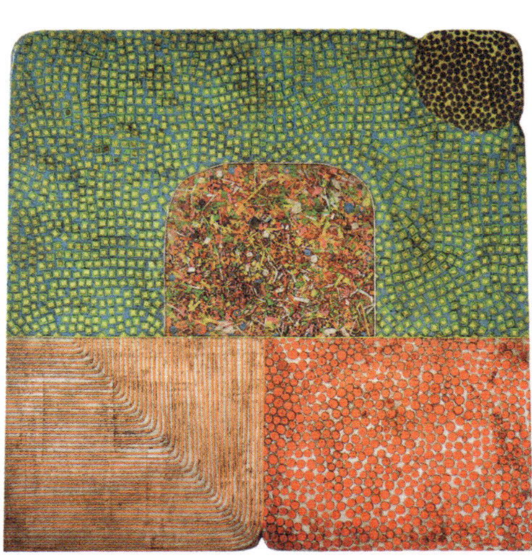
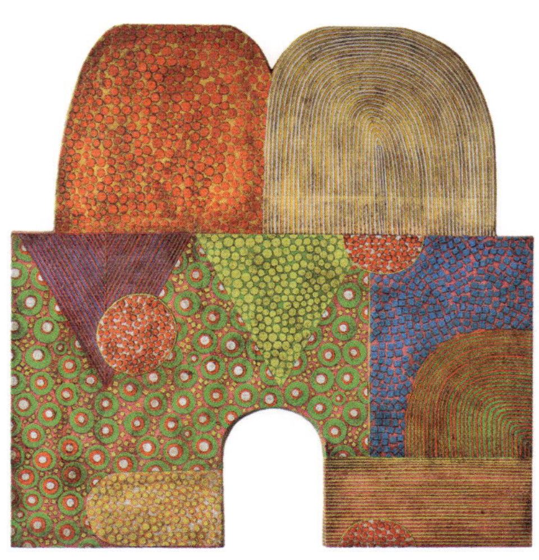
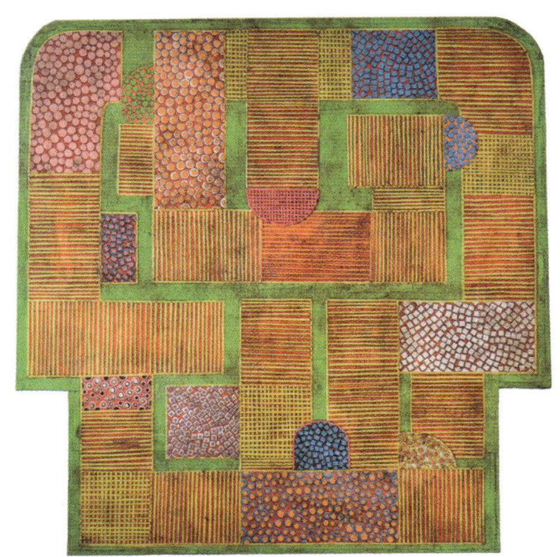
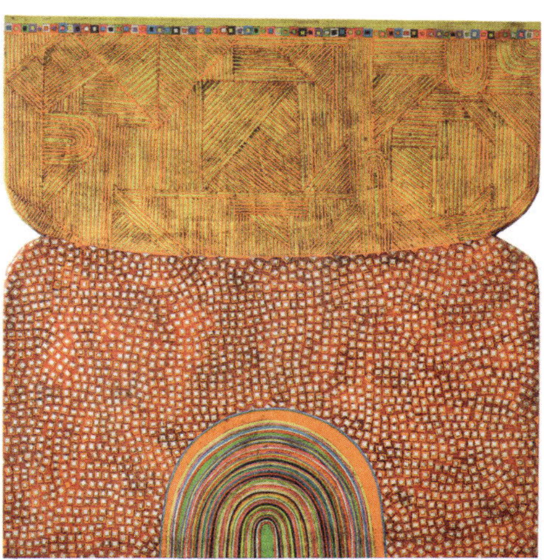

Landscape I, 2015
Paper collage and wax on canvas
60 × 60 cm (23⅝ × 23⅝ in.)

Landscape IV, 2015
Paper collage and wax on canvas
30 × 30 cm (11⅞ × 11⅞ in.)

Willow II, 2015
Paper collage and wax on canvas
30 × 30 cm (11⅞ × 11⅞ in.)

Silhouette (Pyramid I), 2015
Paper collage and wax on canvas
30 × 30 cm (11⅞ × 11⅞ in.)

Cosmos I–VI, 2015
Paper collage and wax on wood
50 × 50 cm (19¾ × 19¾ in.) each

Ben Venom

Renowned for his bringing together of the soft, safe and slow craft of quilt-making and the tough, loud and fast world of heavy metal – two seemingly opposing forces – is the San Francisco-based artist Ben Venom. He creates large-scale quilts into which bold motifs, taken from recycled T-shirts and imagery inspired by vintage tattoos, motorcycle gangs and the occult, are incorporated. By re-contextualizing heavy-metal imagery in textiles he invites the viewer to consider these genres with fresh eyes.

Venom's interest in quilts was sparked after seeing the exhibition 'Quilts of Gee's Bend' at the De Young Museum in San Francisco in 2006. At the time he was a student at the San Francisco Art Institute and was already making large sewn flags and banners that were combined with elements of screenprinting. He had also been invited to exhibit a work in Berlin, and thought that a quilt would be easier to ship than a framed piece, and submitted one into which he had incorporated a selection of heavy-metal T-shirts. Quilting to him was the logical step in developing his work, both conceptually and practically.

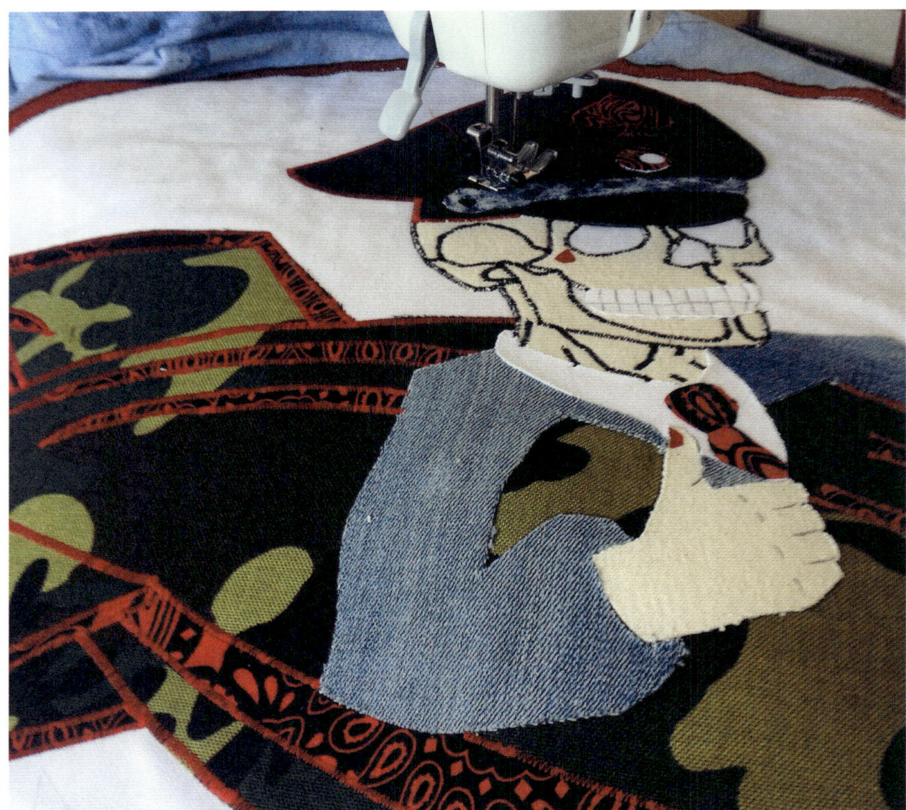

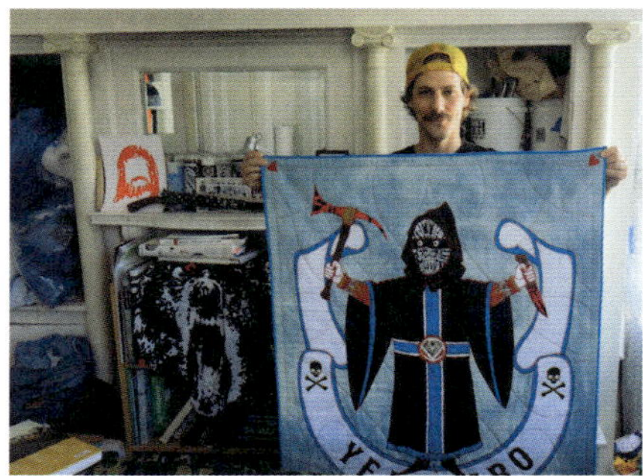

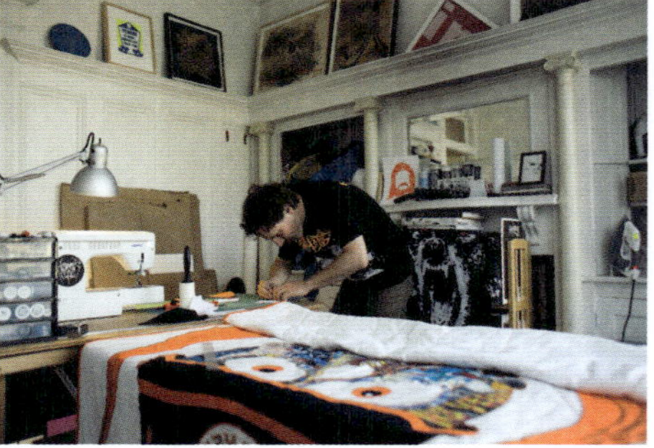

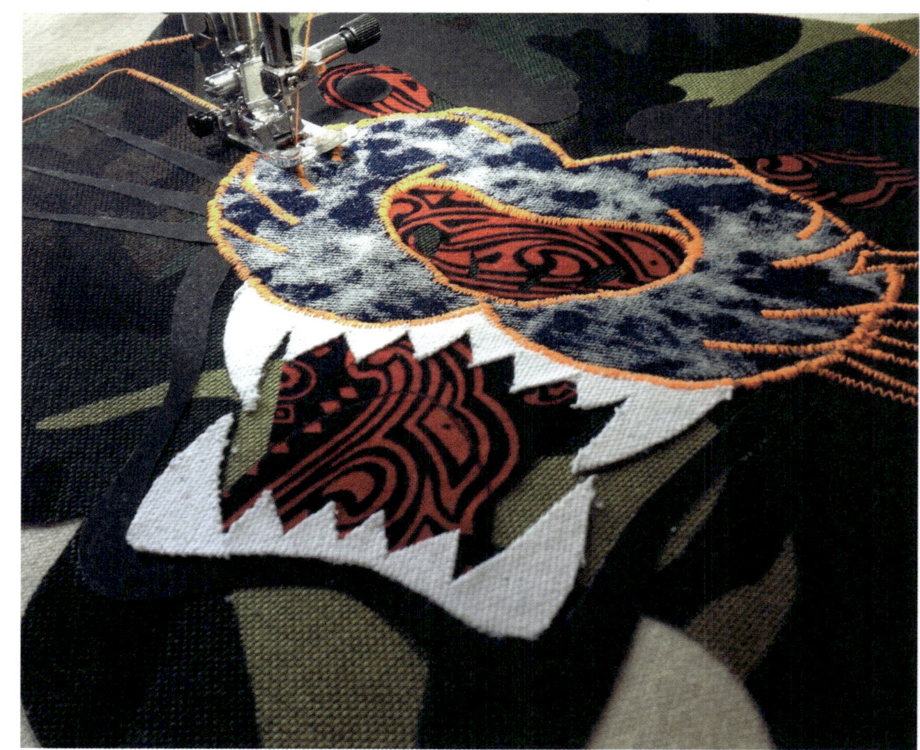

In on the Kill Taker in progress, *c.* 2012

The artist at work.

Bad Kitty jacket in progress, *c.* 2014

The artist holding up *Arrested Motion, c.* 2013

OPPOSITE
Night Lurker, 2012
Handmade quilt with heavy-metal T-shirts
68.6 × 48.3 cm (27 × 19 in.)

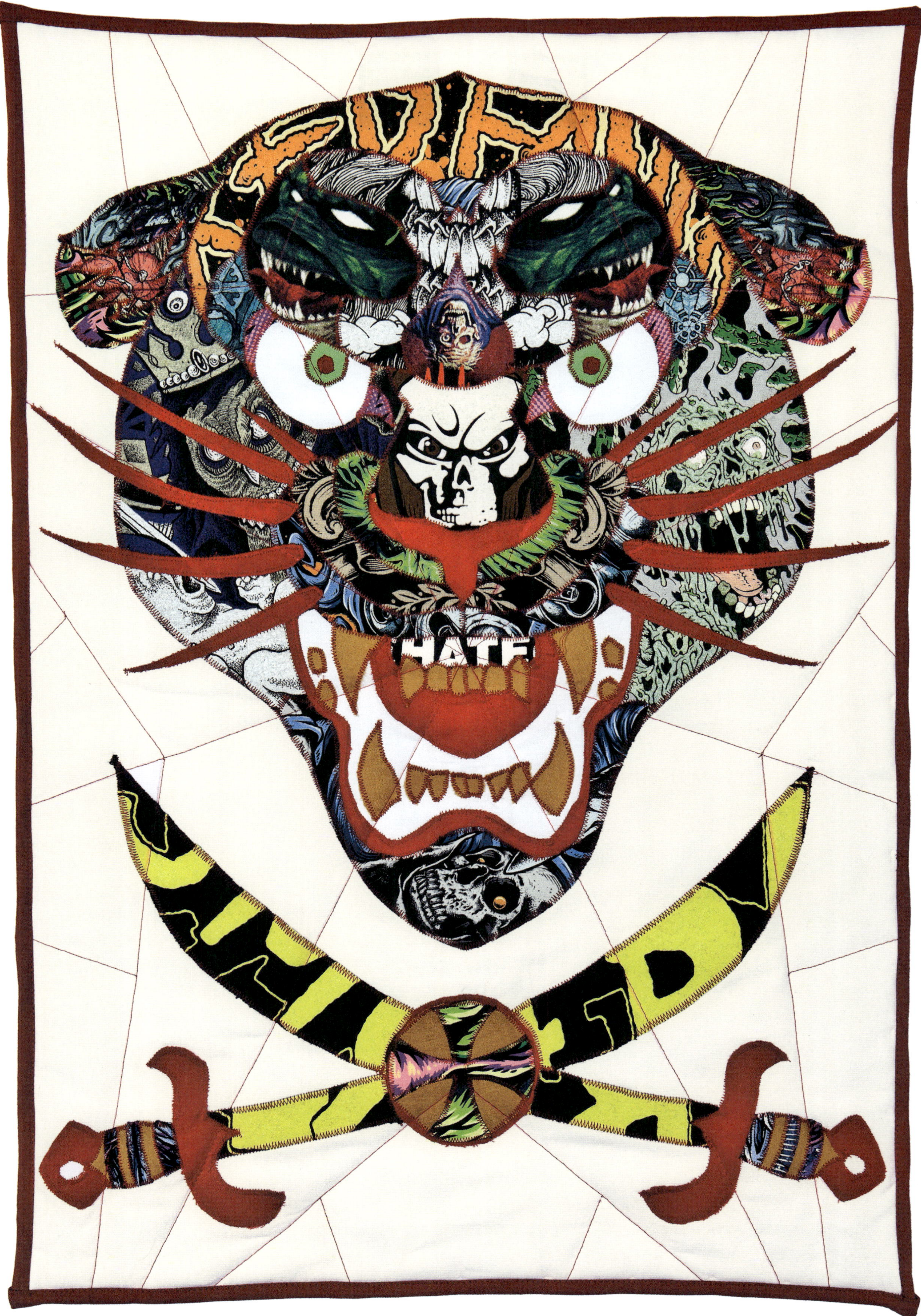

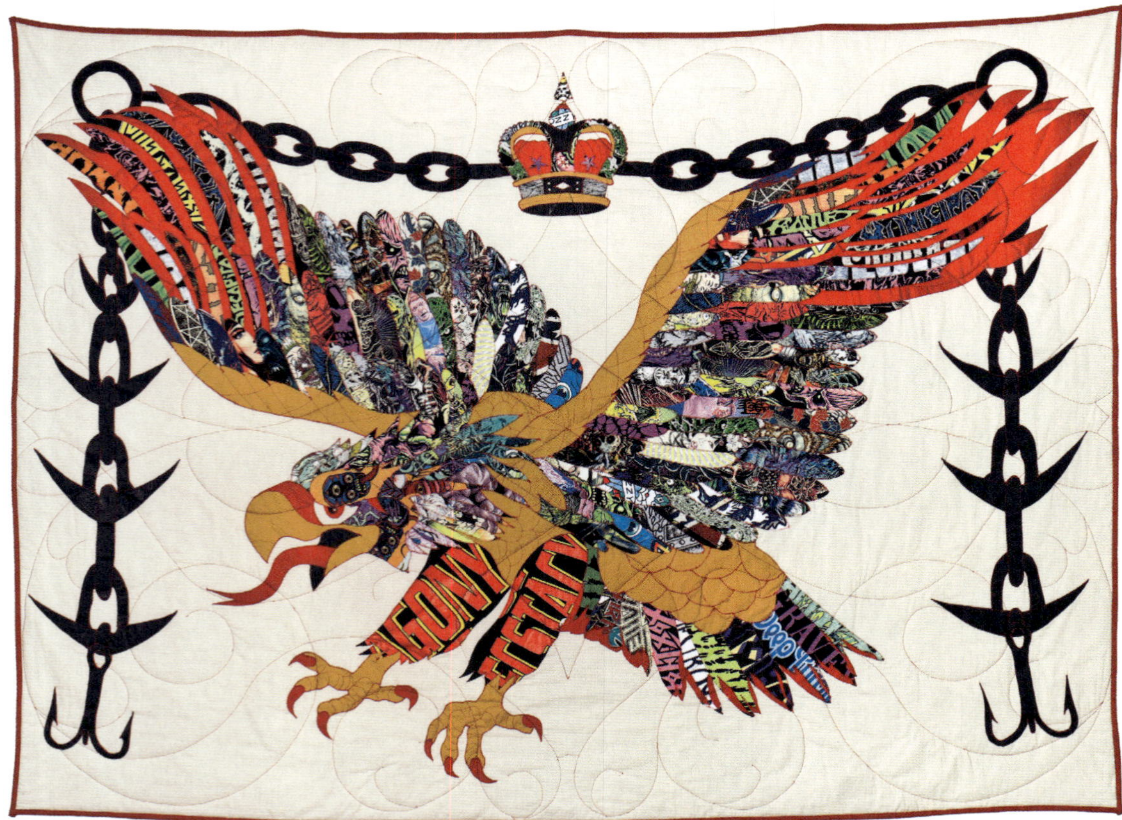

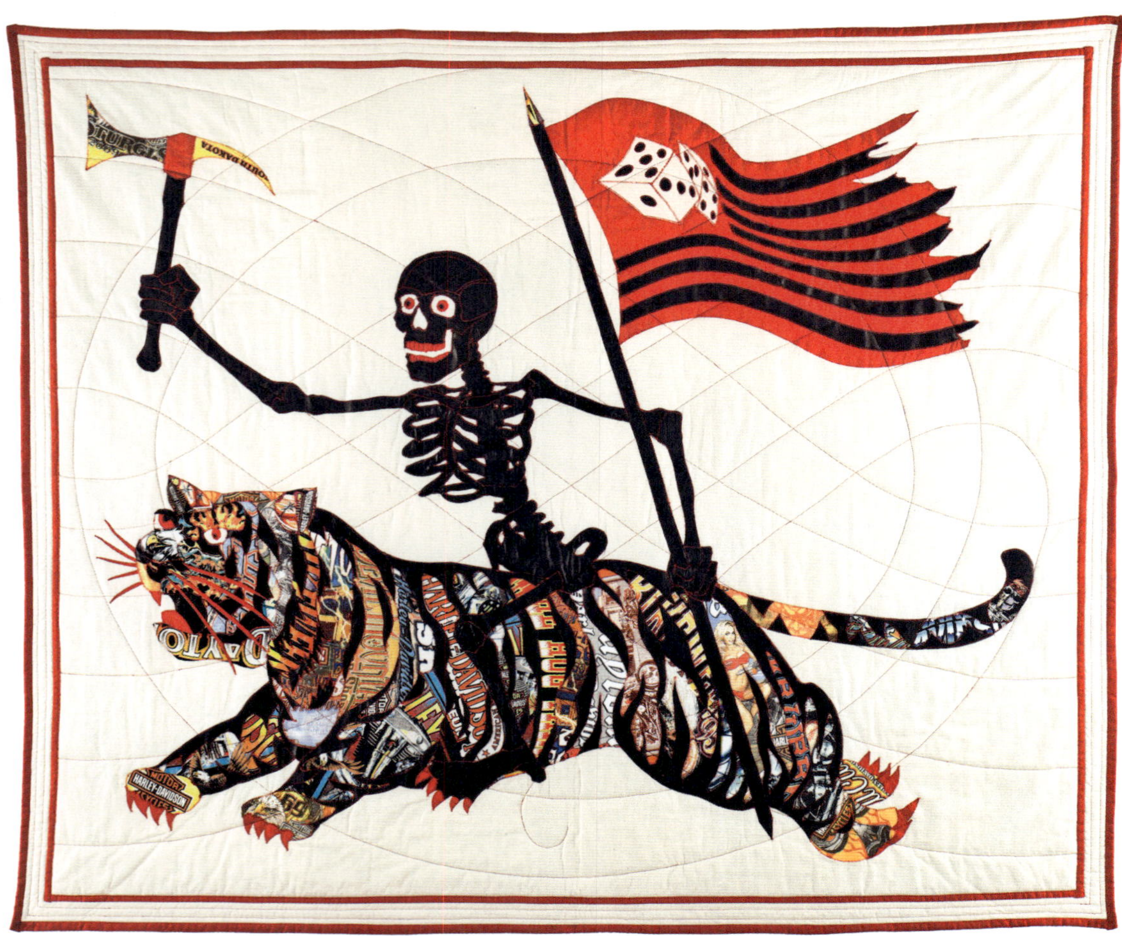

Untitled, 2013
Handmade quilt with heavy-metal T-shirts and leather
149.8 × 210.8 cm (59 × 83 in.)

Into the Night, 2013
Handmade quilt with Harley Davidson T-Shirts and leather
149.8 × 180.3 cm (59 × 71 in.)

OPPOSITE
Untitled, c. 2013
Handmade quilt with heavy-metal T-shirts
68.6 × 48.3 cm (27 × 19 in.)

Since then he has been integrating his own T-shirts into his artworks, juxtaposing them with other materials in order to breathe new life into them. Each piece begins with a preparatory drawing, which is then refined digitally, in Photoshop or Illustrator. After this Venom cuts fabric into pre-determined shapes and sizes, before piecing them together like a puzzle. The finished patchworks seem to go beyond the realms of their constituent parts and into the arena of mythology and the occult, albeit with a sense of humour, with the artist simultaneously mocking and paying tribute to these themes while also elevating them to new heights.

While this process is now finely honed within his practice, he is not overly concerned by the immaculateness of the final outcome; instead embracing mistakes for their ability to highlight the rawness of the medium with which he works. Ultimately, he states, his ambition 'is to create work that is not only inspiring, aesthetically pleasing, but also functional. At the end of the day my art can be worn as fashion or keep you warm at night.'

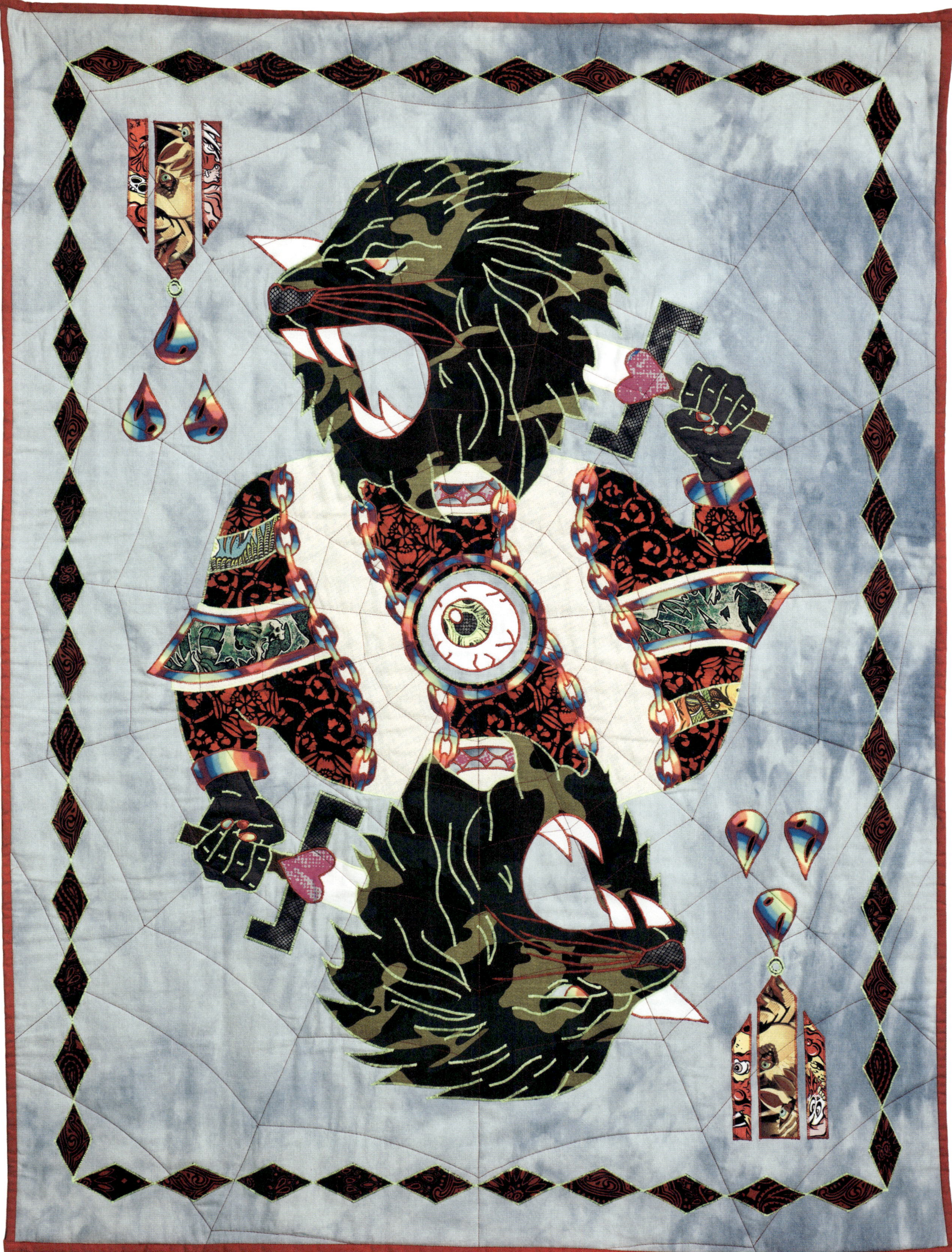

Websites

44flavours
www.44flavours.com

Ibrahim Ahmed III
www.ibrahimahmediii.com

Aryz
www.aryz.es

Bault
http://bault.tumblr.com
https://instagram.com/bault_

Diana Beltrán Herrera
www.dianabeltranherrera.com

Bonar
www.lebonnard.com

Borondo
gonzaloborondo.com

Jason Botkin
www.jasonbotkin.com

Luciano Calderon
www.lucianocalderon.com

Ricardo Cavolo
www.ricardocavolo.com

Cern
http://cernesto.com

David Côté
https://instagram.com/thedavidcote

El Curiot
www.facebook.com/El.Curiot

Marat Danilyan
http://morik1.livejournal.com

Carlos Donjuán
http://carlosdonjuan.com

Dulk
www.dulk.es

Franco Fasoli
www.francofasoli.com.ar

Rune Fisker
www.runefisker.com

Danny Fox
www.white-cake.com

Ugo Gattoni
www.ugogattoni.fr

Robert Hardgrave
http://roberthardgrave.com

Harold Hollingsworth
http://haroldhollingsworth.blogspot.co.uk
http://haroldhollingsworth.tumblr.com

Agostino Iacurci
www.agostinoiacurci.com

Knarf
http://lumpenpack.tumblr.com

Diogo Machado
www.addfuel.com

David Méndez Alonso
http://www.davidmendezalonso.com

Gustavo Ortiz
http://gustavoortiz.com

Pastel
http://pastelfd.com.ar

Pejac
http://pejac.es

Raymond Lemstra
www.raymondlemstra.nl

Mafia
http://holymafia.tumblr.com
https://instagram.com/mafia_tabak
http://wandblatt.tumblr.com

Morcky
www.morcky.com

Jim Pluk
http://plukart777.blogspot.co.uk
http://jimpluk.tumblr.com

João Ruas
www.joaoruas.com

Sainer
www.behance.net/sainer
https://instagram.com/sainer_etam

Rob Sato
www.robsato.com

Ricardo Solís
www.ricardosolisart.com

Le Super Demon
lesuperdemon.blogspot.com

T-Wei
t-wei.tumblr.com
www.behance.net/t-wei

Fuco Ueda
www.fucoueda.com

Ben Venom
www.benvenom.com

Mark Francis Williams
www.markfranciswilliams.com

Irena Zablotska
www.zablotska.com

Ernest Zacharevic
www.ernestzacharevic.com

Zio Ziegler
www.zioziegler.com

Bibliography

Borondo, *Momento Mori*, Rome, 2015

Ricardo Cavolo, *101 Artists to Listen to Before you Die*, London, 2015

Danny Fox, *As He Bowed His Head to Drink*, London, 2015

Ugo Gattoni, *Bicycle*, London, 2012

Robert Hardgrave, *Magic Beans*, Los Angeles, 2008

Ana Ibarra and Marc Valli, *Walk the Line: The Art of Drawing*, London, 2013

Raymond Lemstra, *Big Mother*, No. 4, London, 2014

Jim Pluk, *Josefina*, Cambridge, 2015

—, *Fenn*, Barcelona, 2015

Zio Ziegler, *Color with Zio*, London, 2016

Author Biography

Tristan Manco is an author, art consultant and graphic designer based in Bath in the UK. He currently teaches BA (Hons) Illustration at the Plymouth College of Art.

Previous publications include *Stencil Graffiti* (2002), *Street Logos* (2004), *Graffiti Brasil* (2005), *Street Sketchbook* (2007), *Street Sketchbook: Journeys* (2010), *Raw + Material + Art* (2012) and *Big Art/Small Art* (2014), all published by Thames & Hudson. Manco frequently contributes to art and design publications and is a consultant for clients such as Wahaca.

Photo Acknowledgments

a = above, b = below, l = left, r = right, c = centre

All images courtesy of the artist, unless otherwise indicated: p. 10, photograph by Bruno Lopes; p. 70 (a, c), photographs by Marcello Scopelliti; p. 132 (c, bl, br), photographs by Jack Whitefield; pp. 188–89, photographs by Bruno Lopes; p. 201 (al), photograph by Randy Dodson; p. 208, photographs by Hamdy Reda; p. 216 (a), photograph by Julie Aramburu; p. 216 (cl), photograph by Laura Aurallan; p. 216 (cr), photograph by Fabiano Caputo; p. 216 (b), photograph © BlindEyeFactory; pp. 217–19, photographs by Diego de Miguel Heredero; p. 220 (a), photograph by Benedetta Pam Photos; p. 220 (bl), photograph by Diego de Miguel Heredero; p. 220 (br), photograph by Marco Miccoli; p. 228 (bl, bc, br), photographs by Elizabetta Riccio; p. 234 (al, c), photographs by Rui Soares; p. 234 (ar), photograph by Ricardo C. Mendes; pp. 234 (b), 235, photographs by Hugo Moura; p. 236, photograph by Federico Andres; p. 237 (al), photograph by Dom Poirier; p. 237 (ar), photograph by Tiago Fonseca; p. 237 (c), photograph by Rui Gaiola; p. 237 (b), photograph by Lara Seixo Rodrigues; pp. 238–39, photograph by Federico Andres; p. 250 (cr), photograph by Ryan Van Der Hout.

Acknowledgments

An enormous thank you to all the contributing artists for inspiring this book and for their kind patience and generosity in its production.

Thanks also to the following for their invaluable help in the making of this book: Jamie Camplin, Iris Eisenlohr, Olivia Manco, Chiara Mariani, Charlotte Pyatt, Maximiliano Ruiz and Aaron Shutt.

OVERLEAF
Carlos Donjuán
Untitled, from the 'Sour Grapes' series, 2012
Giclée print
50 × 40 cm (20 × 16 in.)

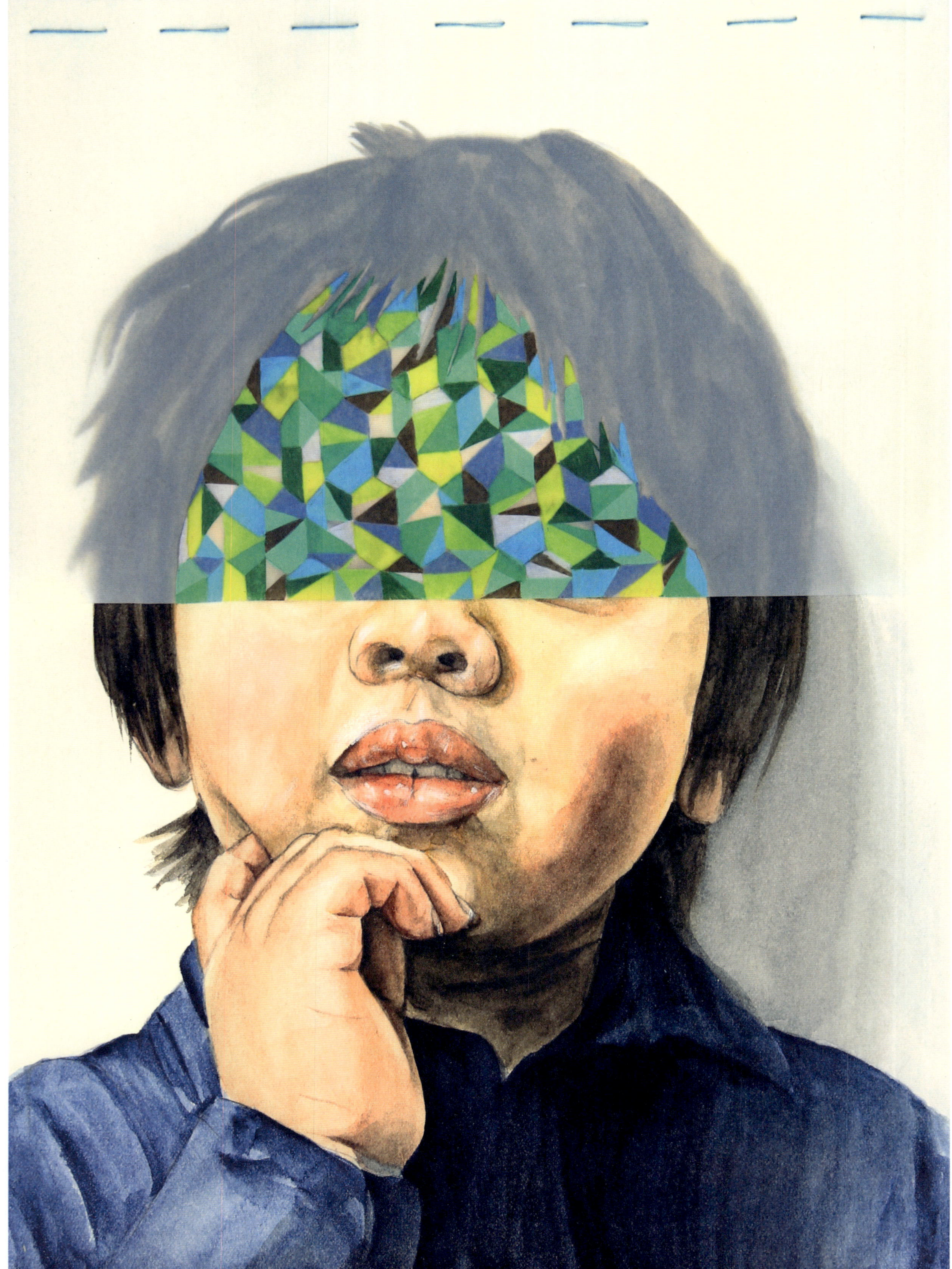